THE BELLARMINE SERIES

Published by the Jesuit Fathers of
Heythrop College

General Editor
EDMUND F. SUTCLIFFE, S.J.
*Professor of Old Testament Exegesis and Hebrew
at Heythrop College*

BY THE SAME AUTHOR

FRIEDRICH NIETZSCHE, PHILOSOPHER OF CULTURE, 1942, SECOND IMPRESSION, 1945—THE BELLARMINE SERIES, NO. 7

ARTHUR SCHOPENHAUER, PHILOSOPHER OF PESSIMISM, 1946, SECOND IMPRESSION, 1947—THE BELLARMINE SERIES, NO. 11

A HISTORY OF PHILOSOPHY, VOL. I: GREECE AND ROME, 1946, REVISED EDITION, 1947—THE BELLARMINE SERIES, NO. 9

VOL. II: MEDIAEVAL PHILOSOPHY, AUGUSTINE TO SCOTUS, 1950—THE BELLARMINE SERIES, NO. 12

ST. THOMAS AND NIETZSCHE, 1944—AQUINAS PAPER, NO. 2
EXISTENTIALISM AND MODERN MAN, 1948—AQUINAS PAPER, NO. 9
MEDIEVAL PHILOSOPHY, 1952—HOME STUDY BOOKS

THE BELLARMINE SERIES

A list of volumes with Press appreciations will be found at the end of this book.

THE BELLARMINE SERIES XIV

A
HISTORY OF PHILOSOPHY

VOLUME III
OCKHAM TO SUÁREZ

BY
FREDERICK COPLESTON, S.J.
*Professor of the History of Philosophy
at Heythrop College*

LONDON
BURNS OATES & WASHBOURNE LTD.
Publishers to the Holy See
1953

De Licentia Superiorum Ordinis:
E. HELSHAM, S.J.
Praep. Prov. Angliae

Nihil Obstat:
J. L. RUSSELL, S.J.
Censor Deputatus

Imprimatur:
✠ JOSEPH
Archiepiscopus Birmingamiensis

Birmingamiae
die 4 Januarii 1952

PRINTED IN GREAT BRITAIN BY JARROLD AND SONS LTD
NORWICH, FOR BURNS OATES AND WASHBOURNE LTD
28 ASHLEY PLACE, LONDON, S.W.1

First published 1953

CONTENTS

Chapter	Page
FOREWORD	ix

I. INTRODUCTION 1
   Thirteenth century—Fourteenth century contrasted with thirteenth—Philosophies of the Renaissance—Revival of Scholasticism.

PART I
THE FOURTEENTH CENTURY

II. DURANDUS AND PETRUS AUREOLI 24
   James of Metz—Durandus—Petrus Aureoli—Henry of Harclay—The relation of these thinkers to Ockhamism.

III. OCKHAM (1) 43
   Life—Works—Unity of thought.

IV. OCKHAM (2) 49
   Ockham and the metaphysic of essences—Peter of Spain and the terminist logic—Ockham's logic and theory of universals—Real and rational science—Necessary truths and demonstration.

V. OCKHAM (3) 62
   Intuitive knowledge—God's power to cause intuitive knowledge of a non-existent object—Contingency of the world-order—Relations—Causality—Motion and time—Conclusion.

VI. OCKHAM (4) 77
   The subject-matter of metaphysics—The univocal concept of being—The existence of God—Our knowledge of God's nature—The divine ideas—God's knowledge of future contingent events—The divine will and omnipotence.

VII. OCKHAM (5) 96
   That an immaterial and incorruptible soul is the form of the body cannot be philosophically proved—The plurality of really distinct forms in man—The rational soul possesses no really distinct faculties—The human person—Freedom—Ockham's ethical theory.

VIII. OCKHAM (6) 111
   The dispute on evangelical poverty, and the doctrine of natural rights—Political sovereignty is not derived from the spiritual power—The relation of the people to their ruler—How far were Ockham's political ideas novel or revolutionary?—The pope's position within the Church.

v

CONTENTS

Chapter	Page
IX. THE OCKHAMIST MOVEMENT: JOHN OF MIRECOURT AND NICHOLAS OF AUTRECOURT	122

The Ockhamist or nominalist movement—John of Mirecourt—Nicholas of Autrecourt—Nominalism in the universities—Concluding remarks.

X. THE SCIENTIFIC MOVEMENT 153

Physical science in the thirteenth and fourteenth centuries—The problem of motion; impetus and gravity—Nicholas Oresme; the hypothesis of the earth's rotation—The possibility of other worlds—Some scientific implications of nominalism; and implications of the impetus theory.

XI. MARSILIUS OF PADUA 168

Church and State, theory and practice—Life of Marsilius—Hostility to the papal claims—The nature of the State and of law—The legislature and the executive—Ecclesiastical jurisdiction—Marsilius and 'Averroism'—Influence of the *Defensor pacis*.

XII. SPECULATIVE MYSTICISM 181

Mystical writing in the fourteenth century—Eckhart—Tauler—Blessed Henry Suso—Ruysbroeck—Denis the Carthusian—German mystical speculation—Gerson.

PART II
THE PHILOSOPHY OF THE RENAISSANCE

XIII. THE REVIVAL OF PLATONISM 207

The Italian Renaissance—The northern Renaissance—The revival of Platonism.

XIV. ARISTOTELIANISM 217

Critics of the Aristotelian logic—Aristotelianism—Stoicism and scepticism.

XV. NICHOLAS OF CUSA 231

Life and works—The influence of Nicholas's leading idea on his practical activity—The *coincidentia oppositorum*—'Instructed ignorance'—The relation of God to the world—The 'infinity' of the world—The world-system and the soul of the world—Man, the microcosm; Christ—Nicholas's philosophical affiliations.

XVI. PHILOSOPHY OF NATURE (1) 248

General remarks—Girolamo Cardano—Bernardino Telesio—Francesco Patrizzi—Tommaso Campanella—Giordano Bruno—Pierre Gassendi.

XVII. PHILOSOPHY OF NATURE (2) 265

Agrippa von Nettesheim—Paracelsus—The two Van Helmonts—Sebastian Franck and Valentine Weigel—Jakob Böhme—General remarks.

CONTENTS

Chapter	Page
XVIII. THE SCIENTIFIC MOVEMENT OF THE RENAISSANCE	275

General remarks on the influence of science on philosophy—Renaissance science; the empirical basis of science, controlled experiment, hypothesis and astronomy, mathematics, the mechanistic view of the world—The influence of Renaissance science on philosophy.

XIX. FRANCIS BACON 292

English philosophy of the Renaissance—Bacon's life and writings—The classification of the sciences—Induction and 'the idols'.

XX. POLITICAL PHILOSOPHY 310

General remarks—Niccoló Machiavelli—St. Thomas More—Richard Hooker—Jean Bodin—Joannes Althusius—Hugo Grotius.

PART III

SCHOLASTICISM OF THE RENAISSANCE

XXI. A GENERAL VIEW 335

The revival of Scholasticism—Dominican writers before the Council of Trent; Cajetan—Later Dominican writers and Jesuit writers—The controversy between Dominicans and Jesuits about grace and free will—The substitution of 'philosophical courses' for commentaries on Aristotle—Political and legal theory.

XXII. FRANCIS SUÁREZ (1) 353

Life and works—The structure and divisions of the *Disputationes metaphysicae*—Metaphysics as the science of being—The concept of being—The attributes of being—Individuation—Analogy—God's existence—The divine nature—Essence and existence—Substance and accident—Modes—Quantity—Relations—*Entia rationis*—General remarks—Étienne Gilson on Suárez.

XXIII. FRANCIS SUÁREZ (2) 380

Philosophy of law and theology—The definition of law—Law (*lex*) and right (*ius*)—The necessity of law—The eternal law—The natural law—The precepts of the natural law—Ignorance of natural law—The immutability of the natural law—The law of nations—Political society, sovereignty and government—The contract theory in Suárez—The deposition of tyrants—Penal laws—Cessation of human laws—Custom—Church and State—War.

XXIV. A BRIEF REVIEW OF THE FIRST THREE VOLUMES . 406

Greek philosophy; the pre-Socratic cosmologies and the discovery of Nature, Plato's theory of Forms and idea of God, Aristotle and the explanation of change and movement, neo-Platonism and Christianity—The importance for mediaeval philosophy of the discovery of Aristotle—Philosophy and theology—The rise of science.

CONTENTS

APPENDICES

                                                                                                   Page

I. Honorific Titles applied to Philosophers treated of in this Volume 427

II. A Short Bibliography 428

    Index 448

FOREWORD

THE first part of this volume is concerned with the philosophy of the fourteenth century. A good deal in the history of the philosophical thought of this period is still obscure, and no definitive account of it can be written until we have at our disposal a much greater number of reliable texts than are at present available. However, in publishing the account contained in this volume I am encouraged by the thought that the learned Franciscan scholar, Father Philotheus Boehner, who is doing so much to shed light on the dark places of the fourteenth century, was so kind as to read the chapters on Ockham and to express appreciation of their general tone. This does not mean, of course, that Father Boehner endorses all my interpretations of Ockham. In particular he does not agree with my view that analysis discloses two ethics implicitly contained in Ockham's philosophy. (This view is in any case, as I hope I have made clear in the text, a conjectural interpretation, developed in order to account for what may seem to be inconsistencies in Ockham's ethical philosophy.) And I do not think that Father Boehner would express himself in quite the way that I have done about Ockham's opinions on natural theology. I mention these differences of interpretation only in order that, while thanking Father Boehner for his kindness in reading the chapters on Ockham, I may not give the impression that he agrees with all that I have said. Moreover, as proofs were already coming in at the time the chapters reached Father Boehner, I was unable to make as extensive a use of his suggestions as I should otherwise wish to have done. In conclusion I should like to express the hope that when Father Boehner has published the texts of Ockham which he is editing he will add a general account of the latter's philosophy. Nobody would be better qualified to interpret the thought of the last great English philosopher of the Middle Ages.

CHAPTER I

INTRODUCTION

Thirteenth century—Fourteenth century contrasted with thirteenth—Philosophies of the Renaissance—Revival of Scholasticism.

1. IN the preceding volume I traced the development of mediaeval philosophy from its birth in the pre-mediaeval period of the early Christian writers and Fathers through its growth in the early Middle Ages up to its attainment of maturity in the thirteenth century. This attainment of maturity was, as we have seen, largely due to that fuller acquaintance with Greek philosophy, particularly in the form of Aristotelianism, which took place in the twelfth century and the early part of the thirteenth. The great achievement of the thirteenth century in the intellectual field was the realization of a synthesis of reason and faith, philosophy and theology. Strictly speaking, of course, one should speak of 'syntheses' rather than of 'a synthesis', since the thought of the thirteenth century cannot legitimately be characterized with reference to one system alone; but the great systems of the period were, in spite of their differences, united by the acceptance of common principles. The thirteenth century was a period of positive constructive thinkers, of speculative theologians and philosophers, who might criticize one another's opinions in regard to this or that problem, but who at the same time were agreed in accepting fundamental metaphysical principles and the mind's power of transcending phenomena and attaining metaphysical truth. Scotus, for example, may have criticized St. Thomas's doctrines of knowledge and of analogy in certain points; but he criticized it in what he regarded, rightly or wrongly, as the interests of objectivity of knowledge and of metaphysical speculation. He considered that St. Thomas had to be corrected or supplemented in certain points; but he had no intention of criticizing the metaphysical foundations of Thomism or of undermining the objective character of philosophic speculation. Again, St. Thomas may have thought that more must be allowed to the unaided power of the human reason than was allowed to it by St. Bonaventure; but neither of these theologian-philosophers

doubted the possibility of attaining certain knowledge concerning the metaphenomenal. Men like St. Bonaventure, St. Thomas, Giles of Rome, Henry of Ghent and Duns Scotus were original thinkers; but they worked within the common framework of an ideal synthesis and harmony of theology and philosophy. They were speculative theologians and philosophers and were convinced of the possibility of forming a natural theology, the crown of metaphysics and the link with dogmatic theology; they were uninfected by any radical scepticism in regard to human knowledge. They were also realists, believing that the mind can attain an objective knowledge of essences.

This thirteenth-century ideal of system and synthesis, of harmony between philosophy and theology, can be viewed perhaps in relation to the general framework of life in that century. Nationalism was growing, of course, in the sense that the nation-States were in process of formation and consolidation; but the ideal of a harmony between papacy and empire, the supernatural and natural focuses of unity, was still alive. In fact, one can say that the ideal of harmony between papacy and empire was paralleled, on the intellectual plane, by the ideal of harmony between theology and philosophy, so that the doctrine as upheld by St. Thomas of the indirect power of the papacy in temporal matters and of the State's autonomy within what was strictly its own sphere was paralleled by the doctrine of the normative function of theology in regard to philosophy together with the autonomy of philosophy in its own sphere. Philosophy does not draw its principles from theology, but if the philosopher reaches a conclusion which is at variance with revelation, he knows that his reasoning is at fault. Papacy and empire, especially the former, were unifying factors in the ecclesiastical and political spheres, while the pre-eminence of the university of Paris was a unifying factor in the intellectual sphere. Moreover, the Aristotelian idea of the cosmos was generally accepted and helped to lend a certain appearance of fixity to the mediaeval outlook.

But though the thirteenth century may be characterized by reference to its constructive systems and its ideal of synthesis and harmony, the harmony and balance achieved were, at least from the practical standpoint, precarious. Some ardent Thomists would be convinced, no doubt, that the synthesis achieved by St. Thomas should have been universally accepted as valid and ought to have been preserved. They would not be prepared to admit that the balance and harmony of that synthesis were intrinsically precarious. But they would be prepared, I suppose, to admit that in practice it was scarcely to be expected that the Thomist synthesis, once achieved, would win universal and lasting acceptance. Moreover, there are, I think, elements inherent in the Thomist synthesis which rendered it, in a certain sense, precarious, and which help to explain the development of philosophy in the fourteenth century. I want now to illustrate what I mean.

The assertion that the most important philosophical event in mediaeval philosophy was the discovery by the Christian West of the more or less complete works of Aristotle is an assertion which could, I think, be defended. When the work of the translators of the twelfth century and of the early part of the thirteenth made the thought of Aristotle available to the Christian thinkers of western Europe, they were faced for the first time with what seemed to them a complete and inclusive rational system of philosophy which owed nothing either to Jewish or to Christian revelation, since it was the work of a Greek philosopher. They were forced, therefore, to adopt some attitude towards it: they could not simply ignore it. Some of the attitudes adopted, varying from hostility, greater or less, to enthusiastic and rather uncritical acclamation, we have seen in the preceding volume. St. Thomas Aquinas's attitude was one of critical acceptance: he attempted to reconcile Aristotelianism and Christianity, not simply, of course, in order to avert the dangerous influence of a pagan thinker or to render him innocuous by utilizing him for 'apologetic' purposes, but also because he sincerely believed that the Aristotelian philosophy was, in the main, true. Had he not believed this, he would not have adopted philosophical positions which, in the eyes of many contemporaries, appeared novel and suspicious. But the point I want to make at the moment is this, that in adopting a definite attitude towards Aristotelianism a thirteenth-century thinker was, to all intents and purposes, adopting an attitude towards *philosophy*. The significance of this fact has not always been realized by historians. Looking on mediaeval philosophers, especially those of the thirteenth century, as slavish adherents of Aristotle, they have not seen that Aristotelianism really meant, at that time, philosophy itself. Distinctions had already been drawn, it is true, between theology and philosophy; but it was the full appearance of Aristotelianism on the scene which showed the mediaevals the power and scope, as it were, of philosophy. Philosophy, under the guise of Aristotelianism, presented itself to their gaze as something which was not merely theoretically but also in historical fact independent of theology. This being so, to adopt an attitude towards Aristotelianism was, in effect, to adopt an attitude, not simply towards Aristotle as distinguished, for example, from Plato (of whom the mediaevals really did not know very much), but rather towards philosophy considered as an autonomous discipline. If we regard in this light the different attitudes adopted towards Aristotle in the thirteenth century, one obtains a profounder understanding of the significance of those differences.

(i) When the integral Aristotelians (or 'Latin Averroists') adopted the philosophy of Aristotle with uncritical enthusiasm and when they acclaimed Aristotle as the culmination of human genius, they found themselves involved in difficulties with the theologians. Aristotle held, for example, that the world was uncreated, whereas theology affirmed that the world had a beginning through divine creation. Again, Aristotle, as interpreted by Averroes, maintained that the intellect is one in all men and denied personal immortality whereas Christian theology maintained personal immortality. In face of these obvious difficulties the integral Aristotelians of the faculty of arts at Paris contended that the function of philosophy is to report faithfully the tenets of the philosophers. Therefore there was no contradiction involved in saying at the same time that philosophy, represented by Aristotle, taught the eternity of the world and the unicity of the human soul, while truth, represented by theology, affirmed the creation of the world in time and each man's possession of his individual rational soul.

This plea on the part of the integral Aristotelians or 'Averroists' that they were simply reporting the tenets of Aristotle, that is, that they were acting simply as historians, was treated by the theologians as a mere subterfuge. But, as I remarked in my second volume, it is difficult to ascertain what the mind of the Averroists really was. If, however, they really meant to do no more than report the opinions of past thinkers, and if they were sincere in affirming the truth of Christian revelation and theology, it would seem that their attitude must have been more or less this. Philosophy represents the work of the human reason reflecting on the natural order. Reason, personified by Aristotle, tells us that in the natural course of events time could have had no beginning and that the intellect would naturally be one in all men. That time had no beginning would thus be a philosophical truth; and the same must be said of monopsychism. But theology, which deals with the supernatural order, assures us that God by His divine power created the world in time and miraculously gave to each individual man his own immortal intellectual soul. It is not that something can be a fact and not a fact at the same time: it is rather that something would be a fact, were it not for God's miraculous intervention which has ensured that it is not a fact.

In regard to creative activity the position is, of course, exactly the same whether the integral Aristotelians of the faculty of arts at Paris were simply reporting Aristotle's teaching as they interpreted it, without reference to its truth or falsity, or whether they were affirming it as true. For in either case they did not add anything, at any rate not intentionally. It was the philosophers of the faculty of theology who were the productive and creative thinkers inasmuch as they felt compelled to examine Aristotelianism critically and, if they accepted it in the main, to rethink it critically. But the point I am trying to make is rather this. The position adopted by the integral Aristotelians implied a radical separation between theology and philosophy. If their own account of their activity is to be taken at its face value, they equated philosophy with history, with reporting the opinions of former philosophers. Philosophy understood in this sense is obviously independent of theology, for theology cannot affect the fact that certain opinions have been held by certain thinkers. If, on the other hand, the theologians were right in thinking that the integral Aristotelians really meant to assert the truth of the offending propositions, or if these propositions were asserted as propositions which would have been true, had not God intervened, the same conclusion concerning philosophy's complete independence of theology is implied. As the philosopher would be concerned merely with the natural course of events, he would be justified in drawing conclusions which conflicted with theological doctrine, since he would simply be asserting what would have been the case, had the natural course of events prevailed. Theology could tell us that a conclusion reached by philosophy did not represent the facts; but the theologian would not be justified in saying that the philosopher's reasoning was wrong simply because the conclusion at which he arrived was theologically unacceptable. We may learn from theology that the natural course of events has not been followed in some particular case; but that would not affect the question what the natural course of events is or would have been.

The most obviously salient features of the integral Aristotelianism or 'Averroism' of the thirteenth century were its slavish adherence to Aristotle and the rather desperate devices adopted by its adherents to square their position with the demands of theological orthodoxy. But implicit in integral Aristotelianism was a sharp separation between philosophy and theology, and an assertion of the former's complete independence. It is true that one should not over-emphasize this line of thought. The separation between theology and philosophy which was implicit in fourteenth-century Ockhamism did not derive from thirteenth-century 'Averroism'. But the appearance on the scene of the Aristotelian system in the thirteenth century was the factor which made it possible to give serious attention to the question of synthesis or separation, precisely because it led to the emergence of something which could be either synthesized or separated.

(ii) St. Thomas Aquinas recognized the distinction between philosophy and theology, in regard to both method and subject-matter. As I pointed out in the last volume, he took this distinction seriously. Though theology tells us that the world did not exist from eternity but had a beginning, no philosopher, according to St. Thomas, has ever adequately demonstrated this fact. The alleged proofs of the world's eternity are invalid, but so are the alleged proofs of the statement that the world did not exist from eternity. In other words, philosophy has not succeeded in solving the question whether the world was or was not created from eternity, though revelation does give us the answer to the question. This is an example of the real distinction which exists between philosophy and theology. On the other hand, St. Thomas certainly did not think that the philosopher could arrive, by valid rational argument, at any conclusion incompatible with Christian theology. If a philosopher arrives at a conclusion which contradicts, explicitly or implicitly, a Christian doctrine, that is a sign that his premisses are false or that there is a fallacy somewhere in his argument. In other words, theology acts as an external norm or as a kind of signpost, warning the philosopher off a cul-de-sac or blind alley. But the philosopher must not attempt to substitute data of revelation for premisses known by the philosophic reason. Nor can he make explicit use of dogma in his arguments. For philosophy is intrinsically autonomous.

In practice, this attitude meant that the philosopher who adopted it philosophized in the light of the faith, even if he did not make formal and explicit use of the faith in his philosophy. The maintenance of this attitude was, moreover, facilitated by the fact that the great thinkers of the thirteenth century were primarily theologians: they were theologian-philosophers. At the same time, once philosophy was recognized as an intrinsically autonomous discipline, it was only to be expected that it should tend in the course of time to go its own way and that it should, as it were, chafe at its bonds and resent its position as handmaid of theology. And indeed, once it had become a normal proceeding for philosophers to be primarily, and even exclusively, philosophers, it was natural that philosophy's alliance with theology should tend to disappear. Furthermore, when the philosophers had no firm belief in revelation, it was only to be expected that the positions of theology and philosophy should be reversed, and that philosophy should tend to subordinate theology to herself, to incorporate the subject-matter of theology in philosophy or even to exclude theology altogether. These developments lay, indeed, well in the future; but they may be said, without absurdity at least, to have had their remote origin in the appearance of the Aristotelian system on the scene in the early thirteenth century.

These remarks are not intended to constitute an evaluation of the Aristotelian philosophy; they are meant to be a historical interpretation of the actual course of development taken by philosophic thought. No doubt, they are somewhat too summary and do not allow for the complexity of philosophic development. Once philosophy had been recognized as an autonomous discipline, that process of self-criticism which would seem to be essential to philosophy set in, and, not unnaturally, the criticism, as it grew, undermined the foundations of the synthesis achieved in the thirteenth century. That is one of the reasons why I spoke of that synthesis as 'precarious'. Whatever one may think of the truth or falsity of Aristotelian metaphysics, for example, it was not to be expected that philosophic thought should stop at a particular point: criticism was, from the practical standpoint, inevitable. But there is a second factor to bear in mind. Once a closely-knit theological-philosophical synthesis had been achieved, in which philosophical terms and categories were used for the expression of theological truths, it was not unnatural that some minds should feel that faith was in danger of being rationalized and that Christian theology had become unduly contaminated with Greek and Islamic metaphysics. Such minds might feel that the mystical rather than the philosophical approach was what was needed, especially in view of the wrangling of the Schools on points of theoretical rather than of primarily religious significance and interest. This second line of thought would also tend to dissolve the thirteenth-century synthesis, though the approach was different from that of thinkers who concentrated on philosophical problems and undermined the synthesis by extensive and far-reaching criticism of the philosophic positions characteristic of that synthesis. We shall see how both lines of thought manifested themselves in the fourteenth century.

(iii) To turn to a different field, namely that of political life and thought. It would obviously be absurd to suggest that there was ever anything but a precarious harmony and balance between the ecclesiastical and civil powers in the Middle Ages: no profound knowledge of mediaeval history is required to be well aware of the constantly recurring disputes between pope and emperor and of the quarrels between popes and kings. The thirteenth century was enlivened by these disputes, especially by those between the emperor Frederick II and the Holy See. Nevertheless, although both parties sometimes made extravagant claims in their own favour, the quarrels were, so to speak, family quarrels: they took place within that mediaeval framework of papacy and empire which found a theoretical expression in the writings of Dante. Moreover, as far as the commonly held political theory was concerned, the distinction between the two powers was recognized. St. Thomas Aquinas who, living in Paris, was more concerned with kingdoms than with the empire, recognized the intrinsically autonomous character of temporal sovereignty, though he naturally also recognized the indirect power of the Church in temporal affairs which follows from the recognition of the superiority of the supernatural function of the Church.[1] If one keeps to the plane of theory, one can speak, therefore, of a balance or harmony between the two powers in the thirteenth century, provided that one does not obscure the fact that in practical life the harmony was not so very apparent. The plain fact is that those popes who entertained grandiose ambitions in regard to temporal power were unable to realize those ambitions, while

[1] The use of the phrase 'indirect power' involves an interpretation of Thomas's doctrine.

emperors who wished to do exactly as they chose without paying any attention to the Holy See were also unable to fulfil their desires. Triumphs on either side were temporary and not lasting. A certain balance, of a somewhat precarious nature, was therefore achieved.

At the same time, however, national kingdoms were becoming consolidated and the centralized power of national monarchs gradually increased. England had never been subject, in any practical sense, to the mediaeval emperor. Moreover, the empire was primarily a German affair; France, for instance, was independent; and the course taken by the dispute between Boniface VIII and Philip the Fair of France at the close of the thirteenth century showed clearly enough the position of France in relation both to the Holy See and to the empire. This growth of national kingdoms meant the emergence of a factor which would eventually destroy the traditional balance of papacy and empire. In the fourteenth century we witness the reflection, on the plane of theory, of the civil authority's growing tendency to assert its independence of the Church. The emergence of the strong national States, which became such a prominent feature of post-mediaeval Europe, began in the Middle Ages. They could hardly have developed in the way they did without the centralization and consolidation of power in the hands of local monarchs; and the process of this centralization and consolidation of power was certainly not retarded by the humiliation to which the papacy was exposed in the fourteenth century through the 'Babylonish captivity', when the popes were at Avignon (1305–77), and through the succeeding calamity of the 'Great Schism', which began in 1378.

The Aristotelian theory of the State could be, and was, utilized within the framework of the two-powers scheme by a thirteenth-century thinker like St. Thomas. This facilitated the theoretical recognition of the State as an intrinsically autonomous society, though it had to be supplemented by a Christian idea of the end of man and of the status and function of the Church. This 'addition' was not, however, simply an addition or juxtaposition; for it profoundly modified, by implication at least, the Greek outlook on the State. Conversely, by emphasizing the Aristotelianism in mediaeval political theory the position of the State could be stressed in such a way as practically to reverse the typical mediaeval conception of the proper relation between the two powers. We can see an example of this in the fourteenth century in the political theory of Marsilius of Padua. To say this is not to say, however, that Marsilius's theory was due to the Aristotelian philosophy: it was due much more, as we shall see later, to reflection on concrete historical events and situations. But it does mean that the Aristotelian theory of the State was a double-edged weapon; and that it not only could be but was utilized in a manner foreign to the mind of a theologian-philosopher like Aquinas. Its use represented, indeed, the growing political consciousness; and the phases of its use expressed the phases of the growth of that consciousness in concrete historical development.

2. If the thirteenth century was the period of creative and original thinkers, the fourteenth century may be called, in contrast, the period of Schools. The Dominicans naturally tended to adhere to the doctrines of St. Thomas Aquinas: and a series of injunctions by various Dominican Chapters encouraged them to do so. A number of works on the texts of St. Thomas appeared. Thus, at the request of Pope John XXII, Joannes Dominici composed an *Abbreviatio* or compendium of the *Summa theologica*, which he finished in 1331, while another Dominican, Benedict of Assignano (d. 1339), wrote a *Concordance*, in which he tried to show how the doctrine of the *Summa theologica* harmonized with that of St. Thomas's commentary on the *Sentences*. Then there were the commentators on, or interpreters of, St. Thomas, Dominicans like Hervaeus Natalis (d. 1323), who wrote a *Defensa doctrinae D. Thomae* and attacked Henry of Ghent, Duns Scotus and others, or John of Naples (d. 1330). But it was the fifteenth century, with John Capreolus (c. 1380-1444), rather than the fourteenth century, which was distinguished for achievement in this field. Capreolus was the most eminent commentator on St. Thomas before Cajetan (1468-1534).

Besides the Thomists there were the Scotists, who formed a rival school to the former, though Duns Scotus was not, in the fourteenth century, the official Doctor of the Franciscans in the same way that St. Thomas was the official Doctor of the Dominicans. In addition, there were the Hermits of St. Augustine, who followed the teaching of Giles of Rome. Henry of Ghent also had his followers, though they did not form a compact school.

In the fourteenth century these groups together with those who followed other thirteenth-century thinkers more or less closely represented the *via antiqua*. They lived on the thought of the preceding century. But at the same time there arose and spread in the fourteenth century a new movement, associated for ever with the name of William of Ockham. The thinkers of this new movement, the *via moderna*, which naturally possessed all the charm of 'modernity', opposed the realism of the earlier schools and became known as the 'nominalists'. This appellation is in some respects not very apposite, since William of Ockham, for example, did not deny that there are universal concepts in some sense; but the word is universally employed and will doubtless continue to be employed. There is not much point, then, in attempting to change it, though a better name is 'terminists'. The logicians of the new movement gave great attention to the logical status and function of terms. It is true that they strongly opposed and criticized the realism of earlier philosophers, particularly that of Duns Scotus; but it would be an over-simplification of their anti-realism to say that it consisted in attributing universality to 'names' or words alone.

It would, however, be a grossly inadequate description if one contented oneself with saying that the fourteenth-century nominalists attacked the realism of the thirteenth-century philosophers. The nominalist movement possessed a significance and an importance which cannot be adequately expressed by reference to one particular controversy. It constituted the wedge which was driven between theology and philosophy, and which broke apart the synthesis achieved in the thirteenth century. The nominalist spirit, if one may so speak, was inclined to analysis rather than to synthesis, and to criticism rather than to speculation. Through their critical analysis of the metaphysical ideas and arguments of their predecessors the nominalists left faith hanging in the air, without (so far as philosophy is concerned) any rational basis. A broad generalization of this sort has, of course, the defects attaching to such generalizations; it does not apply to all thinkers who were influenced by nominalism; but it indicates the result of the more extreme tendencies in the movement.

Philosophy can hardly live without the analytic and critical spirit: at least, critical analysis is one of the 'moments' of philosophic thought, and it is natural that it should follow a period of constructive synthesis. As we have seen, the spirit was present, to a certain extent, in the thought of Duns Scotus, who maintained, for example, that the proofs of the soul's immortality are not absolutely conclusive and that a number of the divine attributes often held to be demonstrable cannot really be demonstrated. But it must be noted that Scotus was a metaphysician who argued as a metaphysician. It is true that he was, like other mediaeval metaphysicians, a logician; but the logician had not, with him, begun to take the place of the metaphysician: his system belongs to the group of thirteenth-century metaphysical syntheses. In the fourteenth century, however, a change can be observed. Metaphysics, while not abandoned, tends to give place to logic; and questions which were formerly treated as metaphysical questions are treated primarily as logical questions. When William of Ockham tackles the subject of universals, he places the emphasis on the logical aspects of the question, on the *suppositio* and *significatio terminorum* rather than on the ontological aspects. Ockham seems to have been convinced of his fidelity to the exigencies of the Aristotelian logic; and one can even say that it was in the name of the Aristotelian logic, or of what he regarded as such, that Ockham criticized the metaphysics of predecessors like Duns Scotus and Thomas Aquinas. One can, of course, devote oneself to logical studies without troubling about metaphysics, and some of the Oxford logicians of the fourteenth century seem to have done so. But one can also go on to criticize metaphysical arguments and proofs in the name of logic, and this is what Ockham did. As we shall see, he to all intents and purposes undermined the natural theology and metaphysical psychology of his predecessors. In his opinion, the alleged proofs or demonstrations of God's attributes or of the spirituality and immortality of the soul either rest on principles the truth of which is not self-evident or terminate in conclusions which do not strictly follow from the relevant premisses. Ockham admitted, indeed, that some metaphysical arguments are 'probable'; but this simply illustrates the tendency in the fourteenth century to substitute probable arguments for demonstrations.

This substitution of probable arguments was connected, of course, with the nominalist tendency to doubt or to deny the validity of inferring from the existence of one thing the existence of another. Ockham stressed the primacy of intuition of the existent individual thing. In regard to a thing's existence the first question to ask, then, is whether we intuit it as existent. In the case of the spiritual soul, for example, Ockham would deny that we have any such intuition. The question then arises whether we can argue with certainty to the existence of the spiritual soul from the intuitions we do have. Ockham did not think this possible. He did not indeed make a purely phenomenalistic analysis of causality: he used the principle himself in metaphysics: but the later 'extremists', like Nicholas of Autrecourt, did give such an analysis. The result was that they questioned our knowledge of the existence of material substance, and probably also of the spiritual soul. In fact, no logical inference from the existence of one thing to the existence of another could amount to a 'demonstration' or cogent proof. In this way the whole metaphysical system of the thirteenth century was discredited.

This thoroughgoing criticism of the preceding metaphysical systems obviously involved a breach in the synthesis of theology and philosophy which had been a characteristic of those systems. St. Thomas, for example, even if he treated the philosophical arguments for the existence of God in works which were only in part philosophical, as distinct from theological, was certainly convinced that valid metaphysical arguments can be given for God's existence. These arguments belong to the *praeambula fidei*, in the sense that the acceptance of divine revelation logically presupposes the knowledge that a God exists who is capable of revealing Himself, a knowledge which can be gained in abstraction from theology. But if, as a number of the fourteenth-century philosophers believed, no cogent proof or demonstration of God's existence can be given, the very existence of God has to be relegated to the sphere of faith. Two consequences follow. First of all, theology and philosophy tend to fall apart. Of course, this consequence might be avoided, were the whole idea of philosophic 'proof' to be revised, but if the choice lies between demonstration and faith, and if the demonstrability of the 'preambles' of faith is denied, the consequence can scarcely be avoided. Secondly, if the important problems of traditional metaphysics, problems which linked philosophy with theology and religion, are relegated to the sphere of faith, philosophy tends to take on more and more a 'lay' character. This consequence did not become very apparent with Ockham himself, since he was a theologian as well as a philosopher, but it became more apparent with certain other fourteenth-century thinkers, like Nicholas of Autrecourt, who belonged to the faculty of arts.

To say that a thirteenth-century philosopher like St. Thomas was preoccupied with 'apologetics' would be untrue and anachronistic. None the less, though not preoccupied with apologetics in the way some Christian thinkers of a later age have been, he was certainly concerned with the relation between philosophy and revelation. Alive to the contemporary currents of thought and to the controversies of his time, he was prepared neither to reject the new Aristotelian metaphysics in the name of Christian tradition nor to pursue philosophic reflection without any regard to its bearing on Christian theology. He was careful to synthesize dogmatic theology on the one hand with his philosophy on the other, and to show the link between them. When we come to William of Ockham in the fourteenth century however, we find a marked absence of any concern for 'apologetics'. We find, indeed, a theologian who considered that his predecessors had obscured or overlaid Christian truths with false metaphysics; but we find also a philosopher who was quite content to apply his principles in a logical and consistent manner, without appearing to care, or perhaps fully to realize, the implications in regard to the synthesis between theology and philosophy. Truths which he believed but which he did not think could be philosophically proved he relegated to the sphere of faith. By assigning to the sphere of faith the truth that there exists an absolutely supreme, infinite, free, omniscient and omnipotent Being, he snapped the link between metaphysics and theology which had been provided by Aquinas's doctrine of the provable *praeambula fidei*. By making the moral law dependent on the free divine choice he implied, whether he realized it or not, that without revelation man can have no certain knowledge even of the present moral order established by God. The best that man could do, unaided by revelation, would presumably be to reflect on the needs of human nature and human society and follow the dictates of his practical reason, even though those dictates might not represent the divine will. This would imply the possibility of two ethics, the moral order established by God but knowable only by revelation, and a provisional and second-class natural and non-theological ethic worked out by the human reason without revelation. I do not mean to say that Ockham actually drew this conclusion from his authoritarian conception of the moral law; but it was, I think, implicit in that conception. To make these observations is not of itself, of course, to make a statement either in favour of or against the validity of Ockham's philosophical arguments; but it is as well to draw attention to the lack of apologetic preoccupations in Ockham. He was a theologian and a philosopher and a political and ecclesiastical pamphleteer; but he was not an 'apologist', not even in the senses in which Aquinas can reasonably be called an 'apologist', and still less in the modern sense of the word.

Some philosophers in the fourteenth century endeavoured to bridge the threatening gap between theology and philosophy by extending Henry of Ghent's theory of 'illumination'. Thus Hugolino of Orvieto (d. 1373), a Hermit of St. Augustine, distinguished certain degrees of illumination, and maintained that Aristotle, for example, was enlightened by a special divine illumination which enabled him to know something of God and of certain of His attributes. Others, however, turned to mysticism and concentrated their attention on a speculative treatment of the relation of the world to God and, in particular, of the relation of the human soul to God. This movement of speculative mysticism, the chief representative of which was the German Dominican Meister Eckhart, was, as we shall see later, very far from being simply a reaction to the arid wranglings of the Schools or a flight from scepticism to the safe haven of piety; but it was, none the less, a feature of the fourteenth century, quite distinct from the more academic philosophy of the universities.

An important feature of fourteenth-century university life, particularly at Paris, was the growth of science. Something will be said about this later on, though only a brief treatment of this theme can be expected in a history of philosophy. The development of mathematical and scientific studies by such fourteenth-century figures as Nicholas of Oresme, Albert of Saxony and Marsilius of Inghen is generally associated with the Ockhamist movement; and thus it is regarded as a feature of the fourteenth, as contrasted with the thirteenth, century. There is certainly truth in this contention, not so much because William of Ockham showed any particular interest in empirical science or because the fourteenth-century scientists accepted all the Ockhamist positions as because the Ockhamist philosophy should, of its very nature, have favoured the growth of empirical science. William of Ockham had a strong belief in the primacy of intuition, that is, in the primacy of intuition of the individual thing: all real knowledge is ultimately founded on intuitive knowledge of individual existents. Moreover, the only adequate ground for asserting a causal relation between two phenomena is observation of regular sequence. These two theses tend of themselves to favour empirical observation and a fresh approach to scientific questions. And in point of fact we do find that the leading figures in fourteenth-century science were associated in some way, though sometimes rather loosely, with the 'modern way'.

At the same time one is not justified in asserting without qualification that a rudimentary appreciation of physical science was peculiar to the fourteenth century, as contrasted with the thirteenth, or that the scientific studies associated with the Ockhamist movement were the direct progenitors of Renaissance science. Already in the thirteenth century interest had been taken in the Latin translations of Greek and Arabic scientific works, and original observations and experiments had been made. We have only to think of men like Albert the Great, Peter of Maricourt and Roger Bacon. In the following century criticism of Aristotle's physical theories coupled with further original reflection and even experiment led to the putting forward of new explanations and hypotheses in physics; and the investigations of the physicists associated with the Ockhamist movement passed in the fifteenth century to northern Italy. The science of the universities of northern Italy certainly influenced the great scientists of the Renaissance, like Galileo; but it would be a mistake to think that Galileo's work was nothing but a continuation of 'Ockhamist' science, though it would be also a mistake to think that it was not influenced by the latter. For one thing, Galileo was able to achieve his results only through a use of mathematics which was unknown in the fourteenth century. This use was facilitated by the translation, at the time of the Renaissance, of works by Greek mathematicians and physicists; and Galileo was stimulated to apply mathematics to the solution of problems of motion and mechanics in a way for which the mediaeval scientists did not possess the necessary equipment. The use of mathematics as the special means of disclosing the nature of physical reality led to a transformation in physical science. The old way of common-sense observation was abandoned in favour of a very different approach. Though it may sound strange to say so, physical science became less 'empirical': it was set free not only from Aristotelian physical theories but also from the common-sense idea of an observational method which had tended to prevail among earlier physicists. It is true that some continuity can be observed between thirteenth- and fourteenth-century science, and between fourteenth-century science and that of the Renaissance; but that does not alter the fact that in the last period a revolution in physical science took place.

3. Mention of the Renaissance of the fifteenth and sixteenth centuries probably still conjures up for some minds the idea of a sudden and abrupt transition and awakening, when the learning and literature of the ancient world were made available, when education began, when men began to think for themselves after the intellectual slavery of the Middle Ages, when the invention of printing made the wide dissemination of books at last possible, when the discovery of new lands broadened men's horizons and opened up new sources of wealth, and when the discovery of gunpowder conferred an inestimable blessing upon mankind.

Such a view is, of course, a considerable exaggeration. As far as the recovery of ancient literature, for example, is concerned, this began centuries before the Italian Renaissance; while in regard to thinking for oneself, it does not require a very profound knowledge of mediaeval philosophy to realize that there was plenty of original thinking in the Middle Ages. On the other hand, one should not emphasize the element of continuous transition so much that one implies that the Renaissance does not form a recognizable period or that its achievements were negligible. It is a question of looking at the matter in the light of our present knowledge of the Middle Ages and of correcting false impressions of the Renaissance, and not a question of suggesting that the word 'Renaissance' is a mere word, denoting no reality. Something more on this subject will be said at a later stage; at the moment I wish to confine myself to a few introductory remarks on the philosophies of the Renaissance.

When one looks at mediaeval philosophy, one certainly sees variety; but it is a variety within a common pattern, or at least it is a variety set against a common and well-defined background. There was certainly original thought; but none the less one gets the impression of a common effort, of what one may call teamwork. The thirteenth-century philosophers criticized one another's opinions; but they accepted not only the same religious faith but also, for the most part, the same metaphysical principles. One thus obtains the impression of a philosophical development which was carried on by men of independent minds but which was at the same time a common development, to which the individual philosophers made their several contributions. Even in the fourteenth century the *via moderna* was so widespread a movement as to grow in the course of time into a more or less hardened 'school', taking its place along with Thomism, Scotism and Augustinianism.

When one looks at Renaissance philosophy, however, one is faced at first sight with a rather bewildering assortment of philosophies. One finds for instance Platonists, Aristotelians of various kinds, anti-Aristotelians, Stoics, sceptics, eclectics and philosophers of nature. One can separate the philosophies into various general currents of thought, it is true, even if it is rather difficult to know to which current one should assign a particular thinker; but the over-all impression is one of a pullulating individualism. And this impression is, in many respects, correct. The gradual breakdown of the framework of mediaeval society and the loosening of the bonds between men which helped to produce a more or less common outlook; the transition to new forms of society, sometimes separated from one another by religious differences; the new inventions and discoveries; all this was accompanied by a marked individualism in philosophic reflection. The feeling of discovery, of adventure, was in the air; and it was reflected in philosophy. To say this is not to retract what I have already said about the inadequacy of regarding the Renaissance as without roots in the past. It had its roots in the past and it passed through several phases, as we shall see later; but this does not mean that a new spirit did not come into being at the time of the Renaissance, though it would be more accurate to say that a spirit which had manifested itself to a certain extent at an earlier date showed an outburst of vitality at the time of the Renaissance. For example, the recovery of the classical literature had started at a much earlier date, within the Middle Ages, as has already been remarked; but historians, while rightly emphasizing this fact, have also rightly pointed out that in regard to the Renaissance the important point is not so much that numbers of fresh texts were made available as that the texts were read in a new light. It was a question of appreciating the texts and the thought therein contained for themselves and not just as possible sources of Christian edification or disedification. The bulk of Renaissance thinkers, scholars and scientists were, of course, Christians; and it is as well to remember the fact; but none the less the classical revival, or perhaps rather the Renaissance phase of the classical revival, helped to bring to the fore a conception of autonomous man or an idea of the development of the human personality which, though generally Christian, was more 'naturalistic' and less ascetic than the mediaeval conception. And this idea favoured the growth of individualism. Even among writers who were devout

Christians one can discern the conviction that a new age for man was beginning. This conviction was not due simply to classical studies, of course; it was due to the complex of historical changes which were taking place at the Renaissance.

It was at the time of the Renaissance that the works of Plato and Plotinus were translated, by Marsilius Ficinus; and in the earlier phase of the period an attempt was made to form a philosophical synthesis of Platonic inspiration. The Platonic philosophers were, for the most part, Christians; but, very naturally, Platonism was looked on as a kind of antithesis to Aristotelianism. At the same time another group of humanists, influenced by the Latin classical literature, attacked the Aristotelian logic and Scholastic abstractions in the name of good taste, realism and the feeling for the concrete, rhetoric and literary exposition. A new idea of education by means of classical literature rather than by abstract philosophy was taking shape. Polite and humanistic scepticism was represented by Montaigne, while Justus Lipsius revived Stoicism and Pierre Gassendi Epicureanism. The Aristotelians of the Renaissance, apart from the Scholastics, were meanwhile divided among themselves into the Averroists and those who favoured the interpretation of Aristotle given by Alexander of Aphrodisias. These latter favoured an interpretation of Aristotle's psychology which led to the denial of human immortality, even the impersonal immortality admitted by the Averroists. Pomponazzi, the chief figure of this group, drew the conclusion that man has a purely terrestrial moral end. At the same time he professed to be a believing Christian and so had to make a rigid division between theological and philosophical truth.

The philosophies which took the form of revivals of classical thought tended to accustom people to an idea of man which had no very obvious connection with Christianity and which was sometimes frankly naturalistic, even if the authors of these naturalistic pictures of man were generally Christians. An analogous process of development went on in regard to the philosophy of nature. Whereas certain forms of Oriental thought would scarcely favour the study of nature, owing to the notion that the phenomenal world is illusion or mere 'appearance', Christian philosophy favoured in a sense the investigation of nature, or at least set no theoretical bar to it, because it regarded the material world not only as real but also as the creation of God, and so as worthy of study. At the same time the emphasis laid by a Christian theologian, philosopher and saint like Bonaventure on the religious orientation of man led to a natural concentration on those aspects of the material world which could be most easily looked on not only as manifestations of God but also as means to elevate the mind from the material to the spiritual. The saint was not particularly interested in studying the world for its own sake: he was much more interested in detecting in it the mirror of the divine. Nevertheless, Christian philosophy, apart from this natural concentration of interest, was not radically hostile to the study of the world; and in the case of thirteenth-century philosophers like St. Albert the Great and Roger Bacon we find a combination of the spiritual outlook with an interest in the empirical study of nature. In the fourteenth century we find this interest in scientific studies growing, in association with the Ockhamist movement and favoured by the rift which was introduced into the thirteenth-century synthesis of theology and philosophy. The way was being prepared for a philosophy of nature which, while not necessarily anti-Christian, emphasized nature as an intelligible totality governed by its own immanent laws. It might perhaps be better to say that the way was being gradually prepared for the scientific study of nature, which was in the course of time, though only at a later period, to shed the name of 'natural philosophy' or 'experimental philosophy' and to become conscious of itself as a separate discipline, or set of disciplines, with its own method or methods. But at the time of the Renaissance we find a number of philosophies of nature arising which stand apart from the development of physical science as such, in that they are characterized by a marked speculative trait which sometimes manifested itself in fanciful and bizarre ideas. These philosophies varied from the Christian and strongly Platonic or neo-Platonic philosophy of a Nicholas of Cusa to the pantheistic philosophy of a Giordano Bruno. But they were marked by common characteristics, by a belief, for example, in nature as a developing system which was infinite, or potentially infinite, and which was regarded either as the created infinite, mirroring the uncreated and divine infinite, or as itself in some sense divine. God was certainly not denied; but the emphasis was placed, in varying degrees with different philosophers, on nature itself. Nature tended to be looked on as the macrocosm and man as the microcosm. This was, indeed, an old idea, going back to Greek times; but it represented a change of emphasis from that characteristic of the mediaeval outlook. In other words, there was a tendency to regard nature as an autonomous system, even though nature's dependence on God was not denied. The bizarre and fantastic aspects of some of these philosophies may tend to make one impatient of them and their authors; but they are of importance in that they marked the rise of a new direction of interest and because of the fact that they formed a kind of mental background against which the purely scientific study of nature could go forward. Indeed, it was against the background of these philosophies, which were the ancestors of philosophies like those of Spinoza and Leibniz, rather than against the background of fourteenth-century Ockhamism, that the great advances of the scientific phase of the Renaissance were achieved. Not infrequently the philosophers anticipated speculatively hypotheses which the physicists were to verify or confirm. Even Newton, it may be remembered, looked upon himself as a philosopher.

When we turn to the Renaissance scientists, we find them interested primarily in knowledge for its own sake. But at the same time it was a characteristic of some Renaissance thinkers to emphasize the practical fruits of knowledge. The new scientific discoveries and the opening up of the new world naturally suggested a contrast between a knowledge of nature, gained by study of her laws and making possible a use of nature for man's benefit, and the older abstract discipline which seemed devoid of practical utility. Study of final causes gets one nowhere; study of efficient causes enables one to control nature and to extend man's dominion over nature. The best-known expression of this outlook is to be found in the writings of Francis Bacon (d. 1626), who, though often assigned to 'modern philosophy', may reasonably be assigned to the Renaissance period. (Distinctions of this sort are to a certain extent a matter of personal choice, of course.) It would be a mistake to father this sort of attitude on the great scientific figures; but it is an attitude which has come to dominate a great part of the modern mentality. One can detect it even in some of the political thinkers of the Renaissance. Machiavelli (d. 1527), for example, neglecting theoretical problems of sovereignty and of the nature of the state in favour of 'realism' wrote his *Prince* as a text for princes who wanted to know how to conserve and augment their power.

Finally, one has to consider the great scientific figures, like Kepler and Galileo, who laid the foundations of the classical science of the modern era, the Newtonian science, as it is often known. If the first phase of the Renaissance was that of Italian humanism, the last was that of the growth of modern science. This development came to exercise a profound influence not only on philosophy but also on the modern mentality in general. But of this influence it will be more proper to speak in other volumes.

4. Martin Luther was very strongly anti-Aristotelian and anti-Scholastic; but Melanchthon, his most eminent disciple and associate, was a humanist who introduced into Lutheran Protestantism a humanistic Aristotelianism set to the service of religion. The Reformers were naturally much more concerned with religion and theology than with philosophy; and men like Luther and Calvin could hardly be expected to have very much sympathy with the predominantly aesthetic attitude of the humanists, even though Protestantism stressed the need for education and had to come to terms with humanism in the educational field.

However, though humanism, a movement which was unsympathetic to Scholasticism, began in Catholic Italy, and though the greatest figures of humanism in northern Europe, Erasmus above all, but also men like Thomas More in England, were Catholics, the late Renaissance witnessed a revival of Scholasticism, a brief treatment of which I have included in the present volume. The centre of this revival was, significantly, Spain, a country which was not much affected either by the religious upheavals and divisions which afflicted so much of Europe or, indeed, by Renaissance philosophy. The revival came at the end of the fifteenth century, with Thomas de Vio (d. 1534), known as Cajetan, De Sylvestris (d. 1520) and others; and in the sixteenth century we find two principal groups, the Dominican group, represented by writers like Francis of Vitoria (d. 1546), Dominic Soto (d. 1560), Melchior Cano (d. 1566), and Dominic Báñez (d. 1640), and the Jesuit group, represented, for example, by Toletus (d. 1596), Molina (d. 1600), Bellarmine (d. 1621), and Suárez (d. 1617). The most important of these late Scholastics is probably Suárez, of whose philosophy I shall give a more extended treatment than in the case of any of the others.

The themes treated by the Renaissance Scholastics were for the most part those themes and problems already set by preceding mediaeval Scholasticism; and if one looks at the extensive works of Suárez, one finds abundant evidence of the author's very wide knowledge of preceding philosophies. The rise of Protestantism naturally led the Scholastic theologians to discuss relevant theological problems which had their repercussions in the field of philosophy; but the Scholastics were not much affected by the characteristically Renaissance philosophies. A thinker like Suárez bears more resemblance to the theologian-philosophers of the thirteenth century than to the intellectual free-lances of the Renaissance. Yet, as we shall see later, contemporary movements influenced Suárez in two ways at least. First, the old philosophical method of commenting on a text was abandoned by him in his *Metaphysical Disputations* for a continuous discussion in a more modern, even if, it must be confessed, somewhat prolix style. Philosophy came to be treated, not in predominantly or largely theological works, but in separate treatises. Secondly, the rise of national states was reflected in a fresh development of political theory and of the philosophy of law, of a much more thorough character than anything produced by mediaeval Scholasticism. In this connection one thinks naturally of the study of international law by the Dominican Francis of Vitoria and of Suárez' treatise on law.

PART I
THE FOURTEENTH CENTURY

CHAPTER II
DURANDUS AND PETRUS AUREOLI

*James of Metz—Durandus—Petrus Aureoli—Henry of Harclay
—The relation of these thinkers to Ockhamism.*

1. ONE is naturally inclined to think that all the theologians and philosophers of the Dominican Order in the late Middle Ages followed the teaching of St. Thomas Aquinas. In 1279 those who did not embrace Thomism were forbidden by the Chapter of Paris to condemn it, and in 1286 the same Chapter enacted that non-Thomists should be removed from their chairs. In the following century the Chapters of Saragossa (1309) and of Metz (1313) made it obligatory to accept the teaching of St. Thomas (who was not canonized until 1323). But these enactments did not succeed in making all Dominicans conform. Leaving out of account Meister Eckhart, whose philosophy will be discussed in the chapter on speculative mysticism, one may mention among the dissentients James of Metz, though his two commentaries on the *Sentences* of Peter Lombard, which seem to have been composed the one before 1295 and the other in 1302, antedated the official imposition of Thomism on members of the Order.

James of Metz was not an anti-Thomist in the sense of being an opponent of St. Thomas's teaching in general; nor was he a philosophic revolutionary; but he did not hesitate to depart from the teaching of St. Thomas and to question that teaching when he saw fit. For example, he did not accept the Thomist view of matter as the principle of individuation. It is form which gives unity to the substance and so constitutes it; and we must accordingly recognize form as the principle of individuation, since individuality presupposes substantiality. James of Metz appears to have been influenced by thinkers like Henry of Ghent and Peter of Auvergne. Thus he developed Henry's idea of the 'modes of being' (*modi essendi*). There are three modes of being, that of substance, that of real accident (quantity and quality) and that of relation. The modes are distinct from one another; but they are not things which together with their foundations make up composite beings. Thus relation is a mode of being which relates a substance or an absolute accident to the term of the relation: it is not itself a thing. Most relations, like similarity, for example, or equality, are mental: the causal relation is the only 'real' relation, independent of our thought. James was something of an eclectic; and his divagations from the teaching of St. Thomas called forth criticism and reproof from the pen of Hervé Nédellec,[1] a Dominican who published a *Correctorium fratris Jacobi Metensis*.

2. Durandus (Durand de Saint-Pourçain) was much more of an *enfant terrible* than was James of Metz. Born between 1270 and 1275, he entered the Dominican Order and did his studies at Paris, where he is supposed to have followed the lectures of James of Metz. At the beginning of the first edition of his commentary on the *Sentences* he laid down the principle that the proper procedure in speaking and writing of things which do not touch the Faith is to rely on reason rather than on the authority of any Doctor however famous or grave. Armed with this principle Durandus proceeded on his way, to the displeasure of his Dominican colleagues. He then published a second edition of his commentary, omitting the offending propositions; but nothing was gained thereby, for the first edition continued in circulation. The Dominican Chapter of Metz condemned his peculiar opinions in 1313, and in 1314 a commission presided over by Hervé Nédellec censured 91 propositions taken from the first edition of Durandus's commentary. The latter, who was at this time a lecturer at the papal court of Avignon, defended himself in his *Excusationes*; but Hervé Nédellec pursued the attack in his *Reprobationes excusationum Durandi* and followed it up by attacking Durandus's teaching at Avignon. In 1316 the Dominican General Chapter at Montpellier, considering that a 'remedy' should be provided for this shocking state of affairs, drew up a list of 235 points on which Durandus had differed from the teaching of St. Thomas. In 1317 Durandus became Bishop of Limoux, being translated to Puy in 1318 and finally to Meaux in 1326. Strengthened by his episcopal position, he published, sometime after 1317, a third edition of his commentary on the *Sentences*, in which he returned, in part, to the positions he had once retracted. One can safely assume that he had always continued to hold the theories in question. As a matter

---

[1] i.e. Hervaeus Natalis, who became Master-General of the Dominicans in 1318.

of fact, though possessed of an independent spirit in regard to St. Thomas's teaching, Durandus was not a revolutionary. He was influenced by the doctrine of Henry of Ghent, for example, while on some points he spoke like an Augustinian. In 1326, when Bishop of Meaux, he was a member of the commission which censured 51 propositions taken from William of Ockham's commentary on the *Sentences*. He died in 1332.

One of Durandus's opinions which offended his critics concerned relations. For Durandus, as for James of Metz, relation is a *modus essendi*, a mode of being. Henry of Ghent, as we have seen, had distinguished three modes of being, that of a substance, that of an absolute accident (quantity and quality) which inheres in a substance, and that of a relation. A relation was regarded by Henry as being a kind of internal tendency of a being towards another being. As far as the real being of a relation is concerned, then, it is reducible to the being of a substance or of a real accident; and the Aristotelian categories are to be regarded as comprising substance, quantity, quality, relation, and the six subdivisions of relation. This doctrine of the three basic modes of being was adopted by James of Metz and Durandus. As the modes of being are really distinct, it follows that the relation is really distinct from its foundation. On the other hand, as the relation is simply the foundation or subject in its relatedness to something else,[1] it cannot properly be a 'thing' or 'creature'; at least, it cannot enter into composition with its foundation.[2] There is a real relation only when a being related to another possesses an objective, internal exigency for this relatedness. This means that there is a real relation, so far as creatures are concerned, only when there is real dependence; and it follows therefore that the causal relation is the only real relation in creatures.[3] Similarity, equality and all relations other than the causal relation are purely conceptual; they are not real relations.

Durandus applied this doctrine to knowledge. The act of knowing is not an absolute accident which inheres in the soul, as St. Thomas thought; it is a *modus essendi* which does not add anything to the intellect or make it more perfect. 'It must be said

---

[1] The relation is a *modus essendi ad aliud, qui est ipse respectus relationis*. 1 *Sent*. (A), 33, 1.
[2] *Relatio est alia res a suo fundamento, et tamen non facit compositionem*. Ibid.
[3] *Relata realia ex natura sui fundamenti habent inter se necessariam coexigentiam ratione fundamenti*. Ibid. (A), 31, 1. *In creaturis realis relatio requirit dependentiam in relato*. Ibid. (A), 30, 2.

that sensation and understanding do not imply the addition to the sense and the intellect of anything real which enters into composition with them.'[1] Sensation and understanding are immanent acts which are really identical with the sense and the intellect. Why did Durandus hold this? Because he considered that to maintain that the soul, when it enters into cognitive relation with an object, receives accidents by way of addition is to imply that an external object can act on a spiritual principle or a non-living object on a living subject, a view which he calls 'ridiculous'. Durandus's thought on this matter is clearly of Augustinian inspiration. For example, one of the reasons why St. Augustine maintained that sensation is an act of the soul alone was the impossibility of a material thing acting on the soul. The object is a *conditio sine qua non*, but not a cause, of knowledge; the intellect itself is the cause.

From this theory of knowledge as a relation Durandus drew the conclusion that the whole apparatus of cognitive *species*, in the sense of accidental forms, can be dispensed with. It follows also that it is unnecessary to postulate an active intellect which is supposed to abstract these *species*. Similarly, Durandus got rid of 'habits' in the intellect and will, and he followed the Augustinian tradition in denying any real distinction between intellect and will.

The principal reason why Durandus got into trouble over his doctrine of relations was its application to the doctrine of the Trinity. In the first edition of his commentary on the *Sentences*[2] he asserted that there is a real distinction between the divine essence or nature and the divine relations or Persons, though in the second passage referred to he speaks with some hesitation. This opinion was condemned by the commission of 1314 as 'entirely heretical'. Durandus tried to explain away his assertions, but Hervé Nédellec drew attention to his actual words. In the Avignon *Quodlibet* he admitted that one could not properly speak of a real distinction between the divine nature and the divine internal relations: the latter are *modi essendi vel habendi essentiam divinam* and the distinction is only *secundum quid*. A renewed attack by Hervé Nédellec followed this change, and in the final edition of the commentary Durandus proposed another view.[3] There are, he says, three possible theories. First, essence and relation, though not two things, differ in that they are not the

---

[1] *Quaestio de natura cognitionis* (ed. J. Koch), p. 18.
[2] 1 *Sent.* (A), 13, 1, and 33, 1.   [3] 1 *Ibid.* (C), 33, 1.

same 'adequately and convertibly'. Secondly, essence and relation differ as thing and 'mode of possessing the thing'. This was the view of Henry of Ghent, James of Metz and, formerly, of Durandus himself. Thirdly, essence and relation differ *formaliter ex natura rei*, although they are identically the same thing. Durandus adopts this third view, that of Scotus, though he adds that he does not understand what *formaliter* means unless this view contains the other two. The first view is included, in that essence and relation, while they are the same thing, are not the same thing 'adequately and convertibly'. The second view is also included, namely that essence and relation differ as *res et modus habendi rem*. In other words, Durandus's opinion did not undergo any very startling change.

It used to be said that Durandus was a pure conceptualist in regard to universals and that he thus helped to prepare the way for Ockhamism. But it is now clear that he did not deny that there was some real foundation in things for the universal concept. He held, indeed, that it is 'frivolous to say that there is universality in things, for universality cannot be in things, but only singularity';[1] but the unity of nature which is thought by the intellect as being common to a multiplicity of objects exists really in things, though not as an objective universal. Universality belongs to concepts, but the nature which is conceived by the intellect as a universal exists really in individual things.

Durandus certainly rejected a considerable number of theories which had been maintained by St. Thomas. We have seen that he denied the doctrines of *species* and of habits or dispositions, and the real distinction between intellect and will. Moreover, in regard to the immortality of the soul he followed Scotus in saying that it is not demonstrable; or, at least, that it is difficult to demonstrate in a rigorous manner. But, as already mentioned, he was not a revolutionary even if he was an independent and critical thinker. His psychology was largely Augustinian in character and inspiration, while even his doctrine of relations was founded on that of Henry of Ghent. And in regard to universals he did not reject the position maintained by the mediaeval Aristotelians. In other words, the former picture of Durandus as a closely-related predecessor of William of Ockham has had to be abandoned, though it is true, of course, that he employed the principle of economy, known as 'Ockham's razor'.

[1] 2 *Sent.*, 3, 7, 8.

3. **Petrus Aureoli** (Pierre d'Auriole) entered the Order of Friars Minor and studied at Paris. After having lectured at Bologna (1312) and Toulouse (1314) he returned to Paris where he received the doctorate of theology in 1318. In 1321 he became Archbishop of Aix-en-Provence. He died shortly afterwards, in January 1322. His first philosophical work was the uncompleted *Tractatus de principiis naturae*, which dealt with questions of natural philosophy. His main work, a commentary on the *Sentences* of Peter Lombard, was published in two successive editions. We have also his *Quodlibeta*.

Petrus Aureoli takes his stand firmly on the statement that everything which exists is, by the very fact that it exists, an individual thing. Speaking of the dispute concerning the principle of individuation, he asserts that in reality there is no question at all to discuss, 'since every thing, by the very fact that it exists, exists as an individual thing' (*singulariter est*).[1] Conversely, if anything is common or universal or can be predicated of a plurality of objects, it is shown by that very fact to be a concept. 'Therefore to seek for something whereby an extramental object is rendered individual is to seek for nothing.'[2] For this is tantamount to asking in what way an extramental universal is individualized, when in point of fact there is no such thing as an extramental universal which could be individualized. The metaphysical problem of individuation is thus no problem at all. There is no universal outside the mind. But this does not mean that God cannot create a number of individuals of the same species; and we know, in fact, that He has done so. Material things have forms, and certain of these forms possess a quality which we call 'likeness' (*similitudo*). If it is asked what sort of a thing (*quale quid*) Socrates is, the answer is that he is a man: there is a quality of likeness in Socrates and Plato of such a kind that though there is nothing in Socrates which is in Plato, there is not in Plato anything to which there cannot be a likeness in Socrates. 'I and you are not the same; but I can be such as you are. So the Philosopher says that Callias, by generating Socrates, generates a similar being.'[3] The extramental foundation of the universal concept is this quality of likeness. Petrus Aureoli does not deny, then, that there is an objective foundation for the universal concept: what he does deny is that there is any common

---

[1] 2 *Sent.*, 9, 3, 3, p. 114, a A. Pagination is given according to the 1596 edition (Rome).
[2] *Ibid.*
[3] *Ibid.*, p. 115, a F.

reality which exists extramentally. As to immaterial forms, these can also be alike. Hence there is no reason why several angels should not belong to the same species.

The intellect, as active, assimilates to itself this likeness and, as passive, is assimilated to it, thus conceiving the thing, that is, producing an 'objective concept' (*conceptus obiectivus*). This concept is intramental, of course, and, as such, it is distinct from the thing; but on the other hand it is the thing as known. Thus Petrus Aureoli says that when the intellectual assimilation takes place 'the thing immediately receives *esse apparens*'. If the assimilation is clear, the thing will have a clear *esse apparens* or phenomenal existence; if the assimilation is obscure, the *esse apparens* will be obscure. This 'appearance' is in the intellect alone.[1] 'From the fact that a thing produces an imperfect impression of itself in the intellect, there arises the generic concept, by which the thing is conceived imperfectly and indistinctly, while from the fact that the same thing produces a perfect impression of itself in the intellect there arises the concept of (specific) difference, by which the thing is conceived in its specific and distinct existence.'[2] The 'objective' diversity of concepts is the result of the formal diversity of the impression made by one and the same object on one and the same mind. 'Therefore if you ask in what the specific unity of humanity consists, I say that it consists in humanity, not in animality, but in humanity as conceived. And in this way it is the same as the objective concept of man. But this unity exists in potency and inchoately in the extramental thing, inasmuch as the latter is capable of causing in the intellect a perfect impression like to the impression caused by another thing.'[3]

Every extramentally existing thing is individual; and it is 'nobler' to know it directly in its unique individuality than to know it by means of a universal concept. The human intellect, however, cannot grasp, directly and primarily, the thing in its incommunicable individuality, though it can know it secondarily, by means of the imagination: primarily and immediately it apprehends the form of the material thing by means of a universal concept.[4] But to say that the intellect knows the thing 'by means of a universal concept' does not mean that there is a *species intelligibilis* in the Thomist sense which acts as a *medium quo* of

[1] 2 *Sent.*, 3, 2, 4, p. 30, c F. [2] *Ibid.*, p. 66, b D.
[3] *Ibid.*, 9, 2, 3, p. 109, b A B. [4] *Ibid.*, 11, 4, 2, pp. 142–5.

knowledge. 'No real form is to be postulated as existing subjectively in the intellect, or in the imagination . . . but that form which we are conscious of beholding when we know the rose as such or the flower as such is not something real impressed subjectively on the intellect, or on the imagination; nor is it a real subsistent thing; it is the thing itself as possessing *esse intentionale*. . . .'[1] Petrus Aureoli thus dispenses with the *species intelligibilis* as *medium quo* of knowledge and insists that the intellect knows the thing itself directly. This is one reason why Étienne Gilson can say that Petrus Aureoli 'admits no other reality than that of the knowable object' and that his solution does not consist of eliminating the *species intelligibilis* in favour of the concept, but in suppressing even the concept.[2] On the other hand, the thing which is known, that is, the object of knowledge, is the extramental thing as possessing *esse intentionale* or *esse apparens*; and it acquires this *esse intentionale* through 'conception' (*conceptio*). The thing as possessing *esse intentionale* is thus the concept (that is to say, the 'objective concept' as distinguished from the 'subjective concept' or psychological act as such); and it follows that the concept is the object of knowledge. 'All understanding demands the placing of a thing in *esse intentionali*', and this is the *forma specularis*.[3] 'The thing posited in *esse apparenti* is said to be conceived by the act of the intellect, indeed, it is the intellectual concept; but a concept remains within the conceiver, and is (owes its being to) the conceiver. Therefore the thing as appearing depends effectively on the act of the intellect, both in regard to production and in regard to content.'[4] Dr. B. Geyer can say, then, that 'the *species*, the *forma specularis*, is thus, according to Aureoli, no longer the *medium quo* of knowledge, as with Thomas Aquinas, but its immediate object'.[5] But, even if Petrus Aureoli may speak on occasion as though he wished to maintain a form of subjective idealism, he insists, for example, that 'health as conceived by the intellect and health as it is present extramentally are one and the same thing in reality (*realiter*), although they differ in their mode of being, since in the mind health has *esse apparens et intentionale*, while extramentally, in the body, it has *esse existens et reale*. . . . They differ in mode of being (*in modo essendi*), although they are one and the same thing.'[6]

---

[1] 1 *Sent.*, 9, 1, p. 319, a B.　　　[2] *La philosophie au moyen âge*, p. 632.
[3] 1 *Sent.*, 9, 1, p. 320, a B.　　　[4] *Ibid.*, p. 321, b B C.
[5] *Die patristische und scholastische Philosophie*, p. 526.
[6] 1 *Sent.*, 9, 1, p. 321, a D E.

'Hence it is clear that things themselves are conceived by the mind, and that that which we intuit is not another *forma specularis*, but the thing itself as having *esse apparens*; and this is the mental concept or objective idea (*notitia obiectiva*).'[1]

Knowledge, for Petrus Aureoli, is rooted in the perception of the concrete, of actually existing things. But a thing as known *is* the thing as having *esse apparens et intentionale*; it *is* the concept. According to the degree of clarity in the knowledge of the thing there arises a generic or specific concept. Genera and species, considered as universals, do not, however, exist extramentally, and are to be regarded as 'fabricated' by the mind. Petrus Aureoli may thus be called a 'conceptualist' inasmuch as he rejects any extramental existence on the part of universals; but he cannot rightly be called a 'nominalist', if 'nominalism' is taken to involve a denial of the objective similarity of natures. This is not to say, however, that he does not speak, more or less frequently, in an ambiguous and even inconsistent fashion. His idea of logic may be said to favour nominalism in that the logician is said to deal with words (*voces*). 'Therefore the logician considers them ("second intentions"), not as *entia rationis*, for it belongs to the metaphysician to decide about real being and conceptual being, but in so far as they are reduced to speech. . . .'[2] But, though the doctrine that logic is concerned with words (*voces*) may seem, if taken by itself, to favour nominalism, Petrus Aureoli adds that the logician is concerned with words as expressing concepts. 'The word, as well as the concept (*ut expressiva conceptus*), is the subject-matter of logic.'[3] In his logic, says Petrus Aureoli, Aristotle always implies that he is considering words as expressing concepts.[4] Moreover, speech, which expresses concepts, is the subject of truth and falsity: it is the sign of truth and falsity (*voces enim significant verum vel falsum in ordine ad conceptum*).[5] The theory of the *suppositio*, as formed in the terministic logic, may be implied in Petrus Aureoli's idea of logic; but he was not a 'nominalist' in metaphysics. It is true that he emphasized the qualitative similarity of things rather than the similarity of nature or essence; but he does not seem to have denied essential similarity as the foundation of the specific concept: rather did he presuppose it.

We have seen that for Petrus Aureoli conceptual knowledge is of the extramental thing in its likeness to other things rather than

---

[1] 1 *Sint.*, 9, 1, p. 321, b B.   [2] *Ibid.*, 23, 2, p. 539, a F–b A.
[3] *Prologus in Sent.*, 5, p. 66, a D.   [4] *Ibid.*, a F.   [5] *Ibid.*, a E.

of the thing precisely as individual. But it is better, he insists, to know the individual thing in its individuality than to know it by means of a universal concept. If the human intellect in its present state knows things rather *per modum abstractum et universalem* than precisely in their individuality, this is an imperfection. The individual thing can make an impression on the senses in such a way that there is sense-knowledge or intuition of the individual thing as individual; but the material thing cannot make an impression of this sort on the immaterial intellect; its form is known abstractly by the intellect, which cannot directly and immediately attain the individual thing as individual. But this does not alter the fact that an intellectual intuition or knowledge of the individual thing as individual would be more perfect than abstract and universal knowledge. 'For the knowledge which attains to the thing precisely as the thing exists is more perfect than knowledge which attains to the thing in a manner in which the thing does not exist. But it is clear that a universal thing does not exist, except in individual things and through individual things, as the Philosopher says against Plato, in the seventh book of the *Metaphysics*. . . . It is quite clear that science, which apprehends essences (*quidditates*), does not apprehend things precisely as they exist . . . but knowledge of this precise individual is knowledge of the thing as it exists. Therefore, it is nobler to know the individual thing as such (*rem individuatam et demonstratam*) than to know it in an abstract and universal way.'[1] It follows that even if the human intellect cannot have that perfect knowledge of individual things which must be attributed to God, it should approach as near thereto as possible by keeping in close contact with experience. We should adhere to 'the way of experience rather than to any logical reasonings, since science arises from experience'.[2] Petrus Aureoli also stressed inner experience of our psychic acts, and he frequently appeals to inner experience or introspection to support his statements about knowledge, volition and psychic activity in general. He shows a strong 'empiricist' bent in his treatment of universals, in his insistence on keeping close to experience, and in his interest in natural science, which is shown by the examples he takes from Aristotle and his Islamic commentators; but

[1] 1 *Sent.*, 35, 4, 2, p. 816, b C–E.
[2] *Prologus in Sent.*, prooemium, 3, p. 25, a F. Petrus Aureoli is here arguing that it is possible for an act of intuition to exist in the absence of the object. This view was also held by Ockham. The remark about keeping close to experience is incidental in the context; but it is none the less significant and enunciates a principle.

Dreiling's investigation led him to conclude that 'the empiricist tendency of Aureoli has a centripetal rather than a centrifugal direction and is turned towards the psychic life more than towards external nature'.[1]

Mention of Petrus Aureoli's appeals to introspection or inner experience leads one on to discuss his idea of the soul. First of all, it can be proved that the soul is the form of the body, in the sense that the soul is an essential part of man which together with the body makes up man. Indeed, 'no philosopher ever denied this proposition'.[2] But it cannot be proved that the soul is the form of the body in the sense that it is simply the forming and termination of matter (*formatio et terminatio materiae*) or that it makes the body to be a body. 'This has not yet been demonstrated, either by Aristotle or by the Commentator or by any other Peripatetic.'[3] In other words, it can be proved, according to Petrus Aureoli, that the soul is an essential part of man and that it is the principal part (*pars principalior*) of man; but it cannot be proved that it is simply that which makes matter to be a human body or that its relation to the body is analogous to the shape of a piece of copper. If a piece of copper is shaped into a statue, its figure may be called a form; but it is no more than the termination (*terminatio*) or figure of the copper; it is not a distinct nature. The human soul, however, is a distinct nature.

Now, Petrus Aureoli declared that a substantial form is simply the actuation of matter (*pura actuatio materiae*) and that, together with matter, it composes one simple nature.[4] It follows that if the human soul is a distinct nature and is not simply the actuation of matter, it is not a form in the same way and in the same sense that other forms are forms. 'I say, therefore, in answer to the question that it can be demonstrated that the soul is the form of the body and an essential part of us, though it is not the actuation and perfection of the body in the way that other souls are.'[5] The spiritual soul of man and the soul or vital principle of a plant, for example, are not forms in a univocal sense.

On the other hand, the Council of Vienne (1311–12) had just laid down that the intellectual or rational soul of man is 'truly, *per se* and essentially the form of the body'. So, after asserting that the human soul is not the form of the body in the same sense in which other forms which inform matter are forms, Petrus

[1] *Der Konzeptualismus . . . des Franziskanererzbischofs Petrus Aureoli*, p. 197.
[2] 2 *Sent.*, 16, 1, 1, p. 218, b.   [3] *Ibid.*, p. 219, a B.
[4] *Ibid.*, 12, 2, 1, p. 174, b D.   [5] *Ibid.*, 15, 1, 1, p. 223, a F.

Aureoli goes on to say that 'the ninth decree of the sacred Council of Vienne' has asserted the opposite, namely that 'the soul is the form of the body, just like other forms or souls'.[1] In face of this embarrassing situation Petrus Aureoli, while adhering to his position that it cannot be proved that the human soul is the form of the body in the same way that other souls are forms, declares that though this cannot be proved, it is nevertheless known by faith. He makes a comparison with the doctrine of the Trinity. This doctrine cannot be philosophically proved, but it has been revealed and we accept it on faith.[2] He allows that it cannot be demonstrated that the human soul is *not* the form of the body in the same sense that other souls are the forms of their respective matters; but he refuses to allow that it can be demonstrated that the soul *is* the form of the body in this sense. He obviously thought that reason inclines one to think that the human soul and the souls of brutes or plants are forms in an equivocal sense; and he remarks that the teaching of the Saints and Doctors of the Church would not lead one to expect the doctrine laid down by the Council; but, none the less, he accepts the Council's doctrine, as he understands it, and draws a strange conclusion. 'Although it cannot be demonstrated that the soul is the form of the body in the way that other forms (are forms of their respective matters), yet it must be held, as it seems to me, that, just as the shape of wax is the form and perfection of wax, so the soul is simply the actuation and forming of the body in the same way as other forms. And just as no cause is to be sought why from the wax and its shape there results one thing, so no cause is to be sought why from the soul and body there results one thing. Thus the soul is simply the act and perfection of matter, like the shape of the wax ... I hold this conclusion precisely on account of the decision of the Council, which, according to the apparent sense of the words, seems to mean this.'[3]

The Fathers of the Council would have been startled to hear this interpretation put on their words; but, as he interpreted the Council's decision in this way and accepted it in this sense, Petrus Aureoli obviously found himself in considerable difficulty on the subject of the human soul's immortality. 'Faith holds that the soul is separated (i.e. outlives the body); but it is difficult to see how this can be done if the soul is assumed to be like other forms, simply the actuation of matter. I say, however, that just as God

---

[1] 2 *Sent.*, 15, 1, 2, p. 223, b A–C.   [2] *Ibid.*, b E–F.   [3] *Ibid.*, p. 224, b D–F.

can separate accidents from the subject (i.e. substance), although they are no more than actuations of the subject, so He can miraculously separate the soul, although it is simply the actuation of matter.'[1] It is, indeed, necessary to say that in forms or 'pure perfections' there are degrees. If the form is extended, it can be affected (and so corrupted) by a natural extended agent; but if the form is unextended, then it cannot be affected (and so corrupted) by a natural extended agent. Now the human soul, although it is *pura perfectio materiae*, cannot be affected (i.e. corrupted) by a natural extended agent; it can be 'corrupted' only by God. This is not, however, a very satisfactory answer to the difficulty which Petrus Aureoli created for himself by his interpretation of the Council of Vienne; and he declares that our minds are not capable of understanding how the soul is naturally incorruptible if it is what the Council stated it to be.[2]

Petrus Aureoli obviously did not think that the natural immortality of the human soul can be philosophically demonstrated; and he seems to have been influenced by the attitude adopted by Duns Scotus in this matter. Various arguments have been produced to prove that the human soul is naturally immortal; but they are scarcely conclusive.[3] Thus some people have argued 'from the proportion of the object to the power' or faculty. The intellect can know an incorruptible object. Therefore the intellect is incorruptible. Therefore the substance of the soul is incorruptible. But the reply might be made that in this case the eye would be incorruptible (presumably because it sees the incorruptible heavenly bodies) or that our intellect must be infinite and uncreated because it can know God, who is infinite and uncreated. Again, others argue that there is a 'natural desire' to exist for ever and that a natural desire cannot be frustrated. Petrus Aureoli answers, like Scotus though more summarily, that the brutes too desire to continue in existence inasmuch as they shun death. The argument, if valid, would thus prove too much. Others, again, argue that justice requires the rewarding of the good and the punishment of the wicked in another life. 'This argument is moral and theological, and moreover, it is not conclusive.' For it might be answered that sin is its own punishment and virtue its own reward.

Petrus Aureoli proceeds to give some arguments of his own; but

---

[1] 2 *Sent.*, 15, 1, 2, p. 226, a E–F.   [2] *Ibid.*, p. 226, a F–b B.
[3] *Ibid.*, 19, 1, p. 246, b D.

he is not very confident as to their probative force. 'Now I give my arguments, but I do not know if they are conclusive.'[1] First of all, man can choose freely, and his free choices are not affected by the heavenly bodies nor by any material agent. Therefore the principle of this operation of free choice also is unaffected by any material agent. Secondly, we experience in ourselves immanent, and therefore spiritual operations. Therefore the substance of the soul is spiritual. But the material cannot act on the spiritual or destroy it. Therefore the soul cannot be corrupted by any material agent.

If man is truly free, it follows, according to Petrus Aureoli, that a judgment concerning a future free act is neither true nor false. 'The opinion of the Philosopher is a conclusion which has been thoroughly demonstrated, namely that no singular proposition can be formed concerning a future contingent event, concerning which proposition it can be conceded that it is true and that its opposite is false, or conversely. No proposition of the kind is either true or false.'[2] To deny this is to deny an obvious fact, to destroy the foundation of moral philosophy and to contradict human experience. If it is now true that a certain man will perform a certain free act at a certain future time, the act will necessarily be performed and it will not be a free act, since the man will not be free to act otherwise. If it is to be a free act, then it cannot now be either true or false that it will be performed.

To say this may appear to involve a denial of the 'law' that a proposition must be either true or false. If we are going to say of a proposition that it is not true, are we not compelled to say that it is false? Petrus Aureoli answers that a proposition receives its determination (that is, becomes true or false) from the being of that to which it refers. In the case of a contingent proposition relating to the future that to which the proposition refers has as yet no being: it cannot, therefore, determine the proposition to be either true or false. We can say of a given man, for example, that on Christmas day he will either drink wine or not drink wine, but we cannot affirm separately either that he will drink wine or that he will not drink wine. If we do, then the statement is neither true nor false: it cannot become true or false until the man actually drinks wine on Christmas day or fails to do so. And Petrus Aureoli appeals to Aristotle in the *De Interpretatione* (9) in support of his view.

[1] 2 *Sent.*, 19, 1, p. 247, a.   [2] 1 *Sent.*, 38, 3, p. 883, b C–D.

As to God's knowledge of future free acts, Petrus Aureoli insists that God's knowledge does not make a proposition concerning the future performance or non-performance of such acts either true or false. For example, God's foreknowledge of Peter's denial of his Master did not mean that the proposition 'Peter will deny his Master' was either true or false. Apropos of Christ's prophecy concerning Peter's threefold denial Petrus Aureoli observes: 'therefore Christ would not have spoken falsely, even had Peter not denied Him thrice'.[1] Why not? Because the proposition, 'you will deny Me thrice', could not be either true or false. Aureoli does not deny that God knows future free acts; but he insists that, although we cannot help employing the word 'foreknowledge' (*praescientia*), there is no foreknowledge, properly speaking, in God.[2] On the other hand, he rejects the view that God knows future free acts as present. According to him, God knows such acts in a manner which abstracts from past, present and future; but we cannot express the mode of God's knowledge in human language. If the problem of the relation of future free acts to God's knowledge or 'foreknowledge' of them is raised, the problem 'cannot be solved otherwise than by saying that foreknowledge does not make a proposition concerning a future contingent event a true proposition';[3] but this does not tell us what God's 'foreknowledge' is positively. 'We must bear in mind that the difficulty of this problem arises either from the poverty of human language, which cannot express statements save by propositions referring to present, past and future time, or from the condition of our mind, which is always involved in time (*qui semper est cum continuo et tempore*).'[4] Again, 'it is very difficult to find the right way of expressing the knowledge which God has of the future. . . . No proposition in which a reference is made to the future expresses the divine foreknowledge properly: indeed, such a proposition is, strictly speaking, false. . . . But we can say that it (a contingent event) was eternally known to God by a knowledge which neither was distant from that event nor preceded it', although our understanding is unable to grasp what this knowledge is in itself.[5]

It should be noted that Petrus Aureoli is not embracing the opinion of St. Thomas Aquinas, for whom God, in virtue of His eternity, knows all things as present. He admits that God knows

[1] 1 *Sent.*, 38, 3, p. 888, a B.   [2] *Ibid.*, p. 889, b A.   [3] *Ibid.*, 39, 3, p. 901, a C.
[4] *Ibid.*, a F–b A.   [5] *Ibid.*, p. 902, a F–b B.

all events eternally; but he will not allow that God knows them as present; he objects to any introduction of words like 'present', 'past' and 'future' into statements concerning God's knowledge, if these statements are meant to express the actual mode of God's knowledge. What it comes to, then, is that Petrus Aureoli affirms God's knowledge of future free acts and at the same time insists that no proposition relating to such future acts is either true or false. Exactly how God knows such acts we cannot say. It is perhaps needless to add that Petrus Aureoli rejects decisively any theory according to which God knows future free acts through the determination or decision of His divine will. In his view a theory of this kind is incompatible with human freedom. Thomas Bradwardine, whose theory was directly opposed to that of Petrus Aureoli, attacked him on this point.

Petrus Aureoli's discussion of statements concerning God's knowledge which involve a reference, explicit or implicit, to time serves as an illustration of the fact that mediaeval philosophers were not so entirely blind to problems of language and meaning as might perhaps be supposed. The language used about God in the Bible forced upon Christian thinkers at a very early date a consideration of the meaning of the terms used; and we find the mediaeval theories of analogical predication worked out as a response to this problem. The precise point which I have mentioned in connection with Petrus Aureoli should not be taken as an indication that this thinker was conscious of a problem to which other mediaeval philosophers were blind. Whether one is satisfied or not with mediaeval discussions and solutions of the problem, one could not justifiably claim that the mediaevals did not even suspect the existence of the problem.

4. Henry of Harclay, who was born about 1270, studied and taught in the university of Oxford, where he became Chancellor in 1312. He died at Avignon in 1317. He has sometimes been spoken of as a precursor of Ockhamism, that is to say of 'nominalism'; but in reality the type of theory concerning universals which he defended was rejected by Ockham as unduly realist in character. It is quite true that Henry of Harclay refused to allow that there is any common nature existing, as common, in members of the same species, and he certainly held that the universal concept as such is a production of the mind; but his polemics were directed against Scotist realism, and it was the Scotist doctrine of the *natura communis* which he rejected. The nature of any given man

is his individual nature, and it is in no way 'common'. However, existent things can be similar to one another, and it is this similarity which is the objective foundation of the universal concept. One can speak of abstracting something 'common' from things, if one means that one can consider things according to their likeness to one another. But the universality of the concept, its predicability of many individuals, is superimposed by the mind: there is nothing objectively existing in a thing which can be predicated of any other thing.

On the other hand, Henry evidently thought of the universal concept as a confused concept of the individual. An individual man, for example, can be conceived distinctly as Socrates or Plato, or he may be conceived 'confusedly' not as this or that individual, but simply as 'man'. The similarity which makes this possible is, of course, objective; but the genesis of the universal concept is due to this confused impression of individuals, while the universality, formally considered, of the concept is due to the work of the mind.

5. It is clear enough that the three thinkers, some of whose philosophical ideas we have considered in this chapter, were not revolutionaries in the sense that they set themselves against the traditional philosophical currents in general. For example, they did not manifest any marked preoccupation with purely logical questions and they did not show that mistrust of metaphysics which was characteristic of Ockhamism. They were, indeed, in varying degrees critical of the doctrine of St. Thomas. But Henry of Harclay was a secular priest, not a Dominican; and in any case he showed no particular hostility towards Thomism, though he rejected St. Thomas's doctrine concerning the principle of individuation, affirmed the older theory of a plurality of formal principles in man and protested against the attempt to make a Catholic of the 'heretical' Aristotle. Again, Petrus Aureoli was a Franciscan, not a Dominican, and he was not under any obligation to accept the teaching of St. Thomas. Of these three philosophers, then, it is only Durandus whose departures from Thomism might be called 'revolutionary'; and, even in his case, his opinions can be called 'revolutionary' only in regard to his position as a Dominican and to the obligation on the members of his Order of following the teaching of St. Thomas, the Dominican Doctor. In this restricted sense he might be called a revolutionary: he was certainly independent. Hervé Nédellec, the Dominican theologian who wrote

against Henry of Ghent and James of Metz, conducted a prolonged warfare against Durandus, while John of Naples and Peter Marsh (Petrus de Palude), both Dominicans, drew up a long list of points on which Durandus had offended against the teaching of Aquinas.[1] Bernard of Lombardy, another Dominican, also attacked Durandus; but his attack was not sustained like that of Hervé Nédellec; he admired and was partly influenced by Durandus. A sharp polemic (the *Evidentiae Durandelli contra Durandum*) came from the pen of Durandellus who was identified for a time with Durandus of Aurillac but who may have been, according to J. Koch, another Dominican, Nicholas of St. Victor.[2] But, as we have seen, Durandus did not turn against or reject the thirteenth-century tradition as such: on the contrary, his interests were in metaphysics and in psychology much more than in logic, and he was influenced by speculative philosophers like Henry of Ghent.

But, though one can hardly call Durandus or Petrus Aureoli a precursor of Ockhamism, if by this one means that the shift of emphasis from metaphysics to logic, coupled with a critical attitude towards metaphysical speculation as such, is a feature of their respective philosophies, yet it is probably true that in a broad sense they helped to prepare the way for nominalism and that they can be called, as they often have been called, transition-thinkers. It is perfectly true that Durandus, as has already been mentioned, was a member of the commission which censured a number of propositions taken from Ockham's commentary on the *Sentences*; but though this fact obviously manifests his personal disapproval of Ockham's teaching it does not prove that his own philosophy had no influence at all in favouring the spread of Ockhamism. Durandus, Petrus Aureoli and Henry of Harclay all insist that only individual things exist. It is true that St. Thomas Aquinas held precisely the same; but Petrus Aureoli drew from it the conclusion that the problem of a multiplicity of individuals within the same species is no problem at all. Quite apart from the question whether there is or is not such a problem, the resolute denial that there is a problem facilitates, I think, the taking of further steps on the road to nominalism which Petrus Aureoli himself did not take. After all, Ockham regarded his theory of universals as simply the logical conclusion of the truth that only individuals exist. Again, though it can be said with truth that Durandus's assertion that universality

---

[1] On this subject see J. Koch: *Durandus de S. Porciano O.P.*, in *Beiträge zur Gesch. des Mittelalters*, 26, 1, pp. 199 ff., Münster i. W., 1927.
[2] *Ibid.*, pp. 340-69.

belongs only to the concept and Petrus Aureoli's and Henry of Harclay's assertions that the universal concept is a fabrication of the mind and that universality has *esse obiectivum* only in the concept do not constitute a rejection of moderate realism, yet the tendency shown by Petrus Aureoli and Henry of Harclay to explain the genesis of the universal concept by reference to a confused or less clear impression of the individual does facilitate a breakaway from the theory of universals maintained by Thomas Aquinas. Further, cannot one see in these thinkers a tendency to wield what is known as 'Ockham's razor'? Durandus sacrificed the Thomist cognitive *species* (that is 'species' in its psychological sense) while Petrus Aureoli often made use of the principle *pluralitas non est ponenda sine necessitate* in order to get rid of what he regarded as superfluous entities. And Ockhamism belonged, in a sense, to this general movement of simplification. In addition, it carried further that spirit of criticism which one can observe in James of Metz, Durandus and Petrus Aureoli. Thus I think that while historical research has shown that thinkers like Durandus, Petrus Aureoli and Henry of Harclay cannot be called 'nominalists', there are aspects of their thought which enable one to link them in some degree to the general movement of thought which facilitated the spread of Ockhamism. Indeed, if one accepted Ockham's estimation of himself as a true Aristotelian and if one looked on Ockhamism as the final overthrow of all vestiges of non-Aristotelian realism, one could reasonably regard the philosophers whom we have been considering as carrying a step further the general anti-realist movement which culminated in Ockhamism. But it would be necessary to add that they were still more or less moderate realists and that in the eyes of the Ockhamists they did not proceed far enough along the anti-realist path. Ockham certainly did not regard these thinkers as 'Ockhamists' before their time.

CHAPTER III

OCKHAM (1)

Life—Works—Unity of thought.

1. WILLIAM OF OCKHAM was probably born at Ockham in Surrey, though it is possible that he was simply William Ockham and that his name had nothing to do with the village. The date of his birth is uncertain. Though usually placed between 1290 and 1300, it is possible that it took place somewhat earlier.[1] He entered the Franciscan Order and did his studies at Oxford, where he began the study of theology in 1310. If this is correct, he would have lectured on the Bible from 1315 to 1317 and on the *Sentences* from 1317 to 1319. The following years, 1319–24, were spent in study, writing and Scholastic disputation. Ockham had thus completed the studies required for the *magisterium* or doctorate; but he never actually taught as *magister regens*, doubtless because early in 1324 he was cited to appear before the pope at Avignon. His title of *inceptor* (beginner) is due to this fact that he never actually taught as doctor and professor; it has nothing at all to do with the founding of a School.[2]

In 1323 John Lutterell, former Chancellor of Oxford, arrived at Avignon where he brought to the attention of the Holy See a list of 56 propositions taken from a version of Ockham's commentary on the *Sentences*. It appears that Ockham himself, who appeared at Avignon in 1324, presented another version of the commentary, in which he had made some emendations. In any case the commission appointed to deal with the matter did not accept for

---

[1] As he seems to have been ordained subdeacon in February 1306, he was most probably born before 1290; according to P. Boehner, about 1280.
[2] P. Boehner follows Pelster in interpreting *inceptor* in the strict sense, that is to say, as meaning someone who had fulfilled all the requirements for the doctorate, but who had not taken up his duties as an actual professor. If this interpretation is accepted it is easy to explain how the *Venerabilis Inceptor* could sometimes be called *doctor*, and even *magister*; but the word *inceptor* should not, I think, be so explained as to imply that the man to whom it was applied was, or might be, an actual doctor. The word was used for a candidate for the doctorate, a 'formed bachelor', and though Ockham was qualified to take the doctorate, he does not appear to have actually taken it. As to his honorific title, *Venerabilis Inceptor*, the first word was applied to him as founder of 'nominalism', while the second, as we have seen, referred simply to his position at the time his studies at Oxford came to an end. Incidentally, there is no evidence whatever that he ever studied at Paris or took the doctorate there.

condemnation all the propositions complained of by Lutterell: in its list of 51 propositions it confined itself more or less to theological points, accepting 33 of Lutterell's propositions and adding others of its own. Some propositions were condemned as heretical, others, less important, as erroneous but not heretical; but the process was not brought to a final conclusion, perhaps because Ockham had in the meantime fled from Avignon. It has also been conjectured that the influence of Durandus, who was a member of the commission, may have been exerted in Ockham's favour, on one or two points at least.

At the beginning of December 1327 Michael of Cesena, the Franciscan General, arrived at Avignon, whither Pope John XXII had summoned him, to answer for his attacks on the papal Constitutions concerning evangelical poverty. At the instance of the General Ockham interested himself in the poverty dispute, and in May 1328 Michael of Cesena, who had just been re-elected General of the Franciscans, fled from Avignon, taking with him Bonagratia of Bergamo, Francis of Ascoli and William of Ockham. In June the pope excommunicated the four fugitives, who joined the Emperor Ludwig of Bavaria at Pisa and went with him to Munich. Thus there began Ockham's participation in the struggle between emperor and pope, a struggle in which the emperor was also assisted by Marsilius of Padua. While some of Ockham's polemics against John XXII and his successors, Benedict XII and Clement VI, concerned theological matters, the chief point of the whole dispute was, of course, the right relation of the secular to the ecclesiastical power, and to this point we shall return.

On October 11th, 1347, Ludwig of Bavaria, Ockham's protector, suddenly died, and Ockham took steps to reconcile himself with the Church. It is not necessary to suppose that his motives were merely prudential. A formula of submission was prepared but it is not known if Ockham actually signed it or whether the reconciliation was ever formally effected. Ockham died at Munich in 1349, apparently of the Black Death.

2. The commentary on the first book of the *Sentences* was written by Ockham himself, and the first edition of this *Ordinatio*[1] seems to have been composed between 1318 and 1323. The commentaries on the other three books of the *Sentences* are *reportationes*, though they also belong to an early period. Boehner

---

[1] The word *ordinatio* was used to denote the text or the part of a text which a mediaeval lecturer actually wrote or dictated with a view to publication.

thinks that they were composed before the *Ordinatio*. The *Expositio in librum Porphyrii*, the *Expositio in librum Praedicamentorum*, the *Expositio in duos libros Elenchorum* and the *Expositio in duos libros Perihermenias* appear to have been composed while Ockham was working on his commentary on the *Sentences* and to have antedated the first *Ordinatio* though not the *Reportatio*. The text of these logical works, minus the *In libros Elenchorum*, in the 1496 Bologna edition is entitled *Expositio aurea super artem veterem*. The *Expositio super octo libros Physicorum* was composed after the commentary on the *Sentences* and before the *Summa totius logicae*, which was itself composed before 1329. As to the *Compendium logicae*, its authenticity has been questioned.

Ockham also composed *Summulae in libros Physicorum* (or *Philosophia naturalis*) and *Quaestiones in libros Physicorum*. As to the *Tractatus de successivis*, this is a compilation made by another hand from an authentic work of Ockham, namely the *Expositio super libros Physicorum*. Boehner makes it clear that it can be used as a source for Ockham's doctrine. 'Almost every line was written by Ockham, and in this sense the *Tractatus de successivis* is authentic.'[1] The authenticity of the *Quaestiones diversae: De relatione, de puncto, de negatione*, is also doubtful.

Theological works by Ockham include the *Quodlibeta VII*, the *Tractatus de Sacramento Altaris* or *De Corpore Christi* (which seems to contain two distinct treatises) and the *Tractatus de praedestinatione et de praescientia Dei et de futuris contingentibus*. The authenticity of the *Centiloquium theologicum* or *summa de conclusionibus theologicis* has not been proved. On the other hand, the arguments adduced to prove that the work is unauthentic do not appear to be conclusive.[2] To Ockham's Munich period belong among other works the *Opus nonaginta dierum*, the *Compendium errorum Ioannis papae XXII*, the *Octo quaestiones de potestate papae*, the *An princeps pro suo succursu, scilicet guerrae, possit recipere bona ecclesiarum, etiam invito papa*, the *Consultatio de causa matrimoniali* and the *Dialogus inter magistrum et discipulum de imperatorum et pontificum potestate*. The last-named work is Ockham's chief political publication. It consists of three parts, composed at different times. But it has to be used with care,

[1] *Tractatus de successivis*, edit. Boehner, p. 29.
[2] See E. Iserloh: *Um die Echtheit des Centiloquium; Gregorianum*, 30 (1949), 78–103.

as many opinions for which Ockham does not make himself responsible are canvassed in it.

3. Ockham possessed an extensive knowledge of the work of the great Scholastics who had preceded him and a remarkable acquaintance with Aristotle. But even though we can discern anticipations in other philosophers of certain theses of Ockham, it would appear that his originality is incontestable. Though the philosophy of Scotus gave rise to certain of Ockham's problems and though certain of Scotus's views and tendencies were developed by Ockham, the latter constantly attacked the system of Scotus, particularly his realism; so that Ockhamism was a strong reaction to, rather than a development of, Scotism. No doubt Ockham was influenced by certain theories of Durandus (those on relations, for example) and Petrus Aureoli; but the extent of such influence, such as it was, does little to impair Ockham's fundamental originality. There is no adequate reason for challenging his reputation as the fountainhead of the terminist or nominalist movement. Nor is there, I think, any cogent reason for representing Ockham as a mere Aristotelian (or, if preferred, as a mere would-be Aristotelian). He certainly tried to overthrow Scotist realism with the help of the Aristotelian logic and theory of knowledge, and further he regarded all realism as a perversion of true Aristotelianism; but he also endeavoured to rectify the theories of Aristotle which excluded any admission of the liberty and omnipotence of God. Ockham was not an 'original' thinker in the sense of one who invented novelties for the sake of novelty, though his reputation as a destructive critic might lead one to suppose that he was; but he was an original thinker in the sense that he thought out his problems for himself and developed his solutions thoroughly and systematically.

The question has been raised and discussed[1] whether or not Ockham's literary career must be regarded as falling into two more or less unconnected parts and, if so, whether this indicates a dichotomy in his character and interests. For it might seem that there is little connection between Ockham's purely logical and philosophical activities at Oxford and his polemical activities at Munich. It might appear that there is a radical discrepancy between Ockham the cold logician and academic philosopher and Ockham the impassioned political and ecclesiastical controversialist. But such a supposition is unnecessary. Ockham was an

[1] See, for example, Georges de Lagarde (cf. *Bibliog.*), IV, pp. 63-6; V, pp. 7 ff.

independent, bold and vigorous thinker, who showed a marked ability for criticism; he held certain clear convictions and principles which he was ready to apply courageously, systematically and logically; and the difference in tone between his philosophical and polemical works is due rather to a difference in the field of application of his principles than to any unreconciled contradiction in the character of the man. No doubt his personal history and circumstances had emotional repercussions which manifested themselves in his polemical writings; but the emotional overtones of these writings cannot conceal the fact that they are the work of the same vigorous, critical and logical mind which composed the commentary on the *Sentences*. His career falls into two phases, and in the second phase a side of Ockham manifests itself which had no occasion to show itself in the same way during the first phase; but it seems to me an exaggeration to imply that Ockham the logician and Ockham the politician were almost different personalities. It is rather that the same personality and the same original mind manifested itself in different ways according to the different circumstances of Ockham's life and the different problems with which he was faced. One would not expect the exile of Munich, his Oxford career cut short and the ban of excommunication on his head, to have treated the problems of Church and State in exactly the same way that he treated the problem of universals at Oxford; but on the other hand one would not expect the exiled philosopher to lose sight of logic and principle and to become simply a polemical journalist. If one knew sufficient of Ockham's character and temperament, the apparent discrepancies between his activities in the two phases would, I think, seem quite natural. The trouble is that we really know very little of Ockham the man. This fact prevents one from making any categorical assertion that he was not a kind of split or double personality; but it seems more sensible to attempt to explain the different aspects of his literary activity on the supposition that he was not a split personality. If this can be done, then we can apply Ockham's own razor to the contrary hypothesis.

As we shall see, there are various elements or strands in Ockham's thought. There are the 'empiricist' element, the rationalist and logical elements, and the theological element. It does not seem to me very easy to synthesize all the elements of his thought; but perhaps it might be as well to remark immediately that one of Ockham's main preoccupations as a philosopher was to purge

Christian theology and philosophy of all traces of Greek necessitarianism, particularly of the theory of essences, which in his opinion endangered the Christian doctrines of the divine liberty and omnipotence. His activity as a logician and his attack on all forms of realism in regard to universals can thus be looked on as subordinate in a sense to his preoccupations as a Christian theologian. This is a point to bear in mind. Ockham was a Franciscan and a theologian: he should not be interpreted as though he were a modern radical empiricist.

CHAPTER IV

OCKHAM (2)

Ockham and the metaphysic of essences—Peter of Spain and the terminist logic—Ockham's logic and theory of universals—Real and rational science—Necessary truths and demonstration.

1. AT the end of the last chapter I mentioned Ockham's preoccupation as a theologian with the Christian doctrines of the divine omnipotence and liberty. He thought that these doctrines could not be safeguarded without eliminating the metaphysic of essences which had been introduced into Christian theology and philosophy from Greek sources. In the philosophy of St. Augustine and in the philosophies of the leading thirteenth-century thinkers the theory of divine ideas had played an important part. Plato had postulated eternal forms or 'ideas', which he most probably regarded as distinct from God but which served as models or patterns according to which God formed the world in its intelligible structure; and later Greek philosophers of the Platonic tradition located these exemplary forms in the divine mind. Christian philosophers proceeded to utilize and adapt this theory in their explanation of the free creation of the world by God. Creation considered as a free and intelligent act on God's part, postulates in God an intellectual pattern or model, as it were, of creation. The theory was, of course, constantly refined; and St. Thomas took pains to show that the ideas in God are not really distinct from the divine essence. We cannot help using language which implies that they are distinct; but actually they are ontologically identical with the divine essence, being simply the divine essence known by God as imitable externally (that is, by creatures) in different ways. This doctrine was the common doctrine in the Middle Ages up to and including the thirteenth century, being considered necessary in order to explain creation and to distinguish it from a purely spontaneous production. Plato had simply postulated universal subsistent forms; but though the Christian thinkers, with their belief in divine providence extending to individuals, admitted ideas of individuals in God, they retained the originally Platonic notion of universal ideas. God creates man, for example, according to His universal idea of human nature. From

this it follows that the natural moral law is not something purely arbitrary, capriciously determined by the divine will: given the idea of human nature, the idea of the natural moral law follows.

Correlative to the theory of universal ideas in God is the acceptance of some form of realism in the explanation of our own universal ideas. Indeed, the former would never have been asserted without the latter; for if a class-word like 'man' were devoid of any objective reference and if there were no such thing as human nature, there would be no reason for ascribing to God a universal idea of man, that is, an idea of human nature. In the second volume of this work an account has been given of the course of the controversy concerning universals in the Middle Ages up to the time of Aquinas; and there it was shown how the early mediaeval form of ultra-realism was finally refuted by Abelard. That only individuals exist came to be the accepted belief. At the same time the moderate realists, like Aquinas, certainly believed in the objectivity of real species and natures. If X and Y are two men, for example, they do not possess the same individual nature; but none the less each possesses his own human nature or essence, and the two natures are similar, each nature being, as it were, a finite imitation of the divine idea of human nature. Duns Scotus proceeded further in the realist direction by finding a formal objective distinction between the human nature of X and the X-ness of X and between the human nature of Y and the Y-ness of Y. Yet, though he spoke of a 'common nature', he did not mean that the actual nature of X is individually the same as the actual nature of Y.

William of Ockham attacked the first part of the metaphysic of essences. He was, indeed, willing to retain something of the language of the theory of divine ideas, doubtless largely out of respect for St. Augustine and tradition; but he emptied the theory of its former content. He thought of the theory as implying a limitation of the divine freedom and omnipotence, as though God would be governed, as it were, and limited in His creative act by the eternal ideas or essences. Moreover, as we shall see later, he thought that the traditional connection of the moral law with the theory of divine ideas constituted an affront to the divine liberty: the moral law depends ultimately, according to Ockham, on the divine will and choice. In other words, for Ockham there is on the one hand God, free and omnipotent, and on the other hand creatures, utterly contingent and dependent. True, all orthodox Christian thinkers of the Middle Ages held the same; but the point is that according to Ockham the metaphysic of essences was a non-Christian invention which had no place in Christian theology and philosophy. As to the other part of the metaphysic of essences Ockham resolutely attacked all forms of 'realism', especially that of Scotus, and he employed the terminist logic in his attack; but, as we shall see, his view of universals was not quite so revolutionary as is sometimes supposed.

Mention will be made later of Ockham's answer to the question, in what sense is it legitimate to speak of ideas in God; at present I propose to outline his logical theory and his discussion of the problem of universals. It must be remembered, however, that Ockham was a gifted and acute logician with a love for simplicity and clarity. What I have been saying about his theological preoccupations should not be taken to mean that his logical inquiries were simply 'apologetic': I was not trying to suggest that Ockham's logic can be waved aside as informed by interested and extrinsic motives. It is rather that in view of some of the pictures which have been given of Ockham it is as well to bear in mind the fact that he *was* a theologian and that he did have theological preoccupations: remembrance of this fact enables one to form a more unified view of his intellectual activity than is otherwise possible.

2. I have said that Ockham 'employed the terminist logic'. This was not a tendentious statement, but it was meant to indicate that Ockham was not the original inventor of the terminist logic. And I wish to make some brief remarks about its development before going on to outline Ockham's own logical theories.

In the thirteenth century there naturally appeared a variety of commentaries on the Aristotelian logic and of logical handbooks and treatises. Among English authors may be mentioned William of Shyreswood (d. 1249), who composed *Introductiones ad logicam*, and among French authors Lambert of Auxerre and Nicholas of Paris. But the most popular and influential work on logic was the *Summulae logicales* of Peter of Spain, a native of Lisbon, who taught at Paris and later became Pope John XXI. He died in 1277. At the beginning of this work we read that 'dialectic is the art of arts and the science of sciences' which opens the way to the knowledge of the principles of all methods.[1] A similar statement of the fundamental importance of dialectic was

---
[1] Ed. Bochenski, p. 1.

made by Lambert of Auxerre. Peter of Spain goes on to say that dialectic is carried on only by means of language, and that language involves the use of words. One must begin, then, by considering the word, first as a physical entity, secondly as a significant term. This emphasis on language was characteristic of the logicians and grammarians of the faculty of arts.

When Peter of Spain emphasized the importance of dialectic, he meant by 'dialectic' the art of probable reasoning; and in view of the fact that some other thirteenth-century logicians shared this tendency to concentrate on probable reasoning as distinct from demonstrative science on the one hand and sophistical reasoning on the other, it is tempting to see in their works the source of the fourteenth-century emphasis on probable arguments. No doubt there may have been a connection; but one must remember that a thinker like Peter of Spain did not abandon the idea that metaphysical arguments can give certainty. In other words, Ockham was doubtless influenced by the emphasis placed by the preceding logicians on dialectic or syllogistic reasoning leading to probable conclusions; but that does not mean that one can father on his predecessors his own tendency to look on arguments in philosophy, as distinct from logic, as probable rather than demonstrative arguments.

A number of the treatises in Peter of Spain's *Summulae logicales* deal with the Aristotelian logic; but others deal with the 'modern logic' or logic of terms. Thus in the treatise headed *De suppositionibus* he distinguishes the *significatio* from the *suppositio* of terms. The former function of a term consists in the relation of a sign to the thing signified. Thus in the English language the term 'man' is a sign, while in the French language the term 'homme' has the same sign-function. But in the sentence 'the man is running' the term 'man', which already possesses its *significatio*, acquires the function of standing for (*supponere pro*) a definite man, whereas in the sentence 'man dies' it stands for all men. One must thus, says Peter, distinguish between *significatio* and *suppositio*, inasmuch as the latter presupposes the former.

Now, this logic of terms, with its doctrine of signs and of 'standing-for', undoubtedly influenced William of Ockham, who took from his predecessors much of what one might call his technical equipment. But it does not follow, of course, that Ockham did not develop the terminist logic very considerably. Nor does it follow that Ockham's philosophical views and the use to which he put the terminist logic were borrowed from a thinker like Peter of Spain. On the contrary, Peter was a conservative in philosophy and was very far from showing any tendency to anticipate Ockham's 'nominalism'. To find the antecedents of the terminist logic in the thirteenth century is not the same thing as attempting to push back the whole Ockhamist philosophy into that century: such an attempt would be futile.

The theory of supposition was, however, only one of the features of fourteenth-century logic. I have given it special mention here because of the use made of it by Ockham in his discussion of the problem of universals. But in any history of mediaeval logic prominence would have to be given to the theory of consequences or of the inferential operations between propositions. In his *Summa Logicae*[1] Ockham deals with this subject after treating in turn of terms, propositions and syllogisms. But in the *De puritate artis logicae*[2] of Walter Burleigh the theory of consequences is given great prominence, and the author's remarks on syllogistics form a kind of appendix to it. Again, Albert of Saxony in his *Perutilis Logica* treats syllogistics as part of the general theory of consequences, though he follows Ockham in starting his treatise with a consideration of terms. The importance of this development of the theory of consequences in the fourteenth century is the witness it bears to the growing conception of logic as formalistic in character. For this feature of the later mediaeval logic reveals an affinity, which was for long disregarded or even unsuspected, between mediaeval and modern logic. Research into the history of mediaeval logic has not indeed yet reached the point at which an adequate account of the subject becomes possible. But further lines for reflection and research are indicated in Father Boehner's little work, *Mediaeval Logic*, which is mentioned in the Bibliography. And the reader is referred to this work for further information.

3. I turn now to Ockham's logic, with special attention to his attack on all realist theories of universals. What has been said in the preceding section will suffice to show that the ascription to Ockham of various logical words and notions should not necessarily be taken to imply that he invented them.

(i) There are various kinds of terms, traditionally distinguished from one another. For example, some terms refer directly to a

[1] Edited by P. Boehner, O.F.M. The Franciscan Institute, St. Bonaventure, N.Y. and E. Nauwelaerts, Louvain. *Pars prima*, 1951.
[2] Edited by P. Boehner, O.F.M. *Ibid.*, 1951.

reality and have a meaning even when they stand by themselves. These terms ('butter', for instance) are called categorematic terms. Other terms, however, like 'no' and 'every' acquire a definite reference only when standing in relation to categorematic terms, as in the phrases 'no man' and 'every house'. These are called syncategorematic terms. Again, some terms are absolute, in the sense that they signify a thing without reference to any other thing, while other terms are called connotative terms, because, like 'son' or 'father', they signify an object considered only in relation to some other thing.

(ii) If we consider the word 'man', we shall recognize that it is a conventional sign: it signifies something or has a meaning, but that this particular word has that particular meaning or exercises that particular sign-function is a matter of convention. This is easily seen to be the case if we bear in mind the fact that in other languages 'homme' and 'homo' are used with the same meaning. Now, the grammarian can reason about words as words, of course; but the real material of our reasoning is not the conventional but the natural sign. The natural sign is the concept. Whether we are English and use the word 'man' or whether we are French and use the word 'homme', the concept or logical significance of the term is the same. The words are different, but their meaning is the same. Ockham distinguished, therefore, both the spoken word (*terminus prolatus*) and the written word (*terminus scriptus*) from the concept (*terminus conceptus* or *intentio animae*), that is, the term considered according to its meaning or logical significance.

Ockham called the concept or *terminus conceptus* a 'natural sign' because he thought that the direct apprehension of anything causes naturally in the human mind a concept of that thing. Both brutes and men utter some sounds as a natural reaction to a stimulus; and these sounds are natural signs. But 'brutes and men utter sounds of this kind only to signify some feelings or some accidents present in themselves', whereas the intellect 'can elicit qualities to signify any sort of thing naturally'.[1] Perceiving a cow results in the formation of the same idea or 'natural sign' (*terminus conceptus*) in the mind of the Englishman and of the Frenchman though the former will express this concept in word or writing by means of one conventional sign, 'cow', while the latter will express it by means of another conventional sign, 'vache'. This treatment of signs was an improvement on that given by

[1] 1 *Sent.*, 2, 8, Q.

Peter of Spain, who does not seem to give sufficient explicit recognition to the identity of logical significance which may attach to corresponding words in different languages.

To anticipate for a moment, one may point out that when Ockham is called a 'nominalist', it is not meant, or should not be meant, that he ascribed universality to words considered precisely as *termini prolati* or *scripti*, that is, to terms considered as conventional signs: it was the natural sign, the *terminus conceptus*, of which he was thinking.

(iii) Terms are elements of propositions, the term standing to the proposition as *incomplexum* to *complexum*; and it is only in the proposition that a term acquires the function of 'standing for' (*suppositio*). For example, in the statement 'the man is running' the term 'man' stands for a precise individual. This is an instance of *suppositio personalis*. But in the statement 'man is a species' the term 'man' stands for all men. This is *suppositio simplex*. Finally, in the statement '*Man* is a noun' one is speaking of the word itself. This is *suppositio materialis*. Taken in itself the term 'man' is capable of exercising any of these functions; but it is only in a proposition that it actually acquires a determinate type of the functions in question. *Suppositio*, then, is 'a property belonging to a term, but only in a proposition'.[1]

(iv) In the statement 'man is mortal' the term 'man', which is, as we have seen, a sign, stands for things, that is, men, which are not themselves signs. It is, therefore, a term of 'first intention' (*primae intentionis*). But in the statement 'species are subdivisions of genera' the term 'species' does not stand immediately for things which are not themselves signs: it stands for class-names, like 'man', 'horse', 'dog', which are themselves signs. The term 'species' is thus a term of second intention (*secundae intentionis*). In other words, terms of second intention stand for terms of first intention and are predicated of them, as when it is said that 'man' and 'horse' are species.

In a broad sense of 'first intention' syncategorematic terms may be called first intentions. Taken in themselves, they do not signify things; but when conjoined with other terms they make those other terms stand for things in a determinate manner. For example, the term 'every' cannot by itself stand for definite things; but as qualifying the term 'man' in the sentence 'every man is mortal' it makes the term 'man' stand for a definite set of things.

[1] *Summa totius logicae*, 1, 63.

In the strict sense of 'first intention', however, a term of first intention is an 'extreme term' in a proposition, one, that is, which stands for a thing which is not a sign or for things which are not signs. In the sentence 'arsenic is poisonous', the term 'arsenic' is both an 'extreme term' and one which stands in the proposition for something which is not itself a sign. A term of second intention, strictly understood, will thus be a term which naturally signifies first intentions and which can stand for them in a proposition. 'Genus', 'species' and 'difference' are examples of terms of second intention.[1]

(v) Ockham's answer to the problem of universals has been already indicated in effect: universals are terms (*termini concepti*) which signify individual things and which stand for them in propositions. Only individual things exist; and by the very fact that a thing exists it is individual. There are not and cannot be existent universals. To assert the extramental existence of universals is to commit the folly of asserting a contradiction; for if the universal exists, it must be individual. And that there is no common reality existing at the same time in two members of a species can be shown in several ways. For example, if God were to create a man out of nothing, this would not affect any other man, as far as his essence is concerned. Again, one individual thing can be annihilated without the annihilation or destruction of another individual thing. 'One man can be annihilated by God without any other man being annihilated or destroyed. Therefore there is not anything common to both, because (if there were) it would be annihilated, and consequently no other man would retain his essential nature.'[2] As to the opinion of Scotus that there is a formal distinction between the common nature and the individuality, it is true that he 'excelled others in subtlety of judgment';[3] but if the alleged distinction is an objective and not purely mental distinction, it must be real. The opinion of Scotus is thus subject to the same difficulties which were encountered by older theories of realism.

Whether the universal concept is a quality distinct from the act of the intellect or whether it is that act itself is a question of but secondary importance: the important point is that 'no universal is anything existing in any way outside the soul; but everything which is predicable of many things is of its nature in the mind, whether subjectively or objectively; and no universal belongs to

---

[1] *Quodlibet*, 4, 19. [2] 1 *Sent.*, 2, 4, D. [3] *Ibid.*, 2, 6, B.

the essence or quiddity of any substance whatever'.[1] Ockham does not appear to have attached very great weight to the question whether the universal concept is an accident distinct from the intellect as such or whether it is simply the intellect itself in its activity: he was more concerned with the analysis of the meaning of terms and propositions than with psychological questions. But it is fairly clear that he did not think that the universal has any existence in the soul except as an act of the understanding. The existence of the universal consists in an act of the understanding and it exists only as such. It owes its existence simply to the intellect: there is no universal reality corresponding to the concept. It is not, however, a fiction in the sense that it does not stand for anything real: it stands for individual real things, though it does not stand for any universal thing. It is, in short, a way of conceiving or knowing individual things.

(vi) Ockham may sometimes imply that the universal is a confused or indistinct image of distinct individual things; but he was not concerned to identify the universal concept with the image or phantasm. His main point was always that there is no need to postulate any factors other than the mind and individual things in order to explain the universal. The universal concept arises simply because there are varying degrees of similarity between individual things. Socrates and Plato are more similar to one another than either is to an ass; and this fact of experience is reflected in the formation of the specific concept of man. But we have to be careful of our way of speaking. We ought not to say that 'Plato and Socrates agree (share) in something or in some things, but that they agree (are alike) by some things, that is, by themselves and that Socrates agrees with (*convenit cum*) Plato, not in something, but by something, namely himself'.[2] In other words, there is no nature common to Socrates and Plato, *in* which they come together or share or agree; but the nature which is Socrates and the nature which is Plato are alike. The foundation of generic concepts can be explained in a similar manner.

(vii) The question might well be raised how this conceptualism differs from the position of St. Thomas. After all, when Ockham says that the notion that there are universal things corresponding to universal terms is absurd and destructive of the whole philosophy

---

[1] 1 *Sent.*, 2, 8, Q.
[2] *Ibid.*, 2, 6, E E. *Respondeo quod conveniunt (Socrates et Plato) aliquibus, quia seipsis, et quod Socrates convenit cum Platone non in aliquo sed aliquo, quia seipso.*

of Aristotle and of all science,[1] St. Thomas would agree. And it was certainly St. Thomas's opinion that while the natures of men, for example, are alike there is no common nature considered as a thing in which all individual men have a share. But it must be remembered that St. Thomas gave a metaphysical explanation of the similarity of natures; for he held that God creates things belonging to the same species, things, that is, with similar natures, according to an idea of human nature in the divine mind. Ockham, however, discarded this theory of divine ideas. The consequence was that for him the similarities which give rise to universal concepts are simply similarities, so to speak, of fact: there is no metaphysical reason for these similarities except the divine choice, which is not dependent on any divine ideas. In other words, although St. Thomas and William of Ockham were fundamentally at one in denying that there is any *universale in re*, the former combined his rejection of ultra-realism with the Augustinian doctrine of the *universale ante rem*, whereas the latter did not.[2]

Another, though less important, difference concerns the way of speaking about universal concepts. Ockham, as we have seen, held that the universal concept is an act of the understanding. 'I say that the first intention as well as the second intention is truly an act of the understanding, for whatever is saved by the fiction can be saved by the act.'[3] Ockham appears to be referring to the theory of Petrus Aureoli, according to which the concept, which is the object appearing to the mind, is a 'fiction'. Ockham prefers to say that the concept is simply the act of the understanding. 'The first intention is an act of the understanding signifying things which are not signs. The second intention is the act signifying first intentions.'[4] And Ockham proceeds to say that both first and second intentions are truly real entities, and that they are truly qualities subjectively existent in the soul. That they are real entities, if they are acts of the understanding, is clear; but it seems rather odd perhaps to find Ockham calling them qualities. However, if his various utterances are to be interpreted as consistent with one another, he cannot be supposed to mean that universal concepts are qualities really distinct from the acts of understanding. 'Everything which is explained through positing something distinct from the act of understanding can be explained without positing such a distinct thing.'[5] In other words, Ockham

---

[1] *Expositio aurea*, 3, 2, 90, R.　　[2] See vol. II, p. 154.　　[3] *Quodlibet*, 4, 19.
[4] *Ibid.*　　[5] *Summa totius logicae*, 1, 12.

is content to talk simply about the act of the understanding; and he applies the principle of economy to get rid of the apparatus of abstracting *species intelligibiles*. But though there is certainly a difference between the theory of Aquinas and that of Ockham in this respect, it must be remembered that Aquinas insisted strongly that the *species intelligibilis* is not the object of knowledge: it is *id quo intelligitur* and not *id quod intelligitur*.[1]

4. We are now in a position to consider briefly Ockham's theory of science. He divides science into two main types, real science and rational science. The former (*scientia realis*) is concerned with real things, in a sense to be discussed presently, while the latter (*scientia rationalis*) is concerned with terms which do not stand immediately for real things. Thus logic, which deals with terms of second intention, like 'species' and 'genus', is a rational science. It is important to maintain the distinction between these two types of science: otherwise concepts or terms will be confused with things. For example, if one does not realize that Aristotle's intention in the *Categories* was to treat of words and concepts and not of things, one will interpret him in a sense quite foreign to his thought. Logic is concerned with terms of second intention, which cannot exist *sine ratione*, that is, without the mind's activity; it deals, therefore, with mental 'fabrications'. I said earlier that Ockham did not much like speaking of universal concepts as fictions or fictive entities; but the point I then had in mind was that Ockham objected to the implication that what we know by means of a universal concept is a fiction and not a real thing. He was quite ready to speak of terms of second intention, which enter into the propositions of logic, as 'fabrications', because these terms do not refer directly to real things. But logic, which is rational science, presupposes real science; for terms of second intention presuppose terms of first intention.

Real science is concerned with things, that is, with individual things. But Ockham also says that 'real science is not always of things as the objects which are immediately known'.[2] This might seem to be a contradiction; but Ockham proceeds to explain that any science, whether real or rational, is only of propositions.[3] In other words, when he says that real science is concerned with things, Ockham does not mean to deny the Aristotelian doctrine that science is of the universal; but he is determined to hold to the other Aristotelian doctrine that it is only individuals which exist.

---

[1] Cf. *S.T.*, 1, 76, 2, *ad* 4; 1, 85, 2. [2] 1 *Sent.*, 2, 4, M. [3] *Ibid.*

Real science, then, is concerned with universal propositions; and he gives as examples of such propositions 'man is capable of laughter' and 'every man is capable of training'; but the universal terms stand for individual things, and not for universal realities existing extramentally. If Ockham says, then, that real science is concerned with individual things by means of terms (*mediantibus terminis*), he does not mean that real science is unconnected with actual existents which are individual things. Science is concerned with the truth or falsity of propositions; but to say that a proposition of real science is true is to say that it is verified in all those individual things of which the terms of the proposition are the natural signs. The difference between real and rational science consists in this, that 'the parts, that is, the terms of the propositions known by real science stand for things, which is not the case with the terms of propositions known by rational science, for these terms stand for other terms'.[1]

5. Ockham's insistence on individual things as the sole existents does not mean, therefore, that he rejects science considered as a knowledge of universal propositions. Nor does he reject the Aristotelian ideas of indemonstrable principles and of demonstration. As regards the former, a principle may be indemonstrable in the sense that the mind cannot but assent to the proposition once it grasps the meaning of the terms, or it may be indemonstrable in the sense that it is known evidently only by experience. 'Certain first principles are not known through themselves (*per se nota* or analytic) but are known only through experience as in the case of the proposition "all heat is calefactive".'[2] As to demonstration, Ockham accepts the Aristotelian definition of demonstration as a syllogism which produces knowledge; but he proceeds to analyse the various meanings of 'know' (*scire*). It may mean the evident understanding of truth; and in this sense even contingent facts, such as the fact that I am now sitting, can be known. Or it may mean the evident understanding of necessary, as distinct from contingent, truths. Or, thirdly, it may mean 'the understanding of one necessary truth through the evident understanding of two necessary truths; ... and it is in this sense that "knowing" is understood in the aforementioned definition'.[3]

This insistence on necessary truths must not be taken to mean that for Ockham there can be no scientific knowledge of contingent things. He did not think, indeed, that an affirmative and assertoric

[1] 1 *Sent.*, 2, 4, O.   [2] *Summa totius logicae*, 3, 2.   [3] *Ibid.*

proposition concerning contingent things and referring to present time (that is, in relation to the speaker) can be a necessary truth; but he held that affirmative and assertoric propositions which include terms standing for contingent things can be necessary, if they are, or can be considered as equivalent to, negative or hypothetical propositions concerning possibility.[1] In other words, Ockham regarded necessary propositions including terms standing for contingent things as equivalent to hypothetical propositions, in the sense that they are true of each thing for which the subject-terms stands *at the time of the existence of that thing*. Thus the proposition, 'every X is Y' (where X stands for contingent things and Y for possessing a property) is necessary if considered as equivalent to 'if there is an X, it is Y' or 'if it is true to say of anything that it is an X, it is also true to say of it that it is Y'.

Demonstration for Ockham is demonstration of the attributes of a subject, not of the existence of the subject. We cannot demonstrate, for example, that a certain kind of herb exists; but we may be able to demonstrate the proposition that it has a certain property. True, we can know by experience that it has this property, but if we merely know the fact because we have experienced it, we do not know the 'reason' of the fact. If, however, we can show from the nature of the herb (knowledge of which presupposes experience, of course) that it necessarily possesses this property, we have demonstrative knowledge. To this sort of knowledge Ockham attached considerable importance: he was very far from being a despiser of the syllogism. 'The syllogistic form holds equally in every field.'[2] Ockham did not mean by this, of course, that all true propositions can be proved syllogistically; but he considered that in all matters where scientific knowledge is obtainable syllogistic reasoning holds good. In other words, he adhered to the Aristotelian idea of demonstrative 'science'. In view of the fact that Ockham is not infrequently called an 'empiricist' it is as well to bear in mind the 'rationalist' side of his philosophy. When he said that science is concerned with propositions he did not mean that science is entirely divorced from reality or that demonstration is incapable of telling us anything about things.

---

[1] *Summa totius logicae*, 3, 2.   [2] 1 *Sent.*, 2, 6, D.

CHAPTER V

OCKHAM (3)

Intuitive knowledge—God's power to cause intuitive 'knowledge' of a non-existent object—Contingency of the world-order—Relations—Causality—Motion and time—Conclusion.

1. SCIENCE, according to Ockham, is concerned with universal propositions, and syllogistic demonstration is the mode of reasoning proper to science in the strict sense: an assent in science is an assent to the truth of a proposition. But this does not mean that for Ockham scientific knowledge is *a priori* in the sense of being a development of innate principles or ideas. On the contrary, intuitive knowledge is primary and fundamental. If we consider, for example, the proposition that the whole is greater than the part, we shall recognize that the mind assents to the truth of the proposition as soon as it apprehends the meaning of the terms; but this does not mean that the principle is innate. Without experience the proposition would not be enunciated; nor should we apprehend the meaning of the terms. Again, in a case where it is possible to demonstrate that an attribute belongs to a subject it is by experience or intuitive knowledge that we know that there is such a subject. Demonstration of a property of man, for example, presupposes an intuitive knowledge of men. 'Nothing can be known naturally in itself unless it is known intuitively.'[1] Ockham is here arguing that we cannot have a natural knowledge of the divine essence as it is in itself, because we have no natural intuition of God; but the principle is a general one. All knowledge is based on experience.

What is meant by intuitive knowledge? 'Intuitive knowledge (*notitia intuitiva*) of a thing is knowledge of such a kind that one can know by means of it whether a thing is or not; and if it is, the intellect immediately judges that the thing exists and concludes evidently that it exists, unless perchance it is hindered on account of some imperfection in that knowledge.'[2] Intuitive knowledge is thus the immediate apprehension of a thing as existent, enabling the mind to form a contingent proposition concerning the existence of that thing. But intuitive knowledge is also knowledge of such

[1] *1 Sent.*, 3, 2, F.   [2] *Prol. Sent.*, 1, 2.

a kind that 'when some things are known, of which the one inheres in the other or is locally distant from the other or is related in some other way to the other, the mind straightway knows, by virtue of that simple apprehension of those things, whether the thing inheres or does not inhere, whether it is distant or not, and so with other contingent truths.... For example, if Socrates is really white, that apprehension of Socrates and whiteness by means of which it can be known evidently that Socrates is white is intuitive knowledge. And, in general, every simple apprehension of a term or of terms, that is, of a thing or things, by means of which some contingent truths, especially concerning the present, can be known, is intuitive knowledge.'[1] Intuitive knowledge is thus caused by the immediate apprehension of existent things. The concept of an individual thing is the natural expression in the mind of the apprehension of that thing, provided that one does not interpret the concept as a *medium quo* of knowledge. 'I say that in no intuitive apprehension, whether sensitive or intellectual, is the thing placed in any state of being which is a medium between the thing and the act of knowing. That is, I say that the thing itself is known immediately without any medium between itself and the act by which it is seen or apprehended.'[2] In other words, intuition is immediate apprehension of a thing or of things leading naturally to the judgment that the thing exists or to some other contingent proposition about it, such as 'it is white'. The guarantee of such judgments is simply evidence, the evident character of the intuition, together with the natural character of the process leading to the judgment. 'I say, therefore, that intuitive knowledge is proper individual knowledge . . . because it is naturally caused by one thing and not by another, nor can it be caused by another thing.'[3]

It is clear that Ockham is not speaking simply of sensation: he is speaking of an intellectual intuition of an individual thing, which is caused by that thing and not by anything else. Moreover, intuition for him is not confined to intuition of sensible or material things. He expressly says that we know our own acts intuitively, this intuition leading to the formation of propositions like 'there is an understanding' and 'there is a will'.[4] 'Aristotle says that nothing of those things which are external is understood, unless first it falls under sense; and those things are only sensibles according to him.

[1] *Prol. Sent.*, 1, 2.   [2] 1 *Sent.*, 27, 3, K.
[3] *Quodlibet*, 1, 13.   [4] *Ibid.*, 1, 14.

And this authority is true in regard to those things; but in regard to spirits it is not.'[1] As intuitive knowledge precedes abstractive knowledge, according to Ockham, we can say, using a later language, that for him sense-perception and introspection are the two sources of all our natural knowledge concerning existent reality. In this sense one can call him an 'empiricist'; but on this point he is no more of an 'empiricist' than any other mediaeval philosopher who disbelieved in innate ideas and in purely *a priori* knowledge of existent reality.

2. We have seen that for Ockham intuitive knowledge of a thing is caused by that thing and not by any other thing. In other words, intuition, as immediate apprehension of the individual existent, carries its own guarantee. But, as is well known, he maintained that God could cause in us the intuition of a thing which was not really there. 'Intuitive knowledge cannot be caused naturally unless the object is present at the right distance; but it could be caused supernaturally.'[2] 'If you say that it (intuition) can be caused by God alone, that is true.'[3] 'There can be by the power of God intuitive knowledge (*cognitio intuitiva*) concerning a non-existent object.'[4] Hence among the censured propositions of Ockham's we find one to the effect that 'intuitive knowledge in itself and necessarily is not more concerned with an existent than with a non-existent thing, nor does it regard existence more than non-existence'. This is doubtless an interpretative summary of Ockham's position; and since it appears to contradict his account of the nature of intuitive knowledge as distinct from abstractive knowledge (in the sense of knowledge which abstracts from the existence or non-existence of the things for which the terms in the proposition stand), the following remarks may help to make his position clearer.

(i) When Ockham says that God could produce in us intuition of a non-existent object, he is relying on the truth of the proposition that God can produce and conserve immediately whatever He normally produces through the mediation of secondary causes. For example, the intuition of the stars is normally and naturally produced in us by the actual presence of the stars. To say this is to say that God produces in us intuitive knowledge of the stars by means of a secondary cause, namely the stars themselves. On Ockham's principle, then, God could produce this intuition directly, without the secondary cause. He could not do this if it

---

[1] *Quodlibet*, 1, 14.   [2] *2 Sent.*, 15, E.   [3] *Quodlibet*, 1, 13.   [4] *Ibid.*, 6, 6.

would involve a contradiction; but it would not involve a contradiction. 'Every effect which God causes through the mediation of a secondary cause He can produce immediately by Himself.'[1]

(ii) But God could not produce in us evident knowledge of the proposition that the stars are present when they are not present; for the inclusion of the word 'evident' implies that the stars really are present. 'God cannot cause in us knowledge such that by it a thing is seen evidently to be present although it is absent, for that involves a contradiction, because such evident knowledge means that it is thus in fact as is stated by the proposition to which assent is given.'[2]

(iii) Ockham's point seems to be, then, that God could cause in us the act of intuiting an object which was not really present, in the sense that He could cause in us the physiological and psychological conditions which would normally lead us to assent to the proposition that the thing is present. For example, God could produce immediately in the organs of vision all those effects which are naturally produced by the light of the stars. Or one can put the matter this way. God could not produce in me the actual vision of a present white patch, when the white patch was not present; for this would involve a contradiction. But He could produce in me all the psycho-physical conditions involved in seeing a white patch, even if the white patch was not really there.

(iv) To his critics, Ockham's choice of terms seemed to be confusing and unfortunate. On the one hand, after saying that God cannot cause evident knowledge that a thing is present when it is not present, he adds that 'God can cause a "creditive" act by which I believe that an absent is present', and he explains that 'that "creditive" idea will be abstractive, not intuitive'.[3] This seems to be fairly plain sailing, if it can be taken as meaning that God could produce in us, in the absence of the stars, all the psycho-physical conditions which we would naturally have in the presence of the stars, and that we would thereby have a knowledge of what the stars are (so far as this can be obtained by sight), though the knowledge could not properly be called 'intuition'. On the other hand, Ockham seems to speak of God as being able to produce in us 'intuitive knowledge' of a non-existent object, though this knowledge is not 'evident'. Moreover, he does not seem to mean simply that God could produce in us intuitive knowledge of the nature of the object; for he allows that 'God can produce an

[1] *Quodlibet*, 6, 6.   [2] *Ibid.*, 5, 5.   [3] *Ibid.*

assent which belongs to the same species as that evident assent to the contingent proposition, "this whiteness exists", when it does not exist'.[1] If God can properly be said to be capable of producing in us assent to a proposition affirming the existence of a non-existent object, and if this assent can properly be called not only a 'creditive act' but also 'intuitive knowledge', then one can only suppose that it is proper to speak of God as capable of producing in us intuitive knowledge which is not in fact intuitive knowledge at all. And to say this would seem to involve a contradiction. To qualify 'intuitive knowledge' by the words 'not evident' would appear to amount to a cancellation of the former by the latter.

Possibly these difficulties are capable of being cleared up satisfactorily, from Ockham's point of view, I mean. For example, he says that 'it is a contradiction that a chimera be seen intuitively'; but 'it is not a contradiction that that which is seen is nothing in actuality outside the soul, so long as it can be an effect or was at some time an actual reality'.[2] If God had annihilated the stars, He could still cause in us the act of seeing what had once been, so far as the act is considered subjectively, just as He could give us a vision of what will be in the future. Either act would be an immediate apprehension, in the first case of what has been and in the second case of what will be. But, even then, it would be peculiar to imply that if we assented to the proposition, 'these things exist *now*', the assent could be produced by God, unless one were willing to say that God could deceive us. Presumably this was the point to which exception was taken by Ockham's theological opponents, and not the mere assertion that God could act directly on our sense organs. However, it must be remembered that Ockham distinguished evidence, which is objective, from certitude as a psychological state. Possession of the latter is not an infallible guarantee of possession of the former.

(v) In any case one must remember that Ockham is not speaking of the natural course of events. He does not say that God acts in this way as a matter of fact: he simply says that God could act in this way in virtue of His omnipotence. That God is omnipotent was not, however, for Ockham a truth which can be philosophically proved: it is known only by faith. If we look at the matter from the purely philosophical point of view, therefore, the question of God's producing in us intuitions of non-existent objects simply does not come up. On the other hand, what Ockham has to say

[1] *Quodlibet*, 5, 5.   [2] *Ibid.*, 6, 6.

on the matter admirably illustrates his tendency, as a thinker with marked theological preoccupations, to break through, as it were, the purely philosophic and natural order and to subordinate it to the divine liberty and omnipotence. It illustrates, too, one of his main principles, that when two things are distinct there is no absolutely necessary connection between them. Our act of seeing the stars, considered as an act, is distinct from the stars themselves: it can therefore be separated from them, in the sense that divine omnipotence could annihilate the latter and conserve the former. Ockham's tendency was always to break through supposedly necessary connections which might seem to limit in some way the divine omnipotence, provided that it could not be shown to his satisfaction that denial of the proposition affirming such a necessary connection involved the denial of the principle of contradiction.

3. Ockham's insistence on intuitive knowledge as the basis and source of all our knowledge of existents represents, as we have seen, the 'empiricist' side of his philosophy. This aspect of his thought may also be said to be reflected in his insistence that the order of the world follows the divine choice. Scotus had made a distinction between God's choice of the end and His choice of the means, as though one could speak significantly of God 'first' willing the end and 'then' choosing the means. Ockham, however, rejected this way of speaking. 'It does not seem to be well said that God wills the end before that which is (ordered) to the end, because there is not there (in God) such a priority of acts, nor are there (in God) such instants as he postulates.'[1] Apart from the anthropomorphisms of such language it seems to impair the utter contingency of the order of the world. The choice of the end and the choice of the means are both utterly contingent. This does not mean, of course, that we have to picture God as a sort of capricious superman, liable to alter the world-order from day to day or from moment to moment. On the supposition that God has chosen a world-order, that order remains stable. But the choice of the order is in no way necessary: it is the effect of the divine choice and of the divine choice alone.

This position is intimately associated, of course, with Ockham's concern for the divine omnipotence and liberty; and it may appear out of place to speak of it as in any way reflecting the 'empiricist' aspect of his philosophy, since it is the position of a theologian.

[1] 1 *Sent.*, 41, 1, E.

But what I meant was this. If the order of the world is entirely contingent on the divine choice, it is obviously impossible to deduce it *a priori*. If we want to know what it is, one must examine what it is in fact. Ockham's position may have been primarily that of a theologian; but its natural effect would be to concentrate attention on the actual facts and to discourage any notion that one could reconstruct the order of the world by purely *a priori* reasoning. If a notion of this kind makes its appearance in the pre-Kantian continental rationalism of the classical period of 'modern' philosophy, its origin is certainly not to be looked for in fourteenth-century Ockhamism: it is to be associated, of course, with the influence of mathematics and of mathematical physics.

4. Ockham's tendency, then, was to split up the world, as it were, into 'absolutes'. That is to say, his tendency was to split up the world into distinct entities, each of which depends on God but between which there is no necessary connection: the order of the world is not logically prior to the divine choice, but it is logically posterior to the divine choice of individual contingent entities. And the same tendency is reflected in his treatment of relations. Once granted that there exists only individual distinct entities and that the only kind of distinction which is independent of the mind is a real distinction in the sense of a distinction between separate or separable entities, it follows that if a relation is a distinct entity, distinct, that is, from the terms of the relation, it must be really distinct from the terms in the sense of being separate or separable. 'If I held that a relation were a thing, I should say with John (Scotus) that it is a thing distinct from its foundation, but I should differ (from him) in saying that every relation differs really from its foundation . . . because I do not admit a formal distinction in creatures.'[1] But it would be absurd to hold that a relation is really distinct from its foundation. If it were, God could produce the relation of paternity and confer it on someone who had never generated. The fact is that a man is called a 'father' when he has generated a child; and there is no need to postulate the existence of a third entity, a relation of paternity, linking father to child. Similarly Smith is said to be like Brown because, for example, Smith is a man and Brown is a man or because Smith is white and Brown is white: it is unnecessary to postulate a third entity, a relation of similarity, in

[1] 2 *Sent.*, 2, H.

addition to the 'absolute' substances and qualities; and if one does postulate a third entity, absurd conclusions result.[1] Relations are names or terms signifying absolutes; and a relation as such has no reality outside the mind. For example, there is no order of the universe which is actually or really distinct from the existent parts of the universe.[2] Ockham does not say that a relation is identical with its foundation. 'I do not say that a relation is really the same as its foundation; but I say that a relation is not the foundation but only an "intention" or concept in the soul, signifying several absolute things.'[3] The principle on which Ockham goes is, of course, the principle of economy: the way in which we speak about relations can be analysed or explained satisfactorily without postulating relations as real entities. This was, in Ockham's view, the opinion of Aristotle. The latter would not allow, for example, that every mover is necessarily itself moved. But this implies that relations are not entities distinct from absolute things; for, if they were, the mover would receive a relation and would thus be itself moved.[4] Relations are thus 'intentions' or terms signifying absolutes; though one must add that Ockham restricts the application of this doctrine to the created world: in the Trinity there are real relations.

This theory naturally affected Ockham's view of the relation between creatures and God. It was a common doctrine in the Middle Ages among Ockham's predecessors that the creature has a real relation to God, although God's relation to the creature is only a mental relation. On Ockham's view of relations, however, this distinction becomes in effect null and void. Relations can be analysed into two existent 'absolutes'; and in this case to say that between creatures and God there are different kinds of relation is simply to say, so far as this way of speaking is admissible, that God and creatures are different kinds of beings. It is perfectly true that God produced and conserves creatures and that the latter could not exist apart from God; but this does not mean that the creatures are affected by a mysterious entity called an essential relation of dependence. We conceive and speak about creatures as essentially related to God; but what actually exists is God on the one hand and creatures on the other, and there is no need to postulate any other entity. Ockham distinguishes various senses in which 'real relation' and 'mental relation' can be understood;[5]

---

[1] Cf. *Expositio aurea*, 2, 64, V. [2] 1 *Sent.*, 30, 1, S. [3] *Ibid.*, 30, 1, R.
[4] *Expositio aurea*, 2, 64, R. [5] 1 *Sent.*, 30, 5.

and he is willing to say that the relation of creatures to God is a 'real' and not a 'mental' relation, if the statement is taken to mean, for example, that a stone's production and conservation by God is real and does not depend on the human mind. But he excludes any idea of there being any additional entity in the stone, in addition, that is, to the stone itself, which could be called a 'real relation'.

One particular way in which Ockham tries to show that the idea of real relations distinct from their foundations is absurd deserves special mention. If I move my finger, its position is changed in regard to all the parts of the universe. And, if there are real relations distinct from their foundation, 'it would follow that at the movement of my finger the whole universe, that is, heaven and earth, would be at once filled with accidents'.[1] Moreover, if, as Ockham says, the parts of the universe are infinite in number, it would follow that the universe is peopled with an infinite number of fresh accidents whenever I move my finger. This conclusion he considered absurd.

For Ockham, then, the universe consists of 'absolutes', substances and absolute accidents, which can be brought into a greater or lesser local approximation to one another, but which are not affected by any relative entities called 'real relations'. From this it would seem to follow that it is futile to think that one could read off, as it were, a mirror of the whole universe. If one wants to know anything about the universe, one must study it empirically. Very possibly this point of view should be regarded as favouring an 'empiricist' approach to knowledge of the world; but it does not follow, of course, that modern science actually developed against a mental background of this sort. Nevertheless, Ockham's insistence on 'absolutes' and his view of relations may reasonably be said to have favoured the growth of empirical science in the following way. If the creature is regarded as having a real essential relation to God, and if it cannot be properly understood without this relation being understood, it is reasonable to conclude that the study of the way in which creatures mirror God is the most important and valuable study of the world, and that a study of creatures in and for themselves alone, without any reference to God, is a rather inferior kind of study, which yields only an inferior knowledge of the world. But if creatures are 'absolutes', they can perfectly well be studied without any

[1] 2 *Sent.*, 2, G.

reference to God. Of course, as we have seen, when Ockham spoke of created things as 'absolutes' he had no intention of questioning their utter dependence on God; his point of view was very much that of a theologian; but none the less, if we can know the natures of created things without any advertence to God, it follows that empirical science is an autonomous discipline. The world can be studied in itself in abstraction from God, especially if, as Ockham held, it cannot be strictly proved that God, in the full sense of the term 'God', exists. In this sense it is legitimate to speak of Ockhamism as a factor and stage in the birth of the 'lay spirit', as M. de Lagarde does. At the same time one must remember that Ockham himself was very far from being a secularist or modern 'rationalist'.

5. When one turns to Ockham's account of causality one finds him expounding the four causes of Aristotle. As to the exemplary cause, which, he says, Seneca added as a fifth type of cause, 'I say that strictly speaking nothing is a cause unless it is a cause in one of the four ways laid down by Aristotle. So the idea or exemplar is not strictly a cause; though, if one extends the name "cause" to (cover) everything the knowledge of which is presupposed by the production of something, the idea or exemplar is a cause in this sense; and Seneca speaks in this extended sense.'[1] Ockham accepts, then, the traditional Aristotelian division of causes into the formal, material, final and efficient causes; and he affirms that 'to any type of cause there corresponds its own (type of) causation'.[2]

Moreover, Ockham did not deny that it is possible to conclude from the characteristics of a given thing that it has or had a cause; and he himself used causal arguments. He did, however, deny that the simple knowledge (*notitia incomplexa*) of one thing can provide us with the simple knowledge of another thing. We may be able to establish that a given thing has a cause; but it does not follow that we thereby gain a simple and proper knowledge of the thing which is its cause. The reason of this is that the knowledge in question comes from intuition; and the intuition of one thing is not the intuition of another thing. This principle has, of course, its ramifications in natural theology; but what I want to emphasize at the moment is that Ockham did not deny that a causal argument can have any validity. It is true that for him two things are always really distinct when the concepts of the two things are distinct, and that when two things are distinct God could create

[1] 1 *Sent.*, 35, 5, N.   [2] 2 *Sent.*, 3, B.

the one without the other; but, given empirical reality as it is, one can discern causal connections.

But, though Ockham enumerates four causes in the traditional manner and though he does not reject the validity of causal argument, his analysis of efficient causality has a marked 'empiricist' colouring. In the first place he insists that, though one may know that a given thing has *a* cause, the only way in which we can ascertain that this definite thing is the cause of that definite thing is by experience: we cannot prove by abstract reasoning that X is the cause of Y, where X is one created thing and Y is another created thing. In the second place the experiential test of a causal relation is the employment of the presence and absence methods or the method of exclusion. We are not entitled to assert that X is the cause of Y, unless we can show that when X is present Y follows and that when X is absent, whatever other factors may be present, Y does not follow. For example, 'it is proved that fire is the cause of heat, since, when fire is there and all other things (that is, all other possible causal factors) have been removed, heat follows in a heatable object which has been brought near (the fire) . . . (Similarly) it is proved that the object is the cause of intuitive knowledge, for when all other factors except the object have been removed intuitive knowledge follows'.[1]

That it is by experience we come to know that one thing is the cause of another is, of course, a common-sense position. So, for the matter of that, is Ockham's idea of the test which should be applied in order to ascertain whether A, B or C is the cause of D or whether we have to accept a plurality of causes. If we find that when A is present D always follows, even when B and C are absent, and that when B and C are present but A is absent D never follows, we must take it that A is the cause of D. If, however, we find that when A alone is present D never follows, but that when A and B are both present D always follows, even though C is absent, we must conclude that both A and B are causal factors in the production of D. In calling these positions common-sense positions I mean that they are positions which would naturally commend themselves to ordinary common sense and that there is nothing revolutionary about either position in itself: I do not mean to suggest that from the scientific point of view the matter was adequately stated by Ockham. It does not need very much reflection to see that there are cases in which the supposed cause

[1] 1 *Sent.*, 1, 3, N.

of an event cannot be 'removed', in order to see what happens in its absence. We cannot, for example, remove the moon and see what happens to the movement of the tides in the absence of the moon, in order to ascertain whether the moon exercises any causal influence on the tides. However, that is not the point to which I really want to draw attention. For it would be absurd to expect an adequate treatment of scientific induction from a thinker who was not really concerned with the matter and who showed comparatively little interest in matters of pure physical science; especially at a time when science had not attained that degree of development which would appear to be required before reflection on scientific method can really be valuable. The point to which I draw attention is rather this, that in his analysis of efficient causality Ockham shows a tendency to interpret the causal relation as invariable or regular sequence. In one place he distinguishes two senses of cause. In the second sense of the word an antecedent proposition may be called a 'cause' in relation to the consequent. This sense does not concern us, as Ockham expressly says that the antecedent is not the cause of the consequent in any proper sense of the term. It is the first sense which is of interest. 'In one sense it (cause) means something which has another thing as its effect; and in this sense that can be called a cause on the positing of which another thing is posited and on the non-positing of which that other thing is not posited.'[1] In a passage like this Ockham seems to imply that causality means regular sequence and does not seem to be talking simply of an empirical test which should be applied to ascertain whether one thing is actually the cause of another thing. To state without more ado that Ockham reduced causality to regular succession would be incorrect; but he does seem to show a tendency to reduce efficient causality to regular succession. And, after all, to do so would be very much in harmony with his theological view of the universe. God has created distinct things; and the order which prevails between them is purely contingent. There are regular sequences as a matter of fact; but no connection between two distinct things can be said to be necessary, unless one means by necessary simply that the connection, which depends on God's choice, is always observable in fact. In this sense one can probably say that Ockham's theological outlook and his tendency to give an empiricist account of efficient causality went hand in hand. However, as God has

---

[1] 1 *Sent.*, 41, 1, F.

created things in such a way that a certain order results, we can predict that the causal relations we have experienced in the past will be experienced in the future, even though God by the use of His absolute power *could* interfere with the order. This theological background is, of course, generally absent from modern empiricism.

6. It is clear that Ockham utilized his razor in his discussion of causality, just as in that of relations in general. He utilized it too in his treatment of the problem of motion. Indeed, his use of the razor or principle of economy was often connected with the 'empiricist' side of his philosophy, inasmuch as he wielded the weapon in an effort to get rid of unobservable entities the existence of which was not, in his opinion, demanded by the data of experience (or taught by revelation). His tendency was always towards the simplification of our view of the universe. To say this is not to say, of course, that Ockham made any attempt to reduce things to sense-data or to logical constructions out of sense-data. Such a reduction he would doubtless have regarded as an over-simplification. But, once granted the existence of substance and absolute accidents, he made an extensive use of the principle of economy.

Employing the traditional Aristotelian division of types of movement, Ockham asserts that neither qualitative alteration nor quantitative change nor local motion is anything positive in addition to permanent things.[1] In the case of qualitative alteration a body acquires a form gradually or successively, part after part, as Ockham puts it; and there is no need to postulate anything else but the thing which acquires the quality and the quality which is acquired. It is true that the negation of the simultaneous acquisition of all the parts of the form is involved; but this negation is not a thing; and to imagine that it is is to be misled by the false supposition that to every distinct term or name there corresponds a distinct thing. Indeed, if it were not for the use of abstract words like 'motion', 'simultaneity', 'succession', etc., the problems connected with the nature of motion would not create such difficulty for people.[2] In the case of quantitative change it is obvious, says Ockham, that nothing is involved save 'permanent things'. As to local motion, nothing need be postulated except a body and its place, that is, its local situation. To be moved locally 'is first to have one place, and afterwards, without any other thing being postulated, to have another place, without any intervening state

[1] 2 *Sent.*, 9, C, D, E.   [2] *Tractatus de successivis*, ed. Boehner, p. 47.

of rest, ... and to proceed thus continuously.... And consequently the whole nature of motion can be saved (explained) by this without anything else but the fact that a body is successively in distinct places and is not at rest in any of them.'[1] In the whole of his treatment of motion, both in the *Tractatus de successivis*[2] and in the commentary on the *Sentences*[3] Ockham makes frequent appeal to the principle of economy. He does the same when dealing with sudden change (*mutatio subita*, that is, substantial change), which is nothing in addition to 'absolute' things. Of course, if we say that 'a form is acquired by change' or 'change belongs to the category of relation', we shall be tempted to think that the word 'change' stands for an entity. But a proposition like 'a form is lost and a form is gained through sudden change' can be translated into a proposition like 'the thing which changes loses a form and acquires a form together (at the same moment) and not part after part'.[4]

The principle of economy was invoked too in Ockham's treatment of place and time. Expounding the Aristotelian definitions,[5] he insists that place is not a thing distinct from the surface or surfaces of the body or bodies in regard to which a certain thing is said to be in a place; and he insists that time is not a thing distinct from motion. 'I say that neither time nor any *successivum* denotes a thing, either absolute or relative, distinct from permanent things; and this is what the Philosopher means.'[6] In whichever of the possible senses one understands 'time', it is not a thing in addition to motion. 'Primarily and principally "time" signifies the same as "motion", although it connotes both the soul and an act of the soul, by which it (the soul or mind) knows the before and after of that motion. And so, presupposing what has been said about motion, and (presupposing) that the statements are understood..., it can be said that "time" signifies motion directly and the soul or an act of the soul directly; and on this account it signifies directly the before and after in motion.'[7] As Ockham expressly says that the meaning of Aristotle in the whole of this chapter about time is, in brief, this, that 'time' does not denote

---

[1] *Tractatus de successivis*, ed. Boehner, p. 46.
[2] This treatise is a compilation; but it is a compilation from Ockham's authentic writings. See p. 45.
[3] 2, 9. [4] Cf. *Tractatus de successivis*, ed. Boehner, pp. 41–2.
[5] For the Aristotelian definitions of place and time see, for example, the first volume of this history, *Greece and Rome*, pp. 321–2.
[6] 2 *Sent.*, 12 D.
[7] *Tractatus de successivis*, ed. Boehner, p. 111.

any distinct thing outside the soul beyond what 'motion' signifies,[1] and as this is what he himself held, it follows that in so far as one can distinguish time from motion it is mental, or, as Ockham would say, a 'term' or 'name'.

7. As a conclusion to this chapter one can remind oneself of three features of Ockham's 'empiricism'. First, he bases all knowledge of the existent world on experience. We cannot, for example, discover that A is the cause of B, or that D is the effect of C, by *a priori* reasoning. Secondly, in his analysis of existent reality, or of the statements which we make about things, he uses the principle of economy. If two factors will suffice to explain motion, for example, one should not add a third. Lastly, when people do postulate unnecessary and unobservable entities, it is not infrequently because they have been misled by language. There is a striking passage on this matter in the *Tractatus de successivis*.[2] 'Nouns which are derived from verbs and also nouns which derive from adverbs, conjunctions, prepositions, and in general from syncategorematic terms . . . have been introduced only for the sake of brevity in speaking or as ornaments of speech; and many of them are equivalent in signification to propositions, when they do not stand for the terms from which they derive; and so they do not signify any things in addition to those from which they derive. . . . Of this kind are all nouns of the following kind: negation, privation, condition, perseity, contingency, universality, action, passion, . . . change, motion, and in general all verbal nouns deriving from verbs which belong to the categories of *agere* and *pati*, and many others, which cannot be treated now.'

[1] *Tractatus de successivis*, ed. Boehner, p. 119.   [2] *Ibid.*, p. 37.

CHAPTER VI

OCKHAM (4)

*The subject-matter of metaphysics—The univocal concept of being
—The existence of God—Our knowledge of God's nature—The
divine ideas—God's knowledge of future contingent events—The
divine will and omnipotence.*

1. OCKHAM accepts the statement of Aristotle that being is the
subject of metaphysics; but he insists that this statement must
not be understood as implying that metaphysics, considered in a
wide sense, possesses a strict unity based on its having one subject-
matter. If Aristotle and Averroes say that being is the subject
of metaphysics, the statement is false if it is interpreted as meaning
that all the parts of metaphysics have being as their subject-
matter. The statement is true, however, if it is understood as
meaning that 'among all the subjects of the different parts of
metaphysics being is first with a priority of predication (*primum
primitate praedicationis*). And there is a similarity between the
question, what is the subject of metaphysics or of the book of
categories and the question who is the king of the world or who is
the king of all Christendom. For just as different kingdoms have
different kings, and there is no king of the whole (world), though
sometimes these kings may stand in a certain relation, as when one
is more powerful or richer than another, so nothing is the subject
of the whole of metaphysics, but here the different parts have
different subjects, though these subjects may have a relation to
one another.'[1] If some people say that being is the subject of
metaphysics, while others say that God is the subject of metaphysics, a distinction must be made, if both statements are to be
justified. Among all the subjects of metaphysics God is the primary
subject as far as primacy of perfection is concerned; but being is
the primary subject as far as primacy of predication is concerned.[2]
For the metaphysician, when treating of God, considers truths
like 'God is good', predicating of God an attribute which is
primarily predicated of being.[3] There are, then, different branches
of metaphysics, or different metaphysical sciences with different
subjects. They have a certain relationship to one another, it is

[1] *Prol. Sent.*, 9, N.   [2] *Ibid.*   [3] *Ibid.*, D, D.

77

true; and this relationship justifies one in speaking of 'metaphysics' and in saying, for example, that being is the subject-matter of metaphysics in the sense mentioned, though it would not justify one's thinking that metaphysics is a unitary science, that is, that it is numerically one science.

2. In so far as metaphysics is the science of being as being it is concerned not with a thing but with a concept.[1] This abstract concept of being does not stand for a mysterious something which has to be known before we can know particular beings: it signifies all beings, not something in which beings participate. It is formed subsequently to the direct apprehension of existing things. 'I say that a particular being can be known, although those general concepts of being and unity are not known.'[2] For Ockham being and existing are synonymous: essence and existence signify the same, though the two words may signify the same thing in different ways. If 'existence' is used as a noun, then 'essence' and 'existence' signify the same thing grammatically and logically; but if the verb 'to be' is used instead of the noun 'existence', one cannot simply substitute 'essence', which is a noun, for the verb 'to be', for obvious grammatical reasons.[3] But this grammatical distinction cannot properly be taken as a basis for distinguishing essence and existence as distinct things: they are the same thing. It is clear, then, that the general concept of being is the result of the apprehension of concrete existing things; it is only because we have had direct apprehension of actual existents that we can form the general concept of being as such.

The general concept of being is univocal. On this point Ockham agrees with Scotus, so far as the use of the word 'univocal' is concerned. 'There is one concept common to God and creatures and predicable of them';[4] 'being' is a concept predicable in a univocal sense of all existent things.[5] Without a univocal concept we could not conceive God. We cannot in this life attain an intuition of the divine essence; nor can we have a simple 'proper' concept of God; but we can conceive God in a common concept predicable of Him and of other beings.[6] This statement must, however, be properly understood. It does not mean that the univocal concept of being acts as a bridge between a direct apprehension of creatures and a direct apprehension of God. Nor does it mean that one can form the abstract concept of being and

---
[1] 3 *Sent.*, 9, T.   [2] 1 *Sent.*, 3, 1, E.
[3] *Quodlibet*, 2, 7; *Summa totius logicae*, 3, 2.
[4] 1 *Sent.*, 2, 9, P.   [5] *Ibid.*, X.   [6] *Ibid.*, P.

deduce therefrom the existence of God. The existence of God is known in other ways, and not by an *a priori* deduction. But without a univocal concept of being one would be unable to conceive the existence of God. 'I admit that the simple knowledge of one creature in itself leads to the knowledge of another thing in a common concept. For example, by the simple knowledge of a whiteness which I have seen I am led to the knowledge of another whiteness which I have never seen, inasmuch as from the first whiteness I abstract a concept of whiteness which refers indifferently to them both. In the same way from some accident which I have seen I abstract a concept of being which does not refer more to that accident than to substance, nor to the creature more than to God.'[1] Obviously, my seeing a white patch does not assure me of the existence of any other white patch; nor did Ockham ever imagine that it could do so. To say that it could would be in flagrant contradiction with his philosophical principles. But, according to him, my seeing a white patch leads to an idea of whiteness which is applicable to other white patches when I see them. Similarly, my abstraction of the concept of being from apprehended existent beings does not assure me of the existence of any other beings. Yet unless I had a common concept of being I could not conceive of the existence of a being, God, which, unlike white patches, cannot be directly apprehended in this life. If, for example, I have no knowledge of God already and then I am told that God exists, I am able to conceive His existence in virtue of the common concept of being, though this does not mean, of course, that I have a 'proper' concept of the divine being.

Ockham was very careful to state his theory of the univocal concept of being in a way which would exclude any pantheistic implication. We must distinguish three types of univocity. In the first place a univocal concept may be a concept which is common to a number of things which are perfectly alike. In the second place a univocal concept may be a concept common to a number of things which are like in some points and unlike in other points. Thus man and ass are alike in being animals; and their matters are similar, though their forms are different. Thirdly, a univocal concept may mean a concept which is common to a plurality of things which are neither accidentally nor substantially alike; and it is in this way that a concept common to God and the creature is univocal, since they are alike neither substantially nor

[1] 3 *Sent.*, 9, R.

accidentally.¹ In regard to the contention that the concept of being is analogous and not univocal, Ockham observes that analogy can be understood in different ways. If by analogy is meant univocity in the third sense mentioned above, then the univocal concept of being may, of course, be called 'analogous';² but, since being as such is a concept and not a thing, there is no need to have recourse to the doctrine of analogy in order to avoid pantheism. If by saying that there can be a univocal concept of being predicable of God as well as of creatures, one meant to imply either that creatures are modes, as it were, of a being identified with God, or that God and creatures share in being, as something real in which they participate, then one would be forced either into accepting pantheism or into reducing God and creatures to the same level; but the doctrine of univocity does not imply anything of the kind, since there is no reality corresponding to the term 'being' when it is predicated univocally. Or, rather, the corresponding reality is simply different beings which are simply conceived as existing. If one considered these beings separately, one would have a plurality of concepts, for the concept of God is not the same as the concept of the creature. And in this case the term 'being' would be predicated equivocally, not univocally. Equivocation does not belong to concepts but to words, that is, to spoken or written terms. As far as the concept is concerned, when we conceive a plurality of beings we either have one concept or a number of concepts. If a word corresponds to one concept, it is used univocally; if it corresponds to several concepts, it is used equivocally. There is, then, no room for analogy, either in the case of concepts or in that of spoken or written words. 'There is no analogical predication, as contradistinguished from univocal, equivocal and denominative predication.'³ In fact, as denominative (that is, connotative) predication is reducible to univocal or to equivocal predication, one must say that predication must be either univocal or equivocal.⁴

3. But, though God can be conceived in some way, can it be philosophically shown that God exists? God is indeed the most perfect object of the human intellect, the supreme intelligible reality; but He is certainly not the first object of the human intellect in the sense of being the object which is first known.⁵ The primary object of the human mind is the material thing or embodied nature.⁶

¹ 3 *Sent.*, 9, Q. ² *Ibid.*, R. ³ *Ibid.*, E. ⁴ *Expositio aurea*, 2, 39, V.
⁵ 1 *Sent.*, 3, 1, D. ⁶ *Ibid.*, F.

We possess no natural intuition of the divine essence; and the proposition that God exists is not a self-evident proposition as far as we are concerned. If we imagine someone enjoying the vision of God and making the statement 'God exists', the statement may seem to be the same as the statement 'God exists' made by someone in this life who does not enjoy the vision of God. But though the two statements are verbally the same, the terms or concepts are really different; and in the second case it is not a self-evident proposition.[1] Any natural knowledge of God must, therefore, be derived from reflection on creatures. But can we come to know God from creatures? And, if so, is this knowledge certain knowledge?

Given Ockham's general position in regard to the subject of causality, one could hardly expect him to say that God's existence can be proved with certainty. For if we can only know of a thing that it has *a* cause, and if we cannot establish with certainty by any other way than by actual experience that *A* is the cause of *B*, we could not establish with certainty that the world is caused by God, if the term 'God' is understood in a recognized theistic sense. It is not very surprising, then, to find Ockham criticizing the traditional proofs of God's existence. He did not do so in the interests of scepticism, of course, but rather because he thought that the proofs were not logically conclusive. It does not follow, however, that once given his attitude scepticism, agnosticism or fideism, as the case might be, would not naturally follow.

As the authenticity of the *Centiloquium theologicum* is doubtful, it would scarcely be appropriate to discuss the treatment of the 'first mover' argument which is given by the author of that work. It is sufficient to say that the author refuses to allow that the basic principle of this Aristotelian-Thomist argument is either self-evident or demonstrable.[2] In fact, there are exceptions to the principle, inasmuch as an angel, and the human soul too, moves itself; and such exceptions show that the alleged principle cannot be a necessary principle and that it cannot form a basis for any strict proof of God's existence, especially as it cannot be proved that an infinite regress in the series of movers is impossible. The argument may be a probable argument in the sense that it is more probable that there is a first unmoved mover than that there is no such first unmoved mover; but it is not a certain argument. This criticism follows the line already suggested by Scotus; and even

---
[1] 1 *Sent.*, 3, 4, D, F.
[2] This principle is that whatever is moved is moved by another (*quidquid movetur ab alio movetur*).

if the work in which it occurs is not a work of Ockham, the criticism would seem to be in harmony with Ockham's ideas. Moreover, there can be no question of his having accepted St. Thomas's *manifestior via* as a certain argument for God's existence, as distinct from the existence of a first mover in a general sense. The first mover might be an angel or some being less than God, if we mean by 'God' an infinite, unique and absolutely supreme being.[1]

The proof from finality also goes by the board. Not only is it impossible to prove that the universe is ordered to one end, God,[2] but it cannot even be proved that individual things act for ends in a way which would justify any certain argument to God's existence. In the case of things which act without knowledge and will, all that we are warranted in saying is that they act because of a natural necessity: it makes no sense to say that they act 'for' an end.[3] Of course, if one presupposes God's existence, one can then speak of inanimate things as acting for ends, that is, for ends determined by God, who created their natures;[4] but if a statement is based on the presupposition of God's existence, it cannot itself be used to prove God's existence. As to agents endowed with intelligence and will, the reason for their voluntary actions is to be found in their own wills; and it cannot be shown that all wills are moved by the perfect good, God.[5] In fine, it is impossible to prove that there is in the universe an immanent teleological order, the existence of which makes it necessary to assert God's existence. There is no order distinct from 'absolute' natures themselves; and the only way in which one could prove God's existence would be as efficient cause of the existence of finite things. Is it, however, possible to do so?

In the *Quodlibet* Ockham states that one must stop at a first efficient cause and not proceed to infinity: but he adds immediately that this efficient cause might be a heavenly body, since 'we know by experience that it is the cause of other things'.[6] He says expressly not only that 'it cannot be proved by the natural reason that God is the immediate efficient cause of all things', but also that it cannot be proved that God is the mediate efficient cause of any effect. He gives as one reason of this the impossibility of proving that there exist any things other than corruptible things. It cannot be proved, for instance, that there is a spiritual and immortal soul in man. And the heavenly bodies can cause

---
[1] Cf. *Quodlibet*, 7, 22–3.   [2] *Ibid.*, 4, 2.
[3] *Summulae in libros physicorum*, 2, 6.
[4] 2 *Sent.*, 3, NN; *Quodlibet*, 4, 1.   [5] 1 *Sent.*, 1, 4, E.   [6] *Quodlibet*, 2, 1.

corruptible things, without its being possible to prove that the heavenly bodies themselves are caused by God.

However, in the commentary on the *Sentences*, Ockham gives his own version of the proof from efficient causality. It is better, he says, to argue from conservation to conserver rather than from product to producer. The reason for this is that 'it is difficult or impossible to prove against the philosophers that there cannot be an infinite regress in causes of the same kind, of which one can exist without the other'.[1] For example, Ockham does not think that it can be strictly proved that a man does not owe his total being to his parents, and they to their parents, and so on indefinitely. If it is objected that even in the case of an infinite series of this kind the infinite series would itself depend for its production on a being intrinsic to the series, Ockham answers that 'it would be difficult to prove that the series would not be possible unless there were one permanent being, on which the whole infinite series depended'.[2] He therefore prefers to argue that a thing which comes into being (that is, a contingent thing) is conserved in being as long as it exists. It can then be asked whether the conserver is itself dependent for its conservation or not. But in this case we cannot proceed to infinity, because an infinite number of *actual* conservers is, says Ockham, impossible. It may be possible to admit an infinite regress in the case of beings which exist one after the other, since in this case there would not be an actually existent infinity; but in the case of actual conservers of the world here and now, an infinite regress would imply an actual infinity. That an actual infinity of this sort is impossible is shown by the arguments of philosophers and others, which are 'reasonable enough' (*satis rationabiles*).

But even though reasonable arguments can be adduced for the existence of God as first conserver of the world, the unicity of God cannot be demonstrated.[3] It can be shown that there is some ultimate conserving being in *this* world; but we cannot exclude the possibility of there being another world or other worlds, with its or their own relatively first beings. To prove that there is a first efficient cause which is more perfect than *its* effects is not the same thing as proving the existence of a being which is superior to every other being, unless you can first prove that every other being is the effect of one single cause.[4] The unicity of God is known with certainty only by faith.

---
[1] 1 *Sent.*, 2, 10, O.   [2] *Ibid.*   [3] *Quodlibet*, 1, 1.   [4] 1 *Sent.*, 35, 2, C.

In answer, therefore, to the question whether Ockham admitted any philosophical proof of God's existence one must first make a distinction. If by 'God' one means the absolutely supreme, perfect, unique and infinite being, Ockham did not think that the existence of such a being can be strictly proved by the philosopher. If, on the other hand, one means by 'God' the first conserving cause of this world, without any certain knowledge about the nature of that cause, Ockham did think that the existence of such a being can be philosophically proved. But, as this second understanding of the term 'God' is not all that is usually understood by the term, one might just as well say, without further ado, that Ockham did not admit the demonstrability of God's existence. Only by faith do we know, as far at least as certain knowledge is concerned, that the supreme and unique being in the fullest sense exists. From this it would seem to follow, as historians have argued, that theology and philosophy fall apart, since it is not possible to prove the existence of the God whose revelation is accepted on faith. But it does not follow, of course, that Ockham himself was concerned to separate theology from philosophy. If he criticized the traditional proofs of God's existence, he criticized them from the point of view of a logician, and not in order to break apart the traditional synthesis. Moreover, though it may be tempting to a modern philosopher to depict Ockham as assigning to theological propositions a purely 'emotional' significance by relegating a large number of the propositions of traditional metaphysics to dogmatic theology, this would be an inaccurate interpretation of his position. When he said, for example, that theology is not a science, he did not mean that theological propositions are not informative propositions or that no theological syllogism can be a correct piece of reasoning: what he meant was that since the premisses of theological arguments are known by faith the conclusions too fall within the same sphere, and that since the premisses are not self-evident the arguments are not scientific demonstrations in the strict sense of 'scientific demonstration'. Ockham did not deny that a probable argument can be given for God's existence. What he denied was that the existence of God as the unique absolutely supreme being can be philosophically 'demonstrated'.

4. If the existence of God as the absolutely supreme being cannot be strictly proved by the natural reason, it is obvious that it cannot be proved that there is an infinite and omnipotent being, creator of all things. But the question may be raised whether,

given the concept of God as the absolutely supreme being, it can then be demonstrated that God is infinite and omnipotent. Ockham's answer to this question is that attributes like omnipotence, infinity, eternity or the power to create out of nothing cannot be demonstrated to belong to the divine essence. His reason for saying this is a technical one. *A priori* demonstration involves the use of a middle term to which the predicate in question belongs in a prior manner. But in the case of an attribute like infinity there can be no middle term to which infinity belongs; and so there can be no demonstration that God is infinite. It may be said that concepts like infinity or the power of creating out of nothing can be demonstrated to belong to the divine essence by using their definitions as middle terms. For example, one can argue in this way. Anything which can produce something from nothing is capable of creating. But God can produce something from nothing. Therefore God can create. A syllogism of this kind, says Ockham, is not what is meant by a demonstration. A demonstration in the proper sense increases knowledge; but the syllogism just mentioned does not increase knowledge, since the statement that God produces or can produce something from nothing is precisely the same as the statement that God creates or can create. The syllogism is useless unless one knows the meaning of the term 'create'; but if we know the meaning of the term 'create' we know that the statement that God can produce something from nothing is the statement that God can create. Thus the conclusion which is professedly demonstrated is already assumed: the argument contains the fallacy of begging the question.[1]

On the other hand, there are some attributes which can be demonstrated. We can argue, for example, as follows. Every being is good: but God is a being: therefore God is good. In a syllogism of this sort there is a middle term, a concept common to God and creatures. But the term 'good' must here be understood as a connotative term, as connoting a relation to the will, if the argument is to be a demonstration. For if the term 'good' is not taken as a connotative term, it is simply synonymous with the term 'being'; and in this case we learn nothing at all from the argument. No attribute can be demonstrated to belong to a subject, unless the conclusion of the demonstration is *dubitabilis*, that is, unless one can significantly raise the question whether the

[1] *Prol. Sent.*, 2, D, D.

attribute is to be predicated of the subject or not. But if the term 'good' is taken not as a connotative term but as synonymous with 'being', we could not know that God is a being and significantly raise the question whether God is good. It is not required, of course, that the attribute predicated of a subject should be really distinct from a subject. Ockham rejected the Scotist doctrine of a formal distinction between the divine attributes, and maintained that there is no distinction. But we do not possess an intuition of the divine essence; and though the realities represented by our concepts of the divine essence and attributes are not distinct we can argue from one concept to another provided that there is a middle term. In the case of concepts common to God and creatures there is a middle term.

But in our knowledge of God's nature what is it precisely that constitutes the term of our cognition? We do not enjoy intuitive knowledge of God, which it is beyond the scope of the human intellect to attain by its own efforts. Nor can there be any natural 'abstractive' knowledge of God as He is in Himself, since it is impossible for us by our natural powers to have an abstractive knowledge of something in itself without an intuitive knowledge of that thing. It follows, therefore, that in our natural state it is impossible for us to know God in such a way that the divine essence is the immediate and sole term of the act of knowing.[1] Secondly, we cannot in our natural state conceive God in a simple concept, proper to Him alone. For 'no thing can be known by us through our natural powers in a simple concept proper to itself, unless the thing is known in itself. For otherwise we could say that colour can be known in a concept proper to colours by a man born blind.'[2] But, thirdly, God can be conceived by us in connotative concepts and in concepts which are common to God and creatures, like being. As God is a simple being, without any internal distinction save that between the three divine Persons, proper quidditative concepts (*conceptus quidditativi*) would be convertible; and so they would not be distinct concepts. If we can have distinct concepts of God, this is due to the fact that our concepts are not proper quidditative concepts of God. They are not convertible because they are either connotative concepts, like the concept of infinity which connotes the finite negatively, or concepts common to God and creatures, like the concept of wisdom. It is only a proper quidditative concept which corresponds

[1] 1 *Sent.*, 2, 9, P.   [2] *Ibid.*, R.

to a single reality. A connotative concept connotes a reality other than the subject of which it is predicated; and a common concept is predicable of other realities than the one of which it is in fact predicated. Moreover, the common concepts which we predicate of God are due to a reflection on other realities than God and presuppose them.

An important consequence follows. If we have, as we do have, distinct concepts of God, a simple being, our conceptual knowledge of the divine nature is a knowledge of concepts rather than a knowledge of God as He is. What we attain is not the divine essence but a mental representation of the divine essence. We can form, it is true, a composite concept which is predicable of God alone; but this concept is a mental construction; we cannot have a simple concept proper to God which would adequately mirror the divine essence. 'Neither the divine essence . . . nor anything intrinsic to God nor anything which is really God can be known by us without something other than God being involved as object.'[1] 'We cannot know in themselves either the unity of God . . . or His infinite power or the divine goodness or perfection; but what we know immediately are concepts, which are not really God but which we use in propositions to stand for God.'[2] We know the divine nature, then, only through the medium of concepts; and these concepts, not being proper quidditative concepts, cannot take the place of an immediate apprehension of the essence of God. We do not attain a reality (*quid rei*), but a nominal representation (*quid nominis*). This is not to say that theology is not true or that its propositions have no meaning; but it is to say that the theologian is confined to the sphere of concepts and mental representation and that his analyses are analyses of concepts, not of God Himself. To imagine, for example, as Scotus did, that because we conceive divine attributes in distinct concepts these attributes are formally distinct in God is to misunderstand the nature of theological reasoning.

The foregoing inadequate account of what Ockham has to say on the subject of our knowledge of the divine nature really belongs to an account of his theological rather than of his philosophical ideas. For if the existence of God as the absolutely supreme being cannot be firmly established by the philosopher, it is obvious that the philosopher cannot give us any certain knowledge of God's nature. Nor can the theologian's reasoning, according to Ockham,

[1] 1 *Sent.*, 3, 2, F. [2] *Ibid.*, M.

give us certain knowledge of God's nature. As far as the analysis of concepts goes, an unbeliever could perform the same analysis as is performed by the believing theologian. What gives us certain knowledge of the truth of theological propositions is not the theologian's reasoning as such, nor his demonstrations, so far as demonstration is possible for him, but God's revelation accepted on faith. The theologian can reason correctly from certain premises; but so can the unbeliever. The former, however, accepts the premises and the conclusions on faith; and he knows that the propositions are true, that is, that they correspond to reality. But he knows this by faith; and his knowledge is not, in the strict sense, 'science'. For there is no intuitive knowledge lying at the basis of his reasoning. Ockham did not intend to question the truth of theological dogmas: he set out to examine the nature of theological reasoning and theological concepts, and he treated his problems from the point of view of a logician. His theological nominalism was not, in his own mind, equivalent to agnosticism or scepticism: it was rather, in intention at any rate, a logical analysis of a theology which he accepted.

But though Ockham's discussion of our knowledge of God's nature belongs more properly to the theological than to the philosophical sphere, it has its place in a discussion of his philosophy, if only for the reason that in it he deals with matters which preceding mediaeval philosophers had considered to fall within the metaphysician's competence. Similarly, though the philosopher as such could scarcely, in Ockham's eyes, establish anything with certainty about the divine 'ideas', this topic had been a salient feature of the traditional mediaeval metaphysics, and Ockham's treatment of it is closely linked with his general philosophic principles. It is desirable, therefore, to say something about it here.

5. In the first place there cannot be any plurality in the divine intellect. The divine intellect is identical with the divine will and the divine essence. We may speak about 'the divine will', 'the divine intellect' and 'the divine essence'; but the reality referred to is one single and simple being. Hence, talk about the 'divine ideas' cannot be taken to refer to realities in God which are in any way distinct either from the divine essence or from one another. If there were a distinction at all, it would be a real distinction; and a real distinction cannot be admitted. In the second place,

it is quite unnecessary, and also misleading, to postulate divine ideas as a kind of intermediary factor in creation. Apart from the fact that if the divine ideas are in no way distinct from the divine intellect, which is itself identical with the divine essence, they cannot be an intermediary factor in creation, God can know creatures and create them without the intervention of any 'ideas'.[1] Ockham makes it clear that in his opinion the theory of ideas in God is simply a piece of anthropomorphism. It also involves a confusion between *quid rei* and *quid nominis*.[2] The upholders of the theory would certainly admit that there is not a real distinction either between the divine essence and the divine ideas or between the ideas themselves but that the distinction is a mental distinction; yet they talk as though the distinction of ideas in God were prior to the production of creatures. Moreover, they postulate in God ideas of universals, which as a matter of fact do not correspond to any reality. In fine, Ockham applies the principle of economy to the theory of divine ideas in so far as this theory implies that there are ideas in God which are distinct from creatures themselves, whether the ideas are interpreted as real or as mental relations. It is unnecessary to postulate such ideas in God to explain either His production of or His knowledge of creatures.

In one sense, therefore, Ockham may be said to have rejected the theory of divine ideas. But this does not mean that he was prepared to declare that St. Augustine was in error or that there was no acceptable interpretation of the theory. On the contrary, as far as verbal acceptance was concerned, he must be said to have accepted the theory. But the meaning which he attaches to the statements he makes has to be clearly understood, if he is not to be judged guilty of flagrant self-contradiction. He asserts, for instance, that there is an infinite number of distinct ideas; and this assertion appears at first hearing to be in obvious contradiction with his condemnation of any ascription of distinct ideas to God.

In the first place, the term 'idea' is a connotative term. It denotes directly the creature itself; but it connotes indirectly the divine knowledge or knower. 'And so it can be predicated of the creature itself that it is an idea but not of the knowing agent nor of the knowledge, since neither the knowledge nor the knower is

[1] Cf. 1 *Sent.*, 35, 5, C.
[2] In other words, Ockham considered that the upholders of the theory had been misled by language, confusing words or names with things.

an idea or pattern.'[1] We can say, then, that the creature itself is the idea. 'The ideas are not in God subjectively and really; but they are in Him only objectively, that is, as certain things which are known by Him, for the ideas are the things themselves which are producible by God.'[2] In other words, it is quite sufficient to postulate God on the one hand and creatures on the other hand: the creatures as known by God are the 'ideas', and there are no other ideas. The creature as known from eternity by God can be considered as the pattern or exemplar of the creature as actually existent. 'The ideas are certain known patterns (*exempla*); and it is by reference to them that the knower can produce something in real existence. . . . This description does not fit the divine essence itself, nor any mental relation, but the creature itself. . . . The divine essence is not an idea . . . (Nor is the idea either a real or a mental relation) . . . Not a real relation, since there is no real relation on God's part to the creature; and not a mental relation, both because there is no mental relation of God to the creature to which the name "idea" could be given and because a mental relation cannot be the exemplar of the creature, just as an *ens rationis* cannot be the exemplar of a real being.'[3] But if creatures themselves are the ideas, it follows that 'there are distinct ideas of all makable things, as the things themselves are distinct from one another'.[4] And thus there are distinct ideas of all the essential and integral parts of producible things, like matter and form.[5]

On the other hand, if the ideas are the creatures themselves, it follows that the ideas are of individual things, 'since individual things alone are producible outside (the mind) and no others'.[6] There are, for example, no divine ideas of genera; for the divine ideas are creatures makable by God, and genera cannot be produced as real existents. It follows, too, that there are no ideas of negations, privations, evil, guilt and the like, since these are not and cannot be distinct things.[7] But, as God can produce an infinity of creatures, we must say that there is an infinite number of ideas.[8]

Ockham's discussion of the theory of divine ideas illuminates both the general mediaeval outlook and his own mentality. The respect for St. Augustine in the Middle Ages was too great for it to be possible for a theologian simply to reject one of his main theories. We find, then, the language of the theory being retained

[1] 1 *Sent.*, 35, 5, E.   [2] *Ibid.*, G.   [3] *Ibid.*, E.   [4] *Ibid.*, G.
[5] *Ibid.*   [6] *Ibid.*   [7] *Ibid.*   [8] *Ibid.*

and used by Ockham. He was willing to speak of distinct ideas and of these ideas as patterns or exemplars of creation. On the other hand, using the principle of economy and determined to get rid of anything which might seem to come between the omnipotent Creator and the creature so as to govern the divine will, he pruned the theory of all Platonism and identified the ideas with creatures themselves as producible by God and as known by God from eternity as producible. From the philosophical point of view he fitted the theory to his general philosophy by eliminating universal ideas, while from the theological point of view he safeguarded, as he thought, the divine omnipotence and eliminated what he considered to be the contamination of Greek metaphysics. (Having identified the ideas with creatures he was able, however, to observe that Plato acted rightly in neither identifying the ideas with God nor placing them in the divine mind.) This is not to say, of course, that Ockham's use of the language of the Aristotelian theory was insincere. He postulated the theory, in so far as it could be taken to mean simply that creatures are known by God, for one of the main traditional reasons, namely that God creates rationally and not irrationally.[1] But at the same time it is clear that in Ockham's hands the theory was so purged of Platonism that to all intents and purposes it was rejected in its original form. Abelard, while rejecting ultra-realism, had retained the theory of universal ideas in God, largely out of respect for St. Augustine; but Ockham eliminated these universal divine ideas. His version of the theory of ideas is thus consistent with his general principle that there are only individual existents and with his constant attempt to get rid of any other factors which could be got rid of. It might be said, of course, that to speak of producible creatures as known by God from all eternity ('things were ideas from eternity; but they were not actually existent from eternity')[2] is to admit the essence of the theory of ideas; and this is, in fact, what Ockham thought and what justified him, in his opinion, in appealing to St. Augustine. But it is perhaps questionable if Ockham's theory is altogether consistent. As he would not confine God's creative power in any way, he had to extend the range of 'ideas' beyond the things actually produced by God; but to do this is, of course, to admit that the 'ideas' cannot be identified with creatures that have existed, do exist and will exist; and to admit this is to come very close to the Thomist theory, except that no ideas of universals

[1] Cf. 1 *Sent.*, 35, 5, E.   [2] *Ibid.*, M.

are admitted. The conclusion that should probably be drawn is not that Ockham made an insincere use of the language of a theory which he had really discarded, but rather that he sincerely accepted the theory, though he interpreted it in such a way as to fit in with his conviction that only individuals exist or can exist and that universal concepts belong to the level of human thought and are not to be attributed to God.

6. When it comes to discussing the divine knowledge Ockham shows a marked and, indeed, very understandable reluctance to make assertions concerning a level of cognition which lies entirely outside our experience.

That God knows, besides Himself, all other things cannot be proved philosophically. Any proof would rest principally on God's universal causality; but, apart from the fact that it cannot be proved by means of the principle of causality that a cause knows its immediate effect, it cannot be proved philosophically that God is the immediate cause of all things.[1] Probable arguments can be given for saying that God knows some things other than Himself; but the arguments are not conclusive. On the other hand, it cannot be proved that God knows nothing other than Himself; for it cannot be proved that every act of cognition depends on its object.[2] Nevertheless, though it cannot be philosophically proved that God is omniscient, that is, that He knows not only Himself but also all other things as well, we know by faith that He is.

But, if God knows all things, does this mean that He knows future contingent events, in the sense of events which depend on free wills for their actuality? 'I say to this question that it must be held without any doubt that God knows all future contingent events with certainty and evidence. But it is impossible for any intellect in our present state to make evident either this fact or the manner in which God knows all future contingent events.'[3] Aristotle, says Ockham, would have said that God has no certain knowledge of any future contingent events for the following reason. No statement that a future contingent event depending on free choice will happen or will not happen is true. The proposition that it either will or will not happen is true; but neither the statement that it will happen nor the statement that it will not happen is true. And if neither statement is true, neither statement can be known. 'In spite of this reason, however, we must hold that God evidently knows all future contingents. But the way (in which

---

[1] 1 *Sent.*, 35, 2, D.   [2] *Ibid.*   [3] *Ibid.*, 38, 1, L.

God knows them) I cannot explain.'[1] But Ockham goes on to say that God does not know future contingent events as present to Him,[2] or by means of ideas as media of knowledge, but by the divine essence itself, although this cannot be proved philosophically. Similarly in the *Tractatus de praedestinatione et de praescientia Dei et de futuris contingentibus*[3] Ockham states: 'So I say that it is impossible to express clearly the way in which God knows future contingent events. However, it must be held that He does (know them), though contingently.' By saying that God knows future contingent facts 'contingently' Ockham means that God knows them as contingent and that His knowledge does not make them necessary. He goes on to suggest that 'the divine essence is intuitive knowledge which is so perfect and so clear that it is itself evident knowledge of all past and future events, so that it knows which part of a contradiction will be true and which part false'.[4]

Thus Ockham affirms that God does not merely know that, for example, I shall choose tomorrow either to go for a walk or to stop at home and read; He knows which alternative is true and which false. This affirmation is not one that can be proved philosophically: it is a theological matter. As to the mode of God's knowledge, Ockham does not offer any suggestion beyond saying that the divine essence is such that God does know future contingent facts. He does not have recourse to the expedient of saying that God knows which part of a disjunctive proposition concerning a future contingent event is true because He determines it to be true: he very sensibly admits that he cannot explain how God knows future contingent events. It is to be noted, however, that Ockham is convinced that one part of a disjunctive proposition concerning such an event is true, and that God knows it as true. This is the important fact from the purely philosophical point of view: the relation of God's knowledge of future free events to the theme of predestination does not concern us here. It is an important fact because it shows that Ockham did not admit an exception to the principle of excluded middle. Some fourteenth-century philosophers did admit an exception. For Petrus Aureoli, as we have seen, propositions which either affirm or deny that a definite contingent event will happen in the future are neither true nor false.

[1] 1 *Sent.*, 38, 1, M.
[2] St. Thomas held that future contingent events are present to God in virtue of His eternity and that He knows them as present.
[3] Ed. Boehner, p. 15.　　　　[4] *Ibid.*

Petrus Aureoli did not deny that God knows future contingent events; but he maintained that as God's knowledge does not look forward, as it were, to the future, it does not make an affirmative or a negative statement which concerns a definite free act in the future either true or false. One can say, then, that he admitted an instance of a 'three-valued' logic, though it would, of course, be an anachronism to depict him as elaborating such a logic. This is not the case, however, with William of Ockham, who does not admit any propositions to be neither true nor false. He rejected Aristotle's arguments designed to show that there are such propositions, though there are one or two passages which seem at first sight to support Aristotle's point of view. Moreover, in the *Summa totius logicae*[1] Ockham expressly states, in opposition to Aristotle, that propositions about future contingent events are true or false. Again, in the *Quodlibet*[2] he maintains that God can reveal knowledge of affirmative propositions concerning future contingent events, because such propositions are true. God made revelations of this sort to the prophets; though precisely how it was done 'I do not know, because it has not been revealed to me.' One cannot say, then, that Ockham admitted an exception to the principle of excluded middle. And because he did not admit an exception he was not faced with the problems of reconciling the admission with the divine omniscience.

7. If the terms 'will', 'intellect' and 'essence' are understood in an absolute sense, they are synonymous. 'If some name were used to signify precisely the divine essence and nothing else, without any connotation of anything else whatever, and similarly if some name were used to signify the divine will in the same manner, those names would be simply synonymous names; and whatever was predicated of the one could be predicated of the other.'[3] Accordingly, if the terms 'essence' and 'will' are taken absolutely, there is no more reason to say that the divine will is the cause of all things than that the divine essence is the cause of all things: it comes to the same thing. However, whether we speak of the 'divine essence' or of the 'divine will', God is the immediate cause of all things, though this cannot be demonstrated philosophically.[4] The divine will (or the divine essence) is the immediate cause of all things in the sense that without the divine causality no effect would follow, even though all other conditions and dispositions were present. Moreover, the power of God is unlimited, in the

[1] 2, 32.   [2] 4, 4.   [3] 1 *Sent.*, 45, 1, C.   [4] *Ibid.*, G.

sense that He can do all that is possible. But to say that God cannot do what is intrinsically impossible is not to limit God's power; for it makes no sense to speak of doing or making what is intrinsically impossible. However, God can produce every possible effect, even without a secondary cause; He could, for instance, produce in the human being an act of hatred of Himself, and if He were to do so He would not sin.[1] That God can produce every possible effect, even without the concurrence of a secondary cause, cannot be proved by the philosopher; but it is none the less to be believed.

The divine omnipotence cannot, then, be philosophically proved. But once it is assumed as an article of faith the world appears in a special light. All empirical causal relations, that is, all regular sequences, are seen as contingent, not only in the sense that causal relations are matters for experiential verification and not for *a priori* deduction, but also in the sense that an external agent, namely God, can always produce B without employing A as secondary cause. Of course, in all mediaeval systems of thought the uniformity and regularity of natural processes were regarded as contingent, inasmuch as the possibility of God's miraculous intervention was admitted by all Christian thinkers. But the metaphysic of essences had conferred on Nature a comparative stability of which Ockham deprived it. With him relations and connections in nature were really reduced to the co-existence or successive existence of 'absolutes'. And in the light of the divine omnipotence, believed on faith, the contingency of relations and of order in nature was seen as the expression of the all-powerful will of God. Ockham's view of nature, taken in isolation from its theological background, might reasonably be regarded as a stage on the path to a scientific view of nature through the elimination of the metaphysical; but the theological background was not for Ockham himself an irrelevant excrescence. On the contrary, the thought of the divine omnipotence and liberty pervaded, explicitly or implicitly, his whole system; and in the next chapter we shall see how his convictions on this matter influenced his moral theory.

[1] 1 *Sent.*, 42, 1, G

CHAPTER VII

OCKHAM (5)

That an immaterial and incorruptible soul is the form of the body cannot be philosophically proved—The plurality of really distinct forms in man—The rational soul possesses no really distinct faculties—The human person—Freedom—Ockham's ethical theory.

1. JUST as Ockham criticized the traditional proofs of God's existence, so also did he criticize a number of the proofs advanced by his predecessors in psychology. We experience acts of understanding and willing; but there is no compelling reason to attribute these acts to an immaterial form or soul. We experience these acts as acts of the form of the body; and, as far as experience takes us, we might reasonably conclude that they are the acts of an extended and corporeal form.[1] 'Understanding by intellectual soul an immaterial and incorruptible form which is wholly in the whole and wholly in every part (of the body), it cannot be known evidently either by arguments or by experience that there is such a form in us or that the activity of understanding belongs to a substance of this kind in us, or that a soul of this kind is the form of the body. I do not care what Aristotle thought about this, for he seems to speak always in an ambiguous manner. But these three things we hold only by faith.'[2] According to Ockham, then, we do not experience the presence of an immaterial and incorruptible form in ourselves; nor can it be proved that the acts of understanding which we do experience are the acts of such a form. And even if we could prove that the acts of understanding which we experience are the acts of an immaterial substance, it would not follow that this substance is the form of the body. And if it cannot be shown by philosophic reasoning or by experience that we possess immaterial and incorruptible souls, it obviously cannot be shown that these souls are created directly by God.[3] Ockham does not say, of course, that we do not possess immortal souls: what he says is that we cannot prove that we possess them. That we do possess them is a revealed truth, known by faith.

2. But though Ockham accepted on faith the existence of an

[1] *Quodlibet*, 1, 12.   [2] *Ibid.*, 1, 10.   [3] *Ibid.*, 2, 1.

immaterial and incorruptible form in man, he was not prepared to say that this form informs matter directly. The function of matter is to support a form; and it is clear that the matter of the human body has a form. But the corruptibility of the human body shows that it is not an incorruptible form which informs matter immediately. 'I say that one must postulate in man another form in addition to the intellectual soul, namely a sensitive form, on which a natural agent can act by way of corruption and production.'[1] This sensitive form or soul is distinct from man's intellectual soul and, unless God wills otherwise, it perishes with the body.[2] There is only one sensitive form in an animal or in a man; but it is extended in such a way that 'one part of the sensitive soul perfects one part of matter, while another part of the same soul perfects another part of matter'.[3] Thus the part of the sensitive soul which perfects the organ of sight is the power of seeing, while the part which perfects the organ of hearing is the power of hearing.[4] In this sense, then, we can speak of sensitive powers which are really distinct from one another; for 'the accidental dispositions which are of necessity required for the act of seeing are really distinct from the dispositions which are of necessity required for the act of hearing'.[5] This is clear from the fact that one can lose the power of sight, for example, without losing the power of hearing. But if we mean by 'powers' forms which are the eliciting principles of the various acts of sensation, there is no need to postulate really distinct powers corresponding to the various organs of sense: the principle of economy can be applied. The one eliciting principle is the sensitive form or soul itself, which is extended throughout the body and works through the different sense-organs.

In one place Ockham speaks as follows. 'According to the opinion which I consider the true one there are in man several substantial forms, at least a form of corporeity and the intellectual soul.'[6] In another place he says that though it is difficult to prove that there are or are not several substantial forms in man, 'it is proved (that there are) in the following way, at least in regard to the intellectual soul and the sensitive soul, which are distinct in man'.[7] His remark about the difficulty of proof is explained in the *Quodlibet*,[8] where he says that it is difficult to prove that the sensitive and intellectual souls are distinct in man 'because it cannot be proved from self-evident propositions'. But this does

---

[1] 2 *Sent.*, 22, H.   [2] *Quodlibet*, 2, 10.   [3] 2 *Sent.*, 26, E.   [4] *Ibid.*
[5] *Ibid.*, D.   [6] *Ibid.*, 9, C C.   [7] 4 *Sent.*, 7, F.   [8] 2, 10.

not prevent his going on to offer arguments based on experience, such as the argument that we can desire a thing with the sensitive appetite, while at the same time we turn away from it with the rational will. As to the fact that in one place he seems to insist on the intellectual soul and the form of corporeity, whereas in another place he seems to insist on the presence in man of intellectual and sensitive souls, the apparent inconsistency seems to be explicable in terms of the two contexts. In any case Ockham clearly maintained the existence in man of three distinct forms. He argues not only that the intellectual soul and the sensitive soul are distinct in man,[1] but also that the sensitive soul and the form of corporeity are really distinct both in men and brutes.[2] In maintaining the existence of a form of corporeity in man Ockham was, of course, continuing the Franciscan tradition; and he gives the traditional theological argument, that the form of corporeity must be postulated in order to explain the numerical identity of Christ's dead body with His living body, though he gives other arguments as well.

In saying that there is in man a form of corporeity and in maintaining that the intellectual soul does not inform prime matter directly Ockham was continuing, then, a traditional position, in favour of which he rejected that of St. Thomas. Moreover, though he maintained the doctrine of the plurality of substantial forms, he did not deny that man, taken in his totality, is a unity. 'There is only one total being of man, but several partial beings.'[3] Nor did he deny that the intellectual soul is the form of the body, though he did not think that this can be proved philosophically. Hence it can hardly be said that Ockham contradicted the teaching of the Council of Vienne (1311), since the Council did not assert that the rational or intellectual soul informs prime matter directly. The majority of the members of the Council themselves held the doctrine of the form of corporeity; and when they declared that the rational soul informs the body directly they left the question entirely open whether or not the body which is informed by the rational soul is constituted as a body by its own form of corporeity or not. On the other hand, the Council had clearly intended to defend the unity of the human being against the implications of Olivi's psychological theories;[4] and it is at least questionable whether Ockham's teaching satisfied this demand.

---

[1] *Quodlibet*, 2, 10; 2 *Sent.*, 22, H.   [2] *Quodlibet*, 2, 11.
[3] *Ibid.*, 2, 10.   [4] See vol. II of this history, pp. 451-3.

It must be remembered that for Ockham a real distinction meant a distinction between things which can be separated, at least by the divine power: he rejected the Scotist doctrine of formal objective distinctions, that is, of objective distinctions between different 'formalities' of one and the same thing, which cannot be separated from one another. When discussing the question whether the sensitive soul and the intellectual soul are really distinct in man, he remarks that the sensitive soul of Christ, though always united to the Deity, remained where God pleased during the time between Christ's death and the resurrection. 'But whether it remained with the body or with the intellectual soul God alone knows; yet both can well be said.'[1] If, however, the sensitive form is really separable from man's rational form and from his body, it is difficult to see how the unity of man can be preserved. It is true, of course, that all the mediaeval Christian thinkers would have admitted that the rational soul is separable from the body: they obviously could not do otherwise. And it might be argued that to assert the separability of the sensitive from the rational soul does not impair man's unity any more than does the assertion that man's rational soul is separable from his body. However, one is entitled to say at least that Ockham's doctrine of the real distinction between the sensitive and rational souls in man makes it harder to safeguard the unity of man than does Scotus's doctrine of the formal distinction. Ockham, of course, disposed of Scotus's formal distinction by means of the principle of economy, and he supported his theory of the real distinction between the sensitive and rational souls by an appeal to experience. It was, indeed, for similar reasons that Scotus maintained the formal distinction; but he seems to have realized better than Ockham the fundamental unity of man's intellectual and sensitive life. In certain respects he appears to have been less influenced by Aristotle than was Ockham, who envisaged the possibility at any rate of the rational soul's being united to the body more as a mover than as a form, though, as we have seen, he accepted on faith the doctrine that the intellectual soul is the form of the body.

3. Though Ockham asserted the existence in man of a plurality of forms, really distinct from one another, he would not admit a real distinction between the faculties of a given form. We have already seen that he refused to allow that the sensitive soul or form possesses powers which are really distinct from the sensitive

[1] *Quodlibet*, 2, 10.

soul itself and from one another, unless by 'powers' one means simply accidental dispositions in the various sense-organs. He also refused to allow that the rational soul or form possesses faculties which are really distinct from the rational soul itself and from one another. The rational soul is unextended and spiritual; and it cannot have parts or ontologically distinct faculties. What is called the intellect is simply the rational soul understanding, and what we call the will is simply the soul willing. The rational soul produces acts; and the intellectual power or faculty 'does not signify only the essence of the soul, but it connotes the act of understanding. And similarly in the case of the will.'[1] In one sense, then, intellect and will are really distinct, that is, if we are taking them as connotative terms; for an act of understanding is really distinct from an act of willing. But if we are referring to that which produces the acts, intellect and will are not really distinct. The principle of economy can be applied in the elimination of really distinct faculties or principles.[2] There is one rational soul, which can elicit different acts. As to the existence of an active intellect distinct from the passive intellect there is no compelling reason for accepting it. The formation of universal concepts, for example, can be explained without postulating any activity of the intellect.[3] Nevertheless, Ockham is prepared to accept the active intellect on account of the authority 'of the saints and philosophers',[4] in spite of the fact that the arguments for its existence can be answered and that in any case no more than probable arguments can be given.

4. In asserting a plurality of substantial forms in man and in denying at the same time that intellect and will are really distinct faculties Ockham remained faithful to two features of the Franciscan tradition. But the doctrine of the plurality of forms in man traditionally meant an acceptance of the form of corporeity in addition to the one human soul, not a breaking-up, as it were, of the soul into distinct forms in Ockham's sense of distinction. His substitution of the real distinction, involving separability, for Scotus's formal objective distinction was scarcely compatible with the assertion of the unity of the human being. Yet in discussing human personality Ockham insisted on this unity. The person is a *suppositum intellectuale*, a definition which holds good for both created and uncreated persons.[5] A *suppositum* is 'a complete

---

[1] 2 *Sent.*, 24, L. [2] *Ibid.*, K. [3] *Ibid.*, 25, O.
[4] *Ibid.*, A A. [5] 1 *Sent.*, 25, J.

being, incommunicable by identity, incapable of inhering in anything, and not supported (*sustentatum*) by anything'.[1] The words 'a complete being' exclude from the class of *supposita* all parts, whether essential or integral, while the words 'incommunicable by identity' exclude the divine essence, which, though a complete being, is 'communicated' identically to the divine Persons. The phrase 'incapable of inhering in anything' excludes accidents, while 'not supported (Ockham means "taken up" or "assumed") by anything' excludes the human nature of Christ, which was assumed by the second Person and is consequently not a person. In the commentary on the *Sentences* Ockham defines 'person' as 'an intellectual and complete nature, which is neither supported (*nec sustentatur*, is not assumed) by anything else nor is able, as a part, to form with another thing one being'.[2] In the case of the three divine Persons each *suppositum intellectuale* or Person is constituted by the divine essence and a relation.[3]

The human person, then, is the total being of man, not the rational form or soul alone. It is in virtue of the rational form that a human being is a *suppositum intellectuale* as distinct from any other kind of *suppositum*; but it is the whole man, not the rational form alone, which constitutes the human person. Ockham, therefore, maintains with St. Thomas that the human soul in the state of separation from the body after death is not a person.[4]

5. One of the principal characteristics of a rational creature is freedom.[5] Freedom is the power 'by which I can indifferently and contingently produce an effect in such a way that I can cause or not cause that effect, without any difference in that power having been made'.[6] That one possesses this power cannot be proved by *a priori* reasoning, but 'it can, however, be known evidently through experience, that is, through the fact that every man experiences that however much his reason dictates something his will can will it or not will it'.[7] Moreover, the fact that we blame and praise people, that is, that we impute to them the responsibility for their actions, or for some of their actions, shows that we accept freedom as a reality. 'No act is blameworthy unless it is in our power. For no one blames a man born blind, for he is blind by sense (*caecus sensu*). But if he is blind by his own act, then he is blameworthy.'[8]

[1] *Quodlibet*, 4, 11. [2] 3 *Sent.*, 1, B; cf. 1 *Sent.*, 23, 1, C.
[3] 1 *Sent.*, 25, 1, J. [4] *Ibid.*, 23, 1, C. [5] *Ibid.*, 1, 3, U.
[6] *Quodlibet*, 1, 16. [7] *Ibid.* [8] 3 *Sent.*, 10, H.

According to Ockham, the will is free to will or not to will happiness, the last end; it does not will it necessarily. This is clear in regard to the last end considered in the concrete, that is to say, God. 'No object other than God can satisfy the will, because no act which is directed to something other than God excludes all anxiety and sadness. For, whatever created object may be possessed, the will can desire something else with anxiety and sadness.'[1] But that the enjoyment of the divine essence is possible to us cannot be proved philosophically; it is an article of faith.[2] If then we do not know that the enjoyment of God is possible, we cannot will it. And even if we know by faith that it is possible, we can still will it or not will it, as is clear from experience. What is more, we do not will necessarily even perfect happiness in general. For the intellect may believe that perfect happiness is not possible for man and that the only condition possible for us is the one in which we actually find ourselves. But if the intellect can believe that perfect happiness is impossible, it can dictate to the will that it should not will something which is impossible and incompatible with the reality of human life. And in this case the will is able not to will what the intellect says that it should not will. The judgment of the intellect is, indeed, erroneous; but though 'the will does not necessarily conform to the judgment of the reason, it can conform with the judgment of the reason, whether that judgment be right or erroneous'.[3]

In emphasizing the freedom of the will in the face of the judgment of the intellect Ockham was following in the common tradition of the Franciscan philosophers. But it may be remarked that his view on the will's freedom even in regard to the willing of happiness in general (*beatitudo in communi*) fitted in very much with his ethical theory. If the will is free to will or not to will happiness, it would scarcely be possible to analyse the goodness of human acts in terms of a relation to an end which is necessarily desired. And in point of fact Ockham's ethical theory was, as we shall see presently, markedly authoritarian in character.

It is only to be expected that Ockham would insist that the will is free to elicit an act contrary to that to which the sensitive appetite is strongly inclined.[4] But he admitted, of course, the existence of habits and inclinations in the sensitive appetite and in the will.[5] There is some difficulty, he says, in explaining how it

---

[1] 1 *Sent.*, 1, 4, S. [2] *Ibid.*, E. [3] *Ibid.*, 1, 6, P.
[4] 3 *Sent.*, 10, D. [5] Cf. 3 *Sent.*, 4, M; 3 *Sent.*, 10, D; 4 *Sent.*, 12, C.

is that habits are formed in a free power like the will as a result of repeated acts of the sensitive appetite; but that they are formed is a matter of experience. 'It is difficult to give the cause why the will is more inclined not to will an object which causes pain in the sensitive appetite.' The cause cannot be found in a command of the intellect, because the intellect can equally well say that the will should will that object as that it should not will it. But 'it is obvious through experience that even if the intellect says that death should be undergone for the sake of the State, the will is naturally, so to speak, inclined to the contrary'. On the other hand, we cannot simply say that the cause of the will's inclination is pleasure in the sensitive appetite. For, 'however intense may be the pleasure in the sensitive appetite, the will can, in virtue of its freedom, will the opposite'. 'And so I say that there does not seem to be any other cause for the will's natural inclination except that such is the nature of the matter; and this fact becomes known to us through experience.'[1] In other words, it is an undoubted fact of experience that the will is inclined to follow the sensitive appetite; but it is difficult to give a satisfactory theoretical explanation of the fact, though this does not alter the nature of the fact. If we indulge the sensitive appetite in a certain direction, a habit is formed, and this habit is reflected in what we can call a habit in the will, and this habit grows in strength if the will does not react sufficiently against the sensitive appetite. On the other hand, it remains in the will's power to act against habit and inclination, even if with difficulty, because the will is essentially free. A human act can never be attributed simply to habit and inclination; for it is possible for the will to choose in a manner contrary to the habit and inclination.

6. A created free will is subject to moral obligation. God is not, and cannot be, under any obligation; but man is entirely dependent upon God, and in his free acts his dependence expresses itself as moral obligation. He is morally obliged to will what God orders him to will and not to will what God orders him not to will. The ontological foundation of the moral order is thus man's dependence on God, as creature on Creator; and the content of the moral law is supplied by the divine precept. 'Evil is nothing else than to do something when one is under an obligation to do the opposite. Obligation does not fall on God, since He is not under any obligation to do anything.'[2]

---

[1] 3 *Sent.*, 13, U.   [2] 2 *Sent.*, 5, H.

This personal conception of the moral law was closely connected with Ockham's insistence on the divine omnipotence and liberty. Once these truths are accepted as revealed truths, the whole created order, including the moral law, is viewed by Ockham as wholly contingent, in the sense that not only its existence but also its essence and character depend on the divine creative and omnipotent will. Having got rid of any universal idea of man in the divine mind, Ockham was able to eliminate the idea of a natural law which is in essence immutable. For St. Thomas man was contingent, of course, in the sense that his existence depends on God's free choice; but God could not create the particular kind of being which we call man and impose on him precepts irrespective of their content. And, though he considered, for exegetic reasons connected with the Scriptures, that God can dispense in the case of certain precepts of the natural law, Scotus was fundamentally of the same mind as St. Thomas.[1] There are acts which are intrinsically evil and which are forbidden because they are evil: they are not evil simply because they are forbidden. For Ockham, however, the divine will is the ultimate norm of morality: the moral law is founded on the free divine choice rather than ultimately on the divine essence. Moreover, he did not hesitate to draw the logical consequences from this position. God concurs, as universal creator and conserver, in any act, even in an act of hatred of God. But He could also cause, as total cause, the same act with which He concurs as partial cause. 'Thus He can be the total cause of an act of hatred of God, and that without any moral malice.'[2] God is under no obligation; and therefore He could cause an act in the human will which would be a morally evil act if the man were responsible for it. If the man were responsible for it, he would commit sin, since he is obliged to love God and not hate Him; but obligation, being the result of divine imposition, cannot affect God Himself. 'By the very fact that God wills something, it is right for it to be done.... Hence if God were to cause hatred of Himself in anyone's will, that is, if He were to be the total cause of the act (He is, as it is, its partial cause), neither would that man sin nor would God; for God is not under any obligation, while the man is not (in the case) obliged, because the act would not be in his own power.'[3] God can do anything or order anything which does not involve logical contradiction. Therefore, because,

---

[1] On Scotus's moral theory, see vol. II of this history, pp. 545-50.
[2] 2 *Sent.*, 19, P.   [3] 4 *Sent.*, 9, E-F.

according to Ockham, there is no natural or formal repugnance between loving God and loving a creature in a way which has been forbidden by God, God could order fornication. Between loving God and loving a creature in a manner which is illicit there is only an extrinsic repugnance, namely the repugnance which arises from the fact that God has actually forbidden that way of loving a creature. Hence, if God were to order fornication, the latter would be not only licit but meritorious.[1] Hatred of God, stealing, committing adultery, are forbidden by God. But they could be ordered by God; and, if they were, they would be meritorious acts.[2] No one can say that Ockham lacked the courage to draw the logical conclusions from his personal theory of ethics.

Needless to say, Ockham did not mean to suggest that adultery, fornication, theft and hatred of God are legitimate acts in the present moral order; still less did he mean to encourage the commission of such acts. His thesis was that such acts are wrong because God has forbidden them; and his intention was to emphasize the divine omnipotence and liberty, not to encourage immorality. He made use of the distinction between the absolute power (*potentia absoluta*) of God, by which God could order the opposite of the acts which He has, as a matter of fact, forbidden, and the *potentia ordinata* of God, whereby God has actually established a definite moral code. But he explained the distinction in such a way as to make it clear not only that God could have established another moral order but that He could at any time order what He has actually forbidden.[3] There is no sense, then, in seeking for any more ultimate reason of the moral law than the divine *fiat*. Obligation arises through the encounter of a created free will with an external precept. In God's case there can be no question of an external precept. Therefore God is not obliged to order any kind of act rather than its opposite. That He has ordered this and forbidden that is explicable in terms of the divine free choice; and this is a sufficient reason.

The authoritarian element in Ockham's moral theory is, very naturally, the element which has attracted the most attention. But there is another element, which must also be mentioned. Apart from the fact that Ockham analyses the moral virtues in dependence on the Aristotelian analysis, he makes frequent use of the Scholastic concept of 'right reason' (*recta ratio*). Right reason is depicted as the norm, at least the proximate norm, of

---

[1] 3 *Sent.*, 12, AAA. [2] 2 *Sent.*, 19, O. [3] Cf. *Opus nonaginta dierum*, c. 95.

morality. 'It can be said that every right will is in conformity with right reason.'[1] Again, 'no moral virtue, nor any virtuous act, is possible unless it is in conformity with right reason; for right reason is included in the definition of virtue in the second book of the *Ethics*'.[2] Moreover, for an act to be virtuous, not only must it be in accordance with right reason but it must also be done because it is in accordance with right reason. 'No act is perfectly virtuous unless in that act the will wills that which is prescribed by right reason because it is prescribed by right reason.'[3] For if one willed that which is prescribed by right reason simply because it is pleasant or for some other motive, without regard to its being prescribed by right reason, one's act 'would not be virtuous, since it would not be elicited in conformity with right reason. For to elicit an act in conformity with right reason is to will what is prescribed by right reason on account of its being so prescribed.'[4] This insistence on motive was not, of course, a sudden outbreak of 'puritanism' on Ockham's part: Aristotle had insisted that for an act to be perfectly virtuous it must be done for its own sake, that is, because it is the right thing to do. We call an act just, he says, if it is what the just man would do; but it does not follow that a man is just, that is, that he has the virtue of justice, simply because he does the act which the just man would do in the circumstances. He has to do it as the just man would do it; and this includes doing it because it is the just thing to do.[5]

Right reason, then, is the norm of morality. A man may be mistaken in what he thinks is the dictate of right reason; but, even if he is mistaken, he is obliged to conform his will to what he believes to be prescribed by right reason. In other words, conscience is always to be followed, even if it is an erroneous conscience. A man may, of course, be responsible for his having an erroneous conscience; but it is also possible for him to be in 'invincible ignorance', and in this case he is not responsible for his error. In any case, however, he is bound to follow what happens to be the judgment of his conscience. 'A created will which follows an invincibly erroneous conscience is a right will; for the divine will wills that it should follow its reason when this reason is not blameworthy. If it acts against that reason (that is, against an

---

[1] 1 *Sent.*, 41, K.
[2] 3 *Sent.*, 12, NN. For the reference to Aristotle's *Ethics*, cf. *Nicomachean Ethics*, 1107, a.
[3] 3 *Sent.*, 12, CCC.   [4] *Ibid.*, CCC–DDD.
[5] Cf. *Nicomachean Ethics*, 1105, a b.

invincibly erroneous conscience), it sins. . . .'[1] A man is morally obliged to do what he in good faith believes to be right. This doctrine, that one is morally obliged to follow one's conscience, and that to follow an invincibly erroneous conscience, so far from being a sin, is a duty, was not a new doctrine in the Middle Ages; but Ockham expressed it in a clear and unequivocal manner.

It would seem, then, at least at first sight, that we are faced with what amounts to two moral theories in Ockham's philosophy. On the one hand there is his authoritarian conception of the moral law. It would appear to follow from this conception that there can be only a revealed moral code. For how otherwise than through revelation could man know a moral code which depends entirely on God's free choice? Rational deduction could not give us knowledge of it. On the other hand there is Ockham's insistence on right reason, which would seem to imply that reason can discern what is right and what is wrong. The authoritarian conception of morality expresses Ockham's conviction of the freedom and omnipotence of God as they are revealed in Christianity, while the insistence on right reason would seem to represent the influence on his thought of Aristotle's ethical teaching and of the moral theories of his mediaeval predecessors. It might seem, then, that Ockham presents one type of ethical theory in his capacity as theologian and another type in his capacity as philosopher. It has thus been maintained that in spite of his authoritarian conception of the moral law Ockham promoted the growth of a 'lay' moral theory represented by his insistence on reason as the norm of morality and on the duty of doing what one in good faith believes to be the right thing to do.

That there is truth in the contention that two moral theories are implicit in Ockham's ethical teaching can hardly, I think, be denied. He built on the substructure of the Christian-Aristotelian tradition, and he retained a considerable amount of it, as is shown by what he says about the virtues, right reason, natural rights and so on. But he added to this substructure a superstructure which consisted in an ultra-personal conception of the moral law; and he does not seem fully to have realized that the addition of this superstructure demanded a more radical recasting of the substructure than he actually carried out. His personal conception of the moral law was not without precedents in Christian

[1] 3 *Sent.*, 13, O.

thought; but the point is that in the twelfth and thirteenth centuries a moral theory had been elaborated in close association with metaphysics, which ruled out any view of the moral law as dependent simply and solely on the divine will. In retaining a good deal of the former moral theory, while at the same time asserting an authoritarian interpretation of the moral law, Ockham was inevitably involved in difficulties. Like other Christian mediaeval thinkers he accepted, of course, the existence of an actual moral order; and in his discussion of such themes as the function of reason or the existence of natural rights[1] he implied that reason can discern the precepts, or at least the fundamental precepts, of the moral law which actually obtains. At the same time he insisted that the moral order which actually obtains is due to the divine choice, in the sense that God could have established a different moral order and that He could even now order a man to do something contrary to the moral law which He has established. But, if the present moral order is dependent simply and solely on the divine choice, how could we know what it is save through God's revelation? It would seem that there can be only a revealed ethic. Yet Ockham does not appear to have said that there can be only a revealed ethic: he seems to have thought that men, without revelation, are able to discern the moral law in some sense. In this case they can presumably discern a prudential code or a set of hypothetical imperatives. Without revelation men could see that certain acts fit human nature and human society and that other acts are harmful; but they could not discern an immutable natural law, since there is no such immutable natural law, nor could they know, without revelation, whether the acts they thought right were really the acts ordered by God. If reason cannot prove conclusively God's existence, it obviously cannot prove that God has ordered this rather than that. If, therefore, we leave Ockham's theology out of account, it would seem that we are left with a non-metaphysical and non-theological morality, the precepts of which cannot be known as necessary or immutable precepts. Hence perhaps Ockham's insistence on the following of conscience, even an erroneous conscience. Left to himself, that is, without revelation, man might perhaps elaborate an ethic of the Aristotelian type; but he could not discern a natural law of the type envisaged by St. Thomas, since Ockham's authoritarian conception of the moral law, coupled with his 'nominalism', would rule this out.

[1] On this subject, see the following chapter.

In this sense, then, one is probably justified in saying that two moralities are implicit in Ockham's teaching, namely an authoritarian ethic and a 'lay' or non-theological ethic.

It is one thing, however, to say that the two ethical systems are implicit in Ockham's moral teaching; and it is another thing to suggest that he intended to promote an ethic divorced from theology. One could say with far more justice that he intended the very opposite; for he evidently considered that his predecessors had obscured the doctrines of the divine omnipotence and liberty through their theories of an immutable natural law. As far as the interpretation of Ockham's own mind is concerned, it is clear that it is the personal side of his moral theory which has to be stressed. One has only to look at a passage like the following wherein he says that the reason why an act elicited contrary to the dictate of conscience is a wrong act is that 'it would be elicited contrary to the divine precept and the divine will which wills that an act should be elicited in conformity with right reason'.[1] In other words, the ultimate and sufficient reason why we ought to follow right reason or conscience is that God wills that we should do so. Authoritarianism has the last word. Again, Ockham speaks of an act 'which is intrinsically and necessarily virtuous *stante ordinatione divina*'.[2] In the same section he says that 'in the present order (*stante ordinatione quae nunc est*) no act is perfectly virtuous unless it is elicited in conformity with right reason'. Such remarks are revealing. A necessarily virtuous act is only relatively so, that is, if God has decreed that it should be virtuous. Given the order instituted by God, it follows logically that certain acts are good and others bad; but the order itself is dependent on God's choice. It possesses a certain stability, and Ockham did not imagine that God is constantly changing His orders, so to speak; but he insists that its stability is not absolute.

One can, then, sum up Ockham's position on more or less the following lines. The human being, as a free created being which is entirely dependent on God, is morally obliged to conform his will to the divine will in regard to that which God commands or prohibits. Absolutely speaking, God could command or prohibit any act, provided that a contradiction is not involved. Actually God has established a certain moral law. As a rational being man can see that he ought to obey this law. But he may not know what God has commanded; and in this case he is morally obliged to do

---

[1] 3 *Sent.*, 13, C. [2] *Ibid.*, 12, CCC.

what he honestly believes to be in accordance with God's commands. To act otherwise would be to act contrary to what is believed to be the divine ordinance; and to do this is to sin. It is not clear what Ockham thought of the moral situation of the man who has no knowledge of revelation, or even no knowledge of God's existence. He appears to imply that reason can discern something of the present moral order; but, if he did mean this, it is difficult to see how this idea can be reconciled with his authoritarian conception of morality. If the moral law is dependent simply on the divine choice, how can its content be known apart from revelation? If its content can be known apart from revelation, how can it be dependent simply on the divine choice? It would seem that the only way of escaping this difficulty is to say that what can be known apart from revelation is simply a provisional code of morality, based on non-theological considerations. But that Ockham actually had this notion clearly in mind, which would imply the possibility of a purely philosophic and second-rank ethic, as distinct from the divinely-imposed and obligatory ethic, I should not care to affirm. He thought in terms of the ethical code commonly accepted by Christians, though he went on to assert that it was dependent on the free divine choice. Very probably he did not clearly realize the difficulties created by his authoritarian conception.

CHAPTER VIII

OCKHAM (6)

The dispute on evangelical poverty, and the doctrine of natural rights—Political sovereignty is not derived from the spiritual power—The relation of the people to their ruler—How far were Ockham's political ideas novel or revolutionary?—The pope's position within the Church.

1. IT would be a mistake to suppose that Ockham was a political philosopher in the sense of a man who reflects systematically on the nature of political society, sovereignty and government. Ockham's political writings were not written to provide an abstract political theory; they were immediately occasioned by contemporary disputes involving the Holy See, and Ockham's immediate object was to resist and denounce what he regarded as papal aggression and unjustified absolutism; he was concerned with relations between pope and emperor and between the pope and the members of the Church rather than with political society and political government as such. Ockham shared in the respect for law and custom and in the dislike for arbitrary and capricious absolutism which were common characteristics of the mediaeval philosophers and theologians: it would be wrong to suppose that he set out to revolutionize mediaeval society. It is true, of course, that Ockham was led to lay down general principles on the relations of Church and State and on political government; but he did this mainly in the course of conducting controversies on concrete and specific points of dispute. For example, he published the *Opus nonaginta dierum* about the year 1332 in defence of the attitude of Michael of Cesena in regard to the dispute on evangelical poverty. Pope John XXII had condemned as heretical a doctrine on evangelical poverty which was held by many Franciscans and had deprived Michael of his post as General of the Franciscan Order. Counterblasts from Michael, who, together with Bonagratia of Bergamo and Ockham had taken refuge with the emperor, Ludwig of Bavaria, elicited from the pope the bull *Quia vir reprobus* (1329) in which Michael's doctrines were again censured and the Franciscans were rebuked for daring to publish tracts criticizing papal pronouncements. Ockham retaliated by subjecting the bull to

close scrutiny and trenchant criticism in the *Opus nonaginta dierum*. This publication was occasioned, therefore, not by any purely theoretical consideration of the position of the Holy See, but by a concrete dispute, that concerning evangelical poverty; it was not composed by a political philosopher in hours of cool reflection but by a participant in a heated controversy. Ockham criticized the papal pronouncements as themselves heretical and was able to refer to the erroneous opinion of John XXII concerning the beatific vision. He was thus writing primarily as a theologian.

But though Ockham wrote the *Opus nonaginta dierum* for the specific purpose of defending his Franciscan colleagues against papal condemnation, and though he devoted a good deal of his attention to discovering heresies and errors in the pope's pronouncements, he discussed the poverty question in the manner which one would expect of a philosopher, a man accustomed to close and careful reasoning. The result is that one can find in the work Ockham's general ideas on, for example, the right of property, though it must be confessed that it is not easy to settle the question exactly which of the opinions discussed are Ockham's own opinions, since he writes in a much more restrained and impersonal manner than one might expect in a polemical writer involved in a heated controversy.

Man has a natural right to property. God gave to man the power to dispose of the goods of the earth in the manner dictated by right reason, and since the Fall right reason shows that the personal appropriation of temporal goods is necessary.[1] The right of private property is thus a natural right, willed by God, and, as such, it is inviolable, in the sense that no one can be despoiled of this right by an earthly power. The State can regulate the exercise of the right of private property, the way in which property is transferred in society, for example; but it cannot deprive men of the right against their will. Ockham does not deny that a criminal, for instance, can legitimately be deprived of his freedom to acquire and possess property; but the right of property, he insists, is a natural right which does not depend in its essence on the positive conventions of society; and without fault on his own part or some reasonable cause a man cannot be forcibly deprived of the exercise of the right, still less of the right itself.

Ockham speaks of a right (*ius*) as being a legitimate power

---

[1] *Opus nonaginta dierum*, c. 14.

(*potestas licita*), a power in conformity with right reason (*conformis rationi rectae*), and he distinguishes legitimate powers which are anterior to human convention from those which depend on human convention. The right of private property is a legitimate power which is anterior to human convention, since right reason dictates the institution of private property as a remedy for the moral condition of man after the Fall. Inasmuch as a man is permitted to own property and use it and to resist anyone who tries to wrest his property from him, he has a right to private property, for that permission (*licentia*) comes from the natural law. But not all natural rights are of the same kind. There are, first, natural rights which are valid until a contrary convention is made. For example, the Roman people have, according to Ockham, the right to elect their bishop: this follows from the fact that they are under an obligation to have a bishop. But the Roman people may cede this right of election to the Cardinals, though the right of the Roman people must again be exercised if for any reason election by the Cardinals becomes impossible or impracticable. Conditional natural rights of this sort are examples of what Ockham calls rights flowing from the natural law understood in the third sense.[1] Secondly, there are natural rights which obtained in the state of humanity before the Fall, though 'natural right' in this sense means simply the consequence of a perfection which once existed and no longer exists; it is conditional on a certain state of human perfection. Thirdly, there are rights which share in the immutability of moral precepts, and the right of private property is one of these rights. In the *Breviloquium* Ockham declares that 'the aforementioned power of appropriating temporal things falls under a precept and is reckoned to belong to the sphere of morality (*inter pure moralia computatur*)'.

But a further distinction is required. There are some natural rights in the third sense named (Ockham's *primus modus*) which are so bound up with the moral imperative that nobody is entitled to renounce them, since renunciation of the right would be equivalent to a sin against the moral law. Thus everyone has the duty of preserving his own life, and he would sin against the moral law by starving himself to death. But if he is obliged to maintain his life, he has a right to do so, a right which he cannot renounce. The right of private property, however, is not of this kind. There is, indeed, a precept of right reason that temporal

[1] *Dialogus*, 22, 6.

goods should be appropriated and owned by men; but it is not necessary for the fulfilment of the precept that every individual man should exercise the right of private property, and he can, for a just and reasonable cause, renounce all rights to the possession of property. Ockham's main point in this connection is that the renunciation must be voluntary, and that when it is voluntary it is legitimate.

Pope John XXII had maintained that the distinction between merely using temporal things and having the right to use them was unreal. His principle was that 'he who, without a right, uses something uses it unjustly'. Now, the Franciscans were admittedly entitled to use temporal things like food and clothing. Therefore they must have a right over them, a right to use them, and it was unreal to pretend that it was the Holy See which possessed all these things without the Franciscans having any right at all. The reply was made that it is quite possible to renounce a right to property and at the same time to use legitimately those things of which the ownership has been renounced. The Franciscans renounced all rights of property, even the right of use: they were not like tenants who, without owning a field, have the right to use it and enjoy its fruits, but they enjoyed simply a 'precarious' use of temporal things over which they had no property rights at all. We must distinguish, says Ockham, between *usus iuris*, which is the right of using temporal things without the right over their substance, and *usus facti*, which springs from a mere permission to use the things of another, a permission which is at any moment revocable.[1] The pope had said that the Franciscans could not use food, for example, legitimately without at the same time having a right to do so, without, that is to say, possessing the *usus iuris*; but this is not true, said Ockham; the Franciscans have not the *usus iuris* but only the *usus facti*; they have the *usus nudus* or mere use of temporal things. Mere permission to use them does not confer a right to use them, for the permission is always revocable. The Franciscans are *usuarii simplices* in a strict sense; their use of temporal things is permitted or tolerated by the Holy See, which possesses both the *dominium perfectum* and the *dominium utile* (or, in Ockham's phrase, *usus iuris*) over these things. They have renounced all property rights whatsoever, and this is true evangelical poverty, after the example of Christ and the Apostles, who neither individually nor in common possessed

[1] Cf. *Opus nonaginta dierum*, c. 2.

any temporal things (an opinion which John XXII declared to be heretical).

The actual dispute concerning evangelical poverty does not concern the history of philosophy; but it has been mentioned in order to show how Ockham's preoccupation with a concrete dispute led him to institute an inquiry concerning rights in general and the right of property in particular. His main point was that the right of private property is a natural right, but that it is a right which a man may voluntarily renounce, and that this renunciation may even include the right of use. From the philosophical point of view the chief interest of the discussion lies in the fact that Ockham insisted on the validity of natural rights which are anterior to human conventions, especially in view of the fact that he made the natural law dependent on the divine will. It may appear a gross inconsistency to say on the one hand that the natural law depends on the divine will and on the other hand that there are certain natural rights which share in the fixity of the natural law, and when Ockham asserts, as he does, that the natural law is immutable and absolute he would seem to be underlining the self-contradiction. It is true that, when Ockham asserts the dependence of the moral law on the divine will, he refers primarily to the possibility that God might have created a moral order different from the one He has actually instituted, and, if this were all that he meant, self-contradiction might be avoided by saying that the moral law is absolute and unalterable in the present order. But Ockham meant more than that; he meant that God can dispense from the natural law, or order acts contrary to the natural law, even when the present moral order has been constituted. It may be that the idea of the moral law's dependence on the divine will is more evident in the commentary on the *Sentences* than in Ockham's political works and that the idea of the immutability of the moral law is more evident in the political works than in the commentary on the *Sentences*; but the former idea appears, not only in the commentary, but also in the political works. In the *Dialogus*, for example, he says that there can be no exception from the precepts of the natural law in the strict sense 'unless God specially excepts someone'.[1] The same theme recurs in the *Octo quaestionum decisiones*,[2] and in the *Breviloquium*. The most one can say, then, by way of apology for Ockham, in regard to his consistency or lack of it, is that for him the natural law is

---
[1] *Dialogus*, 1, 3, 2, 24.   [2] 1, 13.

unalterable, given the present order created by God, unless God intervenes to alter it in any particular instance. As a pure philosopher Ockham speaks on occasion as though there were absolute moral laws and human rights; but as a theologian he was determined to maintain the divine omnipotence as he understood it; and as he was theologian and philosopher in one it was scarcely possible for him to reconcile the absolute character of the moral law with his interpretation of the divine omnipotence, an omnipotence known by revelation but unprovable by the philosopher.

2. The dispute about evangelical poverty was not the only dispute in which Ockham was engaged; he was also involved in a dispute between the Holy See and the emperor. In 1323 Pope John XXII attempted to intervene in an imperial election, maintaining that papal confirmation was required, and when Ludwig of Bavaria was elected, the pope denounced the election. But in 1328 Ludwig had himself crowned at Rome, after which he declared the Avignon Pope to be deposed and appointed Nicholas V. (This antipope, however, had to make his submission in 1330, when Ludwig had departed for Germany.) The quarrel between pope and emperor lasted on after the death of John XXII in 1334 through the reign of Benedict XII into that of Clement VI, during whose pontificate Ockham died in 1349.

The immediate point at issue in this dispute was the emperor's independence of the Holy See; but the controversy had, of course, a greater importance than that attaching to the question whether or not an imperial election required papal confirmation; the broader issue of the proper relation between Church and State was inevitably involved. Further, the question of the right relation of sovereign to subjects was also raised, though it was raised primarily in regard to the pope's position in the Church. In this controversy Ockham stoutly supported the independence of the State in relation to the Church and in regard to the Church itself he strongly attacked papal 'absolutism'. His most important political work is the *Dialogus*, the first part of which was composed in the reign of John XXII. The *De potestate et iuribus romani imperii*, written in 1338 during the reign of Benedict XII, was subsequently incorporated in the *Dialogus* as the second treatise of the third part. The first treatise of the third part, the *De potestate papae et cleri*, was written with the purpose of dissociating its author from Marsilius of Padua, and it elicited from the latter the *Defensor minor*. The *Octo quaestionum decisiones super potestatem summi pontificis* was directed, partly at least, against the *De iure regni et imperii* of Leopold of Babenberg, while in the *Breviloquium de principatu tyrannico* Ockham gave a clear exposition of his political views. His last work, *De pontificum et imperatorum potestate*, was a diatribe against the Avignon papacy. Other polemical works include the *Compendium errorum papae*, an early publication which sums up Ockham's grievances against John XXII, and the *An princeps pro suo succursu, scilicet guerrae, possit recipere bona ecclesiarum, etiam invito papa*, which was written perhaps between August 1338 and the end of 1339 and was designed to show that Edward III of England was justified in taking subsidies from the clergy, even contrary to the pope's wishes or directions, in his war against the French.

Turning first to the controversy concerning the relations between Church and State one can remark that for the most part Ockham's thought moved within the older mediaeval political outlook. In other words, he gave little consideration to the relation of national monarch to emperor, and he was more concerned with the particular relations between pope and emperor than between Church and State in general. In view of his position as a refugee at the court of Ludwig of Bavaria this was only to be expected, though it is true, of course, that he could not discuss the immediate issue which interested him personally without extending his attention to the wider and more general issue. And, if one looks at Ockham's polemics from the point of view of their influence and in regard to the historical development of Europe, one can say that he did, in effect, concern himself with the relations of Church and State, for the position of the emperor in relation to a national monarch like the king of England was little more than a certain pre-eminence of honour.

In maintaining a clear distinction between the spiritual and temporal powers Ockham was not, of course, propounding any revolutionary theory. He insisted that the supreme head in the spiritual sphere, namely the pope, is not the source of imperial power and authority, and also that papal confirmation is not required in order to validate an imperial election. If the pope arrogates to himself, or attempts to assume, power in the temporal sphere, he is invading a territory over which he has no jurisdiction. The authority of the emperor derives, not from the pope, but from his election, the electors standing in the place of the people. There can be no doubt but that Ockham regarded political power as deriving from God through the people, either immediately, in the event of the people directly choosing a sovereign, or mediately, if the people have agreed, explicitly or implicitly, to some other way of transmitting political authority. The State needs a government and the people cannot avoid choosing a sovereign of some kind, whether emperor, monarch or magistrates; but in no case is the authority derived from, or dependent on, the spiritual power. That Ockham did not intend his denial of the pope's supreme power in temporal matters to apply only in favour of the emperor is made abundantly clear; for example, by the *An princeps pro suo succursu*. All legitimate sovereigns enjoy authority which is not derived from the pope.

3. But, as we have already seen, if Ockham supported the independence of temporal princes in relation to the Church, so far as temporal matters were concerned, he did not reject the temporal authority of the papacy in order to support political absolutism. All men are born free, in the sense that they have a right to freedom, and, though the principle of authority, like the principle of private property, belongs to the natural law, they enjoy a natural right to choose their rulers. The method of choosing a ruler and of transmitting authority from one ruler to his successor depends on human law, and it is obviously not necessary that every successive ruler should be elected; but the fundamental freedom of man to choose and appoint the temporal authority is a right which no power on earth can take from him. The community can, of course, of its own free will establish a hereditary monarchy; but in this case it voluntarily submits itself to the monarch and his legitimate successors, and if the monarch betrays his trust and abuses his authority, the community can assert its freedom by deposing him. 'After the whole world spontaneously consented to the dominion and empire of the Romans, the same empire was a true, just and good empire'; its legitimacy rested on its free acceptance by its subjects.[1] Nobody should be placed over the community except by its choice and consent; every people and State is entitled to elect its head if it so wills.[2] If there were any people without a ruler in temporal affairs, the pope would have neither the duty nor the power of appointing rulers for that people, if they wished to appoint their own ruler or rulers.[3]

4. These two important points, namely the independence of the

---

[1] *Dialogus*, 2, 3, 1, 27.   [2] *Ibid.*, 2, 3, 2, 6.
[3] *Opus nonaginta dierum*, 2, 4.

temporal power and the freedom of the people to settle their own form of government if they so choose, were not in themselves novelties. The idea of the two swords, for example, represented the common mediaeval outlook, and when Ockham protested against the tendency of certain popes to arrogate to themselves the position and rights of universal temporal monarchs, he was simply expressing the conviction of most mediaeval thinkers that the spiritual and temporal spheres must be clearly distinguished. Again, all the great mediaeval theologians and philosophers believed in natural rights in some sense and would have rejected the notion that princes possess absolute and unrestricted power. The mediaevals had a respect for law and custom and thoroughly disliked arbitrary power; and the idea that rulers must govern within the general framework of law expressed the general mediaeval outlook. It is difficult to say exactly how St. Thomas Aquinas regarded the problem of the derivation of the sovereign's authority; but he certainly thought of it as limited, as having a definite purpose, and he certainly considered that subjects are not bound to submit to tyrannical government. He recognized that some governments do, or may, derive their authority immediately from the people (ultimately from God); and, though there is no very clear indication that he regarded all governments as necessarily deriving their authority in this manner, he maintained that there can be a resistance to tyranny which is justified and is not to be accounted sedition. A ruler has a trust to fulfil, and if he does not fulfil it but abuses his trust, the community is entitled to depose him. There is good reason, then, for saying, as has been said, that in regard to dislike of arbitrary power and in regard to insistence on law, the principles of Ockham did not substantially differ from those of St. Thomas.

However, even though Ockham's insistence on the distinction of the spiritual and temporal powers and on the fundamental rights of subjects in a political community was not novel, still less revolutionary, if considered as expressing abstract principles, it does not follow that the manner in which he conducted his controversy with the papacy was not part of a general movement which can be called revolutionary. For the dispute between Ludwig of Bavaria and the papacy was one incident in a general movement of which the dispute between Philip the Fair and Boniface VIII had been an earlier symptom; and the direction of the movement, if looked at from the point of view of concrete historical development, was towards the complete independence of the State from the Church, even in spiritual matters. Ockham's thought may have moved within the old categories of papacy and empire, but the gradual consolidation of centralized national States was leading to a breakdown of the balance between the two powers and to the emergence of a political consciousness which found partial expression in the Reformation. Moreover, Ockham's hostility to papal absolutism even within the spiritual sphere, when viewed in the light of his general remarks on the relation of subjects to rulers, was bound to have implications in the sphere of political thought as well. I now turn to his ideas on the pope's position within the Church; though it is worth while noticing beforehand that, though Ockham's ideas on Church government concerned the ecclesiastical sphere and heralded the Conciliar Movement which was to be proximately occasioned by the Great Schism (1378–1417), these ideas were also part of the wider movement which ended in the disintegration of mediaeval Christendom.

5. It is entirely unnecessary to say more than a few words on the subject of Ockham's polemic against the position of the pope within the Church, as this subject belongs to Church history, not to the history of philosophy; but, as already mentioned, the further implications of his ideas on the subject make it desirable to say something about them. Ockham's main contention was that papal absolutism within the Church was unjustified, that it was detrimental to the good of Christendom, and that it should be checked and limited.[1] The means which Ockham suggested for limiting papal power was the establishment of a General Council. Possibly drawing on his experience and knowledge of the constitutions of the mendicant Orders he envisaged religious corporations such as parishes, chapters and monasteries sending chosen representatives to provincial synods. These synods would elect representatives for the General Council, which should include layfolk as well as clergy. It is to be noted that Ockham did not look on the General Council as an organ of infallible doctrinal pronouncements, even if he thought that it was more likely to be right than the pope alone, but as a limitation to and a check on papal absolutism: he was concerned with ecclesiastical politics, with constitutionalizing the papacy, rather than with purely theological matters. He did not deny that the pope is the successor

---

[1] Ockham did not deny papal supremacy as such; he rejected what he called 'tyrannical' supremacy.

of St. Peter and the Vicar of Christ, nor did he wish, in principle, to destroy the papal government of the Church; but he regarded the Avignon papacy as going beyond its brief, so to speak, and as being unfit to govern without decisive checks and limitations. No doubt he held heterodox opinions; but his motive in making these suggestions was that of combating the actual exercise of arbitrary and unrestrained power, and that is why his ideas on the constitutionalization of the papacy had implications in the political sphere, even if his ideas, when looked at in relation to the immediate future, must be regarded as heralding the Conciliar Movement.

CHAPTER IX

THE OCKHAMIST MOVEMENT: JOHN OF MIRECOURT AND NICHOLAS OF AUTRECOURT

The Ockhamist or nominalist movement—John of Mirecourt—Nicholas of Autrecourt—Nominalism in the universities—Concluding remarks.

1. THE phrase 'Ockhamist Movement' is perhaps something of a misnomer. For it might be understood as implying that William of Ockham was the sole fountainhead of the 'modern' current of thought in the fourteenth century and that the thinkers of the movement all derived their ideas from him. Some of these thinkers, like the Franciscan Adam Wodham or Goddam (d. 1358), had indeed been pupils of Ockham, while others, like the Dominican Holkot (d. 1349), were influenced by Ockham's writings without, however, having actually been his pupils. But in some other cases it is difficult to discover how far a given philosopher owed his ideas to Ockham's influence. However, even if from one point of view it may be preferable to speak of the 'nominalist movement' rather than of the 'Ockhamist Movement', it cannot be denied that Ockham was the most influential writer of the movement; and it is only just that the movement should be associated with his name. The names 'nominalism' and 'terminism' were used synonymously to designate the *via moderna*; and the salient characteristic of terminism was the analysis of the function of the term in the proposition, namely the doctrine of *suppositio* or standing-for. As has already been indicated, the theory of *suppositio* can be found in logicians before Ockham; in the writings of Peter of Spain, for example; but it was Ockham who developed the terminist logic in that conceptualist and 'empiricist' direction which we have come to associate with nominalism. One is justified, therefore, in my opinion, in speaking of the 'Ockhamist Movement', provided that one remembers that the phrase is not meant to imply that Ockham was the direct source of all the developments of that movement.

The development of the terminist logic forms one of the aspects of the movement. In this connection one may mention Richard Swineshead and William Heytesbury, both of whom were associated with Merton College, Oxford. The latter, whose logical writings enjoyed a wide circulation, became chancellor of the university of Oxford in 1371. Another popular logician of the fourteenth century was Richard Billingham. But the technical logical studies of the nominalists and of those influenced by the nominalist movement were frequently associated, as were those of Ockham himself, with a destructive attack on the traditional metaphysics, or rather on the proofs offered in the traditional metaphysics. Sometimes these attacks were based on the view that the traditional lines of proof did not amount to more than probable arguments. Thus according to Richard Swineshead the arguments which had been employed to prove the unicity of God were not demonstrations but dialectical arguments, that is to say, arguments which did not exclude the possibility of the opposite being true or which could not, in the language of the time, be reduced to the principle of contradiction. Sometimes emphasis was placed on our supposed inability to know any substance. If we can have no knowledge of any substance, argued Richard Billingham, we cannot prove the existence of God. Monotheism is a matter of faith, not of philosophical proof.

The relegation of propositions like 'God exists', where the term 'God' is understood as denoting the supreme unique Being, to the sphere of faith does not mean that any philosopher doubted the truth of these propositions: it simply means that he did not think that such propositions can be proved. Nevertheless, this sceptical attitude in regard to metaphysical arguments was doubtless combined, in the case of different philosophers, with varying degrees of insistence on the primacy of faith. A lecturer or professor in the faculty of arts might question the validity of metaphysical arguments on purely logical grounds, while a theologian might also be concerned to emphasize the weakness of the human reason, the supremacy of faith and the transcendent character of revealed truth. Robert Holkot, for example, postulated a 'logic of faith', distinct from and superior to natural logic. He certainly denied the demonstrative character of theistic arguments. Only analytic propositions are absolutely certain. The principle of causality, employed in traditional arguments for God's existence, is not an analytic proposition. From this it follows that philosophical arguments for God's existence cannot amount to more than probable arguments. Theology, however, is superior to philosophy; and in the sphere of dogmatic theology we can see the operation of a logic which is superior to the natural logic employed in philosophy. In particular, that the principle of contradiction is transcended in theology is clear, thought Holkot, from the doctrine of the Trinity. My point is, then, not that the theologians who were influenced by the nominalist criticism of metaphysical 'demonstrations' did not support their criticism by an appeal to logic, but rather that this relative scepticism in philosophy must not be taken without more ado as involving a sceptical attitude towards theological statements considered as statements of fact or as a conscious relegation of dogmatic theology to the sphere of conjecture.

Acceptance of this or that nominalist position did not mean, of course, that a given thinker adopted all the positions maintained by William of Ockham. John of Rodington (d. 1348), for example, who became Provincial of the English Franciscans, doubted the demonstrative character of arguments for God's unicity: but he rejected the notion that the moral law depends simply on the divine will. John of Bassolis (d. 1347), another Franciscan, also questioned the demonstrative character of metaphysical proofs for God's existence, unicity and infinity; but he combined this critical attitude with an acceptance of various Scotist positions. Scotism was naturally a powerful influence in the Franciscan Order, and it produced philosophers like Francis of Meyronnes (d. c. 1328), Antoine André (d. c. 1320), the *Doctor dulcifluus*, and Francis de Marcia, the *Doctor succinctus*. It is only to be expected, then, that we should find the Scotist and Ockhamist lines of thought meeting and mingling in thinkers like John of Ripa, who lectured at Paris in the early part of the second half of the fourteenth century, and Peter of Candia (d. 1410). Further, in some cases where a thinker was influenced both by the writings of St. Augustine and by Ockhamism, it is not always easy to judge which influence was the stronger on any given point. For example, Thomas Bradwardine (c. 1290–1349) appealed to St. Augustine in support of his doctrine of theological determinism; but it is difficult to say how far he was influenced by Augustine's writings taken by themselves and how far he was influenced in his interpretation of Augustine by the Ockhamist emphasis on the divine omnipotence and the divine will. Again, Gregory of Rimini (d. 1358), who became General of the Hermits of St. Augustine, appealed to Augustine in support of his doctrines of the primacy of intuition and the 'sign' function of universal terms. But there is difficulty in deciding to what extent he simply adopted Ockhamist positions and then tried to cover them with the mantle of St. Augustine because he himself was a member of the Augustinian Order, and to what extent he really believed that he found in St. Augustine's writings positions which had been suggested to him by Ockham's philosophy. The Dominican Robert Holkot even tried to show that some of his clearly Ockhamist tenets were really not alien to the mind of St. Thomas Aquinas.

Enough has been said to show that Ockhamism or nominalism, which was associated particularly with the secular clergy, penetrated deeply into the religious Orders. Its influence was felt not only in the Franciscan Order, to which Ockham himself had belonged, but also in the Dominican and other Orders. At the same time, of course, the traditional lines of thought were still maintained, especially in an Order which possessed an official Doctor, as the Dominican Order possessed St. Thomas. Take, for example, the Hermits of St. Augustine, who looked on Giles of Rome as their Doctor. We have seen that Gregory of Rimini, who was General of the Order from 1357 until 1358, was influenced by Ockhamism; but Thomas of Strasbourg, who preceded Gregory as General (1345–1357), had tried to protect the Order from nominalist influence in the name of fidelity to Giles of Rome. In point of fact it did not prove possible to keep out or stamp out the influence of nominalism; but the fact that the Order possessed an official Doctor doubtless encouraged a certain moderation in the degree to which the more extreme nominalist positions were accepted by the sympathizers with the *via moderna*.

One common factor among the nominalists or Ockhamists was, as we have seen, the emphasis they laid on the theory of *suppositio*, the analysis of the different ways in which the terms in a proposition stand for things. It is obvious, however, that one is justified in speaking about 'nominalism' or, if preferred, conceptualism only in the case of philosophers who, like Ockham, maintained that a general term or class-name stands in the proposition for individual things, and for individual things alone. Together with this doctrine, namely that universality belongs only to terms in their logical function, the nominalists also tended to maintain that only those propositions which are reducible to the principle of contradiction are absolutely certain. In other words, they held that the truth of a statement is not absolutely certain unless the opposite cannot be stated without contradiction. Now, no statement of a causal relationship can, they thought, be a statement of this kind. In other words, their theory of universals led the nominalists to an empiricist analysis of the causal relation. Moreover, in so far as the inference from phenomena to substance was an inference from effect to cause, this analysis affected also the nominalist view of the substance-accident metaphysic. If, then, on the one hand only analytic propositions, in the sense of propositions reducible to the principle of contradiction, are absolutely certain, while on the other hand statements about causal relations are empirical or inductive generalizations which enjoy at best only a very high degree of probability, it follows that the traditional metaphysical arguments, resting on the employment of the principle of causality and on the substance-accident metaphysic, cannot be absolutely certain. In the case, then, of statements about God's existence, for example, the nominalists maintained that they owed their certainty not to any philosophical arguments which could be adduced in their favour but to the fact that they were truths of faith, taught by Christian theology. This position naturally tended to introduce a sharp distinction between philosophy and theology. In one sense, of course, a sharp distinction between philosophy and theology had always been recognized, namely in the sense that a distinction had always been recognized between accepting a statement as the result simply of one's own process of reasoning and accepting a statement on divine authority. But a thinker like Aquinas had been convinced that it is possible to prove the 'preambles of faith', such as the statement that a God exists who can make a revelation. Aquinas was also convinced, of course, that the act of faith involves supernatural grace; but the point is that he recognized as strictly provable certain truths which are logically presupposed by the act of faith, even if in most actual cases supernatural faith is operative long before a human being comes to understand, if he ever does advert to or understand, the proofs in question. In the nominalist philosophy, however, the 'preambles of faith' were not regarded as strictly provable, and the bridge between philosophy and theology (so far, that is, as one is entitled to speak of a 'bridge' when faith demands supernatural grace) was thus broken. But the nominalists were not concerned with 'apologetic' considerations. In the Christian Europe of the Middle Ages apologetics were not a matter of such concern as they became for theologians and Catholic philosophers of a later date.

In the foregoing summary of the positions of the nominalists I have used the word 'nominalist' to mean the thoroughgoing nominalist or the thinker who developed the potentialities of nominalism or the 'ideal' nominalist, the nominalist *pur sang*. I have remarked earlier that not all those thinkers who were positively affected by the Ockhamist movement and who may in certain respects be called 'nominalists' adopted all the positions of Ockham. But it will be of use, I hope, to give some account of the philosophical ideas of two thinkers associated with the movement, namely John of Mirecourt and Nicholas of Autrecourt, the latter of whom particularly was an extremist. Acquaintance with the philosophy of Nicholas of Autrecourt is an effective means, if further means are still needed, of dispelling the illusion that there was no variety of opinions in mediaeval philosophy about important topics. After outlining the thought of these two men I shall conclude the chapter with some remarks on the influence of nominalism in the universities, especially in the new universities which were founded in the latter part of the fourteenth century and during the fifteenth.

2. John of Mirecourt, who seems to have been a Cistercian (he was called *monachus albus*, 'the white monk'), lectured on the *Sentences* of Peter Lombard at the Cistercian College of St. Bernard in Paris. Of these lectures, which were given in 1344–5, there exist two versions. As a number of his propositions were immediately attacked, John of Mirecourt issued an explanation and justification of his position; but none the less some 41 propositions were condemned in 1347 by the chancellor of the university and the faculty of theology. This led to the publication by John of another work in defence of his position. These two 'apologies', the first explaining or defending 63 suspected propositions, the second doing the same for the 41 condemned propositions, have been edited by F. Stegmüller.[1]

Two types of knowledge are distinguished by John of Mirecourt; and he distinguishes them according to the quality of our assent to different propositions. Sometimes our assent is 'evident', which means, he says, that it is given without fear, actual or potential, of error. At other times our assent is given with fear, actual or potential, of error, as, for example, in the case of suspicion or of opinion. But it is necessary to make a further distinction. Sometimes we give an assent without fear of error

[1] *Recherches de théologie ancienne et médiévale* (1933), pp. 40-79, 192-204.

because we see clearly the evident truth of the proposition to which we assent. This happens in the case of the principle of contradiction and of those principles and conclusions which are ultimately reducible to the principle of contradiction. If we see that a proposition rests upon or is reducible to the principle of contradiction, we see that the opposite of that proposition, its negation that is to say, is inconceivable and impossible. At other times, however, we give an assent without fear of error to propositions the truth of which is not intrinsically evident, though it is assured in virtue of irrefutable testimony. The revealed truths of faith are of this kind. We know, for example, only by revelation that there are three Persons in one God.

Leaving out of account the revealed truths of faith we have, then, so far, propositions to which we assent without fear of error because they are reducible to the primary self-evident principle, the principle of contradiction, and propositions to which we assent with fear of error (for example, 'I think that that object in the distance is a cow'). Assents of the first kind are called by John of Mirecourt *assensus evidentes*, assents of the second kind *assensus inevidentes*. But we must now distinguish two kinds of *assensus evidentes*. First of all, there are evident assents in the strictest and most proper meaning of the phrase. Assent of this kind is given to the principle of contradiction, to principles which are reducible to the principle of contradiction and to conclusions which rest upon the principle of contradiction. In the case of such propositions we have *evidentia potissima*. Secondly, there are assents which are indeed given without fear of error but which are not given in virtue of the proposition's intimate connection with the principle of contradiction. If I give my assent to a proposition based on experience (for example, 'there are stones') I give it without fear of error but I give it in virtue of my experience of the external world, not in virtue of the proposition's reducibility to the principle of contradiction. In the case of such proposition we have, not *evidentia potissima*, but *evidentia naturalis*. John of Mirecourt defines this 'natural evidence' as the evidence by which we give our assent to a thing's existence without any fear of error, this assent being brought about by causes which naturally necessitate our assent.

The above account of John's doctrine on human assents comes from his first apology. He is there explaining the 44th proposition, which had been made an object of attack. The proposition runs as follows: 'It has not been demonstratively proved from propositions which are self-evident or which possess an evidence reducible by us to the certitude of the primary principle that God exists, or that there is a most perfect being, or that one thing is the cause of another thing, or that any created thing has a cause without this cause having its own cause and so on to infinity, or that a thing cannot as a total cause produce something nobler than itself, or that it is impossible for something to be produced which is nobler than anything which (now) exists.' In particular, then, the proofs of God's existence do not rest on self-evident propositions or on propositions which we are capable of reducing to the principle of contradiction, which is the primary self-evident principle. John's adversaries interpreted his doctrine as meaning that no proof of God's existence is of such a kind that it compels assent once it is understood, and that we are not certain, so far as philosophy goes, of God's existence. In answer John observes that the proofs of God's existence rest on experience and that no proposition which is the result of experience of the world is reducible by us to the principle of contradiction. It is clear from his teaching in general, however, that he made one exception to this general rule, namely in the case of the proposition which asserts the existence of the thinker or speaker. If I say that I deny or even doubt my own existence I am contradicting myself, for I cannot deny or even doubt my existence without affirming my existence. On this point John of Mirecourt followed St. Augustine. But this particular proposition stands by itself. No other proposition which is the result of sense-experience, or experience of the external world, is reducible by us to the principle of contradiction. No proposition of this kind, then, enjoys *evidentia potissima*. But John denied that he meant that all such propositions are doubtful. They do not enjoy *evidentia potissima* but they enjoy *evidentia naturalis*. Although propositions founded on experience of the external world are not evident in the same way as the principle of contradiction is evident, 'it does not follow from this that we must doubt about them any more than about the first principle. From this it is clear that I do not intend to deny any experience, any knowledge, any evidence. It is even clear that I hold altogether the opposite opinion to those who would say that it is not evident to them that there is a man or that there is a stone, on the ground that it might appear to them that these things are so without their being really so. I do not mean to deny that these things are evident to us and known by us, but only that they are not known to us by the supreme kind of knowledge (*scientia potissima*).'

Analytic propositions, that is to say propositions which are reducible by analysis to the self-evident principle of contradiction, are thus absolutely certain, and this absolute certainty attaches also to each one's affirmation of his own existence. Apart from this last affirmation all propositions which are the result of and express experimental knowledge of the world enjoy only 'natural evidence'. But what does John of Mirecourt mean by 'natural evidence'? Does this mean simply that we spontaneously give our assent in virtue of a natural unavoidable propensity to assent? If so, does it or does it not follow that the propositions to which we give this kind of assent are certain? John admits that error is possible in the case of some empirical propositions: he could hardly do otherwise. On the other hand he asserts that 'we cannot err in many things (propositions) which accord with our experiences'. Again, he could hardly say anything else, unless he were prepared to admit that his adversaries had interpreted his doctrine correctly. But it seems to be clear that John of Mirecourt accepted the Ockhamist doctrine that sensitive knowledge of the external world could be miraculously caused and conserved by God in the absence of the object. This theme was treated by him at the beginning of his commentary on the *Sentences*. It is probably safe to say, then, that for him 'natural evidence' meant that we naturally assent to the existence of what we sense, though it would be possible for us to be in error, if, that is to say, God were to work a miracle. There is no contradiction in the idea of God working such a miracle. If, therefore, we use the word 'certain' in the sense not only of feeling certain but also of having objective and evident certainty, we are certain of the principle of contradiction and of propositions reducible thereto and each one is certain of his own existence, the infallible character of the intuition of one's own existence being shown by the connection of the proposition affirming one's own existence with the principle of contradiction; but we are not certain of the existence of external objects, however certain we may *feel*. If we care to bring in Descartes' hypothetical 'evil genius', we can say that for John of Mirecourt we are not certain of the existence of the external world, unless God assures us that it exists. All proofs, then, of God's existence which rest upon our knowledge of the external world are uncertain; at least they are not 'demonstrative', in the sense of being reducible to the principle of contradiction or of resting on it. In his first apology John openly says that the opposite of the proposition 'God exists' implies a contradiction; but he goes on to observe that a proposition of this kind does not enjoy the evidence which attaches to the first principle. Why not? Because we arrive at the knowledge expressed in such propositions by reflection on the data of sense-experience, in which we can err, although 'we cannot err in many things (propositions) which accord with our experiences'. Does he mean that we can err in particular empirical judgments, but that we cannot err in regard to a conclusion like the existence of God which follows on the totality of sense-experience rather than on particular empirical judgments? In this case what of the possibility of our having sense-experience when no object is present? This is, no doubt, a limiting possibility and we have no reason to suppose that it is an actuality so far as the totality of sense-experience is concerned; but none the less it remains a possibility. I do not see how the traditional proofs of God's existence can have more than moral certainty or, if you like, the highest degree of probability on John's premises. In his apology he may make an attempt to justify his position by having it both ways; but it seems clear that for him the proofs of God's existence cannot be demonstrative in the sense in which he understands demonstrative. Leaving out of account the question whether John was right or wrong in what he said, he would have been more consistent, I think, if he had openly admitted that for him the proofs of God's existence, based on sense-experience, are not absolutely certain.

The principle of causality, according to John of Mirecourt, is not analytic; that is to say, it cannot be reduced to the principle of contradiction or be shown to depend upon it in such a way that the denial of the principle of causality involves a contradiction. On the other hand it does not follow that we have to doubt the truth of the principle of causality: we have 'natural evidence', even if we have not got *evidentia potissima*. Again the question arises exactly what is meant by 'natural evidence'. It can hardly mean objectively irrefutable evidence, for if the truth of the principle of causality were objectively so clear that it could not possibly be denied and that its opposite was inconceivable, it would surely follow that its evidence is reducible to the evidence of the principle of contradiction. When John speaks of 'causes naturally necessitating assent', it looks very much as though he meant that, though we can conceive the possibility of the principle of causality not being true, we are obliged by nature to think and act in the concrete as though it were true. From this it would appear to follow that for all practical purposes the proofs of God's existence which rest on the validity of the principle of causality are 'evident', but that none the less we can conceive of their not being cogent. Perhaps this means little more than that the proofs of God's existence cannot compel assent in the same way as a mathematical theorem, for example, can compel assent. John's opponents understood him as meaning that one cannot prove God's existence and that God's existence is therefore uncertain; but when he denied that the proofs are demonstrative he was using the word 'demonstrative' in a special sense, and, if his apology represents his real teaching, he did not mean to say that we must be sceptical concerning God's existence. There can, indeed, be little question of his having intended to teach scepticism; but on the other hand it is clear that he did not regard the proofs of God's existence as possessing the same degree of cogency which St. Thomas would have attributed to them.

In criticizing in this way the proofs of God's existence John of Mirecourt showed himself to be a thinker who had his place in the Ockhamist movement. He showed the same thing by his doctrine concerning the moral law. Proposition 51, as contained in the first apology, runs as follows. 'God can cause any act of the will in the will, even hatred of Himself; I doubt, however, whether anything which was created in the will by God alone would be hatred of God, unless the will conserved it actively and effectively.' According to the way of speaking common among the Doctors, says John, hatred of God involves a deformity in the will, and we must not allow that God could, as total cause, cause hatred of Himself in the human will. Absolutely speaking, however, God could cause hatred of Himself in the will, and if He did so, the man in question would not hate God culpably. Again, in the second apology the 25th condemned proposition is to the effect that 'hatred of the neighbour is not demeritorious except for the fact that it has been prohibited by God'. John proceeds to explain that he does not mean that hatred of the neighbour is not contrary to the natural law; he means that a man who hates his neighbour runs the risk of eternal punishment only because God has prohibited hatred of the neighbour. In regard to the 41st proposition of the first apology John similarly observes that nothing can be 'demeritorious' unless it is prohibited by God. It can, however, be contrary to the moral law without being demeritorious.

Needless to say, John of Mirecourt had no intention of denying our duty to obey the moral law; his aim was to emphasize the supremacy and omnipotence of God. Similarly he seems, though extremely tentatively, to have favoured the opinion of St. Peter Damian that God could bring it about that the world should never have been, that is to say, that God could bring it about that the past should not have happened. He allows that this undoing of the fact cannot take place *de potentia Dei ordinata*; but, whereas one might well expect him to appeal to the principle of contradiction in order to show that the undoing of the past is absolutely impossible, he says that this absolute impossibility is not evident to him. 'I was unwilling to lay claim to knowledge which I did not possess' (first apology, proposition 5). He does not say that it is possible for God to bring it about that the past should not have happened; he says that the impossibility of God's doing this is not evident to him. John of Mirecourt was always careful in his statements.

He shows a similar care in the way he hedges over those statements which appear to teach theological determinism and which may betray the influence of Thomas Bradwardine's *De Causa Dei*. According to John, God is the cause of moral deformity, of sin that is to say, just as He is the cause of natural deformity. God is the cause of blindness by not supplying the power of vision; and He is the cause of moral deformity by not supplying moral rectitude. John qualifies this statement, however, by observing that it is perhaps true that while a natural defect can be the total cause of natural deformity, a moral defect is not the total cause of moral deformity because moral deformity (sin), in order to exist, must proceed from a will (first apology, proposition 50). In his commentary on the *Sentences*[1] he first observes that it seems to him possible to concede that God is the cause of moral deformity, and then remarks that the common teaching of the Doctors is the very opposite. But they say the opposite since, in their eyes, to say that God is the cause of sin is to say that God acts sinfully, and that it is impossible for God to act sinfully is clear to John too. But it does not follow from this, he insists, that God cannot be the cause of moral deformity. God causes the moral deformity by not

[1] 2, 3, concl. 3.

supplying moral rectitude; but the sin proceeds from the will, and it is the human being who is guilty. Therefore, if John says that God is not the total cause of sin, he does not mean that God causes the positive element in the act of the will while the human being causes the privation of right order: for him God can be said to cause both, though the privation of right order cannot be realized except in and through a will. The will is the 'effective' cause, not God, though God can be called the 'efficacious' cause in that He wills efficaciously that there should be no rectitude in the will. Nothing can happen unless God wills it, and if God wills it, He wills it efficaciously, for His will is always fulfilled. God causes the sinful act even in its specification as a sinful act of a certain kind; but He does not cause it sinfully.

John considered that the real distinction between accidents and substances is known only by faith. 'I think that except for the faith many would perhaps have said that everything is a substance.'[1] Apparently he affirmed (at least he was understood as affirming) that 'it is probable, as far as the natural light of reason is concerned, that there are no accidents distinct from substance, but that everything is a substance; and except for the faith, this would be or could be probable' (43rd proposition of first apology). For example, 'it can be said with probability that thinking or willing is not something distinct from the soul, but that it is the soul itself' (proposition 42). John defends himself by saying that the reasons for affirming a distinction between substance and accident have more force than the reasons which can be given for denying a distinction; but he adds that he does not know if the arguments for affirming it can rightly be called demonstrations. It is clear that he did not think that these arguments amounted to demonstrations; he accepted the distinction as certain only on faith.

It is difficult to ascertain with any degree of certainty precisely what John of Mirecourt's personal opinions actually were, owing to the way in which he explains away in his apologies what he had said in his lectures on the *Sentences*. When John protests that he is simply retailing other people's opinions or when he remarks that he is merely putting forward a possible point of view without affirming that it is true, is he thoroughly sincere or is he being diplomatic? One can scarcely give any definite answer. However, I turn now to an even more extreme and thoroughgoing adherent of the new movement.

[1] 1 *Sent.*, 19, concl. 6, *ad* 5.

3. Nicholas of Autrecourt, who was born about the year 1300 in the diocese of Verdun, studied at the Sorbonne between 1320 and 1327. In due course he lectured on the *Sentences*, on Aristotle's *Politics*, etc. In 1338 he obtained a Prebend's stall in the Cathedral of Metz. Already in his introductory lecture on the *Sentences* of Peter Lombard, Nicholas had indicated his departure from the thought of previous philosophers, and a continuation of this attitude resulted in a letter from Pope Benedict XII to the Bishop of Paris on November 21st, 1340, in which the latter was instructed to see that Nicholas, together with certain other offenders, put in a personal appearance at Avignon within a month. The pope's death led to a postponement of the investigation of Nicholas's opinions; but after the coronation of Clement VI on May 19th, 1342, the matter was taken up again. The new pope entrusted the examination of Nicholas's opinions to a commission under the presidency of Cardinal William Curti, and Nicholas was invited to explain and defend his ideas. He was given the opportunity of defending himself in the pope's presence, and his replies to the objections brought against his doctrine were taken into account. But when it became clear what the verdict would be Nicholas fled from Avignon; and it is possible, though not certain, that he took refuge for the time being at the court of Ludwig of Bavaria. In 1346 he was sentenced to burn his writings publicly at Paris and to recant the condemned propositions. This he did on November 25th, 1347. He was also expelled from the teaching body of the university of Paris. Of his later life little is known, save for the fact that he became an official of the Cathedral of Metz on August 6th, 1350. Presumably he lived 'happily ever after'.

Of Nicholas's writings we possess the first two letters of a series of nine which he wrote to the Franciscan Bernard of Arezzo, one of his principal critics, and a large part of a letter which he wrote to a certain Aegidius (Giles). We also possess a letter from Aegidius to Nicholas. In addition, the lists of condemned propositions contain excerpts from other letters of Nicholas to Bernard of Arezzo together with some other fragments. All these documents have been edited by Dr. Joseph Lappe.[1] We possess also a treatise by Nicholas which begins *Exigit ordo executionis* and which is referred to as the *Exigit*. It has been edited by J. R. O'Donnell, together with Nicholas's theological writing *Utrum visio creaturae*

---

[1] *Beiträge zur Geschichte der Philosophie des Mittelalters*, VI, 2. References to 'Lappe' in the following account of Nicholas's philosophy are references to this edition, dated 1908.

rationalis beatificabilis per Verbum possit intendi naturaliter.[1] There is further a note by John of Mirecourt about Nicholas's doctrine on causality.[2]

At the beginning of his second letter to Bernard of Arezzo Nicholas remarks that the first principle to be laid down is that 'contradictions cannot be true at the same time'.[3] The principle of contradiction, or rather of non-contradiction, is the primary principle, and its primacy is to be accepted both in the negative sense, namely that there is no more ultimate principle, and in the positive sense, namely that the principle positively precedes and is presupposed by every other principle. Nicholas is arguing that the principle of non-contradiction is the ultimate basis of all natural certitude, and that while any other principle which is put forward as the basis of certitude is reducible to the principle of non-contradiction, the latter is not reducible to any other principle. If any principle other than the principle of non-contradiction is proposed as the basis of certitude, that is, if a principle which is not reducible to the principle of non-contradiction is proposed as the basis of certitude, the proposed principle may appear to be certain but its opposite will not involve a contradiction. But in this case the apparent certitude can never be transformed into genuine certitude. It is only the principle of non-contradiction which bears its own guarantee on its face, so to speak. The reason why we do not doubt the principle of non contradiction is simply that it cannot be denied without contradiction. In order, then, for any other principle to be certain, its denial must involve a contradiction. But in that case it is reducible to the principle of non-contradiction, in the sense that it is certain in virtue of that principle. The principle of non-contradiction must therefore be the primary principle. It is to be remarked that it is not the truth of the principle of non-contradiction which is in question but its primacy. Nicholas tries to show that any genuine certitude rests ultimately on this principle, and he does it by showing that any principle which did not rest on, or was not reducible to, the principle of non-contradiction would not be genuinely certain.

Any certitude which we have in the light of the principle of non-contradiction is, says Nicholas, genuine certitude, and not even the divine power could deprive it of this character. Further, all genuinely certain propositions possess the same degree of evidence.

---

[1] *Mediaeval Studies*, vol. 1, 1939, pp. 179-280. References to the *Exigit* in the following pages are references to this edition.
[2] Lappe, p. 4.   [3] *Ibid*, 6*, 33.

It makes no difference whether a proposition is immediately or mediately reducible to the principle of non-contradiction. If it is not reducible to the principle of non-contradiction, it is not certain; and if it is reducible, it is equally certain, whether it is immediately or mediately reducible. In geometry, for example, a proposition is not less certain because it happens to be the conclusion of a long chain of reasoning, provided that it is rightly demonstrated in the light of the primary principle. Apart from the certitude of faith there is no other certitude than the certitude of the principle of non-contradiction and of propositions which are reducible to that principle.

In a syllogistic argument, then, the conclusion is certain only if it is reducible to the principle of non-contradiction. What is the necessary condition of this reducibility? The conclusion, says Nicholas, is reducible to the primary principle only if it is identical with the antecedent or with a part of what is signified by the antecedent. When this is the case it is impossible to affirm the antecedent and deny the conclusion or to deny the conclusion and affirm the antecedent without contradiction. If the antecedent is certain, the conclusion is also certain. For example, in the inference 'all X's are Y, therefore this X is Y' the conclusion is identical with part of what is signified by the antecedent. It is impossible, without contradiction, to affirm the antecedent and deny the conclusion. That is, if it is certain that all X's are Y, it is certain that any particular X is Y.

How does this criterion of certitude affect factual knowledge? Bernard of Arezzo maintained that because God can cause an intuitive act in the human being without the co-operation of any secondary cause we are not entitled to argue that a thing exists because it is seen. This view was similar to that of Ockham, though Bernard apparently did not add Ockham's qualification that God could not produce in us evident assent to the existence of a non-existent thing, since this would involve a contradiction. Nicholas maintained, though, that Bernard's view led to scepticism, for on his view we should have no means of achieving certitude concerning the existence of anything. In the case of immediate perception the act of perception is not a sign from which we infer the existence of something distinct from the act. To say, for example, that I perceive a colour is simply to say that the colour appears to me: I do not see the colour and then infer its existence. The act of perceiving a colour and the act of being aware that I perceive a colour are one and the same act: I do not perceive a colour and then have to find some guarantee that I actually do perceive a colour. Immediate cognition is its own guarantee. A contradiction would be involved in saying that a colour appears and at the same time that it does not appear. In his first letter to Bernard, Nicholas says, therefore, that in his opinion 'I am evidently certain of the objects of the five senses and of my acts.'[1] Against what he regarded as scepticism, then, Nicholas maintained that immediate cognition, whether it takes the form of sense-perception or of perception of our interior acts, is certain and evident; and he explained the certitude of this knowledge by identifying the direct act of perception and the self-conscious awareness of this act of perception. In this case a contradiction would be involved in affirming that I have an act of perception and in denying that I am aware that I have an act of perception. The act of perceiving a colour is the same as the appearing of the colour to me, and the act of perceiving the colour is identical with the act of being aware that I perceive a colour. To say that I perceive a colour and to say that the colour does not exist or that I am not aware that I perceive a colour would involve me in a contradiction.

Nicholas thus admitted as certain and evident not only analytic propositions but also immediate perception.[2] But he did not think that from the existence of one thing we can infer with certainty the existence of another thing. The reason why we cannot do this is that in the case of two things which are really different from one another it is possible without logical contradiction to affirm the existence of the one thing and deny the existence of the other. If B is identical either with the whole of A or with part of A, it is not possible without contradiction to affirm the existence of A and deny that of B; and if the existence of A is certain the existence of B is also certain. But if B is really distinct from A no contradiction is involved in affirming A's existence and yet at the same time denying the existence of B. In the second letter to Bernard of Arezzo Nicholas makes the following assertion. 'From the fact that something is known to exist it cannot be inferred evidently, with, that is, evidence reducible to the first principle or to the certitude of the first principle, that another thing exists.'[3]

---

[1] Lappe, 6*, 15–16.   [2] Cf. *Exigit*, p. 235.
[3] Lappe, 9*, 15–20.

THE OCKHAMIST MOVEMENT

Bernard of Arezzo tried to counter Nicholas's assertion by what he evidently regarded as common-sense examples to the contrary. For instance, there is a white colour. But a white colour cannot exist without a substance. Therefore there is a substance. The conclusion of this syllogism is, said Bernard, certain. Nicholas's answer was on the following lines. If it is assumed that whiteness is an accident, and if it is assumed that an accident inheres in a substance and cannot exist without it, the conclusion is indeed certain. In the first place, however, the example would be irrelevant to the discussion. For what Nicholas asserted was that one cannot infer with certainty the existence of one thing from the existence of another. In the second place the assumptions that whiteness is an accident and that an accident necessarily inheres in a substance render the argument hypothetical. If whiteness is an accident and if an accident necessarily inheres in a substance, then, given this whiteness, there is a substance in which it inheres. But Nicholas would not admit that there is any compelling reason why these assumptions should be accepted. Bernard's argument conceals its assumptions. It does not show that one can argue with certainty from the existence of one thing to the existence of another thing, for Bernard has assumed that whiteness inheres in a substance. The fact that one sees a colour warrants one's concluding that a substance exists, only if one has assumed that a colour is an accident and that an accident necessarily inheres in a substance. But to assume this is to assume what has to be proved. Bernard's argument is therefore a concealed vicious circle.

Nicholas commented in a similar manner on another example brought by Bernard in order to show that one can argue with certainty from the existence of one thing to the existence of another thing. Fire is applied to tow, and there is no obstacle; therefore there will be heat. Either, said Nicholas, the consequent is identical with the antecedent or with part of it or it is not. In the first case the example would be irrelevant. For the argument would not be an argument from the existence of one thing to the existence of another thing. In the second case there would be two different propositions of which the one could be affirmed and the other denied without contradiction. 'Fire is applied to tow and there is no obstacle' and 'there will not be heat' are not contradictory propositions. And if they are not contradictory propositions the conclusion cannot be certain with the certitude which comes from reducibility to the first principle. Yet this, as has been agreed, is the only certitude.

From this position of Nicholas, that the existence of one thing cannot with certainty be inferred from that of another, it follows that no proposition which asserts that because A happens B will happen or that because B exists A exists, where A and B are distinct things, is or can be certain. Apart, then, from the immediate perception of sense-data (colours, for example) and of our acts no empirical knowledge is or can be certain. No causal argument can be certain. We doubtless believe in necessary connections in nature; but logic cannot detect them, and propositions which state them cannot be certain. What, then, is the reason of our belief in causal connections? Nicholas apparently explained this in terms of the experience of repeated sequences which gives rise to the expectation that if B has followed A in the past it will do so again in the future. Nicholas, it is true, affirmed that we cannot have probable knowledge that B will follow A in the future, unless we have evident certitude that at some time in the past B has followed A; but he did not mean that we cannot have probable knowledge that B will follow A in the future, unless we have evident certitude in the past of a necessary causal connection between A and B. What he meant, in terms of his own example in his second letter to Bernard, was that I cannot have probable knowledge that if I put my hand to the fire it will become warm, unless I have evident certitude of warmth in my hand having followed my putting my hand to the fire in the past. 'If it was once evident to me when I put my hand to the fire that I became warm, it is now probable to me that if I put my hand to the fire I should become warm.'[1] Nicholas considered that repeated experience of the coexistence of two things or of the regular sequence of distinct events increases the probability, from the *subjective* point of view, of similar experiences in the future; but repeated experience does not add anything to the objective evidence.[2]

It is clear that Nicholas considered that the possibility of God acting immediately as a causal agent, without, that is, using any secondary cause, rendered it impossible to argue with absolute certainty from the existence of one created thing to the existence of another created thing. He also argued against Bernard that on the principles enunciated by the latter it would be equally

---

[1] Lappe, 13*, 9–12.   [2] *Exigit*, p. 237.

impossible. But the main interest of Nicholas's discussion of causality lies in the fact that he did not simply argue from the universally admitted doctrine of the divine omnipotence (universally admitted as a theological doctrine at any rate) but approached the question on a purely philosophical level.

It is to be noted that Nicholas did not deny that we can have certitude concerning the coexistence of appearances of A and B. All that is required is that we should actually have the two perceptions at once. But he did deny that one can infer with certainty the existence of the non-apparent from the existence of an appearance. He would not allow, then, that one can infer with certainty the existence of any substance. In order to know with certainty the existence of any material substance we should have either to perceive it directly, intuitively, or to infer its existence with certainty from the appearances or phenomena. But we do not perceive material substances, according to Nicholas. If we did, even the uneducated (the *rustici*) would perceive them. And this is not the case. Moreover, we cannot infer their existence with certainty, for the existence of one thing cannot be logically deduced from the existence of another thing.

In his ninth letter to Bernard, Nicholas asserted that 'these inferences are not evident: there is an act of understanding: therefore there is an intellect; there is an act of willing: therefore there is a will'.[1] This statement suggests that according to Nicholas we have no more certainty of the soul's existence as a substance than we have of material substances. Elsewhere, however, he states that 'Aristotle never had evident knowledge of any substance other than his own soul, understanding by "substance" something different from the objects of our five senses and from our formal experience.'[2] Again, 'we have no certitude concerning a substance joined to matter other than our soul'.[3] Statements like this have led some historians to conclude that Nicholas admitted that we have certitude about the knowledge of the soul as a spiritual substance. They accordingly interpret his remarks about our not being entitled to infer the existence of the intellect from the existence of acts of understanding and the existence of the will from the existence of acts of volition as an attack on the faculty psychology. This is certainly a possible interpretation, though it might be considered odd if Nicholas directed his attack simply against the theory of distinct faculties

---

[1] Lappe, 34*, 7–9.   [2] *Ibid.*, 12*, 20–3.   [3] *Ibid.*, 13*, 19–20.

which had already been subjected to criticism by William of Ockham, for example. But the *Exigit*[1] seems to imply, though it does not say so clearly, that we have no direct awareness of the soul. And in this case it would appear to follow, on Nicholas's premisses, that we have no natural knowledge of the soul's existence as a substance. The statement that Aristotle had no certain knowledge of any substance other than his own soul may be analogous to the assertion in the fifth letter to Bernard of Arezzo that we do not know with certainty that there is any efficient cause other than God. For his general position shows that in Nicholas's opinion we have no natural or philosophical certain knowledge that even God is an efficient cause. It is true that if the parallel between the two statements is pushed, it would seem to follow that Aristotle, according to Nicholas, enjoyed the certainty of faith about the existence of his soul as a spiritual substance; and Nicholas cannot possibly have meant to say this. But it is not necessary to interpret his remarks so strictly. However, it is difficult to be sure whether he did or did not make an exception in favour of our knowledge of our own souls from his general view that we have no certain knowledge of the existence of substances considered as distinct from phenomena.

It is evident that in his critique of causality and substance Nicholas anticipated the position of Hume; and the similarity is all the more striking if he did in fact deny that we have any certain knowledge of the existence of any substance, material or spiritual. But Dr. Weinberg is undoubtedly right, I think, in pointing out that Nicholas was not a phenomenalist. Nicholas thought that one cannot infer with certainty the existence of a non-apparent entity from the existence of phenomena; but he certainly did not think this means that one can infer its non-existence. In the sixth letter to Bernard he laid it down that 'from the fact that one thing exists, it cannot be inferred with certainty that another thing does not exist'.[2] Nicholas did not say that only phenomena exist or that affirmations of the existence of metaphenomenal entities are nonsensical. All he said was that the existence of phenomena does not enable us to infer with certainty the existence of the metaphenomenal or non-apparent. It is one thing to say, for example, that we are unable to prove that there is anything in a material object other than what appears to the senses, and it is another thing to say that there actually is no substance. Nicholas was not

---

[1] p. 225.   [2] Lappe, 31*, 16-17.

a dogmatic phenomenalist. I do not mean to imply by this that Hume was a dogmatic phenomenalist, for he was not, whatever objections his (and Nicholas's) critical analyses of causality and substance may be open to. My point is simply that one must not conclude from Nicholas's denial of the demonstrability of the existence of substances that he actually denied the existence of all substances or said that their non-existence could be proved.

It is obvious enough that Nicholas's critique of causality and substance had important repercussions in regard to his attitude towards the traditional philosophical theology. Although Nicholas does not say so in clear and explicit terms, it would seem to follow from his general principles that it is not possible to prove the existence of God as efficient cause. In the fifth letter to Bernard he remarks that God may be the sole efficient cause, since one cannot prove that there is any natural efficient cause. But to say that God may be the sole efficient cause is not to say that He is the sole efficient cause or, indeed, that He can be proved to be an efficient cause at all. Nicholas meant merely that for all we know or can establish to the contrary God may be the sole efficient cause. As to our being able to prove that God actually is efficient cause, this is excluded by the general principle that we cannot infer with certainty the existence of one thing from the existence of another thing.

The causal or cosmological argument for God's existence could not, then, be a demonstrative argument on Nicholas's premises. Nor could St. Thomas's fourth or fifth arguments be admitted as proofs yielding certain conclusions. We cannot, says Nicholas in the fifth letter to Bernard, prove that one thing is or is not nobler than another thing. Neither inspection of one thing nor comparison of two or more things is able to prove a hierarchy of degrees of being from the point of view of value. 'If anything whatever is pointed out, nobody knows evidently that it may not exceed all other things in value.'[1] And Nicholas does not hesitate to draw the conclusion that if by the term 'God' we understand the noblest being, nobody knows with certainty whether any given thing may not be God. If, then, we cannot establish with certainty an objective scale of perfection, St. Thomas's fourth argument obviously cannot be considered a demonstrative argument. As to the argument from finality, St. Thomas's fifth argument, this is ruled out by Nicholas's statement in the same letter that 'no one

[1] Lappe, 33*, 12–14.

knows evidently that one thing is the end (that is, final cause) of another'.[1] One cannot establish by inspection or analysis of any one thing that it is the final cause of another thing, nor is there any way of demonstrating it with certainty. We see a certain series of events, but final causality is not demonstrable.

Nicholas did, however, admit a probable argument for God's existence. Assuming as probable that we have an idea of the good as a standard for judging about the contingent relations between things,[2] and assuming that the order of the universe is such that it would satisfy a mind operating with the criterion of goodness and fitness, we can argue first that all things are so interconnected that one thing can be said to exist for the sake of another and secondly that this relationship between things is intelligible only in the light of the hypothesis that all things are subjected to an ultimate end, the supreme good or God. It might well appear that an argument of this kind would be no more than an entirely unfounded hypothesis, and that it could not, on Nicholas's own principles, amount to a probable argument. But Nicholas did not deny that we can have some sort of evidence enabling us to form a conjectural hypothesis which may be more or less probable, though it may not be certain as far as we are concerned. It might be true; it might even be a necessary truth; but we could not know that it was true, though we could believe it to be true. Besides theological belief, that is, faith in revealed truths, there is room for a belief which rests on arguments that are more or less probable.

Nicholas's probable argument for God's existence was part of the positive philosophy which he put forward as probable. It is not, in my opinion, worth while going into this philosophy in any detail. Apart from the fact that it was proposed as a probable hypothesis, its various parts are by no means always consistent with one another. One may mention, however, that for Nicholas the corruptibility of things is probably inconsistent with the goodness of the universe. Positively expressed this means that things are probably eternal. In order to show that this supposition cannot be ruled out by observation Nicholas argued that the fact that we see B succeeding A does not warrant our concluding that A has ceased to exist. We may not see A any more, but we do not see that A does not exist any more. And we cannot establish by reasoning that it does not any longer exist. If we could, we could establish by reasoning that nothing exists which is not observed,

---

[1] Lappe, 33*, 18-19. [2] *Exigit*, p. 185.

and this we cannot do. The Aristotelian doctrine of change is by no means certain. Moreover, the corruption of substances can be explained much better on an atomistic hypothesis than on Aristotelian principles. Substantial change may mean simply that one collocation of atoms is succeeded by another, while accidental change may mean the addition of fresh atoms to an atomic complex or the subtraction of some atoms from that complex. It is probable that the atoms are eternal and that precisely the same combinations occur in the periodic cycles which eternally recur.

As to the human soul, Nicholas maintained the hypothesis of immortality. But his suggestions on this matter are closely connected with a curious explanation of knowledge. As all things are eternal, it may be supposed that in knowledge the soul or mind enters into a temporary union with the object of knowledge. And the same can be said of imagination. The soul enters into a state of conjunction with images, but the images themselves are eternal. This hypothesis throws light, in Nicholas's opinion, on the nature of immortality. We may suppose that to good souls noble thoughts come after death, while to bad souls come evil thoughts. Or we may suppose that good souls enter into union with a better collection of atoms and are disposed to better experiences than they received in their previous embodied states, while evil souls enter into union with worse atoms and are disposed to receive more evil experiences and thoughts than in their previous embodied states. Nicholas claimed that this hypothesis allowed for the Christian doctrine of rewards and punishments after death; but he added a prudential qualification. His statements were, he said, more probable than the statements which had for a long time seemed probable. None the less, someone might turn up who would deprive his own statements of probability; and in view of this possibility the best thing to do is to adhere to the Biblical teaching on rewards and punishments. This line of argument was called in the *Articles of Cardinal Curti* a 'foxy excuse' (*excusatio vulpina*).[1]

Nicholas's positive philosophy was obviously at variance on some points with Catholic theology. And indeed Nicholas did not hesitate to say that his statements were more probable than the contradictory assertions. But one must interpret this attitude with some care. Nicholas did not state that his doctrines were true and the opposite doctrines false: he said that if the propositions which

[1] Lappe, 39*, 8.

were contradictory to his own were considered simply in regard to their probability, that is, as probable conclusions of reason, they were less probable than his own statements. For example, the theological doctrine that the world has not existed from eternity is for him certainly true, if it is considered as a revealed truth. But if one attends simply to the philosophical arguments which can be adduced in favour of its truth, one must admit, according to Nicholas, that they are less probable than the philosophical arguments which can be adduced in favour of the contradictory proposition. One is not entitled, however, to conclude that the contradictory proposition is not true. For all we know it may even be a necessary truth. Probability has to be interpreted in terms of the natural evidence available to us at any given moment, and a proposition may be for us more probable than its contradictory even though it is in fact false and its contradictory true. Nicholas did not propose a double-truth theory; nor did he deny any defined doctrines of the Church. What his subjective attitude was is a matter about which we cannot be sure. Pierre d'Ailly asserted that a number of Nicholas's propositions were condemned out of envy or ill-will; and Nicholas himself maintained that some statements were attributed to him which he did not hold at all or which he did not hold in the sense in which they were condemned. It is difficult to judge how far one is justified in taking his protestations at their face-value and how far one should assume that his critics were justified in dismissing these protestations as 'foxy' excuses. There can be little doubt, I think, that he was sincere in saying that the philosophy which he put forward as 'probable' was untrue in so far as it conflicted with the teaching of the Church. At least there is no real difficulty in accepting his sincerity on this point, since apart from any other consideration it would have been quite inconsistent with the critical side of his philosophy if he had regarded the conclusions of his positive philosophy as certain. On the other hand, it is not so easy to accept Nicholas's protestation that the critical views expounded in his correspondence with Bernard of Arezzo were put forward as a kind of experiment in reasoning. His letters to Bernard hardly give that impression, even if the possibility cannot be excluded that the explanation which he offered to his judges represented his real mind. After all, he was by no means the only philosopher of his time to adopt a critical attitude towards the traditional metaphysics, even if he went further than most.

It is, however, quite clear that Nicholas meant to attack the philosophy of Aristotle and that he considered his own positive philosophy to be a more probable hypothesis than the Aristotelian system. He declared that he was himself very astonished that some people study Aristotle and the Commentator (Averroes) up to a decrepit old age and forsake moral matters and the care of the common good in favour of the study of Aristotle. They do this to such an extent that when the friend of truth rises up and sounds a trumpet to rouse the sleepers from slumber they are greatly afflicted and rush upon him like armed men to deadly combat.[1]

Mention of 'moral matters' and of the 'common good' leads one to inquire what Nicholas's ethical and political teaching was. We have not much to go upon here. But it seems clear that he maintained the Ockhamist theory of the arbitrary character of the moral law. There is a condemned proposition of his to the effect that 'God can order a rational creature to hate Him, and that the rational creature merits more by obeying this precept than by loving God in obedience to a precept. For he would do so (that is, hate God) with greater effort and more against his inclination.'[2] As to politics, Nicholas is said to have issued a proclamation that whoever wanted to hear lectures on Aristotle's *Politics* together with certain discussions about justice and injustice which would enable a man to make new laws or to correct laws already in existence, should repair to a certain place where he would find Master Nicholas of Autrecourt, who would teach him all these things.[3] How far this proclamation constitutes evidence of Nicholas's serious concern for the common welfare and how far it is the expression of a love of notoriety it is difficult to say.

I have given an account of the philosophical ideas of John of Mirecourt and Nicholas of Autrecourt in a chapter on the 'Ockhamist Movement'. Is this procedure justified? Nicholas's positive philosophy, which he put forward as probable, was certainly not the philosophy of William of Ockham; and in this respect it would be quite wrong to call him an 'Ockhamist'. As to his critical philosophy, it was not the same as that of Ockham, and Nicholas cannot be properly called an 'Ockhamist', if by this term is meant a disciple of Ockham. Moreover, the tone of Nicholas's writing is different from that of the Franciscan theologian. None the less, Nicholas was an extreme representative of that critical movement of thought which was a prominent feature of fourteenth-century

---

[1] Cf. *Exigit*, pp. 181-2.   [2] Lappe, 41*, 31-4.   [3] *Ibid.*, 40*, 26-33.

philosophy and which finds expression in one aspect of Ockhamism. I have indicated earlier that I use the term 'Ockhamist Movement' to denote a philosophical movement which was characterized, in part, by a critical attitude towards the presuppositions and arguments of the traditional metaphysics, and if the term is used in this sense, one can, I think, justifiably speak of John of Mirecourt and Nicholas of Autrecourt as belonging to the Ockhamist movement.

Nicholas of Autrecourt was not a sceptic, if by this term we mean a philosopher who denies or questions the possibility of attaining any certain knowledge. He maintained that certainty is obtainable in logic and in mathematics and in immediate perception. In modern terms he recognized as certain both analytic propositions (the propositions which are now sometimes called 'tautologies') and basic empirical statements, though one must add the proviso that for Nicholas we can have evident immediate knowledge without that knowledge being expressed in a proposition. On the other hand, propositions involving the assertion of a causal relation in the metaphysical sense or propositions based on an inference from one existent to another he regarded not as certain propositions but rather as empirical hypotheses. One must not, however, turn Nicholas into a 'logical positivist'. He did not deny the significance of metaphysical or theological statements: on the contrary, he presupposed the certitude of faith and admitted revelation as a source of absolute certainty.

4. I announced my intention of concluding this chapter with some remarks on the influence of the new movement in the universities, especially in the universities which were founded in the latter part of the fourteenth century and during the fifteenth.

In 1389 a statute was passed at the university of Vienna requiring of students in the faculty of arts that they should attend lectures on the logical works of Peter of Spain, while later statutes imposed a similar obligation in regard to the logical works of Ockhamist authors like William Heytesbury. Nominalism was also strongly represented in the German universities of Heidelberg (founded in 1386), Erfurt (1392) and Leipzig (1409) and in the Polish university of Cracow (1397). The university of Leipzig is said to have owed its origin to the exodus of nominalists from Prague, where John Hus and Jerome of Prague taught the Scotist realism which they had learnt from John Wycliffe (c. 1320–84). Indeed, when the Council of Constance condemned the theological errors of John Hus in 1415, the nominalists were quick to argue that Scotist realism had also been condemned, though this was not actually the case.

In the first half of the fifteenth century a rather surprising revival of the philosophy of St. Albert the Great took place. The nominalists seem to have left Paris early in the century, partly owing to the conditions brought about by the Hundred Years War, though Ehrle was doubtless correct in connecting the revival of 'Albertism' with the return of the Dominicans to Paris in 1403. They had left the city in 1387. The supremacy of Albertism did not last very long, however, because the nominalists returned in 1437 after the city had been liberated from the English. On March 1st, 1474, King Louis XI issued a decree prohibiting the teaching of nominalism and ordering the confiscation of nominalist books; but in 1481 the ban was withdrawn.

In the fifteenth century, then, nominalism was strongly entrenched at Paris, Oxford and many German universities; but the older traditions continued to hold their ground in certain places. This was the case in the university of Cologne, which was founded in 1389. At Cologne the doctrines of St. Albert and St. Thomas were in possession. After the condemnation of John Hus the Prince Electors asked the university to adopt nominalism on the ground that the more old-fashioned realism easily led to heresy, even though it was not evil in itself. But in 1425 the university replied that while it remained open to anyone to adopt nominalism if he chose, the doctrines of St. Albert, St. Thomas, St. Bonaventure, Giles of Rome and Duns Scotus were above suspicion. In any case, said the university, the heresies of John Hus did not spring from philosophical realism but from the theological teaching of Wycliffe. Further, if realism were forbidden at Cologne the students would leave the university.

With the university of Cologne one must associate that of Louvain, which was founded in 1425. The statutes of 1427 required of candidates for the doctorate that they should take an oath never to teach the doctrines of Buridan, Marsilius of Inghen, Ockham or their followers; and in 1480 professors who expounded Aristotle in the light of the Ockhamist theories were threatened with suspension from office.

The adherents of the 'ancient way', therefore, were by no means completely routed by the nominalists. Indeed, in the middle of the fourteenth century realism gained a foothold at Heidelberg.

Moreover, they could boast of some eminent names. Chief among them was John Capreolus (*c.* 1380–1444), a Dominican who lectured for a time at Paris and later at Toulouse. He set out to defend the doctrines of St. Thomas against the contrary opinions of Scotus, Durandus, Henry of Ghent and all adversaries in general, including the nominalists. His great work, which was completed shortly before his death at Rodez and which earned for him the title of *Princeps thomistarum*, was the *Libri IV defensionum theologiae divi Thomae de Aquino*. Capreolus was the first of the line of distinguished Dominican Thomists and commentators on St. Thomas, which included at a later period men like Cajetan (d. 1534) and John of St. Thomas (d. 1644).

In the Italian universities a current of Averroistic Aristotelianism was represented at Bologna in the first half of the fourteenth century by thinkers like Thaddaeus of Parma and Angelo of Arezzo and passed to Padua and Venice where it was represented by Paul of Venice (d. 1429), Cajetan of Thiene (d. 1465), Alexander Achillini (d. 1512) and Agostino Nipho (d. 1546). The first printed edition of Averroes appeared at Padua in 1472. Something will be said later, in connection with the philosophy of the Renaissance, about the controversy between those who followed Averroes' interpretation of Aristotle and those who adhered to the interpretation given by Alexander of Aphrodisias, and about the condemnation of 1513. The Averroists have been mentioned here simply as an illustration of the fact that the *via moderna* should not be regarded as having swept all before it in the fourteenth and fifteenth centuries.

Nevertheless, nominalism possessed that attraction which comes from modernity and freshness, and it spread widely, as we have seen. A notable figure among fifteenth-century nominalists was Gabriel Biel (*c.* 1425–95), who taught at Tübingen and composed an epitome of Ockham's commentaries on the *Sentences* of Peter Lombard. Biel's work was a methodical and clear exposition of Ockhamism, and though he did not pretend to be more than a follower and exponent of Ockham he exercised a considerable influence. Indeed, the Ockhamists at the universities of Erfurt and Wittenberg were known as *Gabrielistae*. It is perhaps interesting to note that Biel did not interpret Ockham's moral theory as meaning that there is no natural moral order. There are objects or ends besides God which can be chosen in accordance with right reason, and pagan philosophers like Aristotle, Cicero and Seneca were able to accomplish morally good and virtuous acts. In virtue of his 'absolute power' God could, indeed, command acts opposed to the dictates of the natural reason; but this does not alter the fact that these dictates can be recognized without revelation.

5. Finally one may recall that the Ockhamist Movement or nominalism had various aspects. On the purely logical side it was partly a development of the logic of terms and of the theory of *suppositio* as found in pre-Ockhamist logicians like Peter of Spain. This terminist logic was used by William of Ockham in order to exclude all forms of realism. The problem of universals was treated from a logical rather than an ontological point of view. The universal is the abstract term considered according to its logical content, and this term stands in the proposition for individual things, which are the only things which exist.

This terminist logic had not of itself any sceptical consequences in regard to knowledge, nor did Ockham regard it as having any such consequences. But together with the logical aspect of nominalism one must take into account the analysis of causality and the consequences of this analysis in regard to the epistemological status of empirical hypotheses. In the philosophy of a man like Nicholas of Autrecourt we have seen a sharp distinction drawn between analytic or formal propositions, which are certain, and empirical hypotheses, which are not and cannot be certain. With Ockham this view, so far as he held it, was closely connected with his insistence on the divine omnipotence: with Nicholas of Autrecourt the theological background was very much less in evidence.

We have seen, too, how the nominalists (some more than others) tended to adopt a critical attitude towards the metaphysical arguments of the older philosophers. This attitude was fully explicit in an extremist like Nicholas of Autrecourt, since it was made to rest on his general position that one cannot infer with certainty the existence of one thing from the existence of another thing. Metaphysical arguments are probable rather than demonstrative.

But, whatever one may be inclined to think on one or two cases, this critical attitude in regard to metaphysical speculation was practically always combined with a firm theological faith and a firm belief in revelation as a source of certain knowledge. This firm belief is particularly striking in the case of Ockham himself. His view that it is possible to have what would be, from the psychological point of view, intuition of a non-existent thing and his theory about the ultimate dependence of the moral law on the divine choice were not expressions of scepticism but of the tremendous emphasis he placed on the divine omnipotence. If one attempts to turn the nominalists into rationalists or even sceptics in the modern sense, one is taking them out of their historical setting and severing them from their mental background. In the course of time nominalism became one of the regular currents in Scholastic thought; and a theological chair of nominalism was erected even in the university of Salamanca.

But nominalism suffered the fate of most philosophical schools of thought. It obviously began as something new; and whatever one's opinion concerning the various tenets of the nominalists may be, it can hardly be denied that they had something to say. They helped to develop logical studies and they raised important problems. But in the course of time a tendency to 'logic-chopping' showed itself, and this can perhaps be connected with their reserved attitude towards metaphysics. Logical refinements and exaggerated subtlety tended to drain off the energies of the later nominalists; and when philosophy received a fresh impetus at the time of the Renaissance this impetus did not come from the nominalists.

CHAPTER X

THE SCIENTIFIC MOVEMENT

Physical science in the thirteenth and fourteenth centuries—The problem of motion; impetus and gravity—Nicholas Oresme; the hypothesis of the earth's rotation—The possibility of other worlds—Some scientific implications of nominalism; and implications of the impetus theory.

1. FOR a long time it was widely supposed that there was no respect for experience in the Middle Ages and that the only ideas on science which the mediaevals possessed were adopted uncritically from Aristotle and other non-Christian writers. Science was assumed to have started again, after centuries of almost complete quiescence, at the time of the Renaissance. Then it was found that a considerable interest had been taken in scientific matters during the fourteenth century, that some important discoveries had been made at that time, that various theories had been fairly widely held which did not derive from Aristotle and that certain hypotheses which were usually associated with the Renaissance scientists had been proposed in the late Middle Ages. At the same time a better knowledge of late mediaeval philosophy suggested that the scientific movement of the fourteenth century should be connected with Ockhamism or nominalism, largely on the ground that Ockham and those who belonged more or less to the same movement of thought insisted on the primacy of intuition or of immediate experience in the acquisition of factual knowledge. It was not that Ockham himself was thought to have shown much interest in scientific matters; but his insistence on intuition as the only basis of factual knowledge and the empiricist side of his philosophy were thought to have given a powerful impetus to scientific interests and investigations. This view of the matter could be fitted into the traditional outlook inasmuch as Ockham and the nominalists were supposed to have been resolute anti-Aristotelians.

It is not at all my intention to attempt to deny that there is truth in this interpretation of the facts. Although Ockham cannot possibly be called simply 'anti-Aristotelian' without qualification, since in some matters he regarded himself as the true interpreter of Aristotle, his philosophy was in certain important respects undoubtedly at variance with Aristotle's, and it is clear that some thinkers who belonged to the nominalist movement were extremely hostile to Aristotelianism. Moreover, it is probably true to say that Ockhamist insistence on experience as the basis of our knowledge of existent things favoured the growth of empirical science. It may be difficult to assess an epistemological theory's positive influence on the growth of science; but it is reasonable to think that the doctrine of the primacy of intuition would naturally encourage such growth rather than discourage it. Moreover, if one assumes that causes cannot be discovered by *a priori* theorizing but that recourse must be had to experience in order to discover them, this assumption is calculated to turn the mind towards the investigation of the empirical data. No doubt, it can be said with justice that science does not consist in 'intuition' or in merely observing the empirical data; but the point is not that Ockhamism provided a theory of scientific method but rather that it helped to create an intellectual climate which facilitated and tended to promote scientific research. For by directing men's minds to the facts or empirical data in the acquisition of knowledge it at the same time directed them away from passive acceptance of the opinions of illustrious thinkers of the past.

But though it would be improper to discount the connection of fourteenth-century science with Ockhamism it would be equally improper to attribute its growth to Ockhamism as a sufficient cause. In the first place it is not clear to what extent one can legitimately speak of the fourteenth-century physicists as 'Ockhamists', even if one uses the term in a wide sense. One of the leading figures who took an interest in physical theories was John Buridan, who was for a time rector of the university of Paris and died about 1360. This theologian, philosopher and physicist was influenced by the terminist logic and by certain views which were held by Ockham; but he was by no means an unqualified nominalist. Apart from the fact that in his official capacity as rector he was associated with the condemnation of nominalist theories in 1340 he maintained, for example, in his writings that it is possible to prove the existence of one thing from the existence of another thing and that consequently it is possible to prove the existence of God. Albert of Saxony was rather more of an Ockhamist. Rector of the university of Paris in 1353 he became in 1365 the first rector of the university of Vienna. In the same year he was appointed bishop of Halberstadt. He died in that post in 1390. In logic he followed Ockham; but he was certainly not an extreme adherent of the *via moderna*. It is true that he held that the certitude given by experience cannot be absolute; but it would appear that his view of the hypothetical character of empirical statements was due more to the conviction that God can miraculously 'interfere' with the natural order than to any other consideration. Marsilius of Inghen (d. 1396), who was rector of the university of Paris in 1367 and 1371 and first rector of the university of Heidelberg in 1386, was indeed, a declared adherent of the *via moderna*; but he seems to have tempered the nominalist position on universals with a dose of realism, and he thought that the metaphysician can prove the existence and unicity of God. As for Nicholas Oresme, who taught at Paris and died as bishop of Lisieux in 1382, he was much more of a physicist than a philosopher, though he had, of course, theological and philosophical interests.

One can say then, I think, that the leading figures in the scientific movement of the fourteenth century had in most cases affiliations with the Ockhamist Movement. And if one is going to use the term 'nominalist' to denote those who adopted the Ockhamist or terminist logic, one can call them 'nominalists'. But it would be a mistake to suppose that they all adhered to Ockham's views on metaphysics; and it would be still more of a mistake to suppose that they shared the extremist philosophical position of a thinker like Nicholas of Autrecourt. Indeed, Buridan and Albert of Saxony both attacked Nicholas. It is fairly clear, however, that the *via moderna* in philosophy did stimulate, though it did not cause, the scientific developments of the fourteenth century.

That the nominalist movement cannot be accounted the sufficient cause of the growth of science in the fourteenth century is clear from the fact that fourteenth-century science was to a considerable extent a continuation of and growth from thirteenth-century science. I have mentioned that modern research has brought to light the reality of scientific progress in the fourteenth century. But research is also bringing to light the scientific investigations which were pursued in the thirteenth century. These investigations were stimulated mainly by the translations of Greek and Arabic scientific works; but they were none the less real. Mediaeval science was doubtless primitive and rudimentary if we compare it with the science of the post-Renaissance era; but there is no longer any excuse for saying that there was no science in the Middle Ages outside the fields of theology and philosophy. Not only was there a scientific development in the Middle Ages but there was also a continuity in some degree between the science of the late Middle Ages and the science of the Renaissance. It would be foolish to belittle the achievements of the Renaissance scientists or to make out that their hypotheses and discoveries were all anticipated in the Middle Ages. But it is also foolish to depict Renaissance science as being without historical antecedents and parentage.

In the thirteenth century a number of thinkers had insisted on the need for observation or 'experience' in scientific study. In the preceding volume of this history mention was made in this connection of St. Albert the Great (1206–80), Peter of Maricourt (exact dates unknown), Robert Grosseteste (c. 1175–1253) and of Roger Bacon (c. 1212–after 1292). Peter of Maricourt, who stimulated Bacon's interest in scientific matters, is notable for his *Epistola de magnete*, which was utilized by William Gilbert in the second half of the sixteenth century. Grosseteste wrote on optics and tried to improve the theory of refraction contained in Greek and Arabic writings. Optics constituted also one of Bacon's special interests. The Silesian scientist, mathematician and philosopher Witelo wrote on the same subject in his *Perspectiva*. This work was composed in dependence on the writings of the Islamic scientist Alhazen; and Kepler later supplied some developments on Witelo's ideas in his *Ad Vitellionem paralipomena* (1604). The Dominican Theodoric of Freiberg (d. c. 1311) developed a theory in explanation of the rainbow on an experimental basis, which was adopted by Descartes;[1] and another Dominican, Jordanus Nemorarius, made discoveries in mechanics.

But though the thirteenth-century physicists insisted on the need for observation in scientific research, and though a man like Roger Bacon was quick to see the practical purposes to which scientific discoveries could be put, they were by no means blind to the theoretical aspects of scientific method. They did not regard science as consisting in the mere accumulation of empirical data; nor did they concentrate simply on real or imagined practical results. They were interested in explaining the data. Aristotle had held that scientific knowledge is obtained only when one is in a position to show how the observed effects follow from their

---

[1] Theodoric's explanation of the shape of the bow was correct, though he failed to explain the colours.

causes; and for Grosseteste and Bacon this meant in large part being able to give a mathematical deduction of the effects. Hence the great emphasis placed by Bacon on mathematics as the key to other sciences. Furthermore, whereas Aristotle had not given any very clear indication how a knowledge of the 'causes' is to be actually obtained, Grosseteste and Bacon showed how the elimination of explanatory theories which are incompatible with the facts helped one to arrive at this knowledge. In other words, they saw not only that an explanatory hypothesis could be arrived at by examining the common factors in different instances of the phenomenon under investigation, but also that it is necessary to verify this hypothesis by considering what results should follow if the hypothesis were true and by then experimenting in order to see if these expectations are actually fulfilled.

Fourteenth-century science was therefore not an entirely new development: it was a continuation of the scientific work of the preceding century, just as this work was itself a continuation of the scientific studies made by Greek and Arab physicists and mathematicians. But in the fourteenth century other problems came into prominence, especially the problem of motion. And the consideration of this problem in the fourteenth century might have suggested a conception of scientific hypotheses which, had it been subsequently accepted by Galileo, might have gone a long way towards preventing the latter's clash with the theologians.

2. In Aristotle's account of motion a distinction was made between natural and unnatural motion. An element like fire is naturally light and its natural tendency is to move upwards towards its natural place, while earth is heavy and has a natural movement downwards. But one can take a naturally heavy thing and throw it upwards, a stone, for example; and so long as the stone is moving upwards its motion is unnatural. Aristotle considered that this unnatural motion requires an explanation. The obvious answer to the question why the stone moves upwards is that it is thrown upwards. But once the stone has left the hand of the person who throws it it continues to move upwards for some time. Aristotle's answer to the question why this happens was that the person who throws the stone and so starts it on its upward course moves not only the stone but also the surrounding air. This air moves the air higher up and each portion of the air which is moved carries the stone with it until the successive movements of portions of air become so weak that the stone's natural tendency to downward

motion is able at length to reassert itself. The stone then begins to move towards its natural place.

This account of unnatural or violent motion was rejected by William of Ockham. If it is the air which moves a flying arrow, then if two arrows meet in flight we shall have to say that at that moment the same air is causing movements in opposite directions; and this cannot be the case.[1] On the other hand, one cannot suppose that a stone which is thrown upwards continues to move in virtue of some power or quality imparted to it. There is no empirical evidence of the existence of any such quality distinct from the projectile. If there were such a quality it could be conserved by God apart from the projectile; but it would be absurd to suppose that this can be done. Local motion does not involve anything beyond a 'permanent thing' and the term of the motion.[2]

Ockham thus rejected the idea of a quality impressed on the projectile by the agent as an explanation of motion; and to this extent he may be said to have anticipated the law of inertia. But the physicists of the fourteenth century were not content to say that a thing moves because it is in motion: they preferred to adopt the theory of impetus, which had been put forward by Philoponus in the early part of the sixth century and which had been already adopted by the Franciscan Peter John Olivi (*c.* 1248-98), who spoke of the impulse (*impulsus*) or 'inclination' that is given to the projectile by the moving agent. This quality or energy in virtue of which a stone, for example, continues to move after it has left the hand of the thrower until it is overcome by the resistance of the air and the weight of the stone was called *impetus* by the fourteenth-century physicists. They supported the theory empirically, in that they maintained that it was better adapted than the Aristotelian theory for 'saving the appearances'. For example, John Buridan held that Aristotle's theory of motion was unable to explain the movement of a spinning top, whereas this could be explained on the impetus theory. The spinning top, he said, stays in one place; it does not leave its place, which could then be filled by air which would move the top. But though the fourteenth-century physicists attempted to support the impetus theory empirically or to verify it, they did not confine themselves to purely physical considerations but introduced philosophical questions stated in the traditional categories. For example, in his *Abbreviationes super VIII libros physicorum* Marsilius of Inghen

---

[1] 2 *Sent.*, 18, J.   [2] *Ibid.*, 9, E.

raised the question, to what category or *praedicamentum* should impetus be assigned. He did not supply any very definite answer to this question; but he clearly thought that there are different kinds of impetus. For some projectiles move upwards, others downwards, some straight forwards, others in a circle. Again, although Albert of Saxony declared that the question whether impetus is a substance or an accident is a question for the metaphysician rather than for the physicist, he himself asserted that it is a quality, that is to say an accident. In any case it is clear that these physicists regarded impetus as something distinct from and impressed upon the projectile or moving body: they did not follow William of Ockham in his denial of any such distinct reality.

An interesting application of the impetus theory was made in regard to the movement of the heavenly bodies. In his commentary on the *Metaphysics*[1] Buridan maintained that God imparted to the heavenly bodies an original impetus which is the same in kind as the impetus in virtue of which terrestrial bodies move. There is no need to suppose that the heavenly bodies are made of a special element (the quintessence or fifth element), which can only move with a circular motion. Nor is it necessary to postulate Intelligences of the spheres to account for the spheres' movements. Motion on earth and motion in the heavens can be explained in the same way. Just as a man imparts an impetus to the stone which he throws into the air, so God imparted impetus to the heavenly bodies when He created them. The reason why the latter continue to move while the stone eventually falls to the earth is simply that the stone encounters resistance whereas the heavenly bodies do not. The impetus of the stone is gradually overcome by the air's resistance and the force of gravity; and the operation of these factors results in the stone's eventually moving towards its natural place. But although the heavenly bodies are not composed of some special matter of their own these factors do not operate in their case: gravity, in the sense of a factor which makes a body tend towards the earth as its natural place, operates only in regard to bodies within the terrestrial sphere.

This theory of impetus was adopted, to all intents and purposes, by Albert of Saxony, Marsilius of Inghen and Nicholas Oresme. The first-named, however, tried to give a clear account of what is meant by gravity. He made a distinction between the centre of gravity in a body and the centre of its volume. These are not

[1] 12, 9.

necessarily the same. In the case of the earth they are different, as the earth's density is not uniform; and when we talk about the 'centre of the earth' in connection with gravity it is the earth's centre of gravity which is meant. The tendency of a body to move towards its natural place may, then, be taken to mean its tendency to unite its own centre of gravity with the earth's centre of gravity or 'the centre of the earth'. A body's 'gravity' means this tendency. It is noteworthy that this 'explanation' is a physical account: it is not an account in terms of 'ultimate causes' but a positive account of what happens or is thought to happen.

3. The wider implications of the impetus theory will be briefly discussed later in this chapter. At the moment I wish to mention one or two other developments connected with problems of motion.

Nicholas Oresme, who was one of the most independent and outstanding of the mediaeval physicists, made several discoveries in the sphere of dynamics. He found, for example, that when a body moves with a uniformly increasing velocity the distance which it travels is equal to the distance travelled in the same time by a body which moves with a uniform velocity equal to that attained by the first body at the middle instant of its course. Furthermore, he tried to find a way of expressing successive variations of intensity which would make it easy to understand and compare them. The way he suggested was that of representing them by means of graphs, making use of rectangular co-ordinates. Space or time would be represented by a straight base line. On this line Nicholas erected vertical lines, the length of which corresponded to the position or the intensity of the variable. He then connected the ends of the vertical lines and so was able to obtain a curve which represented the fluctuations in intensity. This geometrical device obviously prepared the way for further mathematical developments. But to depict Nicholas as the founder of analytic geometry, in the sense of ascribing to him the developments of Descartes, would be an exaggeration. For the geometrical presentation suggested by Nicholas had to be superseded by the substitution of numerical equivalents. This does not mean, however, that his work was not of importance and that it did not represent an important stage in the development of applied mathematics. He does not appear, however, to have realized very clearly the difference between symbol and reality. Thus in his treatise *De uniformitate et difformitate intensionum* he implies that heat of varying intensity is actually composed of geometrical

THE SCIENTIFIC MOVEMENT

particles of pyramidal structure, a notion which recalls to mind the statement in Plato's *Timaeus* that the particles of fire possess pyramidal form, as pyramids have 'the sharpest cutting edges and the sharpest points in every direction'.[1] Indeed, in the treatise *Du ciel et du monde*,[2] he shows plainly enough his predilection for Plato.

One of the problems discussed by Nicholas was that of the earth's movement. The matter had apparently already been discussed at an earlier date, for Francis of Meyronnes, a Scotist who wrote early in the fourteenth century, asserts that 'a certain doctor' maintained that if it was the earth which moved rather than the heavens it would be a 'better arrangement' (*melior dispositio*). Albert of Saxony dismissed as insufficient the arguments offered in favour of the hypothesis that the earth rotates daily on its axis; but Nicholas Oresme, who discussed the hypothesis at some length, gave it a more favourable reception, even if in the end he preferred not to accept it.

In his treatise *Du ciel et du monde* Nicholas maintained first of all that direct observation cannot afford a proof that the heaven or firmament rotates daily while the earth remains at rest. For the appearances would be precisely the same if it were the earth and not the heaven which rotated. For this and other reasons 'I conclude that one could not show by any experience that the heaven was moved with a daily motion and the earth was not moved in this way.'[3] As to other arguments adduced against the possibility of the earth's daily rotation, replies can be made to them all. For example, from the fact that parts of the earth tend to their 'natural place' with a downward movement it does not follow that the earth as a whole cannot rotate: it cannot be shown that a body as a whole may not have one simple movement while its parts have other movements.[4] Again, even if the heaven does rotate, it does not necessarily follow that the earth is at rest. When a mill-wheel rotates, the centre does not remain at rest, except for a mathematical point which is not a body at all.[5] As to arguments drawn from the Scriptures, one must remember that the Scriptures speak according to a common mode of speech and that they are not necessarily to be regarded as making a scientific statement in some particular case. From the statement in the Bible that the sun was stopped in its course[6] one is no more entitled to draw the

---

[1] *Timaeus*, 56a.   [2] 62d., p. 280
[3] 140a, p. 273. References are to the edition by A. D. Menut and A. J. Denomy.
[4] 140d–141a, p. 275.   [5] 141b, p. 276.   [6] *Josue*, 10, 13

scientific conclusion that the heaven moves and that the earth does not than one is entitled to draw from phrases like 'God repented' the conclusion that God can actually change His mind like a human being.[1] In view of the fact that it is sometimes said or implied that this interpretation of the relevant Scriptural assertions was invented by theologians only when the Copernican hypothesis had been verified and could no longer be rejected, it is interesting to note the clear statement of it by Nicholas Oresme in the fourteenth century.

Furthermore, one can give positive reasons in support of the hypothesis that the earth rotates. For example, it is reasonable to suppose that a body which receives influence from another body should itself move to receive this influence, like a joint being roasted at the fire. Now, the earth receives heat from the sun. It is reasonable, then, to suppose that the earth moves in order to receive this influence.[2] Again, if one postulates the rotation of the earth one can 'save the appearances' much better than on the opposite hypothesis, since if one denies the earth's movement one has to postulate a great number of other movements in order to explain the empirical data.[3] Nicholas draws attention to the fact that Heraclitus Ponticus (Heraclides of Pontus) had put forward the hypothesis of the earth's movement; so it was not a new idea. Nevertheless, he himself ends by rejecting this hypothesis, 'notwithstanding the reasons to the contrary, for they are conclusions which are not evidently conclusive'.[4] In other words, he is not prepared to abandon the common opinion of the time for a hypothesis which has not been conclusively proved.

Nicholas had a critical mind and he was certainly no blind adherent of Aristotle. He saw that the problem was one of 'saving the appearances'; and he asked which hypothesis would account for the empirical data in the most economical manner. It appears to me to be fairly clear that, in spite of his eventual acceptance of the commonly held opinion, he considered the hypothesis of the earth's daily rotation on its axis to meet all requirements better than the opposite hypothesis. The same could not be said about Albert of Saxony, however, who rejected the theory of the earth's rotation on the ground that it did not save the appearances. Like Francis of Meyronnes, he seems to have thought that the theory claimed that all the movements of

---

[1] 141d–142a, pp. 276–7. [2] 142b, p. 277.
[3] 143c–d, p. 278. [4] 144b, p. 279.

the heavenly bodies could be eliminated if the earth were regarded as rotating; and he pointed out that the movements of the planets could not be eliminated in this way. Buridan also rejected the theory of the earth's rotation, though he discussed it quite sympathetically. It was Nicholas Oresme who saw clearly that the theory would only eliminate the diurnal rotation of the 'fixed' stars and would still leave the planets in motion. Some of the reasons he proposed in favour of the theory were good reasons, but others were not; and it would be an extravagance to depict Nicholas as having given a clearer and profounder exposition of the hypothesis of the earth's movement than the astronomers of the Renaissance, as Pierre Duhem was inclined to do. It is obvious, however, that men like Albert of Saxony and Nicholas Oresme can properly be called the precursors of the Renaissance physicists, astronomers and mathematicians. In so calling them Duhem was quite justified.

4. One of the questions discussed in the *Du ciel et du monde* is whether there could be other worlds besides this one. According to Nicholas, neither Aristotle nor anyone else has shown that God could not create a plurality of worlds. It is useless to argue from the unicity of God to the unicity of the world: God is not only one and unique but also infinite, and if there were a plurality of worlds none of them would be, as it were, outside the divine presence and power.[1] Again, to say that if there were another world, the element of earth in the other world would be attracted to this earth as to its natural place is no valid objection: the natural place of the element of earth in the other world would be in the other world and not in this.[2] Nicholas concludes, however, that although no sufficient proofs have been adduced by Aristotle or anyone else to show that there could not be other worlds in addition to this one, there never has been, is not and never will be any other corporeal world.[3]

5. The existence of a certain interest in scientific study during the thirteenth century has been mentioned earlier in this chapter; and the conclusion was then drawn that the scientific work of the succeeding century cannot be ascribed simply to the association of some of the fourteenth-century physicists with the Ockhamist movement. It is true, of course, that certain philosophical positions maintained by Ockham himself or by other followers of the *via moderna* were calculated to influence the conceptions of

---

[1] 38b–c, p. 243.   [2] 38a–b, p. 243.   [3] 39b–c, p. 244.

scientific method and of the status of physical theories. The combination of a 'nominalist' or conceptualist view of universals with the thesis that one cannot argue with certainty from the existence of one thing to the existence of another thing would naturally lead to the conclusion that physical theories are empirical hypotheses which can be more or less probable but which cannot be proved with certainty. Again, the emphasis laid by some philosophers on experience and observation as the necessary basis of our knowledge of the world might well encourage the view that the probability of an empirical hypothesis depends on the extent of its verification, that is, on its ability to explain or account for the empirical data. One might perhaps be tempted to suggest that the philosophy of the nominalist movement could have led to the conclusion that physical theories are empirical hypotheses which involve a certain amount of 'dictation' to nature and *a priori* construction, but which depend for their probability and utility on the extent to which they can be verified. A theory is constructed on the basis of empirical data, it might have been said, but it is a mental construction on the basis of those data. Its object, however, is to explain the phenomena, and it is verified in so far as it is possible to deduce from it the phenomena which are actually observed in ordinary life or which are obtained by artificial and purposive experiment. Moreover, that explanatory theory will be preferable which succeeds in explaining the phenomena with the least number of assumptions and presuppositions and which thus best satisfies the principle of economy.

But it is one thing to say that conclusions of this sort might have been suggested by the new movement in philosophy during the fourteenth century, and it is another thing to say that they were actually drawn. On the one hand, philosophers like Ockham do not seem to have shown any particular interest in questions of scientific theory and method as such, while on the other hand the physicists appear to have been more interested in their actual scientific research and speculations than in reflection on the underlying theory and method. This is, after all, only what one would expect. Reflection on scientific method and theory can hardly reach a high degree of development until physical science has itself progressed to a considerable extent and has reached a stage which prompts and stimulates reflection on the method employed and its theoretical presuppositions. We certainly do find in the thought of the fourteenth-century physicists some elements of the scientific theory which might have been suggested by contemporary philosophical developments. For example, Nicholas Oresme clearly regarded the function of any hypothesis about the world's rotation as being that of 'saving the appearances' or accounting for the observable data, and he clearly regarded as preferable the hypothesis which best satisfied the principle of economy. But the fourteenth-century physicists did not make in any very clear manner that kind of distinction between philosophy and physical science which the philosophy of the Ockhamist movement would appear to facilitate. As we have seen, the affiliations of the several physicists with the nominalist movement in philosophy were not by any means always as close as has sometimes been imagined. Moreover, the use of the principle of economy, as found in the physical speculations of Nicholas Oresme, for example, was already known in the thirteenth century. Robert Grosseteste, for instance, realized quite well that the more economical hypothesis is to be preferred to the less economical. He also realized that there is something peculiar about a mathematical explanation in astronomical physics, in that it does not provide knowledge of causes in a metaphysical sense. One has, then, to be careful in ascribing to the exclusive influence of the Ockhamist movement ideas in fourteenth-century science which, in the abstract, might perhaps have been the result of that movement. The idea of a scientific theory involving *a priori* mental construction could hardly arise except in a post-Kantian intellectual climate; and even the idea of physical theories as being concerned with 'saving the appearances' does not seem to have received special attention from or to have been specially developed by fourteenth-century nominalists.

It is true, however, that one can see a new view of the world coming to birth in the fourteenth century and that this was facilitated by the adoption of the theory of impetus in the explanation of movement. As we have seen, according to this theory celestial dynamics were explained on the same principle as terrestrial dynamics. Just as a stone continues to move after it has left the hand of the thrower, because a certain impetus has been imparted to it, so the celestial bodies move in virtue of an impetus originally imparted to them by God. On this view the first mover, God, appears as efficient rather than as final cause. By saying this I do not mean to imply that men like Nicholas Oresme and Albert of Saxony denied that God is final as well as efficient cause: I mean rather that the impetus theory which they adopted facilitated a shift of emphasis from the Aristotelian idea of God causing the movements of the heavenly bodies by 'drawing' them as final cause to the idea of God as imparting at creation a certain impetus in virtue of which these bodies, encountering no resistance, continued to move. This view might easily suggest that the world is a mechanical or quasi-mechanical system. God set the machine going, as it were, when He created it, after which it continues working on its own without further divine 'interference' save the activity of conservation and concurrence. If this idea were developed, God's function would appear to be that of a hypothesis for explaining the source of movement in the universe. And it would be natural to suggest that consideration of final causes should be excluded from physical science in favour of consideration of efficient causes, as Descartes, for example, insisted.

It must be repeated that I am not attempting to father all the ideas mentioned above on the physicists of the fourteenth century. They were concerned with the problem of motion as a particular problem rather than with drawing broad conclusions from it. And they were certainly not deists. None the less, one can see in the adoption of the impetus theory a step on the road towards a new conception of the material world. Or it might be better to say that it was a step on the road towards the development of physical science as distinct from metaphysics. It facilitated the growth of the idea that the material world can be considered as a system of bodies in motion in which impetus or energy is transmitted from body to body while the sum of energy remains constant. But it is one thing to state that the world, as considered by the physicist, can be regarded in this light, and it is another thing to say that the physicist, in his capacity as physicist, can give an adequate account of the world as a whole. When Descartes later insisted on the exclusion of consideration of final causes by what we would call the physical scientist and the astronomer, he did not say (nor did he think) that consideration of final causes has no place in philosophy. And the physicist-philosophers of the fourteenth century certainly did not say anything of the kind. It is conceivable that reflection on their scientific theories could have prompted them to make a clearer distinction between the world of the physicist and the world of the philosopher than they actually did; but in point of fact the idea that there is a rigid distinction between science and philosophy was an idea of much later growth. Before this idea could develop, science itself had to attain a very much richer and fuller development. In the thirteenth and fourteenth centuries we see the beginnings of empirical science in Christian Europe but only the beginnings. Still, it is as well to realize that the foundations of modern science were laid in mediaeval times. And it is as well also to realize that the development of empirical science is in no way alien in principle to the Christian theology which formed the mental background in the Middle Ages. For if the world is the work of God it is obviously a legitimate and worth-while object of study.

CHAPTER XI

MARSILIUS OF PADUA

Church and State, theory and practice—Life of Marsilius—Hostility to the papal claims—The nature of the State and of law—The legislature and the executive—Ecclesiastical jurisdiction—Marsilius and 'Averroism'—Influence of the Defensor pacis.

1. THE standard political idea of the Middle Ages was the idea of the two swords, of Church and Empire as two intrinsically independent Powers. In other words, the normal mediaeval theory, as presented by St. Thomas, was that Church and State were distinct societies, the former being concerned with man's supernatural well-being and his attainment of his last end, the latter with man's temporal well-being. As man has but one final end, a supernatural end, the Church must be considered superior to the State in point of value and dignity; but that does not mean that the Church is a glorified State enjoying direct jurisdiction in the temporal affairs of particular States, for, on the one hand, the Church is not a State and, on the other hand, each of them, the Church and the State, is a 'perfect' society.[1] All authority of man over man comes ultimately from God; but God wills the existence of the State as well as that of the Church. States existed before the Church, and the institution of the Church by Christ did not abrogate the State or subordinate the State, in the conduct of its own affairs, to the Church.

This view of Church and State is part and parcel of the harmonious philosophical structure achieved in the thirteenth century and associated especially with the name of St. Thomas Aquinas. But it is obvious enough that in practice a harmony of two Powers is inherently unstable, and in point of fact the disputes between papacy and empire, Church and State, loom large on the stage of mediaeval history. The Byzantine emperors had not infrequently attempted to interfere in purely doctrinal questions and to settle these questions by their own decisions; the western emperors did not attempt to usurp the teaching function of the Church, but they

[1] A 'perfect' society is a self-sufficing society, possessing in itself all the means required for attaining its end.

frequently quarrelled with the papacy over questions of jurisdiction, investiture and so forth, and we find first one side, then the other, gaining ground or giving ground, according to circumstances and according to the personal strength and vigour of the leaders on either side and their personal interest in advancing and maintaining practical claims. But we are not concerned here with the inevitable frictions and practical disputes between popes and emperors or kings: we are concerned only with the wider issues of which these practical disputes were, in part, the symptoms. (I say 'in part' because in the concrete historical life of the Middle Ages disputes between Church and State were in practice inevitable, even when no fundamentally conflicting theories about the relations of the two Powers were involved.) Whether one calls these wider issues 'theoretical' or 'practical' depends largely on one's point of view; it depends, I mean, on whether or not one regards political theory as simply an ideological reflection of concrete historical developments. I do not think, however, that any simple answer to the question is feasible. It is an exaggeration to say that theory is always simply the pale reflection of practice, exercising no influence on practice; and it is an exaggeration to say that political theory is never the reflection of actual practice. Political theory both reflects and influences practice, and whether one should emphasize the active or the passive element can be decided only by unprejudiced examination of the case under discussion. One cannot legitimately affirm *a priori* that a political theory like that of Marsilius of Padua, a theory which emphasized the independence and sovereignty of the State and which formed the antithesis to Giles of Rome's theoretical justification of the attitude of Pope Boniface VIII, was no more than the pale reflection of economic and political changes in the concrete life of the later Middle Ages. Nor is one entitled to affirm *a priori* that theories like that of Marsilius of Padua were the chief factor responsible for the practical disturbance of the harmonious balance between the Powers in so far as there ever was a harmonious balance in the sphere of practice—and for the emergence of sharply defined national entities with claims which amounted to that of complete autonomy. If one states either of these positions *a priori*, one is stating a theory which itself needs justification, and the only justification which could possibly be given would have to take the form of an examination of the actual historical data. In my opinion there are elements of truth in both theories; but it is not possible in a history of philosophy adequately to discuss the problem how far a given political theory was an ideological epiphenomenon of concrete historical changes or how far it played a part in actively influencing the course of history. In what follows, then, I wish to outline the ideas of Marsilius of Padua without committing myself to any decided opinion concerning the actual influence of these ideas or their lack of it. To form a decided opinion in virtue of a preconceived general theory is not, I think, a proper proceeding; and to discuss an actual example in sufficient detail is not possible in a general work. If, then, I expound Marsilius' ideas in a rather 'abstract way', this should not be taken to mean that I discount the influence of actual historical conditions in the formation of these ideas. Nor should incidental remarks concerning the influence of historical conditions on Marsilius' thought be taken to mean that I subscribe to the Marxist thesis concerning the nature of political theory. I do not believe in general *a priori* principles of interpretation to which the facts of history have to be fitted; and this holds for the anti-Marxist as well as for the Marxist theories.

2. It is uncertain in what year Marsilius of Padua was born. It would seem that he gave himself to the study of medicine; but in any case he went to Paris, where he was rector of the university from September 1312 until May 1313. The subsequent course of events is by no means clear. It appears that he returned to Italy and studied 'natural philosophy' with Peter of Abano from 1313 to the end of 1315. He may then have visited Avignon, and it appears from bulls of 1316 and 1318 that he was offered benefices at Padua. At Paris he worked on the *Defensor pacis*, with the collaboration of his friend John of Jandun, the book being finished on June 24th, 1324. His enmity towards the papacy and the 'clericals' must have begun at a considerably earlier date, of course; but in any case the book was denounced, and in 1326 Marsilius of Padua and John of Jandun fled from Paris and took refuge at Nuremberg with Ludwig of Bavaria, whom Marsilius accompanied to Italy, entering Rome in his entourage in January 1327. In a papal bull of April 3rd, 1327, Marsilius and John were denounced as 'sons of perdition and fruits of malediction'. The presence of Marsilius at his court was an obstacle to the success of Ludwig's attempts at reconciliation, first with John XXII, then with Benedict XII; but Ludwig had a high opinion of the author of the *Defensor pacis*. The Franciscan group did not share this opinion, and

Ockham criticized the work in his *Dialogus*, a criticism which led to the composition of the *Defensor minor*. Marsilius also published his *De iurisdictione imperatoris in causis matrimonialibus*, which was designed to serve the emperor in a practical difficulty concerning the projected marriage of his son. Marsilius maintained that the emperor could, on his own authority, dissolve an existing marriage and also dispense from the impediment of consanguinity. These two works were composed about 1341–2. A discourse of Clement VI, dated April 10th, 1343, asserts that the 'heresiarchs', Marsilius of Padua and John of Jandun, were both dead; but the exact date of Marsilius' death is unknown. (John of Jandun died considerably earlier than Marsilius.)

3. In his book on Marsilius of Padua[1] Georges de Lagarde finds the key to his mentality, not in a passion for religious reformation nor in a passion for democracy, but in an enthusiastic love for the idea of the lay State or, negatively, in a hatred of ecclesiastical interference in State affairs, that is to say, in a hatred of the doctrines of papal supremacy and of independent ecclesiastical jurisdiction. This is, I think, quite true. Possessed by an ardent enthusiasm for the autonomous State, the idea of which he supported by frequent references to Aristotle, Marsilius set out to show that the papal claims and the ecclesiastical jurisdiction laid down in the Canon Law involve a perversion of the true idea of the State and that they have no foundation in the Scriptures. His examination of the natures of Church and State and of their mutual relations leads him to a theoretical reversal of hierarchy of Powers: the State is completely autonomous and supreme.

But Marsilius was not simply pursuing an abstract theory. It appears that at one time he permitted himself to be lured from the quiet paths of science by the invitations of the Duke of Verona, Can Grande della Scala, and by Matteo Visconti of Milan. In any case his sympathies lay with the Ghibelline party, and he considered that the papal policy and claims were responsible for the wars and miseries of northern Italy. He lays at the door of the popes, who have disturbed the peace with their excommunications and interdicts, the responsibility for the wars, the violent deaths of thousands of the faithful, the hatred and contention, the moral corruption and crimes, the devastated cities and uncared for countryside, the churches abandoned by their pastors, and the

---
[1] *Naissance de l'esprit laïque;* Cahier II, *Marsile de Padoue.*

whole catalogue of evils which afflict the Italian City-States.[1] He may, no doubt, have exaggerated the situation: but the point I wish to make is that Marsilius was not simply theorizing in the abstract; his starting-point was a concrete historical situation, and his interpretation of this concrete situation reflected itself in his political theory. Similarly, in his account of the State as it ought to be we see an idealized reflection of the contemporary north-Italian republic, just as the Platonic and Aristotelian political theories were, to a greater or less extent, the idealization of the Greek City-State. The ideal of the empire, which is so prominent in Dante's political thought, is without any real effect on Marsilius' thought.

When, therefore, in the first *Dictio* of the *Defensor pacis* Marsilius discusses the nature of the State and draws on the teaching of Aristotle, it must be remembered that his thought is not moving in the purely abstract sphere but that it reflects his interpretation of and his enthusiasm for the Italian City-State. It may even be that the more abstract passages and the more Aristotelian parts are due to the influence of his collaborator, John of Jandun. Again, when in the second *Dictio* he discusses the Scriptural foundation, or lack of foundation, of the papal claims and of the independent ecclesiastical jurisdiction demanded by the Canon Law, it must be remembered that there is no real evidence that he had ever studied Civil Law and that his knowledge of Canon Law and of papal pronouncements did not, in spite of what some writers have maintained, amount to much more than knowledge of a Collection of Canons of the pseudo-Isidore and the bulls of Boniface VIII, Clement V and John XXII. He may have been acquainted with the Decree of Gratian; but the passages which are adduced as evidence of a knowledge of Gratian are too vague to serve as a proof of anything which could truly be called 'knowledge'. When Marsilius fulminated against the papal claims, he had primarily in mind the papal supremacy as conceived by Boniface VIII and those who shared his outlook. This is not to say, of course, that Marsilius did not deliver a general attack on the Church and its claims; but it is as well to remember that this attack had its roots in enmity towards the specific claims of specific ecclesiastics. When one reads in the third and concluding *Dictio* the summary of Marsilius' position, one should bear in mind both the historical situation which gave rise to and was reflected in

[1] *Def. pacis*, 2, 26, 19.

necessary with a view to preventing malice on the part of judges and arbiters.[1] Marsilius gives, indeed, several definitions of law. For example, law is the knowledge or doctrine or universal judgment concerning the things which are just and useful to the State's life.[2] But knowledge of these matters does not really constitute law unless a coercive precept is added touching their observance. In order that there should be a 'perfect law' there must be knowledge of what is just and useful and of what is unjust and harmful; but the mere expression of such knowledge is not law in the proper sense unless it is expressed as a precept backed up by sanctions.[3] Law is, therefore, a preceptive and coercive rule, fortified by sanctions applicable in this life.[4]

It would seem to follow from this that law concerns the objectively just and useful, that is to say, what is just and useful in itself, with a logical priority to any positive enactment and that Marsilius implicitly accepts the idea of natural law. So he does to a certain extent. In the second *Dictio*[5] he distinguishes two meanings of natural law. First, it may mean those statutes of the legislator on the rightness and obligatory character of which practically all people agree; for example that parents are to be honoured. These statutes depend on human institution; but they are called natural laws inasmuch as they are enacted by all nations. Secondly, 'there are certain people who call "natural law" the dictate of right reason in regard to human acts, and natural law in this sense they subsume under divine law'. These two senses of natural law, says Marsilius, are not the same; the phrase is used equivocally. In the first case natural law denotes the laws which are enacted in all nations and are practically taken for granted, their rightness being recognized by all: in the second case it denotes the dictates of right reason, which include dictates not universally recognized. From this it follows that 'certain things are licit according to human law which are not licit according to divine law, and conversely'.[6] Marsilius adds that licit and illicit are to be interpreted according to divine rather than human law when the two conflict. In other words, he does not simply deny the existence of natural law in the sense in which St. Thomas would understand it; but he pays little attention to the concept. His philosophy of law represents a transition stage on the way to the rejection of natural law in St. Thomas's sense.

That there is a shift of emphasis and a change in attitude is

[1] I, 11. [2] I, 10, 3. [3] I, 10, 5. [4] 2, 8, 5. [5] 12, 7–8. [6] 2, 12, 9.

clear from the fact, already indicated, that Marsilius was unwilling to apply the word 'law' in a strict sense to any precept which is not fortified by sanctions applicable in this life. It is for this reason that he refused to allow that the law of Christ (*Evangelica Lex*) is law properly speaking: it is rather a speculative or operative doctrine, or both.[1] He speaks in the same strain in the *Defensor minor*.[2] Divine law is compared with the prescriptions of a doctor, it is not law in the proper sense. As natural law in the sense of the Thomist philosophy is expressly said by Marsilius to be reckoned under divine law, it, too, cannot be said to be law in the same sense that the law of the State is law. Thus, although Marsilius does not deny outright the Thomist conception of natural law, he implies that the standard type of law is the law of the State, and his doctrine points towards the conclusion that the law of the State is autonomous and supreme. As Marsilius subordinated Church to State, it would seem that he tended towards the idea that it is the State alone which can judge whether or not a given law is consonant with the divine law and is an application of it; but, on the other hand, as he reserved the name of law in the proper sense to the positive law of the State and refused it to divine law and to natural law in the Thomist sense, one might equally well say that his thought tended towards the separation of law and morality.

5. Law in the proper sense being human law, the law of the State, who precisely is the legislator? The legislator or first efficient cause of law is the people, the totality of citizens, or the more weighty part (*pars valentior*) of the citizens.[3] The more weighty part is estimated according to quantity and quality of persons: it does not necessarily mean a numerical majority, but it must, of course, be legitimately representative of the whole people. It can be understood either in accordance with the actually obtaining customs of States or it may be determined according to the opinions expressed by Aristotle in the sixth book of the *Politics*.[4] However, since there are practical difficulties in the way of the multitude's drawing up the laws, it is suitable and useful that the drawing up of laws should be entrusted to a committee or commission, which will then propose the laws for acceptance or rejection by the legislator.[5] These ideas of Marsilius reflect in large part the theory, if not always the practice, of the Italian republics.

The next point for consideration is the nature, origin and scope

[1] 2, 9, 3.   [2] 1, 4.   [3] 1, 12, 3.   [4] 1, 12, 4.   [5] 1, 13, 8.

of executive power in the State, the *pars principans*. The office of the prince is to direct the community according to the norms set by the legislator; his task is to apply and enforce the laws. This subordination of the prince to the legislator is best expressed when the executive power is conferred on each successive prince by election. Election is, in itself at least, preferable to hereditary succession.[1] In each State there should be a supreme executive power, though it does not necessarily follow that this power should be in the hands of one man.[2] Supremacy means that all other powers, executive or judicial, must be subordinate to the prince; but the supremacy is qualified by the assertion that if the prince transgresses the laws or fails seriously in the duties of his office he should be corrected, or if necessary removed from office, by the legislator or by those appointed by the legislature for this task.[3]

Marsilius' dislike of tyranny and his preference for the election of the executive reflect his concern with the well-being of the Italian City-State, while the concentration of supreme executive and judicial power in the hands of the prince reflects the general consolidation of power in the European States. It has been maintained that Marsilius envisaged a clear separation of powers; but though he separated the executive from the legislative power, he subordinated the judiciary to the executive. Again, it is true that he admitted in a sense the sovereignty of the people; but the later theory of the social contract has no clear explicit foundation in Marsilius' political theory. The subordination of the executive power to the legislature is supported by practical considerations touching the good of the State rather than by a philosophic theory of the social contract.

6. In discussing the nature of the State Marsilius has in view, of course, his coming attack on the Church. For example, the concentration of executive and judicial power, without exception, in the hands of the prince is designed to deprive the Church of all 'natural' foundations to its claims. It remains to be seen if the Church can support her claims from the data of revelation; and this subject is considered in the second part of the *Defensor pacis*. The transition from the first to the second part[4] consists of the statements that the State can function and that its parts can discharge their proper tasks only if the State is in a condition of peace and tranquillity; that it cannot be in this condition if the prince is interfered with or suffers aggression; and that the Church

[1] I, 15, 3; cf. I, 16. [2] I, 17, 2, [3] I, 18. [4] I, 19.

has in fact disturbed the peace by its interference with the rights of the Holy Roman Emperor and of other persons.

After considering various definitions or meanings of the words 'Church', 'temporal', 'spiritual', 'judge' and 'judgment' Marsilius proceeds to argue[1] that Christ claimed no temporal jurisdiction when He was in this world but subjected Himself to the civil power, and that the Apostles followed Him in this. The priesthood, then, has no temporal power. Marsilius goes on in the following chapters to minimize the 'power of the keys' and sacerdotal jurisdiction. As to heresy, the temporal legislator may make it a crime with a view to securing the temporal well-being of the State; but to legislate on this point and to exercise coercion belongs to the State, not to the Church.[2]

After an excursus on absolute poverty, from which he draws the conclusion that Church endowments remain the property of the donor, so that the Church has only the use of them,[3] Marsilius proceeds to attack the divine institution of the papacy. It would be out of place to enter upon a discussion of Marsilius' attempt to disprove the papal claims by reference to the Scriptures; nor does space permit any detailed consideration of his conciliar theory, but it is important to note, first that Marsilius assumes that the Scriptures alone are the rule of faith, and secondly that decisions of General Councils are not regarded by him as having any coercive force unless ratified by the temporal legislator. Canon Law is dismissed as having no weight. A historical treatment of papal encroachments leads up to a consideration of the dispute between John XXII and Ludwig of Bavaria.[4] Mention is made of the state of affairs in Italy and of the excommunication of Matteo Visconti.

In the third part Marsilius gives a brief summary of the conclusions he has reached in the *Defensor pacis*. He makes it quite clear that he is primarily concerned, not with the furtherance of democracy nor with any particular form of government, but rather with the rejection of papal supremacy and ecclesiastical jurisdiction. Moreover, the whole course of the work shows that Marsilius was not content simply with rejecting ecclesiastical interference in temporal matters; he went on to subordinate the Church to the State in all matters. His position was not that of one protesting against the encroachments of the Church on the sphere of the State while admitting the Church as a 'perfect society', autonomous in spiritual affairs: on the contrary, his position was

---

[1] 2, 4.   [2] 2, 10.   [3] 2, 14.   [4] 2, 26.

frankly 'Erastian' and, at the same time, of a revolutionary character. Previté-Orton is obviously quite correct when he says that, in spite of disproportions in the work, there is unity of purpose and idea in the *Defensor pacis*. 'Everything is subordinated to the main aim, that of the destruction of papal and ecclesiastical power.' In the first part of the work, that which deals with the nature of the State, those themes are discussed and those conclusions are drawn which will serve as foundation for the second part. On the other hand, Marsilius was not animated by a hatred against papal supremacy and ecclesiastical jurisdiction for hatred's sake: as we have seen, his actual starting-point was what he regarded as the deplorable condition of northern Italy. He speaks on occasion about the empire, of course, and he apparently envisages the emperor as ratifying decisions of General Councils; but he was interested above all in the City-State or republic, which he considered to be supreme and autonomous in matters spiritual and temporal. There is, indeed, some excuse for regarding him as a forerunner of Protestantism; his attitude towards the Scriptures and towards the papacy shows as much; but it would be a great mistake to regard his attack on the papacy and on ecclesiastical jurisdiction as having proceeded from religious convictions or zeal. One can, of course, admit that in the course of his writing Marsilius became a 'religious controversialist'; but his religious controversy was undertaken, not for the sake of religion, but in the interests of the State. What characterizes him is his conception of the completely autonomous State. He admitted divine law, it is true; but he also admitted that human law may conflict with divine law, and in this case all subjects of the State, clerics and laymen, must obey human law, though one passage, mentioned earlier, seems to imply that if a law of the State obviously contradicts the law of Christ, the Christian should follow the latter. But since the Church, according to Marsilius, has no fully independent authority to interpret the Scriptures, it would scarcely be possible for the Christian to appeal to the teaching of the Church. In spite of its roots in contemporary history Marsilius' political theory looks forward to conceptions of the nature and function of the State which are modern in character, and which have scarcely brought happiness to mankind.

7. It has been maintained that Marsilius' political theory is 'Averroistic' in character. Speaking of the *Defensor pacis* Étienne Gilson remarks that it is 'as perfect an example of political

Averroism as one could wish'.[1] This Averroism consists in the application to politics of the Averroistic dichotomy between the sphere of faith and the sphere of reason. Man has two ends, a natural end, which is served by the State, utilizing the teaching of philosophy, and a supernatural end, served by the Church, utilizing the data of revelation. As the two ends are distinct, the State is completely independent, and the Church has no title to interfere in political affairs. However, although Gilson stresses the Averroism of John of Jandun, he admits that the *Defensor pacis* is due principally to Marsilius of Padua and that what one actually knows of the Averroism of Marsilius 'does not go beyond an application of the theoretic separation of reason and faith to the domain of politics, where he transmutes it into a strict separation of the spiritual and the temporal, of the Church and the State'.[2]

Maurice De Wulf, on the other hand, held that any collaboration of John of Jandun in the *Defensor pacis* has to be excluded, on the ground of the work's unity of plan and homogeneity of style, and was of the opinion that, although Marsilius had been in contact with Averroistic circles, he was influenced much more by the political writings of Aristotle.[3] The Church is not a true society, at least it is not a 'perfect society' since it has no temporal sanctions at its disposal wherewith to enforce its laws. The Church is little more than an association of Christians who find their true unity in the State; and, though the priesthood is of divine institution, the Church's task, as far as this world is concerned, is to serve the State by creating the moral and spiritual conditions which will facilitate the work of the State.

De Wulf's view of the matter, apart from his rejection of any collaboration on the part of John of Jandun, seems to me to be more in accordance with the tone and spirit of the *Defensor pacis* than the idea that the work is of specifically Averroistic inspiration. Marsilius thought that the Church's claims and activity hindered and disturbed the peace of the State, and he found in the Aristotelian conception of the autonomous and self-sufficing State the key to the solution of the problem, provided that the Church was subordinated to the State. It seems to me that Marsilius was animated much more by regard for what he considered to be the welfare of the State than by theoretical considerations concerning

[1] *La philosophie au moyen âge* (1944), p. 592.
[2] *Ibid.*, p. 691.
[3] *Histoire de la philosophie médiévale*, tome III (1947), p. 142.

the end of man. Nevertheless, this in no way excludes an Averroistic influence on Marsilius' thought and, after all, Averroism was, or professed to be, integral Aristotelianism. Averroes was regarded as the 'Commentator'. Marsilius was influenced by Peter of Abano and was in touch with John of Jandun; and both of these men were animated by the Averroistic veneration for Aristotle. There was really no homogeneous doctrine or set of doctrines which one can call 'Averroism'; and if it is true that 'Averroism' was less a doctrine than an attitude, one can perfectly well admit the 'Averroism' of Marsilius without being thereby compelled to conclude that his inspiration was derived from the Averroists rather than from Aristotle.

8. The *Defensor pacis* was solemnly condemned on April 27th, 1327; but it does not appear that the work was really studied by Marsilius' contemporaries, even by those who wrote against it, though Clement VI affirmed that he, when a cardinal, had submitted the work to a profound examination and had discovered therein 240 errors. Clement VI made this assertion in 1343, and we do not possess his publication. In 1378 Gregory XI renewed the condemnations of 1327; but the fact that the majority of the copies of manuscripts were made at the beginning of the fifteenth century seems to confirm the supposition that the *Defensor pacis* was not widely circulated in the fourteenth century. Those who wrote against the work in the fourteenth century tended to see in it little more than an attack on the independence of the Holy See and the immunity of the clergy: they did not realize its historical importance. In the following century the Great Schism naturally gave an impetus to the diffusion of Marsilius' theories; and these ideas exercised their long-term influence more as a 'spirit' than as precisely the ideas of Marsilius of Padua. It is significant that the first printed edition of the *Defensor pacis* was published in 1517 and that the work was apparently utilized by Cranmer and Hooker.

CHAPTER XII

SPECULATIVE MYSTICISM

Mystical writing in the fourteenth century—Eckhart—Tauler—Blessed Henry Suso—Ruysbroeck—Denis the Carthusian—German mystical speculation—Gerson.

1. ONE is accustomed perhaps to think of the sixteenth century, the century of the great Spanish mystics, as the period which was particularly distinguished for mystical writings. It may, indeed, well be that the works of St. Teresa and St. John of the Cross are the supreme achievements of mystical theology, the theoretical exposition, so far as this is possible, of the experimental knowledge of God; but we must remember that there had been writers on mysticism from early Christian times. We have only to think of St. Gregory of Nyssa and of the Pseudo-Dionysius in the Patristic age, of St. Bernard and of Hugh and Richard, of St. Victor in the twelfth century, and of St. Bonaventure and St. Gertrude in the thirteenth century. And in the fourteenth and fifteenth centuries there was a remarkable flowering of mystical writings. This fact is attested by the works of writers like Eckhart (1260–1327), Tauler (c. 1300–61), Bl. Henry Suso (c. 1295–1366), Ruysbroeck (1293–1381), St. Catherine of Siena (1347–80), Richard Rolle of Hampole (c. 1300–49), Walter Hilton (d. 1396), John Gerson (1363–1429), Denis the Carthusian (1402–71), St. Catherine of Bologna (1413–63) and St. Catherine of Genoa (1447–1510). It is with these mystical writings of the fourteenth and early part of the fifteenth centuries that I am concerned in this chapter; but I am concerned with them only in so far as they seem to be relevant to the history of philosophy; I am not concerned with mystical theology as such. This means that I shall confine my attention to philosophic speculation which appears to have been influenced by reflection on the mystical life; and this in turn means in effect that special consideration will be given to two themes, namely the relation of finite being in general and that of the human soul in particular to God. More concretely, it is writers like Eckhart rather than writers like Richard Rolle whose thought will be discussed. In a work on mystical theology as such, attention would have to be paid to writers who cannot be dealt

with here; but in a work on the history of philosophy, attention can be paid only to those who can reasonably be thought of as 'philosophers' according to some traditional or normal use of the term. I do not mean to imply, however, that the writers whom I propose to discuss in this chapter were primarily interested in theory. Even Eckhart, who was much more given to speculation than Henry Suso, for example, was deeply concerned with the practical intensification of religious life. This practical orientation of the mystical writers is shown partly by their use of the vernacular. Eckhart used both German and Latin, his more speculative work being in the latter language; Henry Suso also used both languages; Tauler preached in German; Ruysbroeck wrote in Flemish; and we possess a large collection of Gerson's French sermons, though he wrote mainly in Latin. A profound affective piety, issuing in a desire to draw others to closer union with God, is characteristic of these mystics. Their analyses of the mystical life are not so detailed and complete as those of the later Spanish mystical writers; but they form an important stage in the development of mystical theology.

One might reasonably be inclined to see in the flowering of mystical writing in the fourteenth century a reaction against logical and abstract metaphysical studies, against what some people call 'objective thinking', in favour of the one thing needful, salvation through union with God. And that there was such a reaction seems to be true enough. On the one hand there were the older philosophical traditions and schools; on the other hand there was the *via moderna*, the nominalist movement. The wranglings of the schools could not transform the heart; nor did they bring a man nearer to God. What more natural, then, than that the religious consciousness should turn to a 'philosophy' or pursuit of wisdom which was truly Christian and which looked to the work of divine grace rather than to the arid play of the natural intellect? The remarks of Thomas à Kempis on this matter are well known and have often been quoted. For example, 'I desire to feel compunction rather than to know its definition'; 'a humble rustic who serves God is certainly better than a proud philosopher who, neglecting himself, considers the movement of the heavens'; 'what is the use of much quibbling about hidden and obscure matters, when we shall not be reproved at the Judgment for being ignorant of them?'; 'and what do genera and species matter to us!'[1] Thomas

[1] *Imitation of Christ*, 1, 1; 1, 2; 1, 3.

à Kempis (1380–1471) belonged to the Brethren of the Common Life, an association founded by Gerard Groot (1340–84), who had been strongly influenced by the ideas of Ruysbroeck. The Brethren were of importance in the educational field, and they devoted special attention to the religious and moral upbringing of their charges.

But it was not only Scholastic aridities and academic wranglings about abstract questions which influenced, by way of reaction, the mystical writers; some of them seem to have been influenced by the Ockhamist tendency to deny the validity of the traditional natural theology and to relegate all knowledge of God, even of His existence, to the sphere of faith. The answer to this was found by the mystics, or by some of them, in an extension of the idea of experience. Thus, though Henry Suso did not deny the validity of a philosophical approach to God, he tried to show that there is a certitude based on interior experience, when this accords with the revealed truths of faith. And, indeed, had not Roger Bacon, who insisted so much on the experimental method in the acquisition of knowledge, included spiritual experience of God under the general heading of experience? The mystics in their turn saw no reason for confining 'experience' to sense-experience or to consciousness of one's internal acts.

From the philosophical point of view, however, the chief point of interest concerning the mystical writers is their speculative rationalization of religious experience, particularly their pronouncements concerning the relation of the soul to God and, in general, of creatures to God. As is not uncommon with mystical writers of earlier and also later times, some of them made statements which were certainly bold and which were likely to arouse the hostile attention of theologians who regarded the literal sense of such statements. The chief offender in this respect was Eckhart, a number of whose propositions were subsequently condemned, though Henry Suso, his disciple, defended his orthodoxy. There has also been controversy concerning statements made by Ruysbroeck and Gerson. In what follows I shall give particular, if brief, consideration to this speculative aspect of the mystics' writings. Though certain statements, especially in Eckhart's case, are unorthodox if understood in an absolutely literal sense, I do not consider that the writers in question had any intention of being unorthodox. Many of their suspect propositions can be paralleled in earlier writers and are to be seen in the light of the neo-Platonic tradition. In any case I consider that the attempt which has been made in certain quarters to find a new 'German theology' in Eckhart and his disciples is a vain attempt.

2. Meister Eckhart was born about 1260 at Hochheim near Gotha. Joining the Dominican Order he studied and then lectured at Paris. After having been Provincial of Saxony and later Vicar-General of the Order, he returned to Paris in 1311, where he lectured until 1314. From Paris he moved to Cologne; and it was the archbishop of that city who in 1326 instituted an inquiry into Eckhart's doctrine. Eckhart appealed to the Holy See; but in 1329, two years after his death, 28 propositions taken from his later Latin writings were condemned by Pope John XXII.

In the *Quaestiones Parisienses*[1] Eckhart raises the question whether in God being (*esse*) and understanding (*intelligere*) are the same. His answer is, of course, in the affirmative; but he proceeds to maintain[2] that it is not because God is that He understands, but that He is because He is intellect and understanding. Understanding or intellection is 'the foundation of His being' or existence. St. John did not say: 'In the beginning was being, and God was being'; he said: 'In the beginning was the Word, and the Word was with God, and the Word was God.' So, too, Christ said: 'I am the Truth.' Moreover, St. John also says that all things were made through the Word; and the author of the *Liber de causis* accordingly concludes that 'the first of created things is being'. It follows that God, who is creator, is 'intellect and understanding, but not being or existence' (*non ens vel esse*). Understanding is a higher perfection than being.[3] In God, then, there is neither being nor existence, formally speaking, since God is the cause of being. Of course, if one likes to call understanding 'being', it does not matter; but in this case it must be understood that being belongs to God because He is understanding.[4] 'Nothing which is in a creature is in God save as in its cause, and it is not there formally. And so, since being belongs to creatures, it is not in God save as in its cause; and thus there is not being in God but the purity of being.'[5] This 'purity of being' is understanding. God may have said to Moses, 'I am who am'; but God was then speaking like someone whom one meets in the dark and questions as to his identity, and who, not wishing to reveal himself, answers, 'I am who I am.'[6] Aristotle observed that the power of vision must

---

[1] Ed. A. Dondaine, O.P., 1936, p. 1.   [2] p. 3.
[3] p. 5.   [4] p. 7.   [5] *Ibid.*   [6] pp. 7–8.

itself be colourless, if it is to see every colour. So God, if He is the cause of all being, must Himself be above being.[1]

In making *intelligere* more fundamental than *esse* Eckhart certainly contradicted St. Thomas; but the general notion that God is not being, in the sense that God is super-being or above being, was a commonplace of the neo-Platonic tradition. The doctrine can be found in the writings of the Pseudo-Dionysius, for example. As we have seen, Eckhart cites the author (in a remote sense) of the *Liber de causis*, namely Proclus; and it is very likely that he was influenced by Theodoric (or Dietrich) of Freiberg (*c.* 1250–*c.* 1311), another German Dominican, who made copious use of Proclus, the neo-Platonist. The neo-Platonic side of the teaching of Albert the Great lived on in the thought of Dominicans like Theodoric of Freiberg, Berthold of Moosburg and Meister Eckhart, though it must be added that what for St. Albert was a relic, as it were, of the past, became for some later thinkers a principal and exaggerated element of their thought. In his (unpublished) commentary on Proclus' *Elementatio theologica* Berthold appealed expressly to Albert the Great.

It has been held that, after having maintained in his earlier works that God is *intelligere* and not *esse*, Eckhart changed his view and later maintained that God is *esse*. This was the opinion of Maurice De Wulf, for example. Others, however, like M. Gilson, will not admit a change of doctrine on Eckhart's part. That Eckhart declared that God is *esse*, existence, is certain. Thus, in the *Opus tripartitum*[2] his first proposition is, *Esse est Deus*. 'God and existence are the same.'[3] And he alludes to the words in the book of Exodus, 'I am who am.' 'God alone is properly speaking being (*ens*), one, true and good.'[4] 'To anyone who asks concerning God what or who He is, the reply is: Existence.'[5] That this sounds like a change of front can hardly be denied; but Gilson argues that Eckhart always emphasized the unity of God and that for him real unity is the property of intelligent being alone; so that the supreme unity of God belongs to Him because He is, above all things, intellect, *intelligere*. Eckhart was certainly understood as seeking a unity in God transcending the distinction of Persons; and one of the condemned propositions (24) runs as follows. 'Every distinction is alien to God, whether in Nature or in Persons. Proof: the Nature itself is one, this one thing, and any

---
[1] p. 9.   [2] *Prologus generalis;* ed. H. Bascour, O.S.B., 1935.
[3] p. 12.   [4] p. 21.   [5] p. 22.

of the Persons is one and the same thing as the Nature.' The statement and condemnation of this proposition means, of course, that Eckhart was understood by the theologians who examined his writings as teaching that the distinction of Persons in the Godhead is logically posterior to the unity of Nature in such a way that unity transcends trinity. Henry Suso defended Eckhart by observing that to say that each of the divine Persons is identical with the divine Nature is the orthodox doctrine. This is perfectly correct. The examining theologians, however, understood Eckhart to mean that the distinction of Persons from one another is a secondary 'stage', as it were, in the Godhead. But I am not concerned with the orthodoxy or unorthodoxy of Eckhart's trinitarian doctrine: I wish merely to draw attention to the emphasis he laid on the unity of the Godhead. And it is Gilson's contention that this perfect unity belongs to God, according to Eckhart's constant opinion, in virtue of God's being primarily *intelligere*. The pure divine essence is *intelligere*, which is the Father, and it is from the fecundity of this pure essence that there proceed the Son (*vivere*) and the Holy Spirit (*esse*).

The truth of the matter seems to be that there are various strands in Eckhart's thought. When he comments on the words, 'I am who am', in the *Expositio libri Exodi*, he observes that in God essence and existence are the same and that the identity of essence and existence belongs to God alone. In every creature essence and existence are distinct, and it is one thing to ask about the existence of a thing (*de annitate sive de esse rei*) and another to ask about its quiddity or nature. But in the case of God, in whom existence and essence are identical, the fit reply to anyone who asks who or what God is, is that God exists or is. 'For existence is God's essence.'[1] This doctrine is obviously the Thomist doctrine, learnt and accepted by the Dominican. But in the very passage mentioned Eckhart speaks of the 'emanation' of Persons in the Godhead and uses the very neo-Platonic expression *monas monadem gignit*. Moreover, the tendency to find in God a unity without distinction, transcending the distinction of Persons, a tendency to which I have referred above, is also of neo-Platonic inspiration, as is also the doctrine that God is above being. On the other hand, the notion that *intelligere* is the supreme divine perfection seems to be original: in the Plotinian scheme the One is

---

[1] Meister Eckhart, *Die lateinischen Werke: erster Band*, fasc. 2, pp. 98–100, Stuttgart-Berlin, 1938.

above intellect. Probably it is not possible to harmonize these different strands perfectly; but it is not necessary to suppose that when Eckhart stressed the identity of existence and essence in God he was consciously renouncing his 'former' view that God is *intelligere* rather than *esse*. In the *Expositio libri Genesis* he says: 'the nature of God is intellect, and for Him to be is to understand'; *natura Dei est intellectus, et sibi esse est intelligere*.[1]

However, whether he changed his opinion or not, Eckhart made some rather bold statements in connection with the characterization of God as existence, *esse*. For example, 'outside God there is nothing, inasmuch as it would be outside existence'.[2] God is creator but He does not create 'outside' Himself. A builder makes a house outside himself, but it is not to be imagined that God threw, as it were, or created creatures outside Himself in some infinite space or vacuum.[3] 'Therefore God created all things, not to stand outside Himself or near and beside Himself, like other craftsmen, but He called (them) from nothingness, that is, from non-existence, to existence, which they found and received and had in Him. For He Himself is existence.'[4] There is nothing outside the first cause; for to be outside the first cause would mean being outside existence; since the first cause is God, and God is being and existence. The doctrine that 'outside' God there is nothing is certainly susceptible of an orthodox interpretation: if, that is to say, it is taken as tantamount to the denial of the creature's independence of God. Moreover, when Eckhart declares that, though creatures have their specific natures from their forms, which make them this or that kind of being, their *esse* does not proceed from the form but from God, he might seem to be simply insisting on the facts of divine creation and divine conservation. But he goes further than this and declares that God is to the creature as act to potency, as form to matter, and as *esse* to *ens*, implying apparently that the creature exists by the existence of God. Similarly he says that nothing so lacks distinction as that which is constituted and that from which and through which and by which it is constituted and subsists; and he concludes that nothing so lacks distinction (*nihil tam indistinctum*) as the one God or Unity and the multiplicity of creatures (*creatum numeratum*).

---

[1] Meister Eckhart, *Die lateinischen Werke: erster Band*, fasc. 1, p. 52, Stuttgart-Berlin, 1937.
[2] *Opus tripartitum, Prologus generalis;* ed. H. Bascour, O.S.B., p. 18.
[3] *Ibid.*, p. 16. [4] *Ibid.*

Now, if these propositions are taken in isolation, it is no wonder that Eckhart should be regarded as teaching a form of pantheism. But there is no justification for taking these texts in isolation, if we wish, that is to say, to discover what Eckhart meant. He was accustomed to use antinomies, to state a thesis and give reasons for it, and then to state an antithesis and give reasons for it. Obviously both sets of statements must be taken into consideration if Eckhart's meaning and intention are to be understood. For example, in the case in point the thesis is that nothing is so distinct from the created as God is. One of the reasons given is that nothing is so distant from anything as is the opposite of that thing. Now, 'God and the creature are opposed as the One and Unnumbered is opposed to number, the numbered and the numerable. Therefore nothing is so distinct (as God) from any created being.' The antithesis is that nothing is so 'indistinct' from the creature as God is; and reasons are given for saying this. It is pretty clear that Eckhart's line of thought was as follows. It is necessary to say that God and creatures are utterly different and opposed; but if one *simply* says this, one is implying what is not true; at least one is stating what is not the whole truth; for the creature exists only by and through God, without whom it is nothing at all.

For an understanding of Eckhart's antinomies one can profitably consult Otto Karrer's *Meister Eckhart*,[1] where he cites texts and appends explanatory notes. Karrer may endeavour in an exaggerated manner to assimilate Eckhart's teaching to that of St. Thomas, but his remarks serve to correct an exaggerated view of Eckhart's departures from St. Thomas. For example, Eckhart states that God alone is and that creatures are nothing and also that God is not being; that all creatures are God and also that all creatures are nothing; that no things are so unlike as Creator and creature and that no things are so like as Creator and creature; that God is in all things and also that God is above all things; that God is in all things as their being and also that God is outside all things. That God alone is and that creatures are nothing means simply that in comparison with God creatures are as nothing. In the Augustinian *Soliloquies*[2] occurs the statement that 'only of the Immortal can one really say that He is', and St. Anselm asserts[3] that in a certain sense God alone is. The statement that all creatures are God refers primarily to their eternal presence in God,

---

[1] Munich, 1926. [2] I, 29. [3] *Proslog.*, 27, and *Monol.*, 31.

in the divine intellect, while the statement that they are nothing means that they are nothing apart from God. The doctrine that God and creatures are both like and unlike implies the theory of analogy and it has its roots in the Pseudo-Dionysian *Divine Names*.[1] St. Thomas affirmed[2] that the creature is like God but that God should not be said to be like the creature. God as immanent is in all things by 'power, presence and essence', but He is also above all things, or transcends all things, since He is their creator out of nothing and in no way depends on them. Thus, in his ninth German sermon[3] Eckhart says: 'God is in all creatures ... and yet He is above them.' In other words, there is no adequate reason for finding pantheism in his thought, even though a considerable number of statements, taken in isolation, would seem to imply that he was a pantheist. What draws one's attention in his thought is the bold way in which he juxtaposes his theses and antitheses rather than the isolated statements, which are frequently commonplaces of mediaeval philosophy and can be discovered in Augustine or the Pseudo-Dionysius or the Victorines or even St. Thomas. As Karrer observes, one can find apparent antinomies even in St. Thomas. For instance, in the *Summa theologica*[4] St. Thomas says that God is above all things (*supra omnia*) and yet in all things (*in omnibus rebus*); that God is in things and yet that all things are in God; that nothing is distant from God and yet that things are said to be distant from God. One condemned proposition of Eckhart begins, 'all creatures are one pure nothingness'; and to say that his intentions were not heterodox is not, of course, to question the legitimacy of the ecclesiastical action which was taken, since it is obvious enough that the propositions in question could easily be misinterpreted, and what was condemned was the proposition as it stood taken in its literal or natural sense but not necessarily as the author understood and meant it. The proposition in question was condemned as 'badly sounding, rash and suspected of heresy', and Rome could hardly judge of it in any other way when it was presented for theological comment and judgment. To realize this, one has only to read the following passage in the fourth German sermon.[5] 'All creatures are a pure nothing. I do not say that they are little or something; they are a pure nothing.' But he goes on to

---

[1] 9, 6.   [2] *Summa theologica*, 1, 4, 3, *ad* 4.
[3] Meister Eckhart, *Die deutschen Werke: erster Band, Meister Eckhart's Predigten*, fasc. 2, p. 143.
[4] 1, 8, 1, *ad* 1 ff.   [5] *Op. cit.*, fasc. 1, pp. 69–70.

explain what he means. 'All creatures have no being, as their being depends on the presence of God. If God turned away from creatures for one moment, they would be reduced to nothing.' The historian of philosophy, however, is concerned with the author's intended meaning, not with the theological 'note' to be attached to isolated propositions; and it is, I think, to be regretted that some historians have apparently allowed the boldness of some of Eckhart's propositions to blind them both to the general context and meaning and to the history of the propositions in question.

Eckhart also made some strange statements concerning the act of creation. In the *Expositio libri Genesis* he says, with reference to the statement that God created 'in the beginning', that this 'beginning' is the 'now' of eternity, the indivisible 'now' (*nunc*) in which God is eternally God and the eternal emanation of the divine Persons takes place.[1] He goes on to say that if anyone asks why God did not create the world before He did, the answer is that He could not do so; and He could not do so because He creates the world in the same 'now' in which He is eternally God. It is false to imagine that God awaited, as it were, a moment in which to create the world. To put the matter crudely, in the same 'now' in which God the Father exists and generates His coeternal Son He also creates the world. At first hearing at least this sounds as though Eckhart meant to teach that creation is from eternity, that it is coeternal and bound up with the generation of the Son. Indeed, the first three condemned propositions show clearly that the examining theologians understood him in this sense.

It may be, of course, that Eckhart meant the eternity of creation to refer to the object of the creative act, the actual world, and not only to the act of creation as it is in God. This is certainly the natural interpretation of many of the statements he makes. But in this case are we also to take with absolute literalness his statement that 'creation' and every work of God is simultaneously perfected and finished in the very beginning of creation?[2] If so, would not this imply that there is no time and that the Incarnation, for instance, took place at the beginning of creation? It seems to me that Eckhart was thinking of creation as the work of God who is not in time. God created in the beginning, he says, 'that is, in Himself', since God Himself is the *Principium*.[3] For God there is

[1] Meister Eckhart, *Die lateinischen Werke; erster Band*, fasc. 1, p. 50, Stuttgart-Berlin, 1937.
[2] *Opus tripartitum, Prologi*, p. 18; ed. H. Bascour, O.S.B.   [3] *Ibid.*, p. 14.

no past or future; for Him all things are present. So He may rightly be said to have completed His work at the moment of creation. God is the beginning and end of all things, 'the first and the last'; and since God is eternal, existing in one eternal 'now', He must be conceived as eternally creating all things in that eternal 'now'. I am not suggesting that Eckhart's statements, taken as they stand, were correct from the theological point of view; but he seems to me to have been looking at the creation of the world from what one might call God's point of view and to have been insisting that one should not imagine that God created the world 'after' a time in which there was no world. As to the connection of creation with the generation of the Son, Eckhart was thinking of the words of St. John:[1] 'All things were made by him (the Word): and without him was made nothing that was made.' Coupling these words with the statement contained in the first verse of the first chapter of Genesis, 'In the beginning God created heaven and earth', and understanding 'beginning' with reference to God, that is to say, as referring to God's eternal 'now', he says that God created the world simultaneously with the generation of the Son, by whom 'all things were made'. This would certainly seem to imply that there was no beginning of time and to amount to a denial of creation in time; but in the *Expositio libri Genesis*,[2] after referring to the Platonic Ideas or *rationes rerum* and saying that the Word is the *ratio idealis*, he goes on to quote Boethius and says that God created all things *in ratione et secundum rationem idealem*. Again, the 'beginning' in which God created heaven and the earth is the *intellectus* or *intelligentia*. It is possible, then, that Eckhart did not mean that the object of the creative act, the actual world, is eternal, but rather that God eternally conceived and willed creation in and through the Word. This, in any case, is what he later said he had meant. 'Creation, indeed, and every act of God is the very essence of God. Yet it does not follow from this that if God created the world from eternity, the world on this account exists from eternity, as the ignorant think. For creation in the passive sense is not eternal, just as the created itself is not eternal.'[3] Eckhart obviously utilized sayings like that of St. Albert the Great: 'God created from eternity, but the created is not from eternity,'[4] and of St. Augustine: 'In the eternal Word dost Thou

---

[1] 1, 3.   [2] *Die lateinischen Werke: erster Band*, fasc. 1, pp. 49-50.
[3] Cf. Daniels, *Eine lateinische Rechtfertigungsschrift des Meister Eckhart*, p. 10, n. 8. *Beiträge*, 23, 5, Münster i.W., 1923.
[4] Commentary on the *Celestial Hierarchy* of the Pseudo-Dionysius, 4.

speak eternally all that Thou speakest; and yet not all exists at once and from eternity that Thou effectest in speaking.'[1]

We seem perhaps to have strayed far from Eckhart the mystic. But the mystic aims at union with God, and it is not unnatural that a speculative mystic like Eckhart should emphasize the immanence of God in creatures and their dwelling in God. He did not deny God's transcendence; he affirmed it. But he certainly used exaggerated expressions and ambiguous expressions in stating the relations of creatures in general to God. A like boldness and proneness to exaggeration can be seen in his statements concerning the relation of the human soul in particular to God. In the human soul there is an element, which he called *archa* and which is uncreated. This element is the intelligence.[2] In virtue of *intelligere* the soul is deiform, since God Himself is *intelligere*. But the supreme mystical union with God does not take place through the activities of love and knowledge, which are activities of the soul and not the essence of the soul: it takes place in the innermost recess of the soul, the 'spark' or *scintilla animae*, where God unites the soul to Himself in a hidden and ineffable manner. The intellect apprehends God as Truth, the will as the Good: the essence of the soul, however, its citadel (*bürgelin*), is united with God as *esse*. The essence of the soul, also called its 'spark' (*vünkelin* or *scintilla*) is simple; it is on it that the image of God is stamped; and in the mystical union it is united with God as one and simple, that is to say, with the one simple divine essence transcending the distinction of Persons.[3] Eckhart thus preaches a mystical union which reminds one of Plotinus' 'flight of the alone to the Alone', and one can see the parallelism between his psychology and his metaphysic. The soul has a simple, unitary ground or essence and God has a simple essence transcending the distinction of Persons: the supreme mystical union is the union of the two. But this doctrine of a ground of the soul which is superior to the intelligence as a power does not necessarily mean that the soul's presence is not, in a higher sense, intellect. Nor does the doctrine that the ground of the soul is united with God as *esse* necessarily mean that the *esse* is not *intelligere*. In other words, I do not think that the mystical teaching of Eckhart necessarily contradicts Gilson's view that the statement that God is *esse* involves no break with the earlier statements that God is *intelligere*. The Sermons seem to make it

[1] *Conf.*, 11, 7.   [2] Cf. twelfth German sermon, pp. 197–8. Cf. p. 189, n. 3.
[3] Cf. Meister Eckhart, *Die deutschen Werke: erster Band, Meister Eckhart's Predigten*, fasc. 1, pp. 24–45. Stuttgart-Berlin, 1936.

clear that Eckhart did not change his opinion. He speaks of the ground of the soul as intellect.

Of the union mystically effected between God and the soul Eckhart speaks in an extremely bold way. Thus in the German sermon on the text, 'the just shall live for evermore; and their reward is with the Lord',[1] he declares that 'we are wholly transformed and changed into God'. And he goes on to say that, just as the bread is changed into the Body of Christ, so is the soul changed into God in such a way that no distinction remains. 'God and I we are one. By knowledge I take God into myself; by love I enter into God.' Just as fire changes wood into itself, 'so we are transformed into God'. So too in the following sermon[2] Eckhart says that just as the food which I eat becomes one with my nature so do we become one with the divine nature.

Not unnaturally, statements of this kind did not pass unnoticed. The statement that there is something uncreated in the soul was censured, and the statement that we are wholly transformed into God in a manner similar to that of the transformation of bread into Christ's Body was condemned as heretical. In his self-justification Eckhart admitted that it is false to say that the soul or any part of it is uncreated; but he protested that his accusers had overlooked his having declared that the supreme powers of the soul were created in and with the soul.[3] In point of fact Eckhart had implied that there is something uncreated in the soul, and it is not to be wondered at that his words led to trouble; but he maintained that by 'uncreated' he meant 'not created *per se*, but concreated' (with the soul). Moreover, he had said not that the soul is uncreated but that if the whole soul were essentially and totally intellect, it would be uncreated. It is, however, difficult to see how he could maintain this, unless by 'intellect' he meant the ground of the soul, which is the image of God. In this case he may have meant that the soul, if totally and essentially the image of God (*imago Dei*), would be indistinguishable from the Word. This seems to be its probable meaning.

As to the statement that 'we are transformed and changed into God', Eckhart admits that it is an error.[4] Man, he says, is not the 'image of God, the unbegotten Son of God; but he is (made) to the image of God'. He goes on to say that just as many hosts on many altars are turned into the one Body of Christ, though the accidents

---
[1] *Wisdom* 6, 16; *op. cit.*, fasc. 2, pp. 99–115.   [2] *Op. cit.*, p. 119.
[3] Daniels, p. 5, n. 4; p. 17, n. 6.   [4] Daniels, p. 15, n. 1.

of each host remain, so 'we are united to the true Son of God, members of the one head of the Church who is Christ'. In other words, he admits that his original statements were exaggerated and incorrect, and that the comparison of the union of the soul with God to transubstantiation is an analogy, not a parallel. As a matter of fact, however, though Eckhart's statements in his sermons concerning mystical union with God were obviously *male sonantes* as they stood, they are by no means exceptional among mystical writers, even among some whose orthodoxy has never seriously been called in question. Phrases like man becoming God or the transformation of the soul into God can be found in the works of writers of unquestioned orthodoxy. If the mystic wishes to describe the mystical union of the soul with God and its effects, he has to make use of words which are not designed to express any such thing. For example, in order to express the closeness of the union, the elevation of the soul and the effect of the union on the soul's activity, he employs a verb like 'transform' or 'change into'. But 'change into' denotes such processes as assimilation (of food), consumption of material by fire, production of steam from water, heat from energy, and so on, whereas the mystical union of the soul with God is *sui generis* and really requires an altogether new and special word to describe it. But if the mystic coined a brand new word for this purpose, it would convey nothing at all to anyone who lacked the experience in question. Therefore he has to employ words in more or less ordinary use, even though these words inevitably suggest pictures and parallels which do not strictly apply to the experience he is attempting to describe. There is nothing to be surprised at, then, if some of the mystic's statements, taken literally, are inadequate or even incorrect. And if the mystic is also theologian and philosopher, as Eckhart was, inexactitude is likely to affect even his more abstract statements, at least if he attempts to express in theological and philosophical statements an experience which is not properly expressible, employing for this purpose words and phrases which either suggest parallels that are not strict parallels or already possess a defined meaning in theology and philosophy.

Moreover, Eckhart's thought and expression were influenced by a number of different sources. He was influenced, for example, by St. Thomas, by St. Bonaventure, by the Victorines, by Avicenna, by the Pseudo-Dionysius, by Proclus, by the Christian Fathers. He was, too, a deeply religious man who was primarily interested in his theoretical statements and the abstract theory which, though historically conditioned, had its influence in inculcating a certain general mentality and outlook.

4. The first *Dictio* begins with a quotation from Cassiodorus in praise of peace. The quotations from classical writers and from the Bible cause perhaps a first impression of abstraction and antiquity; but very soon, after remarking that Aristotle has described almost all the causes of strife in the State, Marsilius remarks that there is another cause, which neither Aristotle nor any of his contemporaries or predecessors saw or could see.[1] This is a covert reference to Marsilius' particular reason for writing; and thus the actuality of the book makes itself felt at once, despite the borrowings from former writers.

The account of the nature of the State as a perfect or self-sufficing community which is brought into being for the sake of life but exists for the sake of the good life,[2] and the account of the 'parts' of the State[3] depend on Aristotle; but Marsilius adds an account of the priestly 'part' or order.[4] The priesthood is, then, part of the State, and though Christian revelation has corrected error in teaching and provided a knowledge of the salutary truth, the Christian priesthood remains none the less a part of the State. Marsilius' fundamental 'Erastianism' is thus asserted very early in the *Defensor pacis*.

Leaving out of account the cases where God directly appoints the ruler, one can reduce the different types of government to two fundamental types, government which exists by consent of the subjects and government which is contrary to the will of the subjects.[5] The latter type of government is tyrannical. The former type does not necessarily depend on election; but a government which depends on election is superior to a government which does not depend on election.[6] It may be that non-hereditary rule is the best form of elective government, but it does not follow that this form of government is best suited for any particular State.

Marsilius' idea of law, which next comes up for discussion in the *Defensor pacis*, involved a change from the attitude of thirteenth-century thinkers like St. Thomas. In the first place law has its origin, not in the positive function of the State, but in the need of preventing quarrels and strife.[7] Statute law is also rendered

---

[1] I, 3. [2] I, 4. [3] I, 5. [4] I, 5–6.
[5] I, 9, 5. [6] I, 9, 7. [7] I, 5, 7.

man's attitude to and experience of God: he was not primarily a systematic philosopher, and he never systematically thought through and rendered consistent the ideas and phrases which he had found in various authors and the ideas which occurred to him in his own meditations on the Scriptures. If, then, it is asked whether certain statements made by Eckhart are theologically orthodox when taken in isolation and according to their 'natural' meaning, the answer can hardly be any other than a negative answer. Eckhart lived at a time when exactitude and accuracy of expression were expected; and the fact that he made his bold and exaggerated statements in sermons, the hearers of which might easily misunderstand his real intentions, renders the theological censure of certain propositions easily understandable. On the other hand, if it is asked whether Eckhart intended to be heterodox and whether he intended to found a 'German theology', the answer must also be in the negative. Disciples like Henry Suso warmly defended the Master against charges of heresy; and a man like Suso would never have done this had he seen any reason to doubt Eckhart's personal orthodoxy. To my mind it seems absurd either to make of Eckhart a 'German thinker' in revolt against Catholic orthodoxy or to attack the theologians who took exception to certain of his statements as though there were nothing in these statements to which they were entitled to take exception.

3. John Tauler was born at Strasbourg about the year 1300 and entered the Dominican Order at an early age. He did his studies at Paris; but it is clear that he was already more attracted to the mystical writers and to the writers influenced by neo-Platonism than to the logical investigations of contemporary philosophers or the purely abstract metaphysical speculations of the Schoolmen. He is famous as a preacher rather than as a theologian or a philosopher, and his preaching seems to have been especially concerned with the reformation and deepening of the spiritual life of religious and clergy. At the time of the Black Death he ministered heroically to the sick and dying. His writings present an orthodox Catholic and Christocentric mysticism, in distinction from the heretical and pantheistic mystical doctrines which were strenuously propagated at the time by various associations. He died in the city of his birth in the year 1361.

In Tauler's writings we find the same psychological doctrine of the 'spark' or 'foundation' of the soul as in the writings of Eckhart. The image of God resides in this apex or highest part of the soul, and it is by retreating within himself, transcending images and figures, that a man finds God. If a man's 'heart' (*Gemüt*) is turned towards this foundation of the soul, that is to say, if it is turned towards God, his faculties of intellect and will function as they ought; but if his 'heart' is turned away from the foundation of the soul, from the indwelling God, his faculties, too, are turned away from God. In other words, between the foundation of the soul and the faculties Tauler finds a link, *das Gemüt*, which is a permanent disposition of the soul in regard to its foundation or apex or 'spark'.

Tauler not only utilized the writings of St. Augustine, St. Bonaventure and the Victorines, but also those of the Pseudo-Dionysius; and he seems to have read some Proclus. He was also strongly influenced by Eckhart's teaching. But, whereas Eckhart not infrequently spoke in such a way that his orthodoxy was called in question, it would be superfluous to raise any such question in regard to Tauler, who insists on the simple acceptance of revealed truths and whose thought is constantly Christocentric in character.

4. Henry Suso was born at Constance about the year 1295. He entered the Dominican Order and did his studies at Constance (perhaps partly at Strasbourg), after which he went to Cologne. There he made the personal acquaintance of Eckhart, for whom he retained a lasting admiration, affection and loyalty. Returning to Constance he spent some years there, writing and practising extraordinary mortifications and penances; but at the age of forty he began an apostolic life of preaching not only in Switzerland but also in Alsace and the Rhineland. In 1348 he changed his convent at Constance for that at Ulm (driven thereto by calumnies) and it was at Ulm that he died in January, 1366. He was beatified by Gregory XVI in 1831.

Suso's chief concern as writer was to make known the soul's path to the highest union with God: he was above all a practical mystical writer. The more speculative part of his thought is contianed in *The Little Book of Truth* (*Büchlein der Wahrheit*) and in the last eight chapters of his autobiography. *The Little Book of Eternal Wisdom* (*Büchlein der ewigen Weisheit*) is a book of practical mysticism. Suso wrote a Latin version of it, the *Horologium Sapientiae*, which is not a translation but a development. Some letters and at least two certainly authentic sermons have also been preserved.

SPECULATIVE MYSTICISM

Suso warmly defended Eckhart against the charge of confusing God and creatures. He himself is perfectly clear and decisive about the distinction between them. He says indeed that creatures are eternally in God and that, as in God, they are God; but he carefully explains what he means by this. The ideas of creatures are eternally present in the divine mind; but these ideas are identical with the divine essence; they are not forms distinct from one another or from the divine essence. Further, this being of creatures in God is quite distinct from the being of creatures outside God: it is only through creation that 'creatures' exist. One cannot attribute creatureliness to creatures as they are in God. However, 'the creatureliness of any nature is nobler and more useful to it than the being which it has in God'.[1] In all this Suso was not saying anything different from what St. Thomas had taught. Similarly he expressly teaches that creation is a free act of God.[2] He certainly uses the Pseudo-Dionysian (that is to say, neo-Platonic) idea of the overflowing of the divine goodness; but he is careful to observe that this overflowing takes place as a necessary process only within the Godhead, where it is 'interior, substantial, personal, natural, necessary without compulsion, eternal and perfect'.[3] The overflowing in creation is a free act on God's part and is distinct from the eternal procession of the divine Persons. There is, then, no question of pantheism in Suso's thought.

A similar freedom from pantheistic tendencies is clear in Suso's doctrine of the soul's mystical union with God. As with Eckhart and Tauler, the mystical union is said to take place in the 'essence' of the soul, the 'spark' of the soul. This essence or centre of the soul is the unifying principle of the soul's powers, and it is in it that the image of God resides. Through the mystical union, which takes place by supernaturally impressed knowledge and love, this image of God is further actualized. This actualization is called the 'birth of God' (*Gottesgeburt*) or 'birth of Christ' (*Christusgeburt*) in the soul, by means of which the soul is made more like to and more united with the Deity in and through Christ. Suso's mysticism is essentially Christocentric. He speaks of the soul's 'sinking into' God; but he emphasizes the fact that there is not, and never can be, a complete ontological identification of the ground or essence of the soul with the divine Being. Man remains man, even if he becomes deiform: there is no pantheistic absorption of the creature

---
[1] *Book of Truth*, 332, 16.   [2] *Vita*, 21–4, p. 178.
[3] *Ibid.*, 178, 24–179, 7.

in God.[1] As I have said, Suso was strongly influenced by Eckhart, but he was always careful to bring his teaching into clear harmony with the doctrines of Catholic Christianity. It would, indeed, be preferable to say that his mystical teaching sprang from the Catholic tradition of spirituality, and that, as far as Eckhart is concerned, Suso interpreted the latter's teaching in an orthodox sense.

It has been said that Suso's thought differed from Eckhart's in regard to its direction. Eckhart preferred to start with God: his thought moved from the simple divine essence to the Trinity of Persons, especially to the Word or *Logos*, in which he saw the archetype of creation, and so to creatures in the Word. The union of the soul with God appeared to him as a return of the creature to its dwelling-place in the Word, and the highest mystical experience of the soul is the union of its centre with the simple centre or essence of the Godhead. Suso, however, was less speculatively inclined. His thought moved from the human person to the latter's dynamic union with Christ, the God-Man; and he emphasized strongly the place of the Humanity of Christ in the ascent of the soul to God. In other words, though he often used more or less the same phrases that Eckhart used, his thought was less neo-Platonic than Eckhart's, and he was more strongly influenced than was Eckhart by the affective spirituality and the Christocentric 'bride-mysticism' of St. Bernard.

5. John Ruysbroeck was born in 1293 at the village of Ruysbroeck near Brussels. After some years spent at the latter city he became Prior of the Augustinian convent of Groenendael (Green Valley) in the forest of Soignes near Brussels. He died in 1381. His writings include *The Adornment of the Spiritual Marriage* and *The Book of the Twelve Beguines*. He wrote in Flemish.

Ruysbroeck, who was strongly influenced by the writings of Eckhart, insists on the original presence of the creature in God and on the return to that state of unity. One can distinguish in man a threefold unity.[2] 'The first and highest unity of man is in God.' Creatures depend on this unity for their being and preservation, and without it they would be reduced to nothing. But this relationship to God is essential to the creature and it does not, of itself, make a man really good or bad. The second unity is also natural: it is the unity of man's higher powers inasmuch as these spring from the unity of his mind or spirit. This fundamental

---

[1] Cf. *Vita*, 50 and 51, p. 176.   [2] *Adornment*, 2, 2.

SPECULATIVE MYSTICISM

unity of spirit is the same as the first type of unity, the unity which depends on God; but it is considered in its activity rather than in its essence. The third unity, also natural, is the unity of the senses and of the bodily activities. If in regard to the second natural unity the soul is called 'spirit', in regard to the third it is called 'soul', that is, as vital principle and principle of sensation. The 'adornment' of the soul consists in the supernatural perfection of the three unities; the first through the moral perfection of the Christian; the second through the theological virtues and the gifts of the Holy Spirit; the third through mystical and inexpressible union with God. The highest unification is 'that most high unity in which God and the loving spirit are united without intermediary'.

Like Eckhart Ruysbroeck speaks of 'the most high and superessential Unity of the Divine Nature'. The words recall the writing of the Pseudo-Dionysius. With this supreme Unity the soul, in the highest activity of the mystical life, can become united. But the union transcends the power of reason; it is accomplished by love. In it the ground of the soul is, as it were, lost in the ineffable abyss of the Godhead, in the Essential Unity to which 'the Persons, and all that lives in God, just give place'.[1]

Not unnaturally, Ruysbroeck's doctrine was attacked, particularly by Gerson. However, that he did not intend to teach pantheism Ruysbroeck made clear in *The Mirror of Eternal Salvation* and in *The Book of the Twelve Beguines*. He was defended by Jan van Schoonhoven (d. 1432), himself a mystic, and Denis the Carthusian did not hesitate to borrow from his writings.

6. Denis the Carthusian, who was born at Rychel in 1402 and died as a Carthusian of Roermond in 1471, does not belong chronologically to the period which is being treated in the first part of this work. For the sake of convenience, however, I shall say a few words about him here.

The 'ecstatic Doctor' had done his higher studies at Cologne, and, for a mystical writer, he was surprisingly interested in Scholastic themes. He composed commentaries on the *Sentences* of Peter Lombard and on Boethius, as well as on the writings of the Pseudo-Dionysius, and he wrote a summary of the orthodox faith according to the works of St. Thomas, a manual of philosophy and theology (*Elementatio philosophica et theologica*) and other theological works. In addition, there are his purely ascetical and mystical treatises. It is clear that he was at first a devoted

---
[1] *Adornment*, 3, 4.

follower of St. Thomas; and his hostility not only towards the nominalists but also towards the Scotists seems to have continued throughout his life. But he gradually moved from the camp of the Thomists to that of the followers of St. Albert, and he was much influenced by the writings of the Dominican Ulric of Strasbourg (d. 1277), who had attended St. Albert's lectures at Cologne. Not only did Denis reject the real distinction between essence and existence, which he had at first defended; but he also abandoned the Thomist view of the rôle of the 'phantasm' in human knowledge. Denis restricted the necessity of the phantasm to the lower levels of knowledge and maintained that the soul can know without recourse to the phantasm its own activity, angels and God. Our knowledge of the divine essence, however, is negative; the mind comes to realize clearly the incomprehensibility of God. In this emphasis on negative but immediate knowledge of God Denis was influenced by the Pseudo-Dionysius and by the writings of Ulric of Strasbourg and other followers of St. Albert. The Carthusian Doctor is a remarkable example of the combination of mystical with Scholastic interests.

7. The German mystics of the Middle Ages (I include Ruysbroeck, although he was a Fleming) drew their mysticism from its roots in the Christian Faith. It is not a question of enumerating sources, of showing the influence of the Fathers, of St. Bernard, of the Victorines, of St. Bonaventure or of trying to minimize the neo-Platonic influences on expression and even on idea, but of realizing the mystics' common belief in the necessity of supernatural grace which comes through Christ. The Humanity of Christ may play a larger part in the thought of Suso, for example, than in that of Eckhart; but the latter, in spite of all his exaggerations, was first and foremost a Christian. There is, then, no real support for the attempt which has been made to discover in the writings of the German mediaeval mystics like Eckhart, Tauler and Suso a 'German mysticism', if by this is meant a mysticism which is not Catholic but one proceeding from 'blood and race'.

On the other hand, the German mystics of the fourteenth century do represent an alliance of Scholasticism and mysticism which gives them a stamp of their own. Grabmann remarked that the combination of practical mysticism and of speculation is ultimately a continuation of St. Anselm's programme, *Credo, ut intelligam.* However, although the speculation of the German mystics grew out of the currents of thought which had inspired the mediaeval Scholastics and which had been systematized in various ways in the thirteenth century, their speculation must be seen in the light of their practical mysticism. If it was partly the circumstances of the education of this or that mystical writer which moulded the framework of his speculation and influenced his choice of theoretic ideas, it was also partly his practical mystical life and his reflection on his spiritual experience which influenced the direction of his speculation. It would be a mistake to think that the doctrine of the *scintilla animae*, the spark of the soul or the essence or ground or apex of the soul, was no more than a stock idea which was adopted mechanically from predecessors and passed on from mystic to mystic. The term *scintilla conscientiae* or *synderesis* occurs in St. Jerome[1] and it reappears in, for example, St. Albert the Great, who means by it a power existing in all men which admonishes them of the good and opposes evil. St. Thomas, who refers to St. Jerome,[2] speaks of synderesis metaphorically, as the *scintilla conscientiae*.[3] The mystics certainly meant something else than synderesis when they spoke of the spark or ground of the soul; but, even granting that, practically all the expressions by which they characterized the ground of the soul were already to be found, according to Denifle, in the writings of Richard of St. Victor. No doubt Denifle's contention is true; but the German mystics made the idea of the ground or spark of the soul one of their leading ideas, not simply because they found it in the writings of a revered predecessor, but because it fitted in with their experience of a mystical union with God transcending the conscious play of acts of intelligence and will. As found in their predecessors, the idea doubtless suggested to them this close union; but their meditation on the idea went hand in hand with their experience.

Possibly certain German writers have gone too far in finding in the combination of speculation with practical mysticism a distinguishing mark of the German mystics. It serves to differentiate them from some mystics, it is true, who were more or less innocent of theoretic speculations; but a similar combination can be seen in the case of the Victorines in the twelfth century and, indeed, in that of Gerson himself, though Gerson had scant sympathy for the line of speculation adopted by Eckhart and Ruysbroeck, as he interpreted it at least. However, there is an added characteristic which is connected with the fact that Eckhart, Tauler and Suso were all members of the Dominican Order, the

---

[1] *P.L.*, 25, 22 AB. [2] *De Veritate*, 16, 1, obj. 1. [3] *Ibid.*, 17, 2, *ad* 3.

Order of Friars Preachers. They disseminated mystical doctrine in their sermons, and attempted, as I have already mentioned, to deepen in this way the general spiritual life, particularly among religious. No doubt one could make a similar observation about St. Bernard, for example, but, particularly in the case of Eckhart, there is a speculative flavour and framework, due to the intervening development of mediaeval philosophy, which is not to be found in St. Bernard's sermons. Moreover, the Germans are more 'rugged', less flowery. The German speculative mysticism is so closely connected with Dominican preaching that it enables one to speak, in this sense, of the 'German mysticism' of the Middle Ages, provided that one does not mean to imply that the German Dominicans were attempting to establish a German religion or a German *Weltanschauung*.

8. John Gerson, who was born in 1363, succeeded Peter d'Ailly as chancellor of the university of Paris in 1395.[1] He has been accounted a nominalist; but his adoption of certain nominalist positions did not proceed from adherence to the nominalist philosophy. He was a theologian and mystical writer rather than a philosopher; and it was in the interests of faith and of theology that he tended in certain matters towards nominalist doctrine. Gerson's chancellorship fell in the period of the Great Schism (1378–1417) and he took a prominent part in the work of the Council of Constance. Much distressed not only at the state of the Church, but also at the condition of university studies and the propagation of doctrines which had, it seemed to him, led to or facilitated the rise of theories like those of Hus, he sought to apply a remedy, not through a dissemination of nominalism as such but through a recall of men to the right attitude towards God. The conflict of systems of philosophy and the curiosity and pride of theologians had, he thought, been responsible for much evil. In his *De modis significandi propositiones quinquaginta* Gerson maintained that the various branches of study had become confused to the detriment of truth, logicians trying to solve metaphysical problems by the *modus significandi* proper to logic, metaphysicians and logicians endeavouring to prove revealed truths or to solve theological problems by methods which are not fitted for dealing with the object of theology. This confusion, thought Gerson, had led to a state of anarchy in the intellectual world and to untrue

[1] Gerson died in 1429. For chronological details, see *La vie et les œuvres de Gerson* by P. Glorieux (Archives d'histoire doctrinale et littéraire du moyen âge, t. 18, pp. 149–92; Paris, 1951).

conclusions. Furthermore, the pride of the Scholastic theologians had engendered curiosity and the spirit of novelty or singularity. Gerson published two lectures *Contra vanam curiositatem in negotio fidei*, against vain curiosity in the matter of faith, in which he drew attention to the part played in Scholastic disputes by love of one's own opinions, envy, the spirit of contention and contempt for the uneducated and the uninitiated. The root fault is the pride of the natural reason which endeavours to exceed its bounds and to solve problems which it is incapable of solving.

It is from this angle that one should regard Gerson's attack on realism. The notion of ideas in God involves a confusion, first of logic with metaphysics, and then of metaphysics with theology. Secondly, it implies that God is not simple, since the realists tend to speak of these *rationes ideales* in God as though they were distinct; and some even speak as though creatures pre-existed in God, that is to say, as though the divine ideas were creatures existing in God. Thirdly, the doctrine of divine ideas, employed in explaining creation, serves only to limit the divine freedom. And why do philosophers and theologians limit the divine freedom? From a desire of understanding that which cannot be understood, a desire which proceeds from pride. The thinkers of the Platonic tradition also speak of God, not primarily as free, but as the Good, and they utilize the principle of the natural tendency of goodness to diffuse itself in order to explain creation. But by doing so they tend to make creation a necessary effect of the divine nature. Again, realist metaphysicians and theologians insist that the moral law in no way depends on the divine will, thus restricting the divine liberty, whereas in point of fact 'God does not will certain actions because they are good; but they are good because He wills them, just as others are bad because He prohibits them.'[1] 'Right reason does not precede the will, and God does not decide to give law to a rational creature because He has first seen in His wisdom that He ought to do so; it is rather the contrary which takes place.'[2] It follows that the moral law is not immutable. Gerson adopted this Ockhamist position in regard to the moral law because he considered that it was the only position consonant with God's liberty. The Platonizing philosophers and theologians, he thought, had abandoned the principle of belief, of humble subjection, for the pride of the understanding. Moreover, he did not fail to draw attention to the realist aspects of the thought of John Hus and of Jerome of

---

[1] *Opera*, 3, col. 13. [2] *Ibid.*, col. 26.

Prague; and he drew the conclusion that the pride of the understanding manifested by the realists leads in the end to open heresy.

Thus Gerson's attack on realism, though it involved him in some positions which were actually held by the nominalists, proceeded rather from religious preoccupations than from any particular enthusiasm for the *via moderna* as such. 'Repent and believe the Gospel'[1] was the text on which Gerson built his two lectures against vain curiosity in the matter of faith. The pride which had invaded the minds of university professors and lecturers had made them oblivious to the need for repentance and to the simplicity of faith. This point of view is obviously more characteristic of a man whose concern is the soul's attitude towards God than of a man who is passionately interested in academic questions for their own sake. Gerson's hostility towards the metaphysics and theology of the realists certainly bears some analogy to Pascal's hostility towards those who would substitute for the God of Abraham and Isaac and Jacob the 'God of the philosophers'.

If we look at the matter from this point of view, it is not surprising to find Gerson expressing his amazement that the Franciscans had abandoned St. Bonaventure for *parvenus* in the intellectual world. St. Bonaventure's *Itinerarium mentis in Deum* he regarded as a book beyond all praise. On the other hand, if we consider Gerson's hostility towards realism, his attacks on Ruysbroeck and his attempt to connect realism with the heresies of John Hus and Jerome of Prague, his enthusiasm for St. Bonaventure might well appear somewhat startling when it is remembered that St. Bonaventure laid great stress on the Platonic doctrine of ideas in its Augustinian form and roundly condemned Aristotle for 'execrating' the ideas of Plato. Gerson's conviction was that the theologians of his time had neglected the Bible and the Fathers, the true sources of theology, in favour of pagan thinkers and of importations from metaphysics which impaired the simplicity of faith. He regarded, however, the Pseudo-Dionysius as the disciple and convert of St. Paul, and considered the Dionysian writings to form part of the well-spring of true wisdom. St. Bonaventure he revered as a man who had consistently drunk of these undefiled waters and who had concerned himself above all with the true wisdom, which is the knowledge of God through Jesus Christ.

In spite, then, of his attack on realism, Gerson's mystical doctrine was deeply influenced by the teaching of the

[1] *St. Mark* 1, 15.

Pseudo-Dionysius. M. André Combes, in his most interesting study of Gerson's relation to the writings and thought of the Pseudo-Dionysius,[1] after showing the authenticity of the *Notulae super quaedam verba Dionysii de Caelesti Hierarchia* and arguing that the work should precede the first lecture against 'vain curiosity' in the *Opera* of Gerson, makes it clear that Gerson was never simply a 'nominalist' and that his ideas were never simply identical with those of Peter d'Ailly (1350-1420), his 'master'. In fact, as M. Combes has shown, Gerson borrowed from the Pseudo-Dionysius not merely an arsenal of terminology, but also the important doctrine of the 'return'. Creatures proceed from God and return to God. How is this return accomplished? By each nature performing those acts which are proper to it. Strictly speaking, says Gerson (in his *Sermo de die Jovis sancta*), it is only the rational creature who returns to God, though Boethius said that all things return to their beginning or principle. But the important point about Gerson's doctrine of the 'return' is the emphasis he lays on the fact that it does not mean an ontological merging of the creature with God. As he regarded the Pseudo-Dionysius as a personal disciple of St. Paul, he was convinced that the Dionysian teaching was perfectly 'safe'. But, realizing that it could be misinterpreted, he considered that the theologian must elucidate the Areopagite's true meaning; and he himself utilized the writings of Hugh of St. Victor and of St. Albert the Great. From this two relevant and important points emerge. First, Gerson by no means condemned or rejected the Scholastic theology as such, which he considered necessary for the right interpretation of the Scriptures, of the Fathers and of St. Paul's disciple. Secondly, when he attacked Ruysbroeck, he was not attacking him for drawing on the teaching of the Pseudo-Dionysius but for misinterpreting and perverting that doctrine. Of course, we know that the Pseudo-Dionysius was not a disciple of St. Paul and that he drew copiously on Proclus; but the point is that Gerson interpreted the Pseudo-Dionysius as if he were not a Platonist. This explains how he could show at the same time a marked hostility towards the Platonizers and a marked predilection for the Pseudo-Dionysius.

Gerson accepted the threefold division of theology given by the Pseudo-Dionysius, symbolic theology, theology in the proper sense, and mystical theology. The threefold division is to be found in St. Bonaventure's *Itinerarium mentis in Deum*;[2] but Gerson

[1] *Jean Gerson, Commentateur Dionysien*, Paris, 1940.   [2] 1, 7.

seems to have drawn the distinction from the Pseudo-Dionysius' writings rather than from St. Bonaventure: at least he consulted the former and cites him as his authority. Mystical theology, he says, is the experimental knowledge of God, in which love, rather than the abstract speculative intellect, is at work, though the highest intellectual function is also involved. The *intelligentia simplex* and the *synderesis* or highest affective power are operative in mystical experience, which is not a rejection but a realization of the highest powers of the soul. Mystical union affects the foundation of the soul; but it is a union which does not dissolve the human personality in the Godhead. Mystical theology, at least if it is understood as mysticism itself rather than as the theory of mysticism, is the crown of theology, because it approaches nearest to the beatific vision, which is the final end of the soul.

The presence of this threefold division in Gerson's thought helps to make it clear that, while emphasizing the primacy of mystical theology, he did not reject theology in the ordinary sense. Nor did he reject philosophy. Whether his bent of mind might have led him to reject all but mystical theology had it not been for the Pseudo-Dionysius, St. Bonaventure and St. Albert is another and not very profitable question. He certainly laid stress on the Scriptures and the teaching of the Fathers and he certainly thought that theologians would do well to pay more attention to those sources; he certainly thought, moreover, that speculative theology contaminated by unwarranted importations from suspect philosophers encouraged pride and vain curiosity; but there is no real evidence for saying either that he rejected all Scholastic development of Scriptural and Patristic teaching or that he rejected a philosophy which observed its due limits. In some ways Gerson is the most interesting representative of the movement of speculative mysticism in the late Middle Ages. He shows us that the movement was primarily inspired by the desire for remedying the evils of the time and for deepening men's religious life: it was by no means a mere counter-blast to nominalist scepticism. As for Gerson's own nominalism, it is truer to say that he adopted and exploited certain nominalist positions in the service of his own primary aim rather than that he was a nominalist. To say that Gerson was a nominalist philosopher who at the same time happened to be a mystic would be to give a false impression of his aims, his theoretical position and his spirit.

PART II

THE PHILOSOPHY OF THE RENAISSANCE

CHAPTER XIII

THE REVIVAL OF PLATONISM

The Italian Renaissance—The northern Renaissance—The revival of Platonism.

1. THE first phase of the Renaissance was the humanistic phase which began in Italy and spread to northern Europe. But it would be absurd to speak as if the Renaissance was a historical period with such clearly-defined temporal limits that one could give the exact dates of its beginning and end. In so far as the Renaissance means or involved a rebirth of literature and a devotion to classical learning and style it may be said to have begun as early as the twelfth century, the century in which John of Salisbury, for example, had declaimed against barbarity in Latin style, the century which saw the humanism of the School of Chartres. It is true that the great theologians and philosophers of the thirteenth century were more concerned with *what* was said and with exactitude of statement than with literary style and grace of expression; but it should not be forgotten that a St. Thomas Aquinas could write hymns which are remarkable for their beauty and that in the same period in which Duns Scotus was composing his somewhat bold and unstylistic commentaries Dante was creating one of the greatest achievements of the Italian language. Dante (1265-1321) certainly wrote from the standpoint of a mediaeval; but in the same century in which Dante died, the fourteenth century, we find Petrarch (1304-74) not only setting himself against the cult of Aristotelian dialectic and promoting the revival of the classical, especially the Ciceronian, style but also favouring through his vernacular sonnets the growth of the spirit of humanistic individualism. Boccaccio (1313-75) also belonged to the fourteenth century; and at the end of the century, in 1396, Manuel Chrysoloras (d. 1415), the first real teacher of classical Greek in the West, began lecturing at Florence.

The political conditions in Italy favoured the growth of the humanistic Renaissance, inasmuch as princely, ducal and ecclesiastical patrons were able to spend large sums of money on the purchase and copying of manuscripts and on the foundation of libraries; and by the time the Renaissance made itself felt in northern Europe the greater part of the Greek and Latin classics had been recovered and made known. But the Italian Renaissance was by no means confined to the recovery and dissemination of texts. A most important feature was the rise of a new style and ideal of education, represented by teachers like Vittorino da Feltre (1378–1446) and Guarino of Verona (1370–1460). The humanistic educational ideal at its best was that of developing the human personality to the full. Ancient literature was regarded as the chief means of education; but moral training, development of character, physical development and awakening of the aesthetic sensibility were not neglected; nor was the ideal of liberal education regarded as in any way incompatible with the acceptance and practice of Christianity.[1] This, however, was the humanistic ideal at its best. In practice the Italian Renaissance became associated to a certain extent with a growth of moral or amoral individualism and with the pursuit of fame; while in the later stages of the Renaissance the cult of classical literature degenerated into 'Ciceronianism', which meant the substitution of the tyranny of Cicero for that of Aristotle. The exchange was scarcely a change for the better. Moreover, while a man like Vittorino da Feltre was a convinced and devout Christian, many figures of the Renaissance were influenced by a spirit of scepticism. While it would be ridiculous to belittle the achievements of the Italian Renaissance at its best, other aspects were symptomatic of the disintegration rather than of the enrichment of the preceding cultural phase. And the degenerate phase of 'Ciceronianism' was no improvement on the broader outlook fostered by a theological and philosophical education.

2. In the Italian Renaissance the ideas of self-development and self-culture were marked features: it was, in large part, an individualistic movement, in the sense that the ideal of social and moral reform was not conspicuous: indeed, some of the humanists were 'pagan' in outlook. The ideal of reform, when it came, did not spring from the Renaissance as such, which was predominantly cultural, aesthetic and literary in character. In northern Europe,

---

[1] The *De liberorum educatione*, published in 1450 by Aeneas Sylvius Piccolomini, later Pope Pius II, was taken in large part from Quintilian's *De Oratore*, which had been discovered in 1416, and from an educational work attributed to Plutarch.

however, the literary Renaissance was allied with efforts to achieve moral and social reformation, and there was a greater emphasis on popular education. The northern Renaissance lacked much of the splendour of the Italian Renaissance and it was less 'aristocratic' in character; but it was more obviously allied with religious and moral purposes and, arising at a later date than the Italian movement, it tended to merge with the Reformation, at least if 'Reformation' is understood in a very broad sense and not merely in the sectarian sense. But though both movements had their peculiar strong points, both tended to lose their original inspiration in the course of time, the Italian movement degenerating into 'Ciceronianism', the northern movement tending to pedantry and 'grammaticism', divorced from a living appreciation of the humanistic aspects of classical literature and culture.

Among the scholars associated with the Renaissance in northern Europe one may mention Rudolf Agricola (1443-85), Hegius (1420-95), who was for a time headmaster of a school at Deventer founded in the fourteenth century by the Brethren of the Common Life, and Jacob Wimpfeling (1450-1528), who made of the university of Heidelberg a centre of humanism in western Germany. But the greatest figure of the northern Renaissance was Erasmus (1467-1536), who promoted the study of Greek and Latin literature, including the Scriptures and the writings of the Fathers, and gave a great impetus to the development of humanistic education. In Great Britain there were ecclesiastics like William of Waynflete (c. 1395-1486), St. John Fisher (1459-1535), who brought Erasmus to Cambridge, John Colet (c. 1467-1519), who founded St. Paul's School in 1512, and Thomas Linacre (c. 1460-1524); and laymen like St. Thomas More (1478-1535). Winchester College was founded in 1382 and Eton in 1440.

The Reformers stressed the need of education; but they were led by religious motives rather than by devotion to the humanistic ideal as such. John Calvin (1509-64), who had studied the humanities in France, drew up an educational curriculum for the schools of Geneva and, since he was religious autocrat of the city, he was able to enforce a system of education on Calvinistic lines. But the most humanistically-minded of the famous continental reformers was Philip Melanchthon (1497-1560), the foremost disciple of Martin Luther (1483-1546). In 1518 Melanchthon became professor of Greek at the university of Wittenberg. The humanism of the Reformers, which was hindered rather than promoted by the religious tenets of strict Protestantism, was not, however, their own discovery; it was derived from the impetus of the Italian Renaissance. And in the Counter-Reformation the humanistic ideal was prominent in the educational system developed by the Society of Jesus, which was founded in 1540 and produced the *Ratio Studiorum* in a definite form in 1599.

3. Through the interest and enthusiasm which it aroused for the literature of Greece and Rome the humanistic phase of the Renaissance not unnaturally inspired a revival of ancient philosophy in its various forms. Of these revived philosophies one of the most influential was Platonism or, to speak more accurately, neo-Platonism. The most remarkable centre of Platonic studies in Italy was the Platonic Academy of Florence, founded by Cosimo de' Medici under the influence of George Gemistus Plethon (d. 1464) who arrived in Italy from Byzantium in 1438. Plethon was an enthusiastic adherent of the Platonic or neo-Platonic tradition, and he composed in Greek a work on the difference between the Platonic and Aristotelian philosophies. His main work, of which only parts have survived, was his νόμων συγγραφή. A kindred spirit was John Argyropoulos (d. 1486), who occupied the chair of Greek at Florence from 1456 until 1471, when he left for Rome, where he numbered Reuchlin among his pupils. One must also mention John Bessarion of Trebizond (1395–1472), who was sent from Byzantium together with Plethon to take part in the Council of Florence (1438–45), at which he laboured to achieve the reunion of the Eastern Church with Rome. Bessarion, who became a cardinal, composed among other works an *Adversus calumniatorem Platonis*, in which he defended Plethon and Platonism against the Aristotelian George of Trebizond, who had written a *Comparatio Aristotelis et Platonis* in answer to Plethon.

It must not be thought that these Platonists were all determined haters of Scholasticism. John Argyropoulos translated into Greek St. Thomas Aquinas's *De ente et essentia*, and Bessarion too had a great respect for the Angelic Doctor. For these Platonists it was not so much a question of setting one philosopher against another, Plato against Aristotle, as of renewing a Platonic, or rather neo-Platonic, view of reality which would unite in itself the valuable elements of pagan antiquity and yet at the same time be Christian. It was the religious side of neo-Platonism, as well as its philosophy of beauty and harmony, which particularly appealed to the Platonists and what they particularly disliked in Aristotelianism was

THE REVIVAL OF PLATONISM

the tendency to naturalism which they detected therein. Plethon looked to the renewal of the Platonic tradition for a renewal of life or a reform in Church and State; and if his enthusiasm for Platonism led him into an attack on Aristotle which even Bessarion considered to be somewhat immoderate, it was what he regarded as the spirit of Platonism and its potentialities for spiritual, moral and cultural renewal which inspired him, rather than a purely academic interest in, for example, the Platonic affirmation and the Aristotelian denial of the theory of Ideas. The Platonists considered that the world of the humanistic Renaissance would greatly benefit in practice by absorbing such a doctrine as that of Man as the microcosm and as the ontological bond between the spiritual and the material.

One of the most eminent scholars of the neo-Platonic movement was Marsilius Ficinus (1433–1499). As a young man he composed two works, the *De laudibus philosophiae* and the *Institutiones platonicae* and these were followed in 1457 by the *De amore divino* and the *Liber de voluptate*. But in 1458 his father sent him to Bologna, to study medicine. Cosimo de' Medici, however, recalled him to Florence and had him taught Greek. In 1462 Marsilius translated the Orphic Hymns and in the following years he translated, at Cosimo's request, the Dialogues and Epistles of Plato and works by Hermes Trismegistus, Iamblichus (*De Secta Pythagorica*), Theo of Smyrna (*Mathematica*) and others. In 1469 appeared the first edition of his commentary on Plato's *Symposium* and commentaries on the *Philebus*, the *Parmenides* and the *Timaeus*. In 1474 he published his *De religione christiana* and his most important philosophical work, the *Theologia platonica*. In the following year appeared the commentary on the *Phaedrus* and the second edition of the commentary on the *Symposium*. The translations of and commentaries on the *Enneads* of Plotinus were published in 1485 and 1486; and in 1489 the *De triplici vita*, Marsilius' last work. Marsilius was an indefatigable worker, and in his translations he aimed above all at literal fidelity to the original: even though he sometimes made mistakes in his translation, there can be no doubt of the benefit he conferred on the men of his age.[1]

Marsilius Ficinus became a priest when he was forty years old, and he dreamed of drawing atheists and sceptics to Christ by

[1] For some remarks on the value of Marsilius' translations of Plato and Plotinus, see J. Festugière, *La philosophie de l'amour de Marsile Ficin*, Appendix I, pp. 141–52.

means of the Platonic philosophy. In his commentary on the *Phaedrus* he declares that the love spoken of by Plato and that spoken of by St. Paul are one and the same, namely the love of the absolute Beauty, which is God. God is both absolute Beauty and the absolute Good; and on this theme Plato and Dionysius the Areopagite (the Pseudo-Dionysius) are in accord. Again, when Plato insisted that we are 'reminded of' eternal objects, the Ideas, by the sight of their temporal and material imitations, was he not saying the same as St. Paul when the latter declares that the invisible things of God are understood by means of creatures? In the *Theologia platonica* the universe is depicted according to the neo-Platonic spirit as a harmonious and beautiful system, consisting of degrees of being which extend from corporeal things up to God, the absolute Unity or One. The place of man as the bond between the spiritual and the material is emphasized; and, though Marsilius thought of Aristotelianism as springing from the same philosophical tradition and inspiration as Platonism, he insisted, both as Christian and as Platonist, on the immortality and divine vocation of the human soul. He naturally adopted leading ideas from St. Augustine, developing the Platonic theory of Ideas (or better, Forms) in an Augustinian sense and insisting on Illumination. We learn nothing save in and through God, who is the light of the soul.

A strongly-marked syncretistic element appears in Marsilius' philosophy, as in that of other Platonists like Plethon. It is not only Plato, Plotinus, Iamblichus and Proclus whose thought is synthesized with that of St. John, St. Paul and St. Augustine, but also Hermes Trismegistus[1] and other pagan figures make their appearance as bearers of the spiritual movement which sprang from an original primitive revelation of the beauty and harmoniously ordered and graded system of reality. Marsilius Ficinus, like other Christian Platonists of the Italian Renaissance, was not only personally captivated by Platonism (in a very wide sense), but he also thought that those minds which had become alienated from Christianity could be brought back to it by being led to view Platonism as a stage in divine revelation. In other words, there was no need to choose between the beauty of classical

---

[1] In the Greco-Roman world a considerable literature, dealing with religious, theosophical, philosophical, medical, astrological and alchemist topics became known as the Hermetic literature. It was attributed in some way to, or placed under the patronage of, the 'thrice-great Hermes', who was the Egyptian god Thoth, identified by the Greeks with Hermes.

thought on the one hand and Christianity on the other; one could enjoy both. One could not, however, enjoy the Platonic-Christian heritage if one fell a victim to Aristotelianism as interpreted by those who set Aristotle against Plato, understood him in a naturalistic sense and denied the immortality of the human soul.

The best-known member of the circle which was influenced by Marsilius Ficinus was probably John Pico della Mirandola (1463-94). John possessed a knowledge of both Greek and Hebrew, and when twenty-four years old he planned to defend at Rome 900 theses against all comers, his object being to show how Hellenism and Judaism (in the form of the Cabbala) can be synthesized in a Platonic-Christian system. The disputation was, however, forbidden by the ecclesiastical authorities. John's tendency to syncretism showed itself also in the composition of an (unfinished) work, *De concordia Platonis et Aristotelis*.

John Pico della Mirandola was strongly influenced by the 'negative theology' of neo-Platonism and the Pseudo-Dionysius. God is the One; but He is above being rather than being.[1] He is indeed all things, in the sense that He comprises in Himself all perfections; but He comprises these perfections in His undivided unity in an ineffable manner which exceeds our understanding.[2] As far as we are concerned, God is in darkness; we approach Him philosophically by denying the limitations of creaturely perfections. Life is one perfection; wisdom is another perfection. Think away the particularity and limitations of these and all other perfections and 'that which remains is God'. This is not to be understood pantheistically, of course; God is the One, transcending the world which He has created.

The world is a harmonious system, consisting of beings belonging to different levels of reality; and John Pico della Mirandola speaks of God as having desired to create someone to contemplate the nature of the world, to love its beauty and to admire its greatness. 'Therefore, all things having been already completed (as Moses and Timaeus testify), He took thought finally to produce man.'[3] But God did not assign to man a fixed and peculiar place in the universe or laws which he was unable to contravene. 'I placed thee in the middle of the world, that thence thou mightest see more easily all that is in the world. We made thee neither a heavenly being nor an earthly being, neither mortal nor immortal,

---

[1] Cf. *De ente et uno*, 4.   [2] *Ibid.*, 5.
[3] *Oratio de hominis dignitate*, ed. E. Garin, p. 104.

in order that thou, as the free and sovereign artificer of thyself, mightest mould and sculpture thyself in the form which thou shouldest prefer. Thou wilt be able to degenerate to (the level of) the lower things, the brutes; thou wilt be able, according to thy will, to be reborn into the (level of) the higher things, the divine.'[1] Man is the microcosm; but he has the gift of freedom, which enables him to descend or to ascend. John was, therefore, hostile to the determinism of the astrologers, against whom he wrote his *In astrologiam libri XII*. His view of man, moreover, is a Christian view. There are three 'worlds' within the world or universe; the infralunar world, 'which brutes and men inhabit'; the celestial world, 'in which the planets shine'; and the super-celestial world, 'the abode of the angels'. But Christ, through the Passion, has opened to man the way into the super-celestial world, the way even to God Himself.[2] Man is the head and synthesis of the lower creation, and Christ is the head of the human race.[3] He is also, as divine Word, the 'beginning in which God made heaven and earth'.[4]

In his work against the astrologers John Pico della Mirandola opposed the magical conception of nature. In so far as astrology involved a belief in the harmonious system of nature and in the interrelatedness of all events, it was, whether true or false, a rational system. But it was not rationally grounded, and it involved, moreover, the belief that every earthly event was determined by the heavenly bodies and the belief that he who possessed a knowledge of certain symbols could by the right use of those symbols influence things. It was against the deterministic view of human actions and against the belief in magic that John set himself. Events are causally governed; but the causes are to be looked for in the natures and forms of the various things in the world, not in the stars, and a magical knowledge and use of symbol is ignorant superstition.

Finally one may mention that John's enthusiasm for Plato and his fondness for citing not only Greek and Islamic authors but also Oriental figures did not mean that he was without any appreciation of Aristotle. As already mentioned, he wrote a work on the agreement of Plato and Aristotle, and in the *Proœmium* to the *De ente et uno* he asserts his belief in this agreement. In the fourth chapter of this work he remarks, for instance, that those who think that Aristotle did not realize, as Plato did, that being is subordinate to

---
[1] *Oratio de hominis dignitate*, p. 106.
[2] *Heptaplus*, ed. E. Garin, pp. 186-8.   [3] *Ibid.*, p. 220.   [4] *Ibid.*, p. 244.

the One and does not include God 'have not read Aristotle', who expressed this truth 'much more clearly than Plato'. Whether John interpreted Aristotle correctly is, of course, another question; but he was certainly no fanatical anti-Aristotelian. As to the Scholastics, he cites them and he speaks of St. Thomas as 'the splendour of our theology'.[1] John was far too much of a syncretist to be exclusive.

In the last years of his life John Pico della Mirandola was influenced by Savonarola (1452-98), who also influenced the former's nephew, John Francis Pico della Mirandola (1469-1533). In his *De praenotionibus* John Francis discussed the criteria of divine revelation, finding the chief criterion in an 'inner light'. In regard to philosophy as such he did not follow his uncle's example of attempting to reconcile Aristotle and Plato: on the contrary, he sharply attacked the Aristotelian theory of knowledge in his *Examen vanitatis doctrinae gentium et veritatis Christianae disciplinae*. He argued that the Aristotelian bases his philosophy on sense-experience, which is supposed to be the source even of those most general principles which are employed in the process of proof. But sense-experience informs one about the conditions of the percipient subject rather than about objects themselves, and the Aristotelian can never proceed from his empiricist basis to a knowledge of substances or essences.

Among other Platonists one may mention Leo Hebraeus (c. 1460-c. 1530), a Portuguese Jew who came to Italy and wrote *Dialoghi d'amore* on the intellectual love of God whereby one apprehends beauty as the reflection of absolute Beauty. His views on love in general gave an impetus to the Renaissance literature on this subject, while his idea of the love of God in particular was not without influence on Spinoza. John Reuchlin (1455-1522) may also be mentioned here. This learned German, who not only was a master of the Latin and Greek languages but also introduced into Germany and promoted the study of Hebrew, studied in France and Italy, where, at Rome, he came under the influence of John Pico della Mirandola. In 1520 he became professor of Hebrew and Greek at Ingolstadt; but in 1521 he moved to Tübingen. Looking on the function of philosophy as the winning of happiness in this life and the next, he had little use for the Aristotelian logic and philosophy of nature. Strongly attracted by the Jewish Cabbala, he considered that a profound knowledge of the divine mysteries

[1] *Heptaplus*, p. 222.

is to be obtained from that source; and he combined his enthusiasm for the Cabbala with an enthusiasm for neo-Pythagorean number-mysticism. In his view Pythagoras had drawn his wisdom from Jewish sources. In other words, Reuchlin, though an eminent scholar, fell a victim to the attractions of the Cabbala and of the fantasies of number-mysticism; and in this respect he is more akin to the German theosophists and occultists of the Renaissance than to the Italian Platonists. However, he was certainly influenced by the Platonic circle at Florence and by John Pico della Mirandola, who also thought highly of Pythagoreanism, and on this account he can be mentioned in relation with Italian Platonism.

It is clear that the revived Platonism of Italy might just as well, or better, be called neo-Platonism. But the inspiration of Italian Platonism was not primarily an interest in scholarship, in distinguishing, for example, the doctrines of Plato from those of Plotinus and in critically reconstituting and interpreting their ideas. The Platonic tradition stimulated and provided a framework for the expression of the Renaissance Platonists' belief in the fullest possible development of man's higher potentialities and in their belief in Nature as the expression of the divine. But though they had a strong belief in the value and possibilities of the human personality as such they did not separate man either from God or from his fellow-men. Their humanism involved neither irreligion nor exaggerated individualism. And though they had a strong feeling for Nature and for beauty, they did not deify Nature or identify it with God. They were not pantheists. Their humanism and their feeling for Nature were characteristic of the Renaissance; but for a pantheistic view of Nature we have to turn to other phases of Renaissance thought and not to the Florentine Academy nor, in general, to Italian Platonism. Nor do we find in the Italian Platonists an individualism which discards the ideas of Christian revelation and of the Church.

CHAPTER XIV
ARISTOTELIANISM

Critics of the Aristotelian logic—Aristotelianism—Stoicism and scepticism.

1. THE Scholastic method and the Aristotelian logic were made objects of attack by a number of humanists. Thus Laurentius Valla or Lorenzo della Valle (1407-57) attacked the Aristotelian logic as an abstruse, artificial and abstract scheme which is able neither to express nor to lead to concrete and real knowledge. In his *Dialecticae disputationes contra Aristotelicos* he carried on a polemic against what he regarded as the empty abstractions of the Aristotelian-Scholastic logic and metaphysic. The Aristotelian logic, in Valla's opinion, is sophistry, depending largely on linguistic barbarism. The purpose of thought is to know things, and knowledge of things is expressed in speech, the function of words being to express in determinate form insight into the determinations of things. Many of the terms employed in the Aristotelian logic, however, do not express insight into the concrete characteristics of things, but are artificial constructions which do not express reality at all. A reform of speech is needed, and logic must be recognized as subordinate to 'rhetoric'. The orators treat all subjects much more clearly and in a profounder and sublimer manner than the confused, bloodless and dry dialecticians.[1] Rhetoric is not for Laurentius Valla simply the art of expressing ideas in beautiful or appropriate language; still less is it the art of persuading others 'rhetorically'; it denotes the linguistic expression of real insight into concrete reality.

Paying more attention to the Stoics and Epicureans than to Plato and Aristotle, Laurentius Valla maintained in his *De voluptate* that the Epicureans were right in emphasizing human striving after pleasure and happiness. But as a Christian he added that the complete happiness of man is not to be found in this life. Faith is necessary for life. For instance, man is conscious of freedom; but human freedom, according to Valla in his *De libero arbitrio*, is, as far as the natural light of reason can see, incompatible with the divine omnipotence. Their reconciliation is a mystery which must be accepted on faith.

[1] *De voluptate*, I, 10.

Laurentius Valla's ideas on logic were taken up by Rudolf Agricola (1443–85) in his *De inventione dialectica*; and a somewhat similar view was maintained by the Spanish humanist Luis Vives (1492–1540). But Vives also deserves mention for his rejection of any slavish adherence to the scientific, medical or mathematical ideas of Aristotle and for his insistence that progress in science depends on direct observation of phenomena. In his *De anima et vita* he demanded recognition of the value of observation in psychology: one should not be content with what the ancients said about the soul. He himself treated in an independent way of memory, affections, etc., and stated, for example, the principle of association.

The importance of 'rhetoric' as a general science was strongly emphasized by Marius Nizolius (1488–1566 or 1498–1576), the author of a famous *Thesaurus Ciceronianus*. In philosophical writings like the *Antibarbarus philosophicus sive de veris principiis et vera ratione philosophandi contra pseudophilosophos* he rejected all undue deference to former philosophers in favour of independence of judgment. Philosophy in the narrow sense is concerned with the characteristics of things and comprises physics and politics, while rhetoric is a general science which is concerned with the meaning and right use of words. Rhetoric thus stands to other sciences as soul to body; it is their principle. It does not mean for Nizolius the theory and art of public speaking; it is the general science of 'meaning', and it is independent of all metaphysics and ontology. Rhetoric shows, for instance, how the meaning of general words, of universal terms, is independent of, or does not demand, the objective existence of universals. The universal term expresses a mental operation by which the human mind 'comprehends' all individual members of a class. There is no abstraction, in the sense of a mental operation whereby the mind apprehends the metaphysical essence of things in the universal concept; rather does the mind express in a universal term its experience of individuals of the same class. In the deductive syllogism the mind does not reason from the general or universal to the particular but rather from the whole to the part; and in induction the mind passes from the parts to the whole rather than from particulars to the universal. In 1670 Leibniz republished Nizolius' *De veris principiis et vera ratione philosophandi contra pseudophilosophos*, praising the author's attempt to free the general forms of thought from ontological presuppositions but criticizing his inadequate notion of induction. Even if, however, Nizolius did attempt to purify logic from metaphysics and to treat it from the linguistic point of view, it seems to me that his substitution of *comprehensio* for *abstractio* and of the relation of part to whole for the relation of particular to universal contributed very little, if anything, to the discussion concerning universals. That it is individuals alone which exist would have been agreed to by all mediaeval anti-realists; but it is not enlightening to say that universals are collective terms which arise by a mental act called *comprehensio*. What is it which enables the mind to 'comprehend' groups of individuals as belonging to definite classes? Is it simply the presence of similar qualities? If this is what Nizolius meant, he cannot be said to have added anything which was not already present in terminism. But he did insist that for factual knowledge we have to go to things themselves and that it is useless to look to formal logic for information about the nature or character of things. In this way his logical views contributed to the growth of the empiricist movement.

The artificial character of the Aristotelian-Scholastic logic was also insisted on by the famous French humanist Petrus Ramus or Pierre de la Ramée (1515-72), who became a Calvinist and perished in the massacre of St. Bartholomew's Eve. True logic is a natural logic; it formulates the laws which govern man's spontaneous and natural thinking and reasoning as expressed in correct speech. It is thus the *ars disserendi* and is closely allied with rhetoric. In his *Institutionum dialecticarum libri III* Petrus Ramus divided this natural logic into two parts, the first concerning 'discovery' (*De inventione*), the second dealing with the judgment (*De iudicio*). As the function of natural logic is to enable one to answer questions concerning things, the first stage of the process of logical thought consists in discovering the points of view or categories which will enable the inquiring mind to solve the question raised. These points of view or categories (Ramus calls them *loci*) include original or underived categories like cause and effect and derived or secondary categories like genus, species, division, definition, etc. The second stage consists in applying these categories in such a way that the mind can arrive at the judgment which answers the question raised. In his treatment of the judgment Petrus Ramus distinguishes three stages; first, the syllogism; secondly, the system, the forming, that is to say, of a systematic chain of conclusions; and thirdly, the bringing of all sciences and knowledge into relation with God. Ramus' logic consisted, therefore, of two main sections, one concerning the concept, the other concerning the judgment; he had little new to offer and as his ideal was that of deductive reasoning, he was unable to make any very positive contribution to the advance of the logic of discovery. His lack of real originality did not, however, prevent his logical writings winning widespread popularity, especially in Germany, where Ramists, anti-Ramists and semi-Ramists carried on a lively controversy.

Men like Laurentius Valla, Nizolius, and Petrus Ramus were strongly influenced by their reading of the classics, especially of Cicero's writings. In comparison with Cicero's orations the logical works of Aristotle and the Scholastics seemed to them dry, abstruse and artificial. In the speeches of Cicero, on the other hand, the natural logic of the human mind was expressed in relation to concrete questions. They stressed, therefore, 'natural' logic and its close association with rhetoric or speech. They certainly contrasted the Platonic dialectic with the Aristotelian logic; but in the formation of their ideas on logic, which should be regarded as expressing a humanistic reaction against Scholasticism, Cicero was actually of greater importance than Plato. Their emphasis on rhetoric, however, coupled with the fact that they retained in practice a good deal of the outlook of the formal logician, meant that they did little to develop the method or logic of science. It is true that one of their watchwords was 'things' rather than abstract concepts; and in this respect they may be said to have encouraged the empiricist outlook; but, in general, their attitude was aesthetic rather than scientific. They were humanists, and their projected reform of logic was conceived in the interests of humanism, that is, of cultured expression and, at a deeper level, of the development of personality, rather than in the interests of empirical science.

2. Turning from the opponents of the Aristotelian-Scholastic logic to the Aristotelians themselves, one may mention first one or two scholars who promoted the study of the writings of Aristotle and opposed the Italian Platonists. George of Trebizond (1395–1484), for instance, translated and commented on a number of Aristotle's works and he attacked Plethon as the would-be founder of a new neo-Platonic pagan religion. Theodore of Gaza (1400–78), who, like George of Trebizond, became a convert to Catholicism, was also an opponent of Plethon. He translated works of Aristotle and Theophrastus; and in his ὅτι ἡ φύσις οὐ βουλεύεται he

ARISTOTELIANISM

discussed the question whether the finality which exists according to Aristotle in nature is really to be ascribed to nature. Hermolaus Barbarus (1454–93) also translated works by Aristotle and commentaries by Themistius. Aristotelian scholars of this sort were for the most part opponents of Scholasticism as well as of Platonism. In the opinion of Hermolaus Barbarus, for example, St. Albert, St. Thomas and Averroes were all philosophical 'barbarians'.

The Aristotelian camp became divided between those who interpreted Aristotle according to the mind of Averroes and those who interpreted him according to the mind of Alexander of Aphrodisias. The difference between them which most excited the attention of their contemporaries was that the Averroists maintained that there is only one immortal intellect in all men while the Alexandrists contended there is no immortal intellect in man. As both parties thus denied personal immortality they excited the hostility of the Platonists. Marsilius Ficinus, for example, declared that both parties did away with religion by denying immortality and divine providence. At the fifth Lateran Council (1512–17) the doctrines of both Averroists and Alexandrists concerning man's rational soul were condemned. In the course of time, however, the former greatly modified the theologically objectionable aspects of Averroism, which tended to become a matter of scholarship rather than of any strict adherence to Averroes's peculiar philosophical ideas.

The centre of the Averroist party was at Padua. Nicoletto Vernias, who lectured at Padua from 1471 to 1499, at first maintained the Averroistic doctrine of one immortal reason in all men; but later on he abandoned his theologically unorthodox view and defended the position that each man has an individual immortal rational soul. The same is true of Agostino Nipho or Augustinus Niphus (1473–1546), a pupil of Vernias and author of commentaries on Aristotle, who first defended the Averroistic doctrine in his *De intellectu et daemonibus* and then later abandoned it. In his *De immortalitate animae*, written in 1518 against Pomponazzi, he maintained the truth of the Thomist interpretation of Aristotle's doctrine against the interpretation given by Alexander of Aphrodisias. One may also mention Alexander Achillini (1463–1512), who taught first at Padua and afterwards at Bologna, and Marcus Antonius Zimara (1460–1532). Achillini declared that Aristotle must be corrected where he differs from the orthodox teaching of the Church, while Zimara, who commented on both Aristotle and Averroes, interpreted the latter's doctrine concerning the human intellect as referring to the unity of the most general principles of knowledge which are recognized by all men in common.

The most important figure of the Alexandrist group was Pietro Pomponazzi (1462-1525), a native of Mantua, who taught successively at Padua, Ferrara and Bologna. But if one wishes to represent Pomponazzi as a follower of Alexander of Aphrodisias, one must add that it was the Aristotelian elements of Alexander's teaching which exercised a distinctive influence on him, rather than Alexander's own developments of Aristotle's doctrine. The aim Pomponazzi seems to have had in mind was to purify Aristotle of non-Aristotelian accretions. That is why he attacked Averroism, which he regarded as a perversion of genuine Aristotelianism. Thus in his *De immortalitate animae* (1516) he takes his stand on the Aristotelian idea of the soul as the form or entelechy of the body and uses it not only against the Averroists but also against those who, like the Thomists, try to show that the human soul is naturally separable from the body and immortal. His main point is that the human soul, in its rational as in its sensitive operations, depends on the body; and in support of his argument and of the conclusion he draws from it he appeals, in accordance with Aristotle's practice, to the observable facts. This is not to say, of course, that Aristotle drew the same conclusion from the observable facts that Pomponazzi drew; but the latter followed Aristotle in appealing to empirical evidence. It was largely because of its incompatibility with the observable facts that he rejected the Averroistic hypothesis concerning the rational soul of man.

Pomponazzi argued that it is an empirically supported fact that all knowledge originates in sense-perception and that human intellection always needs an image or phantasm. In other words, even those intellectual operations which transcend the power of animals are nevertheless dependent on the body; and there is no evidence to show that while the sensitive soul of the animal is intrinsically dependent on the body man's rational soul is only extrinsically dependent. It is perfectly true that the human soul can exercise functions which the animal soul is incapable of exercising; but there is no empirical evidence to show that those higher functions of the human soul can be exercised apart from the body. The human mind, for instance, is certainly characterized by the power of self-consciousness; but it does not possess this power in the way that an independent intelligent substance would possess it, namely as a power of direct and immediate intuition of itself; the human mind knows itself only in knowing something other than itself.[1] Even the beasts enjoy some self-knowledge. 'Nor must we deny that the beasts know themselves. For it seems to be altogether stupid and irrational to say that they do not know themselves, when they love themselves and their species.'[2] Human self-consciousness transcends the rudimentary self-consciousness of the brutes; but it is none the less dependent on the soul's union with the body. Pomponazzi did not deny that intellection is itself non-quantitative and non-corporeal; on the contrary, he affirmed it;[3] but he argued that the human soul's 'participation in immateriality' does not involve its separability from the body. His main objection against the Thomists was that they in his view asserted both that the soul is and that it is not the form of the body. He considered that they did not take seriously the Aristotelian doctrine which they professed to accept; they endeavoured to have it both ways. The Platonists were at least consistent, even if they paid scant attention to the facts of psychology. Pomponazzi's own theory, however, can scarcely be considered immune from inconsistency. While rejecting a materialistic view of the rational soul,[4] he yet refused to allow that one can argue from the immaterial character of the soul's intelligent life to its capacity for existing in a state of separation from the body. Nor is it easy to understand precisely what was meant by phrases like 'participation in immateriality' or *immaterialis secundum quid*. Possibly Pomponazzi's view, if translated into more modern terms, would be that of epiphenomenalism. In any case, his main point was that investigation of the empirical facts does not permit one to state that the human soul possesses any mode of cognition or volition which it can exercise in independence of the body and that its status as form of the body precludes its natural immortality. In order to possess natural immortality its relation to the body would have to be that accepted by the Platonists, and for the truth of the Platonic theory there is no empirical evidence. To this Pomponazzi added some considerations deduced from his acceptance of the notion of a hierarchy of beings. The human rational soul stands midway in the scale; like the lower souls it is

---

[1] *De immortalitate animae*, 10; *Apologia*, 1, 3. [2] *Ibid.*
[3] *De immortalitate animae*, 9. [4] Cf. *Ibid.*, 9-10.

the form of the body, though unlike them it transcends matter in its higher operations; like the separate Intelligences it understands essences, though unlike them it can do so only in and with reference to the concrete particular.[1] It depends for its materials of knowledge on the body, though in its use of the material supplied by sense-perception it transcends matter.

The inconsistency of Pomponazzi's doctrine has been mentioned above; and I do not see how this inconsistency can be denied. It must be remembered, however, that he demanded the fulfilment of two conditions before he would recognize the soul's immortality as rationally established.[2] First of all it must be shown that the intelligence as such, in its nature as intelligence, transcends matter. Secondly it must be shown that it is independent of the body in its acquisition of the materials of knowledge. The first position Pomponazzi accepted; the second he regarded as contrary to the empirical facts. The soul's natural immortality cannot, therefore, be proved by mere reason, since, in order for it to be proved, *both* positions would have to be established.

Pomponazzi also gave consideration to the moral objections which were brought against his doctrine, namely that it was destructive of morality by denying sanctions in the future life, by confining the operation of divine justice to the present life, in which it is obviously not always fulfilled, and, most important of all, by depriving man of the possibility of attaining his last end. As regards the first point Pomponazzi argued that virtue is in itself preferable to all other things and that it is its own reward. In dying for his country or in dying rather than commit an act of injustice or sin a man gains virtue. In choosing sin or dishonour in place of death a man does not win immortality, except perhaps an immortality of shame and contempt in the mind of posterity, even if the coming of inevitable death is postponed a little longer.[3] It is true that many people would prefer dishonour or vice to death if they thought that death ended all; but this shows simply that they do not understand the true nature of virtue and vice.[4] Moreover, this is the reason why legislators and rulers have to have recourse to sanctions. In any case, says Pomponazzi, virtue is its own reward, and the essential reward (*praemium essentiale*), which is virtue itself, is diminished in proportion as the accidental reward (*praemium accidentale*, a reward extrinsic to

[1] On the human mind's knowledge of the universal, see, for example, *Apologia*, 1, 3.
[2] *De immortalitate animae*, 4. [3] *Ibid.*, 14. [4] *Ibid.*

virtue itself) is increased. This is presumably a clumsy way of saying that virtue is diminished in proportion as it is sought with a view to obtaining something other than virtue itself. In regard to the difficulty about divine justice, he asserts that no good action ever goes unrewarded and no vicious action unpunished, since virtue is its own reward and vice its own punishment.[1]

As regards the end of man or purpose of human existence, Pomponazzi insists that it is a moral end. It cannot be theoretical contemplation, which is vouchsafed to few men; nor can it consist in mechanical skill. To be a philosopher or to be a house-builder is not within the power of all;[2] but to become virtuous is within everyone's power. Moral perfection is the common end of the human race; 'for the universe would be completely preserved (*perfectissime conservaretur*) if all men were zealous and perfectly moral, but not if all were philosophers or smiths or house-builders'.[3] This moral end is sufficiently attainable within the bounds of mortal life: the idea of Kant that the attainment of the complete good of man postulates immortality was foreign to the mind of Pomponazzi. And to the argument that man has a natural desire for immortality and that this desire cannot be doomed to frustration, he answers that in so far as there is really a natural desire in man not to die, it is in no way fundamentally different from the animal's instinct to shun death, while if an elicited or intellectual desire is meant, the presence of such a desire cannot be used as an argument for immortality, for it has first to be shown that the desire is not unreasonable. One can conceive a desire for all sorts of divine privileges; but it does not follow that such a desire will be fulfilled.[4]

In his *De naturalium effectuum admirandorum causis sive de incantationibus* (generally known as the *De incantationibus*) Pomponazzi endeavours to give a natural explanation of miracles and wonders. He makes a great deal of astral influences; but his astrological explanations are, of course, naturalistic in character, even if they are erroneous. He also accepted a cyclic theory of history and historical institutions, a theory which he apparently applied even to Christianity itself. But in spite of his philosophical ideas Pomponazzi reckoned himself a true Christian. Philosophy, for example, shows that there is no evidence for the immortality of the human soul; on the contrary, it would lead us to postulate the soul's mortal character; but we know by revelation that the

---

[1] *De immortalitate animae*, 13-14.   [2] *Ibid.*, 14.   [3] *Ibid.*   [4] *Ibid.*, 10.

human soul is immortal. As already mentioned, Pomponazzi's doctrine concerning the soul's mortality was condemned at the fifth Lateran Council and he was attacked in writing by Niphus and others; but he was never involved in any more serious trouble.

Simon Porta of Naples (d. 1555), in his *De rerum naturalibus principiis, De anima et mente humana*, followed Pomponazzi's doctrine concerning the mortality of the human soul; but not all the latter's disciples did so. And we have seen that the Averroist school also tended to modify its original position. Finally we find a group of Aristotelians who can be classified neither as Averroists nor as Alexandrists. Thus Andrew Cesalpino (1519-1603) tried to reconcile the two parties. He is perhaps chiefly remarkable for his botanical work; in 1583 he published a *De plantis libri XVI*. Jacobus Zabarella (1532-89), though a devoted Aristotelian, left many important questions undecided. For instance, if one accepts the eternity of motion and of the world, one can accept an eternal first mover; but if one denies the eternity of motion and of the world, one has no adequate philosophical reason for accepting an eternal first mover. In any case it cannot be demonstrated that the heaven itself is not the supreme being. Similarly, if one regards the soul's nature as form of the body, one will judge it to be mortal; but if one regards its intellectual operations, one will see that it transcends matter. On the other hand, the active intellect is God Himself, using the human passive intellect as an instrument, and the question whether the human soul is immortal or not is left undecided as far as philosophy is concerned. Zabarella was succeeded in his chair at Padua by Caesar Cremoninus (1550-1631) who also refused to allow that one can argue with certainty from the movement of the heaven to the existence of God as mover. In other words the idea of Nature as a more or less independent system was gaining ground; and, indeed, Cremoninus insisted on the autonomy of physical science. He based his own scientific ideas, however, on those of Aristotle and rejected the newer ideas in physics, including the Copernican astronomy. He is said to have been the friend of Galileo who refused to look through a telescope in case he should find it necessary to abandon the Aristotelian astronomy.

The influence of Pomponazzi was strongly felt by Lucilius Vanini (1585-1619), who was strangled and burnt as a heretic at Toulouse. He was the author of an *Amphitheatrum aeternae providentiae* (1615) and of a *De admirandis naturae reginae deaeque mortalium arcanis libri quatuor* (1616). He seems to have embraced a kind of pantheism, though he was accused of atheism, which he was said to have dissembled in his first work.

Apart from the work done by scholars in connection with the text of Aristotle, it cannot, I think, be said that the Aristotelians of the Renaissance contributed much that was valuable to philosophy. In the case of Pomponazzi and kindred figures they may be said to have encouraged a 'naturalistic' outlook; but the growth of the new physics can scarcely be attributed to the influence of the Aristotelians. It was made possible very largely by mathematical developments, and it grew in spite of, rather than because of, the Aristotelians.

In northern Europe Philip Melanchthon (1497–1560), although an associate and collaborator of Martin Luther, who was a determined enemy of Scholastic Aristotelianism, distinguished himself as a humanist. Educated in the spirit of the humanistic movement, he then fell under Luther's influence and rejected humanism; but the fact that this narrowness of outlook did not last very long shows that he was always a humanist at heart. He became the leading humanist of the early Protestant movement and was known as the *Praeceptor Germaniae* because of his educational work. For the philosophy of Aristotle he had a lively admiration, though as a thinker he was somewhat eclectic, his ideal being that of moral progress through the study of classical writers and of the Gospels. He had little interest in metaphysics, and his idea of logic, as given in his logical text-books, was influenced by that of Rudolf Agricola. Aristotle he interpreted in a nominalistic sense; and, though he freely utilized Aristotle in his *Commentarius de anima* (in which ideas drawn indirectly from Galen also make their appearance) and in his *Philosophiae moralis epitome* and *Ethicae doctrinae elementa*, he endeavoured to bring Aristotelianism into harmony with revelation and to supplement it by Christian teaching. A salient aspect of Melanchthon's teaching was his doctrine of innate principles, particularly moral principles, and of the innate character of the idea of God, both of which are intuited by means of the *lumen naturale*. This doctrine was opposed to the Aristotelian view of the mind as a *tabula rasa*.

Melanchthon's utilization of Aristotle was influential in the Lutheran universities, though it did not commend itself to all Protestant thinkers, and there occurred some lively disputes, among which may be mentioned the week's debate at Weimar in

1560 between Flacius and Strigel on freedom of the will. Melanchthon maintained the freedom of the will; but Flacius (Illyricus) considered that this doctrine, supported by Strigel, was at variance with the true theory of original sin. In spite of Melanchthon's great influence there was always a certain tension between rigid Protestant theology and the Aristotelian philosophy. Luther himself did not deny all human freedom; but he did not consider that the freedom left to man after the Fall is sufficient to enable him to achieve moral reform. It was only natural, then, that controversy should arise between those who deemed themselves genuine disciples of Luther and those who followed Melanchthon in his Aristotelianism, which was somewhat of a strange bedfellow for orthodox Lutheranism. In addition, of course, there were, as has been mentioned earlier, the disputes between the Ramists, anti-Ramists and semi-Ramists.

3. Among other revivers of ancient philosophical traditions one may mention Justus Lipsius (1547–1606), author of a *Manuductio ad stoicam philosophiam* and a *Physiologia Stoicorum*, who revived Stoicism, and the famous French man of letters, Michel de Montaigne (1533–92), who revived Pyrrhonic scepticism. In his *Essais* Montaigne revived the ancient arguments for scepticism; the relativity of sense-experience, the impossibility of the intellect's rising above this relativity to the sure attainment of absolute truth, the constant change in both object and subject, the relativity of value-judgments, and so on. Man is, in fine, a poor sort of creature whose boasted superiority to the animals is, to a great extent, a vain and hollow pretension. He should, therefore, submit himself to divine revelation, which alone gives certainty. At the same time Montaigne came to attribute considerable importance to the idea of 'nature'. Nature gives to each man a dominant type of character which is fundamentally unchangeable; and the task of moral education is to awaken and preserve the spontaneity and originality of this endowment of nature rather than to attempt to mould it into a stereotyped pattern by the methods of Scholasticism. But Montaigne was no revolutionary; he thought rather that the form of life embodied in the social and political structure of one's country represents a law of nature to which one should submit oneself. The same is true of religion. The theoretical basis of any given religion cannot be rationally established; but the moral consciousness and obedience to nature form the heart of religion, and these will only be

injured by religious anarchy. In this practical conservatism Montaigne was, of course, faithful to the spirit of Pyrrhonic scepticism, which found in the consciousness of one's ignorance an added reason for adhering to traditional social, political and religious forms. A sceptical attitude in regard to metaphysics in general might seem calculated to lead to an emphasis on empirical science; but, as far as Montaigne himself was concerned, his scepticism was rather that of a cultivated man of letters, though he was influenced too by the moral ideal of Socrates and by the Stoic ideals of tranquillity and of obedience to nature.

Among Montaigne's friends was Pierre Charron (1541–1603), who became a lawyer and later a priest. In his *Trois vérités contre tous les athées, idolâtres, juifs, Mohamétans, hérétiques et schismatiques* (1593) he maintained that the existence of one God, the truth of the Christian religion and the truth of Catholicism in particular are three proved truths; but in his main work, *De la sagesse* (1601), he adopted from Montaigne a sceptical position, though he modified it in the second edition. Man is unable to reach certainty concerning metaphysical and theological truths; but human self-knowledge, which reveals to us our ignorance, reveals to us also our possession of a free will by which we can win moral independence and dominion over the passions. The recognition and realization of the moral ideal is true wisdom, and this true wisdom is independent of dogmatic religion. 'I desire that one should be a good man without paradise and hell; these words are, in my view, horrible and abominable, "if I were not a Christian, if I did not fear God and damnation, I should do this or that".'[1]

Another Pyrrhonist was Francis Sanchez (c. 1552–1632), a Portuguese by birth, who studied at Bordeaux and in Italy and taught medicine first at Montpellier and afterwards at Toulouse. In his *Quod nihil scitur*, which appeared in 1580, Sanchez maintained that the human being can know nothing, if the word 'know' is understood in its full sense, that is to say, as referring to the perfect ideal of knowledge. God alone, who has created all things, knows all things. Human knowledge is based either on sense-perception or on introspection. The former is not reliable, while the latter, though assuring us of the existence of the self, can give no clear idea of it; our knowledge of the self is indefinite and indeterminate. Introspection gives us no picture of the self, and without a picture or image we can have no clear idea. On the other hand

[1] *De la sagesse*, 2, 5, 29.

though sense-perception provides us with definite images, these images are far from giving a perfect knowledge of things. Moreover, as the multiplicity of things forms a unified system, no one thing can be perfectly known unless the whole system is known; and this we cannot know.

But though Sanchez denied that the human mind can attain perfect knowledge of anything, he insisted that it can attain an approximate knowledge of some things and that the way to do so is through observation rather than through the Aristotelian-Scholastic logic. The latter makes use of definitions which are purely verbal, and syllogistic demonstration presupposes principles the truth of which is by no means clear. Of the leading sceptics Sanchez probably came nearest to anticipating the direction which philosophy and science were to take; but he was prevented by his sceptical attitude from making positive and constructive suggestions. For example, his strictures on the old deductive logic would lead one to expect a clear emphasis on the empirical investigation of nature; but his sceptical attitude in regard to sense-perception was a hindrance to his making any valuable positive contribution to the development of natural philosophy. The scepticism of these Renaissance thinkers was doubtless a symptom of the period of transition between mediaeval thought and the constructive systems of the 'modern' era; but in itself it was a blind alley.

CHAPTER XV

NICHOLAS OF CUSA

Life and works—The influence of Nicholas's leading idea on his practical activity—The coincidentia oppositorum—*'Instructed ignorance'—The relation of God to the world—The 'infinity' of the world—The world-system and the soul of the world—Man, the microcosm; Christ—Nicholas's philosophical affiliations.*

1. NICHOLAS OF CUSA is not an easy figure to classify. His philosophy is frequently included under the heading 'mediaeval philosophy', and there are, of course, some good reasons for doing this. The background of his thought was formed by the doctrines of Catholicism and by the Scholastic tradition, and he was undoubtedly strongly influenced by a number of mediaeval thinkers. It was possible, then, for Maurice De Wulf to say of him, when outlining his ideas in the third volume of his history of mediaeval philosophy, that 'in spite of his audacious theories he is only a continuer of the past',[1] and that he 'remains a mediaeval and a Scholastic'.[2] On the other hand, Nicholas lived in the fifteenth century and for some thirty years his life overlapped that of Marsilius Ficinus. Moreover, although one can emphasize the traditional elements in his philosophy and push him back, as it were, into the Middle Ages, one can equally well emphasize the forward-looking elements of his thought and associate him with the beginnings of 'modern' philosophy. But it seems to me preferable to see in him a transition-thinker, a philosopher of the Renaissance, who combined the old with the new. To treat him simply as a mediaeval thinker seems to me to involve the neglect of those elements in his philosophy which have clear affinities with the philosophical movements of thought at the time of the Renaissance and those elements which reappear at a later date in the system of a thinker like Leibniz. Yet even if one decides to classify Nicholas of Cusa as a Renaissance philosopher, there still remains the difficulty of deciding to which Renaissance current of thought his philosophy should be assigned. Is he to be associated with the Platonists on the ground that he was influenced by the neo-Platonic tradition? Or does his view of Nature as in some

[1] p. 207.   [2] p. 211.

sense 'infinite' suggest rather that he should be associated with a philosopher like Giordano Bruno? There are doubtless grounds for calling him a Platonist, if one understands the term in a sufficiently generous way; but it would be peculiar if one included him in the same chapter as the Italian Platonists. And there are doubtless grounds for calling him a philosopher of Nature; but he was before all things a Christian, and he was no pantheist like Bruno. He in no way deified Nature. And he cannot be classified with the scientists, even if he was interested in mathematics. I have therefore adopted the solution of giving him a chapter to himself. And this is, in my opinion, what he deserves. Though having many affiliations, he stands more or less by himself.

Nicholas Kryfts or Krebs was born at Cusa on the Moselle in 1401. Educated as a boy by the Brothers of the Common Life at Deventer, he subsequently studied at the universities of Heidelberg (1416) and Padua (1417–23) and received the doctorate in Canon Law. Ordained priest in 1426, he took up a post at Coblenz; but in 1432 he was sent to the Council of Basle on the business of the Count von Manderscheid, who wanted to become bishop of Trier. Becoming involved in the deliberations of the Council, Nicholas showed himself a moderate adherent of the conciliar party. Later, however, he changed his attitude to the position of the papacy and fulfilled a number of missions on behalf of the Holy See. For example, he went to Byzantium in connection with the negotiations for the reunion of the Eastern Church with Rome, which was accomplished (temporarily) at the Council of Florence. In 1448 he was created cardinal and in 1450 he was appointed to the bishopric of Brixen, while from 1451 to 1452 he acted as Papal Legate in Germany. He died in the August of 1464 at Todi in Umbria.

In spite of his ecclesiastical activities Nicholas wrote a considerable number of works, of which the first important one was the *De concordantia catholica* (1433–4). His philosophical writings include the *De docta ignorantia* and the *De coniecturis* (1440), the *De Deo abscondito* (1444) and the *De quaerendo Deum* (1445), the *De Genesi* (1447), the *Apologia doctae ignorantiae* (1449), the *Idiotae libri* (1450), the *De visione Dei* (1453), the *De possest* (1460), the *Tetralogus de non aliud* (1462), the *De venatione sapientiae* (1463) and the *De apice theoriae* (1464). In addition he composed works on mathematical subjects, like the *De transmutationibus geometricis* (1450), the *De mathematicis complementis* (1453) and the *De mathematica perfectione* (1458), and on theological subjects.

2. The thought of Nicholas of Cusa was governed by the idea of unity as the harmonious synthesis of differences. On the metaphysical plane this idea is presented in his idea of God as the *coincidentia oppositorum*, the synthesis of opposites, which transcends and yet includes the distinct perfections of creatures. But the idea of unity as the harmonious reconciliation or synthesis of opposites was not confined to the field of speculative philosophy: it exercised a powerful influence on Nicholas's practical activity, and it goes a long way towards explaining his change of front in regard to the position in the Church of the Holy See. I think that it is worth while to show how this is the case.

At the time when Nicholas went to the Council of Basle and published his *De concordantia catholica* he saw the unity of Christendom threatened, and he was inspired by the ideal of preserving that unity. In common with a number of other sincere Catholics he believed that the best way of preserving or restoring that unity lay in emphasizing the position and rights of General Councils. Like other members of the conciliar party, he was encouraged in this belief by the part played by the Council of Constance (1414–18) in putting an end to the Great Schism which had divided Christendom and caused so much scandal. He was convinced at that time of the natural rights of popular sovereignty not only in the State but also in the Church; and, indeed, despotism and anarchy were always abhorrent to him. In the State the monarch does not receive his authority directly and immediately from God, but rather from or through the people. In the Church, he thought, a General Council, representing the faithful, is superior to the pope, who possesses only an administrative primacy and may for adequate reasons be deposed by a Council. Though he maintained the idea of the empire, his ideal was not that of a monolithic empire which would override or annul the rights and duties of national monarchs and princes: it was rather that of a federation. In an analogous manner, though he was a passionate believer in the unity of the Church, he believed that the cause of this unity would be better served by a moderate conciliar theory than by an insistence on the supreme position of the Holy See. By saying this I do not mean to imply that Nicholas did not at that time believe that the conciliar theory was theoretically justified or that he supported it only for practical reasons, because he considered that the Church's unity would thus be best preserved and that ecclesiastical reform would stand a better chance of being realized if the supremacy of General Councils was recognized. But these practical considerations certainly weighed with him. Moreover, a 'democratic' view of the Church as a harmonious unity in multiplicity, expressed juridically in the conciliar theory, undoubtedly possessed a strong attraction for him. He aimed at unity in the Church and in the State and between Church and State; but the unity at which he aimed, whether in the Church or in the State, or between Church and State, was not a unity resulting from the annulment of differences.

Nicholas came to abandon the conciliar theory and to act as a champion of the Holy See. This change of view was certainly the expression of a change in his theoretical convictions concerning the papacy as a divine institution possessing supreme ecclesiastical authority and jurisdiction. But at the same time he was certainly influenced by the conviction that the cause which he had at heart, namely the unity of the Church, would not in fact be promoted by belittling the position of the pope in the Church. He came to think that an effective implementation of the conciliar theory would be more likely to result in another schism than in unity, and he came to look on the supreme position of the Holy See as the expression of the essential unity of the Church. All the limited authorities in the Church receive their authority from the absolute or sovereign authority, the Holy See, in a manner analogous to the way in which finite, limited beings receive their being from the absolute infinite, God.

This change of view did not involve the acceptance of extravagant theories, like those of Giles of Rome. Nicholas did not envisage, for example, the subordination of State to Church, but rather a harmonious and peaceful relation between the two powers. It was always at reconciliation, harmony, unity in difference that he aimed. In this ideal of unity without suppression of differences he is akin to Leibniz. It is true that Nicholas's attempts to secure harmonious unity were by no means always successful. His attempts to secure harmony in his own diocese were not altogether felicitous; and the reunion of the Eastern Church with Rome, in which he co-operated, was of brief duration. But Leibniz's somewhat unpractical, and sometimes indeed superficial, plans and ideals of unity were also unrealized in practice.

3. God is, for Nicholas, the *coincidentia oppositorum*, the synthesis of opposites in a unique and absolutely infinite being. Finite things are multiple and distinct, possessing their different natures and qualities while God transcends all the distinctions and oppositions which are found in creatures. But God transcends these distinctions and oppositions by uniting them in Himself in an incomprehensible manner. The distinction of essence and existence, for example, which is found in all creatures, cannot be in God as a distinction: in the actual infinite, essence and existence coincide and are one. Again, in creatures we distinguish greatness and smallness, and we speak of them as possessing attributes in different degrees, as being more or less this or that. But in God all these distinctions coincide. If we say that God is the greatest being (*maximum*), we must also say that He is the least being (*minimum*), for God cannot possess size or what we ordinarily call 'greatness'. In Him *maximum* and *minimum* coincide.[1] But we cannot comprehend this synthesis of distinctions and oppositions. If we say that God is the *complicatio oppositorum et eorum coincidentia*,[2] we must realize that we cannot have a positive understanding of what this means. We come to know a finite thing by bringing it into relation to or comparing it with the already known: we come to know a thing by means of comparison, similarity, dissimilarity and distinction. But God, being infinite, is like to no finite thing; and to apply definite predicates to God is to liken Him to things and to bring Him into a relation of similarity with them. In reality the distinct predicates which we apply to finite things coincide in God in a manner which surpasses our knowledge.

4. It is clear, then, that Nicholas of Cusa laid emphasis on the *via negativa*, the way of negation in our intellectual approach to God. If the process of getting to know or becoming acquainted with a thing involves bringing the hitherto unknown thing into relation with, or comparing it with, the already known, and if God is unlike every creature, it follows that the discursive reason cannot penetrate God's nature. We know of God what He is not rather than what He is. In regard, therefore, to positive knowledge of the divine nature our minds are in a state of 'ignorance'. On the other hand, this 'ignorance' of which Nicholas speaks is not the ignorance of someone who has no knowledge of God or who has never made the effort to understand what God is. It is, of course, the result of human psychology and of the limitations

[1] *De docta ignorantia*, 1, 4.   [2] *Ibid.*, 2, 1.

which necessarily affect a finite mind when confronted by an infinite object which is not an empirically given object. But, in order to possess a real value it must be apprehended as the result of these factors, or at any rate as the result of the infinity of God and the finitude of the human mind. The 'ignorance' in question is not the result of a refusal to make an intellectual effort or of religious indifference: it proceeds from the realization of God's infinity and transcendence. It is thus 'learned' or 'instructed ignorance'. Hence the title of Nicholas's most famous work, *De docta ignorantia*.

It may appear inconsistent to stress the 'negative way' and at the same time to affirm positively that God is the *coincidentia oppositorum*. But Nicholas did not reject the 'affirmative way' altogether. For example, since God transcends the sphere of numbers He cannot be called 'one' in the sense in which a finite thing, as distinct from other finite things, is called 'one'. On the other hand, God is the infinite Being and the source of all multiplicity in the created world; and as such He is the infinite unity. But we cannot have a positive understanding of what this unity is in itself. We do make positive affirmations about God, and we are justified in doing so; but there is no positive affirmation about the divine nature which does not need to be qualified by a negation. If we think of God in terms simply of ideas drawn from creatures our notion of Him is less adequate than the realization that He transcends all our concepts of Him: negative theology is superior to positive or affirmative theology. Superior to both, however, is 'copulative' theology by which God is apprehended as the *coincidentia oppositorum*. God is rightly recognized as the supreme and absolutely greatest Being: He cannot be greater than He is. And as the greatest Being He is perfect unity.[1] But we can also say of God that He cannot be smaller than He is. We can say, therefore, that He is the *minimum*. In fact, He is both the greatest and the smallest in a perfect *coincidentia oppositorum*. All theology is 'circular', in the sense that the attributes which we rightly predicate of God coincide in the divine essence in a manner which surpasses the understanding of the human mind.[2]

The lowest stage of human knowledge is sense-perception. The senses by themselves simply affirm. It is when we come to the level of reason (*ratio*) that there is both affirmation and denial. The discursive reason is governed by the principle of contradiction,

---

[1] *De docta ignorantia*, 1, 5.   [2] *Ibid.*, 1, 21.

the principle of the incompatibility or mutual exclusion of opposites; and the activity of the reason cannot bring us to anything more than an approximate knowledge of God. In accordance with his fondness for mathematical analogies Nicholas compares the reason's knowledge of God to a polygon inscribed in a circle. However many sides one adds to the polygon it will not coincide with the circle, even though it may approximate more and more to doing so. What is more, our knowledge of creatures also is only approximate, for their 'truth' is hidden in God. In fine, all knowledge by means of the discursive reason is approximate, and all science is 'conjecture'.[1] This theory of knowledge was developed in the *De coniecturis*; and Nicholas explained that the highest possible natural knowledge of God is attained not by discursive reasoning (*ratio*) but by intellect (*intellectus*), a superior activity of the mind. Whereas sense-perception affirms and reason affirms and denies, intellect denies the oppositions of reason. Reason affirms X and denies Y, but intellect denies X and Y both disjunctively and together; it apprehends God as the *coincidentia oppositorum*. This apprehension or intuition cannot, however, be properly stated in language, which is the instrument of reason rather than of intellect. In its activity as intellect the mind uses language to suggest meaning rather than to state it; and Nicholas employs mathematical analogies and symbols for this purpose. For example, if one side of a triangle is extended to infinity, the other two sides will coincide with it. Again, if the diameter of a circle is extended to infinity the circumference will coincide in the end with the diameter. The infinite straight line is thus at the same time a triangle and a circle. Needless to say, Nicholas regarded these mathematical speculations as no more than symbols; the mathematical infinite and the absolutely infinite being are not the same, though the former can both serve as a symbol for the latter and constitute an aid to thought in metaphysical theology.[2]

The leading ideas of the *De docta ignorantia* were resumed in the writings which compose the *Idiotae*, and in the *De venatione sapientiae* Nicholas reaffirmed his belief in the idea of 'learned' or 'instructed ignorance'. In this work he reaffirmed also the doctrine contained in the *De non aliud*. God cannot be defined by other terms: He is His own definition. Again, God is not other than anything else, for He defines everything else, in the sense that He alone is the source and conserver of the existence of all things.[3] Nicholas

[1] *De docta ignorantia*, 1, 3.   [2] *Ibid.*, 1, 12.   [3] *De venatione sapientiae*, 14.

also reaffirmed the central idea which he had developed in the *De possest*. 'God alone is *Possest*, because He is in act what He can be.'[1] He is eternal act. This idea he took up again in the *De apice theoriae*, his last work, in which God is represented as *posse ipsum*, the absolute power which reveals itself in creatures. The emphasis laid on this idea has suggested to students of Nicholas's works a change of view on the part of the author. And there is, indeed, a good deal to be said in favour of this interpretation. Nicholas says expressly in *De apice theoriae* that he once thought that the truth about God is found better in darkness or obscurity than in clarity and he adds that the idea of *posse*, of power or being able, is easy to understand. What boy or youth is ignorant of the nature of *posse*, when he knows very well that he can eat, run and speak? And if he were asked whether he could do anything, carry a stone, for example, without the power to do so, he would judge such a question to be entirely superfluous. Now, God is the absolute *posse ipsum*. It would appear, then, that Nicholas felt the need of counterbalancing the negative theology on which he had formerly laid such stress. And we may say perhaps that the idea of *posse*, together with other positive ideas like that of light, of which he made use in his natural theology, expressed his conviction of the divine immanence, while the emphasis on negative theology represented rather his belief in the divine transcendence. But it would be wrong to suggest that Nicholas abandoned the negative for the affirmative way. He makes it quite clear in his last work that the divine *posse ipsum* is in itself incomprehensible and that it is incommensurable with created power. In the *Compendium*,[2] which he wrote a year before the *De apice theoriae*, Nicholas says that the incomprehensible Being, while remaining always the same, shows Himself in a variety of ways, in a variety of 'signs'. It is as though one face appeared in different ways in a number of mirrors. The face is one and the same, but its appearances, which are all distinct from itself, are various. Nicholas may have described the divine nature in various ways, and he may very well have thought that he had overdone the way of negation; but it does not seem that there was any fundamental change in his point of view. God was always for him transcendent, infinite and incomprehensible, even though He was also immanent and even though Nicholas may have come to see the desirability of bringing this aspect of God into greater prominence.

[1] *De venatione sapientiae*, 13.   [2] 8.

5. In speaking of the relation between God and the world Nicholas used phrases which have suggested to some readers a pantheistic interpretation. God contains all things; He is *omnia complicans*. All things are contained in the divine simplicity, and without Him they are nothing. God is also *omnia explicans*, the source of the multiple things which reveal something of Him. *Deus ergo est omnia complicans, in hoc quod omnia in eo; est omnia explicans, in hoc quia ipse in omnibus.*[1] But Nicholas protested that he was no pantheist. God contains all things in that He is the cause of all things: He contains them *complicative*, as one in His divine and simple essence. He is in all things *explicative*, in the sense that He is immanent in all things and that all things are essentially dependent on Him. When he states that God is both the centre and the circumference of the world[2] he is to be interpreted neither in a pantheistic nor in an acosmistic sense. The world is not, says Nicholas, a limited sphere with a definite centre and circumference. Any point can be taken and considered as the world's centre, and it has no circumference. God, then, can be called the centre of the world in view of the fact that He is everywhere or omnipresent and the circumference of the world in that He is nowhere, that is, by local presence. Nicholas was certainly influenced by writers like John Scotus Eriugena, and he employed the same type of bold phrases and statements which Meister Eckhart had employed. But in spite of a strong tendency to acosmism, as far as the literal meaning of some of his statements is concerned, it is clear that he insisted strongly on the distinction between the finite creature and the infinite Godhead.

In phrases which recall to mind the doctrine of John Scotus Eriugena Nicholas explains that the world is a theophany, a 'contraction' of the divine being. The universe is the *contractum maximum* which came into existence through emanation from the *absolutum maximum*.[3] Every creature is, as it were, a created God or God created (*quasi Deus creatus*).[4] Nicholas even goes so far as to say that God is the absolute essence of the world or universe, and that the universe is that very essence in a state of 'contraction' (*Est enim Deus quidditas absoluta mundi seu universi. Universum vero est ipsa quidditas contracta*).[5] Similarly, in the *De coniecturis*[6] Nicholas declares that to say that God is in the world is also to say that the world is in God, while in the *De visione Dei*[7] he speaks of

---

[1] *De docta ignorantia*, 2, 3.   [2] *Ibid.*, 2, 11.   [3] *Ibid.*, 2, 4.
[4] *Ibid.*, 2, 2.   [5] *Ibid.*, 2, 4.   [6] 2, 7.   [7] 12.

God as invisible in Himself but visible *uti creatura est*. Statements of this sort certainly lend themselves to a pantheistic interpretation; but Nicholas makes it clear on occasion that it is a mistake to interpret them in this way. For example, in the *De coniecturis*[1] he asserts that 'man is God, but not absolutely, since he is man. He is therefore a human God (*humanus est igitur Deus*).' He goes on to assert that 'man is also the world' and explains that man is the microcosm or 'a certain human world'. His statements are bold, it is true; but by saying that man is God, though not absolutely, he does not appear to mean more than other writers meant when they called man the image of God. It is clear that Nicholas was deeply convinced of the world's nothingness apart from God and of its relation to God as a mirror of the divine. The world is the *infinitas contracta* and the *contracta unitas*.[2] But this does not mean that the world is God in a literal sense; and in the *Apologia doctae ignorantiae* Nicholas explicitly rejects the charge of pantheism. In the *explicatio Dei* or creation of the world unity is 'contracted' into plurality, infinity into finitude, simplicity into composition, eternity into succession, necessity into possibility.[3] On the plane of creation the divine infinity expresses or reveals itself in the multiplicity of finite things, while the divine eternity expresses or reveals itself in temporal succession. The relation of creatures to the Creator surpasses our understanding; but Nicholas, according to his wont, frequently provides analogies from geometry and arithmetic, which, he believed, made things a bit clearer.

6. But though the world consists of finite things it is in a sense infinite. For example, the world is endless or indeterminate in respect of time. Nicholas agrees with Plato that time is the image of eternity,[4] and he insists that since before creation there was no time we must say that time proceeded from eternity. And if time proceeded from eternity it participates in eternity. 'I do not think that anyone who understands denies that the world is eternal, although it is not eternity.'[5] 'Thus the world is eternal because it comes from eternity and not from time. But the name "eternal" belongs much more to the world than to time since the duration of the world does not depend on time. For if the motion of the heaven and time, which is the measure of motion, were to cease, the world would not cease to exist.'[6] Nicholas thus makes a distinction between time and duration, though he does not develop the

---

[1] 2, 14. [2] *De docta ignorantia*, 2, 4. [3] *Ibid.*
[4] *De venatione sapientiae*, 9. [5] *De ludo globi*, 1. [6] *Ibid.*

NICHOLAS OF CUSA

theme. Time is the measure of motion, and it is thus the instrument of the measuring mind and depends on the mind.[1] If motion disappeared, there would be no time; but there would still be duration. Successive duration is the copy or image of the absolute duration which is eternity. We can conceive eternity only as endless duration. The duration of the world is thus the image of the divine eternity and can be called in some sense 'infinite'. This is a curious line of argument, and it is not easy to see precisely what is meant; but presumably Nicholas meant, in part at least, that the world's duration is potentially endless. It is not the absolute eternity of God, but it has not of itself any necessary limits.

The universe is one, unbounded by any other universe. It is, therefore, in some sense spatially 'infinite'. It is without any fixed centre, and there is no point which one could not choose to regard as the world's centre. There is, of course, no absolute 'up' or 'down' either. The earth is neither the centre of the world nor its lowest and least honourable part; nor has the sun any privileged position. Our judgments in these matters are relative. Everything in the universe moves, and so does the earth. 'The earth, which cannot be the centre, cannot be without any motion.'[2] It is smaller than the sun, but it is larger than the moon, as we know from observation of eclipses.[3] Nicholas does not appear to say explicitly that the earth rotates round the sun, but he makes it clear that both the sun and the earth move, together with all the other bodies, though their velocities are not the same. The fact that we do not perceive the earth's motion is no valid argument against its motion. We perceive motion only in relation to fixed points; and if a man in a boat on a river were unable to see the banks and did not know that the water itself was moving he would imagine that the boat was stationary.[4] A man stationed on the earth may think that the earth is stationary and that the other heavenly bodies are in motion, but if he were on the sun or the moon or Mars he would think the same of the body on which he was stationed.[5] Our judgments about motion are relative: we cannot attain 'absolute truth' in these astronomical matters. In order to compare the movements of the heavenly bodies we have to do so in relation to selected fixed points; but there are no fixed points in actuality. We can, therefore, attain only an approximate or relative knowledge in astronomy.

[1] *De ludo globi*, 2.   [2] *De docta ignorantia*, 2, 11.   [3] *Ibid.*, 2, 12.
[4] *Ibid.*   [5] *Ibid.*

7. The idea of a hierarchy of levels of reality from matter, through organisms, animals and man, up to pure spirits was a leading feature both of Aristotelianism and of the Platonic tradition. But Nicholas, while retaining this idea, laid particular emphasis on the individual thing as a unique manifestation of God. In the first place, no two individual things are exactly alike. By saying this Nicholas did not mean to deny the reality of species. The Peripatetics, he says,[1] are right in saying that universals do not actually exist: only individual things exist, and universals as such belong to the conceptual order. None the less members of a species have a common specific nature which exists in each of them in a 'contracted' state, that is to say, as an individual nature.[2] No individual thing, however, realizes fully the perfection of its species; and each member of a species has its own distinct characteristics.[3]

In the second place, each individual thing mirrors the whole universe. Every existent thing 'contracts' all other things, so that the universe exists *contracte* in every finite thing.[4] Moreover, as God is in the universe and the universe in God, and as the universe is in each thing, to say that everything is in each thing is also to say that God is in each thing and each thing in God. In other words, the universe is a 'contraction' of the divine being, and each finite thing is a 'contraction' of the universe.

The world is therefore a harmonious system. It consists of a multiplicity of finite things; but its members are so related to one another and to the whole that there is a 'unity in plurality'.[5] The one universe is the unfolding of the absolute and simple divine unity, and the whole universe is reflected or mirrored in each individual part. According to Nicholas, there is a soul of the world (*anima mundi*); but he rejects the Platonic view of this soul. It is not an actually existent being distinct from God on the one hand and from the finite things in the world on the other hand. If the soul of the world is regarded as a universal form containing in itself all forms, it has no separate existence of its own. The forms exist actually in the divine Word, as identical with the divine Word, and they exist in things *contracte*,[6] that is, as the individual forms of things. Nicholas evidently understood the Platonists as teaching that universal forms exist in a soul of the world, which is distinct from God, and this view he rejected. In

---

[1] *De docta ignorantia*, 2, 6. [2] *Ibid.*; cf. *De coniecturis*, 21, 3.
[3] *De docta ignorantia*, 3, 1. [4] *Ibid.*, 2, 5. [5] *Ibid.*, 2, 6. [6] *Ibid.*, 2, 9.

the *Idiotae*[1] he says that what Plato called the 'soul of the world' Aristotle called 'nature', and he adds that in his opinion the 'soul of the world' or 'nature' is God, 'who works all things in all things'. It is clear, then, that although Nicholas borrowed from Platonism the phrase 'soul of the world' he did not understand by this an existent being distinct from God and intermediate between God and the world. In his cosmology there is no intermediary stage in creation between the actual infinite, God, and the potential infinite, the created world.

8. Although each finite thing mirrors the whole universe, this is particularly true of man who combines in himself matter, organic life, sensitive animal life and spiritual rationality. Man is the microcosm, a little world, embracing in himself the intellectual and material spheres of reality.[2] 'We cannot deny that man is called the microcosm, that is, a little world'; and just as the great world, the universe, has its soul, so has man his soul.[3] The universe is mirrored in every part, and this is true analogously of man, who is the little universe or world. The nature of man is mirrored in a part like the hand, but it is mirrored more perfectly in the head. So the universe, though mirrored in every part, is mirrored more perfectly in man. Therefore man can be called a 'perfect world, although he is a little world and a part of the great world'.[4] In fact, as uniting in himself attributes which are found separately in other beings man is a finite representation of the divine *coincidentia oppositorum*.

The universe is the *concretum maximum*, while God is the *absolutum maximum*, absolute greatness. But the universe does not exist apart from individual things; and no individual thing embodies all the perfections of its species. The absolute greatness is thus never fully 'contracted' or rendered 'concrete'. We can conceive, however, a *maximum contractum* or *concretum* which would unite in itself not only the various levels of created existence, as man does, but also the Godhead itself together with created nature, though this union 'would exceed all our understanding'.[5] But though the mode of union is a mystery, we know that in Christ divine and human nature have been united without confusion of natures or distinction of persons. Christ, then, is the *maximum concretum*. He is also the *medium absolutum*, not only in the sense that in Him there is a unique and perfect union of the

---

[1] 3, 13.   [2] *De docta ignorantia*, 3, 3.   [3] *De ludo globi*, 1.
[4] *Ibid*.   [5] *De docta ignorantia*, 3, 2.

uncreated and the created, of the divine and human nature, but also in the sense that He is the unique and necessary means by which human beings can be united to God.[1] Without Christ it is impossible for man to achieve eternal happiness. He is the ultimate perfection of the universe,[2] and in particular of man, who can realize his highest potentialities only through incorporation with Christ. And we cannot be incorporated with Christ or transformed into His image save through the Church, which is His body.[3] The *Dialogus de pace seu concordantia fidei* shows that Nicholas was by no means narrow in his outlook and that he was quite prepared for concessions to the Eastern Church for the sake of unity; but his works in general by no means suggest that he favoured sacrificing the integrity of the Catholic faith in order to obtain external unity, profoundly concerned though he was about unity and deeply conscious of the fact that such unity could be obtained only through peaceful agreement.

9. It is clear enough that Nicholas of Cusa made copious use of the writings of preceding philosophers. For example, he often quotes the Pseudo-Dionysius; and it is obvious that he was strongly influenced by the latter's insistence on negative theology and on the use of symbols. He knew, too, the *De divisione naturae* of John Scotus Eriugena, and though Eriugena's influence on his thought was doubtless less than that exercised by the Pseudo-Dionysius (whom he thought of, of course, as the disciple of St. Paul) it is reasonable to suppose that some of his bold statements on the way in which God becomes 'visible' in creatures were prompted by a reading of the ninth-century philosopher's work. Again, Nicholas was certainly influenced by the writings of Meister Eckhart and by the latter's use of startling antinomies. Indeed, a great deal of Nicholas's philosophy, his theory of *docta ignorantia*, for example, his idea of God as the *coincidentia oppositorum*, his insistence on the world as a divine self-manifestation and as the *explicatio Dei*, his notion of man as the microcosm, can be regarded as a development of earlier philosophies, particularly those belonging in a wide sense to the Platonic tradition and those which may be classed as in some sense 'mystical'. His fondness for mathematical analogies and symbolism recalls not only the writings of Platonists and Pythagoreans in the ancient world but also those of St. Augustine and other Christian writers. It is considerations of this sort which provide much justification for those who would

---

[1] *De visione Dei*, 19–21.   [2] *Ibid.*, 21.   [3] *De docta ignorantia*, 3, 12.

class Nicholas of Cusa as a mediaeval thinker. His preoccupation with our knowledge of God and with the world's relation to God points backward, it might be maintained, to the Middle Ages. His whole thought moves, some historians would say, in mediaeval categories and bears the imprint of mediaeval Catholicism. Even his more startling utterances can be paralleled in the case of writers whom everyone would class as mediaevals.

On the other hand, it is possible to go to the opposite extreme and to attempt to push Nicholas forward into the modern period. His insistence on negative theology, for example, and his doctrine of God as the *coincidentia oppositorum* can be assimilated to Schelling's theory of the Absolute as the vanishing-point of all differences and distinctions, while his view of the world as the *explicatio Dei* can be regarded as a foretaste of Hegel's theory of Nature as God-in-His-otherness, as the concrete manifestation or embodiment of the abstract Idea. His philosophy can, that is to say, be considered as an anticipation of German idealism. In addition it is obvious that Nicholas's idea of the mirroring of the universe in each finite thing and of the qualitative difference which exists between any two things reappeared in the philosophy of Leibniz.

It can hardly be denied, I think, that there is truth in both these conflicting points of view. Nicholas's philosophy undoubtedly depended on or utilized to a great extent preceding systems. On the other hand, to point out the similarities between certain aspects of his thought and the philosophy of Leibniz is by no means to indulge in far-fetched analogies. When it comes to connecting Nicholas of Cusa with post-Kantian German speculative idealism the links are clearly more tenuous, and there is more chance of anachronistic assimilations; but it is true that interest in his writings began to show itself in the nineteenth century and that this was largely due to the direction taken in that century by German thought. But if there is truth in both points of view, that is all the more reason, I think, for recognizing in Nicholas a transition-thinker, a figure of the Renaissance. His philosophy of Nature, for example, certainly contained elements from the past, but it represented also the growing interest in the system of Nature and what one may perhaps call the growing feeling for the universe as a developing and self-unfolding system. Nicholas's idea of the 'infinity' of the world influenced other Renaissance thinkers, especially Giordano Bruno, even though Bruno developed

Nicholas's ideas in a direction which was alien to the latter's mind and convictions. Again, however much Nicholas's theory of Nature as the *explicatio Dei* may have been dependent on the Platonic or neo-Platonic tradition, we find in that theory an insistence on the individual thing and on Nature as a system of individual things, none of which are exactly alike, that looks forward, as has already been mentioned, to the Leibnizian philosophy. Furthermore, his rejection of the idea that anything in the world can properly be called stationary and of the notions of any absolute 'centre' or 'up' and 'down' links him with the cosmologists and scientists of the Renaissance rather than with the Middle Ages. It is perfectly true, of course, that Nicholas's conception of the relation of the world to God was a theistic conception; but if Nature is looked on as a harmonious system which is in some sense 'infinite' and which is a developing or progressive manifestation of God, this idea facilitates and encourages the investigation of Nature for its own sake and not simply as a stepping-stone to the metaphysical knowledge of God. Nicholas was not a pantheist, but his philosophy, in regard to certain aspects at least, can be grouped with that of Bruno and other Renaissance philosophers of Nature; and it was against the background of these speculative philosophies that the scientists of the Renaissance thought and worked. One may remark in this connection that Nicholas's mathematical speculations provided a stimulus for Leonardo da Vinci.

In conclusion we may perhaps remind ourselves that though Nicholas's idea of the infinite system of Nature was developed by philosophers like Giordano Bruno and though these speculative natural philosophies formed a background for and stimulus to the scientific investigation of Nature, Nicholas himself was not only a Christian but also an essentially Christian thinker who was preoccupied with the search for the hidden God and whose thought was definitely Christocentric in character. It was in order to illustrate this last point that in dealing with his theory of man as the microcosm I mentioned his doctrine of Christ as the *maximum contractum* and the *medium absolutum*. In his humanistic interests, in his insistence on individuality, in the value he attached to fresh mathematical and scientific studies, and in the combination of a critical spirit with a marked mystical bent he was akin to a number of other Renaissance thinkers; but he continued into the Renaissance the faith which had animated and inspired the great thinkers of the Middle Ages. In a sense his mind was steeped in the new ideas which were fermenting at the time; but the religious outlook which permeated his thought saved him from the wilder extravagances into which some of the Renaissance philosophers fell.

CHAPTER XVI

PHILOSOPHY OF NATURE (1)

General remarks—Girolamo Cardano—Bernardino Telesio—Francesco Patrizzi—Tommaso Campanella—Giordano Bruno—Pierre Gassendi.

1. In the last chapter mention was made of the link between Nicholas of Cusa's idea of Nature and the other philosophies of Nature which appeared at the time of the Renaissance. Nicholas's idea of Nature was theocentric; and in this aspect of his philosophy he stands close to the leading philosophers of the Middle Ages; but we have seen how in his thought the idea of Nature as an infinite system, in which the earth occupies no privileged position, came to the fore. With a number of other Renaissance thinkers there arose the idea of Nature considered as a self-sufficient unity, as a system unified by all-pervading forces of sympathy and attraction and animated by a world-soul, rather than, as with Nicholas of Cusa, as an external manifestation of God. By these philosophers Nature was regarded practically as an organism, in regard to which the sharp distinctions, characteristic of mediaeval thought, between living and non-living and between spirit and matter, lost their meaning and application. Philosophies of this type naturally tended to be pantheistic in character. In certain respects they had an affinity with aspects of the revived Platonism or neo-Platonism of the Renaissance; but whereas the Platonists laid emphasis on the supernatural and on the soul's ascent to God, the philosophers of Nature emphasized rather Nature itself considered as a self-sufficient system. This is not to say that all the Renaissance thinkers who are usually regarded as 'natural philosophers' abandoned Christian theology or looked on themselves as revolutionaries; but the tendency of their thought was to loosen the bonds which bound nature to the supernatural. They tended to 'naturalism'.

It is, however, rather difficult to make general judgments about those Renaissance thinkers whom historians are accustomed to classify as 'natural philosophers' or 'philosophers of Nature'; or perhaps one should say rather that it is dangerous to do so. Among the Italians, for example, one can certainly find affinities between the philosophy of Giordano Bruno and the German romantic philosophy of the nineteenth century. But 'romanticism' is not exactly a characteristic which one would naturally attribute to the thought of Girolamo Fracastoro (1483–1553), who was physician to Pope Paul III and who wrote on medical subjects, as well as composing a work on astronomy, the *Homocentricorum seu de stellis liber* (1535). In his *De sympathia et antipathia rerum* (1542) he postulated the existence of 'sympathies' and 'antipathies' between objects, that is, of forces of attraction and repulsion, to explain the movements of bodies in their relations to one another. The names 'sympathy' and 'antipathy' may appear perhaps to be symptomatic of a romantic outlook; but Fracastoro explained the mode of operation of these forces by postulating *corpuscula* or *corpora sensibilia* which are emitted by bodies and enter through the pores of other bodies. Applying this line of thought to the problem of perception, he postulated the emission of *species* or images which enter the percipient subject. This theory obviously renewed the mechanical theories of perception put forward in ancient times by Empedocles, Democritus and Epicurus, even though Fracastoro did not adopt the general atomistic theory of Democritus. A view of this kind emphasizes the passivity of the subject in its perception of external objects, and in his *Turrius sive de intellectione* (published 1555) he says that understanding (*intellectio*) is but the representation of an object to the mind, the result of the reception of a *species* of the object. From this he drew the conclusion that understanding is probably purely passive. It is true that he also postulated a special power, which he named *subnotio*, of experiencing or apprehending the various impressions of a thing as a totality possessing relations which are present in the object itself or as a meaningful whole. So one is not entitled to say that he denied any activity on the part of the mind. He did not deny the mind's reflective power nor its power to construct universal concepts or terms. Moreover, the use of the term *species* was obviously derived from the Aristotelian-Scholastic tradition. None the less, Fracastoro's theory of perception has a strongly marked 'naturalistic' character. Perhaps it is to be associated with his interests as a medical man.

Fracastoro was a physician, while Cardano was a mathematician and Telesio possessed a wide interest in scientific matters. But though a man like Telesio stressed the need for empirical investigation and research in science he certainly did not confine himself to hypotheses which could be empirically verified but advanced philosophical speculations of his own. It is not always easy to decide whether a given Renaissance thinker should be classified as a philosopher or a scientist: a number of philosophers of the time were interested in science and in scientific investigation, while the scientists were by no means always averse to philosophic speculation. However, those whose personal scientific work was of importance in the development of scientific studies are very reasonably classed as scientists, while those who are noteworthy rather for their speculation than for their personal contribution to scientific studies are classed as philosophers of Nature, even though they may have contributed indirectly to scientific advance by anticipating speculatively some of the hypotheses which the scientists attempted to verify. But the union of philosophic speculation with an interest in scientific matters, sometimes combined with an interest in alchemy and even in magic, was characteristic of the Renaissance thinkers. They had a profound belief in the free development of man and in his creative power and they sought to promote human development and power by varied means. Their minds delighted in free intellectual speculation, in the development of fresh hypotheses and in the ascertaining of new facts about the world; and the not uncommon interest in alchemy was due rather to the hope of thus extending man's power, control and wealth than to mere superstition. With the necessary qualifications one can say that the Renaissance spirit expressed a shift of emphasis from the other-worldly to the this-worldly, from transcendence to immanence, and from man's dependence to man's creative power. The Renaissance was a time of transition from a period in which the science of theology formed the mental background and stimulated men's minds to a period in which the growth of the particular natural sciences was to influence more and more the human mind and human civilization; and some at least of the Renaissance philosophies were fertilizing agents for the growth of science rather than systems of thought which one could be expected to treat very seriously as philosophies.

In this chapter I propose to deal briefly with some of the Italian philosophers of Nature and with the French philosopher, Pierre Gassendi. In the next chapter I shall treat of German philosophers of Nature, excluding Nicholas of Cusa, who has been considered separately.

2. Girolamo Cardano (1501–76) was a mathematician of note

and a celebrated physician, who became professor of medicine at Pavia in 1547. A typically Renaissance figure he combined his mathematical studies and the practice of medicine with an interest in astrology and a strong bent towards philosophical speculation. His philosophy was a doctrine of hylozoism. There is an original, indeterminate matter, filling all space. In addition it is necessary to postulate a principle of production and movement, which is the world-soul. The latter becomes a factor in the empirical world in the form of 'warmth' or light; and from the operation of the world-soul in matter empirical objects are produced, all of which are en-souled and between which there exist relations of sympathy and antipathy. In the process of the world's formation the heaven, the seat of warmth, was first separated from the sublunary world, which is the place of the wet and the cold elements. Cardano's enthusiasm for astrology was expressed in his conviction that the heavens influence the course of events in the sublunary world. Metals are produced in the interior of the earth through the mutual reactions of the three elements of earth, water and air; and not only are they living things but they all tend towards the form of gold. As for what are normally called living things, animals were produced from worms, and the forms of worms proceed from the natural warmth in the earth.

This view of the world as an animate organism or as a unified system animated by a world-soul obviously owed a good deal to the *Timaeus* of Plato, while some ideas, like those of indeterminate matter and of 'forms', derived from the Aristotelian tradition. It might be expected perhaps that Cardano would develop these ideas in a purely naturalistic direction, but he was not a materialist. There is in man an immortal rational principle, *mens*, which enters into a temporary union with the mortal soul and the body. God created a definite number of these immortal souls, and immortality involves metempsychosis. In this view of the immortal mind as something separable from the mortal soul of man one can see the influence of Averroism; and one can probably see the same influence in Cardano's refusal to admit that God created the world freely. If creation was due simply and solely to the divine choice, there was no reason or ground for creation: it was a necessary process rather than the result of God's choice.

But there was more in Cardano's philosophy than a mere antiquarianism or a patching-together of elements taken from different philosophies of the past to make a hylozoistic and animistic system. It is clear that he laid great emphasis on the idea of natural law and on the unity of Nature as a law-governed system; and in this respect his thought was in tune with the scientific movement of the Renaissance, even though he expressed his belief in natural law in terms of ideas and theories taken from philosophies of the past. This conviction in regard to the reign of law comes out clearly in his insistence that God has subjected the heavenly bodies, and bodies in general, to mathematical laws and that the possession of mathematical knowledge is a form of true wisdom. It is represented even by his belief in 'natural magic', for the power of magic rests on the unity of all that is. Naturally, the sense in which words can be said to 'be' and to belong to the realm of causes needs a far clearer analysis than Cardano attempted; but the interest in magic which was one of the characteristics of some of the Renaissance thinkers expresses their belief in the causal system of the universe, even though to us it may seem fantastic.

3. A hylozoistic theory was also maintained by Bernardino Telesio (1509–88) of Cosenza in Calabria, the author of *De natura rerum iuxta propria principia* and the founder of the *Academia Telesiana* or *Cosentina* at Naples. According to Telesio, the fundamental causes of natural events are the warm and cold elements, the opposition between which is concretely represented by the traditional antithesis between heaven and earth. In addition to these two elements Telesio postulated a third, passive matter, which becomes distended or rarefied through the activity of the warm and compressed through the activity of the cold element. In the bodies of animals and men there is present the 'spirit', a fine emanation of the warm element, which passes throughout the body by means of the nerves though it is properly situated in the brain. This idea of 'spirit' goes back to the Stoic theory of the *pneuma* which was itself derived from the medical schools of Greece, and it reappears in the philosophy of Descartes under the name 'animal spirits'.

The 'spirit', which is a kind of psychological substance, can receive impressions produced by external things and can renew them in the memory. The spirit has thus the function of receiving sense-impressions and of anticipating future sense-impressions; and analogical reasoning from case to case is grounded in sense-perception and memory. Reasoning begins, then, with sense-perception and its function is to anticipate sense-perception, in that its conclusions or anticipations of future experience must be empirically verified. Telesio does not hesitate to draw the conclusion that *intellectio longe est sensu imperfectior*.[1] He interpreted geometry, for example, in the light of this theory, namely as a sublimated form of analogical reasoning based on sense-perception. On the other hand, he admitted the idea of empty space, which is not a thing but rather the system of relations between things. Places are modifications of this general order or system of relations.

The fundamental natural drive or instinct in man is that of self-preservation. This is the ruling instinct in animals as well, and even in anorganic matter, which is non-living only in a comparative sense, as is shown by the omnipresence of motion, a symptom of life. (Indeed, all things are gifted with 'perception' in some degree, an idea which was later developed by Leibniz.) It was in terms of this fundamental instinct that Telesio analysed man's emotional life. Thus love and hate are feelings directed respectively towards that which promotes and that which hinders self-preservation, while joy is the feeling attendant on self-preservation. The cardinal virtues, prudence, for example, and fortitude, are all various forms in which the fundamental instinct expresses itself in its fulfilment, whereas sadness and kindred emotions reflect a weakening of the vital impulse. We have here an obvious anticipation of Spinoza's analysis of the emotions.

Telesio did not think, however, that man can be analysed and explained exclusively in biological terms. For man is able to transcend the biological urge to self-preservation: he can even neglect his own happiness and expose himself freely to death. He can also strive after union with God and contemplate the divine. One must postulate, therefore, the presence in man of a *forma superaddita*, the immortal soul, which informs body and 'spirit', and which is capable of union with God.

The professed method of Telesio was the empirical method; for he looked to sense-experience for knowledge of the world and regarded reasoning as little more than a process of anticipating future sense-experience on the basis of past experience. He may thus be regarded as having outlined, even if somewhat crudely, one aspect of scientific method. At the same time he propounded a philosophy which went far beyond what could be empirically verified by sense-perception. This point was emphasized by

[1] *De rerum natura*, 8, 3.

Patrizzi, to whom I shall turn next. But the combination of a hostility towards Scholastic abstractions not only with an enthusiasm for immediate sense-experience but also with insufficiently-grounded philosophical speculations was not uncharacteristic of Renaissance thought, which was in many respects both rich and undisciplined.

4. Although Francesco Patrizzi (1529–97) observed that Telesio did not conform in his philosophical speculations to his own canons of verification he himself was much more given to speculation than was Telesio, the essence of whose philosophy may very possibly lie in its naturalistic aspect. Born in Dalmatia Patrizzi ended his life, after many wanderings, as professor of the Platonic philosophy at Rome. He was the author of *Discussionum peripateticarum libri XV* (1571) and *Nova de universis philosophia* (1591), in addition to a number of other works, including fifteen books on geometry. A determined enemy of Aristotle, he considered that Platonism was far more compatible with Christianity and that his own system was eminently adapted for winning heretics back to the Church. He dedicated his *Nova philosophia* to Pope Gregory XIV. Patrizzi might thus very well have been treated in the chapter on the revival of Platonism; but he expounded a general philosophy of Nature, and so I have chosen to deal briefly with his thought here.

Patrizzi had recourse to the ancient light-theme of the Platonic tradition. God is the original and uncreated light, from which proceeds the visible light. This light is the active, formative principle in Nature, and as such it cannot be called wholly material. Indeed, it is a kind of intermediary being which constitutes a bond between the purely spiritual and the purely material and inert. But besides light it is necessary to postulate other fundamental factors in Nature. One of these is space, which Patrizzi describes in a rather baffling manner. Space is subsistent existence, inhering in nothing. Is it, then, a substance? It is not, says Patrizzi, an individual substance composed of matter and form, and it does not fall within the category of substance. On the other hand it is a substance in some sense; for it inheres in nothing else. It cannot therefore be identified with quantity. Or, if it is, it is not to be identified with any quantity which falls under the category of quantity: it is the source and origin of all empirical quantity. Patrizzi's description of space reminds one rather of that given by Plato in the *Timaeus*. It cannot be called anything definite. It is neither purely spiritual; nor is it on the other hand a corporeal substance: rather is it 'incorporeal body', abstract extension which precedes, logically at least, the production of distinct bodies and which can be logically constructed out of *minima* or points. The idea of the *minimum*, which is neither great nor small but is potentially either, was utilized by Giordano Bruno. Space is filled, according to Patrizzi, by another fundamental factor in the constitution of the world, namely 'fluidity'. Light, warmth, space and fluidity are the four elementary factors or principles.

Patrizzi's philosophy was a curious and bizarre amalgam of neo-Platonic speculation and an attempt to explain the empirical world by reference to certain fundamental material or quasi-material factors. Light was for him partly the visible light, but it was also a metaphysical principle or being which emanates from God and animates all things. It is the principle of multiplicity, bringing the multiple into existence; but it is also the principle of unity which binds all things into a unity. And it is by means of light that the mind is enabled to ascend to God.

5. Another strange mixture of various elements was provided by Tommaso Campanella (1568–1639), a member of the Dominican Order and author of the famous political Utopia, the *City of the Sun* (*Civitas solis*, 1623), in which he proposed, whether seriously or not, a communistic arrangement of society obviously suggested by Plato's *Republic*. Campanella spent a very considerable portion of his life in prison, mainly on account of charges of heresy; but he composed a number of philosophical works, including *Philosophia sensibus demonstrata* (1591), *De sensu rerum* (1620), *Atheismus triumphatus* (1631) and *Philosophia universalis seu metaphysica* (1637). In politics he upheld the ideal of a universal monarchy under the spiritual headship of the pope and the temporal leadership of the Spanish monarchy. The very man who had to undergo a term of imprisonment on the accusation of conspiring against the king of Spain lauded the Spanish monarchy in his *De monarchia hispanica* (1640).

Campanella was strongly influenced by Telesio, and he insisted on the direct investigation of Nature as the source of our knowledge about the world. He tended also to interpret reasoning on the same lines as those laid down by Telesio. But the inspiration of his thought was different. If he emphasized sense-perception and the empirical study of Nature, he did so because Nature is, as he put it, the living statue of God, the mirror or image of God.

There are two main ways of coming to a knowledge of God, first the study with the aid of the senses of God's self-revelation in Nature, and secondly the Bible. That Nature is to be regarded as a manifestation of God was, of course, a familiar theme in mediaeval thought. We have only to think of St. Bonaventure's doctrine of the material world as the *vestigium* or *umbra Dei*; and Nicholas of Cusa, who influenced Campanella, had developed this line of thought. But the Renaissance Dominican laid stress on the actual observation of Nature. It is not primarily a question of finding mystical analogies in Nature, as with St. Bonaventure, but rather of reading the book of Nature as it lies open to sense-perception.

That God's existence can be proved was a matter of which Campanella felt quite certain. And the way he set about proving it is interesting, if only because of its obvious affinity with the teaching of Descartes in the seventeenth century. Arguing against scepticism, Campanella maintained that we can at least know that we do not know this or that, or that we doubt whether this or that is the case. Moreover, in the act of doubting one's own existence is revealed. On this point Campanella is a kind of link between St. Augustine with his *Si fallor, sum*, and Descartes, with his *Cogito, ergo sum*. Again, in the consciousness of one's own existence there is also given the consciousness of what is other than oneself: in the experience of finitude is given the knowledge that other being exists. In love, too, is given the consciousness of the existence of the other. (Perhaps Descartes might have adopted and utilized this point of view to advantage.) I, therefore, exist, and I am finite; but I possess, or can possess, the idea of the infinite reality. This idea cannot be my own arbitrary construction or indeed my construction at all: it must be the effect of God's operation in me. Through reflection on the idea of infinite and independent being I see that God actually exists. In this way knowledge of my own existence as a finite being and knowledge of God's existence as infinite being are closely linked. But it is possible also for man to have an immediate contact with God, which affords the highest possible knowledge open to man and at the same time involves love of God; and this loving knowledge of God is the best way of knowing God.

God is the Creator of all finite beings, and these are composed, according to Campanella, of being and not-being, the proportion of not-being increasing as one descends the scale of perfection. This is certainly a very peculiar way of speaking; but the main idea was derived from the Platonic tradition and was not Campanella's invention. The chief attributes (*primalitates*) of being are power, wisdom and love; and the more not-being is mixed with being, the weaker is the participation in these attributes. As one descends the scale of perfection, therefore, one finds an increasing proportion of impotence or lack of power, of unwisdom and of hatred. But every creature is animate in some sense, and nothing is without some degree of perception and feeling. Moreover, all finite things together form a system, the precondition of which is provided by space; and they are related to one another by mutual sympathies and antipathies. Everywhere we find the fundamental instinct of self-preservation. But this instinct or drive is not to be interpreted in a narrowly and exclusively egoistic sense. Man, for example, is a social being, adapted to life in society. Furthermore, he is able to rise above love of self in the narrow sense to love of God, which expresses his tendency to return to his origin and source.

We come to recognize the primary attributes of being through reflection on ourselves. Every man is aware that he can act or that he has some power (*posse*), that he can know something and that he wills or has love. We then ascribe these attributes of power, wisdom and love to God, the infinite being, in the highest possible degree, and we find them in non-human finite things in varying degrees. This is an interesting point because it illustrates Campanella's tendency to imply that we interpret Nature on an analogy with ourselves. In a sense all knowledge is knowledge of ourselves. We perceive the effects of things on ourselves, and we find ourselves limited and conditioned by things other than ourselves. We attribute to them, therefore, activities and functions analogous to those we perceive in ourselves. Whether this point of view is consistent with Campanella's insistence, under the influence of Telesio, on direct sense-knowledge of Nature is perhaps questionable; but the justification for our interpretation of Nature on an analogy with ourselves he found in the doctrine of man as the microcosm. If man is the microcosm or little world, the world in miniature, the attributes of being as found in man are also the attributes of being in general. If this way of thinking really represents Campanella's mind, it is open to the obvious objection that the theory of man as the microcosm should be a conclusion and not a premiss. But Campanella started, of course, from the view that God is revealed in every creature as in a mirror. If this point of view is adopted, it follows that knowledge of the being best known to us is the key to the knowledge of being in general.

6. The most celebrated of the Italian philosophers of Nature is Giordano Bruno. Born at Nola near Naples in 1548 (hence sometimes called 'the Nolan') he entered the Dominican Order at Naples; but in 1576 he laid aside the habit at Rome after he had been accused of holding heterodox opinions. He then began a life of wandering which took him from Italy to Geneva, from Geneva to France, from France to England, where he gave some lectures at Oxford, from England back again to France and then to Germany. Returning rashly to Italy, he was arrested by the Venetian Inquisition in 1592, and in the following year he was handed over to the Roman Inquisition and spent some years in prison. Finally, as he continued to stand by his opinions, he was burned at Rome on February 17th, 1600.

Bruno's writings include *De umbris idearum* (1582) and the following works in dialogue form: *La cena de le ceneri* (1584), *Della causa, principio e uno* (1584), *De l'infinito, universo e mondi* (1584), *Spaccio della bestia trionfante* (1584), *Cabala del cavallo pegaseo con l'agguiunta dell'asino cillenico* (1585) and *Degl' eroici furori* (1585). Among his other works are three Latin poems, published in 1591, the *De triplici minimo et mensura ad trium speculativarum scientiarum et multarum activarum artium principia libri V*, the *De monade, numero et figura, secretioris nempe physicae, mathematicae et metaphysicae elementa* and the *De immenso et innumerabilibus, seu de universo et mundis libri VIII*.

The starting-point and the terminology of Bruno's thought were furnished, very naturally, by preceding philosophies. He took over the neo-Platonic metaphysical scheme, as mediated by the Italian Platonists and by Nicholas of Cusa. Thus in his *De umbris idearum* he represented Nature with its multiplicity of beings as proceeding from the divine super-substantial unity. There is a hierarchy in Nature from matter upwards to the immaterial, from darkness to light; and Nature is intelligible in so far as it is the expression of the divine ideas. Human ideas, however, are simply shadows or reflections of the divine ideas, though human knowledge is capable of advancement and deepening in proportion as the mind moves upwards from the objects of sense-perception towards the divine and original unity, which in itself, however, is impenetrable by the human intellect.

But this traditional scheme formed little more than the

background of Bruno's thought, against which his own philosophy developed. Though neo-Platonism had always represented the world as a divine 'emanation' or creation and as the reflection of God, it had always stressed the divine transcendence and incomprehensibility. But the inner movement of Bruno's speculation was towards the idea of the divine immanence, and so towards pantheism. He never achieved a complete conciliation of the two points of view; nor did he ever carry through a definite exclusion of one point of view in favour of the other.

In his *Della causa, principio e uno* Bruno asserts God's transcendence and incomprehensibility and His creation of things which are distinct from Him. 'From the knowledge of all dependent things we cannot infer any other knowledge of the first cause and principle than by the rather inefficacious way of traces (*de vestigio*). . . . So that to know the universe is like knowing nothing of the being and substance of the first principle. . . . Behold, then, about the divine substance, both because of its infinity and because of its being extremely remote from its effects . . . we can know nothing save by way of traces, as the Platonists say, or by remote effects, as the Peripatetics say. . . .'[1] The interest soon shifts, however, to the principles and causes in the world, and Bruno brings into prominence the idea of the world-soul as the immanent causal and moving agent. The primary and principal faculty of the world-soul is the universal intellect, which is 'the universal physical efficient agent' and 'the universal form' of the world.[2] It produces natural forms in the world, while our intellects produce universal ideas of these forms. It is the universal form of the world in that it is everywhere present and animates everything. Leather as leather or glass as glass, says Bruno, is not in itself animate in the ordinary sense; but it is united to and informed by the world-soul and it has, as matter, the potentiality of forming part of an organism. Matter, in the sense of Aristotle's 'first matter', is indeed, considered from one point of view, a formless and potential substrate; but considered as the fountain-head and source of forms it cannot be regarded as an unintelligible substrate; ultimately pure matter is the same thing as pure act. Bruno used Nicholas of Cusa's doctrine of the *coincidentia oppositorum* in regard to the world. Starting with the assertion of distinctions he went on to show their relative character. The world consists of distinct things and factors, but in the end it is seen to be 'one, infinite,

[1] *Dialogo secondo, Opere*, 1, pp. 175-6.   [2] *Ibid.*, p. 179.

immobile' (that is, incapable of local motion), one being, one substance.[1] The idea, taken over from Nicholas of Cusa, that the world is infinite is supported by arguments in the *De l'infinito, universo e mondi*. 'I call the universe *tutto infinito*, because it has no margin, limit or surface; I do not call the universe *totalmente infinito*, because any part that we take is finite, and of the innumerable worlds which it contains each is finite. I call God *tutto infinito* because He excludes of Himself all limits and because each of His attributes is one and infinite; and I call God *totalmente infinito* because He is wholly in the whole world and infinitely and totally in each of its parts, in distinction from the infinity of the universe which is totally in the whole but not in the parts, if indeed, in reference to the infinite, they can be called parts.'[2]

Here Bruno draws a distinction between God and the world. He also speaks of God, using the phrases of Nicholas of Cusa, as being the infinite *complicatamente e totalmente* whereas the world is the infinite *explicatamente e non totalmente*. But the tendency of his thought is always to weaken these distinctions or to synthesize the 'antitheses'. In the *De triplici minimo* he speaks of the *minimum* which is found on the mathematical, physical and metaphysical planes. The mathematical *minimum* is the *monas* or unit; the physical *minimum* is the atom or monad, indivisible and in some sense animate, and immortal souls are also 'monads'. Nature is the harmonious self-unfolding system of atoms and monads in their interrelations. Here we have a pluralistic view of the universe, conceived in terms of monads, each of which is in some sense gifted with perception and appetition; and this aspect of Bruno's philosophy anticipates the monadology of Leibniz. But we have already noted his remark that one can hardly speak of 'parts' in relation to the infinite world; and the complementary aspect of his philosophy is represented by his idea of finite things as accidents or *circonstanzie* of the one infinite substance. Again, God is called *Natura naturans* in so far as He is considered in distinction from His manifestations, while He is called *Natura naturata* when considered in His self-manifestation. Here we have the monistic aspect of Bruno's thought which anticipated the philosophy of Spinoza. But as has been already remarked, Bruno never positively abandoned pluralism in favour of monism. It is reasonable to say that the tendency of his thought lay in the

[1] *Dialogo quinto*, pp. 247 ff. [2] *Dialogo primo*, p. 298.

direction of monism; but in actual fact he continued to believe in the transcendent God. He considered, however, that philosophy deals with Nature and that God in Himself is a subject which can be properly treated only in theology, above all by the method of negative theology. One is not justified, then, in stating roundly that Bruno was a pantheist. One can say, if one likes, that his mind tended to move away from the categories of neo-Platonism and of Nicholas of Cusa in the direction of a greater insistence on the divine immanence; but there is no real reason for supposing that his retention of the doctrine of the divine transcendence was a mere formality. His philosophy may be a stage on the road from Nicholas of Cusa to Spinoza; but Bruno himself did not travel to the end of that road.

But Bruno's thought was not inspired simply by the neo-Platonic tradition interpreted in a pantheistic sense; it was also deeply influenced by the astronomical hypothesis of Copernicus. Bruno was not a scientist, and he cannot be said to have contributed to the scientific verification of the hypothesis; but he developed speculative conclusions from it with characteristic boldness, and his ideas acted as a stimulus on other thinkers. He envisaged a multitude of solar systems in limitless space. Our sun is simply one star among others, and it occupies no privileged position: still less does the earth. Indeed, all judgments about position are, as Nicholas of Cusa said, relative; and no one star or planet can be called the centre of the universe in an absolute sense. There is no centre, and there is no absolute up or down. Moreover, from the fact that the earth is inhabited by rational beings we are not entitled to draw the conclusion that it is unique in dignity or that it is the centre of the universe from the valuational point of view: for all we know, the presence of life, even of rational beings like ourselves, may not be confined to this planet. The solar systems rise and perish, but all together they form one developing system, indeed one organism animated by the world-soul. Bruno did not confine himself to maintaining that the earth moves and that judgments of position are relative: he linked up the Copernican hypothesis of the earth's movement round the sun with his own metaphysical cosmology. He thus entirely rejected the geocentric and anthropocentric conception of the universe both from the astronomical point of view and in the wider perspective of speculative philosophy. In his system it is Nature considered as an organic whole which stands in the centre of the picture, and not terrestrial human beings who are *circonstanzie* or accidents of the one living world-substance, even if from another point of view each is a monad, mirroring the whole universe.

In some early writings Bruno dealt with questions concerning memory and logic under the influence of the doctrines of Raymond Lull (d. 1315). We can distinguish ideas in the universal intelligence, in the physical order as forms and in the logical order as symbols or concepts. The task of a developed logic would be to show how the plurality of ideas emerge from the 'one'. But though he may be regarded as in some sense a link between Lull and Leibniz, Bruno is best known for his doctrines of the infinite world-substance and of monads and for his speculative use of the Copernican hypothesis. In regard to the first doctrine he probably exercised some influence upon Spinoza, and he was certainly acclaimed as a prophet by later German philosophers like Jacobi and Hegel. In regard to the theory of monads, which is more apparent in his later works, he certainly anticipated Leibniz in some important points, even though it seems improbable that Leibniz received any substantial direct influence from Bruno in the formation of his ideas.[1] Bruno adopted and utilized many ideas taken from Greek, mediaeval and Renaissance thinkers, especially from Nicholas of Cusa; but he possessed an original mind with a strong speculative bent. His ideas were often far-fetched and fantastic and his thought undisciplined, though he was certainly capable of methodical thinking when he chose; and he played the rôle not only of philosopher but also of poet and seer. We have seen that he cannot be called a pantheist in an unqualified manner; but this does not mean that his attitude towards Christian dogmas was either favourable or respectful. He aroused the disapproval and hostility not only of Catholic theologians but also of Calvinists and Lutherans, and his unhappy end was due not to his championship of the Copernican hypothesis, nor to his attacks on Aristotelian Scholasticism, but to his apparent denial of some central theological dogmas. He did make an attempt to explain away his unorthodoxy by reference to a kind of 'double-truth' theory; but his condemnation for heresy was perfectly understandable, whatever one may think of the physical treatment meted out to him. His ultimate fate has, of course, led some writers to attribute to him a greater philosophic importance than

[1] See note on p. 268.

he possesses; but though some of the encomia which have sometimes been lavished upon him in an uncritical manner were exaggerated, he nevertheless remains one of the leading and most influential thinkers of the Renaissance.

7. The date of Pierre Gassendi's death, 1655, coupled with the fact that he carried on a controversy with Descartes, offers a very good reason for considering his philosophy at a later stage. On the other hand, his revival of Epicureanism justifies one, I think, in including it under the general heading of Renaissance philosophy.

Born in Provence in 1592, Pierre Gassendi studied philosophy there at Aix. Turning to theology, he lectured for a time on the subject and was ordained priest; but in 1617 he accepted the chair of philosophy at Aix, where he expounded more or less traditional Aristotelianism. His interest in the discoveries of the Renaissance scientists, however, led his thought into other paths, and in 1624 there appeared the first book of his *Exercitationes paradoxicae adversus Aristotelicos*. He was at this time a canon of Grenoble. The work was to have been composed of seven books; but, apart from a portion of the second book, which appeared posthumously in 1659, no more than the first book was written. In 1631 he published a work against the English philosopher Robert Fludd (1574–1637), who had been influenced by Nicholas of Cusa and Paracelsus, and in 1642 his objections against Descartes's system were published.[1] In 1645 he was appointed professor of mathematics at the Collège Royal in Paris. While occupying this post he wrote on some physical and astronomical questions, but he is best known for the works which he wrote under the influence of the Epicurean philosophy. His treatise *De vita, moribus et doctrina Epicuri libri VIII* appeared in 1647, and this was followed in 1649 by the *Commentarius de vita, moribus et placitis Epicuri seu animadversiones in decimum librum Diogenis Laertii*. This was a Latin translation of and commentary on the tenth book of Diogenes Laërtius's *Lives of the Philosophers*. In the same year he published his *Syntagma philosophiae Epicuri*. His *Syntagma philosophicum* was published posthumously in the edition of his works (1658). In addition he wrote a number of *Lives*, of Copernicus and Tycho Brahe for example.

Gassendi followed the Epicureans in dividing philosophy into logic, physics and ethics. In his logic, which includes his theory

[1] They are the fifth in the series of objections published in the works of Descartes.

of knowledge, his eclecticism at once becomes apparent. In company with many other philosophers of the time he insisted on the sense-origin of all our natural knowledge: *nihil in intellectu quod non prius fuerit in sensu*. And it was from an empiricist standpoint that he criticized Descartes. But although he spoke as if the senses were the only criterion of evidence he also admitted, as one might well expect of a mathematician, the evidence of the deductive reason. As to his 'physics', this was clearly a combination of very different elements. On the one hand, he revived the Epicurean atomism. Atoms, possessing size, shape and weight (interpreted as an inner propensity to movement) move in empty space. According to Gassendi, these atoms come from a material principle, the substrate of all becoming, which, with Aristotle, he described as 'prime matter'. With the help of atoms, space and motion he gave a mechanistic account of Nature. Sensation, for example, is to be explained mechanically. On the other hand, man possesses a rational and immortal soul, the existence of which is revealed by the facts of self-consciousness and by man's power of forming general ideas and apprehending spiritual objects and moral values. Moreover, the system, harmony and beauty of Nature furnish a proof of the existence of God, who is incorporeal, infinite and perfect. Man, as a being who is both spiritual and material and who can know both the material and the spiritual, is the microcosm. Finally, the ethical end of man is happiness, and this is to be understood as absence of pain in the body and tranquillity in the soul. But this end cannot be fully achieved in this life; it can be perfectly attained only in the life after death.

The philosophy of Gassendi may be regarded as an adaptation of Epicureanism to the requirements of Christian orthodoxy. But there is no good reason for saying that the spiritualistic side of his philosophy was inspired simply by motives of diplomatic prudence and that he was insincere in his acceptance of theism and of the spirituality and immortality of the soul. It may well be that the historical importance of his philosophy, so far as it possesses historical importance, lies in the impulse it gave to a mechanistic view of Nature. But this does not alter the fact that his philosophy, considered in itself, is a curious amalgam of Epicurean materialism with spiritualism and theism and of a rather crude empiricism with rationalism. His philosophizing exercised a considerable influence in the seventeenth century, but it was too unsystematic, too much of a patchwork, and too unoriginal to exercise any lasting influence.

CHAPTER XVII

PHILOSOPHY OF NATURE (2)

Agrippa von Nettesheim—Paracelsus—The two Van Helmonts —Sebastian Franck and Valentine Weigel—Jakob Böhme— General remarks.

IN this chapter I propose to outline the ideas not only of men like Paracelsus, who are naturally labelled philosophers of Nature, but also of the German mystic, Jakob Böhme. The latter would possibly be more accurately classified as a theosophist than as a philosopher; but he certainly had a philosophy of Nature, which in some respects resembles that of Bruno. Böhme was doubtless much more religiously-minded than Bruno, and to classify him as a philosopher of Nature may involve placing the accent in the wrong place; but, as we have already seen, the term 'Nature' often meant a great deal more for a Renaissance philosopher than the system of empirically-given distinct things which are capable of being investigated systematically.

1. The theme of microcosm and macrocosm, which is prominent in the Italian philosophies of Nature, occupies a prominent place in the German philosophies of the Renaissance. A feature of the neo-Platonic tradition, it became one of the cardinal points in the system of Nicholas of Cusa, and his profound influence on Giordano Bruno has already been mentioned. His influence was naturally also felt by the German thinkers. Thus according to Heinrich Cornelius Agrippa von Nettesheim (1486-1535) man unites in himself the three worlds, namely the terrestrial world of the elements, the world of the heavenly bodies and the spiritual world. Man is the ontological bond between these worlds, and this fact explains his ability to know all three worlds: man's range of knowledge depends on his ontological character. Further, the harmonious unity of the three worlds in man, the microcosm, reflects the harmonious unity which exists between them in the macrocosm. Man has his soul, and the universe possesses its soul or spirit (*spiritus mundi*), which is responsible for all production. There are, indeed, sympathies and antipathies between distinct things; but they are due to the presence in things of immanent vital principles which are effluences from the *spiritus mundi*.

Finally, the affinities and connections between things and the presence in them of latent powers form the basis for the magical art: man can discover and utilize these powers in his service. In 1510 Agrippa von Nettesheim published his *De occulta philosophia* and though he decried the sciences, including magic, in his *Declamatio de vanitate et incertitudine scientiarum* (1527), he republished the work on occultism in a revised form in 1533. Like Cardano, he was a physician and, like Cardano again, he was interested in magic. It is not an interest which one would associate with modern doctors; but the combination of medicine with magic in an earlier age is understandable. The physician was conscious of powers and healing properties of herbs and minerals and of his ability to utilize them to a certain extent. But it does not follow that he had a scientific understanding of the processes which he himself employed; and it is hardly to be wondered at if he was attracted by the idea of wresting nature's secrets from her by occult means and employing the hidden powers and forces thus discovered. Magic would appear to him as a kind of extension of 'science', a short-cut to the acquisition of further knowledge and skill.

2. This view of the matter is borne out by the example of that strange figure, Theophrastus Bombast von Hohenheim, commonly known as Paracelsus. Born at Einsiedeln in 1493, he was for a time professor of medicine at Basle. He died at Salzburg in 1541. Medical science, which promotes human happiness and well-being, was for him the highest of the sciences. It depends, indeed, on observation and experiment; but an empirical method does not by itself constitute medicine a science. The data of experience must be systematized. Furthermore, the true physician will take account of other sciences like philosophy, astrology and theology; for man, with whom medical science is concerned, participates in three worlds. Through his visible body he participates in the terrestrial world, the world of the elements, through his astral body in the sidereal world and through his immortal soul (the *mens* or *Fünklein*) in the spiritual and divine world. Man is thus the microcosm, the meeting-place of the three worlds which compose the macrocosm; and the physician will have to take this into account. The world at large is animated by its immanent vital principle, the *archeus*, and an individual organism like man develops under the impulse of its own vital principle. Medical treatment should consist essentially in stimulating the activity of the

archeus, a principle which obviously embodies the truth that the task of the physician is to assist nature to do her work. Indeed, Paracelsus put forward some perfectly sensible medical views. Thus he laid considerable emphasis on the individual and on individual factors in the treatment of disease; no disease, he thought, is ever found in exactly the same form or runs precisely the same course in any two individuals. For the matter of that, his idea that the physician should widen his field of view and take other sciences into account was by no means devoid of value. For it means essentially that the physician should consider man as a whole and should not confine his attention exclusively to physical symptoms and causes and treatment.

In some respects, then, Paracelsus was an enlightened theorist; and he attacked violently the medical practice of the time. In particular, he had no use for slavish adherence to the teaching of Galen. His own methods of procedure were highly empirical, and he can hardly be called a scientific chemist, even though he was interested in chemical specifics and drugs but he had at least an independent mind and an enthusiasm for the progress of medicine. With this interest in medicine, however, he combined an interest in astrology and in alchemy. Original matter consists of or contains three fundamental elements or substances, sulphur, mercury and salt. Metals are distinguished from one another through the predominance of this element rather than that; but since they all consist ultimately of the same element it is possible to transform any metal into any other metal. The possibility of alchemy is thus a consequence of the original constitution of matter.

Although Paracelsus may have tended to mix up philosophical speculation with 'science' and also with astrology and alchemy in a fantastic manner, he drew a sharp distinction between theology on the one hand and philosophy on the other. The latter is the study of Nature, not of God Himself. Yet Nature is a self-revelation of God; and we are thus able to attain to some philosophical knowledge of Him. Nature was originally present in God, in the 'great mystery' or 'divine abyss'; and the process by which the world is built up is one of differentiation, that is, of the production of distinctions and oppositions. We come to know only in terms of oppositions. For example, we come to know joy in its opposition to sorrow, health in its opposition to sickness. Similarly, we come to know good only in opposition to evil and God only in opposition to Satan. The term of the world's development will be the absolute division between good and evil, which will constitute the last judgment.

3. Paracelsus' ideas were developed by the Belgian chemist and physician, John Baptist van Helmont (1577-1644). The two primary elements are water and air, and the fundamental substances, namely sulphur, mercury and salt, proceed from water and can be transmuted into water. Van Helmont made a real discovery, however, when he realized that there are gases which are different from atmospheric air. He discovered that what he called *gas sylvestre* (carbon dioxide), which is emitted by burning charcoal, is the same as the gas given off by fermenting must. He is, therefore, of some importance in the history of chemistry. Further, his interest in this science, combined with his interests in physiology and medicine, prompted him to experiment in the application of chemical methods in preparing drugs. In this matter he carried on the work of Paracelsus. Van Helmont was much more of a careful experimenter than Paracelsus had been; but he shared the latter's belief in and enthusiasm for alchemy. In addition, he took up and developed Paracelsus' vitalistic theory. Each organism has its own general *archeus* or *aura vitalis*, on which are dependent the *archei* of the different parts or members of the organism. Not content with the vital principles, however, he also postulated a power of movement, which he called *blas*. This is of various kinds. There is, for instance, a *blas* peculiar to the heavenly bodies (*blas stellarum*) and another which is found in man, the relation between the *blas humanum* and the human *archeus* being left rather obscure.

John Baptist van Helmont did indeed indulge in speculations about the Fall and its effects on human psychology; but he was concerned primarily with chemistry, medicine and physiology, to which one must add alchemy. His son, however, Francis Mercury Van Helmont (1618-99), with whom Leibniz was acquainted,[1] developed a monadology according to which there are a finite number of imperishable monads. Each monad may be called corporeal in so far as it is passive, and spiritual in so far as it is active and endowed with some degree of perception. The inner sympathies and attractions between monads cause groups of them to form complex structures, each of which is governed by a central monad. In man, for example, there is a central monad, the soul,

[1] It seems probable that at any rate the term 'monad' was adopted by Leibniz from the younger Van Helmont or through a reading of Bruno suggested by Van Helmont.

which rules the whole organism. This soul shares in the imperishable character of all monads; but it cannot achieve the perfection of its development in one lifetime, that is to say, in the period in which it is the controlling and directing power in one particular set or series of monads. It therefore enters into union with other bodies or sets of monads until it has perfected itself. It then returns to God, who is the *monas monadum* and the author of the universal harmony of creation. The mediator between God and creatures is Christ.

The younger Van Helmont regarded his philosophy as a valuable antidote to the mechanistic interpretation of Nature, as represented by Descartes (in regard to the material world) and by the philosophy of Thomas Hobbes. His monadology was a development of Bruno's ideas, though it was doubtless also influenced by the vitalistic doctrines of Paracelsus and the elder Van Helmont. It is obvious that it anticipated in many respects the monadology of a much more talented man, Leibniz, though it would appear that Leibniz arrived independently at his fundamental ideas. There was, however, a second link between Van Helmont and Leibniz, and that was a common interest in occultism and alchemy, though in Leibniz's case this interest was perhaps simply one way in which his insatiable curiosity showed itself.

4. The German mystical tradition found a continuation in Protestantism with men like Sebastian Franck (1499–1542) and Valentine Weigel (1533–88). The former, however, would not normally be called a philosopher. At first a Catholic, he became a Protestant minister, only to abandon his charge and lead a restless and wandering life. He was hostile not only to Catholicism but also to official Protestantism. God is the eternal goodness and love which are present to all men, and the true Church, he thought, is the spiritual company of all those who allow God to operate within them. Men like Socrates and Seneca belonged to the 'Church'. Redemption is not a historical event, and doctrines like those of the Fall and the redemption by Christ on Calvary are no more than figures or symbols of eternal truths. This point of view was obviously theological in character.

Valentine Weigel, however, attempted to combine the mystical tradition with the philosophy of Nature as found in Paracelsus. He followed Nicholas of Cusa in teaching that God is all things *complicite* and that the distinctions and oppositions which are found in creatures are one in Him. But to this he added the curious notion that God becomes personal in and through creation, in the sense that He comes to know Himself in and through man, in so far as man rises above his egotism and shares in the divine life. All creatures, including man, receive their being from God, but all have an admixture of not-being, of darkness, and this explains man's power of rejecting God. The being of man tends necessarily towards God, turning to its source and origin and ground; but the will can turn away from God. When this happens, the resulting inner tension is what is known as 'hell'.

Accepting from Paracelsus the division of the universe into three worlds, the terrestrial, the sidereal or astral and the heavenly, Weigel also accepted the doctrine of the astral body of man. Man has a mortal body, which is the seat of the senses, but he has also an astral body, which is the seat of reason. In addition he has an immortal soul or part to which belongs the *Fünklein* or *Gemüt*, the *oculus intellectualis* or *oculus mentis*. This is the recipient of supernatural knowledge of God, though this does not mean that the knowledge comes from without; it comes from God present in the soul, knowing Himself in and through man. And it is in the reception of this knowledge, and not in any external rite or in any historical event, that regeneration consists.

It is clear, then, that Weigel attempted a fusion of Nicholas of Cusa's metaphysic and Paracelsus' philosophy of Nature with a religious mysticism which owed something to the tradition represented by Meister Eckhart (as is shown by the use of the term *Fünklein*, the spark of the soul) but which was strongly coloured by an individualistic and anti-ecclesiastical type of Protestant piety and which also tended in a pantheistic direction. In some respects his philosophy puts one in mind of themes of later German speculative idealism, though in the case of the latter the markedly religious and pietistic element of Weigel's thought was comparatively absent.

5. The man who attempted in a much more complete and influential manner to combine the philosophy of Nature with the mystical tradition as represented in German Protestantism was that remarkable figure, Jakob Böhme. Born in 1575 at Altseidenberg in Silesia, he at first tended cattle, though he received some education at the town-school at Seidenberg. After a period of wandering he settled at Görlitz in 1599, where he pursued the trade of a shoemaker. He married and attained a considerable degree of prosperity, which enabled him to retire

from his shoemaking business though he subsequently took to making woollen gloves. His first treatise, *Aurora*, was written in 1612, though it was not then published. Indeed, the only works which were published in his lifetime were some devotional writings, which appeared at the beginning of 1624. His *Aurora* was, however, circulated in manuscript, and while this brought him a local reputation it also brought upon him from the Protestant clergy a charge of heresy. His other works include, for example, *Die drei Prinzipien des göttlichen Wesens, Vom dreifachen Leben der Menschen, Von der Gnadenwahl, Signatura rerum* and *Mysterium magnum*. An edition of his works was published at Amsterdam in 1675, considerably later than the year of Böhme's death, which occurred in 1624.

God considered in Himself is beyond all differentiations and distinctions: He is the *Ungrund*,[1] the original ground of all things: He is 'neither light, nor darkness, neither love nor wrath, but the eternal One', an incomprehensible will, which is neither evil nor good.[2] But if God is conceived as the *Ungrund* or Abyss, 'the nothing and the all',[3] the problem arises of explaining the emergence of multiplicity, of distinct existent things. First of all Böhme postulates a process of self-manifestation within the inner life of God. The original will is a will to self-intuition, and it wills its own centre, which Böhme calls the 'heart' or 'eternal mind' of the will.[4] Thus the Deity discovers itself; and in the discovery there arises a power emanating from the will and the heart of the will, which is the moving life in the original will and in the power (or second will) that arises from, but is identical with, the heart of the original will. The three movements of the inner life of God are correlated by Böhme with the three Persons of the Trinity. The original will is the Father; the heart of the will, which is the Father's 'discovery and power', is the Son; and the 'moving life' emanating from Father and Son is the Holy Spirit. Having dealt with these obscure matters in a very obscure way Böhme goes on to show how Nature came into being as an expression or manifestation of God in visible variety. The impulse of the divine will to self-revelation leads to the birth of Nature as it exists in God. In this ideal or spiritual state Nature is called the *mysterium magnum*. It emerges in visible and tangible form in the actual world, which is external to God and is animated by the *spiritus mundi*. Böhme

---
[1] *Von der Gnadenwahl*, 1, 3. [2] *Ibid.*, 1, 3-5.
[3] *Ibid.*, 1, 3. [4] *Ibid.*, 1, 9-10.

proceeds to give a spiritual interpretation of the ultimate principles of the world and of the various elements, including Paracelsus' sulphur, mercury and salt.

As Böhme was convinced that God in Himself is good and that the *mysterium magnum* is also good, he found himself confronted with the task of explaining the evil in the actual world. His solution of this problem was not always the same. In the *Aurora* he maintained that only what is good proceeds from God; but there is a good which remains steadfast (Christ) and a good which falls away from goodness, typified by Satan. The end of history is, therefore, the rectification of this falling-away. Later, however, Böhme stated that the external manifestation of God must be expressed in contraries, which are natural concomitants of life. The *mysterium magnum*, when it unfolds itself in visible variety, expresses itself in contrary qualities:[1] light and darkness, good and evil, are correlative. There is, then, a dualism in the world. Christ reconciled man to God, but it is possible for men to refuse salvation. Finally, Böhme tried to relate evil to a movement in the divine life, which he called the wrath of God. The end of history will then be the triumph of love, involving the triumph of the good.

Böhme's ideas were derived in part from a number of different sources. His meditations on the Scriptures were coloured by the mysticism of Kaspar von Schwenckfeld (1490–1561) and of Valentine Weigel; and we find in his writings a deep piety and an insistence on the individual's relation to God. For the idea of a visible and unified authoritative Church he had evidently little sympathy: he laid all the emphasis on personal experience and inner light. This aspect of his thought would not by itself entitle him to be called a philosopher. So far as he can properly be called a philosopher, the name is justified mainly by his having grappled with two problems of theistic philosophy, namely the problem of the relation of the world to God and the problem of evil. Böhme was obviously no trained philosopher, and he was aware of the inadequacy and obscurity of his language. Moreover, he evidently picked up terms and phrases from his friends and from his reading, which derived mainly from the philosophy of Paracelsus, but which he used to express the ideas fermenting in his own mind. None the less, even though the shoemaker of Görlitz was no trained philosopher, he can be said to have carried on the speculative tradition coming from Meister Eckhart and Nicholas of Cusa

[1] Cf. *Von der Gnadenwahl*, 8, 8.

through the German philosophers of Nature, particularly Paracelsus, a tradition which he impregnated with a strong infusion of Protestant piety. Yet even if one makes due allowance for the handicaps under which he laboured, and even though one has not the slightest intention of questioning his deep piety and the sincerity of his convictions, it may be doubted whether his obscure and oracular utterances throw much light on the problems with which he dealt. No doubt the obscurity is broken through from time to time by rays of light; but his thought as a whole is unlikely to commend itself to those who are not theosophically inclined. It might be said, of course, that Böhme's obscure utterances represent the attempt of a higher kind of knowledge to express itself in inadequate language. But if one means by this that Böhme was struggling to convey solutions to philosophical problems, it has yet to be shown that he actually possessed those solutions. His writings leave one in considerable doubt at any rate whether this could properly be affirmed.

But to cast doubt upon the philosophical value of Böhme's utterances is not to deny their influence. He exercised an influence on men like Pierre Poiret (1646–1719) in France, John Pordage (1607–81) and William Law (1686–1761) in England. More important, however, is his influence on post-Kantian German idealism. Böhme's triadic schemes and his idea of the self-unfolding of God reappear, indeed, in Hegel, though minus Böhme's intense piety and devotion; but it was probably Schelling who, in the later phase of his philosophical development, was most influenced by him. For the German idealist drew on Böhme's theosophy and on his ideas about creation and the origin of evil. Schelling was led to Böhme partly by Franz von Baader (1765–1841), who had himself been influenced by Saint-Martin (1743–1803), an opponent of the Revolution who had translated Böhme's *Aurora* into French. There are always some minds for whom Böhme's teaching possesses an appeal, though many others not unnaturally fail to share this sympathy.

6. We have seen how the Renaissance philosophies of Nature varied considerably in tone and emphasis, ranging from the professedly empiricist theories of some of the Italian philosophers to the theosophy of a Jakob Böhme. We find, indeed, a common emphasis on Nature as the manifestation of the divine and as a revelation of God which is deserving of study. But whereas in one philosophy the accent may be laid predominantly on the empirical

study of Nature itself as given to the senses, in another the accent may be laid on metaphysical themes. For Bruno Nature was an infinite system which can be studied in itself, so to speak; and we saw how he championed enthusiastically the Copernican hypothesis. Yet Bruno was above all things a speculative philosopher. And with Böhme we find the emphasis laid on theosophy and on man's relation to God. It is desirable, indeed, to speak of 'accent' and 'emphasis', since the philosophers not infrequently combined an interest in empirical problems with a bent for somewhat ill-grounded speculations. Furthermore, they often combined with these interests an interest in alchemy, in astrology and in magic. They express the feeling for Nature which was one characteristic of the Renaissance; but in their study of Nature they were inclined to take attractive short-cuts, whether by bold and often bizarre philosophical speculations or by means of occultism or by both. The philosophies of Nature acted as a kind of background and stimulus to the scientific study of Nature; but for the actual development of the sciences other methods were required.

CHAPTER XVIII

THE SCIENTIFIC MOVEMENT OF THE RENAISSANCE

General remarks on the influence of science on philosophy—Renaissance science; the empirical basis of science, controlled experiment, hypothesis and astronomy, mathematics, the mechanistic view of the world—The influence of Renaissance science on philosophy.

1. WE have seen that even in the thirteenth century there was a certain amount of scientific development and that in the following century there was an increased interest in scientific problems. But the results of scholarly researches into mediaeval science have not been such as to necessitate any substantial change of view in regard to the importance of Renaissance science. They have shown that interest in scientific matters was not so alien to the mediaeval mind as has been sometimes supposed, and they have shown that the Aristotelian physics and the Ptolemaic astronomy did not possess that firm and universal hold on the mind of the mediaeval physicist with which they have often been credited; but all this does not alter the fact that science underwent a remarkable development at the time of the Renaissance and that this development has exercised a profound influence on European life and thought.

It is not the business of the historian of philosophy to give a detailed account of the discoveries and achievements of the Renaissance scientists. The reader who desires to acquaint himself with the history of science as such must obviously turn to the relevant literature on the subject. But it would be impossible to by-pass the development of science at the time of the Renaissance, if for no other reason than that it exercised a powerful influence upon philosophy. Philosophy does not pursue an isolated path of its own, without any contact with other factors of human culture. It is simply an undeniable historical fact that philosophic reflection has been influenced by science both in regard to subject-matter and also in regard to method and aims. In so far as philosophy involves reflection on the world philosophic thought will obviously be influenced in some way by the picture of the world that is painted by science and by the concrete achievements of science. This is likely to be the case in some degree in all phases of philosophic development. As to scientific method, when the use of a certain method is seen to lead to striking results it is likely that the thought will occur to some philosophers that the adoption of an analogous method in philosophy might also produce striking results in the way of established conclusions. And this thought is one which actually did influence certain philosophers of the Renaissance period. When, however, it is seen that philosophy does not develop in the same way as science, the realization of the fact is likely to give rise to the question whether the prevalent conception of philosophy should not be revised. Why is it, as Kant asked, that science progresses and that universal and necessary scientific judgments can be made and are made (or seemed to Kant to be made), while philosophy in its traditional form does not lead to comparable results and does not seem to progress in the way that science progresses? Is not our whole conception of philosophy wrong? Are we not expecting of philosophy what philosophy of its very nature cannot give? We should expect of philosophy only what it can give, and in order to see what it can give we have to inquire more closely into the nature and functions of philosophic thought. Again, as the particular sciences develop, each with its particular method, reflection will naturally suggest to some minds that these sciences have successively wrested from philosophy her various chosen fields. It may very understandably appear that cosmology or natural philosophy has given way to physics, the philosophy of the organism to biology, philosophical psychology to scientific psychology, and perhaps even moral philosophy to sociology. In other words, it may appear that for all factual information about the world and existent reality we must turn to direct observation and to the sciences. The philosopher, it may appear, cannot increase our knowledge of things in the way that the scientist can, though he may still perform a useful function in the province of logical analysis. And this is, roughly, what a considerable number of modern philosophers think. It is also possible, of course, to accept the idea that all that can be definitely known falls within the province of the sciences and yet at the same time to maintain that it is the special function of philosophy to raise those ultimate problems which cannot be answered by the scientist or in the way that the scientist answers his problems. And then one gets a different conception, or different conceptions, of philosophy.

THE SCIENTIFIC MOVEMENT OF THE RENAISSANCE

Again, as science develops, reflection on the methods of science will also develop. Philosophers will be stimulated to analyse scientific method and to do for induction what Aristotle did for syllogistic deduction. And so we get the reflections of Francis Bacon at the time of the Renaissance and of John Stuart Mill in the nineteenth century and of many other philosophers in more recent times. Thus the concrete progress of the sciences may lead to the development of a new field of philosophic analysis, which could not have been developed apart from actual scientific studies and achievements, since it takes the form of reflection on the method actually used in science.

Further, one can trace the influence of a particular science on a particular philosopher's thought. One can trace, for example, the influence of mathematics on Descartes, of mechanics on Hobbes, the rise of historical science on Hegel or of biology and the evolutionary hypothesis on Bergson.

In the foregoing sketchy remarks I have strayed rather far from the Renaissance and have introduced philosophers and philosophical ideas which will have to be discussed in later volumes of this history. But my object in making these remarks was simply the general one of illustrating, even if in an inevitably inadequate manner, the influence of science upon philosophy. Science is not, of course, the only extra-philosophical factor which exercises an influence upon philosophic thought. Philosophy is influenced also by other factors in human culture and civilization. So, too, is science for the matter of that. Nor is one entitled to conclude from the influence of science and other factors upon philosophy that philosophic thought is itself powerless to exercise any influence upon other cultural elements. I do not think that this is in fact the case. But the point which is relevant to my present purpose is the influence of science upon philosophy, and it is for this reason that I have stressed it here. Before, however, anything very definite can be said about the influence of Renaissance science in particular on philosophic thought something must be said about the nature of Renaissance science, even though I am only too conscious of the handicaps under which I labour in attempting to discuss the matter.

2. (i) The 'vulgar' notion of the cause which brought about the flowering of Renaissance science is still, I suppose, that at that period men began for the first time, since the beginning of the Middle Ages at any rate, to use their eyes and to investigate

Nature for themselves. Direct observation of the facts took the place of reliance on the texts of Aristotle and other ancient writers, and theological prejudice gave place to immediate acquaintance with the empirical data. Yet only a little reflection is needed to realize the inadequacy of this view. The dispute between Galileo and the theologians is considered, perhaps inevitably, as the representative symbol of the struggle between direct recourse to the empirical data on the one hand and theological prejudice and Aristotelian obscurantism on the other. But it is obvious that ordinary observation will not suffice to convince anyone that the earth moves round the sun: ordinary observation would suggest the contrary. The heliocentric hypothesis doubtless 'saved the appearances' better than the geocentric hypothesis did; but it was a hypothesis. Moreover, it was a hypothesis which could not be verified by the type of controlled experiment which is possible in some other sciences. It was not possible for astronomy to advance very much on the basis of observation alone; the use of hypothesis and of mathematical deduction were also required. It argues, then, a short-sighted view of the achievements of Renaissance science if one ascribes those achievements simply to observation and experiment. As Roger Bacon, the thirteenth-century Franciscan, had insisted, astronomy requires the aid of mathematics.

Yet every science is based in some way on observation and has some connection with the empirical data. It is obvious that a physicist who sets out to ascertain the laws of motion starts in a sense with observed movements; for it is the laws exemplified by movements which he wishes to ascertain. And if the laws which he eventually formulates are entirely incompatible with the observed movements, in the sense that if the laws were true the observed movements would not happen, he knows that he will have to revise his theory of motion. The astronomer does not proceed without any reference at all to empirical data: the chemist starts with the empirical data and makes experiments with existent things: the biologist would not get very far if he paid no attention to the actual behaviour of organisms. The development of physics in comparatively recent times, as interpreted by Eddington, for example, may tend to give the impression that science is not concerned with anything so plebeian as empirical data and that it is a pure construction of the human mind which is imposed upon Nature and constitutes the 'facts'; but unless one is dealing with pure mathematics, from which one cannot expect factual information about the world, one can say that every science rests ultimately on a basis of observation of the empirical data. When a science reaches a high degree of development, the empirical basis may not be so immediately obvious; but it is there none the less. The scientist does not set out to evolve a purely arbitrary theory: rather does he set out to 'explain' phenomena and, where possible, he will test or verify his theory, mediately if not immediately.

The connection of scientific theory with the empirical data is probably always obvious in the case of some sciences, whereas in the case of other sciences it may become far from obvious as the science reaches a high degree of development. But it is likely to be insisted on in the earlier stages of the development of any science, and this is especially the case when explanatory theories and hypotheses are put forward which conflict with long established notions. Thus at the time of the Renaissance, when the Aristotelian physics were being discarded in favour of fresh scientific conceptions, appeal was frequently made to the empirical data and to 'saving the appearances'. We have seen how the philosophers of Nature often stressed the need for the empirical study of the facts, and it scarcely needs pointing out that medicine and anatomy, not to speak of technology and geography, would not have made the progress which they actually did make in the sixteenth and seventeenth centuries without the aid of empirical investigation. One cannot construct a useful map of the world or give a valid account and explanation of the circulation of the blood by purely *a priori* reasoning.

The results of actual observation may be seen particularly in the advance of anatomy and physiology. Leonardo da Vinci (1452–1519), the great artist who was also deeply interested in scientific and mechanical problems and experiments, was gifted with a remarkable flair for anticipating future discoveries, inventions and theories. Thus he anticipated speculatively the discovery of the circulation of the blood, which was made by William Harvey about 1615; and in optics he anticipated the undulatory theory of light. He is also well known for his plans for flying-machines, parachutes and improved artillery. But it is his anatomical observation which is relevant in the present context. The results of this observation were portrayed in a large number of drawings; but as they were not published they did not exercise the influence which they might have done. The influential book in this connection was the *De fabrica humani corporis* (1543) by Andreas Vesalius, in which he recorded his study of anatomy. This work was of considerable importance for the development of anatomy, since Vesalius did not set out to find evidence in support of traditional theories but was concerned to observe for himself and to record his observations. The book was illustrated, and it also contained accounts of experiments made by the author on animals.

(ii) The discoveries in anatomy and physiology by men like Vesalius and Harvey were naturally powerful influences in undermining men's trust in traditional theories and assertions and in directing their minds to empirical investigation. The fact that the blood circulates is a commonplace for us; but it was not by any means a commonplace then. The ancient authorities, like Galen and Hippocrates, knew nothing of it. But the scientific advance of the Renaissance cannot be ascribed simply to 'observation' in the narrow sense: one has to take into account the increased use of controlled experiment. For example, in 1586 Simon Stevin published the account of a deliberately contrived experiment with leaden balls, which refuted Aristotle's assertion that the velocity of falling bodies is proportional to the weight of the bodies. Again, William Gilbert, who published his *De magnete* in 1600, confirmed by experiment his theory that the earth is a magnet possessing poles which are near its geographical poles, though not coincident with them, and that it is to those magnetic poles that the needle of the compass is attracted. He took a spherical loadstone and observed the behaviour or a needle or a piece of iron wire placed on it in successively different positions. On each occasion he marked on the stone the direction in which the wire came to rest, and by completing the circles he was able to show that the wire or needle always came to rest pointing to the magnetic pole.

It was Galileo Galilei (1564–1642), however, who was the foremost exponent of the experimental method among the Renaissance scientists. Born at Pisa, he studied at the university of that city, exchanging the study of medicine, with which he started, for the study of mathematics. After lecturing at Florence he became professor of mathematics first at Pisa (1589) and then at Padua (1592), occupying this last place for eighteen years. In 1610 he went to Florence as mathematician and philosopher to the Grand Duke of Tuscany and as *mathematicus primarius* in the university, though he was free from the obligation of giving courses of lectures in the university. In 1616 began the celebrated affair with the Inquisition about his astronomical views, which ended with Galileo's formal recantation in 1633. The great scientist was indeed held in detention for a time; but his scientific studies were not stopped, and he was able to continue working until he became blind in 1637. He died in 1642, the year in which Isaac Newton was born.

Galileo's name is universally associated with astronomy; but his work was also of great importance in the development of hydrostatics and mechanics. For example, whereas the Aristotelians maintained that it was a body's shape which decided whether it would sink or float in water, Galileo tried to show experimentally that Archimedes was right in saying that it was the density or specific gravity of a body, and not its shape, which determined whether it would sink or float. He also tried to show experimentally that it was not simply the body's density which decided the matter but rather its density as relative to that of the fluids in which it was placed. Again, while at Pisa he confirmed by experiment the discovery already made by Stevin that bodies of different weight take the same time to fall a given distance and that they do not, as the Aristotelians thought, reach the ground at different times. He also endeavoured to establish experimentally the law of uniform acceleration, which had indeed been anticipated by other physicists, according to which the speed of a body's fall increases uniformly with the time, and the law that a moving body, unless acted upon by friction, the resistance of the air or gravity, continues to move in the same direction at a uniform speed. Galileo was especially influenced by his conviction that Nature is essentially mathematical, and hence that under ideal conditions an ideal law would be 'obeyed'. His relatively crude experimental results suggested a simple law, even if they could hardly be said to 'prove' it. They also tended to suggest the falsity of the Aristotelian notion that no body would move unless acted upon by an external force. Indeed, Galileo's discoveries were one of the most powerful influences which discredited the Aristotelian physics. He also gave an impetus to technical advance by, for example, his plans for a pendulum clock, which was later constructed and patented by Huygens (1629–95), and by his invention, or reinvention, of the thermometer.

(iii) Mention of controlled experiment should not be taken to imply that the experimental method was widely practised from the beginning of the sixteenth century. On the contrary, it is the comparative rarity of clear cases in the first half at any rate of the century which makes it necessary to draw attention to it as something which was just beginning to be understood. Now, it is clear that experiment, in the sense of deliberately contrived experiment, is inseparable from the use of tentative hypotheses. It is true that one might devise an experiment simply to see what happens; but in actual practice controlled experiment is devised as a means of verifying a hypothesis. To perform an experiment is to put a question to Nature, and asking that particular question normally presupposes some hypothesis. One would not drop balls of different weight from a tower in order to see whether they do or do not hit the ground at the same time, unless one wished to confirm a preconceived hypothesis or unless one envisaged two possible hypotheses and desired to discover which was correct. It would be wrong to suppose that all Renaissance scientists had a clear conception of the hypothetical character of their theories: but that they used hypotheses is clear enough. It is most obvious in the case of astronomy, to which I now turn.

Nicholas Copernicus (1473-1543), the famous and learned Polish ecclesiastic, was by no means the first to realize that the apparent movement of the sun from east to west is no conclusive proof that it does actually move in this way. As we have seen, this fact had been clearly realized in the fourteenth century. But whereas the fourteenth-century physicists had confined themselves to developing the hypothesis of the earth's daily rotation on its axis, Copernicus argued on behalf of the hypothesis that the rotating earth also rotates round a stationary sun. He thus substituted the heliocentric for the geocentric hypothesis. This is not to say, of course, that he discarded the Ptolemaic system entirely. In particular, he retained the old notion that the planets move in circular orbits, though he supposed that these were 'eccentric'. In order to make his heliocentric hypothesis square with the appearances, he then had to add a number of epicycles. He postulated less than half the number of circles postulated by the Ptolemaic system of his time, and he thus simplified it; but he went about matters in much the same way as his predecessors had done. That is to say, he made speculative additions in order to 'save the appearances'.

There can be little doubt that Copernicus was convinced of the truth of the heliocentric hypothesis. But a Lutheran clergyman

THE SCIENTIFIC MOVEMENT OF THE RENAISSANCE

called Andreas Osiander (1498–1552), to whom the manuscript of Copernicus' *De revolutionibus orbium cœlestium* had been entrusted by Georg Joachim Rheticus of Wittenberg, took it upon himself to substitute a new preface for that written by Copernicus. In this new preface Osiander made Copernicus propose the heliocentric theory as a mere hypothesis or mathematical fiction. In addition he omitted the references to Aristarchus which Copernicus had made; and this omission brought upon Copernicus charges of dishonest plagiarism. Luther and Melanchthon thoroughly disapproved of the new hypothesis; but it did not excite any pronounced opposition on the part of the Catholic authorities. Osiander's preface may have contributed to this, though it must also be remembered that Copernicus had circulated privately his *De hypothesibus motuum coelestium commentariolus* without arousing hostility. It is true that the *De revolutionibus*, which was dedicated to Pope Paul III, was put on the Index in 1616 (*donec corrigatur*), as objections were raised against some sentences which represented the heliocentric hypothesis as a certainty. But this does not alter the fact that the work did not arouse opposition on the part of Catholic ecclesiastical circles when it was first published. In 1758 it was omitted from the revised Index.

Copernicus' hypothesis did not immediately find enthusiastic adherents, however, apart from the Wittenberg mathematicians, Reinhold and Rheticus. Tycho Brahe (1546–1601) opposed the hypothesis and invented one of his own, according to which the sun circles round the earth, as in the Ptolemaic system, while Mercury, Venus, Mars, Jupiter and Saturn circle round the sun in epicycles. The first real improvement on Copernicus' theory was made by John Kepler (1571–1630). Kepler, who was a Protestant, had been convinced by Michael Mästlin of Tübingen that the Copernican hypothesis was true, and he defended it in his *Prodromus dissertationum cosmographicarum seu mysterium cosmographicum*. The work contained, however, Pythagorean speculations concerning the geometrical plan of the world, and Tycho Brahe characteristically suggested that the young Kepler should give more attention to sound observation before indulging in speculation. But he took Kepler as his assistant, and after his patron's death Kepler published the works in which he enunciated his famous three laws. These works were the *Astronomia nova* (1609), the *Epitome astronomiae copernicanae* (1618) and the *Harmonices mundi* (1619). The planets, said Kepler, move in ellipses having the sun as one focus. The radius sector of the ellipse sweeps out equal areas in equal times. Moreover, we can compare mathematically the times required by the various planets to complete their respective orbits by the use of the formula that the square of the time taken by any planet to complete its orbit is proportional to the cube of its distance from the sun. In order to explain the movement of the planets Kepler postulated a motive force (or *anima motrix*) in the sun which emits rays of force, rotating with the sun. Sir Isaac Newton (1642–1727) later showed that this hypothesis was unnecessary, for in 1666 he discovered the law of the inverse square, that the sun's gravitational pull on a planet which is n times the earth's distance from the sun is $1/n^2$ times the pull at the earth's distance, and in 1685 he at last found himself in a position to work out the mathematical calculations which agreed with the demands of observation. But though Newton showed that the movements of the planets can be explained without postulating Kepler's *anima motrix*, the latter had made a most important contribution to the advance of astronomy by showing that the movements of all the then known planets could be accounted for by postulating a number of ellipses corresponding to the number of planets. The old paraphernalia of circles and epicycles could thus be dispensed with. The heliocentric hypothesis was thus greatly simplified.

On the observational side the advance of astronomy was greatly promoted by the invention of the telescope. The credit for the practical invention of the telescope must be given, it seems, to one of two Dutchmen in the first decade of the seventeenth century. Galileo, hearing of the invention, made an instrument for himself. (A Jesuit, Father Scheiner, constructed an improved instrument by embodying a suggestion made by Kepler, and Huygens introduced further improvements.) By using the telescope Galileo was enabled to observe the moon, which revealed itself as having mountains; and from this he concluded that the moon consists of the same sort of material as the earth. He was also able to observe the phases of Venus and the satellites of Jupiter, his observations fitting in very well with the heliocentric, but not with the geocentric, hypothesis. Furthermore, he observed the existence of sunspots, which were also seen by Scheiner. The existence of varying sunspots showed that the sun consisted of changeable matter, and this fact further discredited the Aristotelian cosmology. In general the telescopic observations made by Galileo and others provided empirical confirmation of the Copernican hypothesis. Indeed, observation of the phases of Venus showed clearly the superiority of the heliocentric to the geocentric hypothesis, since they were inexplicable in terms of the Ptolemaic scheme.

Perhaps one should say something at this point about the deplorable clash between Galileo and the Inquisition. Its importance as evidence of the Church's supposed hostility towards science has often been greatly exaggerated. Indeed, the fact that it is to this particular case that appeal is almost always made (the case of Bruno was quite different) by those who wish to show that the Church is the enemy of science should by itself be sufficient to cast doubt on the validity of the universal conclusion which is sometimes drawn from it. The action of the ecclesiastical authorities does not, it is true, reflect credit on them. One could wish that they had all realized more clearly the truth, suggested by Galileo himself in a letter of 1615, envisaged by Bellarmine and others at the time, and clearly affirmed by Pope Leo XIII in his encyclical letter *Providentissimus Deus*, that a Biblical passage like *Josue* 10, 12-13 can be taken as an accommodation to the ordinary way of speaking and not as an assertion of a scientific fact. We all speak of the sun as moving, and there is no reason why the Bible should not employ the same way of speaking, without one's being entitled to draw therefrom the conclusion that the sun rotates round a stationary earth. Moreover, even though Galileo had not proved the truth of the Copernican hypothesis beyond question, he had certainly shown its superiority to the geocentric hypothesis. This fact is not altered by his having laid particular stress on an argument based on a mistaken theory about the ebb and flow of the tides in his *Dialogo sopra i due massimi sistemi del mondo*, the work which precipitated a serious clash with the Inquisition. On the other hand, Galileo obstinately refused to recognize the hypothetical character of his theory. Given his naïvely realist view of the status of scientific hypotheses, it might perhaps have been difficult for him to recognize it; but Bellarmine pointed out that the empirical verification of a hypothesis does not necessarily prove its absolute truth, and if Galileo had been ready to recognize this fact, which is familiar enough today, the whole unfortunate episode with the Inquisition could have been avoided. However, Galileo not only persisted in maintaining the non-hypothetical character of the Copernican hypothesis but was also needlessly provocative into the bargain. Indeed, the clash of personalities played a not unimportant part in the affair. In fine, Galileo was a great scientist, and his opponents were not great scientists. Galileo made some sensible remarks about the interpretation of the Scriptures, the truth of which is recognized today and might well have been recognized more clearly by the theologians involved in the case. But the fault was by no means all on one side. In regard to the status of scientific theories Bellarmine's judgment was better than Galileo's, even though the latter was a great scientist and the former was not. If Galileo had had a better understanding of the nature of scientific hypotheses, and if the theologians in general had not taken up the attitude which they did in regard to the interpretation of isolated Biblical texts, the clash would not have occurred. It did occur, of course, and in regard to the superiority of the heliocentric over the geocentric hypothesis Galileo was undoubtedly right. But no universal conclusion can legitimately be drawn from this case about the Church's attitude to science.

(iv) It is clear that in the astronomy of the Renaissance hypothesis as well as observation played an indispensable rôle. But the fruitful combination of hypothesis and verification, both in astronomy and in mechanics, would not have been possible without the aid of mathematics. In the sixteenth and seventeenth centuries mathematics made considerable progress. A notable step forward was taken when John Napier (1550–1617) conceived the idea of logarithms. He communicated his idea to Tycho Brahe in 1594, and in 1614 he published a description of the general principle in his *Mirifici logarithmorum canonis descriptio*. Shortly afterwards the practical application of the principle was facilitated by the work of Henry Briggs (1561–1630). In 1638 Descartes published an account of the general principles of analytic geometry, while in 1635 Cavalieri, an Italian mathematician, published a statement of the 'method of indivisibles', which had already been used in a primitive form by Kepler. This was, in essence, the first statement of the calculus of infinitesimals. In 1665–6 Newton discovered the binomial theorem, though he did not publish his discovery until 1704. This hesitation in publishing results led to the celebrated dispute between Newton and Leibniz and their respective supporters about priority in discovering the differential and integral calculi. The two men discovered the calculus independently, but although Newton had written a sketch of his ideas in

1669 he did not actually publish anything on the matter until 1704, whereas Leibniz began publication in 1684. These elaborations of the calculus were, of course, much too late to be utilized by the great scientists of the Renaissance, and a man like Galileo had to rely on older and clumsier mathematical methods. But the point is that his ideal was that of developing a scientific view of the world in terms of mathematical formulae. He may be said to have combined the outlook of a mathematical physicist with that of a philosopher. As a physicist he tried to express the foundations of physics and the observed regularities of Nature in terms of mathematical propositions, so far as this was possible. As a philosopher he drew from the success of the mathematical method in physics the conclusion that mathematics is the key to the actual structure of reality. Though partly influenced by the nominalist conception of causality and the nominalist substitution of the study of the behaviour of things for the traditional search for essences, Galileo was also strongly influenced by the mathematical ideas of Platonism and Pythagoreanism; and this influence predisposed him to believe that the objective world is the world of the mathematician. In a well-known passage of his work *Il saggiatore* (6) he declared that philosophy is written in the book of the universe but that 'it cannot be read until we have learnt the language and understood the characters in which it is written. It is written in mathematical language, and its characters are triangles, circles and other geometrical figures, without which it is impossible to understand a single word.'

(v) This aspect of Galileo's idea of Nature expressed itself in a mechanistic view of the world. Thus he believed in atoms and explained change on the basis of an atomist theory. Again, he maintained that qualities like colour and warmth exist as qualities only in the sensing subject: they are 'subjective' in character. Objectively they exist only in the form of the motion of atoms; and they can thus be explained mechanically and mathematically. This mechanistic conception of Nature, based on an atomist theory, was also maintained by Pierre Gassendi, as we saw earlier. It was further developed by Robert Boyle (1627–91), who believed that matter consists of solid particles, each possessing its own shape, which combine with one another to form what are now termed 'molecules'. Finally Newton argued that if we knew the forces which act upon bodies, we could deduce the motions of those bodies mathematically, and he suggested that the ultimate atoms or particles are themselves centres of force. He was concerned immediately only with the movements of certain bodies; but in the preface to his *Philosophiae naturalis principia mathematica* he put forward the idea that the movements of all bodies could be explained in terms of mechanical principles and that the reason why natural philosophers had been unable to achieve this explanation was their ignorance of the active forces in nature. But he took care to explain that it was his purpose to give only 'a mathematical notion of those forces, without considering their physical causes or seats'. Hence when he showed that 'the force' of gravity which causes an apple to fall to the ground is identical with 'the force' which causes the elliptical movements of the planets, what he was doing was to show that the movements of planets and falling apples conform to the same mathematical law. Newton's scientific work enjoyed such a complete success that it reigned supreme, in its general principles that is to say, for some two hundred years, the period of the Newtonian physics.

3. The rise of modern science or, better, of the classical science of the Renaissance and post-Renaissance periods naturally had a profound effect on men's minds, opening up to them new vistas of knowledge and directing them to new interests. No sensible man would wish to deny that the scientific advance of the sixteenth and seventeenth centuries was one of the most important and influential events in history. But it is possible to exaggerate its effect on the European mind. In particular, it is, I think, an exaggeration to imply that the success of the Copernican hypothesis had the effect of upsetting belief about man's relation to God, on the ground that the earth could no longer be regarded as the geographical centre of the universe. That it did have this effect is not infrequently implied, and one writer repeats what another has said on the subject; but any necessary connection between the revolution in astronomy and a revolution in religious belief has yet to be demonstrated. Further, it is a mistake to suppose that the mechanical view of the universe either was or ought logically to have been a bar to religious belief. Galileo, who considered that the application of mathematics to the world is objectively ensured, believed that it was ensured by God's creation of the world as a mathematically intelligible system. It was divine creation which guaranteed the parallelisms between mathematical deduction and the actual system of Nature. Robert Boyle also was convinced of divine creation. And that Newton

was a man of firm piety is well known. He even conceived absolute space as the instrument by which God is omnipresent in the world and embraces all things in His immanent activity. It is true, of course, that the mechanistic view of the world tended to promote deism, which brings in God simply as an explanation of the origin of the mechanical system. But it must be remembered that even the old astronomy, for example, can be regarded as a mechanical system in a sense: it is a mistake to suppose that the scientific advance of the Renaissance suddenly cut away, as it were, the link between the world and God. The mechanical-mathematical view naturally involved the elimination from physics of the consideration of final causes; but, whatever the psychological effect of this change on many minds may have been, the elimination of final causes from physics did not necessarily involve a denial of final causality. It was a consequence of the advance in scientific method in a particular field of knowledge; but this does not mean that men like Galileo and Newton regarded physical science as the sole source of knowledge.

I want to turn, however, to the influence of the new science on philosophy, though I shall confine myself to indicating two or three lines of thought without attempting at this stage to develop them. As a preliminary, one may remind oneself of the two elements of scientific method, namely the observational and inductive side and the deductive and mathematical side.

The first aspect of scientific method, namely observation of the empirical data as a basis for induction, for discovering causes, was stressed by Francis Bacon. But as his philosophy will form the subject of the next chapter I shall say no more about him here. What I want to do at the moment is to draw attention to the connection between the emphasis laid by Francis Bacon on observation and induction in scientific method and the classical British empiricism. It would certainly be quite wrong to regard classical empiricism as being simply the philosophical reflection of the place occupied by observation and experiment in Renaissance and post-Renaissance science. When Locke asserted that all our ideas are based on sense-perception and introspection he was asserting a psychological and epistemological thesis, the antecedents of which can be seen in mediaeval Aristotelianism. But it can legitimately be said, I think, that a powerful impetus was given to philosophical empiricism by the conviction that the contemporary scientific advances were based on actual observation of the empirical data. The scientific insistence on going to the observable 'facts' as a necessary basis for explanatory theory found its correlative and its theoretical justification in the empiricist thesis that our factual knowledge is ultimately based on perception. The use of observation and experiment in science, and indeed the triumphant advance of science in general, would naturally tend, in the minds of many thinkers, to stimulate and confirm the theory that all our knowledge is based on perception, on direct acquaintance with external and internal events.

It was, however, the other aspect of scientific method, namely the deductive and mathematical aspect, which most influenced the continental 'rationalist' philosophy of the post-Renaissance period. The success of mathematics in the solution of scientific problems naturally enhanced its prestige. Not only was mathematics clear and exact in itself, but in its application to scientific problems it also made clear what had formerly been obscure. It appeared as the highroad to knowledge. It is understandable that the certainty and exactitude of mathematics suggested to Descartes, himself a talented mathematician and the chief pioneer in the field of analytic geometry, that an examination of the essential characteristics of the mathematical method would reveal the right method for use in philosophy also. It is understandable also that under the influence of mathematics as a model several of the leading philosophers on the Continent believed that they could reconstruct the world, as it were, in an *a priori* deductive manner with the aid of certain fundamental ideas analogous to the definitions and axioms of mathematics. Thus a mathematical model provided the framework of Spinoza's *Ethica more geometrico demonstrata,* though it scarcely provided its content.

We have seen how the development of astronomy and of mechanics at the time of the Renaissance promoted the growth of a mechanical view of the world. This outlook was reflected in the field of philosophy. Descartes, for example, considered that the material world and its changes can be explained simply in terms of matter, identified with geometrical extension, and motion. At creation God placed, as it were, a certain amount of motion or energy in the world, which is transmitted from body to body according to the laws of mechanics. Animals can be considered as machines. Descartes himself did not apply these mechanistic analogies to the human being as a whole, but some later French thinkers did. In England Thomas Hobbes, who objected against

THE SCIENTIFIC MOVEMENT OF THE RENAISSANCE 291

Descartes that thought is an activity of bodies and that the activity of bodies is motion, believed that just as the behaviour of inanimate bodies can be deduced from certain fundamental ideas and laws so the behaviour of human societies, which are simply organizations of bodies, can be deduced from the properties of these organized groupings of bodies. Mechanics thus furnished a partial model for Descartes and a more complete model for Hobbes.

The foregoing remarks are intentionally brief and summary: they are designed only to indicate some of the lines on which the development of science influenced philosophic thought. Names of philosophers have been introduced who will be treated of in the next volume; and it would be out of place to say more about them here. It may be as well, however, to point out in conclusion that the philosophic ideas which have been mentioned reacted in turn on science. For example, Descartes' conception of organic bodies may have been crude and inadequate, but it probably helped to encourage scientists to investigate the processes and behaviour of organic bodies in a scientific manner. A hypothesis need not be completely true in order to bear fruit in some particular direction.

CHAPTER XIX

FRANCIS BACON

English philosophy of the Renaissance—Bacon's life and writings—The classification of the sciences—Induction and 'the idols'.

1. THE first outstanding philosopher of the post-mediaeval period in England was Francis Bacon: it is his name which is for ever associated with the philosophy of the Renaissance in Great Britain. With the exception of St. Thomas More and Richard Hooker, whose political ideas will be briefly considered in the next chapter, the other British philosophers of the Renaissance merit little more than bare mention. It should, however, be emphasized that the general tone of philosophical thinking in the English universities at the time of the Renaissance was conservative. The Aristotelian-Scholastic logical tradition persisted for many years, especially at Oxford, and it formed the background of John Locke's university education in the seventeenth century. Latin works of logic, like the *Institutionum dialecticarum libri IV* of John Sanderson (1587–1602) or the *Logicae libri V de praedicabilibus* of Richard Crakanthorpe (1569–1624), began to give place to works in the vernacular like *The rule of reason, containing the arte of logique* (1552) by Thomas Wilson or *The philosopher's game* (1563) and the *Arte of reason rightly termed Witcraft* (1573) of Ralph Lever; but such works contained nothing much in the nature of novelty. Sir William Temple (1533–1626) defended the Ramist logic; but he was attacked by Everard Digby (1550–92), who wrote a refutation of Ramism in the name of Aristotelianism. Sir Kenelm Digby (1603–65), who became a Catholic in Paris, where he was acquainted with Descartes, endeavoured to combine the Aristotelian metaphysics with the corpuscular theory of matter. Everard Digby, though an Aristotelian in logic, was influenced by the neo-Platonic ideas of Reuchlin. Similarly, Robert Greville, Lord Brooke (1608–43), was influenced by the Platonic Academy of Florence; and in *The Nature of Truth* he maintained a doctrine of the divine light which helped to prepare the way for the group of Cambridge Platonists. Ideas of Cardinal Nicholas of Cusa and of Paracelsus were represented by Robert Fludd (1574–1637), who

travelled extensively on the Continent and was influenced by the continental Renaissance. In his *Philosophia Mosaica* he depicted God as the synthesis in identity of opposites. In Himself God is incomprehensible darkness; but considered in another aspect He is the light and wisdom which manifests itself in the world, which is the *explicatio Dei*. The world manifests in itself the twofold aspect of God, for the divine light is manifested in, or is the cause of, warmth, rarefaction, light, love, goodness and beauty, while the divine darkness is the origin of cold, condensation, hate and unloveliness. Man is a microcosm of the universe, uniting in himself the two aspects of God which are revealed in the universe. There is in man a constant strife between light and darkness.

2. The leading figure of the philosophy of the Renaissance in England was, however, a thinker who turned consciously against Aristotelianism and who did so not in favour of Platonism or of theosophy but in the name of scientific and technical advancement in the service of man. The value and justification of knowledge, according to Francis Bacon, consists above all in its practical application and utility; its true function is to extend the dominion of the human race, the reign of man over nature. In the *Novum Organum*[1] Bacon calls attention to the practical effects of the invention of printing, gunpowder and the magnet, which 'have changed the face of things and the state of the world; the first in literature, the second in warfare; the third in navigation'. But inventions such as these did not come from the traditional Aristotelian physics; they came from direct acquaintance with nature herself. Bacon certainly represents 'humanism' in the sense that he was a great writer; but his emphasis on man's dominion over nature by means of science distinguishes him sharply from the Italian humanists, who were more concerned with the development of the human personality, while his insistence on going direct to nature, on the inductive method, and his mistrust of speculation distinguish him from the neo-Platonists and the theosophists. Though he did not make positive contributions to science himself and though he was far more influenced by Aristotelianism than he realized, Bacon divined in a remarkable way the technical progress which was to come, a technical progress which, he was confident, would serve man and human culture. This vision was present, in a limited sense, to the minds of the alchemists; but Bacon saw that it was a scientific knowledge of nature, not alchemy

[1] I, 129.

or magic or fantastic speculation, which was to open up to man the path of dominion over nature. Bacon stood not only chronologically but also, in part at least, mentally on the threshold of a new world revealed by geographical discovery, the finding of fresh sources of wealth and, above all, by the advance in natural science, the establishment of physics on an experimental and inductive basis. It must be added, however, that Bacon had, as we shall see, an insufficient grasp and appreciation of the new scientific method. That is why I stated that he belonged mentally 'in part at least' to the new era. However, the fact remains that he did look forward to the new era of scientific and technical achievement: his claim to be a herald or *buccinator* of that era was justified, even if he over-estimated his power of vision.

Francis Bacon was born in 1561 in London. After studying at Cambridge he spent two years in France with the British ambassador and then took up the practice of law. In 1584 he entered Parliament and enjoyed a successful career which culminated in his appointment as Lord Chancellor in 1618 and the reception of the title Baron Verulam. He was created Viscount of St. Albans in 1621; but in the same year he was accused of accepting bribes in his judicial capacity. Found guilty he was sentenced to deprivation of his offices and of his seat in Parliament, a large fine and imprisonment in the Tower. In actual fact, however, he was released from the Tower after a few days and payment of the fine was not exacted. Bacon admitted that he had accepted presents from litigants, though he claimed that his judicial decisions had not been influenced thereby. His claim may or may not be valid; one cannot know the truth about this matter; but in any case it would be an anachronism to expect of a judge in the reigns of Elizabeth and James I precisely the same standard of behaviour which is demanded today. This is not to defend Bacon's behaviour, of course; and the fact that he was brought to trial bears witness to contemporary realization of the fact that his behaviour was improper. But it must be added at the same time that his fall was not brought about simply by a disinterested desire for pure justice on the part of his opponents: partly at least he was the victim of political intrigue and jealousy. In other words, though it is true that Bacon was not a man of profound moral integrity, he was not a wicked man or an iniquitous judge. His reception of presents, as also his behaviour towards Essex, has sometimes been presented in a grossly exaggerated light. It is quite incorrect to regard him as an example of a sort of 'split personality', a man who combined in himself the two irreconcilable characters of the disinterested philosopher and the egoistic politician who cared nothing for the demands of morality. He was by no means a saint like Thomas More; but neither was he an instance of Jekyll and Hyde. His death occurred on April 9th, 1626.

Of the Advancement of Learning appeared in 1606 and the *De sapientia veterum* in 1609. Bacon planned a great work, the *Instauratio magna*, of which the first part, the *De dignitate et augmentis scientiarum*, appeared in 1623. This was a revision and extension of *The Advancement of Learning*. The second part, the *Novum organum*, had appeared in 1620. This had its origin in the *Cogitata et visa* (1607); but it was never completed, a fate which overtook most of Bacon's literary plans. In 1622 and 1623 he published parts of his projected *Historia naturalis et experimentalis ad condendam philosophiam: sive phenomena universi*. The *Sylva sylvarum* and the *New Atlantis* were published posthumously. Numerous other writings include essays and a history of Henry VII.

3. According to Bacon[1] 'that division of human learning is most true which is derived from the threefold faculty of the rational soul'. Taking memory, imagination and reason to be the three faculties of the rational soul, he assigns history to memory, poetry to imagination and philosophy to reasoning. History, however, comprises not only 'civil history', but also 'natural history', and Bacon remarks that 'literary history' should be attended to.[2] Philosophy falls into three main divisions; the first being concerned with God (*de Numine*), the second with nature and the third with man. The first division, that concerned with God, is natural or rational theology; it does not comprise 'inspired or sacred theology', which is the result of God's revelation rather than of man's reasoning. Revealed theology is, indeed, 'the haven and sabbath of all human contemplations',[3] and it is a province of knowledge (*scientia*), but it stands outside philosophy. Philosophy is the work of the human reason, nature being known directly (*radio directo*), God indirectly by means of creatures (*radio refracto*), and man by reflection (*radio reflexo*). Bacon's division of human learning or knowledge according to the faculties of the rational soul is unhappy and artificial; but when he comes to determine the main divisions of philosophy he divides them according to objects: God, nature and man.

---

[1] *De augmentis scientiarum*, 2, 1.   [2] *Ibid.*, 2, 4.   [3] *Ibid.*, 3, 1.

The divisions of philosophy, he says,[1] are like the branches of a tree which are united in a common trunk. This means that there is 'one universal science, which is the mother of the rest' and is known as 'first philosophy'. This comprises both fundamental axioms, like *quae in eodem tertio conveniunt, et inter se conveniunt*, and fundamental notions like 'possible' and 'impossible', 'being' and 'not-being', etc. Natural theology, which is the knowledge of God that can be obtained 'by the light of nature and the contemplation of created things'[2] treats of God's existence and of His nature, but only so far as this is manifested in creatures; and it has as its appendix *doctrina de angelis et spiritibus*. The philosophy of nature Bacon divides into speculative and operative natural philosophy. Speculative natural philosophy is subdivided into *physics* (*physica specialis*) and metaphysics. Metaphysics, as part of natural philosophy, must be distinguished, Bacon says,[3] from first philosophy and natural theology, to neither of which does he give the name 'metaphysics'. What, then, is the difference between physics and metaphysics? It is to be found in the types of causes with which they are respectively concerned. Physics treats of efficient and material causes, metaphysics of formal and final causes. But Bacon presently declares that 'inquiry into final causes is sterile and, like a virgin consecrated to God, produces nothing'.[4] One can say, then, that metaphysics, according to him, is concerned with formal causes. This was the position he adopted in the *Novum organum*.

One is naturally tempted to interpret all this in Aristotelian terms and to think that Bacon was simply continuing the Aristotelian doctrine of causes. This would be a mistake, however, and Bacon himself said that his readers should not suppose that because he used a traditional term he was employing it in the traditional sense. By 'forms', the object of metaphysics, he meant what he called 'fixed laws'. The form of heat is the law of heat. Actually there is no radical division between physics and metaphysics. Physics started with examining specific types of matter or bodies in a restricted field of causality and activity; but it goes on to consider more general laws. Thus it shades off into metaphysics, which is concerned with the highest or widest laws of nature. Bacon's use of Aristotelian terminology is misleading. Metaphysics is for him the most general part of what might otherwise be called physics. Moreover, it is not directed to

[1] *De augmentis scientiarum*, 3, 1. [2] *Ibid.*, 2. [3] *Ibid.*, 4. [4] *Ibid.*, 5.

contemplation but to action. We seek to learn the laws of nature with a view to increasing human control over bodies.

Speculative natural philosophy consisting, then, of physics and metaphysics, what is operative natural philosophy? It is the application of the former; and it falls into two parts, mechanics (by which Bacon means the science of mechanics) and magic. Mechanics is the application of physics in practice, while magic is applied metaphysics. Here again Bacon's terminology is apt to mislead. By 'magic' he does not mean, he tells us, the superstitious and frivolous magic which is as different from true magic as the chronicles about King Arthur are different from Caesar's commentaries: he means the practical application of the science of 'hidden forms' or laws. It is improbable that youth could be suddenly and magically restored to an old man; but it is probable that a knowledge of the true natures of assimilation, bodily 'spirits', etc., could prolong life or even partly restore youth 'by means of diets, baths, unctions, the right medicines, suitable exercises and the like'.[1]

The 'appendix' of natural philosophy is mathematics.[2] Pure mathematics comprises geometry, which treats of continuous abstract quantity, and arithmetic, which treats of discrete abstract quantity. 'Mixed mathematics' comprises perspective, music, astronomy, cosmography, architecture, etc. Elsewhere,[3] however, Bacon remarks that astronomy is rather the noblest part of physics than a part of mathematics. When astronomers pay exclusive attention to mathematics they produce false hypotheses. Even if Bacon did not reject outright the heliocentric hypothesis of Copernicus and Galileo, he certainly did not embrace it. Apologists for Bacon point out that he was convinced that the appearances could be saved either on the heliocentric or on the geocentric hypothesis and that the dispute could not be settled by mathematical and abstract reasoning. Doubtless he did think this; but that does not alter the fact that he failed to discern the superiority of the heliocentric hypothesis.

The third main part of philosophy is the part dealing with man. It comprises *philosophia humanitatis* or anthropology and *philosophia civilis* or political philosophy. The former treats first of the human body and is subdivided into medicine, cosmetics, athletics and *ars voluptuaria*, including, for example, music considered from a certain point of view. Secondly it treats of the human soul,

---
[1] *De augmentis scientiarum*, 5. [2] *Ibid.*, 6. [3] *Ibid.*, 4.

though the nature of the rational, divinely created and immortal soul (*spiraculum*) as distinct from the sensitive soul is a subject which belongs to theology rather than to philosophy. The latter is, however, able to establish the fact that man possesses faculties which transcend the power of matter. Psychology thus leads on to a consideration of logic, *doctrina circa intellectum*, and ethics, *doctrina circa voluntatem*.[1] The parts of logic are the *artes inveniendi, judicandi, retinendi et tradendi*. The most important subdivision of the *ars inveniendi* is what Bacon calls 'the interpretation of nature', which proceeds *ab experimentis ad axiomata, quae et ipsa nova experimenta designent*.[2] This is the *novum organum*. The art of judging is divided into induction, which belongs to the *novum organum*, and the syllogism. Bacon's doctrine concerning the *novum organum* will be considered presently, as also his theory of the 'idols' which forms one of the topics comprised under the heading of the doctrine of the syllogism. In passing it may be mentioned that apropos of pedagogy, which is an 'appendix' of the *ars tradendi*, Bacon observes, 'Consult the schools of the Jesuits: for nothing that has been practised is better than these.'[3] Ethics deals with the nature of human good (*doctrina de exemplari*), not only private but also common, and with the cultivation of the soul with a view to attaining the good (*doctrina de georgica animi*). The part dealing with the common good does not treat of the actual union of men in the State but with the factors which render men apt for social life.[4] Finally *philosophia civilis*[5] is divided into three parts, each of which considers a good which accrues to man from civil society. *Doctrina de conversatione* considers the good which comes to man from association with his fellows (*solamen contra solitudinem*); *doctrina de negotiis* considers the help man receives from society in his practical affairs; and the *doctrina de imperio sive republica* considers the protection from injury which he obtains through government. Or one can say that the three parts consider the three types of prudence; *prudentia in conversando, prudentia in negotiando* and *prudentia in gubernando*. Bacon adds[6] that there are two *desiderata* in the part dealing with government, namely a theory concerning the extension of rule or empire and a science of universal justice, the *de justitia universali sive de fontibus iuris*.

In the ninth and last book of the *De augmentis scientiarum*

[1] *De augmentis scientiarum*, 5, 1.   [2] *Ibid.*, 2.   [3] *Ibid.*, 6, 4.
[4] *Ibid.*, 7, 2.   [5] *Ibid.*, 8, 1.   [6] *Ibid.*, 8, 3.

Bacon touches briefly on revealed theology. Just as we are bound to obey the divine law, he says, even when the will resists; so we are obliged to put faith in the divine word even when reason struggles against it. 'For, if we believe only those things which are agreeable to our reason, we assent to things, not to their Author' (that is to say, our belief is based on the evident character of the propositions in question, not on the authority of God revealing). And he adds that 'the more improbable (*absonum*, discordant) and incredible a divine mystery is, so much the more honour is paid to God through believing, and so much the nobler is the victory of faith'. This is not to say, however, that reason has no part to play in Christian theology. It is used both in the attempt to understand the mysteries of faith, so far as this is possible, and in drawing conclusions from them.

Bacon's outline of philosophy in the *De augmentis scientiarum* is on the grand scale and comprises a very extensive programme. He was undoubtedly influenced by traditional philosophy, probably to a greater extent than he realized; but I have already pointed out that the use of Aristotelian terms by Bacon is no sure guide to the meaning he gave them. And in general one can see a new philosophical outlook taking shape in his writings. In the first place, he eliminated from physics consideration of final causality, on the ground that the search for final causes leads thinkers to be content with assigning specious and unreal causes to events when they ought to be looking for the real physical causes, knowledge of which alone is of value for extending human power. In this respect, says Bacon,[1] the natural philosophy of Democritus was more solid and profound than the philosophies of Plato and Aristotle, who were constantly introducing final causes. It is not that there is no such thing as final causality; and it would be absurd to attribute the origin of the world to the fortuitous collision of atoms, after the manner of Democritus and Epicurus. But this does not mean that final causality has any place in physics. Furthermore, Bacon did not assign to metaphysics a consideration of final causality in the Aristotelian sense. Metaphysics was for him neither the study of being as being nor a contemplation of unmoving final causes: it is rather the study of the most general principles or laws or 'forms' of the material world, and this study is undertaken in view of a practical end. His conception of philosophy was to all intents and purposes naturalistic and

---
[1] *De augmentis scientiarum*, 3, 4.

materialistic. This does not mean that Bacon affirmed atheism or that he denied that man possesses a spiritual and immortal soul. It does mean, however, that he excluded from philosophy any consideration of spiritual being. The philosopher may be able to show that a first Cause exists; but he cannot say anything about God's nature, the consideration of which belongs to theology. Similarly, the subject of immortality is not one which can be treated philosophically. Bacon thus made a sharp division between theology and philosophy, not simply in the sense that he made a formal distinction between them but also in the sense that he accorded full liberty to a materialistic and mechanistic interpretation of Nature. The philosopher is concerned with what is material and with what can be considered from the mechanistic and naturalistic point of view. Bacon may have spoken on occasion in more or less traditional terms about natural theology, for example, but it is clear that the real direction of his thought was to relegate the immaterial to the sphere of faith. Moreover, in spite of his retention of the Aristotelian term 'first philosophy', he did not understand by it precisely what the Aristotelians had understood by it: for him first philosophy was the study of the axioms which are common to the different sciences and of various 'transcendental' concepts considered in their relations to the physical sciences. In a broad sense, Bacon's conception of philosophy was positivistic in character, provided that this is not taken to imply a rejection of theology as a source of knowledge.

4. I turn now to the second part of the *Instauratio magna*, which is represented by the *Novum organum sive indicia vera de interpretatione naturae*. In this work Bacon's philosophical attitude is most clearly revealed. 'Knowledge and human power come to the same thing', for 'nature cannot be conquered except by obeying her'.[1] The purpose of science is the extension of the dominion of the human race over nature; but this can be achieved only by a real knowledge of nature; we cannot obtain effects without an accurate knowledge of causes. The sciences which man now possesses, says Bacon,[2] are useless for obtaining practical effects (*ad inventionem operum*) and our present logic is useless for the purpose of establishing sciences. 'The logic in use is of more value for establishing and rendering permanent the errors which are based on vulgar conceptions than for finding out the truth; so that it is more harmful than useful.'[3] The syllogism consists of

---
[1] I, 3.   [2] I, 11.   [3] I, 12.

propositions; and propositions consist of words; and words express concepts. Thus, if the concepts are confused and if they are the result of over-hasty abstraction, nothing which is built upon them is secure. Our only hope lies in true *induction*.[1] There are two ways of seeking and finding the truth.[2] First, the mind may proceed from sense and from the perception of particulars to the most general axioms and from these deduce the less general propositions. Secondly it may proceed from sense and the perception of particulars to immediately attainable axioms and thence, gradually and patiently, to more general axioms. The first way is known and employed; but it is unsatisfactory, because particulars are not examined with sufficient accuracy, care and comprehensiveness and because the mind jumps from an insufficient basis to general conclusions and axioms. It produced *anticipationes naturae*, rash and premature generalizations. The second way, which has not yet been tried, is the true way. The mind proceeds from a careful and patient examination of particulars to the *interpretatio naturae*.

Bacon does not deny, then, that some sort of induction had been previously known and employed; what he objected to was rash and hasty generalization, resting on no firm basis in experience. Induction starts with the operation of the senses; but it requires the co-operation of mind, though the mind's activity must be controlled by observation. Bacon may have lacked an adequate notion of the place and importance of hypothesis in scientific method; but he saw clearly that the value of conclusions based on observation depend on the character of that observation. This led him to say that it is useless to attempt to graft the new on to the old; we must start again from the beginning.[3] He does not accuse the Aristotelians and Scholastics of neglecting induction entirely but rather of being in too much of a hurry to generalize and to draw conclusions. He thought of them as being more concerned with logical consistency, with ensuring that their conclusions followed in due form from their premisses, than with giving a sure foundation to the premisses on the truth of which the conclusions depended. Of the logicians he says[4] that 'they seem to have given scarcely any serious consideration to induction; they pass it over with a brief mention and hurry on to the formulas of disputation'. He, on the other hand, rejects the syllogism on the ground that induction must take its rise in the observation of

---
[1] 1, 14.   [2] 1, 19 ff.   [3] 1, 31.   [4] *Instauratio magna, distributio operis.*

things, of particular facts or events, and must stick to them as closely as possible. The logicians wing their way at once to the most general principles and deduce conclusions syllogistically. This procedure is admittedly very useful for purposes of disputation; but it is useless for purposes of natural and practical science. 'And so the order of demonstration is reversed';[1] in induction we proceed in the opposite direction to that in which we proceed in deduction.

It might appear that Bacon's insistence on the practical ends of inductive science would itself tend to encourage the drawing of over-hasty conclusions. This was not his intention at least. He condemns[2] the 'unreasonable and puerile' desire to snatch at results which, 'as an Atlanta's apple, hinders the race'. In other words, the establishment of scientific laws by the patient employment of the inductive method will bring greater light to the mind and will prove of more utility in the long run than unco-ordinated particular truths, however immediately practical the latter may seem to be.

But to attain a certain knowledge of nature is not so easy or simple as it may sound at first hearing, for the human mind is influenced by preconceptions and prejudices which bear upon our interpretation of experience and distort our judgments. It is necessary, then, to draw attention to 'the idols and false notions' which inevitably influence the human mind and render science difficult of attainment unless one is aware of them and warned against them. Hence Bacon's famous doctrine of 'the idols'.[3] There are four main types, the idols of the tribe, the idols of the cave or den, the idols of the market-place and the idols of the theatre. 'The doctrines of the idols stands to the interpretation of nature as the doctrine of sophistical arguments stands to common logic.'[4] Just as it is useful for the syllogistic dialectician to be aware of the nature of sophistical arguments, so it is useful for the scientist or natural philosopher to be aware of the nature of the idols of the human mind, that he may be on his guard against their influence.

The 'idols of the tribe' (*idola tribus*) are those errors, the tendency to which is inherent in human nature and which hinder objective judgment. For example, man is prone to rest content with that aspect of things which strikes the senses. Apart from the

---
[1] *Instauratio magna, distributio operis.*   [2] *Ibid.*
[3] *Novum organum,* 1, 38–68.   [4] *Ibid.,* 1, 40.

fact that this tendency is responsible for the neglect of investigation into the nature of those things which, like air or the 'animal spirits', are not directly observable, 'sense is in itself weak and misleading'. For the scientific interpretation of nature it is not enough to rely on the senses, not even when they are supplemented by the use of instruments; suitable experiments are also necessary. Then, again, the human mind is prone to rest in those ideas which have once been received and believed or which are pleasing to it and to pass over or reject instances which run counter to received or cherished beliefs. The human mind is not immune from the influence of the will and affections: 'for what a man would like to be true, to that he tends to give credence'. Further, the human mind is prone to indulge in abstractions; and it tends to conceive as constant what is really changing or in flux. Bacon thus draws attention to the danger of relying on appearances, on the untested and uncriticized data of the senses; to the phenomenon of 'wishful thinking'; and to the mind's tendency to mistake abstractions for things. He also draws attention to man's tendency to interpret nature anthropomorphically. Man easily reads into nature final causes 'which proceed from the nature of man rather than from that of the universe'. On this matter one may recall what he says in his work *Of the Advancement of Learning* (2) concerning the introduction of final causes into physics. 'For to say that the hairs of the eyelids are for a quickset and fence about the sight; or that the firmness of the skins and hides of living creatures is to defend them from the extremities of heat or cold; or that the clouds are for watering of the earth' is 'impertinent' in physics. Such considerations 'stay and slug the ship from farther sailing, and have brought this to pass, that the search of the physical causes hath been neglected and passed in silence'. Although Bacon says, as we have seen, that final causality 'is well inquired and collected in metaphysics', it is pretty clear that he regarded notions like the above as instances of man's tendency to interpret natural activity on an analogy with human purposeful activity.

The 'idols of the den' (*idola specus*) are the errors peculiar to each individual, arising from his temperament, education, reading and the special influences which have weighed with him as an individual. These factors lead him to interpret phenomena according to the viewpoint of his own den or cave. 'For each one has (in addition to the aberrations of human nature in general) a certain individual cave or cavern of his own, which breaks and distorts the light of nature.' Bacon's language designedly recalls Plato's parable of the cave in the *Republic*.

The 'idols of the market-place' (*idola fori*) are errors due to the influence of language. The words used in common language describe things as commonly conceived; and when an acute mind sees that the commonly accepted analysis of things is inadequate, language may stand in the way of the expression of a more adequate analysis. Sometimes words are employed when there are no corresponding things. Bacon gives examples like *fortuna* and *primum mobile*. Sometimes words are employed without any clear concept of what is denoted or without any commonly recognized meaning. Bacon takes as an example the word 'humid', *humidum*, which may refer to various sorts of things or qualities or actions.

The 'idols of the theatre' (*idola theatri*) are the philosophical systems of the past, which are nothing better than stage-plays representing unreal worlds of man's own creation. In general there are three types of false philosophy. First there is 'sophistical' philosophy, the chief representative of which is Aristotle, who corrupted natural philosophy with his dialectic. Secondly, there is 'empirical' philosophy, based on a few narrow and obscure observations. The chemists are the chief offenders here: Bacon mentions the philosophy of William Gilbert, author of *De magnete* (1600). Thirdly there is 'superstitious' philosophy, characterized by the introduction of theological considerations. The Pythagoreans indulged in this sort of thing, and, more subtly and dangerously, Plato and the Platonists.

Bad demonstrations are the allies and support of the 'idols': 'by far the best demonstration is experience'.[1] But it is necessary to make a distinction. Mere experience is not enough; it may be compared to a man groping his way in the dark and clutching at anything which offers, in the hope that he will eventually take the right direction. True experience is planned: it may be compared to the activity of a man who first lights a lamp and sees the way clearly.[2] It is not a question of simply multiplying experiments, but of proceeding by an orderly and methodically inductive process.[3] Nor is true induction the same thing as *inductio per enumerationem simplicem*, which is 'puerile' and leads to precarious conclusions which are arrived at without sufficient examination and often with a total neglect of negative instances.[4]

[1] I, 70.   [2] I, 83.   [3] I, 100.   [4] I, 105.

Bacon seems to have thought, wrongly, that the only form of induction known to the Aristotelians was perfect induction or induction 'by simple enumeration', in which no serious attempt was made to discover a real causal connection. But it is undeniable that insufficient consideration had been paid to the subject of inductive method.

What, then, is true induction, positively considered? Human power is directed to or consists in being able to generate a new form in a given nature. From this it follows that human science is directed to the discovery of the forms of things.[1] 'Form' does not here refer to the final cause: the form or formal cause of a given nature is such that, 'given the form, the nature infallibly follows'.[2] It is the law which constitutes a nature. 'And so the form of heat or the form of light is the same thing as the law of heat or the law of light.'[3] Wherever heat manifests itself it is fundamentally the same reality which manifests itself, even if the things in which heat manifests itself are heterogeneous; and to discover the law governing this manifestation of heat is to discover the form of heat. The discovery of these laws or forms would increase human power. For example, gold is a combination of various qualities or natures, and whoever knew the forms or laws of these various qualities or natures could produce them in another body; and this would infallibly result in the transformation of that body into gold.[4]

The discovery of forms in this sense, that is, of the eternal and unchangeable forms or laws, belongs, however, to metaphysics, to which, as has already been mentioned, the consideration of 'formal causes' properly belongs. Physics are concerned with efficient causes or with the investigation of concrete bodies in their natural operation rather than with the possible transformation of one body into another through a knowledge of the forms of simple natures. The physicist will investigate 'concrete bodies as they are found in the ordinary course of nature'.[5] He will investigate what Bacon calls the *latens processus*, the process of change which is not immediately observable but needs to be discovered. 'For example, in every generation and transformation of bodies inquiry must be made as to what is lost and flies away, what remains and what is added; what is dilated and what is contracted; what is united and what is separated; what is continued and what is cut off; what impels and what hinders; what

[1] 2, 1. [2] 2, 4. [3] 1, 17. [4] 2, 5. [5] *Ibid.*

dominates and what succumbs; and much else besides. Nor are these things to be investigated only in the generation and transformation of bodies but also in all other alterations and motions . . .'[1] The process of natural change depends on factors which are not immediately observed by the senses. The physicist will also investigate what Bacon calls the *latens schematismus*, the inner structure of bodies.[2] 'But the thing will not on that account be reduced to the atom, which presupposes the vacuum and unchanging matter (both of which are false) but to true particles, as they may be found to be.'[3]

We have thus the investigation of the eternal and changeless forms of simple natures, which constitutes metaphysics, and the investigation of the efficient and material causes and of the *latens processus* and *latens schematismus* (all of which relate to 'the common and ordinary course of nature, not to the fundamental and eternal laws'), which constitutes physics.[4] The purpose of both is, however, increase of man's power over nature; and this cannot be fully attained without a knowledge of the ultimate forms.

The problem of induction is, therefore, the problem of the discovery of forms. There are two distinct stages. First, there is the 'eduction' of axioms from experience; and, secondly, there is the deduction or derivation of new experiments from the axioms. In more modern language we should say that a hypothesis must first be formed on the basis of the facts of experience, and then observations which will test the value of the hypothesis must be deduced from the hypothesis. This means, says Bacon, that the primary task is to prepare a 'sufficient and good natural and experimental history', based on the facts.[5] Suppose that one desires to discover the form of heat. First of all one must construct a list of cases in which heat is present (*instantiae convenientes in natura calidi*); for example, the rays of the sun, the striking of sparks from flint, the interior of animals, or nasturtium when chewed. Then we shall have a *tabula essentiae et praesentiae*.[6] After this a list should be made of cases which are as much as possible alike to the first but in which heat is nevertheless absent. For example, 'the rays of the moon and of the stars and of comets are not found to be warm to the sense of touch'.[7] In this way *a tabula declinationis sive absentiae in proximo* will be constructed. Finally what Bacon calls a *tabula graduum* or *tabula comparativae* must be made of cases in which the nature whose form is being investigated

[1] 2, 6.   [2] 2, 7.   [3] 2, 8.   [4] 2, 9.   [5] 2, 10.   [6] 2, 11.   [7] 2, 12.

is present in varying degrees.[1] For example, the heat of animals is increased by exercise and by fever. These tables having been constructed, the work of induction really begins. By comparing the instances we must discover what is always present when a given nature (heat, for example) is present; what is always absent when it is absent; and what varies in correspondence with the variations of that 'nature'.[2] First of all, we shall be able to exclude (as the form of a given nature) what is not present in some instance in which that nature is present or which is present in an instance in which the nature is absent or which does not vary in correspondence with the variations of that nature. This is the process of *rejectio* or *exclusio*.[3] But it simply lays the foundations of true induction, which is not completed until a positive affirmation is arrived at.[4] A provisional positive affirmation is arrived at by comparing the positive 'tables'; and Bacon calls this provisional affirmation a *permissio intellectus* or *interpretatio inchoata* or *vindemiatio prima*.[5] Taking heat as an example, he finds the form of heat in motion or, more exactly, in *motus expansivus, cohibitus, et nitens per partes minores*, expanding and restrained motion which makes its way through the smaller parts.

However, in order to render the provisional affirmation certain further means have to be employed; and the rest of the *Novum organum*[6] is devoted to the first of these, which Bacon calls the way of *praerogativae instantiarum*, privileged cases or instances. One class of privileged case is that of unique cases, *instantiae solitariae*. These are cases in which the nature under investigation is found in things which have nothing in common save their participation in that nature. The plan of the *Novum organum* demands that after treating of the *praerogativae instantiarum* Bacon should go on to treat first of seven other 'helps to the intellect' in true and perfect induction and then of the *latentes processus* and *latentes schematismi* in nature; but in actual fact he gets no further than the completion of his treatment of the *praerogativae instantiarum*.

In the *Nova Atlantis*, which also is an unfinished work, Bacon pictures an island in which is situated Solomon's House, an institute devoted to the study and contemplation 'of the works and creatures of God'. Bacon is informed that 'the purpose of our foundation is the knowledge of the causes and motions and inner virtues in nature and the furthest possible extension of the limits

---

[1] 2, 13. [2] 2, 15. [3] 2, 16–18. [4] 2, 19. [5] 2, 20. [6] 2, 21 ff.

of human dominion'. He is then told of their researches and inventions, among which figure submarines and aeroplanes. All this illustrates Bacon's conviction concerning the practical function of science. But though he performed experiments himself he cannot be said to have contributed much personally to the practical realization of his dreams. He certainly exerted himself to find a patron able and willing to endow a scientific institute of the type of which he dreamed, but he met with no success. This lack of immediate success should not, however, be taken as an indication that Bacon's ideas were unimportant, still less that they were silly. The Scholastic, and in general the metaphysician, will lay much more emphasis on and attach much more value to 'contemplation' (in the Aristotelian sense) than Bacon did; but the latter's insistence on the practical function of science, or of what he called 'experimental philosophy', heralded a movement which has culminated in modern technical civilization, rendered possible by those laboratories and institutes of research and applied science which Bacon envisaged. He vehemently attacked the English universities, for which, in his opinion, science meant at the best mere learning and at the worst mere play with words and obscure terms, and he looked on himself, with his idea of fruitful knowledge, as the herald of a new era. So indeed he was. There has been a strong tendency to depreciate Francis Bacon and to minimize his importance; but the influence of his writings was considerable, and the outlook which he represented has entered profoundly into the western mind. Perhaps it is only fitting, if one can say so without being misunderstood, that the most recent systematic and appreciative study of his philosophy is the work of an American. For my own part I find Bacon's outlook inadequate, if it is considered as a comprehensive philosophy; but I do not see how one can legitimately deny its importance and significance. If one looks upon him as a metaphysician or as an epistemologist, he scarcely bears favourable comparison with the leading philosophers of the classical modern period; but if one looks upon him as the herald of the scientific age he stands in a place by himself.

One of the reasons why Bacon has been depreciated is, of course, his failure to attribute to mathematics that importance in physics which it actually possessed. And it would be difficult, I think, even for his most ardent admirer to maintain successfully that Bacon had a proper understanding of the sort of work which was being accomplished by the leading scientists of his day.

Furthermore, he implies that right use of the inductive method would put all intellects more or less on the same level, as though 'not much is left to acuteness and strength of talent'.[1] It is difficult, he says, to draw a perfect circle without a pair of compasses, but with it anyone can do so. A practical understanding of the true inductive method serves a function analogous to that of the pair of compasses. It was a weakness in Bacon that he did not fully realize that there is such a thing as scientific genius and that its rôle cannot be adequately supplied by the use of a quasi-mechanical method. No doubt he distrusted the illegitimate employment of imagination and fantasy in science, and rightly so; but there is considerable difference between the great scientist who divines a fruitful hypothesis and the man who is capable of making experiments and observations when he has been told on what lines to work.

On the other hand, Bacon was by no means blind to the use of hypothesis in science, even if he did not attach sufficient importance to scientific deduction. In any case the deficiencies in Bacon's conception of method ought not to prevent one giving him full credit for realizing the fact that a 'new organ' was required, namely a developed logic of inductive method. Not only did he realize the need and make a sustained attempt to supply it, but he also anticipated a great deal of what his successor in this matter was to say in the nineteenth century. There are, of course, considerable differences between Bacon's philosophy and that of J. S. Mill. Bacon was not an empiricist in the sense in which Mill was an empiricist, for he believed in 'natures' and in fixed natural laws; but his suggestions as to inductive method contain essentially the canons later formulated by Mill. Bacon may not have made any profound study of the presuppositions of induction. But, then, if induction requires a 'justification', it was certainly not supplied by Mill. Bacon obviously did not solve all problems of induction, nor did he give a final and adequate logical systematization of scientific method; but it would be absurd to expect or to demand that he should have done so. With all his shortcomings the author of the *Novum organum* occupies one of the most important positions in the history of inductive logic and of the philosophy of science.

---

[1] *Novum organum*, 1, 61.

CHAPTER XX

POLITICAL PHILOSOPHY

General remarks—Niccoló Machiavelli—St. Thomas More—Richard Hooker—Jean Bodin—Joannes Althusius—Hugo Grotius.

1. WE have seen that political thought at the close of the Middle Ages still moved, to a great extent, within the general framework of mediaeval political theory. In the political philosophy of Marsilius of Padua we can certainly discern a strong tendency to the exaltation of the self-sufficiency of the State and to the subordination of Church to State; but the general outlook of Marsilius, as of kindred thinkers, lay under the influence of the common mediaeval dislike of absolutism. The conciliar movement aimed at the constitutionalization of ecclesiastical government; and neither Ockham nor Marsilius had advocated monarchic absolutism within the State. But in the fifteenth and sixteenth centuries we witness the growth of political absolutism; and this historical change was naturally reflected in political theory. In England we witness the rise of the Tudor absolutism, which began with the reign of King Henry VII (1485-1509), who was able to establish centralized monarchic power at the close of the Wars of the Roses. In Spain the marriage of Ferdinand and Isabella (1469) united the kingdoms of Aragon and Castile and laid the foundation for the rise of the Spanish absolutism which reached its culmination, so far as imperialistic glory was concerned, in the reign of Charles V (1516-56), who was crowned emperor in 1520 and abdicated in 1556 in favour of Philip II (d. 1598). In France the Hundred Years War constituted a set-back to the growth of national unity and the consolidation of the central power; but when in 1439 the Estates agreed to direct taxation by the sovereign for the purpose of supporting a permanent army, the foundation of monarchic absolutism was laid. When France emerged from the Hundred Years War in 1453, the way was open for the establishment of the absolute monarchy which lasted until the time of the Revolution. Both in England, where absolutism was comparatively short-lived, and in France, where it enjoyed a long life, the rising class of merchants favoured the centralization of power at the expense of

the feudal nobility. The rise of absolutism meant the decay of the feudal society. It meant also the inauguration of a period of transition between mediaeval and 'modern' conceptions of the State and of sovereignty. However, later developments can be left out of account here; it is with the Renaissance that we are concerned; and the Renaissance period was the period in which monarchic absolutism arose in an obvious manner.

This does not mean, of course, that the political theories of the Renaissance period were all theories of monarchic despotism. Catholics and Protestants were at one in regarding the exercise of sovereign power as divinely limited. For example, the famous Anglican writer, Richard Hooker, was strongly influenced by the mediaeval idea of law as divided into eternal, natural and positive law, while a Catholic theorist like Suárez insisted strongly on the unchangeable character of natural law and the indefeasibility of natural rights. The theory of the divine right of kings, as put forward by William Barclay in his *De regno et regali potestate* (1600), by James I in his *Trew Law of Free Monarchies* and by Sir Robert Filmer in his *Patriarcha* (1680), was not so much a theoretical reflection of practical absolutism as an attempt to support a challenged and passing absolutism. This is especially true of Filmer's work, which was largely directed against both Catholic and Protestant opponents of royal absolutism. The theory of the divine right of kings was not really a philosophical theory at all. Philosophers like the Calvinist Althusius and the Catholic Suárez did not regard monarchy as the sole legitimate form of government. Indeed, the theory of the divine right of kings was a passing phenomenon, and it was eminently exposed to the type of ridicule with which John Locke treated it.

But though the consolidation of centralized power and the growth of royal absolutism did not necessarily involve the acceptance of absolutism on the plane of political theory, they were themselves the expression of the felt need for unity in the changing economic and historical circumstances; and this need for unity was indeed reflected in political theory. It was reflected notably in the political and social philosophy of Machiavelli who, living in the divided and disunited Italy of the Renaissance, was peculiarly sensible to the need for unity. If this led him, in one aspect of his philosophy, to emphasize monarchic absolutism, the emphasis was due, not to any illusions about the divine right of kings, but to his conviction that a strong and stable political unity could be secured only in this way. Similarly, when at a later date Hobbes supported centralized absolutism in the form of monarchic government he did not do so out of any belief in the divine right of monarchs or in the divine character of the principle of legitimacy, but because he believed that the cohesion of society and national unity could be best secured in this way. Moreover, both Machiavelli and Hobbes believed in the fundamental egoism of individuals; and a natural consequence of this belief is the conviction that only a strong and unfettered central power is capable of restraining and overcoming the centrifugal forces which tend to the dissolution of society. In the case of Hobbes, whose philosophy will be considered in the next volume of this history, the influence of his system in general on his political theory in particular has also to be taken into account.

The growth of royal absolutism in Europe was also, of course, a symptom of, and a stimulant to, the growth of national consciousness. The rise of the nation-States naturally produced more prolonged reflection on the nature and basis of political society than had been given to this subject during the Middle Ages. With Althusius we find a use of the idea of contract, which was to play so prominent a part in later political theory. All societies, according to Althusius, depend on contract, at least in the form of tacit agreement, and the State is one of the types of society. Again, government rests on agreement or contract, and the sovereign has a trust to fulfil. This contract theory was accepted also by Grotius, and it played a part in the political philosophies of the Jesuits Mariana and Suárez. The theory may be employed, of course, in different ways and with different purposes. Thus Hobbes used it to defend absolutism whereas Althusius employed it in defence of the conviction that political sovereignty is, of necessity, limited. But in itself the theory involves no particular view as to the form of government, though the idea of promise or agreement or contract as the basis of organized political society and of government might seem to stress the moral basis and the moral limitations of government.

The rise of absolutism naturally led to further reflection on the natural law and on natural rights. On this matter Catholic and Protestant thinkers were at one in continuing more or less the typical mediaeval attitude. They believed that an unchangeable natural law exists which binds all sovereigns and all societies and that this law is the foundation of certain natural rights. Thus the appeal to natural rights was allied with a belief in the limitation of sovereign power. Even Bodin, who wrote his *Six livres de la république* with a view to strengthening the royal power, which he considered to be necessary in the historical circumstances, had nevertheless a firm belief in natural law and in natural rights, particularly in the rights of private property. For the matter of that, not even the upholders of the divine right of kings imagined that the monarch was entitled to disregard the natural law: indeed, it would have constituted a contradiction had they done so. The theory of natural law and natural rights could not be asserted without a limitation on the exercise of political power being at the same time implied; but it did not involve an acceptance of democracy.

The Reformation naturally raised new issues in the sphere of political theory, or at least it set these issues in a fresh light and rendered them in certain respects more acute. The salient issues were, of course, the relation of Church to State and the right of resistance to the sovereign. The right of resistance to a tyrant was recognized by mediaeval philosophers, who had a strong sense of law; and it was only natural to find this view perpetuated in the political theory of a Catholic theologian and philosopher like Suárez. But the concrete circumstances in those countries which were affected by the Reformation set the problem in a new light. Similarly, the problem of the relation of Church to State took a new form in the minds of those who did not understand by 'Church' the super-national body the head of which is the pope as Vicar of Christ. One cannot conclude, however, that there was, for example, one clearly defined Protestant view on the right of resistance or one clearly defined Protestant view of the relation of Church to State. The situation was much too complicated to allow of such clearly defined views. Owing to the actual course taken by religious history we find different groups and bodies of Protestants adopting different attitudes to these problems. Moreover, the course of events sometimes led members of the same confession to adopt divergent attitudes at different times or in different places.

Both Luther and Calvin condemned resistance to the sovereign; but the attitude of passive obedience and submission came to be associated with Lutheranism, not with Calvinism. The reason for this was that in Scotland and in France Calvinists were at odds with the government. In Scotland John Knox stoutly defended resistance to the sovereign in the name of religious reform, while in France the Calvinists produced a series of works with the same theme. The best known of these, the *Vindiciae contra tyrannos* (1579), the authorship of which is uncertain, represented the view that there are two contracts or covenants, the one between people and sovereign, the other between the people together with the sovereign and God. The first contract creates the State; the second makes the community a religious body or Church. The point of bringing in this second contract was to enable the author to maintain the people's right not only of resistance to a ruler who tries to enforce a false religion but also of bringing pressure to bear on a 'heretical' ruler.

Owing to historical circumstances, then, some groups of Protestants seemed to those who favoured the idea of submission to the ruler in religious matters to be akin to the Catholics, that is to say, to be maintaining not only the distinction of Church and State but also the superiority of the former to the latter. And to a certain extent this was indeed the case. When ecclesiastical power was combined with secular power, as when Calvin ruled at Geneva, it was a simple matter to preach obedience to the sovereign in religious matters; but in Scotland and France a different situation obtained. John Knox found himself compelled to depart from the attitude of Calvin himself, and in Scotland the Calvinist body by no means considered itself obliged to submit to a 'heretical' sovereign. When, in France, the author of the *Vindiciae contra tyrannos* introduced the idea of the contract, he did so in order to find a ground for corporate Huguenot resistance and, ultimately, for bringing pressure to bear on ungodly rulers; he did not do so in order to support 'private judgment' or individualism or toleration. The Calvinists, in spite of their bitter hostility to the Catholic religion, accepted not only the idea of revelation but also that of invoking the aid of the civil power in establishing the religion in which they believed.

The Reformation thus led to the appearance of the perennial problem of the relation of Church and State in a new historical setting; but, as far as the Calvinists were concerned, there was some similarity at least between the solution they gave to the problem and the solution given by Catholic thinkers. Erastianism or the subordination of Church to State, was indeed a different solution; but neither Calvinists nor Erastians believed in the dissociation of religion from politics. Moreover, it would be a mistake to confuse either the limitations placed by Calvinists on the civil power or the Erastian subordination of Church to State with an assertion of 'democracy'. One could scarcely call the Scottish Presbyterians or the French Huguenots 'democrats', in spite of their attacks on their respective monarchs, while Erastianism could be combined with a belief in royal absolutism. It is true, of course, that religious movements and sects arose which did favour what may be called democratic liberalism; but I am speaking of the two most important of the Reformers, Luther and Calvin, and of the more immediate effects of the movements they inaugurated. Luther was by no means always consistent in his attitude or teaching; but his doctrine of submission tended to strengthen the power of the State. Calvin's teaching would have had the same effect but for historical circumstances which led to a modification of Calvin's attitude by his followers and to a forcing of Calvinists in certain countries into opposition to the royal power.

2. Niccoló Machiavelli (1469–1527) is celebrated for his attitude of indifference towards the morality or immorality of the means employed by the ruler in the pursuit of his political purpose, which is the preservation and increase of power. In *The Prince* (1513), which he addressed to Lorenzo, Duke of Urbino, he mentions such good qualities as keeping faith and showing integrity and then observes that 'it is not necessary for a prince to have all the good qualities I have enumerated, but it is very necessary that he should appear to have them'.[1] If, says Machiavelli, the prince possesses and invariably practises all these good qualities, they prove injurious, though the appearance of possessing these qualities is useful. It is a good thing to appear to be merciful, faithful, humane, religious and upright, and it is a good thing to be so in reality; but at the same time the prince ought to be so disposed that he is able to act in a contrary way when circumstances require. In fine, in the actions of all men, and especially of princes, it is results which count and by which people judge. If the prince is successful in establishing and maintaining his authority, the means he employs will always be deemed honourable and will be approved by all.

It has been said that in *The Prince* Machiavelli was concerned simply to give the mechanics of government, that he prescinded from moral questions and wished simply to state the means by which political power may be established and maintained. No

[1] *The Prince*, 18.

doubt this is true; but the fact remains that he obviously considered the ruler entitled to use immoral means in the consolidation and preservation of power. In the *Discourses* he makes it quite clear that in his opinion it is legitimate in the sphere of politics to use an immoral means in order to attain a good end. It is true that the end which Machiavelli has in mind is the security and welfare of the State; but, quite apart from the immoral character of the implied principle that the end justifies the means, the obvious difficulty arises that conceptions of what is a good end may differ. If morality is to be subordinated to political considerations, there is nothing but the actual possession of power to prevent political anarchy.

This does not mean that Machiavelli had any intention of counselling widespread immorality. He was perfectly well aware that a morally degraded and decadent nation is doomed to destruction; he lamented the moral condition of Italy as he saw it and he had a sincere admiration for the civic virtues of the ancient world. Nor do I think that one is entitled to state without any qualification that he explicitly rejected the Christian conception of virtue for a pagan conception. It is perfectly true that he says in the *Discourses*[1] that the Christian exaltation of humility and contempt of the world has rendered Christians weak and effeminate; but he goes on to say that the interpretation of the Christian religion as a religion of humility and love of suffering is an erroneous interpretation. Still, one must admit that a statement of this kind, when taken in connection with Machiavelli's general outlook, approaches very nearly to an explicit repudiation of the Christian ethic. And if one also takes into account his doctrine of the amoral prince, a doctrine which is at variance with the Christian conscience, whether Catholic or Protestant, one can hardly refrain from allowing that Nietzsche's reading of Machiavelli's mind was not without foundation. When, in *The Prince*,[2] Machiavelli remarks that many men have thought that the world's affairs are irresistibly governed by fortune and God, and when he goes on to say that, although he is sometimes inclined to that opinion, he considers that fortune can be resisted, implying that virtue consists in resisting the power which governs the world, it is difficult to avoid the impression that 'virtue' meant for him something different from what it means for the Christian. He admired strength of character and power to achieve one's ends: in the

[1] 2, 2. [2] 25.

prince he admired ability to win power and keep it: but he did not admire humility and he had no use for any universal application of what Nietzsche would call the 'herd morality'. He took it for granted that human nature is fundamentally egoistic; and he pointed out to the prince where his best interests lay and how he could realize them. The fact of the matter is that Machiavelli admired the unscrupulous though able potentate as he observed him in contemporary political or ecclesiastical life or in historical examples; he idealized the type. It was only through such men, he thought, that good government could be assured in a corrupt and decadent society.

The last sentence gives the key to the problem of the apparent discrepancy between Machiavelli's admiration for the Roman Republic, as manifested in the *Discourses on the First Ten Books of Titus Livius* and the monarchical doctrine of *The Prince*. In a corrupt and decadent society in which man's natural badness and egoism have more or less free scope, where uprightness, devotion to the common good, and the religious spirit are either dead or submerged by license, lawlessness and faithlessness, it is only an absolute ruler who is able to hold together the centrifugal forces and create a strong and unified society. Machiavelli was at one with the political theorists of the ancient world in thinking that civic virtue is dependent on law; and he considered that in a corrupt society reformation is possible only through the agency of an all-powerful lawgiver. 'This is to be taken for a general rule that it happens rarely, or not at all, that any republic or kingdom is either well-ordered at the beginning or completely reformed in regard to its old institutions, if this is not done by one man. It is thus necessary that there should be one man alone who settles the method and on whose mind any such organization depends.'[1] An absolute legislator is necessary, therefore, for the founding of a State and for the reform of a State; and in saying this Machiavelli was thinking primarily of contemporary Italian States and of the political divisions of Italy. It is law which gives birth to that civic morality or virtue which is required for a strong and unified State, and the promulgation of law requires a legislator. From this Machiavelli drew the conclusion that the monarchic legislator may use any prudent means to secure this end and that, being the cause of law and of civic morality, he is independent of both so far as is required for the fulfilment of his political function. The

[1] *Discourses*, I, 9, 2.

moral cynicism expressed in *The Prince* by no means constitutes the whole of Machiavelli's doctrine; it is subordinate to the final purpose of creating or of reforming what he regarded as the true State.

But, though Machiavelli regarded the absolute monarch or legislator as necessary for the foundation or reformation of the State, absolute monarchy was not his ideal of government. In the *Discourses*[1] he roundly asserts that, in respect of prudence and constancy, the people have the advantage and are 'more prudent, more steady and of better judgment than princes'.[2] The free republic, which was conceived by Machiavelli on the model of the Roman Republic, is superior to the absolute monarchy. If constitutional law is maintained and the people have some share in the government, the State is more stable than if it is ruled by hereditary and absolute princes. The general good, which consists, according to Machiavelli, in the increase of power and empire and in the preservation of the liberties of the people,[3] is regarded nowhere but in republics; the absolute monarch generally has regard simply for his private interests.[4]

Machiavelli's theory of government may be somewhat patchwork and unsatisfactory in character, combining, as it does, an admiration for the free republic with a doctrine of monarchic despotism; but the principles are clear. A State, when once well-ordered, will hardly be healthy and stable unless it is a republic, this is the ideal; but in order that a well-ordered State should be founded or in order that a disordered State should be reformed, a monarchic legislator is necessary in practice. Another reason for this necessity is the need for curbing the power of the nobles, for whom Machiavelli, contemplating the Italian political scene, had a particular dislike. They are idle and corrupt, and they are always enemies of civil government and order;[5] they maintain bands of mercenaries and ruin the country. Machiavelli also looked forward to a prince who would liberate and unify Italy, who would 'heal her wounds and put an end to the ravaging and plundering of Lombardy, to the swindling and taxing of the kingdom of Naples and of Tuscany'.[6] In his view the papacy, not having sufficient strength to master the whole of Italy but being strong enough to prevent any other Power from doing so, was responsible for the division of Italy into principalities, with the result that the weak

[1] 1, 58, 61.   [2] *Ibid.*, 8.   [3] *Ibid.*, 1, 29, 5.
[4] *Ibid.*, 2, 2, 3.   [5] *Ibid.*, 1, 55, 7–11.   [6] *The Prince*, 26.

and disunited country was a prey for the barbarians and for anyone who thought fit to invade it.[1]

Machiavelli, as historians have remarked, showed his 'modernity' in the emphasis he laid on the State as a sovereign body which maintains its vigour and unity by power-politics and an imperialistic policy. In this sense he divined the course of historical development in Europe. On the other hand he did not work out any systematic political theory; nor was he really concerned to do so. He was intensely interested in the contemporary Italian scene; he was an ardent patriot; and his writings are coloured through and through by this interest; they are not the writings of a detached philosopher. He also over-estimated the part played in historical development by politics in a narrow sense; and he failed to discern the importance of other factors, religious and social. He is chiefly known, of course, for his amoral advice to the prince, for his 'Machiavellianism'; but there can be little doubt that the principles of state-craft he laid down have not infrequently, even if regrettably, been those actually operative in the minds of rulers and statesmen. But historical development is not conditioned entirely by the intentions and deeds of those who occupy the limelight on the political stage. Machiavelli was clever and brilliant; but he can scarcely be called a profound political philosopher.

On the other hand, one must remember that Machiavelli was concerned with actual political life as he saw it and with what is actually done rather than with what ought to be done from the moral point of view. He expressly disclaims any intention of depicting ideal States[2] and he remarks that if a man lives up consistently to the highest moral principles in political life, he is likely to come to ruin and, if he is a ruler, to fail to preserve the security and welfare of the State. In the preface to the first book of the *Discourses*, he speaks of his new 'way', which, he claims, has been hitherto left untrodden. His method was one of historical induction. From a comparative examination of cause-effect sequences in history, ancient and recent, with due allowance for negative instances, he sought to establish certain practical rules in a generalized form. Given a certain purpose to be achieved, history shows that a certain line of action will or will not lead to the achievement of that purpose. He was thus immediately concerned with political mechanics; but his outlook implied a certain philosophy of history.

---

[1] *Discourses*, 1, 12, 6–8. [2] Cf. *The Prince*, 15.

It implied, for example, that there is repetition in history and that history is of such a nature that it affords a basis for induction. Machiavelli's method was not, of course, altogether new. Aristotle, for example, certainly based his political ideas on an examination of actual constitutions and he considered not only the ways in which States are destroyed but also the virtues which the ruler should pretend to have if he is to be successful.[1] But Aristotle was much more concerned than Machiavelli with abstract theory. He was also primarily interested in political organizations as the setting for moral and intellectual education, whereas Machiavelli was much more interested in the actual nature and course of concrete political life.

3. A very different type of thinker was St. Thomas More (1478–1535), Lord Chancellor of England, who was beheaded by Henry VIII for refusing to acknowledge the latter as supreme head of the Church in England. In his *De optimo reipublicae statu deque nova insula Utopia* (1516) he wrote, under the influence of Plato's *Republic*, a kind of philosophical novel describing an ideal State on the island of Utopia. It is a curious work, combining a sharp criticism of contemporary social and economic conditions with an idealization of the simple moral life, which was scarcely in harmony with the more worldly spirit of the time. More was unacquainted with *The Prince*; but his book was in part directed against the idea of statecraft represented in Machiavelli's work. It was also directed against the growing spirit of commercial exploitation. In these respects it was a 'conservative' book. On the other hand More anticipated some ideas which reappear in the development of modern socialism.

In the first book of his *Utopia* More attacks the destruction of the old agricultural system through the enclosure of land by wealthy and wealth-seeking proprietors. Desire of gain and wealth leads to the conversion of arable land into pasture, in order that sheep may be reared on a wide scale and their wool sold in foreign markets. All this greed for gain and the accompanying centralization of wealth in the hands of a few leads to the rise of a dispossessed and indigent class. Then, with a view to keeping this class in due subjection, heavy and fearful punishments are decreed for theft. But the increased severity of the criminal law is useless. It would be much better to provide the means of livelihood for the indigent, since it is precisely want which drives these people to

---
[1] Cf. *Politics*, 5, 11.

crime. The government, however, does nothing: it is busily engaged in diplomacy and wars of conquest. War necessitates extortionate taxation, and, when war is over, the soldiers are thrown into a community which is already unable to support itself. Power-politics thus aggravates the economic and social evils.

In contrast with an acquisitive society More presents an agricultural society, in which the family is the unit. Private property is abolished, and money is no longer used as a means of exchange. But More did not depict his Utopia as a republic of uneducated peasants. The means of livelihood are assured to all, and the working hours are reduced to six hours a day, in order that the citizens may have leisure for cultural pursuits. For the same reason a slave class sees to the harder and more burdensome work, the slaves consisting partly of condemned criminals, partly of captives of war.

It is sometimes said that More was the first to proclaim the ideal of religious toleration. It must be remembered, however, that in sketching his Utopia he prescinded from the Christian revelation and envisaged simply natural religion. Divergent views and convictions were to be tolerated for the most part, and theological strife was to be avoided; but those who denied God's existence and providence, the immortality of the soul and sanctions in the future life would be deprived of capacity to hold any public office and accounted as less than men. The truths of natural religion and of natural morality might not be called in question, whatever a man might think privately, for the health of the State and of society depended on their acceptance. There can be little doubt that More would have regarded the Wars of Religion with horror; but he was certainly not the type of man who asserts that it is a matter of indifference what one believes.

More had no use at all for the dissociation of morals from politics, and he speaks very sharply of statesmen who rant about the public good when all the time they are seeking their own advantage. Some of his ideas, those concerning the criminal code, for example, are extremely sensible, and in his ideals of security for all and of reasonable toleration he was far ahead of his time. But though his political ideal was in many respects enlightened and practical, in some other respects it can be regarded as an idealization of a past co-operative society. The forces and tendencies against which he protested were not to be stayed in their development by any

Utopia. The great Christian humanist stood on the threshold of a capitalistic development which was to run its course. Yet in due time some at any rate of his ideals were to be fulfilled.

4. More died before the Reformation in England had taken a definite form. In *The Laws of Ecclesiastical Polity* by Richard Hooker (1553–1600) the problem of Church and State finds its expression in the form dictated by religious conditions in England after the Reformation. Hooker's work, which had its influence on John Locke, was written in refutation of the Puritan attack on the established Church of England; but its scope is far wider than that of the ordinary controversial writing of the time. The author treats first of law in general, and on this matter he adheres to the mediaeval idea of law, particularly to that of St. Thomas. He distinguishes the eternal law, 'that order which God before all ages hath set down with Himself for Himself to do all things by',[1] from the natural law. He then proceeds to distinguish the natural law as operative in non-free agents, which he calls 'natural agents', from the natural law as perceived by the human reason and as freely obeyed by man.[2] 'The rule of voluntary agents on earth is the sentence that reason giveth concerning the goodness of those things which they are to do.'[3] 'The main principles of reason are in themselves apparent';[4] that is to say, there are certain general moral principles the obligatory character of which is immediately apparent and evident. A sign of this is the general consent of mankind. 'The general and perpetual voice of men is as the sentence of God Himself. For that which all men have at all times learned Nature herself must needs have taught; and God being the author of Nature, her voice is but His instrument.'[5] Other more particular principles are deduced by reason.

In addition to the eternal law and the natural law there is human positive law. The natural law binds men as men and it does not depend on the State;[6] but human positive law comes into being when men unite in society and form a government. Owing to the fact that we are not self-sufficient as individuals 'we are naturally induced to seek communion and fellowship with others'.[7] But societies cannot exist without government, and government cannot be carried on without law; 'a distinct kind of law from that which hath been already declared'.[8] Hooker teaches that there are two foundations of society; the natural inclination of man to

---

[1] I, 2.   [2] I, 3.   [3] I, 8.   [4] *Ibid.*
[5] *Ibid.*   [6] I, 10.   [7] *Ibid.*   [8] *Ibid.*

live in society, and 'an order expressly or secretly agreed upon, touching the manner of their union in living together. The latter is that which we call the law of a common weal, the very soul of a politic body, the parts whereof are by law animated, held together, and set on work in such actions as the common good requireth.'[1]

The establishment of civil government thus rests upon consent, 'without which consent there were no reason that one man should take upon him to be lord or judge over another'.[2] Government is necessary; but Nature has not settled the kind of government or the precise character of laws, provided that the laws enacted are for the common good and in conformity with the natural law. If the ruler enforces laws without explicit authority from God or without authority derived in the first instance from the consent of the governed, he is a mere tyrant. 'Laws they are not therefore which public approbation hath not made so', at least through 'Parliaments, Councils, and the like assemblies'.[3] How, then, does it come about that whole multitudes are obliged to respect laws in the framing of which they had no share at all? The reason is that 'corporations are immortal: we were then alive in our predecessors, and they in their successors do live still'.[4]

Finally there are 'the laws that concern supernatural duties',[5] 'the law which God Himself hath supernaturally revealed'.[6] Thus Hooker's theory of law in general follows the theory of St. Thomas, with the same theological setting or, rather, with a like reference of law to its divine foundation, God. Nor does he add anything particularly new in his theory of the origin of political society. He introduces the idea of contract or agreement; but he does not represent the State as a purely artificial construction; on the contrary, he speaks explicitly of man's natural inclination to society, and he does not explain the State and government simply in terms of a remedy for unbridled egoism.

When he comes to treat of the Church, Hooker distinguishes between truths of faith and Church government, which is 'a plain matter of action'.[7] The point he tries to develop and defend is that the ecclesiastical law of the Church of England is in no way contrary to the Christian religion or to reason. It ought, therefore, to be obeyed by Englishmen, for Englishmen are Christians and, as Christians, they belong to the Church of England. The assumption is that Church and State are not distinct societies, at least not when the State is Christian. Hooker did not, of course, deny

---

[1] I, 10.   [2] *Ibid.*   [3] *Ibid.*   [4] *Ibid.*   [5] I, 15.   [6] I, 16.   [7] 3, 3.

that Catholics and Calvinists were Christians; but he assumed in a rather naïve fashion that the Christian faith as a whole requires no universal institution. He also assumed that ecclesiastical government was more or less a matter of indifference, a view which would commend itself, for different reasons, neither to Catholics nor to Calvinists.

Hooker is remarkable principally for his continuation of the mediaeval theory and divisions of law. In his political theory he was obviously not an upholder of the divine right of kings or of monarchic despotism. On the other hand, he did not propose his doctrine of consent or contract in order to justify rebellion against the sovereign. Even if he had considered rebellion justified, he would hardly have laboured such a point in a book designed to show that all good Englishmen should conform to the national Church. In conclusion one may remark that Hooker writes for the most part with remarkable moderation of tone, if, that is to say, one bears in mind the prevailing atmosphere of contemporary religious controversy. He was essentially a man of the *via media* and no fanatic.

5. Jean Bodin (1530–96), who had studied law at the university of Toulouse, endeavoured to make a close alliance between the study of universal law and the study of history in his *Methodus ad facilem historiarum cognitionem* (1566). After dividing history into three types he says: 'let us for the moment abandon the divine to the theologians, the natural to the philosophers, while we concentrate long and intently upon human actions and the rules governing them'.[1] His leading interest is revealed by the following statement in his *Dedication*. 'Indeed, in history the best part of universal law lies hidden; and what is of great weight and importance for the best appraisal of legislation—the custom of the peoples, and the beginnings, growth, conditions, changes and decline of all States—are obtained from it. The chief subject matter of this *Method* consists of these facts, since no rewards of history are more ample than those usually gathered about the governmental form of states.' The *Method* is remarkable for its strongly marked tendency to the naturalistic interpretation of history. For example, he treats of the effects of geographical situation on the physiological constitution, and so on the habits, of peoples. 'We shall explain the nature of peoples who dwell to the north and to the south, then of those who live to the east

[1] *Preamble*.

and to the west.'[1] This sort of idea reappears later in the writings of philosophers like Montesquieu. Bodin also evolved a cyclical theory of the rise and fall of States. But the chief importance of Bodin consists in his analysis of sovereignty. Originally sketched in chapter 6 of the *Methodus*, it is treated at greater length in the *Six livres de la république* (1576).[2]

The natural social unit, from which the State arises, is the family. In the family Bodin included not simply father, mother and children, but also servants. In other words he had the Roman conception of the family, with power residing in the *paterfamilias*. The State is a secondary or derived society, in the sense that it is 'a lawful government of several households, and of their common possessions, with sovereign power'; but it is a different kind of society. The right of property is an inviolable right of the family; but it is not a right of the ruler or the State, considered, that is to say, as ruler. The ruler possesses sovereignty; but sovereignty is not the same thing as proprietorship. It is clear, then, that for Bodin, as he says in the *Methodus*,[3] 'the State is nothing else than a group of families or fraternities subjected to one and the same rule'. From this definition it follows that 'Ragusa or Geneva, whose rule is comprised almost within its walls, ought to be called a State' and that 'what Aristotle said is absurd—that too great a group of men, such as Babylon was, is a race, not a State'.[4] It is also clear that for Bodin sovereignty is essentially different from the power of the head of a family and that a State cannot exist without sovereignty. Sovereignty is defined as 'supreme power over citizens and subjects, unrestrained by law'.[5] It involves the power to create magistrates and define their offices; the power to legislate and to annul laws; the power to declare war and make peace; the right of receiving appeals; and the power of life and death. But, though it is clear that sovereignty is distinct from the power of the head of a family, it is not at all clear how sovereignty comes into being, what ultimately gives the sovereign his title to exercise sovereignty and what is the foundation of the citizen's duty of obedience. Bodin apparently thought that most States come into existence through the exercise of force; but he did not consider that force justifies itself or that the possession of physical power *ipso facto* confers sovereignty on its possessor. What does confer legitimate sovereignty is, however, left obscure.

Sovereignty is inalienable and indivisible. Executive functions

---

[1] 5. [2] Enlarged Latin edition, 1584. [3] 6. [4] *Ibid.* [5] *Republic*, 1, 8.

and powers can, of course, be delegated, but sovereignty itself, the possession of supreme power, cannot be parcelled out, as it were. The sovereign is unrestrained by law, and he cannot limit his sovereignty by law, so long as he remains sovereign, for law is the creation of the sovereign. This does not mean, of course, that the sovereign is entitled to disregard the divine authority or the natural law; he cannot, for instance, expropriate all families. Bodin was insistent on the natural right of property, and the communistic theories of Plato and More drew sharp criticism from his pen. But the sovereign is the supreme fount of law and has ultimate and full control over legislation.

This theory of sovereignty must give the impression that Bodin believed simply in royal absolutism, especially if one speaks of the sovereign as 'he'. But though he certainly wished to strengthen the position of the French monarch, since he felt that this was necessary in the historical circumstances, his theory of sovereignty is not in itself bound up with monarchic absolutism. An assembly, for example, can be the seat of sovereignty. Forms of government may differ in different States; but the nature of sovereignty remains the same in all those States, if they are well-ordered States. Moreover, there is no reason why a monarch should not delegate a great deal of his power and govern 'constitutionally', provided that it is recognized that this governmental arrangement depends on the will of the monarch, if, that is to say, sovereignty rests with the monarch. For it does not necessarily follow that because a State happens to have a king, the latter is sovereign. If the king is really dependent on an assembly or parliament, he cannot be called a sovereign in the strict sense.

As historians have pointed out, however, Bodin was by no means always consistent. It was his intention to increase the prestige and insist on the supreme power of the French monarch; and it followed from his theory of sovereignty that the French monarch should be unrestricted by law. But it followed from his theory of natural law that there might be cases when the subject would be not only justified in disobeying a law promulgated by the sovereign but also morally obliged to do so. Moreover, he even went so far as to state that taxation, as it involves an interference with property, requires the assent of the Estates, though the latter, according to the theory of sovereignty, depend for their existence on the sovereign. Again, he recognized certain *leges imperii* or constitutional limitations on the power of the king. In other words, his desire to emphasize the monarch's supreme and sovereign power was at variance with his inclination towards constitutionalism and led him into contradictory positions.

Bodin emphasized the philosophical study of history and he certainly made a sustained attempt to understand history; but he was not altogether free from the prejudices and superstitions of his time. Though he rejected astrological determinism, he nevertheless believed in the influence of the heavenly bodies on human affairs and he indulged in speculations concerning numbers and their relations to governments and States.

In conclusion it may be mentioned that in his *Colloquium heptaplomeres*, a dialogue, Bodin pictures people of different religions living together in harmony. In the midst of historical events which were not favourable to peace among the members of different confessions he supported the principle of mutual toleration.

6. Bodin had given no very clear account of the origin and foundation of the State; but in the philosophy of the Calvinist writer Joannes Althusius (1557–1638) we find a clear statement of the contract theory. In Althusius' opinion a contract lies at the basis of every association or community of men. He distinguishes various types of community; the family, the *collegium* or corporation, the local community, the province and the State. Each of these communities corresponds to a natural need in man; but the formation of any definite community rests upon an agreement or contract whereby human beings agree to form an association or community for their common good in respect of specified purposes. In this way they become *symbiotici*, living together as sharers in a common good. The family, for instance, corresponds to a natural need in man; but the foundation of any definite family rests on a contract. So it is with the State. But a community, in order to attain its purpose, must have a common authority. So we can distinguish a second contract between the community and the administrative authority, a contract which is the foundation of the duties pertaining to either party.

There is a further important point to be made. As each type of community corresponds to a definite human need, the constitution of a wider or more extensive community does not annul or abolish the narrower community: rather is the wider community constituted by the agreement of a number of narrower communities, which themselves remain in existence. The local community, for example, does not annul the families or the corporations composing it; it owes its existence to their agreement and its purpose is distinct from theirs. They are not, therefore, swallowed up by the wider community. Again, the State is immediately constituted by the agreement of provinces rather than directly by a contract between individuals, and it does not render the provinces superfluous or useless. From this a certain federation logically follows. Althusius was far from considering the State as resting on a contract whereby individuals handed over their rights to a government. A number of associations, which, of course, ultimately represent individuals, agree together to form the State and agree on a constitution or law regulating the attainment of the common purpose or good for which the State is formed.

But, if the State is one among a number of communities or associations, what is its distinguishing and peculiar mark? As in Bodin's political theory it is sovereignty (*ius maiestatis*); but, unlike Bodin, Althusius declared that sovereignty rests always, necessarily and inalienably, with the people. This does not mean, of course, that he envisaged direct government by the people; through the law of the State, a law itself resting on agreement, power is delegated to the administrative officers or magistrates of the State. Althusius contemplated a supreme magistrate, who might, of course, though not necessarily, be a king, and 'ephors' who would see that the constitution was observed. But the theory does involve a clear assertion of popular sovereignty. It also involves the right of resistance, since the power of the ruler rests on a contract, and if he is faithless to his trust or breaks the contract, power reverts to the people. When this happens, the people may appoint another ruler, though this will be done in a constitutional manner.

Althusius assumed, of course, the sanctity of contracts, resting on the natural law; and the natural law itself he regarded, in the traditional manner, as resting on divine authority. It was Grotius, rather than Althusius, who re-examined the idea of natural law. But Althusius' political theory is remarkable for its assertion of popular sovereignty and the use made of the idea of contract. As a Calvinist he insisted on the right of resistance to the ruler; but it must be added that he had no idea of religious freedom or of a State which would be officially indifferent to forms of religion. Such a notion was no more acceptable to the Calvinist than to the Catholic.

7. The chief work of Hugo Grotius or Huig de Groot (1583–1645) is his famous *De iure belli ac pacis* (1625). In the *Prolegomena*

to that work[1] he represents Carneades as holding that there is no such thing as a universally obligatory natural law, 'because all creatures, men as well as animals, are impelled by nature towards ends advantageous to themselves'. Each man seeks his own advantage; human laws are dictated simply by consideration of expediency; they are not based upon or related to a natural law, for the latter does not exist. To this Grotius replies that 'man is, to be sure, an animal, but an animal of a superior kind', and 'among the traits characteristic of man is an impelling desire for society, that is, for the social life, not of any and every sort, but peaceful and organized according to the measure of his intelligence. . . . Stated as a universal truth, therefore, the assertion that every animal is impelled by nature to seek only its own good cannot be conceded.'[2] There is a natural social order, and it is the maintenance of this social order which is the source of law. 'To this sphere of law belong the abstaining from that which is another's . . . the obligation to fulfil promises . . .'[3] Furthermore, man is possessed of the power of judging 'what things are agreeable or harmful (as to both things present and things to come) and what can lead to either alternative'; and 'whatever is clearly at variance with such judgment is understood to be contrary also to the law of nature, that is, to the nature of man'.[4]

The nature of man is thus the foundation of law. 'For the very nature of man, which even if we had no lack of anything would lead us into the mutual relations of society, is the mother of the law of nature.'[5] The natural law enjoins the keeping of promises; and as the obligation of observing the positive laws of States arises from mutual consent and promise, 'nature may be considered, so to say, the great-grandmother of municipal law'. In point of fact, of course, individuals are by no means self-sufficient; and expediency has a part to play in the institution of positive law and subjection to authority. 'But just as the laws of each State have in view the advantage of that State, so by mutual consent it has become possible that certain laws should originate as between all States or a great many States; and it is apparent that the laws thus originating had in view the advantage, not of particular States, but of the great society of States. And this is what is called the law of nations, whenever we distinguish that term from the law of nature.'[6] But it is not simply a question of

[1] 5.   [2] *De iure belli ac pacis*, 6.   [3] *Ibid.*, 8.
[4] *Ibid.*, 9.   [5] *Ibid.*, 16.   [6] *Ibid.*, 17.

expediency: it is also a question of natural justice. 'Many hold, in fact, that the standard of justice which they insist upon in the case of individuals within the State is inapplicable to a nation or the ruler of a nation.'[1] But, 'if no association of men can be maintained without law . . . surely also that association which binds together the human race, or binds many nations together, has need of law; this was perceived by him who said that shameful deeds ought not to be committed even for the sake of one's country'.[2] It follows that 'war ought not to be undertaken except for the enforcement of rights; when once undertaken, it should be carried on only within the bounds of law and good faith'.[3]

Grotius is convinced, then, that 'there is a common law among nations, which is valid alike in peace and war'.[4] We have, therefore, the natural law, the municipal law or positive law of States, and the law of nations. In addition, Grotius, a believing Protestant, admits the positive Christian law. 'This, however—contrary to the practice of most men—I have distinguished from the law of nature, considering it as certain that in that most holy law a greater degree of moral perfection is enjoined upon us than the law of nature, alone and by itself, would require.'[5]

Historians generally attribute to Grotius an important rôle in the 'freeing' of the idea of natural law from theological foundations and presuppositions and in naturalizing it. In this respect, it is said, he was much closer than were the Schoolmen to Aristotle, for whom he had a great admiration. It is certainly true to some extent that Grotius separated the idea of natural law from the idea of God. 'What we have been saying would have a degree of validity even if we should concede that which cannot be conceded without the utmost wickedness, that there is no God, or that the affairs of men are of no concern to Him.'[6] But he proceeds to say that the law of nature, 'proceeding as it does from the essential traits implanted in man, can nevertheless rightly be attributed to God, because of His having willed that such traits exist in us'.[7] And he quotes Chrysippus and St. John Chrysostom in support. Moreover he defines the law of nature as follows. 'The law of nature is a dictate of right reason which points out that an act, according as it is or is not in conformity with rational nature, has in it a quality of moral baseness or moral necessity; and that, in consequence, such an act is either forbidden or enjoined by the

---

[1] *De iure belli ac pacis*, 21.   [2] *Ibid.*, 23.   [3] *Ibid.*, 25.   [4] *Ibid.*, 28.
[5] *Ibid.*, 50.   [6] *Prolegomena*, 11.   [7] *Ibid.*, 12.

author of nature, God.'[1] Among his references on this matter he refers to Thomas Aquinas and Duns Scotus, whose remarks, he says, are by no means to be slighted. While, then, it may be true to say that, as a historical fact, Grotius' treatment of the idea of natural law contributed to the 'naturalization' of the idea inasmuch as he was treating law, not as a theologian, but as a lawyer and philosopher of law, it is wrong to suggest that Grotius made any radical break with the position of, say, St. Thomas. What seems to impress some historians is his insistence on the fact that an act enjoined or forbidden by the natural law is enjoined or forbidden by God because it is, in itself, obligatory or wrong. The natural law is unchangeable, even by God.[2] It is not right or wrong because of God's decision that it should be right or wrong. But the notion that the moral quality of acts permitted, enjoined or forbidden by the natural law depends on God's arbitrary *fiat* was certainly not that of St. Thomas. It represents, more or less, the Ockhamist view; but it is in no way necessarily bound up with the attribution of an ultimate metaphysical and 'theological' foundation to the natural law. When Grotius points out[3] the difference between the natural law and 'volitional divine law', he is making a statement with which St. Thomas would gave agreed. It seems to me that it is Grotius' 'modernity', his careful and systematic treatment of law from the standpoint of a lay lawyer and philosopher, which is responsible for the impression that he made a bigger break with the past than he actually did.

In his *Prolegomena*[4] Grotius says, 'I have made it my concern to refer the proofs of things touching the law of nature to certain fundamental conceptions which are beyond question, so that no one can deny them without doing violence to himself'. In the first book[5] he asserts that *a priori* proof, which 'consists in demonstrating the necessary agreement or disagreement of anything with a rational and social nature', is 'more subtle' than *a posteriori* proof, though the latter is 'more familiar'. But later in his work,[6] when treating of the causes of doubt in moral questions, he remarks that 'what Aristotle wrote is perfectly true, that certainty is not to be found in moral questions in the same degree as in mathematical science'. To this statement Samuel Pufendorf took exception.[7] I do not think, therefore, that one ought to lay great

---

[1] I, I, 10, I.   [2] I, I, 10, 5.   [3] I, I, 10, 2.   [4] 39.
[5] I, I, 12, I.   [6] 2, 23, I.   [7] *De jure naturae et gentium*, I, 2, 9–10.

stress on Grotius' place in the movement of philosophical thought which was characterized by emphasis on deduction, an emphasis due to the influence of the success of mathematical science. No doubt he did not escape this influence; but the doctrine that there are self-evident principles of natural morality was by no means new.

'The State', says Grotius,[1] 'is a complete association of free men, joined together for the enjoyment of rights and for their common interests.' The State itself is the 'common subject' of sovereignty, sovereignty being the power 'whose actions are not subject to the legal control of another, so that they cannot be rendered void by the operation of another human will'.[2] The 'special subject is one or more persons, according to the laws and customs of each nation'.[3] Grotius proceeds to deny the opinion of Althusius (who is not named, however) that sovereignty always and necessarily resides in the people. He asks why it should be supposed that the people should be incapable of transferring sovereignty.[4] Though sovereignty is in itself indivisible, in the sense that it means something definite, the actual exercise of sovereign power can be divided. 'It may happen that a people, when choosing a king, may reserve to itself certain powers but may confer the others on the king absolutely.'[5] Divided sovereignty may have its disadvantages, but so has every form of government; 'and a legal provision is to be judged not by what this or that man considers best, but by what accords with the will of him with whom the provision originated'.[6]

As to resistance or rebellion against rulers, Grotius argues that it is quite incompatible with the nature and purpose of the State that the right of resistance should be without limitation. 'Among good men one principle at any rate is established beyond controversy, that if the authorities issue any order that is contrary to the law of nature or to the commandments of God, the order should not be carried out';[7] but rebellion is a different matter. However, if in the conferring of authority the right of resistance was retained or if the king openly shows himself the enemy of the whole people or if he alienates the kingdom, rebellion, that is, resistance by force, is justified.

Grotius teaches that a just war is permissible; but he insists that 'no other just cause for undertaking war can there be excepting

---

[1] I, I, 14, I.   [2] I, 3, 7, I.   [3] I, 3, 7, 3.   [4] I, 3, 8, I.
[5] I, 3, 17, I.   [6] I, 3, 17, 2.   [7] I, 4, I, 3.

injury received'.[1] It is permissible for a State to wage war against another State which has attacked it, or in order to recover what has been stolen from it, or to 'punish' another State, that is, if the other State is obviously infringing the natural or divine law. But preventive war may not be waged unless there is moral certainty that the other State intends attack;[2] nor may it be waged simply for advantage's sake,[3] nor to obtain better land,[4] nor out of a desire to rule others under the pretext that it is for their good.[5] War should not be waged in cases of doubt as to its justice,[6] and, even for just causes, it should not be undertaken rashly:[7] it should only be undertaken in cases of necessity,[8] and peace should always be kept in view.[9] In the actual conduct of war what is permissible can be viewed either absolutely, in relation to the law of nature, or in relation to a previous promise, in relation, that is, to the law of nations.[10] Discussion of the permissible in war with reference to a previous promise is discussion concerning good faith among enemies; and Grotius insists that good faith is always to be kept, because 'those who are enemies do not in fact cease to be men'.[11] For example, treaties should be scrupulously observed. The law of nature binds, of course, all men as men: the law of nations 'is the law which has received its obligatory force from the will of all nations, or of many nations'.[12] It is distinct, therefore, from the law of nature and rests on promise and on custom. 'The law of nations, in fact,' as Dio Chrysostom well observes, 'is the creation of time and custom. And for the study of it the illustrious writers of history are of the greatest value to us.'[13] In other words, custom, consent and contract between States give rise to an obligation just as promises between individuals give rise to an obligation. In the absence of any international authority or tribunal or court of arbitration war between States necessarily takes the place of litigation between individuals; but war should not be waged if it can be avoided by arbitration or conferences (or even lot, says Grotius); and if it cannot be avoided, if, that is to say, it proves to be necessary for the enforcement of rights, it should be waged only within the bounds of good faith and with a scrupulous attention to proper procedure analogous to that observed in judicial processes. It is obvious that Grotius considered 'public war' not as a justifiable instrument of policy, imperialistic ambition or territorial greed, but as something which cannot be avoided in the

[1] 2, 1, 1, 4.   [2] 2, 22, 5.   [3] 2, 22, 6.   [4] 2, 23, 8.   [5] 2, 22, 12.
[6] 2, 23, 6.   [7] 2, 24.   [8] 2, 24, 8.   [9] 3, 25, 2.   [10] 3, 1, 1.
[11] 3, 19, 1, 2.   [12] 1, 1, 14, 1.   [13] 1, 1, 14, 2.

absence of an international tribunal capable of rendering war as unnecessary as law-courts have rendered 'private war'. Nevertheless, just as individuals enjoy the right of self-defence, so do States. There can be a just war; but it does not follow that every means is legitimate even in a just war. The 'law of nations' must be observed.

Grotius was a humanist, a humanitarian and a learned man; he was also a convinced Christian. He desired the healing of the rifts between Christians; and he defended toleration in regard to the different confessions. His great work, *De iure belli ac pacis*, is remarkable, not only for its systematic and its humanitarian character, but also for its dispassionate freedom from bigotry. Its spirit is well expressed in a remark he makes about the Schoolmen. The latter, he says, 'furnish a praiseworthy example of moderation; they contend with one another by means of arguments—not, in accordance with the practice which has lately begun to disgrace the calling of letters, with personal abuse, base offspring of a spirit lacking self-mastery'.[1]

In this chapter I have avoided discussion of treatises on political theory by Scholastic writers, since I propose to treat of Renaissance Scholasticism in the next part of this work. But it may be as well to draw attention here to the fact that Scholastic authors formed an important channel whereby the mediaeval philosophy of law was transmitted to men like Grotius. This is particularly true of Suárez. In addition, the treatments of the 'law of nations' and of war by Vitoria and Suárez were not without influence on non-Scholastic writers of the Renaissance and post-Renaissance periods. One does not wish to depreciate the importance of a man like Grotius, but it is as well to realize the continuity which existed between mediaeval thought and the political and legal theories of the Renaissance period. Moreover, an understanding of the Scholastic philosophies of law helps one to avoid attributing to Grotius and kindred thinkers a degree of 'secularization' of thought which is not, in my opinion, present in their writings. The notion that the Scholastics in general made the natural law dependent on the arbitrary divine will naturally inclines those who hold it to regard a man like Grotius as one who humanized and secularized the concept of natural law. But the notion is incorrect and is based either on ignorance of Scholasticism in general or on an assumption that the peculiar ideas of some of the nominalist school represented the common views of Scholastic philosophers.

[1] *Prolegomena*, 52.

PART III
SCHOLASTICISM OF THE RENAISSANCE

CHAPTER XXI
A GENERAL VIEW

The revival of Scholasticism—Dominican writers before the Council of Trent; Cajetan—Later Dominican writers and Jesuit writers—The controversy between Dominicans and Jesuits about grace and free will—The substitution of 'philosophical courses' for commentaries on Aristotle—Political and legal theory.

1. ONE might perhaps have expected that the life and vigour of Aristotelian Scholasticism would have been finally sapped by two factors, first the rise and spread of the nominalist movement in the fourteenth century and secondly the emergence of new lines of thought at the time of the Renaissance. Yet in the fifteenth and sixteenth centuries there occurred a remarkable revival of Scholasticism, and some of the greatest names in Scholasticism belong to the period of the Renaissance and the beginning of the modern era. The chief centre of this revival was Spain, in the sense that most, though not all, of the leading figures were Spaniards. Cajetan, the great commentator on the writings of St. Thomas, was an Italian but Francis of Vitoria, who exercised a profound influence on Scholastic thought, was a Spaniard, as were also Dominic Soto, Melchior Cano, Dominic Báñez, Gabriel Vásquez and Francis Suárez. Spain was comparatively untouched either by the ferment of Renaissance thought or by the religious dissensions of the Reformation; and it was only natural that a renewal of studies which was carried through predominantly, though not, of course, exclusively, by Spanish theologians should take the form of a revivification, prolongation and development of Scholasticism.

This renewal of Scholastic thought is associated with two religious Orders in particular. First in the field were the Dominicans, who produced noted commentators on St. Thomas like Cajetan and De Sylvestris and eminent theologians and philosophers like Francis of Vitoria, Dominic Soto, Melchior Cano and Dominic Báñez. Indeed, the first stage of the revival of

Scholasticism, namely the stage which preceded the Council of Trent, was in a special degree the work of the Order of Preachers. The Council of Trent began in 1545, and it gave a powerful impulse to the renewal of Scholastic thought. The Council was primarily concerned, of course, with theological doctrines, questions and controversies, but the handling and discussion of these themes involved also a treatment of philosophical matters, in the sense at least that the theologians who assisted at the Council or who discussed the subjects which arose in the Council were necessarily involved to some extent in philosophical discussions. The work of the Dominicans in commenting on the works of St. Thomas and in elucidating and developing his thought was thus reinforced by the impulse contributed by the Council of Trent to the promotion of Scholastic studies. A further enrichment of life was given to Scholasticism by the Society of Jesus, which was founded in 1540 and which is especially associated with the work of the so-called Counter-Reformation, inaugurated by the Council. The Society of Jesus not only made a most important general contribution to the deepening and extension of intellectual life among Catholics through the foundation of numerous schools, colleges and universities but it also played a signal part in the theological and philosophical discussions and controversies of the time. Among the eminent Jesuits of the sixteenth century and the early part of the seventeenth we find names like Toletus, Molina, Vásquez, Lessius, St. Robert Bellarmine and, above all, Francis Suárez. I do not mean to imply that other Orders did not also play a part in the renewal of Scholasticism. There were well-known writers, like the Franciscan, Lychetus, who belonged to other Orders. But it remains true that the two bodies of men who did most for Scholastic thought at the time of the Renaissance were the Dominicans and the Jesuits.

2. Of the Scholastics who died before or shortly after the beginning of the Council of Trent one may mention, for example, Petrus Niger (d. 1477), author of *Clypeum thomistarum*, Barbus Paulus Soncinas (d. 1494), author of an *Epitome Capreoli*, and Dominic of Flanders (d. 1500), who published among other works *In XII libros metaphysicae Aristotelis quaestiones*. These three were all Dominicans. So also was Chrysostom Javelli (c. 1470–c. 1545) who was named Chrysostomus Casalensis after his birthplace. He lectured at Bologna and composed commentaries on the principal works of Aristotle; *Compendium logicae isagogicum*,

In universam naturalem philosophiam epitome, In libros XII metaphysicorum epitome, In X ethicorum libros epitome, In VIII politicorum libros epitome, Quaestiones super quartum meteorum, super librum de sensu et sensato, super librum de memoria et reminiscentia. He also defended Aquinas's exposition of Aristotle in *Quaestiones acutissimae super VIII libros physices ad mentem S. Thomae, Aristotelis et Commentatoris decisae* and in *Quaestiones super III libros de anima, super XII libros metaphysicae.* In addition he wrote *In Platonis ethica et politica epitome* and a *Christiana philosophia seu ethica,* besides publishing a refutation of Pomponazzi's arguments to show that the human soul is naturally mortal. This last theme he took up again in his *Tractatus de animae humanae indeficientia in quadruplici via, sc. peripatetica, academica, naturali et christiana.* He also wrote on the thorny subject of predestination.

Mention should also be made of Francis Sylvester de Sylvestris (*c.* 1474–1528), known as Ferrariensis, who lectured at Bologna and published *Quaestiones* on Aristotle's *Physics* and *De anima, Annotationes* on the *Posterior Analytics* and a commentary on St. Thomas's *Summa contra Gentiles.* But a much more important writer was Cajetan.

Thomas de Vio (1468–1534), commonly known as Cajetan, was born at Gaeta and entered the Dominican Order at the age of sixteen. After studying at Naples, Bologna and Padua he lectured in the university of Padua; and it was there that he composed his treatise on Aquinas's *De ente et essentia.* Subsequently he lectured for a time at Pavia, after which he held various high offices in his Order. In 1508 he was elected Master-General, and in this post he gave constant attention to promoting higher studies among the Dominicans. He was created a cardinal in 1517, and from 1518 to 1519 he was papal legate in Germany. In 1519 he was appointed Bishop of Gaeta. His numerous works include commentaries on the *Summa theologica* of St. Thomas, on the *Categories, Posterior Analytics* and *De anima* of Aristotle, and on the *Praedicabilia* of Porphyry, as well as his writings *De nominum analogia, De subiecto naturalis philosophiae, De conceptu entis, De Dei infinitate* and the already-mentioned *De ente et essentia.* Although Cajetan took part in theological and philosophical controversy he wrote with admirable calm and moderation. He was, however, accused of obscurity by Melchior Cano, who was more influenced than Cajetan by contemporary humanism and care for literary style.

338 SCHOLASTICISM OF THE RENAISSANCE

In his *De nominum analogia* Cajetan developed a view of analogy which has exercised a considerable influence among Thomists. After insisting[1] on the importance of the rôle which analogy plays in metaphysics he goes on to divide analogy into three main kinds. (i) The first kind of analogy, or of what is sometimes called analogy, is 'analogy of inequality'.[2] Sensitive or animal life, for example, is found in a higher degree of perfection in men than in brutes; and in this sense they are 'unequally' animals. But this does not alter the fact, says Cajetan, that animality is predicated univocally of men and brutes. Corporeity is nobler in a plant than in a metal; but plants and metals are bodily things in a univocal sense. This type of analogy is called 'analogy', therefore, only by a misuse of the term. (ii) The second kind of analogy is analogy of attribution,[3] though the only type of this kind of analogy which Cajetan recognized was analogy of extrinsic attribution. An animal, for example, is called healthy because it possesses health formally, while food and medicine are called healthy only because they preserve or restore health in something other than themselves, an animal, for instance. This example may, however, be misleading. Cajetan did not assert that finite things are good, for example, only in the sense in which food is called healthy: he was well aware that each finite thing has its own inherent goodness. But he insisted that if finite things are called good precisely because of their relationship to the divine goodness as their efficient, exemplary or final cause, they are being called good only by extrinsic denomination. And he thought that when an analogous term is predicated of A only because of a relationship which A has to B, of which alone the analogous term is formally predicated, the predication is called analogous only on sufferance, as it were. Analogy in the proper and full sense occurs only in the case of the third kind of analogy. (iii) This third kind of analogy is analogy of proportionality.[4]

Analogy of proportionality can be either metaphorical or non-metaphorical. If we speak of a 'smiling meadow' this is an instance of metaphorical analogy; 'and sacred Scripture is full of this kind of analogy'.[5] But there is analogy of proportionality in the proper sense only when the common term is predicated of both analogates without the use of metaphor. If we say that there is an analogy between the relation of God's activity to His being and the relation of man's activity to his being, there is analogy of proportionality, since an imperfect similarity is asserted as holding

[1] Ch. 1.   [2] *Ibid.*   [3] Ch. 2.   [4] Ch. 3.   [5] *Ibid.*

between these two 'proportions' or relations; but activity is attributed formally and properly to both God and man. Again, we can predicate wisdom of God and man, meaning that an analogy holds between the relation of the divine wisdom to the divine being and the relation of man's wisdom to his being, and we do so without using the word 'wisdom' metaphorically.

According to Cajetan, this kind of analogy is the only kind which obtains between creatures and God; and he made a valiant effort[1] to show that it is capable of yielding a real knowledge of God. In particular, he tried to show that we can argue by analogy from creatures to God without committing the fallacy of equivocation. Suppose an argument like the following. Every pure perfection which is found in a creature exists also in God. But wisdom is found in human beings and it is a pure perfection. Therefore wisdom is found in God. If the word 'wisdom' in the minor premiss means human wisdom, the syllogism involves the fallacy of equivocation, because the word 'wisdom' in the conclusion does not mean human wisdom. In order to avoid this fallacy one must employ the word 'wisdom' neither univocally nor equivocally, that is, neither in one simple sense nor in two distinct senses, but in a sense which contains both uses *proportionaliter*. The conception 'father', for example, as predicated analogously of God and man contains both uses. It is true that we obtain a knowledge of wisdom, for instance, through an acquaintance with human wisdom and then apply it analogously to God; but, says Cajetan,[2] we should not confuse the psychological origin of a concept with its precise content when it is used analogously.

Apart from the obscurity of Cajetan's account of analogy, it is clear, I think, that to lay down rules for the term in order to avoid the fallacy of equivocation is not the same thing as to show that we are objectively justified in using the term in this way. It is one thing to say, for example, that if we assert that there is some similarity between the relation of the divine wisdom to the divine being and the relation of man's wisdom to his being we must not use the term 'wisdom' either univocally or equivocally; but it is another thing to show that we are entitled to speak at all of the divine wisdom. How could this possibly be shown if the only analogy which obtains between creatures and God is analogy of proportionality? It is difficult to see how this kind of analogy can be of any value at all in regard to our knowledge of God, unless the

[1] Ch. 10.   [2] Ch. 11.

analogy of intrinsic attribution is presupposed. Cajetan had doubtless much of value to say on the wrong uses of analogy; but I venture to doubt whether his restriction of analogy, as applied to God and creatures, to analogy of proportionality represents the view of St. Thomas. And it is perhaps a little difficult to see how his position does not lead in the end to agnosticism.

Cajetan criticized Scotism on many occasions, though always politely and temperately. Still more did he criticize the 'Averroism' of his day. But it is worth noting that in his commentary on the *De anima* of Aristotle he allowed that the Greek philosopher had really held the opinion attributed to him by the Averroists, namely that there is only one intellectual and immortal soul in all men and that there is no individual or personal immortality. Cajetan certainly rejected both the Averroist thesis, that there is only one intellectual and immortal soul in all men, and the Alexandrist thesis, that the soul is naturally mortal. But he apparently came to think that the immortality of the human soul cannot be philosophically demonstrated though probable arguments can be adduced to show that it is immortal. In his commentary on the *Epistle to the Romans*,[1] he explicitly says that he has no philosophic or demonstrative knowledge (*nescio* is the word he uses) of the mystery of the Trinity, of the immortality of the soul, of the Incarnation 'and the like, all of which, however, I believe'. If he was ready to couple the immortality of the soul with the mystery of the Trinity in this way, he cannot have thought that the former is a philosophically demonstrable truth. Moreover, in his commentary on *Ecclesiastes*[2] he says explicitly that 'no philosopher has yet demonstrated that the soul of man is immortal: there does not appear to be a demonstrative argument; but we believe it by faith, and it is in agreement with probable arguments' (*rationibus probabilibus consonat*). One can understand, then, his objection to the proposed decree of the fifth Lateran Council (1513) calling upon professors of philosophy to justify the Christian doctrine in their lectures. In Cajetan's opinion this was the task of theologians and not of philosophers.

3. Among the later Dominican writers of the period one can mention first Francis of Vitoria (1480–1546), who lectured at Salamanca and composed commentaries on the *Pars prima* and on the *Secunda secundae* of Aquinas's *Summa theologica*. But he is best known for his political and juridical ideas, and these will be

[1] 9, 23.   [2] 3, 21.

treated later. Dominic Soto (1494-1560), who also lectured at Salamanca, published, among other works, commentaries on Aristotle's logical writings and his *Physics* and *De anima*, as well as on the fourth book of the *Sentences* of Peter Lombard. Melchior Cano (1509-60) is justly celebrated for his *De locis theologicis*, in which he endeavoured to establish the sources of theological doctrine in a systematic and methodic manner. Bartholomew of Medina (1527-81), Dominic Báñez (1528-1604) and Raphael Ripa or Riva (d. 1611) were also outstanding Dominican theologians and philosophers.

Among the Jesuit writers an eminent name is that of Francis Toletus (1532-96), who was a pupil of Dominic Soto at Salamanca and afterwards lectured at Rome, where he was created cardinal. He published commentaries on the logical works of Aristotle and on his *Physics*, *De anima* and *De generatione et corruptione*, as well as on St. Thomas's *Summa theologica*. A set of learned commentaries on Aristotle were published by a group of Jesuit writers, known as the *Conimbricenses* from their connection with the university of Coimbra in Portugal. The chief member of this group was Peter de Fonseca (1548-99), who composed commentaries on the *Metaphysics*, as well as publishing *Institutiones dialecticae* and an *Isagoge philosophica* or introduction to philosophy. Among other Jesuit theologians and philosophers mention should be made of Gabriel Vásquez (c. 1551-1604), who lectured chiefly at Alcalá and Rome, and Gregory of Valentia (1551-1603). Both these men published commentaries on the *Summa theologica* of St. Thomas. Leonard Lessius (1554-1623), however, who lectured at Douai and Louvain, wrote independent works like his *De iustitia et iure ceterisque virtutibus cardinalibus* (1605), *De gratia efficaci, decretis, divinis libertate arbitrii et praescientia Dei conditionata disputatio apologetica* (1610), *De providentia Numinis et animae immortalitate* (1613), *De summo bono et aeterna beatitudine hominis* (1616) and *De perfectionibus moribusque divinis* (1620).

The Franciscan Lychetus (d. 1520) commented on the *Opus Oxoniense* and the *Quodlibeta* of Scotus. It was not until 1593, however, that the latter was declared the official Doctor of the Franciscan Order. Giles of Viterbo (d. 1532), an Augustinian, composed a commentary on part of the first book of the *Sentences* of Peter Lombard. And one must not omit to mention the group of professors associated with the university of Alcalá, founded by Cardinal Ximenes in 1489, who are known as the *Complutenses*,

The leading member of the group was Gaspar Cardillo de Villalpando (1537–81), who edited commentaries on Aristotle in which he tried to establish critically the actual meaning of the text.

4. Perhaps this is the place to say a few words about the famous controversy which broke out in the sixteenth century between Dominican and Jesuit theologians concerning the relation between divine grace and human free will. I do not wish to say much on the subject, as the controversy was primarily of a theological character. But it ought to be mentioned, I think, as it has philosophical implications.

Leaving out of account preliminary stages of the controversy one can start by mentioning a famous work by Luis de Molina (1535–1600), a Jesuit theologian who lectured for many years at the university of Evora in Portugal. This work, entitled *Concordia liberi arbitrii cum gratiae donis, divina praescientia, providentia, praedestinatione et reprobatione*, was published at Lisbon in 1589. In it Molina affirmed that 'efficacious grace', which includes in its concept the free consent of the human will, is not intrinsically different in nature from merely 'sufficient grace'. Grace which is merely sufficient is grace which is sufficient to enable the human will to elicit a salutary act, if the will were to consent to it and co-operate with it. It becomes 'efficacious', if the will does in fact consent to it. Efficacious grace is thus the grace with which a human will does in fact freely co-operate. On the other hand, if God exercises universal and particular providence, He must have infallible knowledge of how any will would react to any grace in any set of circumstances; and how can He know this if an efficacious grace is efficacious in virtue of the will's free consent? In order to answer this question Molina introduced the concept of *scientia media*, the knowledge by which God knows infallibly how any human will, in any conceivable set of circumstances, would react to this or that grace.

It is quite clear that Molina and those who agreed with him were concerned to safeguard the freedom of the human will. Their point of view may perhaps be expressed by saying that we start from what is best known to us, namely human freedom, and that we must explain the divine foreknowledge and the action of grace in such a way that the freedom of the will is not explained away or tacitly denied. If it did not seem fanciful to introduce such considerations into a theological dispute, one might perhaps suggest that the general humanistic movement of the Renaissance was reflected to some extent in Molinism. In the course of the controversy Molinism was modified by Jesuit theologians like Bellarmine and Suárez, who introduced the idea of 'congruism'. 'Congruous' grace is a grace which is congruous with or suited to the circumstances of the case and obtains the free consent of the will. It is opposed to 'incongruous' grace, which for some reason or other is not suited to the circumstances of the case, in that it does not obtain the free consent of the will, though in itself it is 'sufficient' to enable the will to make a salutary act. In virtue of the *scientia media* God knows from eternity what graces would be 'congruous' in regard to any will in any circumstances.

Molina's adversaries, of whom the most important was the Dominican theologian Báñez, started from the principle that God is the cause of all salutary acts and that God's knowledge and activity must be prior to and independent of the human will's free act. They accused Molina of making the power of divine grace subordinate to the human will. According to Báñez, efficacious grace is intrinsically different from merely sufficient grace, and it obtains its effect by reason of its own intrinsic nature. As for Molina's *scientia media* or 'intermediate knowledge', this is a mere term without any corresponding reality. God knows the future free acts of men, even conditional future free acts, in virtue of His predetermining decrees, by which He decides to give the 'physical premotion' which is necessary for any human act. In the case of a salutary act this physical premotion will take the form of efficacious grace.

Báñez and the theologians who agreed with him thus began with metaphysical principles. God, as first cause and prime mover, must be the cause of human acts in so far as they have being. Báñez, it must be emphasized, did not deny freedom. His view was that God moves non-free agents to act necessarily and free agents, when they act as free agents, to act freely. In other words God moves every contingent agent to act in a manner conformable to its nature. According to the Bannezian view, one must begin with assured metaphysical principles and draw the logical conclusions. The Molinist view, according to the Bannezians, was unfaithful to the principles of metaphysics. According to the Molinists on the other hand, it was very difficult to see how the Bannezians could retain human freedom in anything except in name. Moreover, if the idea of a divine concurrence which is logically prior to the free act and which infallibly brings about a certain act was admitted, it was very difficult to see how one is to avoid making God responsible for sin. The Molinists did not think that the distinctions introduced by their opponents in order to avoid the conclusion that God is responsible for sin were of any substantial use for this purpose. *Scientia media* was admittedly a hypothesis; but it was preferable to make this hypothesis rather than to suppose that God knows the future free acts of men in virtue of His predetermining decrees.

The dispute between the Dominicans and the Jesuits induced Pope Clement VIII to set up a special Congregation in Rome to examine the points at issue. The Congregation is known as the *Congregatio de auxiliis* (1598–1607). Both parties had full opportunity to state their respective cases; but the end of the matter was that both opinions were permitted. At the same time the Jesuits were forbidden to call the Dominicans Calvinists, while the Dominicans were told that they must not call the Jesuits Pelagians. In other words, the different parties could continue to propound their own ways of reconciling God's foreknowledge, predestination and saving activity with human freedom, provided that they did not call each other heretics.

5. Cajetan was the first to take Aquinas's *Summa theologica* as a theological text-book instead of the *Sentences* of Peter Lombard; and both Dominicans and Jesuits looked on St. Thomas as their Doctor. Aristotle was still regarded as 'the Philosopher'; and we have seen that Renaissance Scholastics continued to publish commentaries on his works. At the same time there was gradually effected a separation of philosophy from theology more systematic and methodic than that which had generally obtained in the mediaeval Schools. This was due partly to the formal distinction between the two branches of study which had already been made in the Middle Ages and partly, no doubt, to the rise of philosophies which owed nothing, professedly at least, to dogmatic theology. We find, then, the gradual substitution of philosophical courses for commentaries on Aristotle. Already with Suárez (d. 1617) we find an elaborate discussion of philosophical problems in separation from theology; and the order of treating metaphysical themes and problems which had been adopted by Suárez in his *Disputationes metaphysicae* exercised an influence on later Scholastic method. In the freer style of philosophical writing which was inaugurated by Suárez one can doubtless see the influence of Renaissance humanism. I said earlier in this chapter that Spanish Scholasticism was

comparatively unaffected by the Renaissance. But one must make an exception, I think, in regard to literary style. Suárez was, it must be admitted, a diffuse writer; but his work on metaphysics did a great deal to break through the former tradition of writing philosophy in the form of commentaries on Aristotle.

The eminent Dominican theologian and philosopher John of St. Thomas (1589–1644) published his *Cursus philosophicus* before his *Cursus theologicus*, and, to take another Dominican example, Alexander Piny issued a *Cursus philosophicus thomisticus* in 1670. The Carmelite Fathers of Alcalá published a *Cursus artium* in 1624, which was revised and added to in later editions. Among the Jesuits, Cardinal John de Lugo (1583–1660) left an unpublished *Disputationes metaphysicae*, while Peter de Hurtado de Mendoza published *Disputationes de universa philosophia* at Lyons in 1617 and Thomas Compton-Carleton a *Philosophia universa* at Antwerp in 1649. Similarly, both Rodrigo de Arriaga and Francis de Oviedo published philosophical courses, the former at Antwerp in 1632 and the latter at Lyons in 1640. A *Cursus philosophicus* by Francis Soares appeared at Coimbra in 1651, and a *Philosophia peripatetica* by John-Baptist de Benedictis at Naples in 1688. Similar philosophical courses were written by Scotists. Thus John Poncius and Bartholomew Mastrius published respectively a *Cursus philosophicus ad mentem Scoti* (1643) and a *Philosophiae ad mentem Scoti cursus integer* (1678). Among writers belonging to other religious Orders Nicholas of St. John the Baptist, a Hermit of St. Augustine, published his *Philosophia augustiniana, sive integer cursus philosophicus iuxta doctrinam sancti Patris Augustini* at Geneva in 1687, while Celestino Sfondrati, a Benedictine, published a *Cursus philosophicus sangallensis* (1695–9).

In the course of the seventeenth century, then, *Cursus philosophici* tended to take the place of the former commentaries on Aristotle. This is not to say, however, that the former custom was abandoned. Sylvester Maurus (1619–87), for example, a Jesuit theologian and philosopher, published a commentary on Aristotle in 1668. Nor is one entitled to conclude from the change in the method of philosophic writing that the Scholastics of the Renaissance and of the seventeenth century were profoundly influenced by the new scientific ideas of the time. The Franciscan Emmanuel Maignan, who published a *Cursus philosophicus* at Toulouse in 1652, complained that the Scholastics of his time devoted themselves to metaphysical abstractions and subtleties and that some of them, when their opinions on physics were challenged in the name of experience and experiment, replied by denying the testimony of experience. Maignan himself was considerably influenced by Cartesianism and atomism. Honoré Fabri (c. 1607–88), a Jesuit writer, laid particular emphasis on mathematics and physics; and there were, of course, other Scholastics who were alive to the ideas of their time. But if one takes the movement of the Renaissance and post-Renaissance philosophy as a whole, it is fairly obvious that Scholasticism lay somewhat apart from the main line of development and that its influence on non-Scholastic philosophers was restricted. This is not to say that it had no influence; but it is obvious that when we think of Renaissance and post-Renaissance philosophy we do not think primarily of Scholasticism. Generally speaking, the Scholastic philosophers of the period failed to give sufficient attention to the problems raised by, for example, the scientific discoveries of the time.

6. There was, however, at least one department of thought in which the Renaissance Scholastics were deeply influenced by contemporary problems and in which they exercised a considerable influence. This was the department of political theory. I shall say something more in detail later about Suárez' political theory; but I want to make some general remarks here concerning the political theory of the Scholastics of the Renaissance.

The problem of the relation between Church and State did not, as we have already seen, come to an end with the close of the Middle Ages. Indeed, it was in a sense intensified by the Reformation and by the claim of some rulers to possess jurisdiction even in matters of religion. As far as the Catholic Church was concerned a doctrine of full submission to the State was impossible: it was precluded by the position accorded to the Holy See and by the Catholic idea of the Church and her mission. The Catholic theologians and philosophers, therefore, felt called upon to lay down the principles by which the relations between Church and State should be governed. Thus Cardinal Robert Bellarmine maintained in his work on the papal power[1] that the pope, while not possessing a direct power over temporal affairs, possesses an indirect power. Temporal interests must give way to spiritual interests, if a clash arises. This theory of the pope's indirect power in temporal affairs did not mean that Bellarmine regarded the civil ruler as the pope's vicar—the theory excluded any such

[1] *De summo pontifice*, 1581; enlarged as *De potestate summi pontificis*, 1610.

idea; it was simply the consequence of applying the theological doctrine that man's end is a supernatural end, namely the beatific vision of God. The theory was also maintained by Francis Suárez in his *Defensio fidei catholicae* (1613), written against King James I of England.

But though Bellarmine and Suárez rejected the idea that the civil ruler is a vicar of the pope, they did not accept the theory that he derives his sovereignty directly from God, as was asserted by the upholders of the theory of the divine right of kings. And the fact that Suárez argued against this theory in his *Defensio fidei catholicae* was one of the reasons why James I had the book burned. Both Bellarmine and Suárez maintained that the civil ruler receives his power immediately from the political community. They held, indeed, that the civil ruler receives his authority ultimately from God, since all legitimate authority comes ultimately from Him; but it is derived immediately from the community.

One might be perhaps tempted to think that this theory was inspired by the desire to minimize the royal power at a time when the centralized and powerful monarchies of the Renaissance were very much in evidence. What better way of taking the wind out of the sails of the royalists could be devised than that of maintaining that though the monarch's power does not come from the pope it does not come directly from God either, but from the people? What better way of exalting the spiritual power could be found than that of asserting that it is the pope alone who receives his authority directly from God? But it would be a great mistake to regard the Bellarmine-Suárez theory of sovereignty as being primarily a piece of ecclesiastical propaganda or politics. The idea that political sovereignty is derived from the people had been put forward as early as the eleventh century by Manegold of Lautenbach; and the conviction that the civil ruler has a trust to fulfil and that if he habitually abuses his position he may be deposed was expressed by John of Salisbury in the twelfth, Aquinas in the thirteenth, and Ockham in the fourteenth century. Writers like Bellarmine and Suárez simply inherited the general outlook of the earlier Scholastic theologians and philosophers, though the fact that they gave a more formal and explicit statement of the theory that political sovereignty derives from the people was doubtless largely due to reflection on the concrete historical data of their time. When Mariana (d. 1624), the Spanish Jesuit, made his unfortunate statements about the use of tyrannicide as a remedy for political oppression (some of his remarks were interpreted as a defence of the murder of Henry III of France, and this caused his *De rege et regis institutione*, 1599, to be burned by the French Parliament) his principle was simply the principle of the legitimacy of resistance against oppression, which had been commonly accepted in the Middle Ages, though Mariana's conclusions were misguided.[1]

The Renaissance Scholastics were not, however, concerned simply with the position of the civil ruler in regard to the Church on the one hand and the political community on the other: they were concerned also with the origin and nature of political society. As far as Suárez is concerned, it is clear that he regarded political society as resting essentially on consent or agreement. Mariana, who derived the power of the monarch from a pact with the people, regarded the origin of political society as following a state of nature which preceded government; and the main step on the road to organized States and governments he found in the institution of private property. Suárez cannot be said to have followed Mariana in the latter hypothesis of a state of nature. But he found the origin of the State in voluntary consent, on the part of heads of families at least, though he evidently thought that such associations between men had occurred from the beginning.

Suárez may, then, be said to have held a double-contract theory, one contract being between the heads of families, the other between the society so formed and its ruler or rulers. But if one says this, one must realize that the contract theory as held by Suárez did not imply the artificial and conventional character either of political society or of government. His political theory, as we shall see more clearly later, was subordinate to his philosophy of law, in which he maintained the natural character of political society and political government. If we want to know Suárez' political theory, we have to turn primarily to his great treatise *De legibus*, which is above all things a philosophy of law. The idea of natural law, which goes back to the ancient world and which was given a metaphysical foundation by the philosophers of the Middle Ages, is essential to that philosophy and forms the background of his political theory. Political society is natural to man, and government is necessary for society; and as God is the Creator of human

---

[1] The then General of the Jesuits prohibited the teaching by members of the Order of Mariana's doctrine on tyrannicide.

nature both society and government are willed by God. They are not, therefore, purely arbitrary or conventional human contrivances. On the other hand, though Nature requires political society, the formation of determinate political communities normally depends on human agreement. Again, though Nature demands that any society should have some governing principle, Nature has not fixed any particular form of government or designated any particular individual as ruler. In certain instances God has directly designated a ruler (Saul, for instance, or David); but normally it rests with the community to determine the form of government.

The theory that political society rests on some sort of agreement was not altogether new, and one can find anticipations of it even in the ancient world. In the Middle Ages John of Paris, in his *Tractatus de potestate regia et papali* (c. 1303), presupposed a state of nature and held that though primitive men probably did not make any definite contract they were persuaded by their more rational fellows to live together under common law. And Giles of Rome in the thirteenth century had put forward a contract theory as one of the possible explanations of the foundation of political society. With Mariana in the sixteenth century the theory became explicit. In the same century the Dominican Francis of Vitoria implied a contract theory, and he was followed by the Jesuit Molina, though neither made any very explicit statement of the theory. Thus there was a growing tradition of the social contract theory; and Suárez' statement of it must be seen in the light of that tradition. In the course of time, however, the theory became divorced from the mediaeval philosophy of law. This philosophy was taken over, as we have seen, by Richard Hooker, and from him it passed, in a watered-down form, to Locke. But in Hobbes, Spinoza and Rousseau it is conspicuous by its absence, even if the old terms were sometimes retained. There is, then, a very great difference between the contract theory of Suárez and that of Rousseau, for example. And for this reason it may be misleading to speak of a contract theory in Suárez, if, that is to say, one understands by the term the sort of theory held by Rousseau. There was some historical continuity, of course; but the setting, atmosphere and the interpretation of the theory had undergone a fundamental change in the intervening period.

Another problem with which some of the Renaissance Scholastics concerned themselves was that of the relations between individual States. Already at the beginning of the seventh century St. Isidore of Seville in his curious encyclopaedic work, the *Etymologies*, had spoken of the *ius gentium* and of its application to war, making use of texts of Roman lawyers. Again, in the thirteenth century St. Raymund of Peñafort examined the topic of the right of war in his *Summa poenitentiae*, while in the second half of the fourteenth century there appeared works like the *De bello* of John of Legnano, a professor of the university of Bologna. Far better known, however, is Francis of Vitoria (1480–1546). It was very largely to him that the revival of theology in Spain was due, as was testified by pupils like Melchior Cano and Dominic Soto, while the Spanish humanist, Vivés, writing to Erasmus, praised Vitoria highly and spoke of his admiration for Erasmus and his defence of him against his critics. But it is for his studies on international law that Vitoria is known to the world at large.

Vitoria looked on different States as forming in some sense one human community, and he regarded the 'law of nations' as being not merely an agreed code of behaviour but as having the force of law, 'having been established by the authority of the whole world'.[1] His position seems to have been more or less as follows. Society could not hold together without laws the infringement of which renders transgressors liable to punishment. That such laws should exist is a demand of the natural law. There have therefore grown up a number of principles of conduct, for example the inviolability of ambassadors, on which society as a whole is agreed, since it is realized that principles of this kind are rational and for the common good. They are derivable in some way from the natural law and they must be reckoned to have the force of law. The *ius gentium* consists of prescriptions for the common good in the widest sense, which either belong directly to the natural law or are derivable in some way from it. 'What natural reason has established among all nations is called the *ius gentium*.'[2] According to Vitoria, the law of nations confers rights and creates obligations. Sanctions, however, can be applied only through the instrumentality of princes. But it is clear that his conception of international law leads to the idea of an international authority, though Vitoria does not say so.

Applying his ideas to war and to the rights of the Indians in regard to the Spaniards, Vitoria in the *De Indis* makes it clear that in his opinion physical power by itself confers no right to annex the property of others and that Christian missionary zeal confers no

[1] *De potestate civili*, 21.   [2] *Ibid*.

title to make war on the heathen. As regards slavery he adopted the usual position of theologians of the time, namely that slavery is legitimate as a penal measure (corresponding to modern penal servitude). But this concession must not be taken to imply that the Scholastic theologians and philosophers simply accepted the contemporary customs in regard to slavery. The example of the Jesuit Molina is interesting in this matter. Not content with theorizing in his study he went down to the port at Lisbon and questioned the slave-traders. As a result of these frank conversations he declared that the slave-trade was simply a commercial affair and that all the talk about exalted motives, like that of converting the slaves to Christianity, was nonsense.[1] But though he condemned the slave-trade, he admitted the legitimacy of slavery as a penal measure, when, for example, criminals were sent to the galleys in accordance with the penal customs of the time.

Suárez developed the idea of the 'law of nations'. He pointed out that it is necessary to make a distinction between the law of nations and the natural law. The former prohibits certain acts for a just and sufficient reason, and so it can be said to render certain acts wrong, but the natural law does not make acts wrong but prohibits certain acts because they are wrong. That treaties should be observed, for example, is a precept of the natural law rather than of the law of nations. The latter consists of customs established by all, or practically all, nations; but it is unwritten law, and this fact distinguishes it from civil law. Although, for instance, the obligation to observe a treaty once it has been made proceeds from the natural law, the precept that an offer of a treaty, when made for a reasonable cause, should be accepted is not a matter of strict obligation proceeding from the natural law; nor is there any written law about the matter. The precept is an unwritten custom which is in harmony with reason, and it belongs to the 'law of nations'.

The rational basis of the *ius gentium* is, according to Suárez, the fact that the human race preserves a certain unity in spite of the division of mankind into separate nations and States. Suárez did not consider a world-State to be practicable or desirable; but at the same time he saw that individual States are not self-sufficing in a complete sense. They need some system of law to regulate their relations with one another. Natural law does not provide sufficiently for this need. But the conduct of nations has introduced

[1] Cf. *De iustitia*, 1, 2, disp. 34–5.

certain customs or laws which are in accord with the natural law, even though they are not strictly deducible from it. And these customs or laws form the *ius gentium*.

It has been said, not unreasonably, that Vitoria's idea of all nations as forming in some sense a world-community and of the *ius gentium* as law established by the authority of the whole world looked forward to the possible creation of a world-government, whereas Suárez' idea of the *ius gentium* looked forward rather to establishment of an international tribunal which would interpret international law and give concrete decisions without being itself a world-government, which Suárez did not regard as practicable.[1] However this may be, it is clear that in much of their political and legal philosophy the Renaissance Scholastics showed a grasp of concrete problems and a readiness to handle them in a 'modern' way. Men like Vitoria, Bellarmine and Suárez all maintained that political sovereignty is in some sense derived from the people; and they maintained the right of resistance to a ruler who acts tyrannically. Although they naturally thought in terms of contemporary forms of government, they did not consider that the actual form of government is a matter of prime importance. At the same time the fact that their conception of political society and of law was founded on a clear acceptance of the natural moral law constituted its great strength. They systematized and developed mediaeval legal and political philosophy and transmitted it to the seventeenth century. Grotius, for example, was certainly indebted to the Scholastics. Some people would maintain, I suppose, that the legal and political theory of the Renaissance Scholastics constituted a stage in the development from a predominantly theological outlook to a positivist outlook; and as a historical judgment this may be true. But it does not follow that the later secularization of the idea of natural law and its subsequent abandonment to all intents and purposes constituted a philosophical advance in any but a chronological sense.

[1] Cf. *The Catholic Conception of International Law* by J. B. Scott, Ch. XIII.

CHAPTER XXII

FRANCIS SUÁREZ (1)

Life and works—The structure and divisions of the Disputationes metaphysicae—*Metaphysics as the science of being—The concept of being—The attributes of being—Individuation—Analogy—God's existence—The divine Nature—Essence and existence—Substance and accident—Modes—Quantity—Relations—*Entia rationis—*General remarks—Étienne Gilson on Suárez.*

1. FRANCIS SUÁREZ (1548–1617), known as *Doctor eximius*, was born at Granada and studied canon law at Salamanca. He entered the Society of Jesus in 1564 and in due course began his professional career by teaching philosophy at Segovia. Afterwards he taught theology at Avila, Segovia, Valladolid, Rome, Alcalá, Salamanca and Coimbra. Suárez, who was an exemplary and holy priest and religious, was also very much the student, scholar and professor; and his whole adult life was devoted to lecturing, study and writing. He was an indefatigable writer, and his works fill twenty-three volumes in the earlier editions and twenty-eight volumes in the Paris edition of 1856–78. A large number of these works were, of course, concerned with theological questions; and for present purposes his most important writings are the two volumes of *Disputationes metaphysicae* (1597) and his great work *De legibus* (1612). One may also mention his *De Deo uno et trino* (1606) and the *De opere sex dierum* (published posthumously in 1621).

Suárez was convinced that a theologian ought to possess a firm grasp and profound understanding of the metaphysical principles and foundations of speculation. He says explicitly that no one can become a perfect theologian unless he has first laid the firm foundations of metaphysics. Accordingly, in his *Disputationes metaphysicae* he set out to give a complete and systematic treatment of Scholastic metaphysics; and, indeed, the work was the first of its kind. It was incomplete in the sense that metaphysical psychology was omitted; but this was supplied in the *Tractatus de anima* (published posthumously in 1621). Suárez abandoned the order adopted by Aristotle in his *Metaphysics*[1] and divided the

[1] The importance of this change is not diminished, of course, by the fact that we know that Aristotle's *Metaphysics* was not 'a book' but a collection of treatises.

matter systematically into fifty-four disputations, subdivided into sections; though at the beginning he provided a table showing where the themes treated of in the successive chapters of Aristotle's *Metaphysics* were dealt with in his own work. In this work the author's astounding erudition is clearly expressed in his discussions of, or references and allusions to, Greek, Patristic, Jewish, Islamic and Scholastic authors and to Renaissance thinkers like Marsilius Ficinus and Pico della Mirandola. Needless to say, however, Suárez does not confine himself to the historical recital of opinions; his object is always the attainment of a positive and objective answer to the problems raised. He may be prolix, but he is certainly systematic. As an example of a competent non-Scholastic judgment of the work one may quote the following sentence. 'All the important Scholastic controversies are in this work lucidly brought together and critically examined and their results combined in the unity of a system.'[1]

In the present chapter I shall be concerned mainly with the *Disputationes metaphysicae*. In the next chapter I shall treat of the contents of the *Tractatus de legibus ac Deo legislatore in X libros distributus*. This last work summarized and systematized Scholastic legal theories, and in it the author presented his own development of Thomist legal and political theory. In this connection one must mention also Suárez' *Defensio fidei catholicae et apostolicae adversus Anglicanae sectae errores, cum responsione ad apologium pro iure fidelitatis et praefationem monitoriam Serenissimi Jacobi Angliae Regis* (1613). In this book Suárez maintained Bellarmine's theory of the indirect power of the pope in temporal affairs and argued against the notion, dear to James I of England, that temporal monarchs receive their sovereignty immediately from God. As I remarked in the last chapter, James I had the book burned.

2. Before going on to outline some of Suárez' philosophical ideas I want to say something about the structure and arrangement of the *Disputationes metaphysicae*.

In the first disputation (or discussion) Suárez considers the nature of first philosophy or metaphysics, and he decides that it can be defined as the science which contemplates being as being. The second disputation deals with the concept of being, while disputations 3 to 11 inclusive treat of the *passiones entis* or

---

[1] M. Frischeisen-Köhler and W. Moog: *Die Philosophie der Neuzeit bis zum Ende des XVIII Jahrhunderts*, p. 211; vol. III of F. Ueberweg's *Grundriss der Geschichte der Philosophie*, 12th edition.

transcendental attributes of being. Unity in general is the theme of the fourth disputation, while individual unity and the principle of individuation are dealt with in the fifth. The sixth disputation treats of universals, the seventh of distinctions. After considering unity Suárez passes to truth (disputation 8) and falsity (9), while in disputations 10 and 11 he treats of good and evil. Disputations 12 to 27 are concerned with causes; disputation 12 with causes in general, disputations 13 and 14 with the material cause, disputations 15 and 16 with the formal cause, disputations 17 to 22 with efficient causality, and disputations 23 and 24 with final causality, while exemplary causality is the subject of disputation 25. Finally, disputation 26 deals with the relations of causes to effects and disputation 27 with the mutual relations of the causes to one another.

The second volume begins with the division of being into infinite and finite being (disputation 28). Infinite or divine being is treated in the next two disputations, God's existence in disputation 29 and His essence and attributes in disputation 30. In disputation 31 Suárez goes on to consider finite created being in general, and in the following disputation he considers the distinction of substance and accidents in general. Disputations 33 to 36 contain Suárez' metaphysics of substance, and disputations 37 to 53 deal with the various categories of accidents. The last disputation of the work, 54, deals with *entia rationis*.

As has already been indicated, Suárez' *Disputationes metaphysicae* mark the transition from commentaries on Aristotle to independent treatises on metaphysics and to *Cursus philosophici* in general. It is true that one can discern among Suárez' predecessors, as for example with Fonseca, a growing tendency to shake off the bonds imposed by the commentary method; but it was Suárez who really originated the new form of treatment. After his time the *Cursus philosophici* and independent philosophical treatises became common, both inside and outside the Jesuit Order. Moreover, Suárez' decision not to include rational psychology in metaphysics but to treat it on its own and consider it as the highest part of 'natural philosophy'[1] had its influence on succeeding writers like Arriaga and Oviedo, who assigned the theory of the soul to physics rather than to metaphysics.[2]

One feature of Suárez' *Disputationes metaphysicae* which should

[1] *Disp. metaph.*, 1, 2, nn. 19-20.
[2] This classification of psychology was in accordance with Aristotle's remarks in his *De Anima*.

be noticed is that no separation is made in this work between general and special metaphysics. The later distinction between ontology or general metaphysics on the one hand and special metaphysical disciplines like psychology, cosmology and natural theology on the other hand has commonly been ascribed to the influence of Christian Wolff (1679-1754), the disciple of Leibniz, who wrote separate treatises on ontology, cosmology, psychology natural theology, etc. But further investigation into the history of Scholasticism in the second half of the seventeenth century has shown that the distinction between general and special metaphysics and the use of the word 'ontology' to describe the former antedate the writings of Wolff. Jean-Baptiste Duhamel (1624-1706) used the word 'ontology' to describe general metaphysics in his *Philosophia vetus et nova* or *Philosophia universalis* or *Philosophia Burgundica* (1678). This is not to say, however, that Wolff's division of the philosophical disciplines was not of great influence or that the continued use of the word 'ontology' for general metaphysics is not to be ascribed primarily to him.

3. Metaphysics, says Suárez,[1] has as its *obiectum adequatum* being in so far as it is real being. But to say that the metaphysician is concerned with being as being is not the same thing as saying that he is concerned with being as being in complete abstraction from the ways in which being is concretely realized, that is to say, in complete abstraction from the most general kinds of being or *inferiora entis*. After all, the metaphysician is concerned with real being, with being as including in some way the *inferiora entis secundum proprias rationes*.[2] He is concerned, therefore, not only with the concept of being as such but also with the transcendental attributes of being, with uncreated and created, infinite and finite being, with substance and accidents, and with the types of causes. But he is not concerned with material being as such: he is concerned with material things only in so far as knowledge of them is necessary in order to know the general divisions and categories of being.[3] The fact is that the concept of being is analogous, and so it cannot be properly known unless the different kinds of being are clearly distinguished.[4] For instance, the metaphysician is primarily concerned with immaterial, not with material substance; but he has to consider material substance in so far as knowledge of it is necessary in order to distinguish it from immaterial substance and

---

[1] *Disp.*, 1, 1, 24.   [2] 1, 2, 11.   [3] 1, 2, 24.   [4] *Ibid.*

in order to know the metaphysical predicates which belong to it precisely as material substance.[1]

With Suárez, then, as Suarezians at any rate would maintain, the fundamental metaphysical attitude of Thomism persists unchanged. The Aristotelian idea of 'first philosophy' as the study or science of being as being is maintained. But Suárez emphasizes the fact that by being he means real being; the metaphysician is not concerned simply with concepts. Again, though he is concerned primarily with immaterial reality, he is not so exclusively concerned with it that he has nothing to say of material reality. But he considers material reality only from the metaphysical point of view, not from the point of view of a physicist or of a mathematician; Suárez accepted the Aristotelian doctrine of the degrees of abstraction. Again, we may note that Suárez emphasized the analogical character of the concept of being; he would not allow that it is univocal. Lastly, as to the purpose of metaphysics, Suárez is convinced that it is the contemplation of truth for its own sake;[2] he remains in the serene atmosphere of the Aristotelian *Metaphysics* and of St. Thomas and is unaffected by the new attitude towards knowledge which manifested itself in a Francis Bacon.

4. In the second disputation Suárez treats of the concept of being; and he declares that 'the proper and adequate formal concept of being as such is one' and that 'it is different from the formal concepts of other things'.[3] As he goes on to say that this is the common opinion and reckons among its defenders 'Scotus and all his disciples', it might seem that he is making the concept of being univocal and not analogical. It is necessary, then, to say something about Suárez' view on this matter.

In the first place the formal concept of being is one, in the sense that it does not signify immediately any particular nature or kind of thing: it does not signify a plurality of beings according as they differ from one another, but 'rather in so far as they agree with one another or are like to one another'.[4] The concept of being is really distinct from the concept of substance or the concept of accident: it abstracts from what is proper to each.[5] It will not do to say that there is a unity of word alone, for the concept precedes the word and its use.[6] Moreover, 'to the formal concept of being there corresponds an adequate and immediate objective concept, which does not expressly signify either substance or accident, either God

[1] *Disp.*, 1, 2, 5.   [2] 1, 4, 2.   [3] 2, 1, 9.
[4] 2, 1, 9.   [5] 2, 1, 10.   [6] 2, 1, 13.

or creature: it signifies them all in so far as they are in some way like to one another and agree in being.'[1] Does this mean that in a created substance, for instance, there is a form of being which is actually distinct from the form or forms which make it a created substance in particular? No, abstraction does not necessarily require a distinction of things or forms which actually precedes the abstraction: it is sufficient if the mind considers objects, not as each exists in itself, but according to its likeness to other things.[2] In the concept of being as such the mind considers only the likeness of things, not their differences from one another. It is true that a real being is such by its own being which is inseparable from it, that is to say, it is true that a thing's being is intrinsic to it; but this simply means that the concept of being as such does not include its 'inferiors'.

Suárez admits, then, that a concept of being can be formed which is strictly one; and on this matter he ranges himself with Scotus against Cajetan. But he emphasizes the fact that this concept is the work of the mind and that 'as it exists in the thing itself, it is not something actually distinct from the inferiors in which it exists. This is the common opinion of the whole School of St. Thomas.'[3] Why, then, does he insist that the concept of being represents reality? If it represents reality, in what does being as such consist and how does it belong to its inferiors? Does it not seem that if the concept of being as such represents reality, it must represent something in the inferiors, that is, in existent beings, which is distinct from that intrinsic entity or beingness which is peculiar to each? And, if this is not so, does it not follow that the concept of being as such does not represent reality?

Suárez distinguishes 'being' understood as a participle, that is to say, as signifying the act of existing, from 'being' understood as a noun, that is to say, as signifying what has a real essence, whether it actually exists or not. A 'real essence' is one which does not involve any contradiction and which is not a mere construction of the mind. Now, 'being' understood as a participle gives rise to one concept 'common to all actually existent beings, since they are like to one another and agree in actual existence' and this holds good both for the formal and for the objective concepts.[4] We can also have one concept of being understood as a noun, provided that the concept simply abstracts from, and does not exclude, actual existence.

[1] *Disp.*, 2, 2, 8.   [2] 2, 2, 15.   [3] 2, 3, 7.   [4] 2, 4, 4.

It does not appear to me that the repetition of this statement of our ability to form one concept of being provides a very adequate answer to the difficulties which can be raised; but I wish now to indicate why Suárez does not call this concept a univocal concept.

In order that a concept should be univocal, it is not sufficient that it should be applicable in the same sense to a plurality of different inferiors which have an equal relationship to one another.[1] Suárez, therefore, demanded more for a univocal concept than that it should be one concept; he demanded that it should apply to its inferiors in the same way. We can, indeed, form a formal concept of being which is one and which says nothing about the differences of the inferiors; but no inferior is, so to speak, outside being. When the concept of being is narrowed down (*contrahitur*) to concepts of different kinds of being, what is done is that a thing is conceived more expressly,[2] according to its own mode of existence, than it is by means of the concept of being.[3] This does not mean, however, that something is added to the concept of being as though from outside. On the contrary, the concept of being is made more express or determinate. In order that the inferiors should be properly conceived as beings of a certain kind, the concept of being must indeed be contracted: but this means making more determinate what was already contained in the concept. The latter cannot, therefore, be univocal.

5. In the third disputation Suárez proceeds to discuss the *passiones entis in communi*, the attributes of being as such. There are only three such attributes, namely unity, truth and goodness.[4] These attributes do not, however, add anything positive to being. Unity signifies being as undivided; and this undividedness adds to being simply a denial of division, not anything positive.[5] Truth of knowledge (*veritas cognitionis*) does not add anything real to the act itself, but it connotes the object existing in the way that it is represented by the judgment as existing.[6] But truth of knowledge is found in the judgment or mental act and is not the same as *veritas transcendentalis*, which signifies the being of a thing with connotation of the knowledge or concept of the intellect, which represents, or can represent, the thing as it is.[7] This conformity of the thing to the mind must be understood primarily of a relation to the divine mind, and only secondarily of conformity to the

---

[1] 2, 2, 36; 39, 3, 17. [2] *expressius, per maiorem determinationem.*
[3] 2, 6, 7. [4] 3, 2, 3. [5] *Disp.*, 4, 1–2. [6] 8, 2, 9. [7] 8, 7, 25.

human mind.[1] As to goodness, this means the perfection of a thing, though it also connotes in another thing an inclination to or capacity for the aforesaid perfection. This connotation, however, does not add to the thing which is called good anything absolute; nor is it, properly speaking, a relation.[2] None of the three transcendental attributes of being, then, adds anything positive to being.

6. In the fifth disputation Suárez considers the problem of individuation. All actually existing things—all things which can exist 'immediately'—are singular and individual.[3] The word 'immediately' is inserted in order to exclude the common attributes of being, which cannot exist immediately, that is to say, which can exist only in singular, individual beings. Suárez agrees with Scotus that individuality adds something real to the common nature; but he rejects Scotus' doctrine of the *haecceitas* 'formally' distinct from the specific nature.[4] What, then, does individuality add to the common nature? 'Individuality adds to the common nature something which is mentally distinct from that nature, which belongs to the same category, and which (together with the nature) constitutes the individual metaphysically, as an individual *differentia* contracting the species and constituting the individual.'[5] Suárez remarks that to say that what is added is mentally distinct from the specific nature is not the same thing as saying that it is an *ens rationis*; he has already agreed with Scotus that it is *aliquid reale*. In answer, then, to the question whether a substance is individuated by itself Suárez replies that if the words 'by itself' refer to the specific nature as such, the answer is in the negative, but that, if the words 'by itself' mean 'by its own entity or being', the answer is in the affirmative. But it must be added that the thing's entity or being includes not only the *ratio specifica* but also the *differentia individualis*, the two being distinguished from one another by a mental distinction. Suárez emphasizes the fact that he is speaking of created things, not of the divine substance; but among created things he applies the same doctrine to both immaterial and material substances. From this it follows that he rejects the Thomist view of *materia signata* as the only principle of individuation.[6] In the case of a composite substance, composed, that is to say, of matter and form, 'the adequate principle of individuation is this matter and this form in union, the form being the chief principle and sufficient by itself for the composite, as an individual

[1] 8, 7, 28–9. [2] 10, 1, 12. [3] 5, 1, 4. [4] 5, 2, 8–9. [5] 5, 2, 16. [6] 5, 3.

thing of a certain species, to be considered numerically one. This conclusion . . . agrees with the opinion of Durandus and Toletus; and Scotus, Henry of Ghent and the Nominalists do not hold anything substantially different' (*in re non dissentiunt*).[1] It is perfectly true that because our knowledge is founded on experience of sensible things, we often distinguish individuals according to their several 'matters' or according to the accidents, like quantity, which follow on the possession of matter; but if we are considering a material substance in itself, and not in relation simply to our mode of cognition, its individuality must be primarily ascribed to its principal constitutive element, namely the form.[2]

7. Having dealt at length with the doctrine of causes Suárez comes in disputation 28 to the division of being into infinite being and finite being. This division is fundamental; but it can be made 'under different names and concepts'.[3] For example, being can be divided into *ens a se* and *ens ab alio*, into necessary being and contingent being, or into being by essence and being by participation. But these and similar divisions are equivalent, in the sense that they are all divisions of being into God and creatures and exhaust being, as it were.

The question then arises whether being is predicated equivocally, univocally or analogically of God and creatures. Suárez notes[4] that a doctrine of equivocation is wrongly attributed to Petrus Aureoli. The Scotist doctrine, that 'being signifies immediately one concept which is common to God and creatures and which is therefore predicated of them univocally, and not analogically',[5] Suárez rejects. But if being is predicated analogically of God and creatures, is the analogy in question the analogy of proportionality alone, as Cajetan taught, or the analogy of proportionality together with the analogy of attribution, as Fonseca, for example, considered? According to Suárez, the analogy in question cannot be the analogy of proportionality, for 'every true analogy of proportionality includes an element of metaphor', whereas 'in this analogy of being there is no metaphor'.[6] It must be, therefore, analogy of attribution, and, indeed, intrinsic attribution. 'Every creature is being in virtue of a relation to God, inasmuch as it participates in or in some way imitates the being (*esse*) of God, and, as having being, it depends essentially on God, much more than an accident depends on a substance.'[7]

[1] 5, 6, 15. [2] 5, 6, 17. [3] 28, 1, 6. [4] 28, 3, 1.
[5] 28, 3, 2. [6] 28, 3, 11. [7] 28, 3, 16.

8. In the following disputation (29) Suárez considers the question whether God's existence can be known by reason, apart from revelation. First of all he examines the 'physical argument', which is to all intents and purposes the argument from motion as found in Aristotle. Suárez' conclusion is that this argument is unable to demonstrate the existence of God. The principle on which the argument is founded, namely 'every thing which is moved is moved by another' (*omne quod movetur ab alio movetur*), he declares to be uncertain. Some things appear to move themselves, and it might be true of the motion of the heaven that the latter moves itself in virtue of its own form or of some innate power. 'How, then, can a true demonstration, proving God's existence, be obtained by the aid of uncertain principles?'[1] If the principle is rightly understood, it is more probable (*probabilius*) than its opposite, but all the same, 'by what necessary or evident argument can it be proved from this principle that there is an immaterial substance?'[2] Even if it can be shown that a mover is required, it does not follow that there is not a plurality of movers, still less that the mover is immaterial pure act. Suárez' point is that one cannot prove the existence of God as immaterial uncreated substance and pure act by arguments drawn from 'physics'. In order to show that God exists it is necessary to have recourse to metaphysical arguments.

First of all it is necessary to substitute for the principle *omne quod movetur ab alio movetur* the metaphysical principle *omne quod fit, ab alio fit*.[3] The truth of the principle follows from the evident truth that nothing can produce itself. On the basis of this metaphysical principle one can argue as follows.[4] 'Every being is either made or not made (uncreated). But not all beings in the universe can be made. Therefore there is necessarily some being which is not made, but which is uncreated.' The truth of the major premiss can be made evident in this way. A made or produced being is produced by 'something else'. This 'something else' is itself either made or not made. If the latter, then we already have an uncreated being. If the former, then that on which the 'something else' depends for existence is itself either made or not made. In order to avoid an infinite regress or a 'circle' (which would obtain if one said that A was made by B, B by C, and C by A), it is necessary to postulate an uncreated being. In his discussion of the impossibility of an infinite regress[5] Suárez distinguishes *causae per*

[1] 29, I, 7.   [2] 29, I, 8.   [3] 29, I, 20.   [4] 29, I, 21.   [5] 29, I, 25–40.

se subordinatae and *causae per accidens subordinatae*; but he makes it clear that he considers an infinite regress impossible even in the case of the latter. He adopts, then, a different opinion from that of St. Thomas. But he remarks that even if one accepts the possibility of an infinite regress in the series of *causae per accidens subordinatae*, this does not affect the main line of the argument, for the infinite series would be eternally dependent on a higher extrinsic cause. If it were not, there would be no causality or production at all.

This argument, however, does not immediately show that God exists: it has still to be shown that there is only one uncreated being. Suárez argues first of all that 'although individual effects, taken and considered separately, do not show that the maker of all things is one and the same, the beauty of the whole universe and of all things which are in it, their marvellous connection and order sufficiently show that there is one first being by which all things are governed and from which they derive their origin'.[1] Against the objection that there might be several governors of the universe Suárez argues that it can be shown that the whole sensible world proceeds from one efficient cause. The cause or causes of the universe must be intelligent; but several intelligent causes could not combine to produce and govern the one systematically united effect unless they were subordinated to a higher cause using them as organs or instruments.[2] There is, however, another possible objection. Might there not be another universe, made by another uncreated cause? Suárez allows that the creation of another universe would not be impossible, but he observes that there is no reason to suppose that there is another universe. Still, given the possibility, the argument from the universe to the unicity of God holds good, strictly speaking, only for those things which are capable of being known by human experience and reasoning. He concludes, therefore, that an *a priori* proof of the unicity of uncreated being must be given.

The *a priori* proof is not, Suárez notes, *a priori* in the strict sense: it is impossible to deduce God's existence from its cause, for it has no cause. 'Nor, even if it had, is God known by us so exactly and perfectly that we can apprehend Him by means of His own principles, so to speak.'[3] Nevertheless, if something about God has been already proved *a posteriori*, we may be in a position to argue *a priori* from one attribute to another.[4] 'When it has been proved

[1] 29, 2, 7.   [2] 29, 2, 21.   [3] 29, 3, 1.   [4] *Ibid.*

a posteriori that God is necessary self-existent being (*ens a se*), it can be proved *a priori* from this attribute that there cannot be any other necessary self-existent being, and consequently it can be proved that God exists.'[1] In other words, Suárez' argument is that it can be proved that there must be *a* necessary being and that it can then be shown conclusively that there cannot be more than *one* necessary being. How does he show that there can be only one necessary being? He argues that, in order that there may be a plurality of beings having a common nature, it is necessary that the individuality of each should be in some way (*aliquo modo*) outside the essence of the nature. For, if individuality was essential to the nature, the latter would not be multipliable. But in the case of uncreated being it is impossible for its individuality to be in any way distinct from its nature, for its nature is existence itself, and existence is always individual. The foregoing argument is the fourth which Suárez considers.[2] Later on[3] he remarks that 'although some of these arguments which have been considered do not perhaps, when taken separately, so convince the intellect that a froward or ill-disposed man cannot find ways of evading them, none the less all the arguments are most efficacious, and, especially if they are taken together, they abundantly prove the aforesaid truth'.

9. Suárez proceeds to consider the nature of God. He points out at the beginning of disputation 30 that the question of God's existence and the question of God's nature cannot be entirely isolated from one another. He also repeats his observation that, although our knowledge of God is *a posteriori*, we can in some cases argue *a priori* from one attribute to another. After these preliminary remarks he proceeds to argue that God is perfect being, possessing in Himself, as creator, all the perfections which He is capable of communicating. But He does not possess them all in the same way. Those perfections which do not of themselves contain any limitation or imperfection, God possesses 'formally' (*formaliter*). A perfection like wisdom, for example, though it exists in human beings in a finite or imperfect manner, does not include in its formal concept any limitation or imperfection, and it can be predicated formally of God, *salva analogia, quae inter Deum et creaturam semper intercedit*.[4] Perfections of this sort exist 'eminently' (*eminenter*) in God, for creaturely wisdom as such cannot be predicated of God; but there is, none the less, a formal

[1] 29, 3, 2. [2] 29, 3, 11. [3] 29, 3, 31. [4] 30, 1, 12.

analogous concept of wisdom which can be predicated formally, though analogously, of God. In the case, however, of perfections which involve inclusion of the being possessing them in a certain category these can be said to be present in God only *modo eminenti*, and not formally.

In succeeding sections Suárez argues that God is infinite,[1] pure act and without any composition,[2] omnipresent,[3] immutable and eternal, yet free,[4] one,[5] invisible,[6] incomprehensible,[7] ineffable,[8] living, intelligent and self-sufficient substance.[9] He then considers the divine knowledge[10] and the divine will[11] and the divine power.[12] In the section on the divine knowledge Suárez shows that God knows possible creatures and existent things and then remarks that the question of God's knowledge of conditional future contingent events cannot be properly treated without reference to theological sources, even though it is a metaphysical question, 'and so I entirely omit it'.[13] But he allows himself the remark that if statements like, 'if Peter had been here, he would have sinned' have a determinate truth, this truth cannot be unknown to God. That they have determinate truth is 'much more probable' (*multo probabilius*) than that they have not, in the sense that Peter in the example given would either have sinned or not have sinned and that, though we cannot know which would have happened, God can know it. However, as Suárez omits any further treatment of this matter in his metaphysical disputations, I too omit it.

10. Coming to the subject of finite being, Suárez treats first of the essence of finite being as such, of its existence, and of the distinction between essence and existence in finite being. He first outlines the arguments of those who hold the opinion that existence (*esse*) and essence are really distinct in creatures. 'This is thought to be St. Thomas's opinion, which, understood in this sense, has been followed by almost all the early Thomists.'[14] The second opinion mentioned by Suárez is that the creature's existence is 'formally' distinguished from its nature, as a mode of that nature. 'This opinion is attributed to Scotus.'[15] The third opinion is that essence and existence in the creature are distinguished only mentally (*tantum ratione*). This opinion, says Suárez,[16] was held by Alexander of Hales and others, including the nominalists. It is

---

[1] 30, 2. [2] 30, 3–5. [3] 30, 7. [4] 30, 8–9
[5] 30, 10. [6] 30, 11. [7] 30, 12. [8] 30, 13.
[9] 30, 14. [10] 30, 15. [11] 30, 16. [12] 30, 17.
[13] 30, 15, 33. [14] 31, 1, 3. [15] 31, 1, 11. [16] 31, 1, 12.

the opinion he himself defends, provided that 'existence' is understood to mean actual existence and 'essence' actually existing essence. 'And this opinion, if so explained, I think to be quite true.'[1] It is impossible, Suárez states, for anything to be intrinsically and formally constituted as a real and actual being by something distinct from it. From this it follows that existence cannot be distinguished from essence as a mode which is distinct from the essence or nature *ex natura rei*.[2] The right view is this.[3] If the terms 'existence' and 'essence' are understood to refer respectively to actual being (*ens in actu*) and potential or possible being (*ens in potentia*), then there is, of course, a real distinction; but this distinction is simply that between being and not-being, since a possible is not a being and its potentiality for existence is simply logical potentiality, that is, the idea of it does not involve a contradiction. But if 'essence' and 'existence' are understood to mean, as they should be understood to mean in the present controversy, actual essence and actual existence, the distinction between them is a mental distinction with an objective foundation (*distinctio rationis cum fundamento in re*). We can think of the natures or essences of things in abstraction from their existence, and the objective foundation for our being able to do so is the fact that no creature exists necessarily. But the fact that no creature exists necessarily does not mean that when it exists its existence and essence are really distinct. Take away the existence, so to speak, and you cancel the thing altogether. On the other hand, a denial of the real distinction between essence and existence does not, Suárez argues, lead to the conclusion that the creature exists necessarily.

Existence and essence together form an *ens per se unum*; but this composition is a 'composition' in an analogical sense. For it is only really distinct elements that can together form a real composition. The union of essence and existence to form an *ens per se unum* is called a 'composition' only in a sense analogous to the sense in which the union of matter and form, two really distinct elements, is called a composition.[4] Moreover, the union of essence and existence differs from that of matter and form in this point also, that the former is found in all creatures, whereas the latter is confined to bodies. Composition out of matter and form is a physical composition and forms the basis of physical change, whereas composition out of essence and existence is a metaphysical

---

[1] 31, 1, 13.   [2] 31, 6, 9.   [3] 31, 6, 13-24.   [4] 31, 13, 7.

composition. It belongs to the being of a creature, whether spiritual or material. The statement that it is a *compositio rationis* does not contradict the statement that it belongs to the being of a creature, for the reason why it belongs to the being of a creature is not the mental character of the distinction between essence and existence but rather the objective foundation of this mental distinction, namely the fact that the creature does not exist necessarily or of itself (*a se*).

Suárez considers the objection that it follows or seems to follow from his view that the existence of the creature is not received in a potential and limiting element and that consequently it is perfect and infinite existence. If, it is said, existence is not an act which is received in a potential element, it is unreceived, and consequently it is subsistent existence. But, says Suárez,[1] the existence of a creature is limited by itself, by its entity, and it does not need anything distinct from itself to limit it. Intrinsically it is limited by itself; extrinsically or *effective* it is limited by God. One can distinguish two kinds of limitation or contraction, namely metaphysical and physical. 'Metaphysical limitation (*contractio*) does not require an actual real distinction between the limited and limiting factors, but a distinction of concepts with some objective foundation is sufficient; and so we can admit (if we wish to use the language of many people) that essence is made finite and is limited with a view to existence and, conversely, that existence is rendered finite and limited by being the act of a particular essence.'[2] As to physical limitations, an angel does not need any intrinsic principle of limitation other than its simple substance, while a composite substance is limited by its intrinsic component factors or principles. This is equivalent to saying that a composite substance also is limited by itself, since it is not something distinct from those intrinsic component factors taken together in their actuality.

Suárez' view is, then, this. 'Because existence is nothing else than essence constituted in act, it follows that, just as actual essence is formally limited by itself, or by its own intrinsic principles, so also created existence has its limitation from the essence, not because essence is a potentiality in which existence is received, but because existence is in reality nothing else but the actual essence itself.'[3] A great deal has been written in Scholastic circles about the dispute between Suárez and his Thomist

[1] 31, 13, 18.   [2] *Ibid.*   [3] *Ibid.*

opponents on the subject of the distinction between essence and existence; but, whichever side is right, it should at least be clear that Suárez had no intention whatsoever of impairing, so to speak, the contingent character of the creature. The creature is created and contingent, but what is created is an actual essence, that is to say, an existent essence, and the distinction between the essence and its existence is only mental, though this mental distinction is grounded on and made possible by the creature's contingent character. Both Thomists and Suarezians agree, of course, about the creature's contingent character. Where they differ is in the analysis of what it means to be contingent. When the Thomists say that there is a real distinction between essence and existence in the creature, they do not mean that the two factors are separable in the sense that either or both of them could preserve actuality in isolation; and when the Suarezians say that the distinction is a *distinctio rationis cum fundamento in re*, they do not mean that the creature exists necessarily, in the sense that it cannot not exist. However, I do not propose to take sides in the controversy; nor shall I introduce reflections which, in the context of contemporary philosophy in Great Britain, might suggest themselves.

11. Passing to the subject of substance and accident, Suárez remarks[1] that the opinion that the division between substance and accident is a sufficient proximate division of created being is 'so common, that it has been received by all as if it were self-evident. Therefore it needs an explanation rather than a proof. That among creatures some things are substances and others accidents is clear from the constant change and alteration of things.' But being is not predicated univocally of substance and accidents: it is predicated analogically. Now, many people, like Cajetan, think that the analogy in question is the analogy of proportionality alone; 'but I think that the same must be said in this connection as has been said concerning being as common to God and to creatures, namely that there is here no analogy of proportionality, properly speaking, but only analogy of attribution'.[2]

In creatures primary substance (that is, existent substance, as distinguished from the universal or *substantia secunda*) is the same thing as a *suppositum*;[3] and a *suppositum* of rational nature is a person.[4] But Suárez discusses the question whether 'subsistence' (*subsistentia*), which makes a nature or essence a created *suppositum*,

[1] 32, 1, 4.   [2] 32, 2, 12.   [3] 34, 1, 9.   [4] 34, 1, 13.

is something positive, distinct from the nature. According to one opinion existence and subsistence are the same; and that which being a *suppositum* adds to a nature is consequently existence. 'This opinion is now frequently met with among modern theologians.'[1] But Suárez cannot agree with this theory, as he does not believe that existence is really distinct from the actual nature or essence. 'Actual essence and its existence are not really distinct. Therefore, in so far as subsistence is distinct from actual essence, it must be distinct from the existence of that essence.'[2] Therefore being a *suppositum* or having subsistence, which makes a thing independent of any 'support' (that is, which makes a thing a substance) cannot, in so far as it is something added to an actual essence or nature, be the same thing as existence. What, if anything, does subsistence add to an actual essence or nature? Existence as such simply means having actual being: that a being exists does not, of itself, determine whether it exists as a substance or as an accident. 'But subsistence denotes a determinate mode of existing',[3] namely existing as a substance, not inhering in a substance as an accident inheres in a substance. Therefore subsistence does add something. But what it adds is a mode of existing, a way of existing, not existence itself; it determines the mode of existence and gives to the substance its completion *in ratione existendi*, on the level of existence. Having subsistence or being a *suppositum* adds, therefore, to an actual essence or nature a mode (*modus*), and *subsistentia* differs modally (*modaliter*) from the nature of which it is the subsistence as a thing's mode differs from the thing itself.[4] The composition between them is, then, the composition of a mode with the thing modified.[5] Created subsistence is thus 'a substantial mode, finally terminating the substantial nature and constituting a thing as *per se* subsistent and incommunicable'.[6]

12. Here we meet Suárez' idea of 'modes', of which he makes extensive use. For example, he says that probably 'the rational soul, even while joined to the body, has a positive mode of subsistence, and, when it is separated (from the body), it does not acquire a new positive mode of existence, but it is simply deprived of the positive mode of union with the body'.[7] In man, then, not only is there a 'mode' whereby soul and body are conjoined but the soul, even while in the body, also has its own mode of partial

---

[1] 34, 4, 8.   [2] 34, 4, 16.   [3] 34, 4, 24.   [4] 34, 4, 33.
[5] 34, 4, 39.   [6] 34, 5, 1.   [7] 34, 5, 33.

subsistence; and what happens at death is that the mode of union disappears, though the soul retains its own mode of subsistence. In purely material substances both form and matter have their own modes, in addition to the mode of union; but it is the 'partial mode' (*modus partialis*) of the matter alone which is conserved after separation of form and matter. The form of a purely material substance does not, like the human soul, which is the form of the body, preserve any mode of subsistence after the corruption of the substance.[1] A material form has not got its own mode of existence or partial subsistence,[2] but matter has. It follows that God could conserve matter without any form.[3]

13. In his detailed treatment of the different kinds of accidents Suárez gives a good deal of attention to the subject of quantity. First of all, the opinion that quantity is really distinct from material substance must be accepted. 'For although it may not be possible to demonstrate its truth sufficiently by natural reason, it is nevertheless shown to be true by the principles of theology, especially on account of the mystery of the Eucharist. Indeed, the natural reason, enlightened by this mystery, understands that this truth is more in agreement and conformity with the natures themselves of things (than the opposite opinion). Therefore the first reason for this opinion is that in the mystery of the Eucharist God separated quantity from the substances of bread and wine...'[4] This distinction must be a real distinction, for, if the distinction were only modal, quantity could not exist in separation from that of which it is a mode.

Considerations taken from the theology of the Eucharist appear also in Suárez' treatment of the formal effect of quanity (*effectus formalis quantitatis*), which he finds in the quantitative extension of parts as apt to occupy place. 'In the body of Christ in the Eucharist besides the substantial distinction of parts of matter there is also a quantitative extension of parts. For, although the parts of that body are not actually extended in place, they are none the less so extended and ordered in relation to one another that, if they were not supernaturally prevented, they would have to possess actual extension in place. This (first) extension they receive from quantity, and it is impossible for them to be without it if they are not without quantity.'[5]

14. As to relations, Suárez maintains that there are in creatures real relations which constitute a special category.[6] But a real

[1] 34, 5, 35. [2] 34, 5, 42. [3] 34, 5, 36. [4] 40, 2, 8. [5] 40, 4, 14. [6] 47, 1.

relation, although it signifies a real form, is not something actually distinct from every absolute form: it is in reality identified with an absolute form which is related to something else.[1] To take an example. In the case of two white things the one thing has to the other a real relation of similarity. But that real relation is not something really distinct from the thing's whiteness: it is the whiteness itself (considered as an 'absolute form') as similar to the whiteness of another thing. This denial of a real distinction between the relation and its subject[2] does not, says Suárez, contradict the assertion that real relations belong to a category of their own, for 'the distinction between categories is sometimes only a *distinctio rationis cum aliquo fundamento in re*, as we shall say later in regard to action, passion and other categories'.[3]

It is only real relations which can belong to the category of relation; for mental relations (*relationes rationis*) are not real beings and cannot, therefore, belong to the category *ad aliquid*.[4] But it does not follow that all real relations belong to the category of relation. If there are two white things, the one is really like the other; but if one of them is destroyed or ceases to be white, the real relation of similarity also ceases. There are, however, says Suárez, some real relations which are inseparable from the essences of their subjects. For example, it belongs to the essence of an existent creature that it depends on the Creator: 'it does not seem that it can be conceived or exist without a transcendental relation to that on which it depends. It is in this relation that the potentiality and imperfection of a created being as such seem especially to consist.'[5] Again, 'matter and form have a true and real mutual relationship essentially included in their own being; and so the one is defined by its relation to the other'.[6] These relations, called by Suárez *relationes transcendentales*, are not mental relations; they are real; but they cannot disappear while the subject remains, as predicamental relations (that is, relations belonging to the category of relation) can disappear. A predicamental relation is an accident acquired by a thing which is already constituted in its essential being; but a transcendental relation is, as it were (*quasi*), a *differentia* constituting and completing the essence of that thing of which it is affirmed to be a relation.[7] The

---

[1] 47, 2, 22.
[2] The opinion that there is always a real distinction between a real relation and its foundation is 'the opinion of the old Thomists', like Capreolus and Cajetan (47, 2, 2).
[3] 47, 2, 22.   [4] 47, 3, 3.   [5] 47, 3, 12.   [6] 47, 3, 11.   [7] 47, 4, 2.

definition of a predicamental relation is 'an accident, the whole being of which is *ad aliud esse, seu ad aliud se habere, seu aliud respicere*'.[1] This definition might seem to cover also transcendental relations; but 'I think that transcendental relations are excluded by the phrase, *cuius totum esse est esse ad aliud*, if it is understood in the strict sense explained at the end of the preceding section. For those beings which include a transcendental relation are not so related to another thing that their whole being consists simply in a relation to that other thing.'[2] Suárez goes on to argue that a predicamental relation requires a subject, a foundation (for example, the whiteness of a white thing) and a term of the relation.[3] But a transcendental relation does not require these three conditions. For example, 'the transcendental relation of matter to form has no foundation, but it is intimately included in matter itself'.[4]

The two examples of transcendental relation given above, namely the relation of creature to Creator and of matter and form to one another, should not lead one to suppose that, for Suárez, there is a 'mutual' relation between the creature and the Creator. There is a real relation to the Creator on the part of the creature, but the Creator's relation to the creature is a *relatio rationis*.[5] The nominalists hold that[6] God acquires real relations in time, not in the sense that God acquires new perfections but in the sense, for example, that God is really Creator and, as creation took place in time, God becomes related to creatures in time. But Suárez rejects the opinion.[7] If the relation were real, God would acquire an accident in time which is an absurd idea; and it is useless to say that the relation would *assistere Deo*, and not *inesse Deo* (a distinction attributed to Gilbert de la Porrée), for the relation must be in a subject and, if it is not in the creature, it must be in God.

15. Suárez' final disputation (54) is devoted to the subject of *entia rationis*. He tells us that, although he has said in the first disputation that *entia rationis* are not included in the special subject-matter of metaphysics, he thinks that the general principles concerning this topic should be considered. The topic cannot be properly treated except by the metaphysician, even if it belongs to his subject-matter *quasi ex obliquo et concomitanter*.[8]

After distinguishing various possible meanings of the phrase *ens rationis*, Suárez says that, properly speaking, it signifies 'that

[1] 47, 5, 2.   [2] 47, 6, 5.   [3] 47, 6-9.   [4] 47, 4, 2.
[5] 47, 15, 6.   [6] 47, 15, 16.   [7] 47, 15, 17-28.   [8] 54, *introd.*

which has being objectively only in the mind' or 'that which is thought of as being by the mind, although it has no being in itself'.[1] Blindness, for example, has no positive being of its own, though it is 'thought of' as if it were a being. When we say that a man is blind, we do not mean that there is anything positive in the man to which the word 'blindness' is given; we mean that he is deprived of vision. But we think of this deprivation as if it were a being, says Suárez. A purely mental relation is another example of an *ens rationis*. So is a chimera or purely imaginative construction, which cannot have being apart from the mind. Its being consists in being thought or imagined.

Three reasons can be assigned why we form these *entia rationis*. First of all, the human intellect tries to know negations and privations. These are nothing in themselves; but the mind, which has being as its object, cannot conceive that which is in itself nothing except *ad modum entis*, that is, as if it were being. Secondly, our intellect, being imperfect, has sometimes, in its endeavour to know something which it cannot know as it exists in itself, to introduce relations which are not real relations by comparing it to something else. The third reason is the mind's power to construct composite ideas which cannot have an objective counterpart outside the mind, though the ideas of the parts correspond to something extramental. For example, we can construct the idea of a horse's body with a man's head.

There can be no concept of being common to real beings and to *entia rationis*, for existence (*esse*) cannot be intrinsically participated in by the latter. To 'exist' only in the mind is not to exist (*esse*), but to be thought or mentally constructed. Therefore *entia rationis* cannot be said to possess essence. This distinguishes them from accidents. Nevertheless, an *ens rationis* is called *ens* in virtue of 'some analogy' to being, since it is founded in some way on being.[2]

Entia rationis are caused by the intellect conceiving that which has no real act of being as if it were a being.[3] The senses, appetite and will are not causes of *entia rationis*, though the imagination can be; and in this respect 'the human imagination shares in some way the power of the reason', and perhaps it never forms them save with the co-operation of reason.[4]

The three types of *entia rationis* are negations, privations and (purely mental) relations. A negation differs primarily from a

[1] 54, 1, 6.   [2] 54, 1, 9.   [3] 54, 2, 15.   [4] 54, 2, 18.

privation in that, while a privation signifies the lack of a form in a subject naturally apt to possess that form, a negation signifies the lack of a form without there being any natural aptitude to possess that form.[1] For example, blindness is a privation; but a man's lack of wings is a negation. According to Suárez[2] imaginary space and imaginary time, conceived without any 'subject', are negations. The logical relations of, for example, genus and species, subject and predicate, antecedent and consequent, which are 'second intentions', are purely mental and so *entia rationis*, though they are not gratuitously formed but have some objective foundation.[3]

16. In the multitudinous pages of the *Disputationes metaphysicae* Suárez pursues the problems considered into their various ramifications, and he is careful to distinguish the different meanings of the terms employed. He shows himself to be an analytic thinker, in the sense that he is not content with broad generalizations, hasty impressions or universal conclusions based on an insufficient study of the different aspects of the problem at issue. He is thorough, painstaking, exhaustive. One cannot, of course, expect to find in his work an analysis which will satisfy all the demands made by modern analysts: the terms and ideas in which he thought were for the most part traditional in the Schools and were taken for granted. One might, indeed, take various points out of Suárez' writings and express them in the more fashionable terms of today. For example, his observations that to 'exist' only in the mind is not really to exist at all but to be thought or mentally constructed could be translated into a distinction between different types of sentences analysed in reference to their logical meaning as distinct from their grammatical form. One has, however, to take a past thinker in his historical setting, and if Suárez is seen in the light of the philosophical tradition to which he belonged, there can be no doubt that he possessed the gift of analysis in an eminent degree.

That Suárez possessed an analytic mind would hardly, I think, be denied. But it has been maintained that he lacked the power of synthesis. He became immersed in a succession of problems, it is sometimes said, and he gave such a careful consideration to the manifold ways in which these problems had been treated and solved in history that he was unable to see the wood for the trees. Moreover, his great erudition inclined him to eclecticism. He

---

[1] 54, 5, 7.   [2] 54, 5, 23.   [3] 54, 6, 8–9.

borrowed a view here and an opinion there, and the result was a patchwork rather than a system. His critics would not, I think, suggest that he was a superficial eclectic, since it needs no very close acquaintance with his writings to see that he was very far from being superficial; but they do suggest that he was an eclectic in a sense which is incompatible with possessing the gift of synthesis.

The accusation that a given philosopher was not a system-builder is not an accusation which is likely to carry much weight in contemporary philosophical circles. Provided that the accusation does not rest on the fact that the philosopher in question expounded a number of mutually incompatible theses, many modern philosophers would comment, 'so much the better'. However, leaving this aspect of the matter out of account one can ask whether the accusation is in fact true. And in the first place one can ask in what sense Suárez was an eclectic.

That Suárez was an eclectic in some sense seems to me undeniable. He had an extremely extensive knowledge of former philosophies, even if, as is only to be expected, he was sometimes mistaken in his assertions or interpretations. And he could hardly possess this knowledge without being influenced by the opinions of the philosophers he studied. But this does not mean that he accepted other people's opinions in an uncritical manner. If, for example, he accepted the opinion of Scotus and Ockham that there is a confused intellectual intuition of the individual thing, which logically precedes abstraction, he did so because he thought that it was true. And if he questioned the universal applicability of the principle *quidquid movetur ab alio movetur* he did not do so because he was a Scotist or an Ockhamist (he was neither) but because he considered that the principle, considered as a universal principle, is in fact questionable. Moreover, if Suárez was an eclectic, so was Aquinas. The latter did not simply accept Aristotelianism in its entirety; if he had done so, he would have occupied a far less important position in the development of mediaeval philosophy and would have shown himself to be devoid of any spirit of philosophical criticism. Aquinas borrowed from Augustine and other thinkers, as well as from Aristotle. And there is no cogent reason why Suárez should not have followed his example by utilizing what he considered valuable in philosophers who lived at a later date than Aquinas. Of course, if the accusation of eclecticism means simply that Suárez departed from the teaching of St. Thomas on a number of points, he was certainly an eclectic. But the relevant philosophical question would be not so much whether Suárez departed from Aquinas's teaching as whether he was objectively justified in doing so.

That Aquinas was also in some sense an eclectic would presumably be admitted by all. What philosopher is not in some sense an eclectic? But some would still maintain that there is this big difference between the philosophy of St. Thomas and that of Suárez. The former rethought all the positions which he adopted from others and developed them, welding these developments, together with his own original contributions, into a powerful synthesis with the aid of certain fundamental metaphysical principles. Suárez on the other hand juxtaposed various positions and did not create a synthesis.

The truth of this accusation is, however, extremely doubtful. In his preface (*Ad lectorem*) to the *Disputationes metaphysicae* Suárez says that he intends to play the part of philosopher in such a way as to have always before his eyes the truth that 'our philosophy ought to be Christian and the servant of divine theology' (*divinae Theologiae ministram*). And if one regards his philosophical ideas in this light, one can see a synthesis clearly emerging from the mass of his pages. For Aristotle, in the *Metaphysics* at least, God was simply the first unmoved mover: His existence was asserted in order to explain motion. The Christian philosophers, like St. Augustine, introduced the idea of creation, and St. Thomas attempted to weld together Aristotelianism and creationism. Beneath, as it were, the Aristotelian distinction of matter and form St. Thomas discerned the more fundamental distinction of essence and existence, which runs through all finite being. Act is limited by potentiality, and existence, which stands to essence as act to potentiality, is limited by essence. This explains the finitude of creatures. Suárez, however, was convinced that the utter dependence which logically precedes any distinction of essence and existence is itself the ultimate reason of finitude. There is absolute being, God, and there is participated being. Participation in this sense means total dependence on the Creator. This total dependence or contingency is the reason why the creature is limited or finite.[1] Suárez did not explain finitude and contingency in terms of the distinction between existence and essence: he explained this distinction, in the sense, that is, in which he

---

[1] 31, 13, 18.

accepted it, in terms of a finitude which is necessarily bound up with contingency.

It is sometimes said that Suarezianism is an 'essential' philosophy or a philosophy of essence rather than a philosophy of existence, like Thomism. But it would seem difficult to find a more 'existential' situation than the situation of utter dependence which Suárez finds to be the ultimate characteristic of every being other than God. Moreover, by refusing to admit a 'real' distinction between essence and existence in the creature Suárez avoided the danger of turning existence into a kind of essence. Cancel the creature's existence, and its essence is cancelled too. The Thomist would say the same, of course; but this fact suggests perhaps that there is not so great a difference between the Thomist 'real' distinction and the Suarezian conceptual distinction with an objective foundation as might be supposed. The difference lies perhaps rather in the fact that the Thomist appeals to the metaphysical principle of the limitation of act by potentiality, which suggests a view of existence that seems strange to many minds, whereas Suárez founds his distinction simply on creation. The view is at any rate arguable that he carried the 'purification' of Greek philosophy a stage further by bringing the concept of creation and of utter dependence which creation spells more into the centre of the picture. Again, whereas St. Thomas laid stress on the Aristotelian argument from motion in proving God's existence, Suárez, like Scotus, preferred a more metaphysical and less 'physical' line of thought, precisely because the existence of creatures is more fundamental than their movement and because God's creation of finite being is more fundamental than His concurrence in their activity.

There are, moreover, many other ideas in the philosophy of Suárez which follow in some way from, or are connected with, his fundamental idea of dependence or 'participation'. Dependent being is necessarily finite, and as finite it is capable of acquiring further perfection. If it is a spiritual being it can do this freely. But as dependent it needs the divine concurrence even in the exercise of its freedom. And as utterly dependent on God it is subject to the divine moral law and is necessarily ordered to God. Again, as finite perfectible being the free creature is capable not only of acquiring perfection by its own activity, with the divine concurrence, but of receiving a perfection which lifts it above its natural life; as dependent spiritual being it is, as it were, malleable by God and possesses a *potentia obedientialis* for the reception of grace. Further, finite being is multipliable in diverse species and in a plurality of individuals in one species. And in order to explain the multipliability of individuals in a species it is not necessary to introduce the idea of matter as principle of individuation, with all the remnants of 'unpurified' Platonism attaching to that Aristotelian idea.

It has not been my intention in this last section of the present chapter to give my own views on the matters raised, and I do not wish to be understood in this sense. My intention has been rather that of showing that there is a Suarezian synthesis, that the key to it is the idea of 'participation' or dependence in being, and that it was this idea above all which must, Suárez was convinced, be the distinguishing mark of a Christian philosophy. To say this is not, of course, to suggest in any way that the idea is absent from Thomism. Suárez regarded himself as a follower of St. Thomas; and Suarezians do not set Suárez against St. Thomas. What they believe is that Suárez carried on and developed the work of St. Thomas in building up a metaphysical system in profound harmony with the Christian religion.

That the *Disputationes metaphysicae* exercised a wide influence in post-Renaissance Scholasticism scarcely needs saying. But they penetrated also into the Protestant universities of Germany, where they were studied by those who preferred Melanchthon's attitude towards philosophy to that of Luther. Indeed, the *Disputationes metaphysicae* served as a text-book of philosophy in a large number of German universities in the seventeenth century and part of the eighteenth. As for the leading post-Renaissance philosophers, Descartes mentions the work in his reply to the fourth set of objections, though apparently he did not know it at all well. But Leibniz tells us himself that he read the work as if it were a novel while he was still a youth. And Vico studied Suárez for a whole year. Again Suárez' idea of analogy is mentioned by Berkeley in his *Alciphron*.[1] At the present time the *Disputationes metaphysicae* are a living force primarily in Spain, where Suárez is considered one of the greatest, if not the greatest, of the national philosophers. To the modern world at large he is known rather for his *De legibus*, to which I shall turn in the next chapter.

17. Reference has been made in the preceding section to the contention that the metaphysics of Suárez is an essentialist, as

[1] 4, 20.

contrasted with an existentialist, metaphysics. In *Being and Some Philosophers* Professor Étienne Gilson argues that Suárez, following Avicenna and Scotus but proceeding further in the same direction, lost sight of Aquinas's vision of being as the concrete act of existing and tended to reduce being to essence. And Suárez begot Christian Wolff who refers with approval to the Spanish Jesuit in his *Ontologia*. Finally Suárez' influence has corrupted large tracts of neo-Scholasticism. Modern existentialism has protested in the name of existence against the essentialist philosophy. Kierkegaard reacted strongly against the system of Hegel, who is to be numbered, so one gathers, among the spiritual descendants of Suárez. But modern existentialism has no true realization of existence. The consoling conclusion emerges, therefore, that St. Thomas Aquinas is the one true metaphysician.

That the position and character of the analysis of the concept of being which is found in many neo-Scholastic text-books of metaphysics are very largely due to the influence of Suárez can hardly be denied. Nor can it well be denied, I think, that Suárez influenced Wolff and that a number of neo-Scholastic writers were influenced, indirectly at least, by Wolff. But the issues raised by Professor Gilson in his discussion of 'essentialist' metaphysics as contrasted with 'existentialist' metaphysics are so wide and far-reaching that they cannot, in my opinion, be properly treated in the form of a note to Suárez' philosophy. At the close of my *History of Philosophy* I hope to return to the subject in the course of considering the development of western philosophy as a whole. Meanwhile, it must suffice to have drawn the reader's attention to Gilson's estimate of Suárez' philosophy, which can be found in *L'être et l'essence* and *Being and Some Philosophers*, both of which books are listed in the Bibliography.

CHAPTER XXIII

FRANCIS SUÁREZ (2)

Philosophy of law and theology—The definition of law—Law (lex) and right (ius)—The necessity of law—The eternal law—The natural law—The precepts of the natural law—Ignorance of natural law—The immutability of the natural law—The law of nations—Political society, sovereignty and government—The contract theory in Suárez—The deposition of tyrants—Penal laws—Cessation of human laws—Custom—Church and State —War.

1. SUÁREZ' philosophy of law was based on that of St. Thomas Aquinas; but it must, none the less, be judged an original creative development, if one bears in mind its amplitude, thoroughness and profundity. In the philosophy of law Suárez was the mediator between the mediaeval conception of law, as represented by Thomism, and the conditions prevailing at the time he wrote. In the light of those conditions he elaborated a legal philosophy and in connection therewith a political theory which in scope and completeness went beyond anything attained in the Middle Ages and which exercised a profound influence. There can be no doubt that Grotius was seriously indebted to Suárez, even if he did not acknowledge this indebtedness clearly. That he did not do so can be easily understood, if one bears in mind, on the one hand, Suárez' doctrine of political authority and of the right to resist, and on the other hand Grotius' dependence on the King of France at the time that he wrote his *De iure belli ac pacis*.

In his preface to the *De legibus ac Deo legislatore* (1612) Suárez observes that no one need be surprised to find a professional theologian embarking on a discussion of law. The theologian contemplates God, not only as He is in Himself, but also as man's last end. This means that he is concerned with the way of salvation. Now, salvation is attained by free acts and moral rectitude; and moral rectitude depends to a great extent on law considered as the rule of human acts. Theology, then, must comprise a study of law; and, being theology, it is necessarily concerned with God as lawgiver. It may be objected that the theologian, while legitimately giving his attention to divine law, should abstain from concerning himself with human law. But all law derives its authority ultimately from God; and the theologian is justified in treating all types of law, though he does so from a higher point of view than that of the moral philosopher. For example, the theologian considers natural law in its relation of subordination to the supernatural order, and he considers civil law or human positive law with a view to determining its rectitude in the light of higher principles or with a view to making clear the obligations bearing on the conscience in regard to civil law. And Suárez appeals, in the first place, to the example of St. Thomas.

2. Suárez begins by giving a definition of law (*lex*) taken from St. Thomas. 'Law is a certain rule and measure, according to which one is induced to act or is restrained from acting.'[1] He goes on, however, to observe that the definition is too broad. For example, as no mention of obligation is made, no distinction is drawn between law and counsel. It is only after a discussion of the various conditions requisite for law that Suárez finally gives his definition of it as 'a common, just and stable precept, which has been sufficiently promulgated'.[2] Law, as it exists in the legislator, is the act of a just and upright will binding an inferior to the performance of a particular act;[3] and it must be framed for a community. Natural law relates to the community of mankind;[4] but human laws may properly be enacted only for a 'perfect' community.[5] It is also inherent in the nature of law that it be enacted for the common good, though this must be understood in relation to the actual subject-matter of the law, not in relation to the subjective intentions of the legislator, which is a personal factor.[6] Furthermore, it is essential to law that it should prescribe what is just, that is, that it should prescribe acts which can be justly performed by those whom the law affects. It follows from this that a law which is unjust or unrighteous is not, properly speaking, a law at all, and it possesses no binding force.[7] Indeed, an unrighteous law cannot be licitly obeyed, though in cases of doubt as to the righteousness of the law the presumption is in favour of the law. Suárez observes that in order for a law to be just three conditions must be observed.[8] First, it must be enacted, as already mentioned, for the common good, not for private advantage. Secondly, it must be enacted for those in regard to whom the legislator has authority to legislate, that is, for those who are his subjects. Thirdly, law must not proportion

---
[1] *De legibus*, 1, 1, 1; cf. St. Thomas, *S.T.*, Ia, IIae, 90, 1.
[2] *De legibus*, 1, 12, 5.   [3] *Ibid.*, 1, 5, 24.   [4] *Ibid.*, 1, 6, 18.   [5] *Ibid.*, 1, 6, 21.
[6] *Ibid.*, 1, 7, 9.   [7] *Ibid.*, 1, 9, 11.   [8] *Ibid.*, 1, 9, 13.

burdens unequally, in an inequitable manner. The three phases of justice which must characterize the law in regard to its form are, then, legal justice, commutative justice and distributive justice.[1] Law must also, of course, be practicable, in the sense that the acts it enjoins must be practicable.

3. What is the relation between law (*lex*) and right (*ius*)? Strictly speaking, *ius* denotes 'a certain moral power which every man has, either over his own property or with respect to what is due to him'.[2] Thus the owner of a thing has a *ius in re* in regard to that thing actually possessed, while a labourer, for example, has a right to his wages, *ius ad stipendium*. In this sense of the word *ius* is distinct from *lex*. But the term *ius* is often used, says Suárez, in the sense of 'law'.

4. Are laws necessary? Law is not necessary, if by 'necessity' is understood absolute necessity. God alone is a necessary being in an absolute sense, and God cannot be subject to law.[3] But, given the creation of rational creatures, law must be said to be necessary in order that the rational creature may live in a manner befitting his nature. A rational creature is capable of choosing well or ill, rightly or wrongly; and it is susceptible of moral government. In fact, moral government, which is effected through command, is connatural to the rational creature. Given, therefore, rational creatures, law is necessary. It is irrelevant, says Suárez,[4] to argue that a creature may receive the grace of impeccability; for the grace in question does not involve the creature's removal from the state of subjection to law but brings it about that the creature obeys the law without fail.

5. Suárez' treatment of the eternal law is contained in the second book of the *De legibus*.[5] This law is not to be understood as a rule of right conduct imposed by God upon Himself:[6] it is a law of action in regard to the things governed. In regard to all things, irrational as well as rational? The answer depends on the degree of strictness in which the word 'law' is understood. It is true that all irrational creatures are subject to God and are governed by Him; but their subjection to God can be called 'obedience' only in a metaphorical sense, and the law by which God governs them is called a 'law' or 'precept' only metaphorically. In the strict sense, then, 'eternal law' has reference only to rational creatures.[7] It is the moral or human acts of rational creatures which form the

---

[1] *De legibus*, 1, 9, 13. [2] *Ibid.*, 1, 2, 5. [3] *Ibid.*, 1, 3, 2. [4] *Ibid.*, 1, 3, 3.
[5] Chapters 1–4. [6] *De legibus*, 2, 2, 5. [7] *Ibid.*, 2, 2, 13.

proper subject-matter of the eternal law, 'whether the latter commands their performance, prescribes a particular mode of acting, or prohibits some other mode'.[1]

The eternal law is 'a free decree of the will of God, who lays down the order to be observed; either generally, by the separate parts of the universe with respect to the common good . . . or else specifically, by intellectual creatures in their free actions'.[2] It follows that the eternal law, as a freely established law, is not absolutely necessary. This would be inconsistent with the eternity of the law only if nothing which is free could be eternal. The eternal law is eternal and immutable; but it is none the less free.[3] One can, however, distinguish law as it exists in the mind and will of the legislator from law as externally established and promulgated for the subjects. In the first phase the eternal law is truly eternal; but in the second phase it did not exist from eternity, because the subjects did not exist from eternity.[4] This being the case, one must conclude that actual promulgation to subjects is not the essence of eternal law. It is sufficient, for the eternal law to be called 'law', that it should have been made by the legislator to become effective at the proper time. In this respect the eternal law differs from other laws, which are not complete laws until they have been promulgated.[5]

Inasmuch as all created right reason partakes in 'the divine light which has been shed upon us', and inasmuch as all human power comes ultimately from God, all other law is a participation in the eternal law and an effect thereof.[6] It does not follow, however, that the binding force of human law is divine. Human law receives its force and efficacy directly from the will of a human legislator. It is true that the eternal law does not actually bind unless it is actually promulgated; and it is true that it is actually promulgated only through the medium of some other law, divine or human; but, in the case of human law, the obligation to observe it is caused proximately by this human law as enacted and promulgated by legitimate human authority, though fundamentally and mediately it proceeds from the eternal law.[7]

6. Turning to the subject of natural law, Suárez criticizes the opinion of his fellow-Jesuit, Father Vásquez, that rational nature and the natural law are the same. Suárez observes that, although rational nature is indeed the foundation of the objective goodness

---

[1] *De legibus*, 2, 2, 15.   [2] *Ibid.*, 2, 3, 6.   [3] *Ibid.*, 2, 3, 4.   [4] *Ibid.*, 2, 1, 5.
[5] *Ibid.*, 2, 1, 11.   [6] *Ibid.*, 2, 4, 5.   [7] *Ibid.*, 2, 4, 8–10.

of the moral acts of human beings, it does not follow that it should be called 'law'. Rational nature may be called a 'standard'; but the term 'standard' is a term of wider extension than the term 'law'.[1] There is, however, a second opinion, according to which rational nature, considered as the basis of the conformity or non-conformity of human acts with itself, is the basis of natural rectitude, while natural reason, or the power of rational nature to discriminate between acts in harmony with itself and acts not in harmony with itself, is the law of nature.[2] So far as this opinion means that the dictates of right reason, considered as the immediate and intrinsic rule of human acts, is the natural law, it may be accepted. In the strictest sense, however, the natural law consists in the actual judgment of the mind; but the natural reason or the natural light of reason may also be called natural law, for we think of men as permanently retaining that law in their minds, even though they may not be engaged in any specific act of moral judgment. In other words, the question how natural law should be defined is partly a terminological question.[3]

As to the relation of the natural law to God, there are two extreme positions, which are opposed to one another. According to the first opinion, ascribed to Gregory of Rimini, the natural law is not a preceptive law in the proper sense; for it does not indicate the will of a superior but simply makes clear what should be done, as being intrinsically good, and what should be avoided, as being intrinsically evil. The natural law is thus a demonstrative law rather than a preceptive law; and it does not derive from God as legislator. It is, so to speak, independent of God, that is, of God considered as moral legislator. According to the second opinion, however, which is ascribed to William of Ockham, God's will constitutes the whole basis of good and evil. Actions are good or evil simply and solely in so far as they are ordered or prohibited by God.

Neither of these opinions is acceptable to Suárez. 'I hold that a middle course should be taken, this middle course being, in my judgment, the opinion held by St. Thomas and common to the theologians.'[4] In the first place, the natural law is a preceptive and not merely a demonstrative law; for it does not merely indicate what is good or evil, but it also commands and prohibits. But it does not follow from this that the divine volition is the total cause of the good or evil involved in the observance or transgression of the natural law. On the contrary, the divine volition presupposes

[1] *De legibus*, 2, 5, 6.   [2] *Ibid.*, 2, 5, 9.   [3] *Ibid.*, 2, 5, 14.   [4] *Ibid.*, 2, 6, 5.

the intrinsic moral character of certain acts. It is repugnant to reason to say, for example, that hatred of God is wrong simply and solely because it is prohibited by God. The divine volition presupposes a dictate of the divine reason concerning the intrinsic character of human acts. God is, indeed, the author of the natural law; for He is Creator and He wills to bind men to observe the dictates of right reason. But God is not the arbitrary author of the natural law; for He commands some acts because they are intrinsically good and prohibits other acts because they are intrinsically evil. Suárez does not, of course, mean to imply that God is, as it were, governed by a law which is external to His nature. What he means is that God (to speak anthropomorphically) could not help seeing that certain acts are in harmony with rational nature and that certain acts are morally incompatible with rational nature, and that God, seeing this, could not fail to command the performance of the former and prohibit the performance of the latter. It is true that the natural law, taken simply in itself, reveals what is intrinsically good and evil, without any explicit reference to God; but the natural light of reason none the less makes known to man the fact that actions contrary to the natural law are necessarily displeasing to the author and governor of nature. As to the promulgation of the natural law, 'the natural light is of itself a sufficient promulgation'.[1]

7. In the discussion of this matter in the *De legibus*, there is, I think, a certain prolixity and even a certain lack of clarity and exactitude. It is certainly clear that Suárez rejected the authoritarian ethical theory of William of Ockham and that, fundamentally, his own theory follows that of St. Thomas; but it does not seem to me to be made as clear as one could wish in what precise sense the term 'good' is being used. Suárez does, however, clarify the matter somewhat when he discusses the question what is the subject-matter dealt with by natural law.

He distinguishes various types of precepts which belong to the natural law.[2] First of all, there are general and primary principles of morality, such as 'one must do good and shun evil'. Secondly, there are principles which are more definite and specific, like 'God must be worshipped' and 'one must live temperately'. Both these types of ethical propositions are self-evident, according to Suárez. Thirdly, there are moral precepts which are not immediately self-evident but which are deduced from self-evident propositions and

[1] *De legibus*, 2, 6, 24.   [2] *Ibid.*, 2, 7, 5.

become known through rational reflection. In the case of some of these precepts, like 'adultery is wrong', their truth is easily recognized; but in the case of some other precepts, like 'usury is unjust' and 'lying can never be justified', more reflection is required in order to see their truth. Nevertheless, all these types of ethical propositions pertain to the natural law.

But if the natural law enjoins that good must be done, and if all righteous and licit acts are good acts, does it not seem to follow that the natural law enjoins the performance of all acts which are righteous and licit? Now, the act of contracting marriage is a good act. Is it, then, enjoined by the natural law? On the other hand, living according to the counsels of perfection is good. For example, it is good to embrace perpetual chastity. Is it, then, enjoined by the natural law? Certainly not; a counsel is not a precept. But why not? Suárez, developing a distinction made by St. Thomas, explains that, if virtuous acts are considered individually, not every such act falls under a natural precept. He mentions the counsels and contracting marriage.[1] One can also say[2] that all virtuous acts, in respect of the manner in which they should be performed, fall under the natural law, but that, in regard to their actual performance, they are not all absolutely prescribed by the natural law. It might, however, have been simpler to say that the natural law enjoins, not simply the doing of what is good, but the doing of good and the avoidance of evil, in the sense that what is prescribed absolutely is the doing of something good when its omission or the doing of something else would be evil. But the terms 'good' and 'evil' would still need some further clarificatory analysis. Some of the apparent confusion in Suárez' treatment of natural law seems to be due to his using the phrase 'natural law' both in a narrower sense, to mean the law based on human nature as such, and also in a wide sense, to include 'the law of grace'.[3] To embrace the evangelical counsels is certainly not made a matter of obligation by the essential propensities and requirements of human nature: but the life of the counsels is offered to the individual for a supernatural end, and it could become a matter of obligation only if God absolutely commanded an individual to embrace it or if he or she could achieve his or her last end only by embracing it.

Possibly the following may make Suárez' position a little clearer. An act is good if it is in accordance with right reason; and an act is evil if it is not in accordance with right reason. If doing a

---

[1] *De legibus*, 2, 7, 11.   [2] *Ibid.*   [3] Cf. *Ibid.*, 2, 8, 1.

certain act averts a man from his last end, that act is evil and is not in accordance with right reason, which enjoins that the means necessary to the attainment of the last end shall be taken. Now, every concrete human act, that is, every concrete deliberate free act, is in the moral order and is either good or bad: it is either in accordance or not in accordance with right reason.[1] The natural law enjoins, therefore, that every concrete human act should be good and not evil. But to say this is not the same thing as to say that every possible good act should be done. This would scarcely be possible; and in any case omitting to do one good act does not necessarily involve doing a bad act. To take a rather trivial example. If taking some exercise is indispensable for my health and the proper fulfilment of my work, it is in accordance with right reason that I should take some exercise. But it does not follow that I ought to go for a walk; for I might also play golf or swim or do gymnastic exercises. Again, it might be a good thing for a man to become a friar; but it does not follow that he is doing evil if he does not become a friar. He might marry, for example; and to marry is to do a good act, even if, abstractly speaking at least, to become a friar is better. What the moral law enjoins is to do good *and* not to do evil: it does not always order which good act is to be done. The natural law prohibits all evil acts, since the avoidance of evil is necessary for morality; but it does not order all good acts, for to do a particular good act is not always necessary. From the obligation of never sinning there follows the positive obligation of acting well; but this positive obligation is conditional ('if a free act is to be done'), not simply absolute. 'It is a general obligation of doing good, when some act has to be done; and this obligation can be fulfilled by acts which are not absolutely enjoined. Therefore, it is not all good acts which, by virtue of the natural law, fall under a precept.'[2]

8. As to possible ignorance of the natural law, Suárez maintains that no one can be ignorant of the primary or most general principles of the natural law.[3] It is possible, however, to be ignorant of particular precepts, even of those which are self-evident or easily deducible from self-evident precepts. But it does not follow that such ignorance can be guiltless, not at least for any considerable length of time. The precepts of the Decalogue are of this character. Their binding force is so easily recognizable that no

---
[1] *Tractatus de bonitate et malitia humanorum actuum*, 9, 3, 10.
[2] *De Religione, pars secunda*, 1, 7, 3.   [3] *De legibus*, 2, 8, 7.

one can remain in ignorance of it for any considerable length of time without guilt. However, invincible ignorance is possible in regard to those precepts knowledge of which requires greater reflection.

9. Are the precepts of the natural law immutable? Before the question can be profitably discussed, it is necessary to make a distinction.[1] It is possible for a law to become intrinsically defective by becoming harmful instead of useful or irrational instead of rational. It is also possible for a law to be changed by a superior. Again, both intrinsic change and extrinsic change can affect either the law itself or some particular case or application. For instance, a superior might abolish the law as such or he might relax it or dispense from it in some particular case. Suárez first considers intrinsic change; and he maintains[2] that, properly speaking, the natural law cannot undergo any change, either in regard to its totality or in regard to particular precepts, so long as human nature endures, gifted with reason and free will. If rational nature were abolished, natural law would also be abolished in regard to its concrete existence, since it exists in man or flows from human nature. As natural law flows from human nature, as it were, it cannot become injurious with the course of time; nor can it become irrational if it is grounded in self-evident principles. Apparent instances of intrinsic change in particular cases are due simply to the fact that the general terms in which a natural precept is customarily stated do not adequately express the natural precepts themselves. For instance, if a man has lent me a knife and demands it back, I ought to restore to him what is his property; but if he has become a homicidal maniac and I know that he wants to use the knife to murder someone, I ought not to restore it. This does not mean, however, that the precept that deposits should be restored on demand has undergone an intrinsic change in this case; it simply means that the precept, so stated, is an inadequate statement of what is contained in or involved by the precept itself. Similarly, the precept of the Decalogue, 'thou shalt not kill', really includes many conditions which are not explicitly mentioned; for example, 'thou shalt not kill on thine own authority and as an aggressor'.[3]

Can the natural law be changed by authority? Suárez maintains that 'no human power, even though it be the papal power, can abrogate any proper precept of the natural law' (that is, any

---

[1] *De legibus*, 2, 13, 1.   [2] *Ibid.*, 2, 13, 2.   [3] *Ibid.*, 2, 13, 8.

precept properly belonging to the natural law), 'nor truly and essentially restrict such a precept, nor grant a dispensation from it'.[1] A difficulty may seem to arise in regard to property. According to Suárez,[2] nature has conferred on men in common dominion over things, and consequently every man has the power to use those things which have been given in common. It might seem, then, that the institution of private property and of laws against theft either constitute an infringement of the natural law or indicate that the natural law is subject, in some cases at least, to human power. Suárez answers that the law of nature did not positively forbid the division of common property and its appropriation by individuals; the institution of common dominion was 'negative', not positive. Positively considered, the natural law ordains that no one should be prevented from making the necessary use of common property as long as it is common, and that, after the division of property, theft is wrong. We have to distinguish[3] between preceptive laws and the law concerning dominion. There is no preceptive law of nature that things should always be held in common; but there are preceptive laws relating to conditions which are to a certain extent subject to human power. Nature did not divide goods among private individuals; but the private appropriation of goods was not forbidden by natural law. Private property may, therefore, be instituted by human agency. But there are preceptive laws of nature relating to common ownership and to private ownership; and these preceptive laws are not subject to human agency. The power of the State to confiscate property when there is just cause (as in certain criminal cases) must be understood as provided for in the preceptive laws of nature.

In other words, Suárez will not admit that the natural law is subject to human power. At the same time he maintained that Nature gave the things of the earth to all men in common. But it does not follow, he tells us, either that the institution of private property is against the natural law or that it constitutes a change in the natural law. Why not? A matter may fall under the natural law either in a negative sense or in a positive sense (through positive prescription of an action). Now, common ownership was a part of natural law only in a negative sense, in the sense, that is to say, that by virtue of the natural law all property was to be held in common unless men introduced a different provision. The introduction of private property was thus not against the natural law

[1] *De legibus*, 2, 14, 8.   [2] *Ibid.*, 2, 14, 16.   [3] *Ibid.*, 2, 14, 19.

nor did it constitute a change in any positive precept of the natural law.

However, even if men cannot change or dispense from the natural law, has not God the power to do so? In the first place, if God can dispense from any of the precepts of the Decalogue, it follows that He can abrogate the whole law and order those acts which are forbidden by the natural law. Dispensation from the law prohibiting an act would render that act permissible; but, if God can render an otherwise prohibited act permissible, why could He not prescribe it? 'This was the opinion supported by Occam, whom Pierre d'Ailly and Andreas a Novocastro followed.'[1] The opinion is, however, to be rejected and condemned. The commands and prohibitions of God in respect of the natural law presuppose the intrinsic righteousness of the acts commanded and the intrinsic wickedness of the prohibited acts. The notion that God could command man to hate Him is absurd. Either God would be commanding man to hate an object worthy of love or He would have to render Himself worthy of hatred; but either supposition is absurd.

What, then, of Scotus' opinion, that a distinction must be drawn between the precepts of the First Table of the Decalogue and those of the Second Table and that God can dispense in regard to the latter? Suárez observes that, in a sense, it is inaccurate to say that God, according to Scotus, can dispense in the case of certain precepts of the natural law, since Scotus would not allow that all the precepts of the Decalogue belong, at least in the strictest sense, to the natural law. But Suárez rejects the opinion that the precepts of the Second Table do not strictly belong to the natural law. 'The arguments of Scotus, indeed, are not convincing.'[2]

Suárez maintains, then, that God cannot dispense in regard to any of the Commandments. He appeals to St. Thomas, Cajetan, Soto and others.[3] All the Commandments involve one intrinsic principle of justice and obligation. The apparent cases of dispensation of which we read in the Old Testament were not really cases of dispensation at all. For example, when God told the Hebrews to despoil the Egyptians, He was not acting as legislator and giving them a dispensation to steal. He was either acting as supreme lord and transferring dominion over the goods in question from the Egyptians to the Hebrews; or He was acting as supreme judge and awarded the Hebrews proper wages for their work, wages which had been withheld by the Egyptians.[4]

[1] *De legibus*, 2, 15, 3.   [2] *Ibid.*, 2, 15, 12.   [3] *Ibid.*, 2, 15, 16.   [4] *Ibid.*, 2, 15, 20.

10. Suárez goes on to distinguish the natural law from 'the law of nations' (*ius gentium*). In Suárez' opinion, the *ius gentium* does not prescribe any acts as being of themselves necessary for right conduct, nor does it forbid anything as being of itself and intrinsically evil: such prescriptions and prohibitions pertain to the natural law, and not to the *ius gentium*.[1] The two are not, therefore, the same. The *ius gentium* 'is not only indicative of what is evil but also constitutive of evil'.[2] Suárez means that the natural law prohibits what is intrinsically evil whereas the *ius gentium* considered precisely as such does not prohibit intrinsically evil acts (for these are already forbidden by natural law) but prohibits certain acts for a just and sufficient reason and renders the performance of those acts wrong. From this it follows that the *ius gentium* cannot possess the same degree of immutability as the natural law possesses.

The laws of the *ius gentium* are, therefore, positive (not natural) and human (not divine) laws. In this case, however, does it differ from civil law? It is not sufficient merely to say that civil law is the law of one State, while the *ius gentium* is common to all peoples; for a mere difference between greater and less does not constitute a specific difference.[3] Suárez' opinion is that 'the precepts of the *ius gentium* differ from those of the civil law in that they are not established in written form'; they are established through the customs of all or nearly all nations.[4] The *ius gentium* is thus unwritten law; and it is made up of customs belonging to all, or practically all, nations. It can, indeed, be understood in two ways. A particular matter can pertain to the *ius gentium* either because it is a law which the various peoples and nations ought to observe in their relations with each other or because it is a set of laws which individual States observe within their own borders and which are similar and so commonly accepted. 'The first interpretation seems, in my opinion, to correspond most properly to the actual *ius gentium* as distinct from the civil law.'[5]

Of the *ius gentium* understood in this sense Suárez gives several examples. For example, as far as natural reason is concerned it is not indispensable that the power of avenging an injury by war should belong to the State, for men could have established some other means of avenging injury. But the method of war, which is 'easier and more in conformity with nature', has been adopted by custom and is just.[6] 'In the same class I place slavery.' The

---

[1] *De legibus*, 2, 17, 9.   [2] *Ibid.*, 2, 19, 2.   [3] *Ibid.*, 2, 19, 5.
[4] *Ibid.*, 2, 19, 6.   [5] *Ibid.*, 2, 19, 8.   [6] *Ibid.*

institution of slavery (as a punishment for the guilty) was not necessary from the standpoint of natural reason; but, given this custom, the guilty are bound to submit to it, while the victors may not inflict a more severe punishment without some special reason. Again, though the obligation to observe treaties once they have been made proceeds from the natural law, it is a matter pertaining to the *ius gentium* that offers of treaties, when duly made and for a reasonable cause, should not be refused. To act in this way is, indeed, in harmony with natural reason; but it is more firmly established by custom and the *ius gentium*, and so acquires a special binding force.

The rational basis of this kind of *ius gentium* is the fact that the human race, however much it may be divided into different nations and States, preserves a certain unity, which does not consist simply in membership of the human species, but is also a moral and political unity, as it were (*unitatem quasi politicam et moralem*). This is indicated by the natural precept of mutual love and mercy, which extends to all, 'even foreigners'.[1] A given State may constitute a perfect community, but, taken simply by itself, it is not self-sufficient but requires assistance through association and relationship with other States. In a certain sense, then, different States are members of a universal society; and they need some system of law to regulate their relations with one another. Natural reason does not provide sufficiently for this need; but the habitual conduct of nations has introduced certain laws which are in accordance with nature, even if they are not strictly deducible from the natural law.

St. Thomas asserted in the *Summa theologica*[2] that the precepts of the *ius gentium* are conclusions drawn from principles of the natural law and that they differ from precepts of the civil law, which are determinations of the natural law, not general conclusions from it. Suárez interprets this as meaning that the precepts of the *ius gentium* are general conclusions of the natural law, 'not in an absolute sense and by necessary inference, but in comparison with the specific determination of civil and private law'.[3]

11. In the third book of the *De legibus* Suárez turns to the subject of positive human law. He asks first whether man possesses the power to make laws or whether the making of laws by man spells tyranny; and his treatment of this question involves consideration of the State and of political authority.

---
[1] *De legibus*, 2, 19, 9. [2] Ia, IIae, 95, 4. [3] *De legibus*, 2, 20, 2.

Man is a social animal, as Aristotle said, and he has a natural desire to live in community.[1] The most fundamental natural society is, indeed, the family; but the family, though a perfect community for purposes of domestic or 'economic' government, is not self-sufficing. Man stands in further need of a political community, formed by the coalition of families. This political community is necessary, both for the preservation of peace between individual families and for the growth of civilization and culture.

Secondly, in a perfect community (Suárez is here speaking of the political community) there must be a governing power. The truth of this principle would seem to be self-evident, but it is confirmed by analogy with other forms of human society, like the family.[2] Moreover, as St. Thomas indicates,[3] no body can endure unless it possesses some principle the function of which is to provide for the common good. The institution of civil magistracy is thus necessary.

Thirdly, a human magistracy, if it is supreme in its own sphere, has the power to make laws in its own sphere, that is to say, civil or human laws. A civil magistracy is a necessity in a State; and the establishment of laws is one of the most necessary acts of a civil magistracy, if it is to fulfil its governmental and regulative function in the life of the State.[4] This power to make laws belongs to the magistracy which possesses supreme jurisdiction in the State: it is an essential factor in political sovereignty.

The State and political sovereignty are thus natural institutions, in the sense that nature demands their establishment. It may be true that empires and kingdoms have often been established through tyranny and force; but historical facts of this kind are examples of human abuse of power and strength, not of the essential nature of political sovereignty.[5] As to St. Augustine's opinion, that the domination of one man over another is due to the state of affairs brought about by sin, this is to be understood, says Suárez,[6] of that form of dominion which is accomplished by servitude and the exercise of coercion. Without sin there would be no exercise of coercion and no slavery; but there still would be government; at least, 'in so far as directive power is concerned, it would seem probable that this would have existed among men even in the state of innocence'.[7] In this matter Suárez follows St. Thomas.[8] In the *De opere sex dierum*[9] Suárez says that since

---

[1] *De legibus*, 3, 1, 3. [2] *Ibid.*, 3, 1, 4. [3] *De regimine principum*, 1, 1.
[4] *De legibus*, 3, 1, 6. [5] *Ibid.*, 3, 1, 11. [6] *Ibid.*, 3, 1, 12. [7] *Ibid.*
[8] For St. Augustine's opinion see Vol. II of this history, pp. 88–9. [9] 5, 7, 6.

human society is a result not of human corruption but of human nature itself, it appears that men would have been united in a political community even in the state of innocence, had that state continued to exist. Whether there would have been one political community or more is not a question which one can answer. All one can say is that if all men had continued to live in Paradise, there could have been one single political community. Suárez goes on to say that there would have been no servitude in the state of innocence but there would have been government, as this is required for the common good.[1]

But the fact that civil magistracy and government are necessary and that the supreme magistracy in a State has power to make laws, does not mean that the power to make laws is conferred directly and immediately on any individual or group of individuals. On the contrary, 'this power, viewed solely according to the nature of things, resides, not in any individual man, but rather in the whole body of mankind'.[2] All men are born free; and nature has not conferred immediately upon any man political jurisdiction over another.

When, however, it is said that the power of making laws was conferred by Nature immediately upon mankind ('the multitude of mankind'), this must not be understood as meaning that the power was conferred on men regarded simply as an aggregate, without any moral union. We must understand mankind as meaning men gathered together by common consent 'into one political body through one bond of fellowship and for the purpose of aiding one another in the attainment of a single political end'.[3] If regarded in this way, men form 'a single mystical body' which needs a single head.[4]

It is to be added that the power in question does not reside in mankind in such a way that it is one power residing in all existent men, with the consequence that they would all form one single political community. 'On the contrary, that would scarcely be possible, and much less would it be expedient.'[5] It seems, then, that the power of making laws, if it existed in the whole assemblage of mankind, did so only for a brief time: mankind began to be divided into distinct political communities 'soon after the creation of the world'. Once this division had begun to take place, the power to make laws resided in the several political communities.

---

[1] *De legibus*, 5, 7, 11. [2] *Ibid.*, 3, 2, 3. [3] *Ibid.*, 3, 2, 4.
[4] *Ibid.* [5] *Ibid.*, 3, 2, 5.

This power comes from God as its primary source.[1] But how does He confer it? In the first place, it is given by God 'as a characteristic property resulting from nature'. In other words, God does not confer the power by any special act which is distinct from the act of creation. That it results from nature means that natural reason shows that the exercise of the power is necessary for the preservation and proper government of the political community, which is itself a natural society. In the second place, the power does not manifest itself until men have formed a political community. Therefore the power is not conferred by God without the intervention of will and consent on the part of men, that is to say, on the part of those men who, by consent, form themselves together into a perfect society or State. However, once they have formed the community the power is resident therein. It is rightly said, then, to have been immediately conferred by God. Suárez adds[2] that the power does not reside in a given political community in such a way that it cannot be alienated by the consent of that community or forfeited by way of just punishment.

12. It is clear that Suárez regarded political society as originating, essentially, in consent. That a greater or less number of States may have actually originated in other ways is a historical accident, not affecting the essence of the State. But if, to this extent, Suárez may be said to have proposed a theory of the 'social contract', this does not mean that he regarded political society as a purely artificial society, a creation of enlightened egoism. On the contrary, as we have seen, he found the ultimate origin of political society in human nature, that is, in the social character and needs of the human being. The formation of political society is a necessary expression of human nature, even if the formation of a given political community must be said to rest essentially on consent, since nature has not specified what particular communities are to be formed.

Much the same is to be said about his theory of sovereignty or, to restrict oneself to the actual point discussed, the power of making laws which appertains to sovereignty. Nature has not specified any particular form of government, says Suárez;[3] the determination of the form of government depends on human choice. It would be extremely difficult for the whole community as such to make laws directly, and practical considerations point to monarchy

[1] *De legibus*, 3, 3, 4. [2] *Ibid.*, 3, 3, 7. [3] *Ibid.*, 3, 4, 1.

as the best form of government, though it is as a rule expedient, given man's character, 'to add some element of common government'.[1] What this element of common government is to be, depends on human choice and prudence. In any case, whoever holds the civil power, this power has been derived, either directly or indirectly, from the people as a community. Otherwise it could not be justly held.[2] In order that sovereignty may justly be vested in a given individual, 'it must necessarily be bestowed upon him by the consent of the community'.[3] In certain cases God has conferred power directly, as on Saul; but such cases are extraordinary and, as far as regards the mode of imparting power, supernatural. In the case of hereditary monarchy the just possessor derived power from the commonwealth.[4] As to royal power obtained through unjust force, the king in this case possesses no true legislative power, though in the course of time the people may come to give their consent to and acquiesce in his sovereignty, thus rendering it legitimate.[5]

Thus, just as Suárez holds that the formation of a given political community depends on human consent, so he holds that the establishment of a certain government depends on the consent of the political community which confers the sovereignty. He may therefore be said to maintain, in a sense, the double-contract theory. But, just as he holds that the formation of political communities is a requirement of nature, so he holds that the establishment of some government is required by nature. He may tend to lay more emphasis on the idea of consent; indeed, he speaks explicitly of a 'pact or agreement' between the king and the kingdom;[6] but political authority and sovereignty are nevertheless necessary for the proper preservation and government of mankind. Political authority is derived ultimately from God, on whom all dominion depends; but the fact that it is conferred on a definite individual derives from a grant on the part of the State itself: 'the principate itself is derived from men'.[7] In other words, political sovereignty is not in itself simply a matter of convention or agreement, for it is necessary for human life; but the conferring of sovereignty on certain individuals does depend on agreement.

It may be noted in passing that Suárez thought in terms of the monarchic state of his time. The mediaeval idea of the imperial power plays little part in his political theory. In his *Defence of the*

---

[1] *De legibus*, 3, 4, 1. [2] *Ibid.*, 3, 4, 2. [3] *Ibid.* [4] *Ibid.*, 3, 4, 3.
[5] *Ibid.*, 3, 4, 4. [6] *Ibid.*, 3, 4, 5. [7] *Ibid.*, 3, 4, 5.

Catholic and Apostolic Faith[1] Suárez expressly denies that the emperor has universal temporal jurisdiction over all Christians. It is probable, he says, that the emperor never did possess this power; and, even if he did, he has certainly lost it. 'We assume that there are, besides the emperor, a number of temporal kings, like the kings of Spain, France and England, who are entirely independent of the emperor's jurisdiction.'[2] On the other hand, Suárez evidently did not think that a world-State and a world-government were practical possibilities. History shows that there never has been a truly world-wide government. It does not exist, never did exist, and never could have existed.[3] Suárez maintained as we have seen, that the existence of a single political community for all men is morally impossible and that, even if possible, it would be highly inexpedient.[4] If Aristotle was right, as he was, in saying that it is difficult to govern a very large city properly, it would be far more difficult to govern a world-State.

13. What implications did Suárez draw from his doctrine of the pact between monarch and kingdom? Did he hold in particular that the citizens have a right to depose a tyrannical monarch, one who violates his trust?

According to Suárez,[5] the transfer of sovereignty from the State to the prince is not a delegation but a transfer or unlimited bestowal of the whole power which resided in the community. The prince, then, may delegate the power, if he so chooses: it is granted to him absolutely, to be exercised by him personally or through agents, as he thinks most expedient. Moreover, once the power has been transferred to the monarch, he is the vicar of God; and obedience to him is obligatory, according to the natural law.[6] In fact, the transference of power to the monarch makes him superior even to the State which conferred the power, since the State has subjected itself to the monarchy by making the transference.

The monarch cannot, then, be deprived of his sovereignty, since he has acquired ownership of his power. But Suárez immediately adds the qualification, 'unless perchance he lapses into tyranny, on which ground the kingdom may wage a just war against him'.[7] There are two sorts of tyrants.[8] There is the tyrant who has usurped the throne by force and unjustly; and there is the legitimate prince who rules tyrannically in the use he makes of his power. In regard to the first kind of tyrant, the whole State or any

---
[1] 3, 5, 7.   [2] *Ibid.*   [3] *De legibus*, 3, 4, 7.   [4] *Ibid.*, 3, 2, 5.
[5] *Ibid.*, 3, 4, 11.   [6] *Ibid.*, 3, 4, 6.   [7] *Ibid.*
[8] *Defence of the Catholic and Apostolic Faith*, 6, 4, 1.

part of it has the right to revolt against him, for he is an aggressor. To revolt is simply to exercise the right of self-defence.[1] As to the second type of tyrant, namely the legitimate prince who rules tyrannically, the State as a whole may rise against him, for it must be supposed that the State granted him the power on condition that he should govern for the common good and that he might be deposed if he lapsed into tyranny.[2] It is, however, a necessary condition for the legitimacy of such a revolt that the king's rule should be manifestly tyrannical and that the norms pertaining to a just war should be observed. Suárez refers to St. Thomas on this matter.[3] But it is only the whole State which is entitled to rise against a legitimate monarch acting tyrannically; for he cannot, without more ado, be an aggressor against all individual citizens in the way that the unjust usurper is an aggressor. This is not to say, however, that an individual who is the subject of actual tyrannical aggression on the part of a legitimate monarch may not defend himself. But a distinction must be drawn between self-defence and defence of the State.

In his *Defence of the Catholic and Apostolic Faith*[4] Suárez considers the particular question of tyrannicide. A legitimate monarch may not be slain by private authority on the grounds that he rules tyrannically. This is the doctrine of St. Thomas,[5] Cajetan and others. A private individual who kills on his own authority a legitimate monarch who acts tyrannically is a murderer. He does not possess the requisite jurisdiction.[6] As to self-defence, a private individual may not kill the legitimate monarch simply in order to defend his private possessions; but if the monarch tyrannically threatens the citizen's life, he may defend himself, even if the monarch's death results, though regard for the common welfare might, in certain circumstances, bind him in charity to refrain from slaying the monarch, even at the cost of his own life.

In the case of a tyrannical usurper, however, it is licit for the private individual to kill him provided that no recourse can be had to a superior authority and provided that the tyranny and injustice of the usurper's rule are manifest. Other conditions added by Suárez[7] are that tyrannicide is a necessary means for the liberation of the kingdom; that no agreement has been freely entered upon by the usurper and the people; that tyrannicide will not leave the State afflicted with the same or greater evils than

---

[1] *De triplici virtute theologica; de caritate*, 13, 8, 2.   [2] *Ibid.*
[3] *De regimine principum*, 1, 6.   [4] 6, 4.   [5] *De regimine principum*, 1, 6.
[6] *Defence*, 6, 4, 4.   [7] *Ibid.*, 6, 4, 8–9.

before; and that the State does not expressly oppose private tyrannicide.

Suárez thus affirms the right of resistance, which logically follows from his doctrine of the origin and transference of sovereignty. He certainly in no way encouraged unnecessary revolts; but it is easily understandable that his work on the Catholic Faith was most obnoxious to James I of England, who believed in the divine right of kings and the principle of legitimacy.

14. In the fourth book of the *De legibus* (*De lege positiva canonica*) Suárez considers canon law; and in the fifth book he treats *de varietate legum humanarum et praesertim de poenalibus et odiosis*. In connection with penal laws he raises the question of their binding force in conscience. First of all, it is possible for the human legislator to make laws which bind in conscience, even though a temporal penalty for transgression is attached.[1] But do such laws bind in conscience when the legislator has not expressly stated his intention of binding the consciences of his subjects? In Suárez' opinion[2] a law which contains a precept binds in conscience unless the legislator has expressed or made clear his intention not to bind the conscience. (Whether the law binds under pain of mortal or venial sin depends on the matter of the law and other circumstances.) Suárez draws the logical conclusion that just taxation laws bind in conscience, 'like the law in Spain taxing the price of wheat'.[3] It is possible, however, for there to be penal laws which do not bind in conscience in regard to the act to be performed. Whether a law is of this kind, that is, whether a law is merely penal, depends on the intention of the legislator. This intention need not necessarily be expressed in so many words, for it may be made clear by tradition and custom.[4] When a penal law does not actually command or prohibit an act but simply states, for example, that if someone exports wheat he will be fined, it can be presumed to be merely penal unless it is clear from some other consideration that it was meant to bind in conscience.

A human penal law can oblige subjects in conscience to undergo the penalty, even before judicial sentence; but only if the penalty is one that the subject can licitly inflict on himself and provided that it is not so severe or repugnant to human nature that its voluntary performance cannot be reasonably demanded.[5] But

---
[1] *De legibus*, 5, 3, 2. [2] *Ibid.*, 5, 3, 6. [3] *Ibid.*, 5, 3, 10.
[4] *Ibid.*, 5, 4, 8. [5] *Ibid.*, 5, 5, 15.

it does not follow that all penal laws do so oblige in actual fact. If a penal law simply threatens a penalty, it does not oblige the transgressor to undergo the penalty before sentence, whatever the penalty may be:[1] the legislator's intention to oblige the transgressor in conscience to undergo the penalty on his own initiative must be made clear. As to the obligation to undergo the penalty inflicted by judicial sentence, Suárez holds that if some action or co-operation on the part of the guilty man is necessary for the execution of the penalty, he is bound in conscience to perform that act or give that co-operation, provided that the law which he has broken is a just law and that the penalty in question is not immoderate.[2] In this matter, however, common sense has to be used. No one, for example, is obliged to execute himself.[3]

As already mentioned, Suárez considered that taxation laws, if they are just, bind in conscience. He maintained that 'the laws by which such taxes are ordered to be paid, even if no penalty is attached, certainly cannot be called purely penal'.[4] They therefore bind in conscience; and just taxes must be paid in full, even if they have not been demanded, from oversight, for example, unless the legislator's intention to pass a purely penal taxation law is made clear. Regarded in themselves, taxation laws are true moral laws binding in conscience.[5] As for unjust taxation laws, they never bind in conscience, either before or after the demand for the payment of the tax.[6]

15. The sixth book of the *De legibus* is concerned with the interpretation, cessation and change of human laws. It is not always necessary that a law should be revoked by the sovereign before it can be disobeyed licitly. Apart from the fact that a law enjoining anything wrong, anything impossible of fulfilment or anything devoid of any utility is unjust and null from the start,[7] a law may cease to be valid and binding because the adequate end, both intrinsic and extrinsic of the law, has ceased to exist.[8] For example, if a law is passed imposing a tax solely with a view to obtaining money for a specific object, the law lapses, as regards its binding force, when the purpose has been achieved, even if the law has not been revoked. But if the end of a law is not purely extrinsic but is also intrinsic (for example, if a good act is indeed commanded with a view to some specific end but in such a way that the legislator would command that act irrespective of the

---

[1] *De legibus*, 5, 6, 4.   [2] *Ibid.*, 5, 10, 8.   [3] *Ibid.*, 5, 10, 12.   [4] *Ibid.*, 5, 13, 4.
[5] *Ibid.*, 5, 13, 9.   [6] *Ibid.*, 5, 18, 12.   [7] *Ibid.*, 6, 9, 3.   [8] *Ibid.*, 6, 9, 10.

specific end), it cannot, of course, be taken for granted that the law lapses simply because the specified end has been achieved.

16. Suárez writes at length of unwritten law or custom, a matter to which he devotes the seventh book (*De lege non scripta quae consuetudo appellatur*). Custom, considered as a juridical factor, is introduced in default of law: it is unwritten law. But it is only common or public custom which can establish law (that is, custom regarded as law), not private custom, which is the custom of one person or of an imperfect community.[1] Moreover, a custom, to establish law, must be morally good: a custom which is intrinsically evil establishes no law.[2] But the distinction between morally good and bad customs is not the same as that between reasonable and unreasonable customs: a custom might be good in itself, that is, considered simply as a custom, while at the same time it might be unreasonable and imprudent if regarded juridically, namely as establishing law.[3]

For the establishment of a custom a perfect community is required:[4] but it is not necessary for its establishment that it should be observed by literally the whole of the community; it is sufficient if the greater part of the community observes it.[5] How is it established? By a repetition of certain public acts by the people.[6] These acts must, of course, be voluntary acts. The reason for this is that the acts which establish a custom are of effect in doing so only in so far as they manifest the consent of the people.[7] They must, therefore, be voluntary: a custom cannot be validly established by acts done under compulsion or from grave or unjust fear.[8] But it does not follow that the consent of the prince is not necessary for the valid establishment of custom or consuetudinary law. This consent may, however, be given in different ways; either by express consent, or by antecedently permitting the introduction of a custom or by contemporaneous or subsequent confirmation, or by the prince doing nothing to check the custom when he has become aware of it.[9] Tacit consent, then, on the part of the sovereign can be sufficient.

Legitimate custom may have various different effects. It may establish a law; it may serve to interpret an existent law; or it may abrogate a law.[10] As regards the first effect, ten years are necessary and sufficient to establish a legal custom.[11] As to the abrogation of law through custom, a twofold will, the will of the people and the

[1] *De legibus*, 7, 3, 8–10.   [2] *Ibid.*, 7, 6, 4.   [3] *Ibid.*, 7, 6, 7.   [4] *Ibid.*, 7, 9, 3.
[5] *Ibid.*, 7, 9, 12.   [6] *Ibid.*, 7, 10, 1.   [7] *Ibid.*, 7, 12, 1.   [8] *Ibid.*, 7, 12, 10.
[9] *Ibid.*, 7, 13, 6.   [10] *Ibid.*, 7, 14, 1.   [11] *Ibid.*, 7, 15, 2.

will of the prince, is necessary for the attainment of this effect,[1] though a tacit consent on the prince's part can suffice. Custom can even establish penal law.[2] A custom of ten years' standing is required for the abrogation of civil law; but in the case of canon law a period of forty years is required for a custom to be prescriptive against a law.[3]

In the eighth book of the *De legibus* (*De lege humana favorabili*) Suárez deals with privilege, and in the ninth and tenth books with divine positive law. Passing over these topics I propose to say something on Suárez' view of the relation of Church to State.

17. In his *Defence of the Catholic and Apostolic Faith* Suárez discusses and rejects the view that the pope possesses not only supreme spiritual power but also supreme civil power with the consequence that no purely temporal sovereign possesses supreme power in temporal affairs. He appeals to utterances of popes, and then goes on to argue[4] that no just title can be discovered whereby the pope possesses direct jurisdiction in temporal affairs over all Christian States. And without a just title he cannot possess such jurisdiction. There is no evidence that either divine or human law has conferred such jurisdiction on the pope. Suárez recognized, of course, the temporal jurisdiction of the pope as temporal ruler over the Papal States; but he refused to regard other temporal sovereigns as mere vicars of the Holy See. In other words Church and State are distinct and independent societies, even though the end for which the Church exists is higher than that for which the State exists.

But, although the pope does not possess direct or primary civil jurisdiction over temporal sovereigns, he possesses a directive power over them, not merely as individuals but also as sovereigns. In virtue of his spiritual jurisdiction the pope possesses the power of directing temporal princes with a view to a spiritual end.[5] 'By directive power we do not understand simply the power of advising, warning or requesting; for these are not peculiar to superior authority; but we mean a strict power of obliging.'[6] Temporal monarchs are the spiritual subjects of the pope; and the pope's spiritual authority includes the power of directing the monarch in the use of his temporal authority, 'if in any matter he deviates from right reason, or from faith, justice or charity'.[7] This involves an indirect power on the part of the pope over temporal affairs.

[1] *De legibus*, 7, 18, 5.   [2] *Ibid.*, 7, 16, 3.   [3] *Ibid.*, 7, 18, 12.
[4] *Defence*, 3, 5, 11.   [5] *Ibid.*, 3, 22, 1.   [6] *Ibid.*   [7] *Ibid.*, 3, 22, 5.

There may occur a clash between spiritual good and temporal convenience or expediency; and on such occasions the temporal sovereign must yield to the spiritual.[1] The pope should not attempt to usurp direct temporal jurisdiction; but in cases where it is necessary for spiritual good he may interfere, in virtue of his indirect power.

Suárez thus maintained the doctrine of the pope's indirect, though not direct, jurisdiction in the temporal sphere. He also maintained that the pope possesses 'coercive power over temporal princes who are incorrigibly wicked, and especially over schismatics and stubborn heretics'.[2] For directive power without coercive power is inefficacious. This power extends not only to the infliction of spiritual punishments like excommunication but also to the infliction of temporal punishments, such as, in case of necessity, deposition from the throne.[3] As to heathen monarchs, even if the pope does not possess the power to punish them, he has the power to free their Christian subjects from allegiance to them, if the Christians are in danger of moral destruction.[4]

18. Finally something may be said on the subject of Suárez' doctrine concerning war.

War is not intrinsically evil: there can be a just war. Defensive war is permitted; and sometimes it is even a matter of obligation.[5] But certain conditions have to be observed in order that a war should be just. First of all, the war must be waged by a legitimate power; and this is the supreme sovereign.[6] But the pope has the right to insist that matters of dispute between Christian sovereigns should be referred to himself, though the sovereigns are not bound to secure the pope's authorization before making war, unless the pope has expressly said that they must do so.[7]

The second condition for a just war is that the cause of making war should be just. For example, the suffering of a grave injustice which cannot be repaired or avenged in any other way is a just cause for war.[8] A defensive war should be attempted; but before an offensive war is begun, the sovereign should estimate his chances of victory and should not begin the war if he is more likely to lose than to win it.[9] The reason for this proviso is that otherwise the prince would incur the obvious risk of inflicting great injuries on his State. (By 'offensive war' Suárez means, not an 'aggressive war', but a just war freely undertaken. It is

---

[1] *Defence*, 3, 22, 7.   [2] *Ibid.*, 3, 23, 2.   [3] *Ibid.*, 3, 23, 10.
[4] *Ibid.*, 3, 23, 22.   [5] *De triplici virtute theologica; de caritate*, 13, 1, 4.
[6] *Ibid.*, 13, 2, 4.   [7] *Ibid.*, 13, 2, 5.   [8] *Ibid.*, 13, 4, 1.   [9] *Ibid.*, 13, 4, 10.

legitimate to declare war freely in order to repair injuries suffered or to defend the innocent.)

The third condition for a just war is that the war must be properly conducted and that due proportion must be observed throughout its course and in victory. Before beginning a war the prince is bound to call the attention of the sovereign of the other State to the existence of a just cause of war and to ask for adequate satisfaction. If the other offers adequate reparation for the injury done, he is bound to accept it; if he nevertheless attacks, the war will be unjust.[1] During the conduct of the war it is legitimate to inflict on the enemy all losses necessary for the attainment of victory, provided that these losses do not involve intrinsic injury to innocent persons.[2] Finally, after the winning of victory the prince may inflict upon the conquered enemy such penalties as are sufficient for a just punishment; and he may demand compensation for all losses his State has suffered, including those suffered through the war.[3] Indeed, after the war 'certain guilty individuals among the enemy may also be put to death with justice'.[4]

As to the 'innocent', 'it is implicit in the natural law that the innocent include children, women, and all unable to bear arms', while, according to the *ius gentium*, ambassadors are included, and, among Christians, by positive law, religious and priests. 'All other persons are considered guilty; for human judgment looks upon those able to take up arms as having actually done so.'[5] Innocent persons as such may never be slain, for the slaying of them is intrinsically evil; but if victory cannot be achieved without the 'incidental' slaying of the innocent, it is legitimate to slay them.[6] Suárez means that it is legitimate, for example, to blow up a bridge or to storm a town, if such acts are necessary for victory, even though the attacker has reason to think that these acts will involve the death of some innocent persons 'incidentally'. It would not, however, be legitimate to do such acts with the purpose of killing innocent people.

A question in connection with war discussed by Suárez[7] is the question how far the soldiers partaking in it are morally obliged to ascertain whether it is a just or unjust war. His answer, briefly stated, is as follows. Regular soldiers who are subjects of a prince are not bound to make careful investigation before obeying the summons to war: they can assume that the war is just, unless the

---
[1] *De triplici virtute theologica; de caritate*, 13, 7, 3.   [2] *Ibid.*, 13, 7, 6.
[3] *Ibid.*, 13, 7, 7.   [4] *Ibid.*   [5] *Ibid.*, 13, 7, 10.
[6] *Ibid.*, 13, 7, 15.   [7] *Ibid.*, 13, 6, 8–12.

contrary is evident. If they have simply speculative doubts about the justice of the war, they should disregard these doubts; but if the soldiers have practical and convincing reasons for thinking that the justice of the war is extremely doubtful they should make further inquiries. As to mercenaries who are not subjects of the prince who proposes to make war, Suárez argues that, although the common opinion seems to be that they are bound to inquire into the justice of war before enlisting, he himself finds no difference in actual fact between subjects and non-subjects. The general principles are, (*a*) that if the doubt which arises about the justice of a war is purely negative, it is probable that soldiers may enlist without making any further inquiry; and (*b*) that if the doubt is positive, and if both sides advance plausible arguments, those about to enlist should inquire into the truth. If they cannot discover the truth, let them aid him who is probably in the right. In practice 'inquiry' for an ordinary soldier means consulting 'prudent and conscientious men' but if the soldiers form an organized body, they can leave the inquiry and decision to their commander. As to the sovereign who wishes to make war, he is bound, of course, to inquire diligently into the justice of his cause; and he may not go to war if the other side is more probably in the right, let alone if it is morally certain that justice rests with the other side.[1]

[1] *De triplici virtute theologica; de caritate*, 13, 6, 2.

CHAPTER XXIV

A BRIEF REVIEW OF THE FIRST THREE VOLUMES

Greek philosophy; the pre-Socratic cosmologies and the discovery of Nature, Plato's theory of Forms and idea of God, Aristotle and the explanation of change and movement, neo-Platonism and Christianity—The importance for mediaeval philosophy of the discovery of Aristotle—Philosophy and theology—The rise of science.

1. IN the first volume of this *History of Philosophy* I dealt with the philosophy of Greece and Rome. If one regards Greek philosophy as starting in the sixth century B.C. and ending with Justinian's closing of the Athenian Academy in A.D. 529, one can say that it lasted for about a thousand years and that it formed a definite period of philosophic thought with certain more or less well-defined phases.

(i) According to the traditional division, the first phase was that of pre-Socratic philosophy; and it has been customary to depict this phase as characterized predominantly by cosmological speculation. This view has, of course, the authority of Socrates in the *Phaedo*; and Aristotle, who interpreted the thought of previous philosophers largely in terms of his own theory of causes, speaks of the early Greek philosophers as busying themselves with the 'material cause' and of thinkers like Empedocles and Anaxagoras as considering the source of motion or efficient cause. I think that this view of pre-Socratic philosophy, namely that it was predominantly, though certainly not exclusively, cosmological in character, is obviously reasonable and sound. One can express it perhaps by saying that the pre-Socratic philosophers discovered 'Nature', that is, they formed the idea of a cosmos, an organized physical system governed by law. That the cosmos was looked on as divine in some sense, and that one can discern in the theories of the pre-Socratics mythical elements, the connection of which with older cosmogonies can be traced, is true; but there is a world of difference between the mythical cosmogonies and the cosmologies of the pre-Socratic philosophers. There is connection, but there is also difference. The play of imagination and phantasy began to retreat before the reflective work of the mind, based to some degree on empirical data.

It is, I think, important to remember that the pre-Socratic cosmologists represent a pre-scientific phase of thought. There was then no distinction between philosophy and the empirical sciences; nor, indeed, could there have been. The empirical sciences had to attain a certain stage of development before the distinction could well be made; and we may recall that even after the time of the Renaissance 'natural philosophy' or 'experimental philosophy' was used as a name for what we would call 'physical science'. The early Greek philosophers aimed simply at understanding the nature of the world, and their attention was centred on certain problems which aroused their interest and curiosity or, as Aristotle puts it, 'wonder'. Some of these problems were certainly what we would call 'scientific problems', in the sense that they can be profitably dealt with only by the use of scientific method, though the pre-Socratics tried to solve them by the only means in their power, namely by reflection on casual observations and by speculation. In some instances they made brilliant guesses which anticipated scientific hypotheses of a much later date. Anaximander appears to have put forward an evolutionary hypothesis about man's origin, while the atomic theory of Leucippus and Democritus is a notable example of a speculative anticipation of a later scientific hypothesis. According to Aristotle, men first felt wonder at the more obvious things and later raised difficulties and questions about more important matters; and he mentions questions about the sun and the moon and the stars and about the generation of the universe. This statement by Aristotle is worth reflecting on. The 'wonder' of which he speaks was the fountain-head of both philosophy and science. But in the beginning they were not distinguished, and it is only in terms of a later distinction to which we have become thoroughly accustomed, that we classify questions about the sun and moon and stars as scientific questions. It is obvious enough to us that if we wish to learn about the stars, for example, we have to turn to the astronomer for information: we would hardly go to the speculative philosopher for our information. Similarly, we do not think that questions about the physical constitution of matter or about the mechanism of vision (a subject in which Empedocles, for example, interested himself) can be answered by means of arm-chair reflection.

If I were to rewrite the sections about the pre-Socratics in my first volume, I would wish, I think, to give more attention to these aspects of their thought, namely the fact that a number of the questions which they raised were what we would regard as scientific questions and that a number of the theories which they put forward were speculative anticipations of later scientific hypotheses. At the same time it would be incorrect to suggest that the pre-Socratics were nothing but would-be scientists who lacked the method and the requisite technical means for pursuing their real vocation. One might perhaps say something like this about Thales and Anaximenes; but it would be a strange thing to say about Parmenides or even, I think, about Heraclitus. It seems to me that the pre-Socratics, or some of them at least, raised a number of problems which have generally been considered properly philosophical problems. Heraclitus, for example, appears to have raised moral problems which cannot be answered by empirical science. And it is arguable that the drive behind the intellectual activity of some of them was the desire to 'explain' the universe by reducing multiplicity to unity and by discovering the nature of 'ultimate reality', and that they had this drive in common with later speculative philosophers.

I do not think, then, that one is justified in interpreting the pre-Socratics as nothing more than speculative forerunners of science. To do this is to be guilty of a rather cavalier and hasty generalization. At the same time it is only right to draw attention to the fact that some of the main questions which they raised were not questions which can be answered in the way in which the pre-Socratics (unavoidably) tried to answer them. And in this sense it is true to say that they were forerunners of science. It is, I think, also true to say that they were predominantly 'cosmologists' and that a good deal of the field of their cosmological speculation has now been taken over, as it were, by science. But though one can say if one likes that their assumption that Nature is an organized cosmos was a scientific hypothesis, one can just as well say that it was a philosophic hypothesis which lies at the root of all scientific work and research.

(ii) If the early cosmologists discovered Nature, the Sophists, Socrates and Plato discovered Man. It is true, of course, that this statement is inaccurate and exaggerated in at any rate two ways. In the first place, Man was not discovered by the Sophists or by Socrates in the sense that a hitherto unknown island is discovered by an explorer. Nor, for the matter of that, was Nature discovered in this sense by the pre-Socratics. And in the second place, pre-Socratic philosophers, like the Pythagoreans, had theories about

Man, just as Plato had theories about Nature. None the less at the time of Socrates there occurred a shift in philosophic interest and emphasis. And that is why some historians say, and are able to make out a reasonable case for saying, that Greek philosophy began with Socrates. In their view, pre-Socratic philosophy should be regarded as primitive science, not as philosophy at all. Philosophy began with the Socratic ethical analysis. This is not my view of the situation; but it is an arguable position.

But it is not my purpose to say anything further here about the shift of interest from Nature to Man. That there was such a shift of interest in the case of Socrates would not be denied; and I dwelt on this theme in my first volume. What I want to do now is to draw attention to a topic which I did not sufficiently emphasize in that volume, namely the part played by analysis in the philosophies of Socrates and Plato. It might be better, however, to say that I wish now to emphasize the part played by analysis in the philosophy of Plato, since it is an obvious enough fact that Socrates was concerned with analysis. (In saying this I am assuming the truth of the view, represented in my first volume, that Socrates did not invent the theory of Forms or Ideas.)

It seems to me that Plato's theory of values was based very largely on an analysis of ethical propositions and value-statements. And though statements of this kind do seem to me to imply belief in the objectivity of values in some sense, it does not follow that values possess the kind of objectivity which Plato appears to have attributed to them. If one may borrow the language of Husserl, one can say perhaps that Plato carried on a phenomenological analysis of 'essences' without observing the *epoche*, thus confusing descriptive phenomenology with metaphysics. Again, it is a feature of Plato's thought that he drew attention to the differences in logical meaning between different types of sentences. He saw, for example, that in some sentences names are used which do not denote any definite individual thing and that there is a sense in which such sentences can be true even if there are no individual things in existence which correspond to those names. On this basis he developed his theory of Forms in so far as it was extended to generic and specific terms. In doing so he was misled by language and confused logic with metaphysics.

In saying this I am very far from suggesting that Plato's idea of the Good and his theory of exemplarism were worthless and that his theory of Forms was no more than the result of a confusion of logic with metaphysics. His remarks about the Good, obscure though they may be, scarcely lend support to the notion that he postulated the Good simply and solely because he was misled by our use of the word 'good'. But the fact remains that Plato's dialectical and logical approach to the metaphysics of 'Forms' or 'Ideas' is open to very serious objections; and in my first volume I did not, I think, bring out sufficiently either the element of 'linguistic analysis' in Plato's philosophy or his confusion of logic with metaphysics.

But it is possible, I think, to place too much emphasis on the theory of Forms or Ideas in Plato's thought. There is no real evidence, so far as I know, that he ever abandoned this theory; indeed, it seems to me that the available evidence prohibits any such supposition. But at the same time I think that it is true to say that the idea of mind or soul came to play an increasingly important part in Plato's thought. The subject of Plato's theology is notoriously obscure; but it is at least clear that he was the real founder of natural theology. That he attached great importance to the idea of a divine Mind or Soul in the universe is made obvious in the *Laws*; and it is equally clear from the *Timaeus*, even if one has to allow for the 'mythical' character of the contents of that dialogue. This is not to say, of course, that Plato had any clear theistic philosophy: if he had, he certainly did not reveal the fact to his readers. If one means by 'God' the God of Judaeo-Christian monotheism, the evidence would suggest that Plato arrived by different lines of thought at two aspects of God; but it does not suggest, or at least it gives us no solid ground for asserting, that Plato combined those two aspects of Deity, attributing them to one personal Being. Thus the Good may be said to represent what the Christian philosopher calls 'God' under the aspect of exemplary cause, though it does not follow, of course, that Plato would have called the Good 'God'. And the Demiurge of the *Timaeus* and the divine Mind or Soul of the *Laws* may be said to represent God under the aspect of efficient cause, provided that one understands by efficient cause in this connection not a Creator in the full sense but an explanatory cause of the intelligible structure of the empirical world and of the orderly movements of the heavenly bodies. But there is no compelling evidence that Plato ever identified the Good with the being represented by the Demiurge of the *Timaeus*. Nevertheless it is clear that if his theory of Forms was his answer to one problem, his doctrine of a divine Mind or Soul was his answer to another problem; and it would appear that this latter doctrine came to occupy a more important position in his thoughts as time went on.

(iii) In regard to Aristotle, one must emphasize, I think, his attempt to give a rational account of the world of experience and, in particular, his preoccupation with the business of rendering observable change and movement intelligible. (It should be remembered that 'movement' did not mean for Aristotle simply locomotion: it included also quantitative and qualitative change.) One certainly ought not to eliminate or to brush aside the Platonic elements or the metaphysical elements in Aristotle's philosophy, as though they were simply relics of a Platonist phase in his development which he forgot to discard; but it is significant that the God of the *Metaphysics*, the first unmoved mover, was postulated as an explanation of movement in terms of final causality. The God of the *Metaphysics* tends to appear as an astronomical hypothesis.

If one bears in mind Aristotle's preoccupation with the explanation of change and movement, it becomes much easier to account for his radical criticism of the Platonic theory of Forms. As I have already said, Plato's theory certainly lies open to serious objections on logical grounds, and I doubt if his approach to the theory can stand up to criticism, however much value one may wish to attribute to the theory considered in itself and revised. On the other hand, several of Aristotle's criticisms seem to be singularly unimpressive as they stand. Aristotle tended to assume that what Plato was getting at in his theory of Forms was what he, Aristotle, understood by 'forms'; and he then objected that Plato's Forms did not fulfil the function which his own forms fulfilled and that consequently the Platonic theory was absurd. This line of criticism is not a happy one, since it rests on the assumption that Plato's theory was supposed to fulfil the same function which Aristotle's theory of formal causality was intended to fulfil. But if, as I have suggested, one bears in mind Aristotle's preoccupation with the explanation of change and movement and his 'dynamic' outlook, his hostility towards the Platonic theory becomes understandable. His fundamental objection was that the theory was too 'metaphysical'; it was useless, he thought, for explaining the mixture, as it were, of change and stability which we find in things: it was not a hypothesis which had its roots in the empirical data or which was capable of contributing to the explanation of the empirical data or which was verifiable. I do not wish to suggest that

Aristotle was a positivist. But if the word 'metaphysical' is understood as it sometimes is today, namely as referring to altogether unverifiable and gratuitous hypotheses, it is clear that Aristotle considered the Platonic theory to be too 'metaphysical'. I certainly do not think that the theory of exemplary causality has no explanatory function; but it can hardly possess any such function except in connection with the idea of a divine being capable of an activity of which the God of Aristotle's *Metaphysics* was not capable. If one looks at the matter from Aristotle's point of view, one can easily understand his attitude to the Platonic theory. One can also understand how St. Bonaventure in the Middle Ages was able to look on Aristotle as a natural philosopher but not as a metaphysician.

(iv) Plato's Demiurge formed the empirical world, conferring on it an intelligible pattern according to an external exemplar or model: Aristotle's God was the ultimate explanation, as final cause, of movement. For neither of them was God the creator, in the full sense, of empirical beings. The nearest the Greek philosophers came to the idea of creation and to a consideration of the problem of finite existence as such was in neo-Platonism.

But the point about neo-Platonism which I wish to emphasize here is its character as the synthesis of Greek philosophic thought and as a system in which philosophy, ethics and religion were combined. It presented itself as a 'way of salvation', even if as a highly intellectual way of salvation which could appeal only to comparatively few minds. In pre Socratic Pythagoreanism we can already discern the conception of philosophy as a way of salvation, though this aspect of Pythagoreanism may have tended to retreat into the background in proportion as the mathematical studies of the School developed. With Socrates and his theory of virtue as knowledge one can see clearly the idea of philosophy as a way of salvation, and in the thought of Plato the idea is also prominent, though it tends to be overshadowed by the logical and mathematical aspects of his philosophy. Plato was, of course, no pragmatist; but it does not require any great knowledge of his writings in order to realize the importance he attached to the possession of truth for the life of the individual and for society in general. But it is in the later phases of Platonism, especially in neo-Platonism, that the idea of philosophy as a way of salvation becomes so obvious. One has only to think of Plotinus' doctrine of the ethical and religious ascent of man, culminating in ecstatic union with the One. When Porphyry expounded neo-Platonism as a Greek and supposedly intellectually superior rival to Christianity, he was able to do this because in neo-Platonism Greek philosophy had taken on the character of a religion. Stoicism and Epicureanism were both presented as ways of salvation; but though the Stoic ethic certainly possessed a striking nobility, neither system was of a sufficiently high intellectual order to enable it to play the part in the final stages of Greek thought which was actually played by neo-Platonism.

The fact that early Christian writers borrowed terms and ideas from neo-Platonism may tend to make one emphasize the continuity between Greek and Christian thought. And this was the line I took in my first and second volumes. I have no intention of renouncing the validity of this line of thought now; but it is as well to emphasize the fact that there was also a sharp break between Greek and Christian thought. A neo-Platonist like Porphyry realized very clearly the difference between a philosophy which attached little importance to history and for which the idea of an incarnate God was unthinkable and a religion which attached a profound importance to concrete historical events and which was founded on belief in the Incarnation. Moreover, the Christian acceptance of Christ as the Son of God and of a divine revelation in history meant that for the Christian philosophy as such could not be the way of salvation. Christian writers like Clement of Alexandria interpreted philosophy in the literal sense as 'love of wisdom' and regarded Greek philosophy, especially Platonism in a wide sense, as a preparation for Christianity which fulfilled for the Greek world a function analogous to that fulfilled for the Jews by the Law and the Prophets. One is therefore struck by the friendly attitude shown towards Greek philosophy by a Clement of Alexandria as contrasted with the attitude shown by a Tertullian. But if one considers the former attitude a little more closely one will see its implications, namely that the rôle of Greek philosophy has been taken over in a definite manner by the Christian religion. And in point of fact when philosophy really developed in the Christian mediaeval world it tended to be 'academic', a matter for universities and professional logicians. No Christian philosopher really looked on philosophy as a way of salvation; and when mediaeval thinkers are reproached with paying too much attention to logical subtleties it is often forgotten that for them philosophy could not well be anything else than an 'academic' pursuit. When in the modern era one finds the conception of philosophy as a 'way of salvation' showing itself again the conception usually originates either in a disbelief in Christian theology and the desire to find a substitute or, if it is shown by Christian thinkers, in the desire to find an acceptable approach to those who are no longer Christians. The believing Christian looks to religion to be the inspiration of his life and his guide to conduct rather than to philosophy, however interested he may be in the latter.

2. In my second volume I traced the history of philosophy in the Christian world up to the end of the thirteenth century, though I included John Duns Scotus (d. 1308), whose philosophy belongs rather with the great thirteenth-century systems than with the *via moderna* of the fourteenth century. The volume thus covered the Patristic period, the early mediaeval period and the period of constructive metaphysical thinking on the grand scale. The next period, that is to say, the late mediaeval period, has been sketched in the first part of the present volume.

This fourfold division of Christian philosophic thought from the beginning of the Christian era to the close of the Middle Ages is a traditional division, and it is, I think, justified and useful. But it is possible to make an even simpler division by saying that mediaeval philosophy falls into two main periods, the period preceding and the period following the introduction of the Aristotelian *corpus* to western Christendom. In any case I think that it is hardly possible to exaggerate the philosophic importance of this event, namely of the rediscovery of Aristotle. I am speaking primarily as a historian. Philosophers may differ in their evaluations of Aristotelian theories, but there is, I think, no ground for dispute concerning the importance of the rediscovery of Aristotle, considered as a historical event. Apart from the system of John Scotus Eriugena, of which little notice was taken, the early mediaevals possessed nothing which we should be likely to call a philosophical system; and in particular they had no intimate knowledge of any system which owed nothing to Christianity. But the rediscovery of Aristotle and the translation of the leading Islamic thinkers in the second half of the twelfth century and the first part of the thirteenth brought to the knowledge of the Christian mediaeval thinkers for the first time a developed system which was the work of a pagan philosopher and which owed nothing to Christianity. Aristotle therefore naturally tended to mean for them 'philosophy'. It is a great mistake to allow the obstinacy with which some Renaissance Scholastics clung to the physical and scientific ideas of Aristotle to make one think of the discovery of Aristotle as a philosophical disaster. In the Middle Ages Aristotle was, indeed, known as 'the philosopher', and he was so named because his system was for the mediaevals 'philosophy' to all intents and purposes. But his system meant for them 'philosophy' not so much because it was Aristotelian, in the sense in which we distinguish Aristotelianism from Platonism, Stoicism, Epicureanism or neo-Platonism, as because it was the one great system of philosophy of which they possessed an extensive knowledge. It is important to realize this fact. If we speak, for example, of the attempt of St. Thomas to reconcile Aristotelianism with Christian theology, one will realize the nature of the situation better if one makes the experiment of substituting the word 'philosophy' for the word 'Aristotelianism'. When some of the theologians in the thirteenth century adopted a hostile attitude to Aristotle and regarded his philosophy as being in many respects an intellectual menace, they were rejecting independent philosophy in the name of the Christian faith. And when St. Thomas adopted in great measure the Aristotelian system, he was giving a charter to philosophy. He should not be regarded as burdening Christian thought with the system of a particular Greek philosopher. The deeper significance of his action was that he recognized the rights and position of philosophy as a rational study distinct from theology.

It is as well, too, to remind oneself of the fact that the utilization of the new learning in a constructive manner was due to men like St. Thomas and Duns Scotus who were primarily theologians. The rediscovery of Aristotle raised the problem of the relation between theology and philosophy in a form far more acute than it had previously assumed in the Middle Ages. And the only people in the thirteenth century who made a serious attempt to cope with the problem constructively were the theologians. Those professors of the faculty of arts who are often known as the 'Latin Averroists' tended to accept the entire philosophy of Aristotle, as it stood or as interpreted by Averroes, in a slavish manner. And when taxed with the fact that some of Aristotle's doctrines were incompatible with Christian theology, they answered that the philosopher's business is simply to report philosophical opinions. If they were sincere in giving this answer, they equated philosophy with the history of philosophy. If they were not sincere, they accepted

Aristotle in an uncritical and slavish manner. In either case they adopted no constructive attitude. Theologians like St. Thomas on the other hand endeavoured to synthesize Aristotelianism, which, as I have said, meant to all intents and purposes 'philosophy', with the Christian religion. This was not, however, a mere attempt to force Aristotle into a Christian mould, as some critics imagine: it involved a rethinking and development of the Aristotelian philosophy. St. Thomas's work was not a work of ignorant distortion but of original construction. He did not assume the truth of Aristotelianism because it was Aristotelianism and then try to force it into a Christian mould. He was convinced that Aristotelianism, in its main lines, was the result of sound reasoning; and when he attacked the monopsychistic doctrine of the Averroists he attacked it partly on the ground that Averroes had, in his opinion, misinterpreted Aristotle and partly on the ground that monopsychism was false and that it could be shown to be false by philosophic reasoning. It is the second ground which is the most important. If a philosophical theory was incompatible with Christian theology, St. Thomas believed that it was false. But he was well aware that from the philosophic point of view it is not sufficient to say that a theory is false because it is incompatible with Christianity. He was also aware that it is not sufficient to argue that it rested on a misinterpretation of Aristotle. His primary task was to show that the theory rested on bad or inconclusive reasoning. In other words, his rethinking of Aristotelianism was a philosophic rethinking: it did not simply take the form of confronting Aristotelian and supposedly Aristotelian theories with Christian theology and eliminating or changing theories which were incompatible with that theology without any philosophical argument. He was quite prepared to meet both the integral Aristotelians and the anti-Aristotelians on their own ground, namely on an appeal to reasoning. In so doing he developed philosophy as a separate branch of study, separate, that is, from theology on the one hand and from a mere reporting of the words of Aristotle on the other.

One can say, then, that it was due to the rediscovery of Aristotle coupled with the work of the thirteenth-century theologian-philosophers that mediaeval philosophy attained adult stature. Knowledge of the metaphysical and physical works of Aristotle widened the mediaevals' conception of philosophy, which could no longer be looked upon as more or less equivalent to dialectic.

Aristotelianism was thus a fecundating principle of prime importance in the growth of mediaeval philosophy. It is doubtless regrettable that Aristotelian science, especially Aristotelian astronomy, should have come to be accorded the degree of respect which it won for itself in certain quarters; but this does not alter the fact that Aristotle the philosopher was very far from being a paralysing weight and burden round the necks of the mediaeval thinkers. Without him mediaeval philosophy would scarcely have been able to advance as rapidly as it did. For study of the works of Aristotle not only raised the general standard of philosophic thinking and analysis but also greatly extended the field of study of the mediaeval philosophers. For example, knowledge of Aristotle's psychological and epistemological theories led to a prolonged reflection on these themes. And when Aristotle's general position was accepted, as by St. Thomas, new problems arose or old problems were rendered more acute. For if there are no innate ideas and our ideas are formed in dependence on sense-perception, the question arises, how is metaphysics possible, in so far as metaphysics involves thinking and speaking of beings which transcend matter. And what meaning can be attached to terms descriptive of transcendent beings? St. Thomas was aware of these problems and of their origin and he gave some consideration to them, while Scotus also was aware of the need for providing some theoretical justification of metaphysics. Again it is arguable that Aristotle's 'empiricism' was one of the influences which gave rise in the fourteenth century to lines of criticism which tended to undermine the metaphysical systems which had themselves been built on Aristotle's ideas. In fine, whatever one's estimation of the value of Aristotle's theories may be, it is hardly possible to deny the fact that the mediaevals' knowledge of his philosophy acted as a most powerful and wide-ranging influence in stimulating philosophic thought in the Middle Ages. When his ideas came to have a deadening effect on thought, this was due simply to the fact that the living and creative movement of thought which had originally been stimulated by his writings had spent itself, for the time being at least.

But if one emphasizes the importance of Aristotelianism for mediaeval philosophy, one must also remember that the theologian-philosophers of the thirteenth century deepened it considerably from the metaphysical point of view. Aristotle himself was concerned to explain the *how* of the world, that is to say, certain features of the world, especially change or becoming or 'movement'. With a philosopher like St. Thomas, however, there was a shift of emphasis: the problem of the *that* of the world, the problem that is, of the existence of finite beings, became primary. It is perfectly true, of course, as M. Gilson has shown with his customary lucidity, that the Judaeo-Christian doctrine of creation directed attention to this subject; and this obviously took place long before the time of St. Thomas. But the latter gave expression to the primacy of this problem for the Christian metaphysician in his theory of the distinction between essence and existence (or rather in his use of the distinction, since he did not invent it). It is possible, therefore, to call the philosophy of St. Thomas an 'existential' philosophy in a sense in which one can hardly call Aristotle's philosophy 'existential'.

3. The mediaevals always had some knowledge of the Aristotelian logic. And at the time when philosophy meant for most people little more than logic or dialectic it was perfectly understandable that philosophy should be widely regarded as being, in a famous phrase, 'the handmaid of theology'. Logic, according to Aristotle's own view, is an instrument of reasoning, and in the early Middle Ages there was not very much outside the theological sphere to which this instrument could be applied. Although, then, a distinction was drawn between faith and reason, that is, between truths accepted on authority and believed by faith and truths which were accepted as the result of demonstration, the problem of the relation of philosophy to theology was not acute. But when the Aristotelian system as a whole became known in the Christian universities the province of philosophy was extended far beyond the sphere of dialectic. The rise of natural or philosophic theology (which had, of course, its roots in the writings of St. Anselm) and of natural philosophy or cosmology, together with metaphysical psychology, introduced the idea of philosophy as a branch of study distinct from theology and from what would now be called 'science'. It followed, therefore, that Christian thinkers had to give their attention to the proper relation of philosophy to theology.

St. Thomas's views on this matter have been outlined in the second volume of this history, and I do not propose to repeat them here. Let it be sufficient to recall that he gave a charter to philosophy and recognized its intrinsic independence. Naturally, St. Thomas, as a believing Christian, was convinced that a philosophic theory which was incompatible with Christianity was false, for he was far from entertaining the absurd idea that two contradictory propositions could be true at the same time. But, given the truth of Christianity, he was convinced that it could always be shown that a philosophic proposition which was incompatible with Christianity was the result of bad or specious arguments. Philosophers as individual thinkers might go wrong in their reasoning and contradict revealed truth; but philosophy itself could not do so. There is no such thing as an infallible philosopher; but, if there were, his conclusions would always be in harmony with revealed truth, though he would arrive at his conclusions independently of the data of revelation.

This was, of course, a very tidy and convenient view of the relation of philosophy to theology. But one must remark in addition that according to St. Thomas the metaphysician, while unable to demonstrate the revealed mysteries of Christianity, like the Trinity, is able to demonstrate or establish with certainty the 'preambles of faith', such as the existence of a God capable of revealing truths to men. In the fourteenth century, however, as we have seen in the first part of the present volume, a number of philosophers began to question the validity of proofs which St. Thomas had accepted as valid proofs of the 'preambles of faith', that is, as demonstrations of the rational foundations of faith. Their right to criticize any given proof could hardly be questioned legitimately; for analysis and criticism are essential to philosophy. If a philosopher thought, for example, that the principle *omne quod movetur ab alio movetur* could not bear the weight laid on it in St. Thomas's first argument for God's existence, he had every right to say so. On the other hand, if a philosopher questioned the validity of all the proofs for God's existence, it was hardly possible to maintain the close relation between philosophy and theology asserted by St. Thomas, and the problems of the rationality of faith became acute. But no really serious consideration was given to this problem in the fourteenth century. A theologian-philosopher like William of Ockham could question the validity of metaphysical proofs for God's existence without going on to inquire seriously either what the true nature of arguments for God's existence is or what is the rational ground of our belief in God if His existence cannot be demonstrated in the traditional manner. Partly because so many of the leading 'nominalists' were themselves theologians, partly because the general mental background was still provided by Christianity, and partly because the attention of many philosophers was absorbed in logical and analytic problems (and, in Ockham's case, in political and ecclesiastical polemics) the problems raised by the nominalist criticism of traditional metaphysics were not fully grasped or sufficiently discussed. Theology and philosophy were tending to fall apart, but the fact was not clearly recognized.

4. In the first part of the present volume we saw how the *via moderna* spread in the fourteenth and fifteenth centuries. We also saw how in the fourteenth century there were anticipations at least of a new scientific outlook, which developed with striking rapidity at the time of the Renaissance. If the pre-Socratic philosophers discovered Nature, in the sense that they formed the idea of a cosmos or law-governed system, the Renaissance scientists discovered Nature in the sense that they developed the use of scientific method in the discovery of the 'laws' which actually govern natural events. To speak of laws governing Nature may well be open to objection; but the point is not that this or that language was used at the time or that this or that language ought to be used but rather that the Renaissance scientists developed the scientific study of Nature in a way in which it had never been developed before. This meant that physical science attained adult stature. It may have been often known as 'natural philosophy' or 'experimental philosophy', but, terminology apart, the fact remains that through the work of the Renaissance scientists science came to occupy a place of its own alongside theology and philosophy. And with the growth of modern science a great change has gradually taken place in the common estimation of what 'knowledge' is. In the Middle Ages theology and philosophy were universally regarded as 'sciences'; the great figures in university life were the theologians and the philosophers; and it was they who in general estimation were the possessors of knowledge. In the course of time, however, scientific knowledge in the modern sense has come to be popularly regarded as the norm and standard of knowledge; and in many countries neither theologians nor philosophers would be commonly regarded as possessing 'knowledge' in the sense in which scientists are thought to possess it. This attitude towards knowledge has arisen only gradually, of course, and its growth has been fostered by the development of applied and technical science. But the plain fact is that whereas in the Middle Ages philosophy was to all intents and purposes the sole representative of 'scientific'

knowledge outside the sphere of theology, in the post-Renaissance world rival claimants have arisen which in the estimation of many people have wrested from philosophy the title to represent knowledge at all. To mention this view of the matter in connection with Renaissance science is, of course, to anticipate, and it would be inappropriate to discuss the matter at length here. But I have mentioned it in order to show the great importance of the scientific development of the Renaissance period or, rather, one of the ways in which it was important for philosophy. If one can find in the rediscovery of Aristotle a dividing-line in mediaeval philosophy, one can also find in the growth of Renaissance science a dividing-line in the history of European thought.

In view of the fact that the older histories of philosophy were inclined to neglect mediaeval philosophy, of which they knew little, and practically to jump from Aristotle to Descartes, later historians have very rightly emphasized the continuity between Greek philosophy and Christian thought and between mediaeval philosophy and that of the post-Renaissance period. That Descartes, for example, was dependent on Scholasticism for many of his philosophical categories and ideas, that the mediaeval theory of natural law was utilized by Hooker and passed from him in a diluted form to Locke, and that the latter was more dependent on Aristotelianism than he probably realized are now matters of common knowledge among historians. But it is, I think, a mistake so to emphasize the element of continuity that the elements of novelty and change are slurred over. The climate of thought in the post-Renaissance world was not the same as that prevailing in the Middle Ages. The change was due, of course, to a number of different factors working together; but the rise of science was certainly not the least important of those factors. The development of science made it much easier than it formerly had been to consider the world from a point of view which had no obvious connection with theology. If one compares, for instance, St. Bonaventure or even St. Thomas with a philosopher like Descartes one finds at once a considerable difference of outlook and interest, in spite of the fact that all three men were believing Catholics. St. Bonaventure was principally interested in creatures in their relationship to God, as *vestigia Dei*, or in man's case, as the *imago Dei*. St. Thomas, owing to his Aristotelianism, shows a greater interest in creatures from a purely philosophical point of view; but he was above all things a theologian and it is obvious that his primary interest was that of a theologian and a specifically Christian thinker. In the case of Descartes, however, we find an outlook which, though it was the attitude of a man who was a Christian, was what one may call 'neutral' in character. In the post-Renaissance period there were, of course, philosophers who were atheists or at any rate non-Christian: one has only to think of some of the figures of the French Enlightenment. But my point is that after the Middle Ages philosophy tended to become 'lay' in character. A man like Descartes was certainly a good Christian; but one would hardly think of his philosophy as a specifically Christian philosophy, in spite of the influence of his religious beliefs on his philosophic thought. The rise of humanism at the time of the Renaissance, followed by the growth of science, produced fresh interests and lines of thought which, though not necessarily incompatible with theology, could be pursued without any obvious association with or relation to it. This is clear enough in the case of science itself, and the growth of science reacted on philosophy. Or perhaps it is better to say that both the science and the philosophy of the time manifested the growth of the new outlook and fostered it.

But if one stresses the difference between the mediaeval and Renaissance worlds in the climate of thought, it is necessary to qualify this emphasis by drawing attention to the gradual and in large part continuous evolution of the new outlook. A comparatively early mediaeval thinker like St. Anselm was chiefly interested in understanding the faith: for him the primacy of faith was obvious, and what we might call his philosophizing was largely an attempt to understand by the use of reason what we believe. *Credo, ut intelligam.* In the thirteenth century the rediscovery of Aristotelianism greatly widened the interests and horizons of Christian thinkers. Acceptance of Aristotle's physics, however erroneous many of his scientific theories may have been, paved the way for a study of the world for its own sake so to speak. A professional theologian like St. Thomas was naturally not interested in developing what we would call science, not because of any hostility towards such studies but because his interests lay elsewhere. But by the rediscovery of Aristotle and the translations of Greek and Arabic scientific works the ground was prepared for scientific advance. Already in the thirteenth century, and still more in the fourteenth century, we can see the beginning of a scientific investigation of Nature. The ferment of Renaissance philosophy, with its mixture of philosophic speculation and scientific hypothesis, further prepared the way for the rise of Renaissance science. One can say, then, that the rediscovery of Aristotle in the Middle Ages was the remote preparation for the rise of science. But one can, of course, go further still and say that the Christian doctrine of the world's creation by God provided a theological preparation for the advance of science. For if the world is a creation, and if matter is not evil but good, the material world is obviously worth scientific investigation. But scientific investigation could not develop until the right method was found; and for that Christian Europe had to wait many centuries.

The foregoing remarks may possibly sound like an endorsement of Auguste Comte's doctrine of the three stages, as though I meant to say that the theological stage was followed by the philosophical and the philosophical by the scientific stage, in the sense that the later stage supplanted the former, both *de facto* and *de iure*. In regard to the historical facts it has been argued that the development of Greek thought proceeded in the very opposite direction to that demanded by Comte's theory.[1] For the movement was from a primitive 'scientific' stage through metaphysics to theology, rather than from theology through metaphysics to science. However, the development of thought in western Christianity can be used to a certain extent in support of Comte's theory, in so far as the historical facts are concerned. For it might be argued that the primacy of theology was succeeded by a stage characterized by 'lay' philosophical systems, and that this stage has been succeeded by a positivist stage. An interpretation of this sort is certainly open to the objection that it is based on aspects of the development of thought which have been selected in order to support a preconceived theory. For it is clear that the development of Scholastic philosophy did not simply follow the development of Scholastic theology: to a great extent the two developed together. Again, the rise of science in the post-Renaissance world was contemporaneous with a succession of philosophic systems. However, it does seem that at any rate a plausible case can be made out in favour of Comte's interpretation of western thought since the beginning of Christianity. It makes some sense at least to distinguish the Age of Faith, the Age of Reason and the Age of Science, if one is speaking of climates of thought. In the Middle

---

[1] On this subject *The Christian Challenge to Philosophy* by W. H. V. Reade (London, 1951) can profitably be consulted.

Ages religious faith and theology shaped the climate of thought; at the time of the 'Enlightenment' wide sections of the intellectual public placed their trust in 'reason' (though the use of the word 'reason' in this connection stands in need of careful analysis); and in the modern world a positivist climate of thought prevails in a number of countries if one understands 'positivist' and 'positivism' in a wide sense. Yet even if a plausible case can be made out for Comte's theory from the historical point of view, it certainly does not follow that the succession of stages, in so far as there actually was a succession of stages, constitutes a 'progress' in any but a temporal sense of the word 'progress'. In one period theology may be the paramount branch of study and in another period science; but a change in the climate of thought from a theological to a scientific period does not mean that theology is false or that a scientific civilization is an adequate realization of the potentialities of human culture.

It is, however, fairly obvious now that science cannot disprove the validity of faith or of theological beliefs. Physics, for example, has nothing to say about the Trinity or about the existence of God. If many people have ceased to believe in Christianity, this does not show that Christianity is false. And, in general, the relation of science to religion and theology is not one of acute tension: the tension which in the last century was often alleged to exist between them does not really exist at all. The theoretical difficulty arises rather in regard to the relation of philosophy to theology. And this tension existed in germ once philosophy had attained to adult stature. It did not become obvious as long as the leading philosophers were also theologians; but once the rise of science had directed men's thought in fresh directions and philosophers were no longer primarily theologians the tension was bound to become apparent. As long as philosophers thought that they were able to build up a true metaphysical system by a method of their own, the tension tended to take the form of a tension between divergent conclusions and propositions. But now that a considerable number of philosophers believe that the philosopher has no method of his own the employment of which is capable of adding to human knowledge, and that all factual knowledge is derivable from immediate observation and from the sciences, the problem is rather one concerning the rational foundations of faith. In this sense we are back in the situation created in the fourteenth century by the nominalist criticism of traditional metaphysics, though the nature of the problem is clearer now than it was then. Is there such a thing as a valid metaphysical argument? Can there be metaphysical knowledge and, if so, what sort of knowledge is it? Have we 'blind' faith on the one hand and scientific knowledge on the other, or can metaphysics supply a kind of bridge between them? Questions of this sort were implicit in fourteenth-century nominalist criticism, and they are still with us. They have been rendered all the more acute, on the one hand by the constant growth of scientific knowledge since the time of the Renaissance and, on the other hand, by the succession of metaphysical systems in the post-Renaissance and modern worlds, leading to a prevailing mistrust of metaphysics in general. What is the rôle of philosophy? What is its proper relation to science? What is its proper relation to faith and religious belief?

These questions cannot be further developed or discussed now. My object in raising them is simply that of suggesting various points for reflection in considering the later development of philosophic thought. In the next volume I hope to treat of 'modern' philosophy from Descartes to Kant inclusive, and in connection with Kant we shall be faced with an explicit statement regarding these questions and their solution.

APPENDIX I

Honorific titles applied to philosophers treated of in this volume.

DURANDUS:	Doctor modernus, *later* Doctor resolutissimus.
PETRUS AUREOLI:	Doctor facundus.
WILLIAM OF OCKHAM:	Venerabilis inceptor.
ANTOINE ANDRÉ:	Doctor dulcifluus
FRANCIS DE MARCIA:	Doctor succinctus.
JOHN OF MIRECOURT:	Monachus albus.
GREGORY OF RIMINI:	Doctor authenticus.
JOHN RUYSBROECK:	Doctor admirabilis.
DENIS THE CARTHUSIAN:	Doctor ecstaticus.
JOHN GERSON:	Doctor christianissimus.
JAKOB BÖHME:	Philosophus teutonicus.
FRANCIS SUÁREZ:	Doctor eximius.

APPENDIX II
A SHORT BIBLIOGRAPHY
General Works

Boehner, Ph., O.F.M. *Medieval Logic.* Manchester, 1952.
Bréhier, E. *La philosophie du moyen âge*, nouvelle édition corrigée. Paris, 1949.
  Histoire de la philosophie. tome 1, *L'antiquité et le moyen âge.* Paris, 1943. (A treatment of Renaissance philosophy is included in this volume.)
Burckhardt, J. *The Civilization of the Renaissance.* London, 1944.
Carlyle, R. W. and A. J. *A History of Mediaeval Political Theory in the West.* 6 vols. London, 1903–36.
Cassirer, E. *Individuum und Kosmos in der Philosophie der Renaissance.* Berlin, 1927.
Copleston, F. C. *Mediaeval Philosophy.* London, 1952.
Crombie, A. C. *Augustine to Galileo. The History of Science, A.D. 400–1650.* London, 1952. (Unfortunately this work appeared when the present volume was already in proof.)
Curtis, S. J. *A Short History of Western Philosophy in the Middle Ages.* London, 1950.
Dempf, A. *Die Ethik des Mittelalters.* Munich, 1930.
  Metaphysik des Mittelalters. Munich, 1930.
De Wulf, M. *Histoire de la philosophie médiévale.* tome 3, *Aprés le treizième siècle.* Louvain, 1947 (6th edition).
Dilthey, W. *Gesammelte Schriften*, vol. 2 (for Renaissance). Berlin and Leipzig, 1919.
Frischeisen-Köhler, M. and Moog, W. *Die Philosophie der Neuzeit bis zum Ende des XVIII Jahrhunderts.* Berlin, 1924. (This is the third volume of the revised Ueberweg and covers the Renaissance period.)
Geyer, B. *Die patristische und scholastische Philosophie.* Berlin, 1928. (This is the second volume of the revised edition of Ueberweg.)
Gilson, É. *La philosophie au moyen âge.* Paris, 1944. (2nd edition, revised and augmented.)
  The Unity of Philosophical Experience. London, 1938.
  Being and Some Philosophers. Toronto, 1949.
  L'être et l'essence. Paris, 1948.
Grabmann, M. *Die Philosophie des Mittelalters.* Berlin, 1921.
  Mittelalterliches Geistesleben. 2 vols. Munich, 1926 and 1936.

A SHORT BIBLIOGRAPHY

Hauréau, B. *Histoire de la Philosophie scolastique.* 3 vols. Paris, 1872-80.

Hawkins, D. J. B. *A Sketch of Mediaeval Philosophy.* London, 1946.

Hirschberger, J. *Geschichte der Philosophie. I, Altertum und Mittelalter.* Freiburg i. B., 1949.

Picavet, F. *Esquisse d'une histoire générale et comparée des philosophies médiévales.* Paris, 1907 (2nd edition).
Essais sur l'histoire générale et comparée des théologies et des philosophies médiévales. Paris, 1913.

Poole, R. L. *Illustrations of the History of Medieval Thought and Learning.* London, 1920 (2nd edition).

Romeyer, B. *La philosophie chrétienne jusqu'à Descartes.* 3 vols. Paris, 1935-7.

Ruggiero, G. de. *La filosofia del Cristianesimo.* 3 vols. Bari.
Rinascimento, Riforma e Contrariforma. Bari, 1937.

Vignaux, P. *La pensée au moyen âge.* Paris, 1938.

Chapter II: Durandus and Petrus Aureoli

Texts

Durandus

In 4 libros Sententiarum. Various sixteenth-century editions (of 3rd redaction), beginning with the Paris edition of 1508.

Durandi de S. Porciano O.P. Quaestio de natura cognitionis et Disputatio cum anonymo quodam necnon Determinatio Hervaei Natalis O.P. J. Koch (edit.). Münster, 1929; 2nd edition 1929 (Opuscula et textus, 6).

Durandus de S. Porciano, Tractatus de habitibus. Quaestio 4: De subiectis habituum, addita quaestione critica anonymi cuiusdam. J. Koch (edit.). Münster, 1930 (Opuscula et textus, 8).

Petrus Aureoli

In 4 libros Sententiarum. Rome, 1596.

Studies

Dreiling, R. *Der Konzeptualismus in der Universalienfrage des Franziskanererzbischofs Petrus Aureoli (Pierre d'Auriole).* Münster, 1913 (Beiträge, 11, 6.)

Koch, J. *Jakob von Metz, O.P.* Archives d'histoire doctrinale et littéraire du moyen âge, 1929-30 (pp. 169-232).
Durandus de Sancto Porciano O.P. Forschungen zum Streit um Thomas von Aquin zu Beginn des 14 Jahrhunderts, Erster Teil, Literargeschichtliche Grundlegung. Münster, 1927 (Beiträge 26, 1).

Kraus, J. *Die Universalienlehre des Oxforder Kanzlers Heinrich von Harclay in ihrer Mittelstellung zwischen skotistischen Realismus und ockhamistischen Nominalismus.* Divus Thomas (Fribourg, Switzerland), vol. 10 (1932), pp. 36-58 and 475-508 and vol. 11 (1933), pp. 288-314.

Pelster, F. *Heinrich von Harclay, Kanzler von Oxford, und seine Quästionen.* Miscellanea F. Ehrle, vol. 1, pp. 307-56. Rome, 1924.

Teetaert, A. *Pierre Auriol.* Dictionnaire de théologie catholique, vol. 12, cols. 1810-81. Paris, 1934.

Chapters III–VIII: William of Ockham

Texts

Super quattuor libros sententiarum subtilissimae quaestiones. Lyons, 1495.

Quodlibeta septem. Paris, 1487; Strasbourg, 1491.

Expositio aurea et admodum utilis super artem veterem. Bologna, 1496.

Summa totius logicae. Paris, 1948, and other editions, especially: *Summa Logicae. Pars prima.* Ph. Boehner, O.F.M. (edit.). St. Bonaventure, New York, and Louvain, 1951.

Summulae in libros Physicorum. Bologna, 1495 and other editions.

Quaestio prima principalis Prologi in primum librum sententiarum cum interpretatione Gabrielis Biel. Ph. Boehner, O.F.M. (edit.). Paderborn, 1939.

The Tractatus de successivis, attributed to William Ockham. Ph. Boehner, O.F.M. (edit.). St. Bonaventure (New York), 1944.

The Tractatus de praedestinatione et de praescientia Dei et de futuris contingentibus of William Ockham. Ph. Boehner, O.F.M. (edit.). St. Bonaventure (New York), 1945. (This edition also contains a 'Study on the Mediaeval Problem of a Three-valued logic' by the editor.)

Ockham: Selected Philosophical Writings. Ph. Boehner, O.F.M. (edit.). London, 1952.

Gulielmi de Occam Breviloquium de potestate papae (critical edition). L. Baudry (edit.). Paris, 1937.

Gulielmi de Ockham Opera politica, vol. 1. J. O. Sikes (edit.). Manchester, 1940.

Studies

Abbagnano, N. *Guglielmo di Ockham.* Lanciano, 1931.

Amann, E. *Occam.* Dictionnaire de théologie catholique, vol. 11, cols. 864-904. Paris, 1931.

Baudry, L. *Guillaume d'Occam. Sa vie, ses œuvres, ses idées sociales et politiques. I, L'homme et les œuvres.* Paris, 1949.

A SHORT BIBLIOGRAPHY 431

Boehner, Ph., O.F.M. *Ockham's Theory of Truth.* Franciscan
Studies, 1945, pp. 138–61.
Ockham's Theory of Signification. Franciscan
Studies, 1946, pp. 143–70.
Carré, H. M. *Realists and Nominalists* (pp. 101–25). Oxford, 1946.
Giacón, C. *Guglielmo di Occam.* 2 vols. Milan, 1941.
Guelluy, R. *Philosophie et théologie chez Guillaume d'Ockham.* Louvain, 1947.
Hamann, A., O.F.M. *La doctrine de l'église et de l'état chez Occam.* Paris, 1942.
Hochstetter, E. *Studien zur Metaphysik und Erkenntnislehre des Wilhelms von Ockham.* Berlin, 1937.
Lagarde, G. de *Naissance de l'esprit laïque au déclin du moyen âge.* Cahier IV: *Ockham et son temps.* 1942.
V: *Ockham. Bases de départ.* 1946.
VI: *Ockham. La morale et le droit.* 1946.
Martin, G. *Wilhelm von Ockham. Untersuchungen zur Ontologie der Ordnungen.* Berlin, 1949.
Moody, E. A. *The Logic of William of Ockham.* London, 1935.
Vignaux, P. *Nominalisme.* Dictionnaire de théologie catholique, vol. 11, cols. 748–84. Paris, 1931.
Zuidema, S. U. *De Philosophie van Occam in zijn Commentaar op de Sententiën.* 2 vols. Hilversum, 1936.

Chapter IX: The Ockhamist Movement: John of Mirecourt and Nicholas of Autrecourt.

Texts

John of Mirecourt
Birkenmaier, A. *Ein Rechtfertigungsschreiben Johanns von Mirecourt.* Münster, 1922 (Beiträge, 20, 5).
Stegmüller, F. *Die zwei Apologien des Jean de Mirecourt.* Recherches de théologie ancienne et médiévale 1933, pp. 40–79, 192–204.
Nicholas of Autrecourt
Lappe, J. *Nikolaus von Autrecourt.* Münster, 1908 (Beiträge, 6, 1). (This contains correspondence between Nicholas and Bernard of Arezzo and between Nicholas and Giles.)
O'Donnell, J. R. *Nicholas of Autrecourt.* Mediaeval Studies, 1 (1939), pp. 179–280. (This contains an edition of the *Exigit.*)

Studies

Lang, A. *Die Wege der Glaubensbegründung bei den Scholastikern des 14 Jahrhunderts.* Münster, 1931 (Beiträge, 30, 1–2).
Lappe, J. See above.

APPENDIX II

Michalski, C. *Les courants philosophiques à Oxford et à Paris pendant le XIVe siècle.* Bulletin de l'Académie polonaise des Sciences et des Lettres, 1920 (separately, Cracow, 1921).
    Les sources du criticisme et du scepticisme dans la philosophie du XIVe siècle. Cracow, 1924.
Michalski, C. *Le criticisme et le scepticisme dans la philosophie du XIVe siècle.* Bulletin de l'Académie polonaise des Sciences et des Lettres, 1925 (separately, Cracow, 1926).
    Les courants critiques et sceptiques dans la philosophie du XIVe siècle. Cracow, 1927.
O'Donnell, J. R. *The Philosophy of Nicholas of Autrecourt and his appraisal of Aristotle.* Mediaeval Studies, 4 (1942) pp. 97–125.
Ritter, G. *Studien zur Spätscholastik*, 2 vols. Heidelberg, 1921–2.
Vignaux, P. *Nominalisme.* Dictionnaire de théologie catholique, vol. II, cols. 748–84. Paris, 1931.
    Nicholas d'Autrecourt, ibid., cols. 561–87.
Weinberg, J. R. *Nicholas of Autrecourt. A Study in 14th-century Thought.* Princeton, 1948.

Chapter X: The Scientific Movement

Texts

Buridan

Johannis Buridani Quaestiones super libros quattuor de coelo et mundo. A. E. Moody (edit.). Cambridge (Mass.), 1942.
Quaestiones super octo libros physicorum Aristotelis. Paris, 1509.
In metaphysicen Aristotelis quaestiones. Paris, 1480, 1518.
Summulae logicae. Lyons, 1487.
Quaestiones et decisiones physicales insignium virorum Alberti de Saxonia, Thimonis, Buridani. Paris, 1516, 1518. (Contains Buridan's *Quaestiones in libros de Anima* and his *Quaestiones* on Aristotle's *Parva naturalia*.)

Albert of Saxony

Quaestiones super artem veterem. Bologna, 1496.
Quaestiones subtilissimae Alberti de Saxonia super libros Posteriorum. Venice, 1497.
Logica. Venice, 1522.
Sophismata Alberti de Saxonia. Paris, 1489.
Quaestiones in libros de coelo et mundo. Pavia, 1481.
Subtilissimae quaestiones super octo libros physicorum. Padua, 1493.
Quaestiones in libros de generatione (contained in work mentioned last under *Buridan*).

Marsilius of Inghen
Quaestiones Marsilii super quattuor libros sententiarum. Strasbourg, 1501.
Abbreviationes super VIII libros. Venice, 1521.
Egidius cum Marsilio et Alberto de generatione. Venice, 1518.

Nicholas of Oresme
Maistre Nicole Oresme: Le livre du ciel et du monde. A. D. Menut and A. J. Denomy (edit.). Mediaeval Studies, 1941 (pp. 185-280), 1942 (pp. 159-297), 1943 (pp. 167-333). (This Text and Commentary has been published separately. Date unstated.)

Studies
Bochert, E. *Die Lehre von der Bewegung bei Nicolaus Oresme.* Münster, 1934 (Beiträge, 31, 3).
Duhem, P. *Le syèstme du monde: histoire des doctrines cosmologiques de Platon à Copernic.* 5 vols. Paris, 1913-17.
    Études sur Léonard de Vinci. 3 vols. Paris, 1906-13.
Haskins, C. H. *Studies in the History of Mediaeval Science.* Cambridge (Mass.), 1924.
Heidingsfelder, G. *Albert von Sachsen.* Münster, 1926 (Beiträge 22, 3-4).
Maier, A. *Das Problem der intensiven Grösse in der Scholastik.* Leipzig, 1939.
    Die Impetustheorie der Scholastik. Vienna, 1940.
    An der Grenzen von Scholastik und Naturwissenschaft. Studien zur Naturphilosophie des 14 Jahrhunderts. Essen, 1943.
    Die Vorläufer Galileis im 14 Jahrhundert. Rome, 1949.
Michalski, C. *La physique nouvelle et les différents courants philosophiques au XIVe siècle.* Bulletin de l'Académie polonaise des Sciences et des Lettres, 1927 (separately, Cracow, 1928).
Moody, E. A. *John Buridan and the Habitability of the Earth.* Speculum, 1941, pp. 415-25.
Ritter, G. *Studien zur Spätscholastik.* Vol 1, *Marsilius von Inghen und die okkamistische Schule in Deutschland.* Heidelberg, 1921.
Sarton, G. *Introduction to the History of Science.* 3 vols. Washington, 1927-48.
Thorndike, L. *A History of Magic and Experimental Science.* Vols. 3-4, *The fourteenth and fifteenth centuries.* New York, 1934.

Chapter XI: Marsilius of Padua
Texts
The Defensor Pacis of Marsilius of Padua. C. W. Previté-Orton (edit.). Cambridge, 1928.

Marsilius von Padua, Defensor Pacis. R. Scholz (edit.). Hannover, 1933.

Studies

Checchini, A. and Bobbio, N. (edit.). *Marsilio da Padova, Studi raccolti nel VI centenario della morte.* Padua, 1942.

Gewirth, A. *Marsilius of Padua. The Defender of Peace.* Vol. 1, *Marsilius of Padua and Medieval Political Philosophy.* New York, 1951.

Lagarde, G. de *Naissance de l'esprit laïque au déclin du moyen âge.* Cahier II: *Marsile de Padoue.* Paris, 1948.

Previté-Orton, C. W. *Marsiglio of Padua.* Part II: *Doctrines.* English Historical Review, 1923, pp. 1-18.

Chapter XII: Speculative Mysticism

Texts

Eckhart

Meister Eckhart. Die deutschen und lateinischen Werke herausgegeben im Auftrage der Deutschen Forschungsgemeinschaft. Stuttgart, 1936 (in course of publication).

Magistri Eckhardi Opera latina auspiciis Instituti Sanctae Sabinae ad codicum fidem edita. Leipzig.

I. *Super oratione dominica.* R. Klibansky (edit.). 1934.

II. *Opus tripartitum: Prologi.* H. Bascour, O.S.B. (edit.). 1935.

III. *Quaestiones Parisienses.* A. Dondaine, O.P. (edit.). 1936.

Eine lateinische Rechtfertigungsschrift des Meister Eckhart. A. Daniels (edit.). Münster, 1923 (Beiträge, 23, 5).

Meister Eckhart. Das System seiner religiösen Lehre und Lebensweisheit. Textbuch aus den gedrückten und ungedrückten Quellen mit Einführung. O. Karrer (edit.). Munich, 1926.

Tauler

Die Predigten Taulers. F. Vetter (edit.). Berlin, 1910.

Sermons de Tauler. 3 vols. E. Hugueny, P. Théry and A. L. Corin (edit.). Paris, 1927, 1930, 1935.

Bl. Henry Suso

Heinrich Seuse. Deutsche Schriften. K. Bihlmeyer (edit.). 2 vols. Stuttgart, 1907.

L'œuvre mystique de Henri Suso. Introduction et traduction. 4 vols. B. Lavaud, O.P. Fribourg, Switzerland, 1946-7.

Blessed Henry Suso's Little Book of Eternal Wisdom. R. Raby (translator). London, 1866 (2nd edition).

The Life of Blessed Henry Suso by Himself. T. F. Knox (translator). London, 1865.

Ruysbroeck

Jan van Ruusbroec. Werke. Nach der Standardschrift von Groenendal herausgegeben von der Ruusbroec—Gesellschaft in Antwerpen. 2nd edition. 4 vols. Cologne, 1950.

Gerson

Johannis Gersonii opera omnia. 5 vols. M. E. L. Du Pin (edit.). Antwerp, 1706.

Jean Gerson, Commentateur Dionysien. Les Notulae super quaedam verba Dionysii de Caelesti Hierarchia. A. Combes. Paris, 1940.

Six Sermons français inédits de Jean Gerson. L. Mourin (edit.). Paris, 1946.

Studies

Bernhart, J. *Die philosophische Mystik des Mittelalters von ihren antiken Ursprungen bis zur Renaissance.* Munich, 1922.

Bizet, J. A. *Henri Suso et le déclin de la scolastique.* Paris, 1946.

Brigué, L. *Ruysbroeck.* Dictionnaire de théologie catholique, vol. 14, cols. 408–20. Paris, 1938.

Bühlmann, J. *Christuslehre und Christusmystik des Heinrich Seuse.* Lucerne, 1942.

Combes, A. *Jean de Montreuil et le chancelier Gerson.* Paris, 1942.

Connolly, J. L. *John Gerson, Reformer and Mystic.* Louvain, 1928.

Della Volpe, G. *Il misticismo speculativo di maestro Eckhart nei suoi rapporti storici.* Bologna, 1930.

Dempf, A. *Meister Eckhart. Eine Einführung in sein Werk.* Leipzig, 1934.

Denifle, H. *Das geistliche Leben. Deutsche Mystiker des 14 Jahrhunderts.* Salzburg, 1936 (9th edition by A. Auer).

Hornstein, X. de *Les grands mystiques allemands du XIVe siècle. Eckhart, Tauler, Suso.* Lucerne, 1920.

Wautier D'Aygalliers, A. *Ruysbroeck l'Admirable.* Paris, 1923.

Chapter XIII: The Revival of Platonism

Texts

Erasmus. *Opera.* 10 vols. Leyden, 1703–6.

Letters. Latin edition by P. S. Allen, H. S. Allen, H. W. Garrod. 11 vols. Oxford, 1906–47.

Leone Ebreo. *The Philosophy of Love.* F. Friedeberg-Sealey and J. H. Barnes (translators). London, 1937.

Marsilii Ficini Opera. 2 vols. Paris, 1641.

Pico della Mirandola, G. *Opera omnia.* 2 vols. Basle, 1573.
The Renaissance Philosophy of Man (Petrarca, Valla, Ficino, Pico, Pomponazzi, Vives). E. Cassirer, P. O. Kristeller, J. H. Randall, Jr. (edit.). Chicago, 1948.

Studies

Burckhardt, J. *The Civilization of the Renaissance.* London, 1944.
Della Torre, A. *Storia dell' academia platonica di Firenze.* Florence, 1902.
Dress, W. *Die Mystik des Marsilio Ficino.* Berlin, 1929.
Dulles, A. *Princeps concordiae. Pico della Mirandola and the Scholastic Tradition.* Cambridge (Mass.), 1941.
Festugière, J. *La philosophie de l'amour de Marsile Ficin.* Paris, 1941.
Garin, E. *Giovanni Pico della Mirandola.* Florence, 1937.
Gentile, G. *Il pensiero italiano del rinascimento.* Florence, 1940 (3rd edit.).
Hak, H. *Marsilio Ficino.* Amsterdam, Paris, 1934.
Hönigswald, R. *Denker der italienischen Renaissance. Gestalten und Probleme.* Basle, 1938.
Taylor, H. O. *Thought and Expression in the Sixteenth Century.* New York, 1920.
Trinkaus, C. E. *Adversity's Noblemen: The Italian Humanists on Happiness.* New York, 1940.
Woodward, W. H. *Studies in Education during the Age of the Renaissance.* Cambridge, 1906.

Chapter XIV: Aristotelianism

Texts

Laurentius Valla. *Dialecticae disputationes contra Aristotelicos,* 1499. (*Opera.* Basle, 1540.)
Rudolf Agricola. *De inventione dialectica.* Louvain, 1515; and other editions.
Marius Nizolius. *De veris principiis et vera ratione philosophandi contra pseudophilosophos libri IV.* Parma, 1553 (edited by Leibniz under the title *Antibarbarus philosophicus,* Frankfurt, 1671 and 1674).
Petrus Ramus. *Dialecticae partitiones.* Paris, 1543.
    Aristotelicae animadversiones. Paris, 1543.
    Dialectique. Paris, 1555.
Alexander Achillini. *De universalibus.* Bologna, 1501.
    De intelligentiis. Venice, 1508.
    De distinctionibus. Bologna, 1518.

Pietro Pomponazzi. *Opera.* Basle, 1567.
Melanchthon. *Opera.* C. G. Bretschneider and H. E. Bindseil (edit.).
  28 vols. Halle, 1824-60.
   Supplementa Melanchthonia. Leipzig, 1910– .
Montaigne. *Essais.* Numerous editions, the most complete being by
  F. Strowski, P. Gebelin and P. Villey (5 vols.), 1906-33.
Sanchez. *Tractatus philosophici.* Rotterdam, 1649.

Studies

Batistella, R. M. *Nizolio.* Treviso, 1905.
Cassirer, E., Kristeller, P. O. and Randall, J. H. (edit.). *The Renaissance Philosophy of Man (Petrarca, Valla, Ficino, Pico, Pomponazzi, Vives).* Chicago, 1948.
Douglas, C. and Hardie, R. P. *The Philosophy and Psychology of Pietro Pomponazzi.* Cambridge, 1910.
Friedrich, H. *Montaigne.* Berne, 1949.
Giarratano, C. *Il pensiero di Francesco Sanchez.* Naples, 1903.
Graves, F. P. *Peter Ramus and the Educational Reformation of the 16th Century.* London, 1912.
Hönigswald, R. *Denker der italienischen Renaissance. Gestalten und Probleme.* Basle, 1938.
Moreau, P. *Montaigne, l'homme et l'œuvre.* Paris, 1939.
Owen, J. *The Sceptics of the Italian Renaissance.* London, 1893.
Petersen, P. *Geschichte der aristotelischen Philosophie im protestantischen Deutschland.* Leipzig, 1921.
Revista Portuguesa de Filosofia (1951; t. 7, fasc. 2). *Francisco Sanchez no IV Centenário do seu nascimento.* Braga, 1951. (Contains Bibliography of writings about Sanchez.)
Strowski, F. *Montaigne.* Paris, 1906.
Waddington, C. *De Petri Rami vita, scriptis, philosophia.* Paris, 1849.
   Ramus, sa vie, ses écrits et ses opinions. Paris, 1855.

Chapter XV: Nicholas of Cusa

Texts

Nicolai de Cusa Opera Omnia iussu et auctoritate Academiae Heidelbergensis ad codicum fidem edita. Leipzig, 1932– .
Opera. 3 vols. Paris, 1514. Basle, 1565.
Schriften, im Auftrag der Heidelberger Akademie der Wissenschaften in deutscher Uebersetzung herausgegeben von E. Hoffmann. Leipzig, 1936– .
Philosophische Schriften. A. Petzelt (edit.). Vol. 1, Stuttgart, 1949.
De docta ignorantia libri tres. Testo latino con note di Paolo Rotta. Bari, 1913.

The Idiot. San Francisco, 1940.
Des Cardinals und Bischofs Nikolaus von Cusa wichtigste Schriften in deutscher Uebersetzung. F. A. Scharpff. Freiburg i. B., 1862.

Studies

Bett, H. *Nicholas of Cusa.* London, 1932.
Clemens, F. J. *Giordano Bruno und Nicolaus von Cues.* Bonn, 1847.
Gandillac, M. de *La philosophie de Nicolas de Cues.* Paris, 1941.
Gradi, R. *Il pensiero del Cusano.* Padua, 1941.
Jacobi, M. *Das Weltgebäude des Kard. Nikolaus von Cusa.* Berlin, 1904.
Koch, J. *Nicolaus von Cues und seine Umwelt.* 1948.
Mennicken, P. *Nikolaus von Kues.* Trier, 1950.
Rotta, P. *Il cardinale Niccolò di Cusa, la vita ed il pensiero.* Milan, 1928.
    Niccolò Cusano. Milan, 1942.
Schultz, R. *Die Staatsphilosophie des Nikolaus von Kues.* Hain, 1948.
Vansteenberghe, E. *Le cardinal Nicolas de Cues.* Paris, 1920.
    Autour de la docte ignorance. Münster, 1915 (Beiträge, 14, 2–4).

Chapters XVI–XVII: Philosophy of Nature

Texts

Cardano. *Hieronymi Cardani Mediolanensis philosophi et medici celeberrimi opera omnia.* 10 vols. Lyons, 1663.
Telesio. *De natura rerum iuxta propria principia.* Naples, 1586.
Patrizzi. *Discussiones peripateticae.* Basle, 1581.
    Nova de universis philosophia. London, 1611.
Campanella. *Philosophia sensibus demonstrata.* Naples, 1590.
    Prodromus philosophiae. Padua, 1611.
    Atheismus triumphatus. Rome, 1630.
    La città del sole. A Castaldo (edit.). Rome, 1910.
Bruno. *Opere italiane.* G. Gentile (edit.). Bari.
    I. *Dialoghi metafisici.* 1907
    II. *Dialoghi morali.* 1908.
    Opera latine conscripta. I & II. Naples, 1880 and 1886.
    III & IV. Florence, 1889 and 1891.
S. Greenberg. *The Infinite in G. Bruno. With a translation of Bruno's Dialogue: Concerning the Cause, Principle and One.* New York, 1950.
D. W. Singer. *G. Bruno: His Life and Thought. With a translation of*

A SHORT BIBLIOGRAPHY

Bruno's Work: On the Infinite Universe and Worlds. New York, 1950.

Gassendi. *Opera*. Lyons, 1658, Florence, 1727.

Paracelsus. *Four Treatises of Theophrastus von Hohenheim called Paracelsus*. H. E. Sigerist (edit.). Baltimore, 1941.

Paracelsus. *Selected Writings*. Edited with an Introduction by Jolande Jacobi. Translated by Norbert Guterman. London, 1951.

Van Helmont, J. B. *Opera*. Lyons, 1667.

Van Helmont, F. M. *Opuscula philosophica*. Amsterdam, 1690.

The paradoxical discourses of F. M. van Helmont. London, 1685.

Weigel. *Libellus de vita beata*. Halle, 1609.

Der güldene Griff. Halle, 1613.

Vom Ort der Welt. Halle, 1613.

Dialogus de christianismo. Halle, 1614.

Erkenne dich selbst. Neustadt, 1615.

Böhme. *Werke*. 7 vols. K. W. Schiebler (edit.). Leipzig, 1840–7 (2nd edition).

Works. C. J. Barber (edit.). London, 1909– .

Studies

Blanchet, L. *Campanella*. Paris, 1920.

Boulting, W. *Giordano Bruno, His Life, Thought and Martyrdom*. London, 1914.

Cicuttini, L. *Giordano Bruno*. Milan, 1950.

Fiorentino, F. *Telesio, ossia studi storici sull 'idea della natura nel risorgimento italiano*. 2 vols. Florence, 1872–4.

Gentile, G. *Bruno e il pensiero del rinascimento*. Florence, 1920.

Greenberg, S. See under *Texts* (Bruno).

Hönigswald, R. *Denker der italienischen Renaissance. Gestalten und Probleme*. Basle, 1938.

McIntyre, J. L. *Giordano Bruno*. London, 1903.

Peip. A. *Jakob Böhme, der deutsche Philosoph*. Leipzig, 1850.

Penny, A. J. *Studies in Jakob Böhme*. London, 1912.

Introduction to the Study of Jacob Böhme's Writings. New York, 1901.

Sigerist, H. E. *Paracelsus in the Light of Four Hundred Years*. New York, 1941.

Singer, D. W. See under *Texts* (Bruno).

Stillman, J. M. *Theophrastus Bombastus von Hohenheim, called Paracelsus*. Chicago, 1920.

Troilo, E. *La filosofia di Giordano Bruno*. Turin, 1907.

Wessely, J. E. *Thomas Campanellas Sonnenstadt*. Munich, 1900.

Whyte, A. *Jacob Behmen: An Appreciation*. Edinburgh, 1895.

Chapter XVIII: The Scientific Movement of the Renaissance.

Texts

Leonardo da Vinci. *The Literary Works.* J. R. Richter (edit.). Oxford, 1939.
Copernicus. *Gesamtausgabe.* 4 vols.
Tycho Brahe. *Opera omnia.* Prague, 1611, Frankfurt, 1648.
Kepler. *Opera omnia.* 8 vols. Frankfurt, 1858–71.
Galileo. *Opere.* E. Albèri (edit.). Florence, 1842–56.
    Le opere di Galileo Galilei. 20 vols. Florence, 1890–1907.
    Dialogo sopra i due massimi systemi del mondo. Florence, 1632.
    (English translation by T. Salusbury in *Mathematical Collections and Translations.* London, 1661.)
    Dialogues concerning Two New Sciences. H. Crew and A. de Salvio (Translators). Evanston, 1939.

Studies

Aliotta, A. and Carbonara, C. *Galilei.* Milan, 1949.
Armitage, A. *Copernicus, the Founder of Modern Astronomy.* London, 1938.
Burtt, E. A. *The Metaphysical Foundations of Modern Physical Science.* New York, 1936.
Butterfield, H. *Origins of Modern Science.* London, 1949.
Dampier, Sir W. C. *A History of Science.* Cambridge, 1929 (4th edition, 1948).
    A Shorter History of Science. Cambridge, 1944.
Dannemann, F. *Die Naturwissenschaften in ihrer Entwicklung und in ihrem Zusammenhange.* 4 vols. Leipzig, 1910–13.
Dreyer, J. L. E. *Tycho Brahe.* Edinburgh, 1890.
Duhem, P. *Études sur Léonard de Vinci.* Paris, 1906–13.
    Les origines de la statique. Paris, 1905–6.
Fahie, J. J. *Galileo, his Life and Work.* London, 1903.
Grant, R. *Johann Kepler. A Tercentenary Commemoration of his Life and Work.* Baltimore, 1931.
Jeans, Sir J. H. *The Growth of Physical Science.* Cambridge, 1947.
Koyré, A. *Études Galiléennes.* Paris, 1940.
McMurrich, J. P. *Leonardo da Vinci the Anatomist.* London, 1930.
Sedgwick, W. T. and Tyler, H. W. *A Short History of Science.* New York, 1917 (revised edition, 1939).
Stimson, D. *The Gradual Acceptance of the Copernican Theory of the Universe.* New York, 1917.
Strong, E. W. *Procedures and Metaphysics.* Berkeley, U.S.A., 1936.

Taylor, F. Sherwood. *A Short History of Science.* London, 1939.
Science Past and Present. London, 1945.
Galileo and Freedom of Thought. London, 1938.
Thorndike, L. *A History of Magic and Experimental Science.* 6 vols. New York, 1923–42.
Whitehead, A. N. *Science and the Modern World.* Cambridge, 1927 (Penguin, 1938).
Wolf, A. *A History of Science, Technology and Philosophy in the Sixteenth and Seventeenth Centuries.* London, 1935.

Chapter XIX: Francis Bacon

Texts

The Philosophical Works of Francis Bacon. J. M. Robertson (edit.). London, 1905.
Works. R. L. Ellis, J. Spedding and D. D. Heath (edit.). 7 vols. London, 1857–74.
Novum Organum. Edited with introduction and notes by T. Fowler. Oxford, 1889 (2nd edition).
The Advancement of Learning. London (Everyman Series).
R. W. Gibson. *Francis Bacon. A Bibliography.* Oxford, 1950.

Studies

Anderson, F. H. *The Philosophy of Francis Bacon.* Chicago, 1948.
Fischer, Kuno. *Francis Bacon und seine Schule.* Heidelberg, 1923 (4th edition).
Nichol, J. *Francis Bacon, his Life and Philosophy.* 2 vols. London and Edinburgh, 1901.
Sturt, M. *Francis Bacon, a Biography.* London, 1932.

Chapter XX: Political Philosophy

Texts

Machiavelli. *Le Opere di Niccolò Machiavelli.* 6 vols. L. Passerini and G. Milanesi (edit.). Florence, 1873–77.
Tutte le Opere storiche e letterarie di Niccolò Machiavelli. G. Barbèra (edit.). Florence, 1929.
Il Principe. L. A. Burd (edit.). Oxford, 1891.
The Prince. W. K. Marriott (translator). London, 1908 and reprints (Everyman Series).
The Discourse of Niccolò Machiavelli. 2 vols. L. J. Walker, S.J. (translator and editor). London, 1950.
The History of Florence. 2 vols. N. H. Thomson (translator). London, 1906.

APPENDIX II

Machiavelli (*contd.*) *The Works of Nicholas Machiavel.* 2 vols. E. Farneworth (translator). London, 1762. (2nd edition in 4 vols., 1775).
The Historical, Political and Diplomatic Writings of Niccolò Machiavelli. 4 vols. Boston and New York, 1891.

More. *Utopia* (Latin and English). J. H. Lupton (edit.). London, 1895. (There are many other versions, including an English text in the Everyman Series.)
L'Utopie ou le traité de la meilleure forme de gouvernement. Texte latine édite par M. Delcourt avec des notes explicatives et critiques. Paris, 1936.
The English Works. London, 1557. This text is being re-edited and two volumes appeared in 1931 (London), edited by W. E. Campbell and A. W. Reed.
There are various editions of the Latin works. For example, *Opera omnia latina*: Louvain, 1566.

Hooker. *Works.* 3 vols. J. Keble (edit.). Oxford, 1845 (3rd edition).
The Laws of Ecclesiastical Polity, Books I–V. Introduction by Henry Morley. London, 1888.

Bodin. *Method for the Easy Comprehension of History.* B. Reynolds (translator). New York, 1945.
Six livres de la république. Paris, 1566. Latin edition: Paris, 1584. English translation by R. Knolles: London, 1606.

Althusius. *Politica methodice digesta.* Herborn, 1603. Enlarged edition; Groningen, 1610. Modern edition by C. J. Friedrich. Cambridge (Mass.), 1932.

Grotius. *De iure belli ac pacis.* Washington, 1913 (edition of 1625). English translation by F. W. Kelsey and others. Oxford, 1925. (These two vols. together constitute No. 3 of 'The Classics of International Law.')

Studies

Allen, J. W. *A History of Political Thought in the Sixteenth Century.* London, 1928.

Baudrillart, H. *Jean Bodin et son temps.* Paris, 1853.

Burd, L. A. *Florence (II), Machiavelli.* (The Cambridge Modern History, vol. 1, ch. 6.) Cambridge, 1902.

Campbell, W. E. *More's Utopia and his Social Teaching.* London, 1930.

Chambers, R. W. *Thomas More.* London, 1935.

Chauviré, R. *Jean Bodin, auteur de la République.* Paris, 1914.

D'Entrèves, A. P. *Natural Law. An Introduction to Legal Philosophy.* London, 1951.

A SHORT BIBLIOGRAPHY

Figgis, J. N. *Studies of Political Thought from Gerson to Grotius.* Cambridge, 1923 (2nd edition).

Foster, M. B. *Masters of Political Thought.* Vol. I, *Plato to Machiavelli* (Ch. 8, Machiavelli). London, 1942.

Gierke, O. von *Natural Law and the Theory of Society.* 2 vols. E. Barker (translator). Cambridge, 1934.

Johannes Althusius und die Entwicklung der naturrechtlichen Staatstheorien. Breslau, 1913 (3rd edition).

Gough, J. W. *The Social Contract. A Critical Study of its Development.* Oxford, 1936.

Hearnshaw, F. J. C. *The Social and Political Ideas of some Great Thinkers of the Renaissance and the Reformation.* London, 1925.

The Social and Political Ideas of some Great Thinkers in the Sixteenth and Seventeenth Centuries. London, 1926.

Meinecke, F. *Die Idee der Staatsräson.* (Ch. 1, Machiavelli.) Munich, 1929 (3rd edition).

Ritchie, D. G. *Natural Rights.* London, 1916 (3rd edition).

Sabine, G. H. *A History of Political Theory.* London, 1941.

Villari, P. *The Life and Times of Niccolò Machiavelli.* 2 vols. L. Villari (translator). London, 1892.

Vreeland, H. *Hugo Grotius.* New York, 1917.

Chapter XXI: (Scholasticism of the Renaissance) A General View

Texts

A number of titles of works are mentioned in the course of the chapter. Only a very few selected texts will be mentioned here. For fuller biographies the *Dictionnaire de théologie catholique* can be profitably consulted under the relevant names. The standard bibliographical work for writers of the Dominican Order between 1200 and 1700 is *Scriptores Ordinis Praedicatorum* by Quétif-Echard. A photolithographic reprint of the revised Paris edition of 1719–21 is being published by Musurgia Publishers, New York. For Jesuit authors consult Sommervogel-De Backer, *Bibliothèque de la compagnie de Jésus.* Liége, 1852 ff.

Cajetan. *Thomas de Vio Cardinalis Caietanus. Scripta theologica.* Vol. I, *De comparatione auctoritatis papae et concilii cum apologia eiusdem tractatus.* V. M. I. Pollet (edit.). Rome, 1936.

Thomas de Vio Cardinalis Caietanus (1469–1534); *Scripta philosophica:*

Cajetan (*contd.*) *Commentaria in Porphyrii Isagogen ad Praedicamenta Aristotelis.* I. M. Marega (edit.). Rome, 1934.
Opuscula oeconomico-socialia. P. N. Zammit (edit.). Rome, 1934.
De nominum analogia. De conceptu entis. P. N. Zammit (edit.). 1934.
Commentaria in de Anima Aristotelis. Y. Coquelle (edit.). Rome, 1938.
Caietanus . . . in 'De Ente et Essentia' Commentarium. M. H. Laurent (edit.). Turin, 1934.
Cajetan's commentary on Aquinas's *Summa theologica* is printed in the *Opera omnia* (Leonine edition) of St. Thomas.

Bellarmine. *Opera omnia.* 11 vols. Paris, 1870–91.
Opera oratoria postuma. 9 vols. Rome, 1942–8.
De controversiis. Rome, 1832.
Tractatus de potestate summi pontificis in rebus temporalibus. Rome, 1610.

Molina. *De Institia et Iure.* 2 vols. Antwerp, 1615.
Concordia liberi arbitrii cum gratiae donis, divina praescientia, providentia, praedestinatione et reprobatione. Paris, 1876.

Vitoria. *De Indis et de Iure Belli Relectiones.* E. Mys (edit.). Washington, 1917 (Classics of International Law, No. 7).

John of St. Thomas. *Cursus Philosophicus Thomisticus* (edit. Reiser). 3 vols. Turin, 1930–8.
Cursus philosophicus. 3 vols., Paris, 1883.
Joannis a Sancto Thoma O.P. Cursus theologici. Paris, Tournai, Rome, 1931 ff.

Studies

Barcía Trelles, C. *Francisco Suárez, Les théologiens espagnols du XVI siècle et l'école moderne du droit internationale.* Paris, 1933.

Brodrick, J. *The Life and Work of Blessed R. Cardinal Bellarmine.* 2 vols. London, 1928.

Figgis, J. N. See under bibliography for Suárez.

Fritz, G., and Michel, A. Article *Scolastique* (section III) in the Dictionnaire de théologie catholique, vol. 14, cols. 1715–25. Paris, 1939.

Giacón, C. *La seconda scolastica.* I, *I grandi commentatori di san Tommaso;* II, *Precedenze teoretiche ai problemi giuridici;* III, *I Problemi giuridico-politici.* Milan, 1944–50.

Littlejohn, J. M. *The Political Theory of the Schoolmen and Grotius.* New York, 1896.

Régnon, T. de *Bañes et Molina.* Paris, 1883.

A SHORT BIBLIOGRAPHY

Scott, J. B. *The Catholic Conception of International Law. Francisco de Vitoria, Founder of the Modern Law of Nations: Francisco Suárez, Founder of the Philosophy of Law in general and in particular of the Law of Nations.* Washington, 1934.

Smith, G. (edit.). *Jesuit Thinkers of the Renaissance. Essays presented to John F. McCormick, S.J.* Milwaukee, Wis., 1939.

Solana, M. *Historia de la Filosofía Española en el siglo XVI.* Madrid, 1940.

Stegmüller, F. *Geschichte des Molinismus. Band I, Neue Molinaschriften.* Münster, 1935 (Beiträge, 32).

Streitcher, K. *Die Philosophie der spanischen Spätscholastik an den deutschen Universitäten des siebzehnten Jahrhunderts* (in *Gesammelte Aufsätze zur Kulturgeschichte Spaniens*). Münster, 1928.

Vansteenberghe, E. Article *Molinisme* (and bibliography) in the Dictionnaire de théologie catholique, vol. 10, cols. 2094–2187. Paris, 1928.

Chapters XXII–XXIII: Francis Suárez

Texts

Opera. 28 vols. Paris, 1856–78.

Metaphysicarum Disputationum Tomi duo. Salamanca, 1597. (Many editions, up to that of Barcelona, 1883–4.)

Selections from Three Works of Francisco Suárez, S.J. (*De legibus, Defensio fidei catholicae. De triplici virtute theologica.*) 2 vols. Vol. 1, the Latin texts; Vol. 2, the translation. Oxford, 1944. (Classics of International Law, No. 20.)

Among bibliographies one can mention *Bibliografica Suareciana* by P. Mugica. Granada, 1948.

Studies

Aguirre, P. *De doctrina Francisci Suárez circa potestatem Ecclesiae in res temporales.* Louvain, 1935.

Alejandro, J. M. *La gnoseología del Doctor Eximio y la acusación nominalista.* Comillas (Santander), 1948.

Bouet, A. *Doctrina de Suárez sobre la libertad.* Barcelona, 1927.

Bouillard, R. Article *Suárez: théologie pratique.* Dictionnaire de théologie catholique, vol. 14, cols. 2691–2728. Paris, 1939.

Bourret, E. *De l'origine du pouvoir d'après Saint Thomas et Suárez.* Paris, 1875.

Breuer, A. *Der Gottesbeweis bei Thomas und Suárez. Ein wissenschaftlicher Gottesbeweis auf der Grundlage von Potenz und Aktverhältnis oder Abhängigkeitsverhältnis.* Fribourg (Switzerland), 1930.

Conde y Luque, R. *Vida y doctrinas de Suárez.* Madrid, 1909.

Dempf, A. *Christliche Staatsphilosophie in Spanien.* Salzburg, 1937.
Figgis, J. N. *Some Political Theories of the early Jesuits.* (Translations of the Royal Historical Society, XI. London, 1897.)
Studies of Political Thought from Gerson to Grotius. Cambridge, 1923 (2nd edition).
Political Thought in the Sixteenth Century. (The Cambridge Modern History, vol. 3, ch. 22). Cambridge, 1904.
Giacón, C. *Suárez.* Brescia, 1945.
Gómez Arboleya, E. *Francisco Suárez* (1548–1617). Granada, 1947.
Grabmann, M. *Die disputationes metaphysicae des Franz Suárez in ihrer methodischen Eigenart und Fortwirkung (Mittelalterliches Geistesleben,* vol. I, pp. 525–60.). Munich, 1926.
Hellín, J. *La analogía del ser y el conocimiento de Dios en Suárez.* Madrid, 1947.
Iturrioz, J. *Estudios sobre la metafísica de Francisco Suárez, S.J.* Madrid, 1949.
Lilley, A. L. *Francisco Suárez. Social and Political Ideas of some Great Thinkers of the XVIth and XVIIth centuries.* London, 1926.
Mahieu, L. *François Suárez. Sa philosophie et les rapports qu'elle a avec la théologie.* Paris, 1921.
(Replies by P. Descoqs to this work are contained in *Archives de Philosophie,* vol. 2 (pp. 187–298) and vol. 4 (pp. 434–544). Paris, 1924 and 1926.)
Monnot, P. Article *Suárez: Vie et œuvres.* Dictionnaire de théologie catholique, vol. 14, cols. 2638–49. Paris, 1939.
Plaffert, F. *Suárez als Völkerrechtslehrer.* Würzburg, 1919.
Recaséns Siches, L. *La filosofía del Derecho en Francisco Suárez.* Madrid, 1927.
Regout, D. *La doctrine de la guerre juste de saint Augustin à nos jours* (pp. 194–230). Paris, 1934.
Rommen, H. *Die Staatslehre des Franz Suárez.* München-Gladbach, 1927.
Scorraille, R. de. *François Suárez de la Compagnie de Jésus.* 2 vols. Paris, 1911.
Scott, J. B. *The Catholic Conception of International Law. Francisco de Vitoria, Founder of the Modern Law of Nations: Francisco Suárez, Founder of the Modern Philosophy of Law in general and in particular of the Law of Nations.* Washington, 1934.
Werner, K. *Franz Suárez und die Scholastik der letzten Jahrhunderte.* 2 vols. Ratisbon, 1861 and 1889.
Zaragüeta, J. *La filosofía de Suárez y el pensamiento actual.* Granada, 1941.

A SHORT BIBLIOGRAPHY

Among the special issues of periodicals and collected articles devoted to the philosophy of Suárez one may mention the following:

Actas del IV centenario del nacimiento de Francisco Suárez, 1548-1948. 2 vols. Madrid, 1949-50. (Contains articles on Suárez' theological, philosophical and political ideas.)

Archives de philosophie, vol. 18. Paris, 1949.

Pensamiento, vol. 4, número extraordinario, Suárez en el cuarto centenario de su nacimiento (1548-1948). Madrid, 1948. (This number of *Pensamiento* contains valuable studies on the metaphysical, epistemological, political and legal ideas of Suárez.)

Razón y Fe, tomo 138, fascs. 1-4, July-October 1948. Centenario de Suárez, 1548-1948. Madrid, 1948. (Suárez is considered both as theologian and philosopher, but mainly as philosopher.)

The two following works deal mainly with theological aspects of Suárez' thought:

Estudios Eclesiasticos, vol. 22, nos. 85-6, April-September, 1948. Francisco Suárez en el IV centenario de su nacimiento. Madrid, 1948.

Miscelánea Comillas, IX. Homenaje al doctor eximio P. Francisco Suárez, S.J., en el IV centenario de su nacimiento, 1548-1948. Comillas (Santander), 1948.

Among the works published in connection with the third centenary of Suárez' death (1917) one may mention:

Commemoración del tercer centenario del Eximio Doctor español Francisco Suárez, S.J. (1617-1917). Barcelona, 1923.

P. Franz Suárez, S.J. Gedenkblätter zu seinem dreihundertjährigen Todestag (25 September 1617). Beiträge zur Philosophie des P. Suárez by K. Six, etc. Innsbruck, 1917.

Rivista di Filosofia Neo-scolastica, X (1918).

Scritti vari publicati in occasione del terzo centenario della morte di Francesco Suárez, per cura del prof. Agostino Gemelli. Milan, 1918.

Rivière, E. M. and Scorraille, R. de *Suárez et son œuvre. À l'occasion du troisième centenaire de sa mort,* 1617-1917. Vol. 1, La bibliographie des ouvrages imprimés et inédits (E. M. Rivière). Vol. 2, *La Doctrine* (R. de Scorraille). Toulouse-Barcelona, 1918.

INDEX

(The principal references are printed in heavy figures. References followed by an asterisk refer to the Appendices or to a bibliographical note.)

Abbagnano, N. 430*
Abelard, Peter 50, 91
Absolute, the 245
absolute power of God 74, 105, 133, 151
absolutes and relations Ockham 68 ff, 95; *also* 25 f, 371
absolutism, papal and Ockham 111, 116, 119 ff
   political 118 f, **310 ff,** 317 f
   royal 311 f, 315, 326
   See also tyranny
abstraction Ockham 64 f, 79, 86; *also* 33, 219, 301, 303, 357 f
acceleration, law of 281
accidents 24 ff, 36, 70, 74, 134, 139, 159, 355, 368, 371 f
Achillini, Alexander 150, 221, 436*
acosmism 239
act 238; pure 362, 365; limitation of 367, 376 f
Adam Wodham 122
adultery 105
Aegidius *see* Giles
Aeneas Sylvius Piccolomini 208 n.
aesthetics 220
affections 218, 253, 303
agnosticism Ockham 12, 14, 71, 81, 84, 87 f, 108; *also* 123 f, 126, 129 ff, 142 f, 183, 300
Agostino Nipho 150, 221
agreement of mankind 322
Agricola, Rudolf 209, 218, 227, 436*
Agrippa von Nettesheim, Heinrich Cornelius 265 f
Aguirre, P. 445*
Aix-en-Provence 29, 263
Albèri, E. 440*
Albert of Saxony 15, 53, 154 f, 159, 161 f, 165, 432 f*
Albert the Great, St. 16, 20, 149, 185, 191, 200 f, 205 f, 221
Alcalà 341, 345, 353
alchemy 212 n., 250, 267 ff, 274, 293
Alejandro, J. M. 445*
Alexander Achillini 150, 221, 436*
Alexander of Aphrodisias 19, 150, 221 f

Alexander of Hales 365
Alexandrists *see* Alexander of Aphrodisias
Alhazen 156
Aliotta, A. 440*
Allen, J. W. 442*
Allen, P. S. and H. S. 435*
Alsace 196
alteration *see* change, accidental
Althusius, John 311 f, **327 f,** 332, 442 f*
Altseidenberg 270
Amann, E. 430*
ambassadors 350, 404
analogical reasoning 252 f
analogy Cajetan **338 ff,** 444*; Ockham 80; Suárez 356, 359, **361,** 364 ff, 368, 373, 378, 446*; *also* 39, 256 f
   of attribution 338, 361, 368
   of inequality 338
   of proportionality 338, 361, 368
analysis 11, 57, 276, 374, 409 f, 417, 419 f
analytic proposition *see* proposition, analytic
anarchy 229, 233, 316
anatomy 279 f, 440*
Anaxagoras 406
Anaximander 407
Anaximenes 408
Anderson, F. H. 441*
Andreas a Novocastro 390
Angelo of Arezzo 150
angels 30, 200, 214, 223, 296, 367
anima motrix in sun 284
anima mundi see world-soul
animal, irrational *see* brute animals
   A. spirits 252, 303
animism 252
annihilation 56, 66 f
annitas 186
Anselm of Canterbury, St. 188, 200, 418, 422
anthropology 297, 324
anthropomorphism 69, 89, 303
antinomy 188
antipathy 249, 251, 257, 265

448

INDEX

Antoine André 124
Antwerp 345
apologetics 13ff, 51, 126
appearance 30f, 141f, 303
 'saving the A's' 158, 162, 164, 278f, 282, 297
appetite, sensitive 98, 102f
apprehension, simple 63
a priori knowledge *see* innate ideas and knowledge
a priori reasoning Ockham 68, 76, 79, 85; *also* 279, 290
Aquinas, Thomas *see* Thomas Aquinas, St.
Arabian philosophy *see* Islamic philosophy
arbitration 333f; of Pope between Christian rulers 403
archeus 266ff
Archimedes 281
argument well-conducted 334; dialectical 123; probable *see s.v.*
Argyropoulos, John 210
Aristarchus 283
aristocracy 318
Aristotelianism
 and Alexander of Aphrodisias 19, 150, 221f
 Averroists 4ff, 19, 150, 180, 221f, 415f
 and Christianity 3f, 415f
 ethics 107f
 logic Ockham 12, 46, 51f, 59ff; Renaissance humanists 19, 215, 219f; *also* 207, 292, 301, 418
 mediaeval philosophy and 2-7, **414-18**
 metaphysics 7, 28, 59, 74, 81, 145, 215, 242, 292, 377, 417
 natural theology 46, 81, 91, 377
 Ockham and 12, 42, 46, 59f, 74, 81, 91, 105, 107f, 153f
 opposition to 18f, 81, 145, 147, 149, 153f, 207, 210, 213, 215, 217, 227f, 262f, 293, 301, 415, 436*
 physics 2, 16, 145, 226f, 242, 251, 275, 279, 281, 284, 417, 422, 432*
 psychology 19, 34, 215, 222f, 249, 289
 Renaissance A. 18f, 210, 212f, 215, **217-30**, 436f*
 St. Thomas Aquinas and 3, 9, 375ff, **415-18**

Scholasticism and 221, 335, 357
slavish adherence to 3, 6, 226, 275, 278, 415ff
also 263, 292f, 335, 421, 431*
Aristotle
 Averroists *see under* Aristotelianism
 commentaries on 222, 336f, 340ff, 344f, 355, 432*, 444*
 discovery of works 3, **414-18**, 422f
 ethics 105ff
 logic 32, 37, 59, 94, 156f, 217, 220, 304
 metaphysics 33, 71, 75, 77, 141f, 211, 357, **411f**, 432*
 natural theology 92, 163, 376, 412
 Ockham and 69, 77, 94, 96, 99, 153f
 opposition to 147, 204, 211, 215, 220, 254, 299, 304
 physics 157f, 166, 362, 422f, 432*
 political theory 9f, 147, 171ff, 175, 179f, 320, 325, 330
 psychology 4f, 34, 63, 141f, 184, 221f, 340, 444*
 St. Thomas Aquinas and 3, 375, **415-18**
 slavish adherence to 4, 153, 162, 218
 and theology 4, 7, 40, **414-18**
 also 15, 214f, 221, 227, 243, 264, 331, 353f, 406f, 431*
arithmetic 240, 297
Armitage, A. 440*
Arriaga, Rodrigo de 345, 355
arts, school or faculty of 13, 52, 148, 415
assent *see* judgment
assimilation, intellectual 30
assimilation of food 297
association, psychological 218
associations of men *see* social contract; society
astrology 212n., 214, 225, 251, 266f, 274, 327
astronomy
 Copernican 162, 226, 261f, 274 282f, 285f, 288, 297, 440*
 geocentric and heliocentric 161,ff 241, 278, 282-6, 297
 Ptolemaic 275, 282f, 285

astronomy—*contd.*
    also 159, 161, 165f, 241, 246, 249
    261, 263, 281-6, 289f, 297, 407,
    417, 440*
atheism 110, 211, 227, 321, 438*
Athenian academy 406
atom 145, 260, 264, 287f, 306
atomism 145, 249, 264, 287, 299,
    346, 407
attraction
    between bodies 163, 249; between
    monads 268. *See also* gravity
attributes *see* properties; A. of
    being *see* being.
Auer, A. 435*
Augustine of Hippo, St. 27, 49f,
    89ff, 124f, 129, 188, 191, 196,
    212, 244, 256, 375f, 393
Augustinianism 26ff, 58, 204
Augustinian Order 10, 15, 124f,
    341, 345
aura vitalis 268
authority, appeal to 25, 100, 418
authority, international 333f, 350,
    352
    resistance to *see* resistance to
    ruler
    spiritual *see* jurisdiction, spiritual
Averroes 4, 34, 77, 147, 150, 180,
    221f, 15f
Averroism 19, 150, 178ff, 221f,
    251, 340, 416
    integral Aristotelianism and 180,
    415f
    Latin A. 4ff
Avicenna 194, 379
Avignon 25, 39, 43f, 121, 135, 170
Avila 353
axioms 298, 300f, 306

Baader, Franz von 273
Babylon 325
'Babylonish captivity' 9
Bacon, Francis 21, 277, 289, **292-
    309**, 357, **441***
    De augmentis scientiarum 295-300
    Nova Atlantis 307f
    Novum Organum 300-7
Bacon, Roger *see* Roger Bacon
Báñez, Dominic 22, 335, 341, 343,
    444*
Barbèra, G. 441*
Barcía Trelles, C. 444*
Barclay, William 311

Barnes, J. H. 435*
Bartholomew of Medina 341
Bascour, H. 434*
Basle 266
Basle, Council of 232f
Batistella, R. M. 437*
Baudrillart, H. 442*
Baudry, L. 430*
beatific vision 206, 347
beatitude *see* happiness
beauty 212f, 215, 264, 293, 363
Behmen, J. *see* Böhme, Jakob
being 78, 85f, 184f, 252, 257f, 379,
    428*
    attributes of 257, 354ff, 359f
    conceptual B. 32
    degrees of 143, 212f 223, 242,
    256f
    ens rationis see s.v.
    infinite B. *see* infinity
    real B. 32, 356f
    subject of metaphysics 77f, 354,
    356f
    subordinate to the One 214
    being, idea of Ockham **78ff;** Suárez
    354, 356, **357ff,** 379
    analogous 80, 356f, 359, 361, 368
    equivocal 361
    univocal 78ff, 361
belief *see* faith
Bellarmine, Robert *see* Robert
    Bellarmine, St.
Benedict XII, pope 44, 116, 135, 170
Benedict of Assignano 10
Bergson, H. 277
Berkeley, George 378
Bernard of Arezzo 135-43, 146,
    431*
Bernard of Clairvaux, St. 181, 198,
    200, 202
Bernard of Lombardy 41
Bernhart, J. 435*
Berthold of Moosburg 185
Bessarion, John 210f
Bett, H. 438*
Bible, The *see* Scriptures, The Holy
Biel, Gabriel 150
Bihlmeyer, K. 434*
Billingham, Richard 123
Bindseil, H. E. 437*
binomial theorem 286
biology 276ff
Birkenmaier, A. 431*
Bizet, J. A. 435*

INDEX

Blanchet, L. 439*
blas 268
blindness 133, 373f
blood, circulation of the 279f
Bobbio, N. 434*
Boccaccio 207
Bochert, E. 433*
Bodin, Jean 313, **324-7,** 442*
body 252, 255, 290f, 305f
  astral 266, 270
  heavenly BB. *see s.v.*
  human B. 270, 297. *See also* soul and body
  motion of BB. 74f, 166, 287f
  transformation of BB. 305f
Boehner, P. ix, 43n., 44f, 53*, 428*, 430*, 431*
Boethius 191, 199, 205
Böhme, Jakob 265, **270-3,** 274, 427, 439*
Bologna 29, 150, 211, 221f, 336f, 350
Bonagratia of Bergamo 44, 111
Bonaventure, St. 20, 149, 181, 194, 196, 204ff, 256, 412, 421
Boniface VIII, pope 9, 119, 169, 172
Bordeaux 229
botany 226
Bouet, A. 445*
Bouillard, R. 445*
Boulting, W. 439*
Bourret, E. 445*
Boyle, Robert 287f
brain 252
Bréhier, E. 428*
Bretschneider, C. G. 437*
Breuer, A. 445*
Briggs, Henry 286
Brigué, L. 435*
Brixen 232
Brodrick, J. 444*
Brooke, Lord *see* Greville, Robert
Brothers of the Common Life 183, 209, 232
Bruno, Giordano 20, 232, 245f, 249, 255, **258-63,** 265, 269, 274, 285, 438f*
brute animals 223, 251f, 329
  mere machines 290
Bühlmann, J. 435*
Burckhardt, J. 428*
Burd, L. A. 441f*
Buridan, John *see* John Buridan
Burleigh, Walter 53
Burtt, E. A. 440*

Butterfield, H. 440*
Byzantium 210, 232

Cabbala 213, 215f
Cajetan of Thiene 150
Cajetan, Thomas de Vio Cardinal 22, 150, 335, **337-40,** 344, 358, 361, 368, 390, 398, 443f*
calculus 286f
Calvin, John 22, 209, 313ff
Calvinism 262, 313ff, 324, 328
Cambridge 209, 294
Cambridge Platonists 292
Campanella, Tommaso **255-8,** 438f*
Campbell, W. E. 442*
Cano, Melchior 22, 335, 337, 341, 350
Canon law 171f, 177, 399, 402
Capreolus, John 10, 150, 336
Carbonara, C. 440*
Cardano, Girolamo 249, **250-2,** 266, 438*
Carlyle, R. W. and A. J. 428*
Carmelite Order 345
Carneades 329
Carré, H. M. 431*
Cartesianism 346
Cassiodorus 173
Cassirer, E. 436f*
categories 26, 77, 158f, 219, 371
Catherine of Bologna, St. 181
Catherine of Genoa, St. 181
Catherine of Siena, St. 181
Catholicism 145, 200, 229, 231, 244, 262, 269, 311-14, 324, 328, 421. *See also* Church, The Catholic
causae subordinatae per se and *per accidens* 362f
causality, cause 15, 26, 126, 140-3, 148, 157, 214, 252, 287f, 305, 355
  infinite series of CC. 81ff, 129, 362f
  principle of causality 92, 123; not certain 126, 131f, 140; not analytic 123, 131
causality, efficient Ockham **71-4,** 81ff, 95; *also* 21, 143, 165f, 296, 300, 305, 355, 406, 410
  proof of God as efficient cause *see* God, existence of
  as succession 73, 95, 140
cause
  exemplary 71, 355, 410, 412

INDEX

cause—*contd.*
  final 21, 144, 165f, 289, 296, 299, 303, 355, 411. *See also* finality in nature
  first 83, 187, 259, 300. *See also* God, Nature of; first efficient cause
  formal 296, 305, 355, 411
  material 296, 355, 406
  secondary 64f, 95
Cavalieri, B. 286
Centiloquium theologicum 45, 81f
centre of gravity not centre of volume 159f
certitude 52, 66, 127–32, 136–40, 148, 155, 164
  in intuition 63–7, 137f, 148
  in moral matters 331
  restricted to analytic propositions 123, 125, 128, 136f, 151
Cesalpino, Andrew 226
Chambers, R. W. 442*
chance 299, 316
change 74f, 145, 287, 411, 418
  accidental C. 74, 145, 305f, 368
  substantial C. 144f, 305f, 370
Charron, Pierre 229
Chartres, school of 207
Chauviré, R. 442*
Checchini, A. 434*
chemistry 267f, 304
chimera 66, 373
Christ 38, 101, 114, 200, 204, 214, 243f, 246, 269, 272, 413, 435*
  body of, dead 98f
    in Eucharist 370
  subject to civil power 177
  union with 194, 197f, 244
Christendom, unity of 233, 334. *See also* reunion
Christianity 18f, 48, 107, 110, 126, 145, 197, 200, 208, 210, 212ff, 216f, 225, 227, 229, 232, 246, 248, 254, 262, 264, 316, 323f, 350, 413–16, 418–24, 439*
Christian philosophy 19f, 48f, 51, 376, 378, 413f, 423, 429*
Chrysippus 330
Chrysoloras, Manuel 207
Church and State (Theory; for actual relations *see* papacy) Hooker 322ff; Ockham 116–20, 431*; Marsilius of Padua 168f, 171, 176–9; Reformers 313ff; Renaissance Scholastics 346ff; Suárez 402f, 445* *also* 2, 8f, 234, 310
Church, notions of the 269, 272, 313f, 323f
Church of England, the 322ff, 354
Church, the Catholic 168, 179, 194, 202, 216, 233f, 244, 346
  and Marsilius of Padua 172, 176ff
  and science: Copernicus 283; Galileo 281, 285f
  and the State *see* Church and State
Cicero 150, 207ff, 218, 220
Cicuttini, L. 439*
Cistercian Order 127
city-states 172, 176, 178, 325
civilization 250, 277, 393
class, logical 125, 218f
classical literature 18f, 207–10, 220, 227
Clemens, F. J. 438*
Clement VI, pope 44, 116, 135, 171, 180
Clement VIII, pope 344
Clement of Alexandria 413
Coblenz 232
coercion 174, 179, 393. *See also* sanction, legal
cognition *see* knowledge
Coimbra 341, 345, 353
coincidence of opposites 233ff, 243f, 259
  in God 235, 245, 293
Colet, John 209
Cologne 149, 184, 196, 199f
colour 137–40, 185, 287
Combes, A. 205, 435*
commandments, the ten 387f, 390
Common Life, Brothers of the 183, 209, 232
communism 255, 326
community *see* society
compass 280
complexum 55
Complutenses 341
composition 366, 369
comprehensio Nizolius 219
Compton-Carleton, Thomas 345
Comte, A. 423f
concept *see* idea
conceptualism Ockham 56–9; *also* 28, 31f, 41f, 122, 125, 164, 429*
conciliar movement, the 120f, 232ff, 310

INDEX

concurrence, divine 104, 166, 343, 377
concursus *see* concurrence
Conde y Luque, R. 445*
confiscation 389
Congregatio de auxiliis 344
congruism 343
Conimbricenses see Coimbra
Connolly, J. L. 435*
conscience 106–10
consent
  in foundation of society *see* contract
  of mankind in general *see* agreement
consequences, theory of 53
conservation 70, 83f, 104, 166, 187
Constance 196
Constance, Council of 148, 202, 233
contemplation 253, 308, 357
contingency Ockham 50, 60f, 67, 83, 92f, 95, 104; Suárez 368, 376f
contract
  between States 333
  of people with ruler 314, 327, 348
  sanctity of 328, 333
  social C. *see s.v.*
contraction Nicholas of Cusa 239f, 242f
  of concept of being 359
  physical and metaphysical 367
contradiction, principle of 67, 123ff, 128–31, 133, 136–40, 236f
contraries *see* opposites
Copernicus, Nicholas 263, **282f**, 440*. *See also* astronomy, Copernican
Copleston, F. C. 428*
Coquelle, Y. 444*
Corin, A. L. 434*
corporation 323, 327. *See also* society
corpus coeleste see heavenly bodies
corruption and generation 144f, 305f, 370
Cosenza 252
cosmology *see* nature, philosophy of
cosmos *see* world
counsel of perfection 381, 386
Counter-Reformation 210, 336, 429*
Cracow university 148
Crakanthorpe, Richard 292
Cranmer, Thomas 180

creation Ockham 49f, 84f, 89, 91, 104 *also* 187, 190, 259, 270, 376f, 412, 418
  freedom of 49f, 197, 203, 251
  from eternity 190ff, 197, 240
  purpose of 213
  of world 4f, 19, 288, 423. *See also* C. from eternity (above).
  See also God, nature of: Creator
creationism (origin of soul) 96
creatures Ockham 50, 69ff, 80, 89ff, 103; *also* 183, 187–90, 192, 197, 205, 235, 237–40, 242f, 270, 329, 361, **371f**, 376f, 382, 421
  in God and outside God 197f, 203, 242f, 267, 269, 271
  infinite in number 90
  See also finite being; world, and God
'creditive' act 65f
credo ut intelligam 200, 422
Cremoninus, Caesar 226
Crew, H. 440*
crime 321
criminal law *see* law, criminal
criterion of truth 264
criticism in philosophy 7f, 11, 42, 46f, 146ff, 151, 246, 375, 417, 419f, 424f, 432*
Crombie, A. C. 428*
culture 277, 293, 393, 424
Curti, William Cardinal 135, 145
Curtis, S. J. 428*
custom 111, 119, 324, 333, 351f, 391f, 399, **401f**

damnation *see* hell
Dampier, Sir W. C. 440*
Daniels, A. 434*
Dannemann, F. 440*
Dante 172, 207
David, king of Israel 349
da Vinci, Leonardo 246, 279, 433*, 440*
death 36, 103, 253, 370
De auxiliis controversy 342–4
De Benedictis, John Baptist 345
decalogue, the 387f, 390
deception
  by 'evil genius' 130
  by God *see* miracle, miraculous knowledge of non-existent object

deduction 218, 220, 264, 278, 288ff, 302, 306, 309, 332
definition 230
deformity, caused by God 133
deism 289
Delcourt, M. 442*
Della Scala, Can Grande 171
Della Torre, A. 436*
Della Volpe, G. 435*
De Lugo, John Cardinal 345
demerit 131f
demiurge 410, 412
democracy 234, 313, 315
Democritus 249, 299, 407
demonstration 13, 52, 60ff, 84f, 131f, 134, 230, 301, 304, 418
Dempf, A. 428*, 435*, 446*
Denifle, H. 201, 435*
Denis the Carthusian 181, **199f**
Denomy, A. J. 433*
D'Entrèves, A. P. 442*
dependence see contingency; creatures
Descartes, René 130, 156, 166, 252, 256, 263f, 269, 277, 286, 290ff, 378, 421f
Descoqs, P. 446*
desire, natural 36, 225
desire, sensitive 98
despotism 233, 311, 318, 324. See also tyranny
De Sylvestris, Francis (Ferrariensis) 22, 335, 337
determinism 214
theological 124, 133
Deventer 209, 232
De Wulf, M. 179, 185, 231, 428*
dialectic 51f, 217, 220, 304, 410, 416, 418, 436*
dialectical argument 123
Dietrich of Freiberg see Theodoric
difference 356, 358ff, 371
synthesis of D's see coincidence of opposites
Digby, Everard 292
Digby, Sir Kenelm 292
Dilthey, W. 428*
Dio Chrysostom 333
Diogenes Laërtius 263
Dionysius the Areopagite see Pseudo-Dionysius
discovery, scientific 17, 153-6, 268, 279ff, 284, 286, 293f, 298, 305f, 308

logic of 219
disease 267
disposition see habit
distinction 187f, 193, 259, 267, 269, 355, 436*
 D. formalis a parte rei see formal objective D.
 formal objective D. 28, 50, 56, 68, 86, 99f, 360
 real D. 68, 99f
divine right of kings 311ff, 324, 347, 354, 399
divorce, emperor's powers 171
docta ignorantia **235-8**, 244, 437*
doctorate 43, 149
Dominic of Flanders 336
Dominic Soto see Soto, Dominic
Dominican order 10, 22, 24f, 40, 125, 149f, 156, 184f, 195f, 201, 255, 258, 335ff, 340-5, 349, 443*
Dondaine, A. 434*
Douai 341
double truth theories 5f, 19, 146, 262
Douglas, C. 437*
Dreiling, R. 34, 429*
Dress, W. 436*
Dreyer, J. L. E. 440*
Duhamel, J. B. 356
Duhem, Pierre 163, 433*, 440*
Dulles, A. 436*
Duns Scotus, John 1f, 10ff, 28, 36, 46, 50f, 56, 67f, 78, 81, 87, 99f, 104, 149f, 207, 331, 341, 357f, 360f, 365, 375, 379, 390, 414f, 417
Durandellus 41
Durandus of Aurillac 41
Durandus of Saint-Pourçain **25-8**, 40ff, 44, 46, 150, 361, 427, 429*
duration 240f. *See also* time; eternity
dynamics 160
 celestial 159, 165

earth (element) 157, 163
earth, the 160, 241, 261, 280, 288, 433*
 movement in heavens 241, 261, 282f, 285
 rotation of 161ff, 241, 282
Eastern Church, the 210, 232, 244
ecclesiastical power
 spiritual see jurisdiction, spiritual
 temporal see papacy, political jurisdiction

INDEX

Eckhart 15, 181 ff, **184–95,** 196–202, 239, 270, 272, 434 f*
eclecticism 18, 255, 262, 264
  Suárez 374 ff
eclipse 241
economy, principle of Ockham 59, 68 f, 74 ff, 89, 91, 97, 99 f; *also* 28, 42, 164 f
Eddington, Sir Arthur 278
education 19, 22, 183, 208 f, 228, 320, 336, 436 f*
Edward III, king of England 117
egoism 312, 317, 329, 395
Egyptians, spoliation of 390
Ehrle, F. 149
Einsiedeln 266
elements of matter 157, 159, 251 f, 267 f, 272
  transmutation of 267, 305 f
ellipse, 284, 288
Ellis, R. L. 441*
emanation 239, 255, 259
  of divine Persons 186, 190
emotion 253
Empedocles 249, 406
Emperor, Byzantine 168
Emperor, Holy Roman
  and General Council 178
  and papacy 8 f, 44, 111, 116 f, 119, 168 f, 177
  universal jurisdiction of 117, 397
  See also Empire, Holy Roman
Empire, the Holy Roman 168, 172, 178, 233, 396
  and papacy 2, 8 f, 120. *See also* Emperor, Holy Roman
empirical method 253, 266 f, 278 ff, 289, 293
empiricism Ockham 47 f, 61, 64, 67, 70, 72 ff, 76, 122, 153; *also* 33 f, 126, 140, 153, 219 f, 264, 273, 289 f, 304, 309
enclosure of land 320
end justifies the means 316 f
end of man 9, 19, 168, 179 f, 206, 224 f, 347, 380, 386 f
endowments, church 177
energy 166, 290
England 9, 209, 273, 292, 310, 322, 324
  Church of E. *see s.v.*
enlightenment, the 422, 424
ens rationis Suárez 355, 360, **372 ff;** *also* 32

H.P. III—30

Epicureanism 19, 217, 263 f, 413
Epicurus 249, 263, 299. *See also* Epicureanism
epicycles 282 ff
epiphenomenalism 223
epistemology 46, 154, 308, 417, 447*. *See also* knowledge, theory of
epoche 409
equivocation 80, 339, 361
Erasmus 22, 209, 350, 435*
Erastianism 173, 178 f, 314 f
Erfurt university 148, 150
erroneous conscience 106 f
error 130 f, 302 ff
  fear of 127 f
esse
  E. *apparens* 30 ff
  E. *existens et reale* 31
  E. *intentionale* 31 f
  and *intelligere* in God 184–7, 192
essence 50, 287, 358
  and existence Suárez **365–8,** 369, 376 f, 379; *also* 78, 186, 200, 235, 418, 428*, 444*
  in God 186–7, 235
  knowledge of 33, 215, 224
  metaphysic of *see* metaphysic of essence
  E., nature and *suppositum* 368 f
  and relation 27 f
essential philosophy 377 ff
eternity 90 f, 93 n., 190 ff, 240 f
  creation from E. *see s.v.*
  of world *see* world, E. of
ethics Ockham 14, 102, **103–10,** 384; his two ethics ix, 14, 107 ff; *also* 132 ff, 147, 150, 227, 264, 276, 298, 315 ff, 381, 385, 409, 412 f, 428*
  See also natural law
Eton 209
eucharist, the 370
evidence John of Mirecourt 127–32;
  Nicholas of Autrecourt 136, 138, 140 f, 146, 148; *also* 63, 65 f, 264
  cogent E. 132
  natural E. 128–31, 146
evidentia naturalis and *potissima* 128–31, 146
evil 90, 103 ff, 267 f, 272 f, 355
  intrinsic evil 104, 384 f, 390
  moral E. Suárez 382, 384–7, 390 f; *also* 103 f

INDEX

evolution 277, 407
Evora 342
excluded middle, principle of 37, 93 f
exclusion, method of 72
excommunication 403
executive power 176, 325 f
exemplar *see* cause, exemplary; exemplarism
exemplarism 49, 90 f, 409 f, 412
existence Ockham 78 f, 104; Suárez 358, 367, 377, 379; *also* 137, 141, 185, 254
  cessation of 144
  and essence *see* essence
  knowledge of E. *see* existent
  knowledge of coexistence 141
  philosophy of E. 377, 379, 418
  and *subsistentia* 369
  See also esse
existence of one thing inferred from that of another
  impossible Nicholas of Autrecourt **138-43,** 148, 151; *also* 12 f, 164
  possible Buridan 154
existent 78 f, 91 f, 360
  knowledge of 60, 62 ff, 66 ff, 76, 78 f, 91, 360
  knowledge of individual existents *see* singulars, knowledge of
existentialism 379
experience Ockham 33 n., 60 ff, 72, 74, 76, 81, 98 f, 101, 103; *also* 34, 128-31, 137 f, 140 f, 153-6, 164, 183, 215, 249 f, 252 ff, 266, 301, 304, 306, 346, 411
  mystical E. 183, 193 ff, 206
  religious E. 183, 272
  sense E. *see* sense-knowledge
experiment 16, 164, 183, 266, 268, 278-82, 290, 294, 303 f, 308 f, 346
explanation 156-60, 162, 164, 278 f, 282, 290, 297, 408, 411
extension, physical 255, 290, 370
external world, perception of 128 ff, 257. *See also* sense-knowledge.

Fabri, Honoré 346
factual knowledge 137 f, 153, 219, 278 f, 290, 301 f, 424
  See also experience

faculties 97, 141, 295
  not really distinct 99 f
Fahie, J. J. 440*
faith
  above natural knowledge 35, 84, 88, 102
  act of 126
  keeping F. *see* good faith
  also 17, 95 f, 128, 134, 137, 148, 151, 177, 183, 196, 202 ff, 217, 299, 323, 431*
faith and reason
  F. substituted for R. 11, 13 f, 95 f, 123 f, 126, 225, 330, 340, 415
  and moral law 107 f, 110
  also 1, 7, 124, 179, 299, 418, 422-5
fall of man 112 f, 228, 268 f
falsity 32, 355
family, the 321, 325 ff, 393
Farneworth, E. 442*
Fathers of the Church 194, 200, 204 ff, 209
fear
  of God 229
  and voluntary acts 401
federation 233, 328
Ferrara 222
Ferrariensis, Francis *see* De Sylvestris, Francis
Festugière, J. 211 n.*, 436*
feudalism 311
fideism 81, 228
Figgis, J. N. 446*
Filmer, Sir Robert 311
finality in nature 82, 221. *See also* cause, final
finite being 181, 235, 240, 243, 256 f, 260, 355, 361, 365, 376 ff, 418. *See also* creatures
Fiorentino, F. 439*
fire 72, 139 f, 157, 161
first philosophy *see* philosophy, first
first principles 60, 215, 222
  indemonstrable 60
Fischer, K. 441*
Flacius Illyricus 228
Flemish language 182, 198
Florence 207, 210 f, 216, 280, 441*
  Council of 210, 232
Fludd, Robert 263, **292 f**
fluidity 255
Fonseca, Peter de 341, 355, 361

INDEX

force
  physical 287f
  political *see* coercion
form Fr. Bacon 296f, 299, 305ff; *also* 29, 36, 74f, 79, 90, 187, 251, 262, 361
  Corporeal F. 96f
  of corporeity 97f, 100
  corruptible 96f
  Exemplary F. 49. *See also* exemplarism
  extended 96f
  Immaterial F. 30, 96f
  as individuation principle 24
  and mode 370
  Platonic FF. *see* ideas, Platonic
  plurality of FF. 40, 97–100
  relation to matter 371
  Sensitive F. 97–100
  soul as F. *see* soul and body
  Substantial F. 34f, 96ff, 100
  Universal F. 242, 259
forma corporeitatis see form of corporeity
forma specularis 31f
forma superaddita 253
formalities 99
fornication 105
fortune *see* chance
Foster, M. B. 443*
Fowler, T. 441*
Fracastoro, Girolamo 249
France 9, 215, 273, 310, 313f, 326
  French language 182
Franciscan Order 10, 29, 40, 43f, 48, 111f, 114, 122, 124f, 135, 170, 204, 336, 345
Franciscan philosophy 98, 100, 102
Francis de Marcia 124
Francis de Sylvestris (Ferrariensis) *see* De Sylvestris, Francis
Francis of Ascoli 44
Francis of Meyronnes 124, 161f
Francis of Vitoria *see* Vitoria, Francis of
Franck, Sebastian 269
Frederick II, emperor 8
freedom in society 118f, 318, 394
  religious F. *see* toleration
free will Ockham **101–3;** *also* 37, 214, 228f, 377, 380, 445*
  and future acts *see* futuribles
  and God's omnipotence 217

and grace (*de Auxiliis* controversy) 342–4
and judgment of intellect 102
and morality 103, 387
and sensitive appetite 102f
See also determinism
French language 182
Friedeberg-Sealey, F. 435*
Friedrich, C. J. 442*
Friedrich, H. 437*
Frischeisen-Köhler, M. 428*
Fritz, G. 444*
futuribles, knowledge of 37f, 66, 92
  by God *see* God, nature of: foreknowledge

Gabriel Biel 150
Gaeta 337
Galen 227, 267, 280
Galileo 16, 21, 157, 226, 278, **280f,** 287ff, 297, 440f*
  and the Inquisition **284–6**
Gandillac, M. 438*
Garin, E. 436*
Garrod, H. W. 435*
gases 268
Gassendi, Pierre 19, **263f,** 287, 439*
Gebelin, P. 437*
Gemelli, A. 447*
General Council 120, 177f, 233f, 443*. *See also* conciliar movement
generalization *see* induction
generation and corruption 144f, 305f, 370
Geneva 209, 258, 314, 325, 345
genius, scientific 309
Gentile, G. 436*, 438f*
genus 32, 90
geocentric theory *see* astronomy
geography 279, 324
geometry 160, 240, 253f, 283, 287, 297
  analytic 160, 286, 290
George of Trebizond 210, 220
Gerard Groot 183
German language 182, 196
'German theology' 184, 195
German mystical speculation 200ff
Germany 9, 148f, 215, 220, 232, 249, 337, 378, 433*, 437*, 445*
Gerson, John *see* John Gerson

INDEX

Gertrude, St. 181
Gewirth, A. 434*
Geyer, B. 31, 428*
Ghibellines 171
Giacón, C. 431*, 444*, 446*
Giarratano, C. 437*
Gibson, R. W. 441*
Gierke, O. von 443*
Gilbert de la Porrée, 372
Gilbert, William 156, 280, 304
Giles correspondent of Nicholas of Autrecourt 135
Giles of Rome 10, 125, 149, 169, 234, 349
Giles of Viterbo 341
Gilson, É. 31, 178f, 185f, 379, 418, 428*
Giordano Bruno *see* Bruno, Giordano
Glorieux, P. 202n.*
God
    acting without secondary causes 64f, 95, 140
    in Aristotle 411f
    causing intuition of non-existent thing 64ff, 130f, 137
    coincidence of opposites 235, 245, 293
    definition of 237
    final end of all things 102, 165f, 192, 270, 411
    immanent 189, 192, 238, 259, 261
    as light 254f
    manifested in nature (Nicholas of Cusa) 242, 244ff
    subject of metaphysics 77
    as the One 212f, 271
    in Plato 410
    not subject to law 382, 385
    not subject to obligation 103ff
    relation to creatures Eckhart **187–90;** *also* 69, 90, 197, 239f, 242, 372. *See also* similarity and sin *see s.v.*
    transcendent 189, 192, 235f, 238, 259, 261
    union with 182, 192ff, 196–9, 201, 243f, 253, 269,
    wrath of 272
God, existence of Ockham 79, **80–4,** 87; Suárez 355, **362ff,** 446*; *also* 229, 259, 419, 424
    held by faith 14, 84, 87f, 123, 126, 183

provable 13, 79, 154f, 183, 229, 364, 445*. *See also* next entry
known from and in creatures 212, 256f, 264, 267, 295
not provable 13, 71, 84, 123, 129ff, 142f, 419
probable arguments for 83f, 131f, 144, 364
proof from motion 81f, 362, 376
    efficient causality 82f, 143
    finality or order 82, 143f, 363
    grades of being 143
a priori proof 363f
God, nature of
    our knowledge of Nicholas of Cusa **235–8,** 245; Ockham 12, 62, 78f, 81, **84–8;** Suárez 355, **364f;** *also* 200, 213, 227, 339f
    denial or limitation of our knowledge of Ockham 12, 83–8, 92f, 95; *also* 11, 124, 183
    docta ignorantia **235–8,** 244, 437*
    experimental, mystical knowledge 206
    negative knowledge *see via negativa*
    no intuitive knowledge of 78, 81, 86
    act, pure act 238, 362, 365
    conserver 64, 104, 237. *See also* conservation
    creator 84f, 91, 104, 184, 187, 190f, 203, 256, 259, 364, 372
    distinction of attributes 86, 88, 185
    as *esse* and *intelligere* 184–7, 192
    essence 86–9, 93f, 101, 185ff
    essence and existence identical 186f, 235
    eternal 38f, 85, 93n., 190f, 226, 238, 240f, 269, 365
    final end 102, 165f, 192, 270, 411
    first efficient cause 83, 142, 165f, 187, 237, 239, 300, 338, 343
    first mover 165, 226, 343, 376, 411
    foreknowledge Ockham **92–4;** Petrus Aureoli **38f;** *also* 342ff, 365, 430*
    free Ockham 46, 48ff, 67, 95, 104f, 107ff; *also* 197, 203, 240, 365

INDEX

God, nature of—*contd.*
  good 82, 85f, 144, 192, 197, 203, 212, 269, 271f, 338
  immutable 365
  incomprehensible 200, 235, 238, 259, 271, 365. *See also docta ignorantia* (above)
  infinite 84f, 124, 163, 235–8, 257, 260, 264, 365
    infinity not provable 85, 124
  intelligent 38f, 49, 88, 90–4, 184–7, 192, 270f, 343, 365
    knowledge in general *see* intelligent
    of future *see* foreknowledge
  necessary being 361, 364, 382
  omnipotent Ockham 46, 48ff, 66f, 91, **94f**, 104f, 107, 109, 116, 151f; *also* 124, 133, 238, 365
    omnipotence known only by faith 66, 84f, 116
    and human free will 217
  omnipresent 239, 289, 365
  omniscient 92, 94, 229
  personal in and through creation 270
  providence 49, 134, 221, 226, 321, 342
  simplicity 203, 239, 365
  unicity 82ff, 123, 155, 163, 363f
  unity 185f, 212, 236, 242, 365
  will 88, 91, 94, 124, 134, 271, 365
    and man's sin *see* sin
    and moral law *see* natural law, God's will
  wisdom 293
Goddam, Adam *see* Adam Wodham
gold, transformation into 251, 305
Gomez Arboleya, E. 446*
good 85f, 144, 267f, 272, 293, 298, 322, 338, 355, 359f, 409f
  common G. 298, 318, 321, 323, 328, 381, 383, 393f, 398
  God the absolute G. *see* God, nature of: good
  moral G. 384–7, 390
  self-diffusing 203
  temporal and spiritual 168, 403
good faith 315, 330, 333
goods, temporal *see* ownership; private property
Görlitz 270
Gough, J. W. 443*

government 111, 118f, 173, 298, 312, 315–18, 322f, 326, 328, 348f, 393f, 396
  based on contract 312, 314, 323, 337, 348, 396
  church G. 310, 323f
  constitutional G. 310, 326f
  elective G. 173
  forms of G. vary 119, 311f, 326, 332, 349, 352, 395
  world-wide G. *see s.v.*
  See also political authority; ruler
Grabmann, M. 200, 428*, 446*
grace 126, 182, 200, 378
  and free will (*De Auxiliis* controversy) 342–4
Gradi, R. 438*
grammar, grammarians 52, 54, 209
Granada 353
Grant, R. 440*
graphs Nicholas Oresme 160
Gratian 172
Graves, F. P. 437*
gravity 157f, 159f, 163, 280f, 284, 288
  centre of G. not centre of volume 159f
  specific G. 281
  See also attraction
Great Western Schism, the 9, 120, 180, 202, 233
greed 320, 333
Greek language 207–11, 213, 215
Greek philosophy and thought 1, 8, 48f, 91, 210, 212ff, 354, 377, **406–13**, 415, 421, 423
Greenberg, S. 438*
Gregory XI, pope 180
Gregory XIV, pope 254
Gregory XVI, pope 196
Gregory of Nyssa, St. 181
Gregory of Rimini 124f, 384, 427
Gregory of Valentia 341
Grenoble 263
Greville, Robert 292
Groenendael 198
Grosseteste, Robert 156f, 165
Grotius, Hugo 312, **328–34**, 352, 380, 442ff*
Guarino of Verona 208
Guelluy, R. 431*
gunpowder 17, 293
Guterman, N. 439*

INDEX

habit 27f, 102f
haecceitas see individuality
Hak, H. 436*
Halberstadt 155
Hamann, A. 431*
happiness 217, 253, 264, 266, 436*
  eternal H. 244
  purpose of philosophy 215
  willed freely 102
Hardie, R. P. 437*
Harvey, William 279f
Haskins, C. H. 433*
hatred 132, 253, 257, 293
hatred of God 95, 104, 132, 147, 385, 390
Hauréau, B. 429*
Hawkins, D. J. B. 429*
Hearnshaw, F. J. C. 443*
heat 72, 139f, 160, 162, 251, 287, 305ff
Heath, D. D. 441*
heathens see paganism
heaven
  astral 214, 226, 240, 251, 362
  of the just see paradise
heavenly bodies 36f, 82, 214, 252, 268, 327
  influence of see astrology
  movement of 159, 165f, 241, 261, 410
heavy and light matter 157, 280. See also gravity
Hebrew language 213, 215
Hegel, G. W. F. 245, 262, 273, 277, 379
Hegius 209
Heidelberg university 148f, 155, 209, 232
Heidingsfelder, G. 433*
heliocentric theory see astronomy
hell 132, 229, 270
Hellenism 213. See also Greek philosophy and thought
Hellin, J. 446*
Helmont, Van see Van Helmont
Henry III, king of France, murder of 348
Henry VII, king of England 310
Henry VIII, king of England 320
Henry of Ghent 10, 15, 24, 26, 28, 41, 150, 361
Henry of Harclay **39f**, 41f, 430*
Henry Suso, Bl. 181ff, 186, 195, **196-8**, 200f, 434f*

Heraclides of Pontus 162
Heraclitus 408
Heraclitus Ponticus 162
heresy 177, 204, 254f, 262, 271, 403
Hermes Trismegistus 212
Hermetic literature 212 n.
Hermits of St. Augustine see Augustinian Order
Hermolaus Barbarus 221
Hervaeus Natalis 10, 25, 27, 40f, 429* (under Durandus)
Hervé Nédellec see Hervaeus Natalis
Heytesbury, William 122, 148
hierarchy of being see being, degrees of
Hilton, Walter 181
Hippocrates 280
Hirschberger, J. 429*
history 170, 225, 295, 319f, 324, 327, 413, 442*
  Comte's three stages of 423f
  divine H. 324
  historical science 277
  natural H. see s.v.
  philosophy of H. see s.v.
history of philosophy 190, 415, 421
Hobbes, Thomas 269, 277, 290f, 312, 349
Hochheim 184
Hochstetter, E. 431*
Hoffmann, E. 437*
Hohenheim, Theophrastus Bombast von see Paracelsus
Holkot, Robert 122-5
Hönigswald, R. 436*
Hooker, Richard 180, 292, 311, **322ff**, 349, 421, 442*
Hornstein, X. de 435*
Hugh of St. Victor 205. See also Victorines
Hugolino of Orvieto 15
Huguenots 314f
Hugueny, E. 434*
human nature see man
human race, unity of 330, 351, 392
humanism 18f, 22, 216f, 219f, 227, 246, 293, 337, 342, 344, 422, 436*
  Renaissance H. 207-11
Hume, David 142f
humility Machiavelli 316f
Hundred Years War 149, 310
Hurtado de Mendoza, Peter de 345

INDEX

Hus, John 148f, 202ff
Husserl, E. 409
Huygens, Christian 281, 284
hydrostatics 281
hylomorphism 366, 376. *See also* form, matter
   in man *see* soul and body
   and modes 369f
hylozoism 251ff, 257, 259, 261f
hypothesis 151, 157, 161f, 164f, 250, 278f, 282-5, 291, 297, 301, 306, 309, 407f

Iamblichus 211f
idea Petrus Aureoli 30ff; Ockham 54-9, 63, 78ff, 85ff; also 220, 262, 301
   being, I. of *see s.v.*
   Common I. 79, 85ff
   Composite I. 87, 373
   Confused I. 40
   Connotative I. 86f. *See also* term, connotative
   not distinct from intellect 57
   Divine I. *see* ideas, divine
   Formal I. 357
   Innate I. *see s.v.*
   Objective I. 30ff
   Proper I. 78f, 86f
   Simple I. 86f
   Transcendental I. 300
   Universal I. Epistemology *see* ideas, objective validity of
   Ontology *see* universals
   Psychology *see* ideas, universal, existence of; ideas, origin of
   Univocal I. *see* univocal
idea, universal: existence of Ockham **55-9,** 79; Petrus Aureoli **30-3;** *also* 11, 124, 151, 249, 264
idealism
   German 245, 270, 273
   subjective 31
ideas, divine Ockham 50f, 58, **88-92,** 93, 104; *also* 49f, 58, 191, 197, 203f, 258
ideas, objective validity of 28-32, 40, 42, 56f
ideas, origin of 30f, 39f, 42, 100
   dependence on sense 200, 222, 289, 417
ideas, platonic theory of 49, 191, 211f, 242, **409-12**

idols Francis Bacon 298, **302-4**
ignorance
   docta ignorantia (Nicholas of Cusa) *see s.v.*
   invincible 106
   of natural law 387f
illumination, divine 212
image 57, 145, 222, 229f, 249
   I. of God 192f, 195, 197, 240, 421
imagination 30f, 145, 295, 309, 373
imago Dei see image of God
immaterial reality 300, 356f. *See also* spirit
immortality of human soul 212f, 221, 226, 251, 253, 264, 266, 269f, 321, 337
   denied 4, 19, 213, 221-6
   held by faith 11, 35ff, 96, 225, 340
   not provable 28, 36f, 82, 96, 145, 226, 298, 300, 340
imperialism 319, 333
impetus theory **158ff,** 165f, 433*
   I. from God 159, 165f
impulse *see* impetus theory
imputability and free will 101
Incarnation, The 340, 413
inceptor 43
inclination and free will 103
incomplexum 55. See also *notitia incomplexa*
incorruptible beings 36
Index of prohibited books 283
Indians, South American 350
indifferentism 321
indirect power of papacy 2, 8, 346, 354, 402f, 444f*
individualism 18, 207f, 216, 270, 312
individuality (haecceity) 40, 355, 360f, 364
individual, the 29, 33, 40f, 49, 56, 58, 60, 90, 151, 218f, 242f, 246, 267, 360
   all existents are individual 29, 50, 58ff, 90ff, 151, 219, 360
   knowledge of *see* singulars, knowledge of
   and society 328f
individuation, principle of 29, 40, 355, 360f
   matter as principle of 24, 40, 360, 378

INDEX

induction Fr. Bacon 289, 293f, 298, 301f, 304–7, 309; *also* 73, 126, 218f
  historical I. Machiavelli 319f
  inductive method 293, 305ff, 309
  per enumerationem 304f
inertia, law of 158
inference, theory of 53
inferiora entis 356, 358f. *See also* being, idea of
infinite series of causes 81ff, 129, 362f
infinity Nicholas of Cusa 237, 240f, 245; *also* 86, 256, 438f*
  of God *see* God, nature of
  of world *see* world
Ingolstadt 215
innate ideas and knowledge 62, 64, 417
  of God Melanchthon 227
innocence, state of 393f
Inquisition, the 258, 281, 285f
instinct 253
intellect Ockham 54, 57ff, 63, 96, 100; *also* 26f, 30–3, 36, 134, 141, 184, 206, 221f, 226, 249, 291
  active I. 100, 226
  likeness to God 192f
  one in all men 4f, 221, 340, 416
  primary object of 80
  and reason 237
  sense, dependence on 64, 222ff, 252f, 264
  universal I. Bruno 259, 262
  will, action on 102
  will, not distinct from 27
intellectus et ratio 237
intelligence *see* intellect
intelligences, separate 159, 223f
intelligentia simplex 206
intentio animae 54, 69
intentio prima, secunda see intention
intention
  first, second 32, 55f, 58f, 374
  of the mind, 54, 69
international, supranational *see* world-wide
introspection 33f, 63f, 229. *See also* self-knowledge
intuition Ockham 12f, 15, 33n., **62–7**, 71f, 153; Petrus Aureoli 30, 32f; *also* 124, 130, 137f, 140f, 148, 154, 223, 237, 375

certainty of *see* certitude
no human I. of God 78, 81, 86
I. without real object 33n., **64–7**, 130f, 137, 151
inverse square law 284
Iserloh, E. 45n.*
Isidore of Seville, St. 349
Islamic philosophy 8, 33, 214, 354
Italian language 207
Italy 16, 22, 150, 171f, 176ff, 210, 215, 229, 258, 311, 316–19
  Italian Renaissance **207f**, 209–12, 439*
Iturrioz, J. 446*
ius
  ius gentium 350ff, **391f**, 404. *See also* law of nations
  and *lex* 382, 444*
  I. in re, ad rem 382
  See also right

Jacob Wimpfeling 209
Jacobi, F. H. 262
Jacobi, J. 439*
Jacobi, M. 438*
James I, king of England 311, 347, 354, 399
James of Metz **24f**, 26, 28, 41f, 429*
Jan van Schoonhoven 199
Javelli, Chrysostom 336
Jeans, Sir J. H. 440*
Jerome, St. 201
Jerome of Prague 148, 203f
Jesuit Order 22, 210, 298, 312, 336, 341–6, 348n., 349, 353, 355, 443*, 445f*
Jesus Christ *see* Christ
Jews *see* Judaism
Joannes Dominici 10
John St., apostle 212
John XXI, pope *see* Peter of Spain
John XXII, pope 10, 44f, 111f, 114–17, 170, 177, 184
John Buridan 149, 154f, 158f, 163, 432f*
John Capreolus 10, **150**, 336
John Chrysostom, St. 330
John Fisher, St. 209
John Gerson 181ff, 199, 201, **202–6**, 427, 435*, 443*
John Hus 148f, 202ff
John Lutterell 43f

INDEX

John of Bassolis 124
John of Jandun 170 ff, 179 f
John of Legnano 350
John of Mirecourt **127-34**, 136, 431*
John of Montreuil 435*
John of Naples 10, 41
John of Paris 349
John of Ripa 124
John of Rodington 124
John of St. Thomas 150, 345, 444*
John of Salisbury 207, 347
John of the Cross, St. 181
John Scotus Eriugena 239, 244, 414
Jordanus Nemorarius 156
joy 253, 267
Judaism 213, 216, 354, 418
judges, judiciary 174, 176, 294
judgment John of Mirecourt 127-30; also 63, 65 f, 137, 219 f, 359, 384
  obstacles to objective J. 302 f
  value-J. 329, 409
  See also proposition
jurisdiction, spiritual 176 ff, 233 f, 314, 346 f, 402
  and temporal see two swords
jurisdiction, temporal see political authority
jus see ius
justice 106, 147, 224 f, 298, 444*
  commutative, distributive and legal J. 382
  to individuals and nations 330
  of laws see law, conditions of just L.; unjust LL.
Justinian, emperor 406
Justus Lipsius 19, 228

Kant 225, 276, 425
Karrer, Otto 188 f, 434*
Kelsey, F. W. 442*
Kepler, John 21, 156, **283 f**, 286, 440*
keys, power of the see jurisdiction, spiritual
Kierkegaard, S. 379
king see ruler
  divine right of kings see s.v.
Klibansky, R. 434*
Knolles, R. 442*
knowledge John of Mirecourt 127-31; Nicholas of Autrecourt 136-42, 145; Petrus Auroeli 30-3; Ockham 60-7, 71 f, 76; also 26 f, 200, 217, 219, 222 ff, 229 f, 256 ff, 265, 300, 420, 424
Abstractive K. 64 f
A priori K. see innate ideas
Empirical K. 140, 155, 289 f. See also experience
Factual K. 137, 153, 219, 278 f, 290, 301 f, 424
Immediate K. see intuition
Innate K. see innate ideas
Intuitive K. see intuition
practical value 293
Probable K. see probable arguments
of self see self-knowledge
Sense-K. see s.v.
theory of K. 46, 215, 263 f, 431*, 445*. See also epistemology
Knox, John 313 f
Knox, T. F. 435*
Koch, J. 41, 429*, 438*
Koyré, A. 440*
Kraus, J. 430*
Kristeller, P. O. 436 f*

Lagarde, G. de 71, 171, 431*, 434*
Lambert of Auxerre 51
Lang, A. 431*
language 39, 52, 54 f, 76, 89 n., 217 ff, 237, 304, 409 f. See also word
Lappe, J. 135, 431*
La Ramée, Pierre de see Ramus, Petrus
Lateran Council, fifth 221, 226
Latin 19, 182, 207-10, 215, 292
Laurentius Valla **217 f**, 220, 436*
Lavaud, B. 434*
law Hooker 322 ff; Marsilius of Padua 173-6, 178; Suárez **380-405**; also 111, 119, 311, 317, 352, 354, 447*
Canon L. see s.v.
Christ, L. of 175, 178
Christian L. 330. See also Christ, L. of; grace, L. of
Civil L. 351, 381, 391-4
Criminal L. 112, 320 f, 351, 389
definition of 381
Demonstrative L. 384
Divine L. 174 f, 178, 299, 331, 333, 377, 380, 402
Eternal L. 311, 322, **382 f**

INDEX

law—*contd.*
  Grace, L. of 386
  Human L. 174, 178, 322, 329, 380f, 383, 391ff, 399ff
  human nature as basis of L. 329f
  International L. 23, 350, 444*
  Ius Gentium see *s.v.*
  just LL., conditions for 381f
  mediaeval theory of 311, 322, 334, 349, 352, 380
  Moral L.: natural see natural L.; supernatural see Christian L.
  morality, L. divorced from 175
  Municipal L. 330
  Nations, L. of 329f, 333f, 350f, **391f.** See also *ius gentium*
  Natural L. see *s.v.*
  Nature, the L. of = natural L. in Grotius
  Nature, LL. of see *s.v.*
  necessity and origin of 173, 175, 329, 382
  Penal L. **399f,** 402
  philosophy of 23, 174, 331, 334, 348f, 352, 380, 442*, 445f*
  Positive L. 311, 322, 329f, 381, 391f, 402
  Preceptive L. 384
  promulgation of 381, 383, 385
  State, L. of the 329f, 391, 394
  Statute L. 173
  Universal L. 324
  unjust L. 381, 400
  unwritten L. 351, 391, 401
  world-wide L. see *s.v.*
Law, William 273
'lay' spirit see secularism
learning, human 308
  division of 295
  patrons of 208, 308
legislator 175f, 317f, 323, 381, 393ff
Leibniz, G. W. 21, 218, 231, 234, 245f, 253, 260, 262, 268f, 286f, 356, 378, 436* (ref. under Marius Nizolius)
Leipzig university 148
leisure 321
Leo XIII, pope 285
Leo Hebraeus 215, 435*
Leonardo da Vinci 246, 279, 433*, 440*
Leopold of Babenberg 117
Lessius, Leonard 341
Leucippus 407

Lever, Ralph 292
Liber de Causis 184f
liberty see freedom in society; free will
libraries 208
life
  motion a sign of 253
  preservation of see self-preservation
light and heavy matter 157, 280. See also gravity
light (*lux*) 238, 251, 254f, 272, 279
likeness see similarity
likeness of God, *vestigium, umbra Dei* 256, 259, 421
Lilley, A. L. 446*
limitation 367, 376f. See also contraction
Limoux 25
Linacre, Thomas 209
Lipsius, Justus 19, 228
Lisbon 51, 342, 351
Lisieux 155
literary style 207, 217, 337, 345
literature 18, 207ff, 293
Littlejohn, J. M. 444*
local motion see motion
Locke, John 289, 292, 311, 322, 349, 421
logarithms 286
logic Fr. Bacon 298, 300ff, 309; Ockham **53–6,** 59f; Peter of Spain 51ff; also 11f, 32, 122–5, 148, 151f, 202f, **217–20** (critics of the Aristotelian logic), 227, 230, 262f, 292, 409f, 413, 418, 420
  analysis, logical 276
  Aristotelian L. see Aristotle, Aristotelianism
  discovery, L. of 219f, 298, 309
  faith, L. of 123f
  Inductive L. Bacon 298, 301f, 309. See also induction
  mediaeval L. 53, 428, 430ff*
  modern L. 53
  Natural L. 219f
  terminist L. **51–6.** See also terminism
  three-valued L. 94, 430*
logicians 11f, 46ff, 52, 84, 88, 122f, 151, 202, 301f, 413
logos see Word, the divine
Lorenzo, Duke of Urbino 315

INDEX

Lorenzo della Valle **217f**, 220, 436*
Louis XI, king of France 149
Louvain 149, 341
love 215, 253, 256f, 293, 392, 435f*
love of God 104f, 192f, 197ff, 206, 212, 215, 256f
Ludwig IV (of Bavaria), emperor 111, 116f, 119, 135, 170, 177
Lugo, John de 345
Lull, Raymond 262
Lupton, J. H. 442*
Luther, Martin 22, 209, 227f, 283, 313, 315, 378
Lutheranism 22, 227, 262, 313
Lutterell, John 43f
Lychetus, Francis 341
Lyons 345

Machiavelli, Niccolò 21, 311f, **315–20**, 441ff*
McIntyre, J. L. 439*
McMurrich, J. P. 440*
macrocosm, microcosm 265f
man the microcosm *see* man
magic 214, 250, 252, 266, 274, 294, 297, 433*, 441*
magistrate *see* ruler
magnet 156, 280, 293
Mahieu, L. 446*
Maier, A. 433*
Maignan, Emmanuel 345f
man 19, 98–101, 104, 212ff, 228, 240, 244, 253, 268, 270, 297f, 329, 436*
  end of man *see s.v.*
  development of 216, 250
  God, relation to 212, 216, 248, 270, 272, 274, 288. *See also* soul, human
  in Greek philosophy 408f
  as microcosm 20, 211, 214, 240, 243f, 246, 257, 264ff, 293
  three-fold unity of 198, 265.
  See also soul, human
Manderscheid, Count von 232
Manegold of Lautenbach 347
Mantua 222
Manuel Chrysoloras 207
Marega, I. M. 444*
Mariana, Juan 312, 347ff
Marius Nizolius 218ff, 436f*
marriage 386f
  lay dispensation from impediments 171

Marriott, W. K. 441*
Marsh, Peter 41
Marsilius Ficinus 19, **211ff**, 221, 231, 354, 436*
Marsilius of Inghen 149, 155, 158f, 433*
Marsilius of Padua 10, 44, 116, **168–80** (*see* Contents p. vi), 310, 433f*
Martin, G. 431*
Marxism 170
Mästlin, Michael 283
Mastrius, Bartholomew, 345
materialism 264, 291, 300
materia signata 360
mathematics 15f, 68, 148, 156f, 160, 218, 227, 232f, 237, 240, 244, 246, 250ff, 277–80, 283, 286–90, 297, 308, 332, 346, 412
  astronomy 283, 286
  Galileo 280
  laws, mathematical 252
  and nature 281, 284f
  and science 277ff
matter 80, 90, 252, 287, 290, 292, 306, 407, 423
  Anorganic M. 253
  elements of *see s.v.*
  and form 79, 370f
  individuation, M. as principle of *see* individuation
  knowledge of 63, 142
  metaphysics, treatment in 356
  original M. 251, 267
  and partial mode of existence 370
  soul, M. acting on 27, 33, 37
  of sun and moon 284
matter, prime 98, 259, 264
Maurus, Sylvester 345
meaning 39, 52, 54–7, 218, 237, 374, 409, 431*
Meaux 25f
mechanicism 166, 249, 264, 269, 287–91, 300
mechanics 16, 156, 277, 281, 286, 290f, 297
mediaeval philosophy 1, 3, 17, 23, 90, 428f*
  Aristotle, discovery of and 3, 414–18
  Greek thought and 413f
  and law *see* law, mediaeval theory of

mediaeval philosophy—*contd*.
  and modern philosophy 230f, 245, 421ff
  and theology 1-7, 11, 13ff, 88, 95, 107f, 126
  variety in 127
Medici, Cosimo de' 210f
medicine 212n., 218, 229, 249, 251f, 266ff, 279f, 297
Medina, Bartholomew of 341
medium quo 30f, 59, 63
Meinecke, F. 443*
Melanchthon, Philip 22, 209, **227f**, 283, 378, 437*
Melchior Cano *see* Cano, Melchior
memory 218, 252, 295
Mennicken, P. 438*
mens as immortal principle 251, 266
Menut, A. D. 433*
Mercurius Trismegistus 211
merit 105, 147
  demerit 131f
Merton College, Oxford 123
metaphor 338, 361
metaphysic of essence 48-51, 95
metaphysics Fr. Bacon 296f, 299, 303, 305f, 308; Ockham 12-14, 58, **77f**, 84, 88, 108, 123, 431*; Suárez 345, 353-6, **356f**, 379, 445ff*; *also* 1f, 7f, 11-14, 17, 32, 40f, 5?, 58, 123, 148, 155, 202, 204, 274, 308, 338, 409-12, 417-20, 423ff, 428*
  essences, M. of 48-51, 95
  essentialist M. 377ff
  ethics and 108
  existential M. 377, 379
  General and Special M. 356
  object of **77f**, 354, **356f**, 372
  and physics 159f, 165f, 296, 305f, 346, 440*
  and theology 343f, 353
  traditional M. attacked 11-14, 123f, 126, 146, 148, 151f, 217, 420, 424
metempsychosis 251, 269
method
  inductive 293, 305ff, 309
  Mill's MM. 309
  scientific *see s.v.*
Metz 24f, 135
Michael of Cesena 44, 111
Michalski, C. 432f*
Michel, A. *see* Fritz, G.

microcosm 265
  man as M. *see* man
Milanesi, G. 441*
Mill, J. S. 277, 309
  Mill's methods 309
miracle 5, 36, 95, 155, 225
  miraculous knowledge of non-existing object 64-7, 130
mode of God 80
modes of being Durandus 24-8; Suárez **369f**
modern philosophy and thought 230f, 245, 250, 294, 308, 319, 334, 352, 421f, 424
'modern way, the' *see via moderna*
Molina, Luis 342f, 349, 351, 444*
Molinism 343f, 445*. *See also* Molina
monad 186, 260, 262, 268f
monadology 268f
monarch *see* ruler
monarchy 118, 310ff, 317f, 324, 326, 347, 395
  universal M. (Campanella) 255
money 321
monism 260ff
Monnot, P. 446*
monopsychism 4f, 221, 340, 416
monotheism *see* God, nature of; unicity
  a matter of faith 123
Montaigne, Michel de 19, **228f**, 437*
Montesquieu 325
Montpellier 25, 229
Moody, E. A. 431*, 433*
Moog, W. *see* Frischeisen-Köhler
moon, the 241, 284, 407
moral law, the
  natural *see* natural law
  supernatural *see* law, Christian
moral obligation Ockham 103-7, 109; *also* 133, 322, 381, 386f, 390
  of human laws 383
  of penal laws 399f
moral philosophy *see* ethics
morality 224f, 228f, 321, 332, 380, 408
  certainty in moral matters 331
  Machiavelli and 315ff
  right reason as norm or rule of 106, 322, 330, 384, 386f
More, St. Thomas *see* Thomas More, St.

INDEX

Moreau, P. 437*
Morley, H. 442*
Moses 184, 213
motion Ockham 74ff, 81f, 158; also 16, 157, 160, 240f, 246, 249, 268, 278, 281, 287, 290, 307, 362f, 377, 406, 411, 418, 433*
  circular 158f
  of the earth *see* earth, the eternity of 226
  life, M. a sign of 253
  natural and unnatural or violent 157f
  See also heavenly bodies, movement of
Mourin, L. 435*
movement *see* motion
Mugica, P. 445*
multiplicity 187, 236, 240, 242, 255, 271, 364, 378
Munich 44, 46f
Mys, E. 444*
mystery 217, 272
  divine M's. 215, 299, 419
mysticism 8, 15, **181-206** (ch. 12 Speculative mysticism), 244, 246, 256, 269f, 272, 434ff*
  'German M.' **200ff**, 269
  number-M. 216
  Spanish mystics 181f
  transformation into God 193f
myth 406, 410

name 74, 76, 409
  class N. 125
Napier, John 286
Naples 337, 345
nationalism 2, 120, 312
nation-states 2, 9, 23, 120, 169, 233, 312, 349f
  and world-community 351, 392
natura naturans and *naturata* 260
'natural history' 295, 324
natural law Grotius **328-34;** Ockham 50, **103ff,** 107–10, 113, 115f, 118; Suárez 348, 351f, 381, **383-90,** 391f; *also* 132f, 150ff, 174f, 252, 311ff, 321ff, 326, 328, 350, 421, 442*
  dispensation from 389f
  God's will, dependence on, Ockham 14, 50, 104f, **107-10,** 115f;

also 132f, 147, 151f, 203, 331, 334, 384
  ignorance of 387f
  immutability Suárez **388ff;** *also* 115, 203, 312, 331
  independence of 124, 150, 203, 328, 331, 334, 384f
  and rational nature 383f, 388
  and right reason 105f, 174, 330, 384, 386f
natural laws *see* nature, laws of
natural order, the 4ff, 66f, 95, 113, 155
natural philosophy *see* nature, philosophy of
natural theology Ockham ix, 12, 71, 84; *also* 2, 123f, 126, 129, 131f, 142ff, 183, 237, 295f, 300, 356, 410, 418
naturalism 18f, 211, 213, 248–51, 299, 324
nature (as essence) Fr. Bacon 305ff, 309; *also* 34, 82, 95, 187
  common N. 39f, 56ff, 360, 364
  and *suppositum* 368f
  voice of N. from God 322
nature (as totality) Fr. Bacon 293, 295, 297f, 300, 302f, 306ff; *also* 216, 245, 261, 265, 269, 408f
  divine, N. as expression of the 20, 216, 246, 255–8, 260, 264, 267, 271, 273, 293, 406
  dominion over 21, 293, 297, 300, 306ff
  infinite 20, 231, 246, 248, 260
  laws of Fr. Bacon 296f, 299, 305, 309; *also* 252, 281, 420
  mathematical 252, 281, 287f
  organism, N. as 248, 251, 259, 261
  philosophy of *see s.v.*
  study of 19ff, 167, 246, 255ff, 267, 273, 276, 295, 298, 300, 302, 307, 420, 422
  system, N. as 20f, 214, 226, 230, 246, 248, 252, 260, 288, 406, 408, 420
  uniformity of 95
  world-soul *see s.v.*
nature, philosophy of 19f, 29, 232, 246, **248-74** (ch. 16-17; *see* Contents p. vi), 276, 279, 295ff, 299, 302, 304f, 355f, 406ff, 412, 418, 420, 433* 438f*
nature, state of (Mariana) 348f

INDEX

necessary being 361, 364, 382
necessitarianism, Greek 48
necessity in Nature unknowable 140
negations 90, 373f
negative theology, negative way *see via negativa*
neo-Platonism 20, 184ff, 195, 197, 200, 210–13, 220, 246, 248, 255, 258f, 261, 265, 292f, 412f
neo-Pythagoreanism 216
neo-Scholasticism 379
nerves of the body 252
Newton, Sir Isaac 281, **284,** 286–9
Nichol, J. 441*
Nicholas V. antipope 116
Nicholas of Autrecourt 127, **135-48,** 151, 155, 431f*
Nicholas of Cusa **231-47** (*see* Contents, p. vi), 248, 256, 258–63, 265, 269f, 272, 292, 437f*
Nicholas of Oresme 15, 155, 159, **160-3,** 165, 433*
Nicholas of Paris 51
Nicholas of St. John the Baptist 345
Nicholas of St. Victor 41
Nietzsche 316f
Nipho, Agostino 150, 221, 226
Nizolius, Marius 218ff, 436f*
nobles 318
Nola 258
nominalism 11f, 32, 39, 41f, 43n., 46, 53, 55, 88, 108, 122–7, 148–52, 154f, 164f, 182, 200, 202, 204ff, 227, 287, 334f, 361, 365, 372, 419, 424, 430ff*, 445*
and science 153, 155, 164f, 287. *See also* Ockhamism
notitia incomplexa 71
nouns 76
number 236, 327
N-mysticism 216

obligation, moral *see* moral obligation
observation 15f, 156, 164, 218, 255, 266, 277–80, 283ff, 289f, 301, 306, 309, 407, 424
occultism 216, 266, 269
Ockham, Surrey 43
Ockham, William *see* William of Ockham
Ockhamism 6, 28, 39–42, 46, 68, 71, 183, 203, 331, 431–3*

the Ockhamist Movement (ch. 9) 122–52, 431f*
and science 15f, 20f, 72f, 153ff, 163f
See also via moderna
Ockham's razor *see* economy, principle of
O'Donnell, J. R. 135, 431*
Olivi, Peter John 98, 158
omne quod movetur ab alio movetur see Quidquid movetur . . .
One, the 262, 413
God as *see* God
ontology 356, 379
opinion 127
opposites 267, 269, 272
coincidence of *see s.v.*
optics 156, 279
order, and proof of God's existence 363
Order of Preachers *see* Dominican Order
ordinatio 44n.
Oresme, Nicholas of *see* Nicholas of Oresme
organism 268, 291
nature as O. *see* nature (as totality)
Oriental thought and study of nature 19
original sin *see* fall of man
Orphic hymns 211
Osiander, Andreas 283
Oviedo, Francis de 345, 355
Owen, J. 437*
ownership Ockham 112–15; Suárez 389
of power 397
use and right to use 114f. *See also* private property
Oxford 12, 39, 43, 46f, 123, 149, 258, 292, 432*

Padua 150, 170, 221f, 226, 232, 280, 337
paganism 150, 204, 208, 212, 220, 316, 351, 414
Paludanus, Petrus 41
pantheism 20, 79f, 188f, 195, 227, 239f, 248, 259, 261, 270
papacy Marsilius of Padua 170ff, 177f; Nicholas of Cusa 232ff; *also* 318, 346f, 443f*
arbitration 403

INDEX 469

papacy—*contd.*
  and Empire *see s.v.*
  Ockham and 111f, 114, 116–21
  political jurisdiction, no universal 2, 8, 117f, 168, 346, 402f
  indirect power *ibid.* and 354
  property rights of 114, 177
  and State (theory) *see* church and state
  and States (practice) 8f, 111, 402f
papal states 402
Paracelsus 263, **266f,** 268–70, 272f, 292, 439*
paradise
  earthly 394
  heavenly 229
Paris 2, 4f, 15, 29, 43n., 124, 127, 135, 149f, 154f, 170, 184, 195, 202, 263, 432*
Paris, chapter of 24
Parmenides 408
participation 361, 376ff, 383
particulars, knowledge of *see* singulars, knowledge of
Pascal, Blaise 204
Passerini, L. 441*
passiones entis see being, attributes of
past, abolition of, not contradictory 133
patriotism 319
Patristic teaching *see* Fathers of the Church
Patrizzi, Francesco **254f,** 438*
Paul, St. 212
Paul III, pope 249, 283
Paul of Venice 150
Pavia 251, 337
pedagogy 298
Peip, A. 439*
Pelagianism 344
Pelster, F. 43n., 430*
penal law, *see* law, penal
penalty for violation of penal law *see* law, penal
Penny, A. J. 439*
perception 64, 137f, 249, 268, 290, 301
  See also intuition; sense-knowledge
perfection, pure 364f
per se notum 60
person, personality 100f, 208, 216, 220, 228, 293, 368

Peter, St. 38
Peter Aureolus *see* Petrus Aureoli
Peter d'Ailly 146, 202, 205, 390
Peter Damian, St. 133
Peter John Olivi 98, 158
Peter Lombard, 24, 29, 135, 150, 199, 341, 344
Peter Marsh 41
Peter of Abano 170, 180
Peter of Auvergne 24
Peter of Candia 124
Peter of Maricourt 16, 156
Peter of Spain **51–3,** 55, 122, 148, 151
Petersen, P. 437*
Petrarch 207, 436*
Petrus Aureoli **29–39,** 40ff, 46, 58, 93f, 361, 427, 429f*
Petrus de Palude 41
Petrus Niger 336
Petzelt, A. 437*
phantasm 57, 200, 222
phenomenalism 19, 142f
phenomenology 409
phenomenon *see* appearance
Philip IV (the Fair), king of France 9, 119
Philoponus 158
philosophy
  ancilla theologiae 7, 376, 418
  Christian P. *see s.v.*
  courses of 344f, 355
  division of 295f, 356
  Essential P. 377ff
  existence, P. of 377, 379, 418
  first P. 296, 300, 354, 357
  Greek P. *see s.v.*
  handmaid of theology 7, 376, 418
  history, P. of 319, 327
  mathematics and 290
  nature, P. of *see s.v.*
  Renaissance P. *see s.v.*
  salvation, P. as way of 182, 412ff
  schools and systems of 10, 17f, 182, 304, 414f
  and science 20ff, 165f, 250ff, 266, 275ff, 287, **288–91,** 308, 345f, 407ff, **420–5,** 433*, 441*.
    See also Ockhamism and science
  and theology Fr Bacon 295, 298ff, 304; Gerson 203f, 206; Ockham 48f, 67, 73f, 84, 88, synthesis 1–8, 13ff, 49, 376;

philosophy and theology—*contd.*
415f, 418f; separation 5–8, 11, 13f, 19, 48f, 84, 126, 179, 248, 261, 267, 415, 419f; *also* 20, 23, 228, 336, 340, 342, 344, 346, 353, 370, 413f, 421, 423f, 429*, 431*
also 3f, 218, 295, 304
physics Fr. Bacon 294, 296–9, 303, 305f, 308; *also* 16, 21, 68, 154ff, 158ff, 164ff, 226f, 263f, 275f, 278, 287ff, 346, 433*
Aristotelian *see* Aristotle, Aristotelianism
and mathematics 287, 308
physiology 268, 279f
Picavet, F. 429*
Piccolomini, Aeneas Sylvius 208n.
Pico della Mirandola, John **213–15,** 216, 354, 436*
Pico della Mirandola, John Francis 215
Pierre d'Auriole *see* Petrus Aureoli
piety 270, 272f, 289
Piny, Alexander 345
Pisa 44, 280f
Pius II, pope 208n
place 74f, 253, 370
Natural P. 157–61, 163
Plaffert, F. 446*
planets 163, 214, 261, 282–5, 288
Plato 4, 19, 33, 49, 91, 161, 172, 204, 211–17, 220, 240, 243, 299, 326, 337, 408, **409ff,** 412
Republic 255, 304, 320
Timaeus 161, 211, 213, 251, 254, 410
translations of 19, 211
Platonic Academy of Florence 210, 216, 292, 436*
Platonism
Cambridge Platonists 292
and Christianity 210–13, 254, 413
and God 203, 248, 254
ideas, theory of 49, 91, 204, 211, 411f
and mathematics 244, 287
opposition to 91, 203, 205, 378
Renaissance revival of 18ff, **210–16,** 248, 435f*
also 220f, 223, 232, 242, 257ff, 304
pleasure 103, 106, 217

Plethon, George Gemistus 210ff, 220
Plotinus 19, 186, 192, 211f, 216, 412
plurality of forms upheld 40, 97–100
pneuma 252
poetry 295
point 255
Poiret, Pierre 273
political authority Grotius 332; Ockham 111, **116–20;** Suárez **392–9;** *also* 177, 325f
Emperor, no supreme power 397
limitation of 311ff, 332
of pope *see* papacy, political jurisdiction
source of 445*
not immediately from God *see* divine right of kings
ultimately from God 168, 347, 395
immediately from people 176, 233, 323, 328, 332, 347, 352, 394f
not from pope 117f, 168, 346f, 402
See also social contract
political theory Machiavelli 311f, 315 ao, 441ff*; Marsilius of Padua 168–80, 433f*; Ockham 111, 116–19; Suárez 354, 380, 392–405, 444–7*; *also* 8ff, 23, 147, 255, 297f, 428*, 442f*
mediaeval 310ff
Renaissance 310–34 (*see* Contents, p. vii)
Renaissance Scholastics 346–52
politics Ockham 46f, 111f, 120f; *also* 21, 169f, 179, 229
and education 320
and morality 315, 319, 321
religion and 314
Pollet, V. M. I. 443*
Pomponazzi, Pietro 19, 221, **222–6,** 227, 337, 436f*
Poncius, John 345
Poole, R. L. 429*
poor, the 320f
pope
election of 113
Ockham and position of 119–21
See also papacy
Pordage, John 273

Porphyry 337, 413, 444*
Porta, Simon 226
positivism 300, 352, 423f
posse 238
possibility, possibles 61, 95, 366
potentia absoluta Dei and *ordinata* 74, 105, 133, 151
potentia obedientialis 378
potentiality 376f
    active *see* power
    logical 366f
poverty, evangelical 44, 111–16, 177
power 238, 257, 305f, 316f
    all from God 383
    knowledge is P. 300
power, political 310–13, 315f, 318f, 393, 397
    royal 313, 318, 347, 396
powers of man *see* faculties
praeambula fidei 13f, 126, 419
praedicamenta see categories
Prague 148
preambles of faith *see praeambula fidei*
predestination 337, 344, 430*
predetermination 39, 93, 343f
predication 39, 80. See also analogy
prejudices 302
premotion, physical 343
Presbyterians, Scottish 315
pre-Socratic philosophy **406–9**, 412, 420
Previté-Orton, C. W. 178, 434*
pride 203f, 206
priesthood 173, 177, 179
prince *see* ruler
principle
    analytic 60
    of contradiction *see* contradiction, principle of
    of excluded middle, *see* excluded middle, principle of
    first PP. *see s.v.*
    moral PP. 385f
printing 17, 293
private property Ockham 112–15; Suárez 348, **389**, 398; *also* 313, 321, 325f, 348
privation 90, 133f, 373f
privilege 402
probability 126, 145f. *See also* probable arguments

probable arguments 12, 52, 123, 131, 140, 144f, 151
Proclus 185, 194, 196, 205, 212
progress 424
    technical 293
projectile, motion of 157–60. *See also* impetus theory
promises, fulfilment of 329, 333
proof *see* demonstration
properties 61f
property *see* ownership; private property
proposition
    analytic 60, 123, 125, 128ff, 136f, 148, 151
    contingent 62f, 66
    empirical 130f, 148, 151
    hypothetical 61
    necessary 60f
    universal 60
    also 37, 53, 55, 57, 59, 63, 76
Protestantism 22, 178, 209f, 227f, 269ff, 273, 311–14, 378, 437*
providence, divine *see* God, nature of: providence
prudence 298
Pseudo-Dionysius 181, 185, 189, 194, 196f, 199f, 204ff, 212f, 244
psychology Durandus 27f, 41; Ockham 12, **96–103;** *also* 192, 218, 276, 298, 353, 355f, 417f
Pufendorf, S. 331
punishment
    eternal *see* hell
    after death *see* sanction, moral
pure act 362, 365
Puy 25
Pyrrhonism 228f
Pythagoras 216
Pythagoreanism 216, 244, 283, 287, 304, 408, 412

qualitative change *see* change, accidental
qualities, secondary 287
quantitative change 74
quantity 254, 297, **370**
Quétif-Echard 443*
quidditas see essence
quidquid movetur ab alio movetur 81n., 362, 375, 419
quintessence 159
Quintilian 208n.

Raby, R. 435*
Ragusa 325
rainbow 156
Ramists see Ramus, Petrus
Ramus, Petrus **219f,** 228, 292, 436f*
Randall, J. H. 436f*
rationalism 7, 47, 61, 68, 264, 290
Raymond Lull 262
Raymond of Peñafort, St. 350
razor, Ockham's see economy, principle of
Reade, W. H. V. 423n.*
realism (universals) 2, 11, 46, 48, 50f, 56, 149, 151, 155, 203f, 219, 431*
  Exaggerated R. 39, 50, 58, 91
  Moderate R. 42
  Scotist R. 39, 46, 50, 56, 148f, 430*
reason, human 236f, 295, 424
  and faith see faith and reason
  and intellect (*intellectus et ratio*) see intellect
  right R. see s.v.
reasoning 219, 255
  analogical 252f
  a priori see s.v.
  dialectical 123
  probable see probable arguments
  See also demonstration
rebellion 324, 332, **397f.** See also resistance to ruler
Recaséns Siches, L. 446*
recta ratio see right reason
Redemption, the 269
Reed, A. W. 442*
reform
  of Church 211, 234
  of society or State 211, 317
  also 195, 208f, 211, 220, 228, 435*, 437*
Reformation, the 120, 209, 313f, 322, 335, 429*
Reformers, the Protestant 22, 209, 313ff
refraction 156
Régnon, T. de 444*
Regout, D. 446*
regress of causes, infinite 81ff, 128, 362
reincarnation 251, 269
Reinhold, Erasmus 283

relation Durandus 26–8, 46; Ockham 46, 67, **68–71,** 74f, 95, 101; Suárez **370ff,** 373f; also 24f, 253
  foundation, distinction from 26, 68ff, 371
  Mental R. 25, 69, 371, 373f
  Predicamental R. 371f
  Real R. 25, 69f, 370f
  Transcendental R. 371f
relativity
  of motion 241
  of truth 228
religion 178, 182, 209f, 221, 228f, 422
  established by secular power 314
  Natural R. 321
  and science 248, 424f
  See also salvation; theology
religious ideals and practice 182f, 195f, 198, 202ff, 206, 208–11, 216, 247, 270, 288f
  indifferentism 321
  R. toleration see toleration
religious orders and Ockhamism 125
Renaissance, the (see Contents pp. vi–vii)
  humanism 207–11
  Italian R. **207f,** 209–12, 439*
  Literary R., mediaeval origins 207
  Northern R. **208–10,** 265
  and science 21f, 153, **275–91,** 420, 422
republic 178, 318, 442*
  Italian R's 175
  Roman R. 317f
repulsion 249. See also antipathy
resistance to ruler Bodin 324, 326; Grotius 332; Protestants **313ff;** Suárez **397ff;** also 328, 348, 352
responsibility, moral, and free will 101
Reuchlin, John 210, **215f,** 292
reunion of Eastern Church 210, 232, 234, 244
revelation 2, 4, 6f, 13f, 88, 94, 123, 126, 128, 148, 151, 173, 176, 179, 183, 196, 212, 215, 225, 227f, 295, 298, 314, 323, 413, 419
  and moral law 104, 107f, 110
revolt see rebellion
reward see sanction

INDEX

Reynolds, B. 442*
Rheticus, Georg Joachim 283
rhetoric 217-20
Richard Billingham 123f
Richard of St. Victor 201. *See also* Victorines
Richard Rolle of Hampole 181
Richard Swineshead 122f
riches 320
Richter, J. R. 440*
right reason 105-9, 112f, 150, 174, 203, 383
  as norm of morality 106, 322, 330, 384, 386f
rights, natural Ockham 108, 112-16, 119; also 311ff, 443*
rights, renunciation of 113f
Ripa, Raphael 341
Ritchie, D. G. 443*
Ritter, E. 432*
Rivière, E. M. 447*
Robert Bellarmine, St. 285f, 343, 346f, 352, 354, 444*
Robert Grosseteste 156f, 165
Robert Holkot 122-5
Robertson, J. M. 441*
Rodez 150
Roermond 199
Roger Bacon 16, 20, 156f, 183, 278
romanticism 249
Rome
  empire 118
  literature 210
  people's election of bishop 113
  republic 317f
  also 213, 215, 254, 258, 341, 353
Romeyer, B. 429*
Rommen, H. 446*
Rotta, P. 437f*
Rousseau, J. J. 349
Rudolf Agricola 209, 218
Ruggiero, G. de 429*
ruler 118ff, 173, 176, 310-20, 325f, 328, 330, 332, 347ff, 395f
  and custom 401f
  deposition of 118f, 176, 328, 397, 403
  Emperor and national RR. 117, 397
  indirectly subject to pope 346, 402f
  limitations of power 119, 313, 326, 332

H.P. III—31*

resistance to *see* resistance to ruler
royal power 313, 318, 347, 396
source of power *see* political authority
spiritual jurisdiction 346
Ruysbroeck, John 181ff, **198f**, 200f, 204f, 427, 435*
Rychel 199

Sabine, G. H. 443*
sadness 253
Saint-Martin, L. C. de 273
Salamanca 152, 340, 353
Salusbury, T. 440*
salvation 270, 272, 344, 380
  philosophy and 182, 412ff
Salvio, A. de 440*
Salzburg 266
Sanchez, Francis **229f**, 437*
sanction
  legal 174f, 179, 224, 320, 350, 399f
  moral 145, 224, 229, 321
  spiritual 403
Sanderson, John 292
Saragossa, chapter of 24
Sarton, G. 433*
Satan, 267, 272
Saul, king of Israel 349, 396
Savonarola 215
scepticism 18f, 81, 88, 124, 131, 137f, 151f, 206, 208, 211, 228ff, 256, 432*, 437*
Scharpff, F. A. 438*
Scheiner, Christopher 284
Schelling, F. W. 245, 273
Schism, the Western 9, 120, 180, 202, 233
schismatics 403
Scholasticism
  neo-Scholasticism 379
  opposition to 22, 217, 219ff, 227f, 254, 262
  post-Renaissance S. 292, 356, 378
  Renaissance S. 22f, 249, 292, **335-405** (*see* Contents p. vii), 443-6*
  revival of 22f, 335f
Scholastic theology 203, 205f, 353, 423
  and science 345f

Scholasticism—*contd.*
  also 46, 152, 200f, 210, 215, 301, 308, 334, 421, 423, 428f*, 432f*
Schoonhoven, Jan van 199
Schultz, R. 438*
Schwenckfeld, Kaspar von 272
science (notion) (for S. in modern sense *see* S., experimental.) Fr. Bacon 296, 305, 308; Ockham **59f,** 61f, 88; *also* 156f, 219, 420
science, experimental
  Arabian S. 16, 157, 422
  autonomous 20, 166f, 226, 276, 420
  Greek S. 16, 157, 407ff, 422
  Mediaeval S. 153, 155f, 275, 417f, 428*, 433*
  Newtonian S. 22, 287f
  Ockhamism and *see s.v.*
  and philosophy *see s.v.*
  Renaissance S. 16, 21f, 156, 163, 246, 249-53, 263, 275-91 (*see* Contents p. vii), 407, 420f, 423, 440f*
  and theology 161f, 167, 248, 266, 278, 286, 288, 422-5;
  also 15f, 33, 71ff, 153-67 (*see* Contents p. vi), 230, 265ff, 279-81, 294, 300, 308, **420-5,** 428*, 432f*, 440f*
  See also discovery, scientific; scientific method
science, philosophy of 309
scientia media 342ff
scientia potissima 130
scientia rationalis and *realis* 59f
scientific method Fr. Bacon 294, 301f, 304, 306-9; Bacon's Tables (*tabulae*) 306f
  also 73, 156f, 164, 253, 276-81, 289, 407, 420, 423
scintilla animae see soul, human
scintilla conscientiae 201
Scorraille, R. de 446f*
Scotism 10, 39, 99, 124, 200, 340, 345, 357, 361. *See also* realism, Scotist
Scotland 313f
Scott, J. B. 445*
Scotus, John Duns *see* Duns Scotus, John
Scotus Eriugena *see* John Scotus Eriugena
Scriptures, the Holy 39, 104, 145, 161f, 171ff, 177f, 195, 204ff, 209, 256, 272, 285f, 338, 390
secondary qualities 287
secular clergy and nominalism 125
secularism 71, 334, 352, 422f, 431*, 434*
security 321
Sedgwick, W. T. 440*
Segovia 353
self-defence 334, 397f
self-knowledge 129, 138, 200, 223, 229, 256f, 264. *See also* introspection
self-preservation 113, 253, 257
Seneca 71, 150, 269
sensation 27, 33, 63, 97, 199, 249, 252f, 264
sense-knowledge 33, 63ff, 97, 129ff, 137f, 140, 215, 222, 224, 229f, 236f, 252-7, 264, 301
  in absence of real object *see* intuition without real object
  relativity of 228
senses, 97, 99f, 302-3
sentences, meaning of (Plato) 409
separability 68, 99f
Sfondrati, Celestino 345
Sigerist, H. E. 439*
sight *see* vision
sign, 4ff, 58, 60, 124, 137, 238
significatio 52. *See also* meaning
Sikes, J. O. 430*
similarity 25f, 29, 32, 40f, 50, 57f, 68, 79, 219, 242, 358, 361, 371
  between God and creatures 189, 235, 339
sin 107, 110, 113, 224f, 387, 393, 399
  and will of God 103ff, 108f
  God as cause of 133f
  original sin *see* fall of man
  See also evil, moral
Singer, D. W. 438*
singulars, knowledge of Ockham 15, 63; Petrus Aureoli 30, 32f; *also* 375
slavery 321, 351, 391-4
slave-trade 351
Smith, G. 445*
Soares, Francis 345
social contract 176, 312, 327ff, 443*
  to form society 323, 327, 348f, 395f

INDEX

social contract—*contd.*
  of people with ruler 314, 323, 327, 348f, 395ff
socialism 320
society 111, 291, 298, 312, 317, 320-3, 327, 329, 348ff, 392, 443*
  contract of *see* contract; social contract
  natural and necessary 348f, 393f
  origin of *see* social contract
  Perfect S. 168, 173, 179, 381, 392f
  Political S. *see* State
  World-wide S. *see* world-wide
Society of Jesus *see* Jesuit Order
sociology 276
Socrates 229, 269, 406, 408f
Solana, M. 445*
soldiers and morality of a war 404f
Sommervogel and De Backer 443*
Soncinas, Barbus Paulus 336
'sophistical philosophy' 304
sophistical reasoning 52, 302
sophists 408
Sorbonne 135
Soto, Dominic 22, 335, 341, 350, 390
soul 34f, 265, 355, 410
  transmigration of 251, 269
  of the world *see* world-soul
  See also soul, human; spirit
soul and body 251f, 268ff
  S. form of body Petrus Aureoli **34-6;** Ockham **96-9;** *also* 222ff, 226, 253
  and modes 369f
  sensitive F. 97-100
  S. separable from body 99, 101
  S. not separable from body 222ff
soul, human Petrus Aureoli 34-7; *also* 27, 75, 81, 141f, 145, 218, 221, 264f, 297f
  creation of, miraculous 5
  disembodied S. 145, 369
  essence, apex of 192, 195ff, 199, 201, 206
  form of body *see* soul and body
  God, relation to 181, 183, 192ff, 204, 206; *See also* God, union with; man, relation to God
  immaterial 33, 96
  immortal *see* immortality of human soul

Intellectual S. 96-101
scintilla animae 192, 195ff, 201, 266, 270
Sensitive S. 97ff, 298
separated S. *see* disembodied (above)
simple 100, 192
spiritual Ockham 12, 82, 96f, 100; *also* 13, 37, 141f, 222f
transmigration of 251, 269
uncreated element in 193
unicity denied 40, 97-100
sovereign *see* ruler
sovereignty *see* political authority
space 241, 253, **254f,** 257, 261, 264, 289
Spain 22, 310, 335, 350, 378, 399, 445f*
  king of 255
species (class) 32, 50, 57f, 242
  specific nature *see* nature (as essence)
species, cognitive 27, 30f, 42, 59, 249
species intelligibilis 30f, 59
specific unity and individuals 378
Spedding, J. 441*
speech 76, 217, 220. *See also* language; word
spheres, heavenly 159
spinning top 158
Spinoza 21, 215, 253, 260ff, 290, 349
spirit 64, 142, 252, 264, 298, 300, 377
  'animal spirits' 252, 303
  bodily 'spirits' 297
  distinguished from soul 199, 253
  See also soul
spiritual jurisdiction *see* jurisdiction, spiritual
spontaneous generation 251
stars 214, 407
  intuition of 64-7
  motion of 163
State, the Marsilius of Padua 169, 171-3, 175-9; Suárez 389, **392-6,** 402; *also* 2, 9f, 168f, 211, 311f, 317-30, 332f, 346, 352, 438*, 443*, 446*
  authority in *see* political authority
  and Church *see* Church and State (for |theory); papacy and States (for history)

State—contd.
  lay State autonomous 171 ff,
    175–9, 402
  national state see nation-states
  natural institution 393 f
  submission to Luther 313, 315
  world-wide S. see world-wide
statics 440*
stealing see theft
Stegmüller, F. 127, 431*, 445*
Stevin, Simon 280 f
Stillman, J. M. 439*
Stimson, D. 440*
Stoicism 18 f, 217, 228 f, 252, 413
Strasbourg 195 f
Streitcher, K. 445*
Strigel 228
Strong, E. W. 440*
Strowski, F. 437*
Sturt, M. 441*
Suárez, Francis 22 f, 343 ff, **353–405**
  (ch. 22–3. see Contents p.
  vii), 427, 444*, **445 ff***
  De legibus 354, 378, **380–402**
  Disputationes metaphysicae 344,
    353–74, 376, 378, 445 f*
  and essentialist metaphysics 377 ff
  political theory 311 ff, 334, 347 ff,
    392–405
  writings 353
Suárezianism 357, 368, 378
subnotio 249
subsistence (*subsistentia*) 368 ff
substance Suárez 355 ff, 362, **368 f,**
  370; also 24, 74, 96, 134, 141 ff,
  215
  change, substantial see s.v.
  corruption of 145
  Immaterial S. 142, 356, 362
  Material S. 13, 141 f, 356 f, 370
  Primary and Secondary SS. 368
  unknowable 123, 126, 141
succession 75, 240 f
successivum 75
sun, the 241, 261, 282 ff, 407
  anima motrix in sun 284
  stopping the S. (*Jos.* 10, 13) 161 f,
    285
  sunspots 284
  See also astronomy, geocentric
    and heliocentric
supernatural 66 f, 199 f, 248, 270,
  323, 347, 381, 386
suppositio 12, 32, 52 f, 55, 122, 125, 151

suppositum Ockham 100 f; Suárez
  368 f
Swineshead, Richard 122 f
Switzerland 196
syllogism Fr. Bacon 298, 300 ff;
  also 52 f, 61 f, 85, 137, 219, 230
symbolic theology 205
symbols 160, 214, 237, 244, 262,
  269
sympathy 249, 251, 257, 265, 268
syncretism 212 f, 215
synderesis 201, 206
synthesis of differences see coincidence of opposites
synthesis, philosophical
  Aristotelianism with Christianity
    3 f, 415 f
  neo-Platonic 412
  of philosophy and theology see
    philosophy
  Renaissance Platonism 19
  Suárez 374 ff, 378
  Thomas Aquinas 378, 416

Tauler, John 181, **195 f,** 197, 200 f,
  434 f*
taxation 310, 318, 321, 326, **399 f**
Taylor, F. S. 441*
Taylor, H. O. 436*
technology 279
Teetaert, A. 430*
teleology see finality
telescope 226, 284
Telesio, Bernardino 249, **252 ff,**
  255, 257, 438 f*
Temple, Sir William 292
temporal goods see ownership;
  private property
temporal jurisdiction
  papal see papacy, political juris-
    diction
  secular see political authority
Teresa of Jesus, St. 181
term Ockham 52–7, 59–63, 74, 76;
  also 122, 125, 218, 374, 409
  absolute 54
  categorematic 54
  connotative 54, 85 f, 89, 100
  general 125
  syncategorematic 54 f, 76
  universal 57, 125, 218
terminism 11, 46, 122
  terminist logic 11, 32, 51 ff, 56,
    122, 151, 154 f

INDEX

terminus see term
Tertullian 413
testimony 128
Thaddeus of Parma 150
Thales 408
theft 105, 320, 390
Themistius 221
Theo of Smyrna 211
Theodore of Gaza 220
Theodoric of Freiberg 156, 185
theology Ockham 47f, 67, 71, 73f, 84, 87f, 112; Suárez 352f, 370, 380; *also* 22f, 123f, 144ff, 151f, 183, 202–6, 208, 295, 304, 323, 336, 341f, 346, 350, 414ff, 418–24, 445ff*
 'German T.' see s.v.
 Mystical T. 181ff, 205f
 Natural T. see s.v.
 Negative T. 213, 261. See also via negativa
 and philosophy see philosophy
 Protestant T. 228
 and Renaissance 250
 and science see science, experimental
 Symbolic T. 205
theophany 239
Theophrastus 220
theosophy 212n., 216, 265, 273, 293
thermometer 281
Théry, P. 434*
Thomas à Kempis 182
Thomas Aquinas, St.
 agreement with, following of, Suárez 357f, 384ff, 390, 393, 398; *also* 101, 149f, 189, 194, 197, 199f, 210, 215, 322f, 331, 337
 Aristotle, Aristotelianism see Aristotelianism
 criticism of, difference from, Ockham 57ff, 82, 93n., 98, 104, 108; Suárez 365, 376; *also* 1, 12f, 26, 28, 31, 38–42, 132, 173ff, 185, 188f, 200, 221, 340
 official doctor 10, 24, 125, 344
 political theory 2, 8, 119, 168, 173ff, 347, 381, 392f, 398
 Summa theologica 10, 337, 341, 344
 theology and philosophy 1ff, 6, 13ff, 126, **415–19**

also 10, 49f, 207, 336, 375f, 379, 421f, 429*, 445*
Thomas Bradwardine 39, 124, 133
Thomas de Vio, Cardinal Cajetan see Cajetan
Thomas More, St. 22, 209, **320ff**, 326, 442*
Thomas of Strasbourg 125
Thomism 10, 24f, 81, 91, 150, 200, 221ff, 338, 354, 357f, 365, 368, 377f, 380
Thomson, N. H. 441*
Thorndike, L. 433*, 441*
Thoth 212n.
thought
 an activity of bodies 291
 wishful thinking 303
tides 285
time 75f, 240f
 abolition of past 133
Todi 232
toleration, religious 321, 327f, 334
Toletus, Francis 22, 336, 341, 361
top, spinning 158
Torre, A. della 436*
Toulouse 29, 150, 226, 229, 324, 345
Tractatus de successivis see William of Ockham
tradition 154, 228, 279f, 399
 in philosophy 40f, 50, 182, 218, 231, 292, 299
traducianism 83
tranquillity of soul man's end 264
transformation
 of bodies 144f, 305f, 370
 of elements 267, 305f
translations
 from Arabic and Greek 16, 155, 414, 422
 Aristotle 220f
 Plato, Plotinus, etc. 19, 211
transmigration of souls 251, 269
transmutation see transformation
transubstantiation 193f
treaties 333, 351, 392
Trent, Council of 336
tribunal, international 333f, 350, 352
Trinity, the Blessed 27, 35, 69, 101, 128, 185f, 190, 192, 197ff, 271, 340
 and principle of contradiction 124
Trinkaus, C. E. 436*
Troilo, E. 439*

INDEX

truth 32, 60ff, 128, 202, 228, 355, 359, 412, 431*
   God as T. 192
   Necessary T. 60f
   Transcendental T. 359
Tübingen 150, 215
Two Swords, the 119, 168
Tycho Brahe 263, 283, 286, 440*
Tyler, H. W. *see* Sedgwick, W. T.
tyrannicide 348, 398f
tyranny 118f, 173, 176, 323, 332, 393f, **397f**

Ueberweg 428* *see* Frischeisen-Köhler; Geyer
Ulm 196
Ulric of Strasbourg 200
ultra-realism *see* realism, exaggerated
understanding *see* intellect
unity 255, 355, 359, 408
   of Christendom *see s.v.*
   of Church 233f, 244
   of divine nature 199
   of human race 392
   in man 198f
   U. in plurality 242
   Political U. 311f, 317f, 394
   Specific U. 30
universale ante rem, in re 58
universals Durandus 28, 41f; Ockham 12, 41, 48-51, 53, 56-60, 89, 91; Petrus Aureoli 29f, 32f, 41f, 429*; *also* 39, 42, 50, 125f, 151, 155, 218, 242, 355, 430*, 436*
universe *see* world
universities 202, 204, 227, 336, 378, 413, 420
   English 292, 308
   and Ockhamist movement 148ff
univocal 78ff, 338f, 359
unmoved mover 81f, 376
use and right to use 114
usus iuris et usus facti 114

vacuum 306
Valla, Laurentius **217f**, 220, 436*
Valladolid 353
value 143f, 228, 409
Van Helmont, Francis Mercury **268f**, 439*
Van Helmont, John Baptist **268f**, 439*

Vanini, Lucilius 226
Vansteenberghe, E. 438*, 445*
Vásquez, Gabriel 335, 341, 383
velocity 160, 280f
Venice 150, 258
Venus, phases of 284f
verb 76
Verdun, diocese of 135
verification 164, 279, 282, 285, 306
Vernias, Nicoletto 221
Vesalius, Andreas 280
vestigium Dei 256, 259, 421
Vetter, F. 434*
via affirmativa 236, 238
via antiqua 10, 149
via moderna 11, 16f, 122, 125, 150, 155, 163, 182, 204, 414, 420. *See also* Ockhamism
via negativa 200, 213, 235f, 238, 244f, 261
vice *see* sin
Vico, J. B. 378
Victorines, the 181, 189, 194, 196, 200f, 205
Vienna university 148, 154
Vienne, Council of (1311-12) **34-6,** 98
Vignaux, P. 429*, 431f*
Villalpando, Gaspar Cardillo de 342
Villari, P. 443*
Villey, P. 437*
Vinci, Leonardo da 246, 279, 433*, 440*
virtue 106f, 109, 151, 229, 316, 386
   Cardinal VV. 253
   Civic VV. 316f
   its own reward 224
Visconti, Matteo 171, 177
vision 65f, 97, 137, 184, 407
   of God *see* beatific vision
vitalism 268f
Vitoria, Francis of 334f, 340, 349, **350f**, 352, 444f*
Vittorino da Feltre 208
Vives, Luis 218, 350, 436*
Volpe, G. della 435*
voluntarism Ockham 67f, 73, 95. *See also* natural law, dependence on God's will
Vreeland, H. 443*

Waddington, C. 437*
Walker, L. J. 441*
Walter Burleigh 53

INDEX

Walter Hilton 181
war, 293, 310, 321, 330, 333 f, 350, 391, **403ff**, 442*, 444*, 446*
  innocent, killing of 404
  just war, conditions of **332ff, 403f**
  ruler and 403, 405
  soldiers' consciences 404 f
  tyrant, war against 397 f
warmth *see* heat
Wautier d'Aygalliers, A. 435*
wealth 320
Weigel, Valentine **269f,** 272, 439*
Weimar dispute on free will 227
Weinberg, J. R. 142, 432*
Werner, K. 446*
Wessely, J. E. 439*
Whitehead, A. N. 441*
Whyte, A. 439*
will 63, 82, 96, 98, 132 ff, 141, 270, 303
  distinct from intellect? 27, 100
  free *see* free will
  happiness willed freely 102
  and intellect 102, 206
  object of 102
  sense appetite and 103
William Cardinal Curti 135, 145
William Heytesbury 122, 148
William of Ockham ix, 11-15, 26, 28, 33, 39, 41 f, **43-121** (*see* Contents, p. v), 142, 149 f, 153 ff, 158 f, 163, 171, 310, 347, 375, 384 f, 390, 419 f, 427, 430 f*
  Centiloquium theologicum 45, 81f,
  and Ockhamist movement 122, 124 f, 127, 137, 147, 151
  Ockham's razor *see* economy, principle of
  and papacy 111 f, 114-21
  political works 115-17, 430*
  Tractatus de successivis 45, 75 f, 430*
William of Shyreswood 51
William of Waynflete 209
Wilson, Thomas 292
Wimpfeling, Jacob 209
Winchester 209
wisdom 182, 204, 229, 252, 257, 293, 339, 364 f, 413
wishful thinking 303
Witelo 156

Wittenberg 150, 209, 283
Wodham *see* Adam Wodham
Wolf, A. A. 441*
Wolff, Christian 356, 379
wonder, 407
Woodward, W. H. 436*
word 32, 54 f, 59, 74, 80, 89n., 217 f, 252, 301, 304. *See also* language
Word, the divine 191, 193, 198, 214, 242
work 321
world 167, 244, 283, 417 f, 421 f, 433*
  eternity of 4 ff, 144 ff, 226, 240 f.
  See also creation, from eternity
  and God 4 f, 19, 67 f, 73 f, 81 f, 144, 165, **239f;** 245 f, 248, 251, 260, 272, 289, 293, 410 f, 423
  in God *see* creatures, in God
  infinite 70, **240f,** 245, 260, 262
  material W., the 19 f, 166, 423
  as organism 251. *See also* nature (as totality), as organism
  origin of 299
  soul of *see* world-soul
  as system 166, 213 f, 242, 245, 257
  three-fold W. 266, 270
  unicity of 163, 241, 261, 363
world-soul 242 f, 248, 251, 259, 261, 265 f, 271
world-wide
  authority 333 f, 350, 352
  community 392
  government 352, 397
  law 23, 350 ff. *See also* law of nations
  monarchy 255
  State 351 f, 394, **397**
wrath of God 272
wrong *see* evil, moral
Wycliffe, John 148 f

Ximenes, Cardinal 341

Zabarella, Jacobus 226
Zammit, P. M. 444*
Zaragüeta, J. 446*
Zimara, Marcus Antonius 221 f
Zuidema, S. U. 431*

THE BELLARMINE SERIES

★

1. A TWO YEAR PUBLIC MINISTRY. Defended by Father EDMUND F. SUTCLIFFE, S.J., Professor of Holy Scripture at Heythrop College. 8s. 6d.
   Father Sutcliffe 'presents a scholarly view of the relevant evidence.... The book is a very useful contribution to an obscure subject.'—*The Congregational Quarterly.*
   'The author gives a detailed and scholarly treatment of a very difficult question. His work will be of great value to biblical students. The educated laity will also find it most interesting and instructive.'—*The Sign.*
   'The general construction of the work and the marshalling of the arguments should be a joy to all who have the privilege of studying it.'—*Irish News.*
   'Father Sutcliffe's book ... is well worth reading, as it throws much light not only on this problem but on kindred questions of chronology.'—*Buckfast Abbey Chronicle.*

2. MORAL PROBLEMS OF MENTAL DEFECT. By Father J. S. CAMMACK, S.J., Professor of Ethics at Heythrop College. *Out of print.*
   'This valuable study of mental defect makes fascinating reading because of its logical precision and clarity of thought.'—*The Guardian.*
   'Father Cammack is to be thanked and congratulated for his masterly exposition of the problems at issue.'—*Blackfriars.*
   'This is a book to be recommended not only to moral theologians, but to all interested in the moral and social problems of mental defect and delinquency.' —*The Tablet.*
   'The work done is pioneer work, so far as the moral aspect of the problem goes. It is excellently done—balanced, scholarly and most readable.'—*The Irish Ecclesiastical Record.*

3. THE ORACLES OF JACOB AND BALAAM. By Father ERIC BURROWS, S.J., of Campion Hall, Oxford. 10s. 6d.
   'This book ... is a masterpiece of Biblical exegesis.... The author's learning elicits ... a flood of light on Old Testament history and prophecy.'—*The Tablet.*
   'This volume ... bears testimony to his wide studies and keen intellect, and contains much that gives it more than ordinary interest.'—*The Journal of Theological Studies.*
   'The theory ... has never been elaborated with such penetrating detail and insight as in the volume before us.... It is particularly interesting to see how the meaning and significance of verse after verse becomes clear when the zodiacal allusion is explained.'—*The Guardian.*

4. ST. CYPRIAN'S *DE UNITATE*, CHAP. 4, IN THE LIGHT OF THE MANUSCRIPTS. By Father MAURICE BÉVENOT, S.J., Professor of Fundamental Theology at Heythrop College. *Out of print.*
   'This book is one to which all concerned with a fascinatingly difficult textual problem will turn with gratitude.... The tables and collections of data are invaluable.'—*The Times Literary Supplement.*
   'The industry and research of the writer and his elaborate discussion of the manuscripts are worthy of the highest praise.'—*The Guardian.*
   'This painstaking and detailed work ... the most thorough examination of the manuscripts that has yet been made.... Every serious student of Cyprian must go to the book itself.'—A. SOUTER in *The Journal of Theological Studies.*

5. AN INTRODUCTION TO THE STUDY OF ASCETICAL AND MYSTICAL THEOLOGY. The Substance of Seventeen Lectures given at Heythrop College. By the Most Rev. ALBAN GOODIER, S.J., Archbishop of Hierapolis. *Out of print.*
'The concluding section of Archbishop Goodier's book is certainly something which all who value mysticism would be the better for reading carefully. This description of infused prayer, identified here with the Unitive Way, does in fact say what in substance is traditional, yet in a completely fresh way.'—*The Tablet.*
'Archbishop Goodier's description of the inner life of the Christian is worth many a longer and more pretentious work, and may be heartily recommended to all who are seeking to make progress in the spiritual life or to help others to do so. It is the distilled wisdom of one who is master of his subject.'—*The Church Quarterly Review.*

6. THE GOSPEL OF THE INFANCY AND OTHER BIBLICAL ESSAYS. By Father ERIC BURROWS, S.J. *Out of print.*
'This volume is an important contribution to modern biblical studies. . . . These essays display Fr. Burrows's great learning and penetrating vision to the greatest advantage . . . (They) are as brilliant as they are painstaking and learned.—*The Downside Review.*
'The high standard of excellence attained in all the eight papers in the book . . . Fr. Burrows's accustomed brilliance.'—*The Tablet.*

7. FRIEDRICH NIETZSCHE, PHILOSOPHER OF CULTURE. By Father FREDERICK COPLESTON, S.J., Professor of the History of Philosophy at Heythrop College. 1942; [2]1942. *Out of print.*
'Father Copleston's book on Nietzsche is one of the best expositions and discussions of that philosopher in the English language.'—DESMOND MACCARTHY in *The Sunday Times.*
'This book is an exposition . . . of unusual merit . . . . The author neither reads in what is not there nor glosses over the significance of what is there. . Can be recommended as an excellent introduction.'—DR. J. WISDOM in *Mind.*
'This is a book many have, or should have been looking for. A study of Nietzsche from the Christian standpoint, scrupulously fair, and above all unbiassed by the too common desire to make anti-German capital out of Nietzsche by misrepresenting him as a Nazi before Hitler. . . . Such a study was badly needed, and here it is.'—*The Tablet.*

8. THE OLD TESTAMENT AND THE FUTURE LIFE. By Father EDMUND F. SUTCLIFFE, S.J., Professor of Old Testament Exegesis and Hebrew at Heythrop College. 16s. 1946; 1947[2].
'An important study. . . . It will command the attention of the scholar as well as of the general reader . . . the excellence of the work . . . valuable contributions on disputed questions.'—H. H. ROWLEY in *Theology.*
'A book of such intrinsic worth. . . . There could be no question of the importance of the book nor of its substantial scholarly value.'—FATHER KEHOE, O.P., in *The Catholic Herald.*
'No other book on this subject . . . says so much so well in so short a space.' —F. X. PIERCE, S.J., in *Theological Studies.*

9. A HISTORY OF PHILOSOPHY. I. GREECE AND ROME. By Father FREDERICK COPLESTON, S.J., Professor of the History of Philosophy at Heythrop College. 21s. 1946; revised edn. 1947.
'This book will probably be acclaimed . . . as a masterpiece of exposition. I can only say for myself that I shall never willingly read another, and that my only quarrel with (the author) is that he did not write it earlier.'—HUGH ROSS WILLIAMSON in *John O'London's Weekly.*
'The outstanding value of a book which covers its wide ground so adequately, never fails to interest and stimulate by its statements of so many philosophies and judgements upon them, and draws out clearly the lines of ancient thought and their gradual convergence in a developing synthesis.'—*The Tablet.*

10. SEX ENLIGHTENMENT AND THE CATHOLIC. By Father LEYCESTER KING, S.J., Professor of Psychology at Heythrop College. 6s. 1944. *Out of print.*
'At last I have found the Catholic book I have been looking for. . . . You will have the feeling of having your own difficulties discussed with you by a sympathetic psychologist. . . . You are strongly recommended to read it.' —E. J. KING in *The Catholic Herald.*
'Essentially sane and helpful.'—*The Times Literary Supplement.*
'It displays the Church as having neither the Grundy-like obscurantism of the stuffier puritan sects, nor the blatant obsession of the more jovial Paganism, and has much in it to teach and help those not of the Faith.'—*Truth.*

11. ARTHUR SCHOPENHAUER, PHILOSOPHER OF PESSIMISM. By Father FREDERICK COPLESTON, S.J., 12s. 6d. 1946; ²1947.
'No more penetrating study of Schopenhauer nor better dissection both of his philosophy and of the eloquence with which he urged it has appeared in our time.'—*The Times Literary Supplement.*
'This work gives one of the most complete expositions of the philosophy of Schopenhauer yet published.'—*Studies.*

12. A HISTORY OF PHILOSOPHY. II. MEDIAEVAL PHILOSOPHY: AUGUSTINE TO SCOTUS. By Father FREDERICK COPLESTON, S.J., Professor of the History of Philosophy at Heythrop College. 25s. 1950.
'Unquestionably the fullest account of medieval philosophy yet published in English. . . . Fr. Copleston can be relied upon for an accurate account of all the philosophers in the period covered.'—*The Times Literary Supplement.*
'The student or teacher . . . will hardly find a better book in English than the present volume. No reader could fail to admire the ability with which the author has shaped his enormous material into a lucid and scholarly narrative.' —*Philosophy.*

13. EARLY CHRISTIAN BAPTISM AND THE CREED. By Father JOSEPH CREHAN, S.J., Professor of Fundamental Theology at Heythrop College. 1949. 21s.
'Father Crehan has provided a useful contribution to the growing literature on the development of the Credal formularies. He writes with clarity and presents a consistent interpretation of texts and facts.'—*The Times Literary Supplement.*
'L'étude est brillament menée, et dénote une profonde érudition chez son Auteur. Même si elle ne rallie pas toujours tous les suffrages, elle s'impose à l'attention.'—*Revue d'Histoire Ecclésiastique* (Louvain).
'Here is a most erudite and thorough contribution to the history of the doctrine (of Baptism), and even if it were not also suggestive and original, it would possess high value if only as a source-book for the study of the subject.' —C. F. D. MOULE in *Theology.*